*Problem Solving in
Automata, Languages,
and Complexity*

T0350123

Problem Solving in Automata, Languages, and Complexity

Ding-Zhu Du

Ker-I Ko

A Wiley-Interscience Publication

JOHN WILEY & SONS, INC.

New York / Chichester / Weinheim / Brisbane / Singapore / Toronto

Contents

Preface   vii

1 Regular Languages   1

   1.1   Strings and Languages   1
   1.2   Regular Languages and Regular Expressions   8
   1.3   Graph Representations for Regular Expressions   16

2 Finite Automata   23

   2.1   Deterministic Finite Automata   23
   2.2   Examples of Deterministic Finite Automata   28
   2.3   Nondeterministic Finite Automata   38
   2.4   Converting an NFA to a DFA   45
   2.5   Finite Automata and Regular Expressions   53
   2.6   Closure Properties of Regular Languages   58
   2.7   Minimum Deterministic Finite Automata   69
   2.8   Pumping Lemmas   80

3 Context-Free Languages   89

   3.1   Context-Free Grammars   89
   3.2   More Examples of Context-Free Grammars   99
   3.3   Parsing and Ambiguity   109
   3.4   Pushdown Automata   122
   3.5   Pushdown Automata and Context-Free Grammars   132
   3.6   Pumping Lemmas for Context-Free Languages   142

4 Turing Machines 159

4.1	One-Tape Turing Machines	159
4.2	Examples of Turing Machines	166
4.3	Multi-Tape Turing Machines	180
4.4	Church-Turing Thesis	191
4.5	Unrestricted Grammars	193
4.6	Primitive Recursive Functions	200
4.7	Pairing Functions and Gödel Numberings	206
4.8	Partial Recursive Functions	214

5 Computability Theory 225

5.1	Universal Turing Machines	225
5.2	R. E. Sets and Recursive Sets	232
5.3	Diagonalization	241
5.4	Reducibility	246
5.5	Recursion Theorem	258
5.6	Undecidable Problems	266

6 Computational Complexity 281

6.1	Asymptotic Growth Rate	281
6.2	Time and Space Complexity	286
6.3	Hierarchy Theorems	297
6.4	Nondeterministic Turing Machines	304
6.5	Context-Sensitive Languages	314

7 NP-Completeness 323

7.1	NP	323
7.2	Polynomial-Time Reducibility	339
7.3	Cook's Theorem	350
7.4	More NP-Complete Problems	359
7.5	NP-Complete Optimization Problems	370

References 387

Index 389

Preface

Over the past twenty years, automata and formal languages have become the standard introductory theory course in both the undergraduate and graduate curricula of computer science. The subjects studied in such a course include automata theory, formal languages, and models of computation. For a more advanced graduate course, computability theory and computational complexity theory are also covered. Whereas these materials are fundamental in many different areas of computer science, this course also offers a unique opportunity for students to learn various mathematical tools to deal with nonstandard, abstract objects.

This book is designed for such a course, with the emphasis on problem solving. It is commonly recognized that the best, if not the only, way to learn a mathematics subject is through extensive problem-solving experience. By attacking the problems directly, one not only learns techniques and tools to solve the problems, but also consolidates understanding of the underlying concepts. Theory of computation is, by nature, an abstract discipline, and the problem-solving approach appears to be most helpful.

In this book, we collected a rich variety of examples, ranging from elementary questions about basic definitions and concepts, to advanced ones that employ more sophisticated mathematical tools. The proof ideas and techniques are usually explained in a constructive way, often omitting the routine induction proofs. However, for more difficult questions, the complete, rigorous proofs are also presented. A star sign ($\star$) next to an example or an exercise indicates that it is a more advanced question, and may be skipped in the first reading.

Because the emphasis of the book is problem solving, we only include the most common topics in theory of computation: finite-state automata, context-free grammars, Turing machines, recursive and recursively enumerable languages, complexity classes, and NP-completeness. In particular, for formal languages, we limit ourselves to the basics in regular and context-free languages, and omit deterministic context-free languages and various parsing techniques. For computability theory, our approach is a traditional one: we use Turing machines as a basic model, and develop the notion of computability through the rich, flexible language of primitive recursive functions. Comparisons with high-level language constructs are also included, when appropriate.

The authors have used this book in a number of different classes. In a one-semester undergraduate course, we usually cover most of Chapters 1 to 3, and the first half of Chapter 4, skipping most starred examples. In a two-semester sequence, starred examples may be covered, and an additional chapter (e.g., Chapter 7) may be added. In a more advanced graduate course emphasizing computability and complexity theory, we typically cover Chapters 4 to 7, skipping some starred proofs in Chapter 6.

We are grateful to our colleagues and students for their suggestions and criticism on the earlier drafts of this book. We owe special thanks to Xiu-zhen Cheng and Dean Kelley, who read the manuscript carefully and made a number of corrections.

DING-ZHU DU
KER-I KO

1

Regular Languages

1.1 Strings and Languages

The basic object in automata and language theory is a *string*. A string is a finite sequence of *symbols*. For example, the following are three strings and the corresponding sets of symbols in the strings:

strings	{s, t, r, i, n, g}
CS5400	{C, S, 5, 4, 0}
1001	{1, 0}

In a formal theory, it is necessary to fix the set of symbols used to form strings. Such a finite set of symbols is called an *alphabet*. For example, the following are three alphabets:[1]

{a, b, c, ..., x, y, z}	(Roman alphabet)
{0, 1, ..., 9}	(Arabic digits)
{0, 1}	(binary alphabet)

A string over the binary alphabet is called a *binary string*.

---

[1] In general, an alphabet may be defined by a finite set of strings instead of symbols, as long as it satisfies the property that two different finite sequences of its elements form two different strings. For instance, the set {00, 01, 11} is an alphabet, but {00, 0, 1} is not an alphabet because both sequences (0, 0) and (00) form the same string 00. In this book, we do not consider this general type of alphabets, and will only work with alphabets whose elements are single symbols.

1

The *length* of a string x, denoted by $|x|$, is the number of symbols contained in the string. For example, $|\mathtt{strings}| = 7$, $|\mathtt{CS5400}| = 6$, $|\mathtt{1001}| = 4$. The *empty string*, denoted by ε, is a string having no symbol. Clearly, $|\varepsilon| = 0$.

Example 1.1 *How many strings over the alphabet $A = \{a_1, a_2, \ldots, a_k\}$ are there which are of length n, where n is a nonnegative integer?*

Solution. There are n positions in such a string, and each position can hold one of k possible symbols. Therefore, there are k^n strings of length exactly n. □

Let x and y be two strings, and write $x = x_1 x_2 \cdots x_n$ and $y = y_1 y_2 \cdots y_m$, where each x_i and each y_j is a single symbol. Then, x and y are *equal* if and only if (1) $n = m$ and (2) $x_i = y_i$ for all $i = 1, \ldots, n$. For example, $01 \neq 010$ and $1010 \neq 1110$.

The basic operation on strings is *concatenation*. The concatenation $x \cdot y$ of two strings x and y is the string xy, that is, x followed by y. For example, $\mathtt{CS5400}$ is the concatenation of $\mathtt{CS}$ and $\mathtt{5400}$. In particular, we denote $x = x^1$, $xx = x^2, \ldots, \underbrace{x \cdots x}_{k} = x^k$, and define $x^0 = \varepsilon$. (Why is $x^0 = \varepsilon$? The reason is that ε is the identity for the operation of concatenation, and so x^0 satisfies the relation $x^0 x^k = x^{0+k} = x^k$.) For example, $10101010 = (10)^4 = (1010)^2$, $(10)^0 = \varepsilon$. It is obvious that $x^i x^j = x^{i+j}$ for $i, j \geq 0$.

Let x be a string. A string s is a *substring* of x if there exist strings y and z such that $x = ysz$. In particular, when $x = sz$ $(y = \varepsilon)$, s is called a *prefix* of x; and when $x = ys$ $(z = \varepsilon)$, s is called a *suffix* of x. For example, $\mathtt{CS}$ is a prefix of $\mathtt{CS5400}$ and $\mathtt{5400}$ is a suffix of $\mathtt{CS5400}$.

For a string x over alphabet Σ, the *reversal* of x, denoted by x^R, is defined by

$$x^R = \begin{cases} \varepsilon & \text{if } x = \varepsilon, \\ x_n \cdots x_2 x_1 & \text{if } x = x_1 x_2 \cdots x_n, \text{ for } x_1, x_2, \cdots, x_n \in \Sigma. \end{cases}$$

Example 1.2 *For strings x and y, $(xy)^R = y^R x^R$.*

Proof. If $x = \varepsilon$, then $x^R = \varepsilon$ and hence $(xy)^R = y^R = y^R x^R$. If $y = \varepsilon$, then $y^R = \varepsilon$ and hence $(xy)^R = x^R = y^R x^R$. Now, suppose $x = x_1 x_2 \cdots x_m$ and $y = y_1 y_2 \cdots y_n$, with $m, n \geq 1$. Then, $(xy)^R = (x_1 x_2 \cdots x_m y_1 y_2 \cdots y_n)^R = y_n \cdots y_2 y_1 x_m \cdots x_2 x_1 = y^R x^R$. □

Strings are also called *words*. Relations between strings form a theory, called *word theory*. For instance, in word theory, we may be given an equation of strings and are asked to find the solution strings for the variables in the equation.

Example 1.3 *Solve the word equation*

$$x011 = 011x$$

over the alphabet $\{0,1\}$; that is, find the set of strings x over $\{0,1\}$ which satisfy the equation.

Solution. For the equation to hold, either x is the empty string or the string 011 is both a prefix and a suffix of x:

$$011\boxed{x}$$
$$=\boxed{x}011$$

(It is obvious that x cannot be of length 1 or 2.) Let $x = 011y$. Now, remove the first occurrence of 011 from both $011x$ and $x011$, we get $x = y011$. It follows that $011y = y011$. This gives us a recursive solution for x: x is either ε or $x = 011y$ for some other solution y of the equation. It is not hard to see now that $(011)^n$ is a solution to the equation for each $n \geq 0$, and they are the only solutions. □

A *language* is a set of strings. For example, $\{0,1\}$, $\{0^0, 0^1, 0^2, ...\}$, and the set of all English words are languages. Let Σ be an alphabet. We write Σ^* to denote the set of all strings over Σ. Thus, a language L over Σ is just a subset of Σ^*. For any finite language $A \subseteq \Sigma^*$, we write $|A|$ to denote the size (i.e., the number of strings) in A.

The following are some basic operations on languages. (The first four are just set operations. See Figure 1.1.)

Union: If A and B are two languages, then $A \cup B = \{x \mid x \in A \text{ or } x \in B\}$.

Intersection: If A and B are two languages, then $A \cap B = \{x \mid x \in A \text{ and } x \in B\}$.

Subtraction: If A and B are two languages, then $A \setminus B = \{x \mid x \in A \text{ and } x \notin B\}$. ($A \setminus B$ is also denoted by $A - B$ when $B \subseteq A$.)

Complementation: If A is a language over the alphabet Σ, then $\overline{A} = \Sigma^* - A$.

Concatenation: If A and B are two languages, then their concatenation is $A \cdot B = \{ab \mid a \in A, b \in B\}$. We also write AB for $A \cdot B$.

It is clear that concatenation satisfies the associativity law, and so we do not need parentheses when we write the concatenation of more than two languages: $A_1 A_2 \cdots A_k$.

Example 1.4 *(a) If $A = \{0,1\}$ and $B = \{1,2\}$, then $AB = \{01, 02, 11, 12\}$.*

(b) Is it true that if A is of size $n \geq 0$ and B is of size $m \geq 0$ then AB must be of size nm? The answer is no. *For instance, if $A = \{0, 01\}$ and $B = \{1, 11\}$, then $AB = \{01, 011, 0111\}$ has only three elements.*

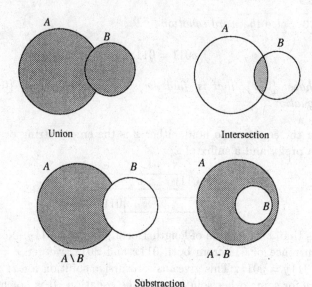

Figure 1.1:   Set operations.

(c) Let $A = \{(01)^n \mid n \geq 0\}$ and $B = \{01, 010\}$. Then,

$$AB = \{(01)^n, (01)^n 0 \mid n \geq 1\}$$
$$ABA = \{(01)^n \mid n \geq 1\} \cup \{(01)^n 0(01)^m \mid m \geq 0, n \geq 1\}. \qquad \square$$

For any language A, we define $A^1 = A$, $A^2 = AA$, and $A^k = AA^{k-1}$ for $k \geq 2$. We also define $A^0 = \{\varepsilon\}$. (Note that $\emptyset$ and $\{\varepsilon\}$ are two different languages: $\emptyset A = \emptyset$ and $\{\varepsilon\}A = A\{\varepsilon\} = A$.) For example, for $\Sigma = \{0, 1\}$, we have $\Sigma^2 = \{00, 01, 10, 11\}$ and, in general, for $k \geq 0$, Σ^k is the set of all strings of length k over Σ. Therefore, $\Sigma^* = \Sigma^0 \cup \Sigma^1 \cup \Sigma^2 \cup \cdots$. The following is the more general star operation based on this formula:

Kleene closure (or *star closure*): For any language A, define

$$A^* = A^0 \cup A^1 \cup A^2 \cup \cdots$$
$$= \{w \mid w \text{ is the concatenation of } 0 \text{ or more strings from } A\}.$$

Example 1.5 *The language $\{0, 10\}^*$ is the set of all binary strings having no substring 11 and ending with 0.*

Proof. It is clear that the concatenation of any number of 0 and 10 must end with 0. Furthermore, it cannot produce a substring 11, since the ending 0's of both strings 0 and 10 separate any two 1's in the concatenated string.

Conversely, let x be a string over $\{0, 1\}$ having no substring 11 and ending with 0. If x contains no occurrence of 1, then x is the concatenation of

$|x|$ many 0's, and so $x \in \{0, 10\}^{|x|} \subseteq \{0, 10\}^*$. Suppose x contains $n \geq 1$ occurrences of 1's. Then, each occurrence of 1 in x must be followed by a 0, for otherwise that symbol 1 is either followed by a 1 or is the last symbol of x, violating the assumption on x. So, we can write x as

$$0 \cdots 0(10)0 \cdots 0(10)0 \cdots 0(10)0 \cdots 0,$$

where $0 \cdots 0$ means zero or more 0's. Thus, x is the concatenation of strings 0 and 10, or, $x \in \{0, 10\}^*$. □

Example 1.6 *Show that for any languages A and B,*

$$(A \cup B)^* = A^*(BA^*)^*.$$

Proof. We observe that every string in $A^*(BA^*)^*$ can be written as the concatenation of strings in $A \cup B$. Indeed, a string x in $A^*(BA^*)^*$ must be in $A^n(BA^*)^m$ for some $n, m \geq 0$. Thus, x can be decomposed into

$$x = x_1 x_2 \cdots x_n y_1 y_2 \cdots y_m,$$

where $x_1, \ldots, x_n \in A$ and $y_1, \ldots, y_m \in BA^*$. Similarly, each y_j, $j = 1, \ldots, m$, can be decomposed into

$$y_j = y_{j,0} y_{j,1} y_{j,2} \cdots y_{j,k_j},$$

with $k_j \geq 0$ and $y_{j,0} \in B$, $y_{j,1}, \ldots, y_{j,k_j} \in A$. Therefore,

$$x = x_1 x_2 \cdots x_n y_{1,0} y_{1,1} \cdots y_{1,k_1} y_{2,0} \cdots y_{2,k_2} \cdots y_{m,k_m}$$

is the concatenation of strings in $A \cup B$. It follows that $A^*(BA^*)^* \subseteq (A \cup B)^*$.

Next, we show that $(A \cup B)^* \subseteq A^*(BA^*)^*$. To do so, consider a general string $x \in (A \cup B)^*$. Again, we can see that $x \in (A \cup B)^n$ for some $n \geq 0$. Thus, we may write

$$x = x_1 x_2 \cdots x_n,$$

for some $x_1, \ldots, x_n \in A \cup B$. Now, assume that $x_{i_1}, x_{i_2}, \ldots, x_{i_k} \in B$, for some $k \geq 0$ and $1 \leq i_1 < i_2 < \cdots < i_k \leq n$, and the other strings x_j, with $j \neq i_1, \ldots, i_k$, are in A. Then, we can write

$$x = y_{i_1} x_{i_1} y_{i_2} x_{i_2} \cdots y_{i_k} x_{i_k} y_{i_{k+1}},$$

where each $y_{i_j} \in A^*$. Thus, $x \in A^*(BA^*)^k \subseteq A^*(BA^*)^*$. It follows that $(A \cup B)^* \subseteq A^*(BA^*)^*$. □

Define the *positive closure* of a language A to be

$$A^+ = A^* A = A \cup A^2 \cup A^3 \cup \cdots.$$

Example 1.7 $A^+ = A^*$ *if and only if* $\varepsilon \in A$.

Proof. Clearly, $A^+ \subseteq A^*$. If $\varepsilon \in A$, then $\{\varepsilon\} = A^0 \subseteq A \subseteq A^+$. Thus, $A^* = A^+$.

Conversely, if $\varepsilon \notin A$, then every string in A^+ has positive length. Thus, A^+ does not contains ε. But, $\varepsilon \in A^*$. Hence, $A^* \neq A^+$. $\square$

For a language A, define the *reversal language* of A to be $A^R = \{x^R \mid x \in A\}$.

Example 1.8 *For languages* A *and* B, $(AB)^R = B^R A^R$ *and* $(A \cup B)^R = A^R \cup B^R$.

Proof.
$$\begin{aligned}
(AB)^R &= \{x^R \mid x \in AB\} \\
&= \{(yz)^R \mid y \in A, z \in B\} \\
&= \{z^R y^R \mid y \in A, z \in B\} \qquad \text{(by Example 1.2)} \\
&= \{z^R \mid z \in B\} \cdot \{y^R \mid y \in A\} \\
&= B^R A^R,
\end{aligned}$$

$$\begin{aligned}
(A \cup B)^R &= \{x^R \mid x \in A \cup B\} \\
&= \{x^R \mid x \in A\} \cup \{x^R \mid x \in B\} \\
&= A^R \cup B^R.
\end{aligned}$$
                  $\square$

$\star$ **Example 1.9** (Arden's Lemma). *Assume that* A, B *are two languages with* $\varepsilon \notin A$, *and* X *is a language satisfying the relation* $X = AX \cup B$. *Then,* $X = A^* B$.

Proof. We use induction to show $X \subseteq A^* B$. First, consider $x = \varepsilon$. If $x \in X$, then $x \in AX \cup B$. Since $\varepsilon \notin A$, we must have $x \in B$ and, hence, $x \in A^* B$.

Next, assume that for all strings w of length less than or equal to n, if $w \in X$ then $w \in A^* B$, and consider a string x of length $n + 1$. If $x \in X = AX \cup B$, then either $x \in B \subseteq A^* B$ or $x = yw$ for some $y \in A$ and $w \in X$. In the second case, we must have $y \neq \varepsilon$ and, hence, $|w| < |x|$. So, by the inductive hypothesis, $w \in A^* B$ and $x \in AA^* B \subseteq A^* B$. This completes the induction step, and it follows that $X \subseteq A^* B$.

Conversely, we use induction to show that $A^n B \subseteq X$ for all $n \geq 0$. For $n = 0$, we have $A^0 B = B \subseteq AX \cup B = X$. For $n > 0$, we have, by the inductive hypothesis, $A^n B = A(A^{n-1} B) \subseteq AX$. Thus, $A^n B \subseteq AX \subseteq AX \cup B = X$. $\square$

$\star$ **Example 1.10** *Assume that languages* $A, B \subseteq \{a, b\}^*$ *satisfy the following two equations:*
$$A = \{\varepsilon\} \cup \{a\}A \cup \{b\}B,$$
$$B = \{\varepsilon\} \cup \{b\}B.$$

Find simple representations for A *and* B.

Proof. We apply Arden's lemma to the second equation, and we get $B = \{b\}^* \cdot \{\varepsilon\} = \{b\}^*$. Then, we apply Arden's lemma to the first equation, and we get

$$A = \{a\}^*(\{\varepsilon\} \cup \{b\}B).$$

Now, substitute $\{b\}^*$ for B, we have

$$A = \{a\}^*(\{\varepsilon\} \cup \{b\}\{b\}^*) = \{a\}^*\{b\}^*. \qquad \square$$

Exercise 1.1

1. Let $A = \{\text{grand}, \varepsilon\}$ and $B = \{\text{mother}, \text{father}\}$. What are AB and A^*B?

2. Let A be a language over $\{a, b\}$ and $x \in \{a, b\}^*$. Find necessary and sufficient conditions in terms of x and A for the equation

$$A^* - \{x\} = A^+.$$

3. For each of the following equations, determine whether it is true for all languages A, B or not. Present a proof or a counterexample.

   (a) $(A^R)^* = (A^*)^R$.
   (b) $(A^+)^* = A^*$.
   (c) $(A \cup A^R)^* = A^* \cup (A^*)^R$.
   (d) $A^2 \cup B^2 = (A \cup B)^2$.
   (e) $A^* \cap B^* = (A \cap B)^*$.

4. (a) Show that, for $k \geq 1$, $\bigcup_{i=0}^{k} A^i = (\{\varepsilon\} \cup A)^k$.
   (b) Show that, for $n \geq 1$, $(A^*)^n = A^*$.
   (c) Assume that $\varepsilon \notin A$. Show that, for $n \geq 1$, $(A^+)^n = A^n A^*$.

5. Prove the following identities on languages A, B, C, D:

   (a) $A(BA)^* = (AB)^*A$.
   (b) $(A \cup B)^* = (A^*B^*)^*$.
   (c) $A(B \cup C) = AB \cup AC$.
   (d) $(A \cup B)C = AC \cup BC$.
   (e) $A^*B(DA^*B \cup C)^* = (A \cup BC^*D)^*BC^*$.

6. Find the shortest string over alphabet $\{0\}$ which is not in $\{\varepsilon, 0, 0^2, 0^5\}^3$.

⋆ 7. Find the general solutions for the equation

$$xy = yx$$

for $x, y \in \{0, 1\}^*$.

⋆ **8.** Solve the following language equations for languages $A, B, C \subseteq \{a, b\}^*$:

$$A = \{a\}C \cup \{b\}B,$$
$$B = \{\varepsilon\} \cup \{b\}A \cup \{a\}C,$$
$$C = \{\varepsilon\} \cup \{a\}A.$$

1.2   Regular Languages and Regular Expressions

The concept of *regular languages* (or, *regular sets*) over an alphabet Σ is defined recursively as follows:

(1) The empty set $\emptyset$ is a regular language.

(2) For every symbol $a \in \Sigma$, $\{a\}$ is a regular language.

(3) If A and B are regular languages, then $A \cup B$, AB, and A^* are all regular languages.

(4) Nothing else is a regular language.

The following are some examples.

Example 1.11 *(a) The set $\{\varepsilon\}$ is a regular language, because $\{\varepsilon\} = \emptyset^*$.*

(b) The set $\{001, 110\}$ is a regular language over the binary alphabet: $\{001, 110\} = (\{0\}\{0\}\{1\}) \cup (\{1\}\{1\}\{0\})$.

(c) From (b) above, we can generalize that every finite language is a regular language. □

When a regular language is obtained through a long sequence of operations of union, concatenation and Kleene closure, its representation becomes cumbersome. For example, it may look like this:

$$(\{0\}^* \cup (\{1\}\{0\}\{0\}^*))\{1\}\{0\}^*((\{0\}\{1\}^*) \cup \{1\}^*). \tag{1.1}$$

To simplify the representations for regular languages, we define the notion of *regular expressions* over alphabet Σ as follows:

(1) $\emptyset$ is a regular expression which represents the empty set.

(2) ε is a regular expression which represents language $\{\varepsilon\}$.

(3) For $a \in \Sigma$, **a** is a regular expression which represents language $\{a\}$.

(4) If r_A and r_B are regular expressions representing languages A and B, respectively, then $(r_A) + (r_B)$, $(r_A)(r_B)$, and $(r_A)^*$ are regular expressions representing $A \cup B$, AB, and A^*, respectively.

(5) Nothing else is a regular expression over Σ.

For example, language $A = \{0\}^*$ has a regular expression $r_A = (\mathbf{0})^*$ and language $B = \{00\}^* \cup \{0\}$ has a regular expression $r_B = (((\mathbf{0})(\mathbf{0}))^*) + (\mathbf{0})$.

For any regular expression r, we let $L(r)$ denote the regular language represented by r.

To further reduce the number of parentheses in a regular expression, we apply the following preference rules to a non-fully parenthesized regular expression:

(1) Kleene closure has the higher preference over union and concatenation.

(2) Concatenation has the higher preference over union.

In other words, we interpret a regular expression like an arithmetic expression, treating union like addition, concatenation like multiplication, and Kleene closure like exponentiation. (This is exactly why we use the symbol $+$ for union, the symbol $\cdot$ for concatenation, and the symbol $*$ for Kleene closure.) Using these rules, we can simplify the above two regular expressions to $r_A = 0^*$ and $r_B = (00)^* + 0$, respectively. The regular expression (1.1) can also be simplified to

$$(0^* + 100^*)10^*(01^* + 1^*).$$

In addition, like the operations $+$ and $\cdot$ in an arithmetic expression, the operations $+$ and $\cdot$ in a regular expression satisfy the *distributive law*: For any regular expressions r, s and t,

$$r(s + t) = rs + rt,$$
$$(r + s)t = rt + st.$$

(See Exercises 5(c), 5(d) of Section 1.1.)

A regular language may have several regular expressions. For example, both $0^*1 + \emptyset$ and 0^*1 represent the same regular set $\{0\}^*\{1\}$. The following are some examples of identities about regular expressions. (When there is no risk of confusion, we use the Roman letter a to denote both the symbol a in the alphabet of the language and the regular expression representing the set $\{a\}$.)

Example 1.12 $a^*(a + b)^* = (a + ba^*)^*$.

Proof. We show that both sides are equal to $(a + b)^*$.

Clearly, both sides are subsets of $(a + b)^*$ since $(a + b)^*$ contains all strings over alphabet $\{a, b\}$. Thus, it suffices to show that both sides contain $(a+b)^*$. Since $\varepsilon \in a^*$, we have $a^*(a + b)^* \supseteq (a + b)^*$. Also, $b \in ba^*$ and it follows that $(a + b)^* \subseteq (a + ba^*)^*$.   □

For convenience, we define an additional notation: $r^+ = rr^*$.

Example 1.13 $(ba)^+(a^*b^* + a^*) = (ba)^*ba^+b^*$.

Proof. $(ba)^+(a^*b^* + a^*) = (ba)^*(ba)a^*(b^* + \varepsilon) = (ba)^*ba^+b^*$.   □

Regular expressions can be a convenient notation to represent regular languages, if one knows how to construct them. The following examples demonstrate some ideas.

Example 1.14 *Find a regular expression for the set of binary expansions of integers which are the powers of 4.*

Solution. The binary expansion of the integer 4^n is $1\underbrace{00\cdots0}_{2n}$. Therefore, it can be represented by $1(00)^*$. □

Example 1.15 *Find a regular expression for the set of binary strings which have at least one occurrence of the substring 001.*

Solution. Such a string can be written as $x001y$, where x and y could be any binary strings. So, we get a regular expression for this set:

$$(0 + 1)^*001(0 + 1)^*.$$ □

Example 1.16 *Find a regular expression for the set A of binary strings which have no substring 001.*

Solution. A string x in this set has no substring 00, except that it may have a suffix 0^k for $k \geq 2$. The set of strings with no substring 00 can be represented by the regular expression

$$(01 + 1)^*(\varepsilon + 0)$$

(cf. Example 1.5). Therefore, set A has a regular expression

$$(01 + 1)^*(\varepsilon + 0 + 000^*) = (01 + 1)^*0^*.$$ □

Example 1.17 *Find a regular expression for the set B of all binary strings with at most one pair of consecutive 0's and at most one pair of consecutive 1's.*

Solution. A string x in B may have one of the following forms:

(1) ε,

(2) $u_1 0$,   (4) $u_1 00 v_1$,   (6) $u_1 00 w_1 11 v_0$,

(3) $u_0 1$,   (5) $u_0 11 v_0$,   (7) $u_0 11 w_0 00 v_1$,

where u_0, u_1, v_0, v_1, w_0, w_1 are strings with no substring 00 or 11, and u_0 ends with 0, u_1 ends with 1, v_0 begins with 0, v_1 begins with 1, w_0 begins with 0 and ends with 1, and w_1 begins with 1 and ends with 0.

Now, observe that these types of strings can be represented by simple regular expressions:

$u_1 0 : (\varepsilon + 0)(10)^*$ $0v_1 : (01)^*(\varepsilon + 0)$ $0w_1 1 : (01)^*$

$u_0 1 : (\varepsilon + 1)(01)^*$ $1v_0 : (10)^*(\varepsilon + 1)$ $1w_0 0 : (10)^*$

(For convenience, we added ε to each case. Note that ε is in B.)

Now, we can combine cases (1), (2), (4), (6) and use the distributive law to simplify it into the following regular expression:

$$(\varepsilon + 0)(10)^*(\varepsilon + (01)^* \, (\varepsilon + 0) + (01)^*(10)^*(\varepsilon + 1))$$
$$= (\varepsilon + 0)(10)^*(01)^*(0 + (10)^*(\varepsilon + 1)).$$

(Note that $\varepsilon + (01)^*\varepsilon = (01)^*$.)

Cases (1), (3), (5), (7) have a symmetric form, and set B has the following regular expression:

$$(\varepsilon + 0)(10)^*(01)^*(0 + (10)^*(\varepsilon + 1)) + (\varepsilon + 1)(01)^*(10)^*(1 + (01)^*(\varepsilon + 0)). \quad \square$$

Example 1.18 *Find a regular expression for the set of all binary strings with the property that none of its prefixes has two more 0's than 1's nor two more 1's than 0's.*

Solution. Consider a string $x = x_1 x_2 \cdots x_n$ in the language, where each x_i is a bit 0 or 1. The given property implies that for any positive integer $i \leq n/2$, $x_{2i-1} \neq x_{2i}$. To see this, we assume, for the sake of contradiction, that there exists a positive integer $i \leq n/2$ such that $x_{2i-1} = x_{2i}$. Let i^* be the smallest such i. Without loss of generality, assume $x_{2i^*-1} = x_{2i^*} = 0$. Then, each pair of $x_1 x_2, x_3 x_4, \ldots, x_{2i^*-3} x_{2i^*-2}$ is either 01 or 10 and, hence, the prefix $x_1 x_2 \cdots x_{2i^*-2}$ has an equal number of 0's and 1's. It follows that the prefix $x_1 x_2 \cdots x_{2i^*-1} x_{2i^*}$ contains two more 0's than 1's, a contradiction. Conversely, any string x satisfying that, for all positive integers $i \leq n/2$, $x_{2i-1} \neq x_{2i}$ belongs to this language, since each pair $x_{2i-1} x_{2i}$ is either 10 or 01.

From this characterization, it is now easy to see that this language can be represented by the regular expression

$$(01 + 10)^*(0 + 1 + \varepsilon). \qquad\qquad \square$$

* Example 1.19 *Find a regular expression for the set of all nonempty strings having no repeated adjacent symbols over the arabic digits.*

Solution. Let us analyze a general string w in the language. It must be of the form

$$\cdots 9 \cdots 9 \cdots 9 \cdots .$$

That is, digits 9 separate the string w into several parts. Each part is a string over $\{0, 1, \ldots, 8\}$, having no repeated adjacent symbols. In addition, except possibly for the first and the last parts, each part is nonempty.

The above analysis suggests us to solve the problem by employing a recursive formula. For $k = 0, 1, \ldots, 9$, let a_k be the kth arabic digit (e.g.,

$a_3 = 3$). Also, for $k = 0, 1, \ldots, 9$, let L_k be the set of all nonempty strings over $\{a_0, \ldots, a_k\}$ having no repeated adjacent symbols. Then, we have

$$L_0 = a_0,$$
$$L_{k+1} = L_k + (\varepsilon + L_k)(a_{k+1}L_k)^* a_{k+1}(\varepsilon + L_k).$$

(Note that if a string in L_{k+1} does not contain a_{k+1}, then it is in L_k.)   □

⋆ **Example 1.20** *Find a regular expression for the set of all strings over alphabet*

$$\left\{ \begin{pmatrix} 0 \\ 0 \\ 0 \end{pmatrix}, \begin{pmatrix} 1 \\ 0 \\ 0 \end{pmatrix}, \begin{pmatrix} 0 \\ 1 \\ 0 \end{pmatrix}, \begin{pmatrix} 0 \\ 0 \\ 1 \end{pmatrix}, \begin{pmatrix} 1 \\ 1 \\ 0 \end{pmatrix}, \begin{pmatrix} 1 \\ 0 \\ 1 \end{pmatrix}, \begin{pmatrix} 0 \\ 1 \\ 1 \end{pmatrix}, \begin{pmatrix} 1 \\ 1 \\ 1 \end{pmatrix} \right\}$$

that represent correct additions over binary expansions of integers, with leading 0's added when necessary. For example, the relation

$$\begin{array}{ccccc} & 0 & 1 & 1 & 0 \\ + & 0 & 1 & 0 & 1 \\ \hline & 1 & 0 & 1 & 1 \end{array}$$

implies that the string

$$\begin{pmatrix} 0 \\ 0 \\ 1 \end{pmatrix} \begin{pmatrix} 1 \\ 1 \\ 0 \end{pmatrix} \begin{pmatrix} 1 \\ 0 \\ 1 \end{pmatrix} \begin{pmatrix} 0 \\ 1 \\ 1 \end{pmatrix}$$

is in the set.

Solution. First, we note that the language is closed under string concatenation; that is, the concatenation of two strings in the language is still in the language. Thus, it suffices to study the minimal strings in the language.

Next, we consider the leftmost symbol. It has four choices:

$$\begin{pmatrix} 0 \\ 0 \\ 0 \end{pmatrix}, \begin{pmatrix} 0 \\ 1 \\ 1 \end{pmatrix}, \begin{pmatrix} 1 \\ 0 \\ 1 \end{pmatrix}, \begin{pmatrix} 0 \\ 0 \\ 1 \end{pmatrix}.$$

In the first three cases, this digit by itself is a minimal string in the language.

Now, we consider the fourth case. Here, the rightmost symbol has only one choice:

$$\begin{pmatrix} 1 \\ 1 \\ 0 \end{pmatrix},$$

and the second rightmost symbol must exist and has four choices:

$$\begin{pmatrix} 0 \\ 0 \\ 1 \end{pmatrix}, \begin{pmatrix} 0 \\ 1 \\ 0 \end{pmatrix}, \begin{pmatrix} 1 \\ 0 \\ 0 \end{pmatrix}, \begin{pmatrix} 1 \\ 1 \\ 1 \end{pmatrix}.$$

If the second rightmost symbol is the first case, then the two rightmost symbols form a minimal string in the language (i.e., the minimal string has length 2 and the second rightmost symbol *is* the leftmost symbol). In the other three cases, the third rightmost symbol must exist and has the same four choices as the second rightmost symbol.

Thus, from the above analysis, we see that this language has the following regular expression:

$$\left[\left(\begin{array}{c} 0 \\ 0 \\ 0 \end{array}\right) + \left(\begin{array}{c} 0 \\ 1 \\ 1 \end{array}\right) + \left(\begin{array}{c} 1 \\ 0 \\ 1 \end{array}\right) + \left(\begin{array}{c} 0 \\ 0 \\ 1 \end{array}\right)\left[\left(\begin{array}{c} 0 \\ 1 \\ 0 \end{array}\right) + \left(\begin{array}{c} 1 \\ 0 \\ 0 \end{array}\right) + \left(\begin{array}{c} 1 \\ 1 \\ 1 \end{array}\right)\right]^* \left(\begin{array}{c} 1 \\ 1 \\ 0 \end{array}\right)\right]^*.$$

$\square$

Mathematical induction is an important proof technique in mathematics. To prove a statement S_n true for all natural numbers $n = 0, 1, \ldots$, we can prove it by induction on n as follows:

1. (*Basis Step*) For $n = 0$, prove that the statement S_0 is true.

2. (*Induction Step*) Suppose that the statement S_n is true for an arbitrary integer $n \geq 0$. Prove that the statement S_{n+1} is true.

We used this proof technique in Example 1.9: To show that $X \subseteq A^*B$, we proved that for each n, if $|w| = n$ then $w \in X \Rightarrow w \in A^*B$.

This induction principle can be generalized to other sets of objects which are defined by an *inductive* (or, *recursive*) *definition*. Since regular languages are defined inductively, this principle can be employed to prove a property Q of regular languages in the following way:

(1) Prove that $\emptyset$ has the property Q.

(2) For each $a \in \Sigma$, prove that $\{a\}$ has the property Q.

(3) Prove that if A and B have the property Q, then each of $A \cup B$, AB, and A^* has the property Q.

Here, steps (1) and (2) serve as the basis step, and step (3) serves as the induction step.

Example 1.21 *For each language L over alphabet Σ, let L' be the set of all suffixes of strings in L, that is, $L' = \{w \mid uw \in L$ for some string $u\}$. Show that if L is a regular language so is L'.*

Solution. We prove this result by induction as follows.

Basis Step (1): $\emptyset' = \emptyset$ is a regular set.

Basis Step (2): For any $a \in \Sigma$, $\{a\}' = \{\varepsilon, a\}$ is a regular set.

Induction Step (3): Suppose that L_1 and L_2 are regular sets with the property that L_1' and L_2' are regular sets. Then, we have

(a) $(L_1 \cup L_2)' = \{w \mid (\exists u)[uw \in L_1 \cup L_2]\}$

$\qquad\qquad\quad = \{w \mid (\exists u)[uw \in L_1]$ or $(\exists u)[uw \in L_2]\}$

$$= \{w \mid (\exists u)[uw \in L_1]\} \cup \{w \mid (\exists u)[uw \in L_2]\} = L_1{}' \cup L_2{}'.$$

(b) $(L_1 L_2)' = \{w \mid (\exists u)[uw \in L_1 L_2]\}$

$\qquad = \{w \mid \text{ either } w \in L_2{}' \text{ or } w = xy \text{ for some } x \in L_1{}', y \in L_2\}$

$\qquad = L_2{}' \cup L_1{}' L_2.$

(c) $(L_1{}^*)' = \left(\bigcup_{i=0}^{\infty} L_1{}^i \right)' = \bigcup_{i=0}^{\infty} (L_1{}^i)'$ \hfill by part (a)

$\qquad = \{\varepsilon\} \cup \left(\bigcup_{i=1}^{\infty} (L_1{}' \cup L_1{}' L_1 \cup \cdots \cup L_1{}' L_1{}^{i-1}) \right)$ \hfill by part (b)

$\qquad = L_1{}' \cdot \left(\bigcup_{i=1}^{\infty} (\{\varepsilon\} \cup L_1 \cup \cdots \cup L_1{}^{i-1}) \right) = L_1{}' L_1{}^*.$

Therefore, $(L_1 \cup L_2)'$, $(L_1 L_2)'$, and $(L_1{}^*)'$ are regular sets. This completes the induction step. \hfill □

Remark. What is wrong with the following proof for part (c) of Example 1.21?

Proof for part (c). From part (a), we know that

$$(L_1{}^*)' = \left(\bigcup_{i=0}^{\infty} L_1{}^i \right)' = \bigcup_{i=0}^{\infty} (L_1{}^i)'.$$

From part (b), we know that each $(L_1^i)'$ is regular for $i \geq 0$. Therefore, $(L_1^*)'$ is the union of regular languages $(L_1^i)'$, for $i = 0, 1, \ldots$, and so it is regular.

In the last step of the above "proof," the rule of

$$[A, B \text{ are regular } \Rightarrow A \cup B \text{ is regular}]$$

has been illegally extended to

$$\left[A_0, A_1, A_2, \ldots \text{ are regular } \Rightarrow \bigcup_{i=0}^{\infty} A_i \text{ is regular} \right].$$

This generalized rule is false. To see this, we note that every language $L \subseteq \Sigma^*$ can be written as the union of an infinite number of regular languages: Let the elements in L be $x_0, x_1, x_2, \ldots$. Then, $L = \{x_0\} \cup \{x_1\} \cup \{x_2\} \cup \cdots$. Thus, the generalized rule would imply that *every* language is regular, which is known to be false (see Section 2.8).

Example 1.22 *Show that every regular language has a regular expression in disjunctive normal form* $\alpha_1 + \alpha_2 + \cdots + \alpha_n$, *in which each* α_i, *for* $i = 1, 2, \cdots, n$, *does not contain the operator* +.

Proof. We prove it by induction.

Basis Step (1): The empty set $\emptyset$ has a regular expression $\emptyset$ in disjunctive normal form.

Basis Step (2): For any symbol a, $\{a\}$ has a regular expression a in disjunctive normal form.

· Induction Step (3): Suppose that language L_1 has a regular expression $\alpha_1 + \alpha_2 + \cdots + \alpha_m$ in disjunctive normal form and language L_2 has a regular expression $\beta_1 + \beta_2 + \cdots + \beta_n$ in disjunctive normal form. Then,

(a) $L_1 \cup L_2$ has a regular expression $\alpha_1 + \cdots + \alpha_m + \beta_1 + \cdots + \beta_n$.

(b) $L_1 L_2$ has a regular expression $(\sum_{i=1}^{m} \alpha_i)(\sum_{j=1}^{n} \beta_j) = \sum_{i=1}^{m} \sum_{j=1}^{n} \alpha_i \beta_j$.

(c) L_1^* has a regular expression $(\sum_{i=1}^{m} \alpha_i)^* = (\alpha_1^* \alpha_2^* \cdots \alpha_m^*)^*$ (cf. Exercise 5(b) of Section 1.1).

Thus, $L_1 \cup L_2$, $L_1 L_2$, and L_1^* all can be represented by regular expressions in disjunctive normal form. This completes the induction proof. □

Exercise 1.2

1. Describe in English the languages expressed by the following regular expressions:

   (a) $(0^*1^*)^*0$.

   (b) $(01^*)^*0$.

   (c) $(00 + 11 + (01 + 10)(00 + 11)^*(01 + 10))^*$.

   (d) $0^* + (0^*1 + 0^*11)(0^+1 + 0^+11)^*0^*$.

2. Simplify the following regular expressions:

   (a) $(00)^*0 + (00)^*$.

   (b) $(0 + 1)(\varepsilon + 00)^+ + (0 + 1)$.

   (c) $(0 + \varepsilon)0^*1$.

3. Construct regular expressions for the following languages over alphabet $\{0, 1\}$:

   (a) The set of all strings whose fifth symbol from right is 0.

   (b) The set of all strings having either 000 or 111 as a substring.

   (c) The set of all strings having neither 000 nor 111 as a substring.

   (d) The set of all strings having no substring 010.

   (e) The set of all strings having an odd number of 0's.

   (f) The set of all strings having an even number of occurrences of substring 011. [*Hint:* First find the regular expression for the set of binary strings having no substring 011.]

4. Show that $(0^2 + 0^3)^* = (0^2 0^*)^*$.

5. Construct a regular expression for the set of all strings over alphabet

$$\left\{ \begin{pmatrix} 0 \\ 0 \\ 0 \end{pmatrix}, \begin{pmatrix} 1 \\ 0 \\ 0 \end{pmatrix}, \begin{pmatrix} 0 \\ 1 \\ 0 \end{pmatrix}, \begin{pmatrix} 0 \\ 0 \\ 1 \end{pmatrix}, \begin{pmatrix} 1 \\ 1 \\ 0 \end{pmatrix}, \begin{pmatrix} 1 \\ 0 \\ 1 \end{pmatrix}, \begin{pmatrix} 0 \\ 1 \\ 1 \end{pmatrix}, \begin{pmatrix} 1 \\ 1 \\ 1 \end{pmatrix} \right\}$$

that represent correct subtractions. For example,

$$
\begin{array}{r}
1\ \ 0\ \ 1\ \ 1 \\
-\ \ 0\ \ 1\ \ 0\ \ 1 \\
\hline
0\ \ 1\ \ 1\ \ 0
\end{array}
$$

implies that string

$$\begin{pmatrix} 1 \\ 0 \\ 0 \end{pmatrix} \begin{pmatrix} 0 \\ 1 \\ 1 \end{pmatrix} \begin{pmatrix} 1 \\ 0 \\ 1 \end{pmatrix} \begin{pmatrix} 1 \\ 1 \\ 0 \end{pmatrix}$$

is in the set.

6. Show that for any regular language L, $L_{odd} = \{x \in L \mid |x| = odd\}$ and $L_{even} = \{x \in L \mid |x| = even\}$ are regular.

7. Show that if L is a regular language, then $L'' = \{u \mid \exists v, uv \in L\}$ is regular.

8. Suppose $h : \Sigma^* \to \Gamma^*$ is a mapping satisfying $h(xy) = h(x)h(y)$ for any $x, y \in \Sigma^*$. Show that if A is a regular set over Σ, then $h(A) = \{h(x) \mid x \in A\}$ is a regular set over Γ. Conversely, if B is a regular set over Γ, then $h^{-1}(B) = \{x \in \Sigma^* \mid h(x) \in B\}$ is a regular set over Σ. [*Hint:* Prove by induction.]

1.3   Graph Representations for Regular Expressions

A *directed graph* (or, *digraph*) is a pair of sets (V, E) such that each element in E is an ordered pair of elements in V. The elements in V are called *vertices*, and the elements in E are called *edges*. An edge (u, v) is *directed*, meaning that it originates at u and goes to v. For this reason, (u, v) is said to be an *in-edge* to v and an *out-edge* from u. A *loop* is an edge which starts and ends at the same vertex; that is, it is both an in-edge and an out-edge for the same vertex. We often draw a diagram for a graph with a small circle representing a vertex and an arrow from circle u to circle v representing an edge (u, v). Figure 1.2 shows a digraph $G = (V, E)$ where $V = \{a, b, c, d\}$ and $E = \{(a, a), (a, b), (b, b), (b, c), (c, a), (c, d)\}$.

A *path* is a finite sequence of vertices, $(v_1, v_2, \cdots, v_k)$, such that there exists an edge from v_i to v_{i+1} for every $i = 1, 2, \cdots, k - 1$. For example, in Figure 1.2, (a, b, c, d) is a path, but (a, c, d) is not a path because no edge exists from a to c. A path starting and ending at the same vertex is called a *cycle*.

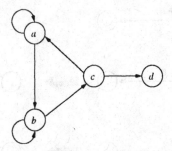

Figure 1.2: A digraph.

In some applications, we would like to assign labels to edges of a digraph. Such a digraph is called a *labeled digraph*. In general, we allow more than one edge from a vertex u to a vertex v, if they have different labels.

There is an interesting way to represent regular expressions by labeled digraphs with labels from $\Sigma \cup \{\varepsilon\}$. For any regular expression r, its labeled digraph representation can be obtained as follows:

1. Initially, we start with two special vertices, the *initial* vertex and the *final* vertex, and draw an edge between them with label r (see Figure 1.3(1)). (In Figure 1.3(1), we draw an arrow with no starting point to the initial vertex and use double circles to denote the final vertex.)

2. Repeat the following until every edge has a label that does not contain operation symbols $+$, $\cdot$, or *:

   Replace each edge with label $f + g$ by two edges with labels f and g, as shown in Figure 1.3(2).

   Replace each edge with label fg by an additional vertex and two edges with labels f and g, as shown in Figure 1.3(3).

   Replace each edge with label f^* by an additional vertex and three edges with labels ε, f, and ε, as shown in Figure 1.3(4).

3. Delete all edges with label $\emptyset$.

For a regular expression r, let $G(r)$ be its graph representation constructed as above. Clearly, each edge in $G(r)$ has a label in $\Sigma \cup \{\varepsilon\}$. Every path in $G(r)$ is associated with a string which is obtained by concatenating all symbols labeling the edges in the path. This representation has the following property:

Theorem 1.23 *Let r be a regular expression. A string x belongs to the language $L(r)$ if and only if there is a path in $G(r)$ from the initial vertex to the final vertex whose associated string is x.*

Proof. Let v_1 be the initial vertex and v_f be the final vertex in $G(r)$. Consider the following statement:

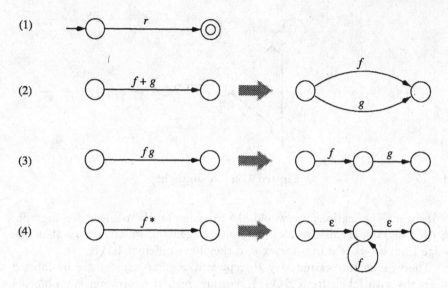

Figure 1.3: Graph $G(r)$ for regular expression r.

S: $x \in L(r)$ if and only if there is a path $(v_1, v_2, ..., v_k = v_f)$ in digraph G such that $x \in L(r_1)L(r_2)\cdots L(r_{k-1})$, where r_i is the label of the edge (v_i, v_{i+1}), $i = 1, \ldots, k-1$.

We claim that statement S holds with respect to the graph G at any stage of the above construction of $G(r)$. First, it is clear that S holds with respect to the graph G at the beginning of the step 2. Next, we observe that, because of the way the edges are replaced, if S holds with respect to a graph G, then it still holds after an edge replacement performed at step 2. Thus, the statement S holds with respect to the graph G at the end of step 2.

At step 3, we delete edges with the label $\emptyset$, and this does not affect statement S, since $L(\emptyset) = \emptyset$. Therefore, at the end of step 3, each edge of $G(r)$ is labeled by exactly one symbol from $\Sigma \cup \{\varepsilon\}$, and statement S implies that $x \in L(r)$ if and only if there is a path in $G(r)$ from v_1 to v_f whose associated string is exactly x.   □

Example 1.24 *Construct $G(r)$ for $r = (11+0)^*(00+1)^*$.*

Solution. The construction is shown in Figure 1.4.   □

In a digraph $G(r)$, an edge with label ε is called an *ε-edge*. For a regular expression r, it is often desirable to construct $G(r)$ with a minimum number of ε-edges while still preserving the property of Theorem 1.23. For instance, in Figure 1.4, the two middle ε-edges can be replaced by a single ε-edge. The following is a simple rule for eliminating redundant ε-edges:

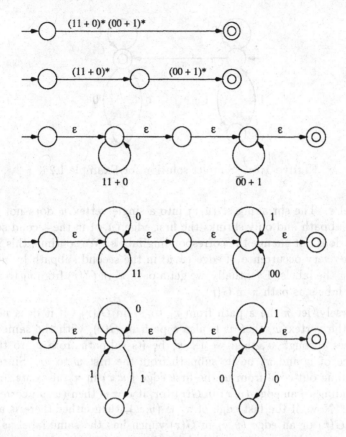

Figure 1.4: Labeled digraph $G(r)$ for $r = (11 + 0)^*(00 + 1)^*$.

★ **Theorem 1.25** *Let r be a regular expression. Then, an ε-edge (u, v) in $G(r)$ which is a unique out-edge from a nonfinal vertex u or a unique in-edge to a noninitial vertex v can be shrunk into a single vertex, still preserving the property of Theorem 1.23. (If one of the endpoints of the ε-edge is the initial vertex or the final vertex, then so is the resulting vertex.)*

Proof. To see why such an ε-edge can be deleted, suppose that an ε-edge (u, v) is the unique out-edge from u, and suppose that u is not the final vertex. Let $G'(r)$ be the graph obtained from $G(r)$ by shrinking the edge (u, v) to a single vertex w. Let v_1 be the initial vertex of $G(r)$ and v_f be the final vertex of $G(r)$. We need to show that for each path π in $G(r)$ from v_1 to v_f, there is a path π' in $G'(r)$ from v_1 to v_f with the same lables as π, and vice versa.

Let π be a path in $G(r)$ from v_1 to v_f. If it does not pass through vertex u, then the same path exists in $G'(r)$ and all their labels remain the same. If π passes through u, then we can divide it into two subpaths, one from v_1 to the first occurrence of u and the other from the first u to v_f. Since (u, v) is the only out-edge from u, the second subpath must start with this edge (u, v),

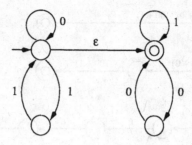

Figure 1.5:   Simpler solution for Example 1.24.

with label ε. The shrinking of (u, v) into a single vertex w does not change the first subpath and only shrinks the first edge (u, v) in the second subpath to w and does not change the corresponding labels. We continue this process to replace every occurrence of edge (u, v) in the second subpath by w, while preserving the labels. Eventually, we get a path π' in $G'(r)$ from v_1 to v_f with the same labels as path π in $G(r)$.

Conversely, let π' be a path from v_1 to v_f in $G'(r)$. If it does not pass through the vertex w, then it is also a path in $G(r)$, with the same labels. If it passes through w, then we let π'_1 be its subpath from v_1 to the first occurrence of w and π'_2 be its subpath from the first w to v_f. Since (u, v) is the unique out-edge from u, the first edge (w, x) in π'_2, if exists, must be corresponding to an edge (v, x) in $G(r)$ (or, if $x = w$ then (w, w) corresponds to (v, v)). Now, if the last edge of π'_1 is (y, w), then either there is an edge (y, u) in $G(r)$ or an edge (y, v) in $G(r)$ which has the same label as (y, w). In the first case, we replace w of π'_1 by the edge (u, v); in the second case, we simply replace the vertex w by the vertex v. Thus, we have eliminated an occurrence of w in π' without changing its total labels. We continue this process to eliminate all occurrences of w and we obatin a path π in $G(r)$ with the same total labels.

At this point, we observe that this path π must start at v_1 and end at v_f: If w is not the final vertex of $G'(r)$, then we have not changed the last vertex of π' and so π and π' end at the same vertex v_f. If w is the final vertex of $G'(r)$, then v must be the final vertex of $G(r)$, since u is known, by assumption, to be a nonfinal vertex. Our replacement process above then lets the last vertex of π be $v = v_f$. This completes the proof for the first half of the theorem. The second half can be proved by a similar argument. $\square$

As an example, we note that the solution to Example 1.24 can be simplified to that as shown in Figure 1.5. It is worth mentioning that we can only apply the rule of Theorem 1.25 to shrink ε-edges one at a time. Indeed, initially all four ε-edges in Figure 1.4 satisfy the condition for shrinking. However, not all can be deleted when we shrink them one by one.

The above simplification can also be done during the construction of $G(r)$.

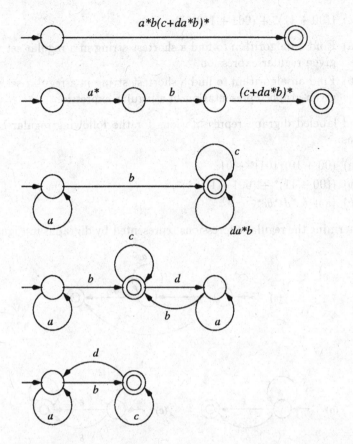

Figure 1.6: Labeled digraph $G(r)$ for $r = a^*b(c + da^*b)^*$.

In fact, if an ε-edge is a unique out-edge from a nonfinal vertex or a unique in-edge to a noninitial vertex when it is created, then it remains so after the replacements are done in the construction.

Example 1.26 *Construct $G(r)$ for $r = a^*b(c + da^*b)^*$.*

Solution. The construction is shown in Figure 1.6. Note that we made an additional simplification at the final step. $\qquad\square$

Exercise 1.3

1. What is the shortest string in each of the following languages? What is the shortest nonempty string in each language?

   (a) $10 + (0 + 11)0^*1$.

   (b) $(00 + 11 + (01 + 10)(00 + 11)^*(01 + 10))^*$.

(c) $((00+11)^* + (001+110)^*)^*$.

2. (a) Find an algorithm to find a shortest string in a regular set with a given regular expression.

    (b) Find an algorithm to find a shortest string in a regular set with a given graph representation of a regular expression.

3. Find labeled digraph representations for the following regular expressions:

    (a) $(00+10)(101)^* + 01$.
    (b) $((00+11)^* + (001+110)^*)^*$.
    (c) $(a + bc^*d)^*bc^*$.

4. Determine the regular expressions represented by digraphs in Figure 1.7.

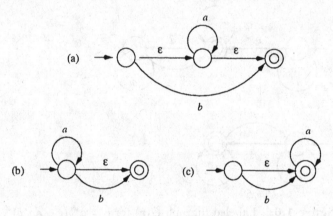

Figure 1.7: Three digraphs for Exercise 4.

5. Find the simplest digraph representing ε.

★ 6. Find counterexamples to show that Theorem 1.25 is incorrect if we remove the requirements that u must be a nonfinal vertex and v must be a noninitial vertex.

2

Finite Automata

2.1 Deterministic Finite Automata

In this section, we introduce a simple machine model, called deterministic finite automata, that will be shown later to recognize exactly the class of regular languages. Intuitively, a *deterministic finite automaton* (DFA) is a simple machine which reads an input string one letter at a time and then, after the input is completely read, decides to accept or to reject the input. A DFA consists of three parts: a tape, a tape head (or, simply, head), and a finite control.

The *tape* is used to store the input data. It is divided into a finite number of cells. Each cell holds a symbol from a given alphabet Σ. The *tape head* scans the tape, reads symbols from the tape, and passes the information to the finite control. At each move of the DFA, the head scans one cell of the tape and reads the symbol in the cell, and then moves to the next cell to the right.

The *finite control* has a finite number of *states* which form the *state set* Q. At the beginning of a move, the control is in one of the states. Then, it determines, from the current state and the symbol read by the tape head, how the state is changed to a new state. More precisely, the change of state at each move is governed by a *state transition function* (or, simply, *transition function*) $\delta : Q \times \Sigma \to Q$. At each move, if the finite control is currently at state $q \in Q$ and the symbol read by the tape head is $a \in \Sigma$, then the finite control changes to the new state $p = \delta(q, a)$.

To complete the description of a DFA, we need to specify two special kinds

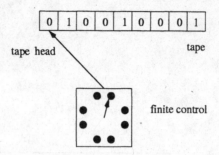

Figure 2.1: A finite automaton.

of states: an *initial state* q_0 at which the DFA begins to work, and a set $F \subseteq Q$ of *final states* at which the DFA certifies that the input is in the language. Thus, a DFA can be represented as a quintuple $M = (Q, \Sigma, \delta, q_0, F)$.

How does a DFA M work exactly? Initially, the DFA M is in the initial state, the tape holds the input string, and the tape head scans the leftmost cell of the tape. Then, the DFA M operates, move by move, according to the transition function δ. The DFA M halts after it reads the symbol in the rightmost cell of the tape and its tape head moves off the tape. When the DFA halts, it *accepts* the input string if it halts in one of the final states. Otherwise, the input string is *rejected*. The set of all strings accepted by a DFA M is denoted by $L(M)$. We also say that the language $L(M)$ is *accepted* by M.

The *transition diagram* of a DFA is an alternative way to represent the DFA. For $M = (Q, \Sigma, \delta, q_0, F)$, the transition diagram of M is a labeled digraph (V, E) satisfying

$$V = Q,$$
$$E = \{q \xrightarrow{a} p \mid p = \delta(q, a)\},$$

where $q \xrightarrow{a} p$ denotes an edge (q, p) with label a. In addition, the initial state of the DFA is pointed to by an arrow without a starting vertex, and every final state is denoted by double circles.

Example 2.1 *Consider a DFA $M = (Q, \Sigma, \delta, q_0, F)$ where $Q = \{q_0, q_1, q_2, q_3\}$, $\Sigma = \{0, 1\}$, $F = \{q_1, q_2\}$, and δ is the function defined by the following table:*

δ	0	1
q_0	q_1	q_3
q_1	q_2	q_3
q_2	q_2	q_2
q_3	q_3	q_3

Then, the transition diagram of M is as shown in Figure 2.2. (A number i in a circle or in double circles denotes the state q_i.)   □

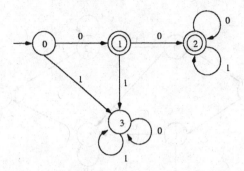

Figure 2.2:   The transition diagram of the DFA of Example 2.1.

Since the transition function δ is well-defined on $Q \times \Sigma$, the transition diagram of the DFA has the property that for every vertex (state) q and every symbol a, there exists *exacly one* edge with label a leaving q. This implies that for each string x, there exists exactly one path starting from q_0 whose labels form the string x. This path is called the *computation path* of the DFA on x. We note that a string x is accepted by M if and only if its computation path ends at one of the final states.

To formally define the notion of a DFA accepting an input string, we extend the transition function δ from the domain $Q \times \Sigma$ to the domain $Q \times \Sigma^*$ by the following inductive definition:

(1) $\delta(q, \varepsilon) = q$,

(2) For any $x \in \Sigma^*$ and $a \in \Sigma$, $\delta(q, xa) = \delta(\delta(q, x), a)$.

With this extension, for any string x, $\delta(q_0, x)$ is the last state in the computation path of the string x. Therefore, we can formally define that $x \in L(M)$ if and only if $\delta(q_0, x) \in F$; that is,

$$L(M) = \{x \in \Sigma^* \mid \delta(q_0, x) \in F\}.$$

Example 2.2 *Consider the DFA M given by Figure 2.2. Determine whether M accepts strings* 000 *and* 010.

Solution. The computation path of the string 000 is the sequence $q_0, \delta(q_0, 0) = q_1, \delta(q_1, 0) = q_2$, and $\delta(q_2, 0) = q_2$. Thus, $\delta(q_0, 000) = q_2 \in F$ and M accepts 000. Similarly, we can find that $\delta(q_0, 010) = q_3 \notin F$, and M rejects 010. □

Example 2.3 *What is the language $L(M)$ accepted by the DFA M of Figure 2.2?*

Solution. We observe that once the DFA M enters state q_3, it will never be able to leave this state, and will reject the input string regardless what the remaining part of the input string is. (We call such a state a *failure* state.) On the other hand, once M enters state q_2, it will never leave this state, and

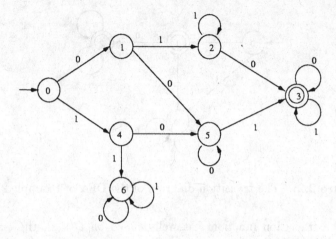

Figure 2.3:   DFA of Example 2.4.

will accept the input string. (We call such a state a *success* state.) From these observations, we see that $L(M)$ consists of the string 0 (which ends at state q_1) and all strings starting with 00. In the regular expression notation,

$$L(M) = 0 + 00(0 + 1)^*.$$ □

Example 2.4 *What is the language $L(M)$ accepted by the DFA M of Figure 2.3?*

Solution. Similar to Example 2.3, q_6 is a failure state and q_3 is a success state. So, we only need to figure out how we can reach q_3 from q_0. There are three kinds of paths from q_0 to q_3:

$$(q_0, q_1, q_2, \ldots, q_2, q_3),$$
$$(q_0, q_1, q_5, \ldots, q_5, q_3),$$
$$(q_0, q_4, q_5, \ldots, q_5, q_3).$$

They correspond with strings beginning with 011^*0, 000^*1 and 100^*1, respectively. So,

$$L(M) = (011^*0 + 000^*1 + 100^*1)(0 + 1)^*.$$ □

Example 2.5 *What is the language $L(M)$ accepted by the DFA M of Figure 2.4?*

Solution. A string x accepted by M is either in 0^* (so, M never leaves state q_0), or is associated with a computation cycle from q_0 to q_0, passing through states q_1, q_2, q_3, q_4 for a finite number of times. Note that the DFA M changes from a state q_i, $0 \le i \le 3$, to a new state q_{i+1} (or from q_4 to q_0) if and only if it reads a symbol 1. Thus, each time M goes from state q_0 to states $q_1, \ldots, q_4$

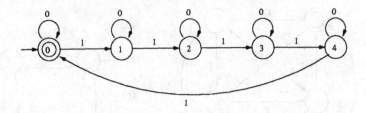

Figure 2.4: DFA of Example 2.5.

then comes back to q_0, it must have read five 1's, with an arbitrary number of 0's in between any two 1's. This means that a string x is accepted by M if and only if the number of occurrences of symbol 1 in x is a multiple of 5. In the form of a regular expression,

$$L(M) = 0^*(10^*10^*10^*10^*10^*)^*.$$ □

Exercise 2.1

1. Consider the DFA M with the transition diagram of Figure 2.5.

   (a) Which state is the initial state of M, and which states are the final states of M?

   (b) For each of the strings 0001, 010101, and 001110101101, find the computation path of M on the string and determine whether M accepts it.

   (c) Among all strings in $(01)^*$, which ones are in $L(M)$?

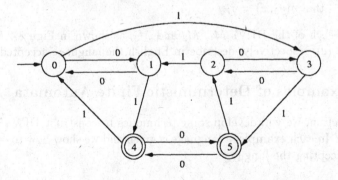

Figure 2.5: DFA of Exercise 1.

2. For integers $n, d \geq 1$, consider a DFA $M_{n,d} = (Q, \Sigma, \delta, q_0, F)$, where $Q = \{q_0, q_1, q_2, \cdots, q_{n-1}\}$, $\Sigma = \{a_0, a_1, \cdots, a_{d-1}\}$, $\delta(q_i, a_k) = q_{(di+k) \bmod n}$, and $F = \{q_1\}$.

   (a) Draw the transition diagram of $M_{n,d}$ with $n = 7$ and $d = 2$.

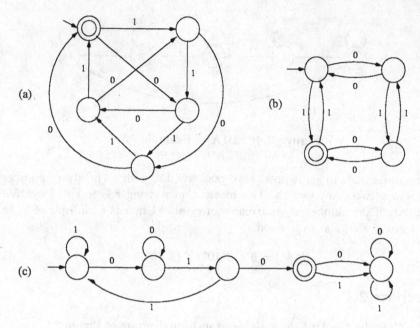

Figure 2.6:   Three DFA's of Exercise 3.

  (b) Suppose $n = 7$, $d = 2$, $a_0 = 0$ and $a_1 = 1$. Find $\delta(q_3, 0101)$ and
      $\delta(q_1, 11010)$.

  (c) Suppose $n = 7$, $d = 2$, $a_0 = 0$ and $a_1 = 1$. Find binary strings x
      and y such that $\delta(q_0, x) = q_5$ and $\delta(q_0, y) = q_6$.

$\star$(d) Show that for any state $q_j \in Q$, there exists a string $x \in \Sigma^*$ such
      that $\delta(q_0, x) = q_j$.

 3. For each of the DFA's M_1, M_2 and M_3, as shown in Figure 2.6(a), (b)
    and (c), respectively, describe in English the language accepted by it.

2.2   Examples of Deterministic Finite Automata

In this section, we will develop some techniques to construct DFA's through
examples. In each example, a language is given and we show how to construct
a DFA accepting the language.

Example 2.6 $(0 + 1)^*$.

Solution. The language $(0 + 1)^*$ contains all binary strings. So, we simply
let the initial state be the final success state. The transition diagram of this
DFA is actually the same as the labeled digraph representation for the regular
expression $(0 + 1)^*$. We show it in Figure 2.7(a). (In a transition diagram, if
two edges have the same starting and ending vertices, we may merge them into

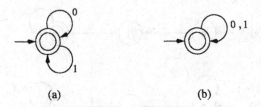

(a)   (b)

Figure 2.7: DFA for $(0+1)^*$.

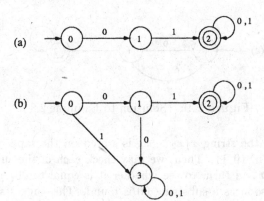

Figure 2.8: Solution to Example 2.7.

one edge and put both labels on the new edge. For instance, the transition diagram of Figure 2.7(a) can be simplified to that of Figure 2.7(b).)   □

Example 2.7 *The set of all binary strings beginning with prefix* 01.

Solution. It is easy to find a regular expression $01(0+1)^*$ for this language. From the regular expression, we can immediately find its labeled digraph representation as shown in Figure 2.8(a). However, it is not the transition diagram of a DFA. Recall that in the transition diagram of a DFA $M = (Q, \Sigma, \delta, q_0, F)$, there is *exactly one* out-edge from state q with label a for each pair of $(q, a) \in Q \times \Sigma$. To satisfy this condition, we add a failure state q_3 and edges $q_0 \xrightarrow{1} q_3$ and $q_1 \xrightarrow{0} q_3$. The complete transition diagram is shown in Figure 2.8(b).   □

Example 2.8 *The set of all binary strings having a substring* 00.

Solution. First, let us note that the regular expression $(0+1)^*00(0+1)^*$ for this set does not indicate where the first pair 00 occurs in the string. On the other hand, the DFA must recognize the substring 00 at its first occurrence. Thus, the above regular expression is not helpful to this problem. Instead, we need to analyze the problem more carefully.

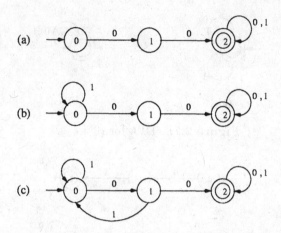

Figure 2.9: Solution to Example 2.8.

Suppose that the string $x_1 x_2 \cdots x_n$ is stored on the tape, where each x_i denotes one bit in $\{0, 1\}$. Then, we may check each of the substrings $x_1 x_2$, $x_2 x_3$, ..., $x_{n-1} x_n$ in turn, to see whether it is equal to 00, and accept the input string as soon as a substring 00 is found. This suggests the following way to construct the required DFA.

Step 1. Build a checker as shown in Figure 2.9(a), with state q_2 being a success state, meaning that if two consecutive 0's are found then the input string is to be accepted. In particular, if $x_1 x_2 = 00$, the the string x is accepted.

Step 2. If $x_1 = 1$, then we give up on substring $x_1 x_2$ and continue to check $x_2 x_3$. So, we need to go back to state q_0; that is, $\delta(q_0, 1) = q_0$. This action is shown in Figure 2.9(b).

Step 3. If $x_1 = 0$ and $x_2 = 1$, then neither $x_1 x_2$ nor $x_2 x_3$ is 00. So, we also need to go back to restart at q_0 to check $x_3 x_4$. That is, we let $\delta(q_1, 1) = q_0$. Figure 2.9(c) shows the complete DFA.   □

In general, suppose that $x_1 x_2 \cdots x_n$ is the string on the tape and we want to check $x_1 \cdots x_k$, $x_2 \cdots x_{k+1}$, ..., $x_{n-k+1} \cdots x_n$ in turn to match a substring $a_1 a_2 \cdots a_k$. Then, we set up $k + 1$ states $q_0, q_1, \ldots, q_k$, with q_i standing for "found $a_1 a_2 \ldots a_i$." At state q_i, if $b = a_{i+1}$, then we define $\delta(q_i, b) = q_{i+1}$. If $b \neq a_{i+1}$, then we define $\delta(q_i, b) = q_j$, where j is the maximum index j such that

$$a_{i-j+2} a_{i-j+3} \cdots a_i b = a_1 a_2 \cdots a_j.$$

That is, we find the longest suffix y of $a_1 \cdots a_i b$ which is a prefix of $a_1 \cdots a_k$ and go to $q_{|y|}$. The following example explains this idea more clearly.

Example 2.9 *The set of all binary strings having the substring* 00101.

Solution. Following the above idea, we first construct a checker as shown in Figure 2.10(a).

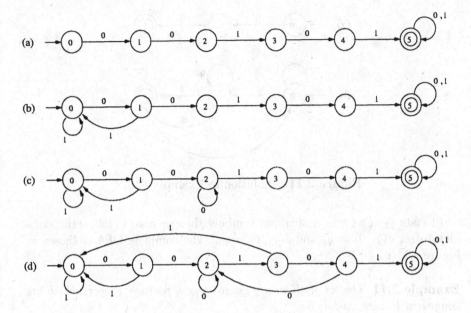

Figure 2.10: Solution to Example 2.9.

Intuitively, for each $i = 0, 1, \ldots, 5$, state q_i means "the past i input symbols just read are $a_1 a_2 \cdots a_i$," where $a_1 a_2 \cdots a_5$ is the target substring 00101. Thus, at state q_0, if we read a new symbol 1, the new string $a_1 \cdots a_i 1 = 1$ (here, $i = 0$) is not a prefix of 00101, and so we need to go back to state q_0. Similarly, if a symbol 1 is read at state q_1, neither the string $a_1 1 = 11$ nor the string 1 is a prefix of 00101, and so we let $\delta(q_1, 1) = q_0$. We upgrade the DFA as shown in Figure 2.10(b).

Now, consider $\delta(q_2, 0)$. The string $a_1 a_2 0 = 000$ is not a prefix of 00101, but the last two symbols $a_2 0 = 00$ *is* a prefix of 00101. That is, if the next three input symbols are 1, 0 and 1, then we should accept the input. So, we define $\delta(q_2, 0) = q_2$ to indicate this partial success. This action is shown in Figure 2.10(c).

Based on the same idea, we define $\delta(q_3, 1) = q_0$ (neither $a_1 a_2 a_3 1 = 0011$ nor any of its suffixes is a prefix of 00101), and $\delta(q_4, 0) = q_2$ (the last two bits of $a_1 a_2 a_3 a_4 0$ are 00 and form a prefix of 00101). The complete DFA is shown in Figure 2.10(d). □

Example 2.10 *The set A of all binary strings ending with 01.*

Solution. Initially, we build a checker as shown in Figure 2.11(a). Again, states q_0 and q_1 indicate "found no prefix of 01" and "found prefix 0 of 01," respectively. Note, however, that although state q_2 is a final state, it is *not* a success state since a string must *end* at state q_2 to be accepted.

Now, following the idea of the last example, it is easy to see that we need to define $\delta(q_0, 1) = q_0$ and $\delta(q_1, 0) = q_1$.

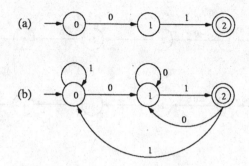

Figure 2.11: Solution to Example 2.10.

At state q_2, if we read more input symbols, then we need to follow the same idea to set $\delta(q_2, 0) = q_1$ and $\delta(q_2, 1) = q_0$. The complete DFA is shown in Figure 2.11(b). □

Example 2.11 *The set of all binary expansions of positive integers which are congruent to zero modulo 5.*

Solution. The idea of this DFA is similar to that of the last two examples. We need to set up five states $q_0, q_1, \ldots, q_4$, with each state q_i meaning "the prefix y of the input string read so far has the property of $y \equiv i \pmod 5$." That is, we need to define $\delta(q_0, x_1 x_2 \cdots x_k) = q_i$ if $x_1 x_2 \cdots x_k \equiv i \pmod 5$.

How do we determine the edges between these five states from this idea? Recall that the transition function δ of a DFA has to satisfy

$$\delta(\delta(q_0, x), a) = \delta(q_0, xa),$$

for any $x \in \{0, 1\}^*$ and any $a \in \{0, 1\}$. Suppose $\delta(q_0, x) = q_i$ and $\delta(q_0, xa) = q_j$. Then, we must have $x \equiv i \pmod 5$ and $xa \equiv j \pmod 5$. Thus,

$$
\begin{aligned}
j &\equiv xa \pmod 5 \\
&\equiv 2 \cdot x + a \pmod 5 \\
&\equiv 2 \cdot i + a \pmod 5.
\end{aligned}
$$

Therefore, we need to define $\delta(q_i, a) = q_j$, where $j \equiv 2i + a \pmod 5$. For instance, $\delta(q_2, 0) = q_4$ and $\delta(q_2, 1) = q_0$. See Figure 2.12 for the other edges. In addition, state q_0 is the unique final state, since $\delta(q_0, x) = q_0$ means $x \equiv 0 \pmod 5$.

Finally, we note that a binary expansion of a positive integer always begins with the symbol 1. So, we need to add a new initial state and a failure state, as shown in Figure 2.12. □

Note that the set $A \cup \{1\}$, where A is the set defined in Example 2.10, may be regarded as the set of binary expansions of integers congruent to 1 modulo

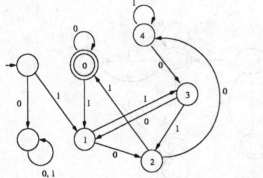

Figure 2.12: DFA for Example 2.11.

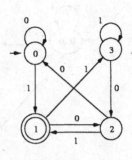

Figure 2.13: DFA for set $A \cup \{1\}$.

4, with leading zeros allowed. Using the idea of the above example, we get a new DFA for set $A \cup \{1\}$ as shown in Figure 2.13. Note that the states q_0 and q_2 in this DFA can be merged into one, and the simplifed DFA is just the one shown in Figure 2.11(b), except that the initial state has been changed (to state q_1 of Figure 2.11(b)).

Example 2.12 *The set of all binary strings having a substring* 00 *or ending with* 01.

Solution. This language is the union of two languges $(0 + 1)^*00(0 + 1)^*$ and $(0+1)^*01$. In Examples 2.8 and 2.10, we have already constructed two DFA's for these two languages. To check whether an input string x belongs to the union of these two languages, we can run these two DFA's in parallel. For example, suppose $x = 0101$. In the first DFA M_1 shown in Figure 2.9(c), the computation path of x is $(q_0, q_1, q_0, q_1, q_0)$, and in the second DFA M_2 in Figure 2.11(b), the computation path is $(q_0, q_1, q_2, q_1, q_2)$. Since the second path ends at a final state, x is accepted in this parallel simulation.

One idea on how to build a DFA for the union of these two languages is, then, to combine the two DFA's into one such that, at each step, the new DFA would keep track of the computation paths of both DFA's. This suggests us to consider a *product automaton* $M = M_1 \times M_2$ as follows: Assume that the first DFA is $M_1 = (Q_1, \Sigma, \delta_1, q_0, F_1)$ and the second DFA is $M_2 = (Q_2, \Sigma, \delta_2, q_0, F_2)$. (Note that Q_1 and Q_2 may have states of the same name but playing different roles in two DFA's.) Then, the state set Q of M is the cross product of the state sets of M_1 and M_2; that is, $Q = Q_1 \times Q_2$. We denote each member of Q as $[q_i, q_j]$, where $q_i \in Q_1$ and $q_j \in Q_2$. The initial state of M is $[q_0, q_0]$. At each state $[q_i, q_j]$ in Q, we simulate both computations of M_1 and M_2 in parallel by

$$\delta([q_i, q_j], a) = [\delta_1(q_i, a), \delta_2(q_j, a)].$$

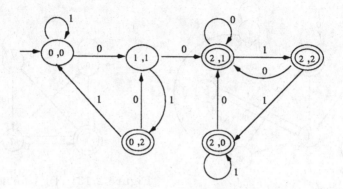

Figure 2.14: Product DFA for Example 2.12.

For instance, the computation path of $x = 0101$ in this product automaton is $[q_0, q_0], [q_1, q_1], [q_0, q_2], [q_1, q_1], [q_0, q_2]$. Furthermore, if $q_i \in F_1$ or $q_j \in F_2$, then we let $[q_i, q_j] \in F$. That is, $F = (F_1 \times Q_2) \cup (Q_1 \times F_2)$.

From the above description, it is clear that M accepts the union of the DFA's M_1 and M_2. We show this product DFA M in Figure 2.14, where each vertex with the label (i, j) denotes the state $[q_i, q_j]$.

Two facts about this DFA are worth mentioning: First, since states $[q_0, q_1]$, $[q_1, q_0]$ and $[q_1, q_2]$ are unreachable from the initial state $[q_0, q_0]$, we omitted them in Figure 2.14. Second, states $[q_2, q_1]$, $[q_2, q_0]$ and $[q_2, q_2]$ can be merged into a single success state, since all three states are final states and there is no way to leave these three states once we get there. There are some general techniques of simplifying DFA's. We will discuss these techniques in Section 2.7.   □

The above method can also be applied to the problems of finding the intersections or the differences of two languages which are accepted by DFA's. All we need is to construct the product DFA of the two given DFA's and choose different sets of final states. This method can also be generalized to construct the product DFA of three, four, or any finite number of DFA's.

Example 2.13 *The set of all binary strings having a substring* 00 *and ending with* 01.

Solution 1. This language is the intersection of two languages $(0+1)^*00(0+1)^*$ and $(0+1)^*01$. In Example 2.12, we constructed a product DFA to accept the union of these two languages. Here, we can use the same product DFA, except that we will define the set F of final states to consist of states in which both components are final states; that is, $F = F_1 \times F_2$. The transition diagram of the resulting DFA is just like that of Figure 2.14, except that the final set consists of only one state $[q_2, q_2]$.   □

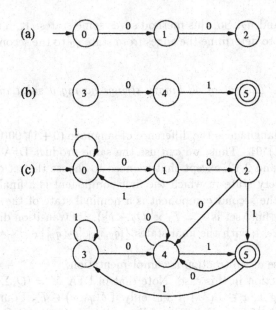

Figure 2.15: The second solution to Example 2.13.

Solution 2. We can also use the *checker* method of Example 2.8 to construct a DFA for this set. First, we note that if a string x has a substring 00 and a suffix 01, then the occurrence of 00 must come before that of 01. So, we set up the two checkers as shown in Figure 2.15(a) and 2.15(b). Intuitively, states q_0, q_1 and q_2 are like those in Figure 2.9. State q_3 means that "substring 00 has been found and no prefix of 01 is found," and state q_4 means that "substring 00 has been found and prefix 0 of 01 has also been found." Note that the out-edges from state q_2 are not determined yet, since finding the substring 00 does not imply the string being accepted.

Now we add additional edges to the checkers as in Examples 2.8 and 2.10. It is easy to see that we need to define $\delta(q_0, 1) = \delta(q_1, 1) = q_0$, since we are still at the first stage of checking substring 00.

Next, we have $\delta(q_2, 1) = q_5$, which is a final state, since, at state q_2, we have just seen a substring 00 and the second 0 plus the new symbol 1 form the required suffix 01. We also let $\delta(q_2, 0) = q_4$, since q_4 is the state at which stubstring 00 has been found *and* a symbol 0 has just been read.

The actions at states q_3, q_4 and q_5 are just like those in Figure 2.11. That is, we add

$$\delta(q_3, 1) = q_3, \quad \delta(q_4, 0) = q_4,$$
$$\delta(q_5, 0) = q_4, \quad \delta(q_5, 1) = q_3.$$

The complete DFA is shown in Figure 2.15(c).

Note that, in Solution 1, the number of states in the product DFA M is, in general, the product of the number n_1 of states in M_1 and the number n_2 of states in M_2. In Solution 2 here, the number of states is, in general, only the sum of n_1 and n_2. So, this method saves some states. It, however, needs some heuristics to determine the edges from state q_2 to the second part of the DFA.   □

Example 2.14 *The set of all binary strings having a substring* 00 *but not ending with* 01.

Solution. This language is the difference of language $(0+1)^*00(0+1)^*$ minus language $(0+1)^*01$. Thus, we can use the same product DFA as we did in Examples 2.12 and 2.13, except that we need to choose the set of final states to consist of every state in which the first component is a final state of the first DFA and the second component is a nonfinal state of the second DFA; that is, our new final set is $F = F_1 \times (Q_2 - F_2)$. Its transition diagram is like that of Figure 2.14, with the final states $\{[q_2, q_0], [q_2, q_1]\}$.   □

A special case of subtraction is complementation: $\overline{A} = \Sigma^* - A$. There is a simpler construction in this case. Note that in DFA $M = (Q, \Sigma, \delta, q_0, F)$, for any input string x, $x \in L(M)$ if and only if $\delta(q_0, x) \in F$. Equivalently, $x \notin L(M)$ if and only if $\delta(q_0, x) \notin F$. It follows that the DFA $(Q, \Sigma, \delta, q_0, Q - F)$ accepts the complement of $L(M)$.

Example 2.15 *The set L of all binary strings in which every block of four consecutive symbols contains a substring* 01.

Solution. The condition "every block of four consecutive symbols contains a substring 01" is a *global* condition, which appears difficult to verify. By considering the complement $\overline{L}$, we turn this condition into a simpler *local* condition: $\overline{L}$ contains binary strings with a substring 0000, 1000, 1100, 1110, or 1111. We first construct a DFA accepting $\overline{L}$ and then change all final states into nonfinal states and all nonfinal states into final states. A solution is shown in Figure 2.16.   □

The above four examples established the following properties of the class of languages accepted by DFA's.

Theorem 2.16 *The class of languages accepted by DFA's is closed under union, intersecton, subtraction, and complementation.*

Exercise 2.2

1. For each of the following languages, construct a DFA that accepts the language:

   (a) The set of binary strings beginning with 010.
   (b) The set of binary strings ending with 101.
   (c) The set of binary strings beginning with 10 and ending with 01.

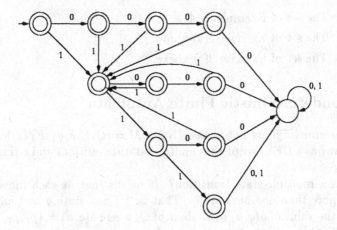

Figure 2.16: Solution to Example 2.15.

(d) The set of binary strings having a substring 010 or 101.

(e) The set of binary strings in which the last five symbols contain at most three 0's.

(f) The set of binary strings w in which $\#_1(w) + 2\#_0(w)$ is divisible by 5, where $\#_a(w)$ is the number of occurrences of the symbol a in string w.

(g) The set of strings over the alphabet $\{1, 2, 3\}$ in which the sum of all symbols is divisible by 5.

(h) The set of strings over the alphabet $\{0, 1, 2\}$ which are the ternary expansions (base-3 representations) of positive integers which are congruent to 2 modulo 7.

(i) The set of binary strings in which every block of four symbols contains at least two 0's.

(j) The set of binary strings in which every substring 010 is followed immediately by substring 111.

2. For each of the following languages, use the product automaton method to construct a DFA that accepts the language:

   (a) The set of binary strings beginning with 010 or ending with 101.

   (b) The set of binary strings having a substring 010 but not having a substring 101.

   (c) The set of binary strings beginning with 010, ending with 101 and having a substring 0000.

3. For each of the following languages, use the *checker method* to construct a DFA that accepts the language:

   (a) The set of Example 2.12.

(b) The set of Example 2.14.

(c) The set of Exercise 2(a) above.

(d) The set of Exercise 2(c) above.

2.3 Nondeterministic Finite Automata

A *nondeterministic finite automaton* (NFA) $M = (Q, \Sigma, \delta, q_0, F)$ is defined in the same way as a DFA except that multiple-state transitions and ε-transitions are allowed.

What is a multiple-state transition? It means that at each move, there could be more than one next state. That is, for any state q and any input symbol a, the value of $\delta(q, a)$ is a subset of Q, where $\delta(q, a) = \{p_1, p_2, \ldots, p_k\}$ means that the next state from state q, after reading a, can be any one of p_1, p_2, ..., or p_k. A special case is that $\delta(q, a)$ could be the empty set $\emptyset$. This means that the machine has no next state and *hangs*, and the input is rejected regardless of what remaining input symbols are. It is the equivalent of going to a *failure* state in a DFA.

In addition to multiple-state transitions, we also allow ε-transitions (or, ε-moves) in an NFA. An ε-transition is a move in which the tape head does not do anything (it neither reads nor moves), but the state can be changed. In other words, we allow a transition like $\delta(q, \varepsilon) = \{p_1, ..., p_k\}$, which means that state q can be changed to any one of p_1, p_2, ..., or p_k, without reading a symbol from the input.

Therefore, the transition function δ is, formally, a function of the form

$$\delta : Q \times (\Sigma \cup \{\varepsilon\}) \to 2^Q,$$

where 2^Q denotes the collection of all subsets of Q. The following is an example of a transition function of an NFA M_1:

$\delta(q, a)$	0	1	ε
q_0	$\emptyset$	$\{q_0, q_1\}$	$\{q_1\}$
q_1	$\{q_2\}$	$\{q_1, q_2\}$	$\emptyset$
q_2	$\{q_2\}$	$\emptyset$	$\{q_1\}$

NFA's, like DFA's, can also be represented by transition diagrams. In the transition diagram, we still use a vertex to represent a state and a labeled edge to represent a move, except that we allow multiple edges from one vertex to other vertices with the same label. That is, if $\delta(q, a) = \{p_1, p_2, \ldots, p_k\}$, then we draw k edges from state q to each of $p_1, p_2, \ldots, p_k$, and each with a label a. For instance, the transition diagram of the transition function of M_1 above is as shown in Figure 2.17. (We also made $F = \{q_2\}$.)

On an input x, an NFA may have more than one computation path. For instance, for NFA M_1 shown in Figure 2.17, the input 01 has the following

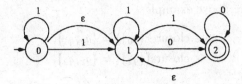

Figure 2.17: The transition diagram of an NFA.

three computation paths:

$$q_0 \xrightarrow{\varepsilon} q_1 \xrightarrow{0} q_2 \xrightarrow{\varepsilon} q_1 \xrightarrow{1} q_1,$$
$$q_0 \xrightarrow{\varepsilon} q_1 \xrightarrow{0} q_2 \xrightarrow{\varepsilon} q_1 \xrightarrow{1} q_2,$$
$$q_0 \xrightarrow{\varepsilon} q_1 \xrightarrow{0} q_2 \xrightarrow{\varepsilon} q_1 \xrightarrow{1} q_2 \xrightarrow{\varepsilon} q_1.$$

Note that in the last two paths, after the NFA reads all input symbols 01, it can choose to halt in state q_2 or to use the ε-move to move to state q_1.

In general, the computation paths for an input x form a *computation tree* since they all start with the same state q_0 and then branch out to different states. Figure 2.18 shows the computation tree of the NFA M_1 on input 01. (In Figure 2.18, we added an edge $q_2 \xrightarrow{\varepsilon} q_2$ to indicate that the second path ends at q_2.)

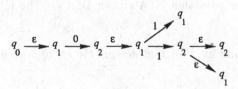

Figure 2.18: The computation tree of input 01.

Some of these computation paths lead to final states and some do not. How do we define the notion of an NFA accetping an input in such a situation? The answer is that the NFA accepts an input x if *at least* one computation path on x leads to a final state. For instance, in the above example, since the second computation path ends at state $q_2 \in F$ after the NFA reads the input 01, the string 01 is accepted by the NFA M_1.

To formally define the notion of an NFA M accepting an input x, we need to define the notion of ε-*closure*. The ε-closure of a subset $A \subseteq Q$ is the set of states that can be reached from a state q in A by ε-moves (including the move from q to q). That is,

$$\varepsilon\text{-closure}(A) = \{p \in Q \mid p \in A \text{ or } (\exists q_0, q_1, \ldots, q_m)\, [q_0 \in A,$$
$$q_m = p, \text{ and } q_{i+1} \in \delta(q_i, \varepsilon), i = 0, \ldots, m-1]\}.$$

For instance, in the above example,

$$\varepsilon\text{-closure}(\{q_0\}) = \{q_0, q_1\},$$
$$\varepsilon\text{-closure}(\{q_2\}) = \{q_1, q_2\}.$$

Now, we extend the transition function δ to the domain $2^Q \times (\Sigma \cup \{\varepsilon\})$ by

$$\delta(A, a) = \varepsilon\text{-closure}\left(\bigcup_{q \in \varepsilon\text{-closure}(A)} \delta(q, a) \right),$$

and then further extend it to the domain $2^Q \times \Sigma^*$ as follows:

$$\delta(A, \varepsilon) = \varepsilon\text{-closure}(A),$$
$$\delta(A, xa) = \delta(\delta(A, x), a), \quad \text{if } x \in \Sigma^* \text{ and } a \in \Sigma.$$

For instance, in the above example, we have $\delta(\{q_0\}, 0) = \{q_1, q_2\}$, and $\delta(\{q_1, q_2\}, 1) = \{q_1, q_2\}$. Therefore, $\delta(\{q_0\}, 01) = \{q_1, q_2\}$. Note that $\delta(\{q_0\}, x)$ is the set of all leaves in all computation paths of x.

We can now formally define that an NFA $M = (Q, \Sigma, \delta, q_0, F)$ *accepts input* x if $\delta(\{q_0\}, x) \cap F \neq \emptyset$. For an NFA M, we let $L(M)$ denote the set of all strings accepted by M; that is

$$L(M) = \{x \in \Sigma^* \mid \delta(\{q_0\}, x) \cap F \neq \emptyset\}.$$

It is often easier to design NFA's than DFA's. The following are some examples.

Example 2.17 *Find an NFA that accepts the set of binary strings having a substring* 010.

Solution. We show the NFA M in Figure 2.19. Note that it is just the checker for substring 010 plus two loops from state q_0 to q_0 with labels 0 and 1. These two loops allow the machine to *wait* until it successfully checks the substring 010. With these two *waiting* loops, we do not need to define $\delta(q_1, 0) = q_1$ and $\delta(q_2, 1) = q_0$, as we did in a DFA. Instead, we simply let $\delta(q_1, 0) = \delta(q_2, 1) = \emptyset$.

We also show, in Figure 2.20, the *computation tree* of M on input $x = 1001010$. Note that there are two occurrences of 010 in x and so there are two different accepting paths for x. $\qquad\square$

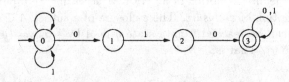

Figure 2.19: NFA for Example 2.17.

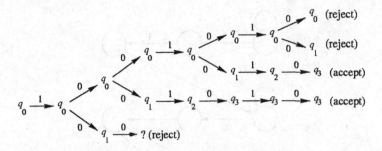

Figure 2.20: The computation tree of input 1001010.

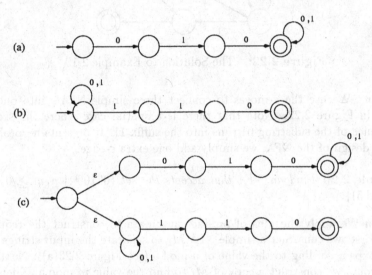

Figure 2.21: Solution to Example 2.18.

Example 2.18 *Find an NFA that accepts the set of binary strings beginning with* 010 *or ending with* 110.

Solution. The set of binary strings beginning with 010 is accepted by the NFA of Figure 2.21(a). The set of binary strings ending with 110 is accepted by the NFA of Figure 2.21(b). Note that the final state q_3 has no outlet; that is, $\delta(q_3, 0) = \delta(q_3, 1) = \emptyset$. So, if a computation path of a string x reaches state q_3 before x is completely read, it is a *rejecting* path (but that does not imply that x is rejected).

Now, we combine these two NFA's by adding an initial state and two ε-edges to the two old initial states to form the final NFA, as shown in Figure 2.21(c).   □

Example 2.19 *Find an NFA that accepts the set of binary strings with at least two occurrences of substring* 01 *and ends with* 11.

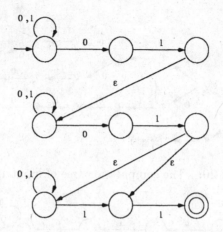

Figure 2.22:   The Solution to Example 2.19.

Solution. We use the ε-moves to connect three simple NFA's into one, as shown in Figure 2.22. Note that there is a special case where the second occurrence of the substring 01 runs into the suffix 11. It presents no problem for the design of the NFA; we simply add one extra ε-edge.   □

Example 2.20 *Find an NFA that accepts the set* $\{0^n 10^m \mid n, m \geq 0, n \equiv m \pmod 5\}$.

Solution We apply the idea of product automata to construct the required NFA. First, we construct a simple NFA M_1 to separate the input strings into five groups according to the value of n mod 5 (see Figure 2.23(a)). Next, for each group, we construct a copy of M_1 to find the value m mod 5. Then, we assign final states to each copy of M_1 accordingly. Figure 2.23(b) shows the complete DFA.   □

In Section 2.2, we have seen how to construct a DFA to accept the union or the intersection of the languages accepted by two given DFA's. Can we do this for NFA's? It is actually easier, as demonstrated by Example 2.18, to construct an NFA to accept the union of the languages accepted by two given NFA's. In addition, the following examples show that for given NFA's M_1 and M_2, it is easy to construct NFA's to accept $L(M_1) \cdot L(M_2)$ and $L(M_1)^*$. On the other hand, there is no simple way to construct an NFA for the intersection or the difference of $L(M_1)$ and $L(M_2)$ from two given NFA's M_1 and M_2.

Example 2.21 *Let M_1 and M_2 be two NFA's. Construct an NFA M such that $L(M) = L(M_1) \cdot L(M_2)$.*

Solution. Let $M_1 = (Q_1, \Sigma, \delta_1, q_0^1, F_1)$ and $M_2 = (Q_2, \Sigma, \delta_2, q_0^2, F_2)$ be two NFA's. We construct NFA M as follows: we make a copy of each of M_1 and M_2. Then, we let the initial state q_0^1 of M_1 be the initial state of M and let

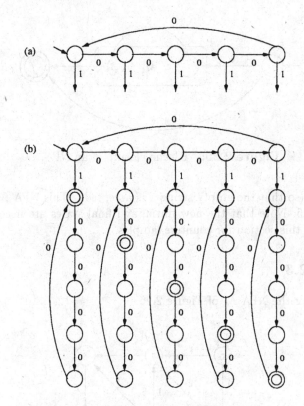

Figure 2.23: Solution to Example 2.20.

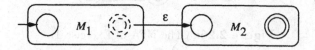

Figure 2.24: Concatenation of two NFA's.

the set F of the final states of M be equal to F_2. We also add an ε-move from each state q in F_1 to the initial state q_0^2 of M_2. We show the construction in Figure 2.24. For convenience, we only show one final state for each of M_1 and M_2. □

Example 2.22 *Let M_1 be an NFA. Construct an NFA M such that $L(M) = L(M_1)^*$.*

Solution. Let $M_1 = (Q_1, \Sigma, \delta_1, q_0, F_1)$ be an NFA. We construct M by adding a new initial state s and a unique final state f. Then, we add an ε-move from s to the initial state q_0 of M_1 and an ε-move from each $q_i \in F_1$ to the new final state f. We also add, from each state $q_i \in F_1$, an ε-move to the initial state q_0 of M_1. Finally, we add an ε-move from the initial state s to the new

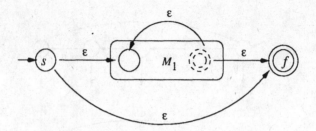

Figure 2.25:   Kleene closure of an NFA.

final state f (so that the empty string ε is accepted). This NFA M is shown in Figure 2.25. Note that the new initial and final states are necessary. See Exercise 4 of this section for counterexamples.   □

Exercise 2.3

1. Consider the NFA M of Figure 2.26.

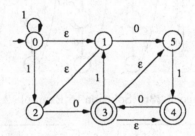

Figure 2.26:   The NFA of Exercise 1.

(a) What are ε-closure($\{q_0\}$) and ε-closure($\{q_1, q_2, q_3\}$)?

(b) What are $\delta(\{q_0\}, 0)$ and $\delta(\{q_2, q_3\}, 1)$?

(c) Draw the computation trees of M on strings $x = 011$ and $y = 101$. Does M accept or reject x and y?

2. For each NFA M shown in Figure 2.27, determine what $L(M)$ is.

3. For each of the following languages, construct an NFA that accepts the language:

(a) The set of binary strings that contain at least three occurrences of substring 010.

(b) The set of binary strings that contain both substrings 010 and 101. [*Hint*: This is equivalent to the set of binary strings that contain *either* a substring 0101 *or* a substring 1010 *or* a substring 010 followed by 101 *or* a substring 101 followed by 010.]

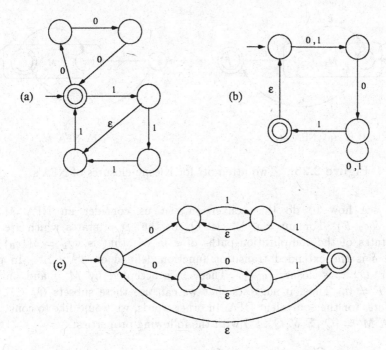

Figure 2.27: Three NFA's of Exercise 2.

(c) The set of binary strings that contain either a substring 010 or a substring 101, and end with 111 or 000.

(d) The set of binary strings of which the $(3n)$th symbol is 0 for each $n \geq 1$.

(e) The set of binary strings x of length $3n$ for some $n \geq 1$, such that, for each $1 \leq k \leq n$, at least one of the $(3k-2)$nd, $(3k-1)$st and $(3k)$th symbols of x is 0.

(f) The set $\{0^n 10^m 10^q \mid q \equiv nm \pmod 5\}$.

4. Prove that the new initial state s and the final state f in the construction of Example 2.22 are necessary. That is, find NFA's M_1 and M_2 such that the NFA's M_1' and M_2' of Figure 2.28 have the property $L(M_1') \neq L(M_1)^*$ and $L(M_2') \neq L(M_2)^*$.

2.4   Converting an NFA to a DFA

Although it is easier to construct, a nondeterministic machine is just an idealized machine which cannot be efficiently implemented in practice, since a real machine can only follow one computation path at a time. For the finite state automata, it is fortunate that there is a simple procedure to convert an NFA to an equivalent DFA which accepts the same language. Thus, the notion of NFA's can be turned into practical use.

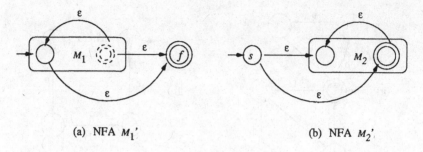

(a) NFA M_1' (b) NFA M_2'

Figure 2.28: Two attempts for Kleene closures of NFA's.

To see how to do this conversion, let us consider an NFA $M = (Q, \Sigma, \delta, q_0, F)$. For any $x \in \Sigma^*$, let Q_x be the set of states which are the end states of the computation paths of x in M; that is, $Q_x = \delta(\{q_0\}, x)$, where δ is the extended transition function defined on $2^Q \times \Sigma^*$. In particular, $Q_\varepsilon = \varepsilon\text{-closure}(\{q_0\})$. Then, x is accepted by M if and only if $Q_x \cap F \neq \emptyset$. Thus, it suggests that we can use these subsets $Q_x \subseteq Q$ as the *states* for the equivalent DFA. In other words, we would like to construct a DFA $M' = (Q', \Sigma, \delta', Q_\varepsilon, F')$ with the following properties:

$$Q' = \{Q_x \mid x \in \Sigma^*\},$$
$$F' = \{Q_x \mid Q_x \cap F \neq \emptyset\},$$
$$\delta'(Q_x, a) = Q_{xa}, \qquad \text{for } x \in \Sigma^*, a \in Sigma.$$

Note that each Q_x is a subset of Q, and so Q' is a finite set. Indeed, $Q' \subseteq 2^Q$ and so $|Q'| \leq 2^{|Q|}$. Furthermore, if $Q_x = Q_y$, then $Q_{xa} = Q_{ya}$ for all $a \in \Sigma$. It follows that the above definition of δ' is well defined. In fact, using the extended transition function δ of M, we know that for any $x \in \Sigma^*$ and $a \in \Sigma$, $\delta'(Q_x, a) = \delta(Q_x, a)$. The above analysis shows that this construction is feasible. We call it the *subset construction* for DFA's. The following are some examples.

Example 2.23 *An NFA* $M = (Q, \{0, 1\}, \delta, q_0, F)$ *is given by* $Q = \{q_0, q_1, q_2, q_3, q_4, q_5\}$, $F = \{q_3, q_4\}$, *and*

δ	0	1	ε
q_0	$\{q_0\}$	$\{q_0, q_2\}$	$\{q_1\}$
q_1	$\{q_5\}$	$\{q_2\}$	–
q_2	$\{q_3\}$	–	–
q_3	–	–	$\{q_4\}$
q_4	$\{q_3\}$	–	–
q_5	–	$\{q_4\}$	–

(See Figure 2.29(a) for the transition diagram of M.) Find a DFA which is equivalent to the NFA M.

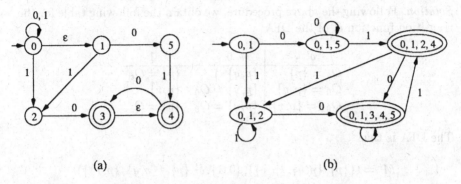

(a)   (b)

Figure 2.29: Converting an NFA to a DFA.

Solution. We construct the DFA M' as follows:

Step 1. We let $Q_\varepsilon = \varepsilon$-closure($\{q_0\}$) as the initial state, and let $F' = \emptyset$ be the set of final states. Let $Q' = \{Q_\varepsilon\}$. If $Q_\varepsilon \cap F \neq \emptyset$, then add Q_ε to F'.

Step 2. Repeat the following until $\delta'(Q_x, a)$ is defined for all $Q_x \in Q'$ and all $a \in \{0, 1\}$:

(1) Select $Q_x \in Q'$ and $a \in \{0, 1\}$ such that $\delta(Q_x, a)$ is not yet defined.

(2) Let $Q_{xa} = \delta(Q_x, a)$.

(3) If $Q_{xa} \notin Q'$, then add Q_{xa} to Q', and also add it to F' if $Q_{xa} \cap F \neq \emptyset$.

The whole process for this example is shown in the following table.

δ'	0	1
$Q_\varepsilon = \{q_0, q_1\}$	$\{q_0, q_1, q_5\}$	$\{q_0, q_1, q_2\}$
$Q_0 = \{q_0, q_1, q_5\}$	$\{q_0, q_1, q_5\} = Q_0$	$\{q_0, q_1, q_2, q_4\}$
$Q_1 = \{q_0, q_1, q_2\}$	$\{q_0, q_1, q_3, q_4, q_5\}$	$\{q_0, q_1, q_2\} = Q_1$
$Q_{01} = \{q_0, q_1, q_2, q_4\}$	$\{q_0, q_1, q_3, q_4, q_5\}$	$\{q_0, q_1, q_2\} = Q_1$
$Q_{10} = \{q_0, q_1, q_3, q_4, q_5\}$	$\{q_0, q_1, q_3, q_4, q_5\} = Q_{10}$	$\{q_0, q_1, q_2, q_4\} = Q_{01}$

Note that, in Step 2, we did not have to consider states Q_{00}, Q_{000}, Q_{001}, and so on, since $Q_{00} = Q_0$ and so $Q_{000} = Q_{00} = Q_0$ and $Q_{001} = Q_{01}$. Similarly, since $Q_{11} = Q_1$, we do not need to consider Q_{11w} for any $w \in \{0, 1\}^*$.

The transition diagram of the DFA M' is shown in Figure 2.29(b). (We write $(i_1, i_2, \ldots, i_m)$ inside a vertex to denote the state $\{q_{i_1}, q_{i_2}, \ldots, q_{i_m}\}$.) $\square$

Example 2.24 *Construct a DFA which is equivalent to the NFA* $M = (\{p, q, r\}, \{0, 1\}, \delta, p, \{q, r\})$, *where*

δ	0	1
p	$\{p, q\}$	$\{p\}$
q	$-$	$\{r\}$
r	$-$	$-$

Solution. Following the above procedure, we obtain the following table for the transition function δ' of the DFA:

δ'	0	1
$Q_\varepsilon = \{p\}$	$\{p, q\}$	$\{p\} = Q_\varepsilon$
$Q_0 = \{p, q\}$	$\{p, q\} = Q_0$	$\{p, r\}$
$Q_{01} = \{p, r\}$	$\{p, q\} = Q_0$	$\{p\} = Q_\varepsilon$

The DFA is thus

$$M' = (\{\{p\}, \{p, q\}, \{p, r\}\}, \{0, 1\}, \delta', \{p\}, \{\{p, q\}, \{p, r\}\}). \qquad \square$$

From the above construction, we see that for each NFA there exists a DFA accepting the same language accepted by the NFA. Moreover, a DFA is also an NFA. Therefore, we have the following theorem.

Theorem 2.25 *A language is accepted by an NFA if and only if it is accepted by a DFA.*

Theorem 2.25 provides us with an easy tool to construct a DFA for a given language L: we can first construct an NFA for L and then convert it to a DFA. The following are some examples.

Example 2.26 *Let $M = (\{p, q, r, s\}, \{0, 1\}, \delta, p, \{q, s\})$ be an NFA given by*

δ	0	1
p	$\{q, s\}$	$\{q\}$
q	$\{r\}$	$\{q, r\}$
r	$\{s\}$	$\{p\}$
s	$-$	$\{p\}$

Construct an NFA that accepts $\overline{L(M)}$.

Solution. It is hard to figure out the construction of such an NFA M' directly from M. In particular, the naive approach of changing nonfinal states of M to final states and changing final states of M to nonfinal states does not work. This is due to the nature of nondeterminism of the NFA's: It is possible that, for some string x, $Q_x \cap F \neq \emptyset$ and $Q_x \cap (Q - F) \neq \emptyset$; then, x would be accepted by both M and the new NFA M'. (For instance, here we have $Q_{01} = \{p, q, r\}$ and $F = \{q, s\}$, and so the string 01 would be accepted by both M and M'.) Therefore, M' does not accept $\overline{L(M)}$.

Instead, we can apply the subset construction to get the required NFA as follows: We first find a DFA M_D equivalent to M and, then, change final states of M_D to nonfinal states and nonfinal states of M_D to final states to get a new automaton M'. The new automaton we get is actually a DFA.

δ_D	0	1
$Q_\varepsilon = \{p\}$	$\{q,s\}$	$\{q\}$
$Q_0 = \{q,s\}$	$\{r\}$	$\{p,q,r\}$
$Q_1 = \{q\}$	$\{r\}$	$\{q,r\}$
$Q_{00} = \{r\}$	$\{s\}$	$\{p\}$
$Q_{01} = \{p,q,r\}$	$\{q,r,s\}$	$\{p,q,r\}$
$Q_{11} = \{q,r\}$	$\{r,s\}$	$\{p,q,r\}$
$Q_{000} = \{s\}$	$\emptyset$	$\{p\}$
$Q_{010} = \{q,r,s\}$	$\{r,s\}$	$\{p,q,r\}$
$Q_{110} = \{r,s\}$	$\{s\}$	$\{p\}$
$Q_{0000} = \emptyset$	$\emptyset$	$\emptyset$

Figure 2.30: The transition function of M_D in Example 2.26.

For the first step, we obtain $M_D = (Q_D, \{0,1\}, \delta_D, \{p\}, F_D)$, where the set Q_D and the transition function δ_D are as shown in Figure 2.30, and the set of final states is

$$F_D = \{A \subseteq \{p,q,r,s\} \mid A \cap \{q,s\} \neq \emptyset\}$$
$$= \{\{q\}, \{s\}, \{q,s\}, \{q,r\}, \{r,s\}, \{p,q,r\}, \{q,r,s\}\}.$$

Now, the DFA $M' = (Q_D, \{0,1\}, \delta_D, \{p\}, Q_D - F_D)$ accepts $\overline{L(M)}$, where

$$Q_D - F_D = \{\{p\}, \{r\}, \emptyset\}. \qquad \square$$

Example 2.27 *Construct a DFA accepting the set of all binary strings in which the fifth symbol from right is 0.*

Solution. Is is easy to construct an NFA for this language: Just draw a *checker* as shown in Figure 2.31(a). This checker recognizes all strings of length 5 which begins with 0.

Now, we add two loops $q_0 \xrightarrow{0} q_0$ and $q_0 \xrightarrow{1} q_0$ to the checker and this is the required NFA (see Figure 2.31(b)). More formally, this NFA can be expressed as $M = (\{q_0, q_1, \cdots, q_5\}, \{0,1\}, \delta, q_0, \{q_5\})$, with

$$\delta(q_0, 0) = \{q_0, q_1\}, \qquad \delta(q_0, 1) = \{q_0\},$$
$$\delta(q_i, 0) = \delta(q_i, 1) = q_{i+1}, \text{ for } 1 \leq i \leq 4.$$
$$\delta(q_5, 0) = \delta(q_5, 1) = \emptyset.$$

Next, we convert this NFA M to an equivalent DFA $M' = (Q', \{0,1\}, \delta', \{q_0\}, F')$, where

$$Q' = \{q' \mid q' \subseteq \{q_0, q_1, \cdots, q_5\}, q_0 \in q'\},$$
$$F' = \{q' \in Q' \mid q_5 \in q'\},$$

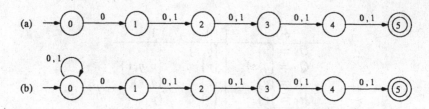

Figure 2.31: Solution to Example 2.27.

and δ' is defined by

$$\delta'(q', 0) = \{q_0, q_1\} \cup \{q_{i+1} \mid q_i \in q' \text{ and } 1 \le i \le 4\}$$
$$\delta'(q', 1) = \{q_0\} \cup \{q_{i+1} \mid q_i \in q' \text{ and } 1 \le i \le 4\}.$$

This DFA M' has totally 32 states. We leave the transition diagram of δ' to the reader.   □

* Example 2.28 *Consider the following multiplication table on* $\{a, b, c\}$:

$\times$	a	b	c
a	c	a	b
b	b	c	a
c	c	b	c

For any string w in $\{a, b, c\}^+$, denote by value(w) *the value obtained by multiplying symbols in w from left to right. For instance, let $w = abcb$. Then, we get*

$$\text{value}(w) = ((a \times b) \times c) \times b = (a \times c) \times b = b \times b = c, \text{ and}$$
$$\text{value}(w^R) = ((b \times c) \times b) \times a = (a \times b) \times a = a \times a = c.$$

Construct an NFA for the set L of all strings w over $\{a, b, c\}$ such that value(w) = value(w^R). *(E.g., $abcb \in L$ and $abb \notin L$.)*

Solution. Define $Q = \{q_s, q_a, q_b, q_c\}$ and $\Sigma = \{a, b, c\}$. First, we define a transition function $\delta : Q \times \Sigma \to Q$ by $\delta(q_s, x) = q_x$ for $x \in \Sigma$, and $\delta(q_x, y) = q_z$ if $x \times y = z$, for $x, y, z \in \Sigma$; that is,

δ	a	b	c
q_s	q_a	q_b	q_c
q_a	q_c	q_a	q_b
q_b	q_b	q_c	q_a
q_c	q_c	q_b	q_c

Clearly, for each $x \in \Sigma$, the DFA $M_x = (Q, \Sigma, \delta, q_s, \{q_x\})$ accepts the set of all strings w over Σ having value(w) = x. We show M_a in Figure 2.32(a).

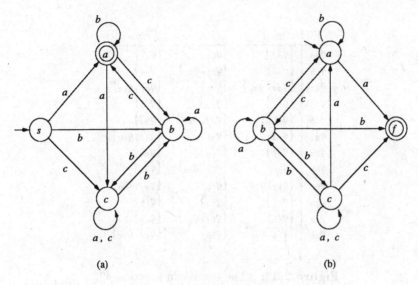

Figure 2.32: Two NFA's for Example 2.28.

Next, we define $Q' = \{q_a, q_b, q_c, q_f\}$ and a transition function $\delta' : Q' \times \Sigma \to 2^{Q'}$ by letting $q_f \in \delta(q_x, x)$ for all $x \in \Sigma$, and $q_x \in \delta(q_z, y)$ if $z = x \times y$, for $x, y, z \in \Sigma$. That is, we change state q_s in Figure 2.32(a) to state q_f, and reverse all arrows in Figure 2.32(a). Then, for each $x \in \Sigma$, the DFA $M'_x = (Q', \Sigma, \delta', q_x, \{q_f\})$ accepts the set of all strings w over Σ having value$(w^R) = x$. Figure 2.32(b) shows the NFA M'_a.

Now, the language L can be described as

$$(L(M_a) \cap L(M'_a)) \cup (L(M_b) \cap L(M'_b)) \cup (L(M_c) \cap L(M'_c)).$$

In Section 2.3, we have seen that it is easy to construct an NFA to accept the union or the concatenation of two languages accepted by two given NFA's. For the intersection of two languages, however, there is no simple way to do it. Here, we are going to use the *product automaton* method introduced in Section 2.2 to do it.

Let $Q'' = Q \times Q'$. To simplify the notation, we will write q_{uv} to denote the state $[q_u, q_v]$ in Q''. Define $\delta'' : Q'' \times \Sigma \to Q''$ by

$$\delta''(q_{uv}, x) = \{q_{wz} \mid q_w = \delta(q_u, x) \text{ and } q_z \in \delta'(q_v, x)\}.$$

We show the complete table for δ'' in Figure 2.33. (Note that $\delta''(q_{xf}, y) = \emptyset$ for all $x, y \in \Sigma$, and so we do not show them in the table.)

Then, for each $x \in \{a, b, c\}$, the NFA $M''_x = (Q'', \Sigma, \delta'', q_{sx}, \{q_{xf}\})$ accepts the language $L(M_x) \cap L(M'_x)$.

Now, to get an NFA accepting $L(M''_a) \cup L(M''_b) \cup L(M''_c)$, we can simply use three copies of M''_a, M''_b, M''_c and add an initial state $\tilde{q}_s$ with three ε-transitions from $\tilde{q}_s$ to the three initial states of the machines M''_a, M''_b, M''_c. More pre-

δ''	a	b	c
q_{sa}	$\{q_{af}\}$	$\{q_{ba}\}$	$\{q_{cb}\}$
q_{sb}	$\{q_{ab}\}$	$\{q_{bf}, q_{bc}\}$	$\{q_{ca}\}$
q_{sc}	$\{q_{aa}, q_{ac}\}$	$\{q_{bb}\}$	$\{q_{cf}, q_{cc}\}$
q_{aa}	$\{q_{cf}\}$	$\{q_{aa}\}$	$\{q_{bb}\}$
q_{ab}	$\{q_{cb}\}$	$\{q_{af}, q_{ac}\}$	$\{q_{ba}\}$
q_{ac}	$\{q_{ca}, q_{cc}\}$	$\{q_{ab}\}$	$\{q_{bf}, q_{bc}\}$
q_{ba}	$\{q_{bf}\}$	$\{q_{ca}\}$	$\{q_{ab}\}$
q_{bb}	$\{q_{bb}\}$	$\{q_{cf}, q_{cc}\}$	$\{q_{aa}\}$
q_{bc}	$\{q_{ba}, q_{bc}\}$	$\{q_{cb}\}$	$\{q_{af}, q_{ac}\}$
q_{ca}	$\{q_{cf}\}$	$\{q_{ba}\}$	$\{q_{cb}\}$
q_{cb}	$\{q_{cb}\}$	$\{q_{bf}, q_{bc}\}$	$\{q_{ca}\}$
q_{cc}	$\{q_{ca}, q_{cc}\}$	$\{q_{bb}\}$	$\{q_{cf}, q_{cc}\}$

Figure 2.33: The transition function δ''.

cisely, the required NFA can be described as $\widetilde{M} = (\widetilde{Q}, \Sigma, \widetilde{\delta}, \widetilde{q}_s, \{q_{af}^a, q_{bf}^b, q_{cf}^c\})$, where

$$\widetilde{Q} = \{q_{uv}^t \mid t \in \{a, b, c\}, q_{uv} \in Q''\} \cup \{\widetilde{q}_s\},$$

and

$$\widetilde{\delta}(\widetilde{q}_s, \varepsilon) = \{q_{sa}^a, q_{sb}^b, q_{sc}^c\},$$
$$\widetilde{\delta}(q_{uv}^t, x) = \{q_{wz}^t \mid q_{wz} \in \delta''(q_{uv}, x)\}, \text{ for } q_{uv} \in Q'', t, x \in \{a, b, c\}. \quad \square$$

Exercise 2.4

1. Convert each of the following NFA's into an equivalent DFA:

   (a) The NFA $M = (\{p, q, r, \}, \{0, 1\}, \delta, p, \{q, r\})$, with

δ	0	1
p	$\{p\}$	$\{p, q\}$
q	$\{r\}$	$-$
r	$-$	$-$

   (b) The NFA M of Figure 2.27(a).
   (c) The NFA M of Figure 2.27(b).
   (d) The NFA M of Figure 2.27(c).

2. For each of the following languages, construct a DFA that accepts the language:

   (a) The set of binary strings that contain both substring 010 and substring 101.

    (b) The set of all binary strings ending with 00 or 01 or 10.

    (c) The set of binary strings that contain both 001 and 110 as substrings or contain neither 001 nor 110 as a substring.

    (d) The set of binary strings in which both the fourth symbol from the right and the fourth from the left symbols are 0. [*Note:* Both strings 0110 and 10101 belong to this set.]

$\star$ **3.** Consider the following multiplication table on $\{a, b, c\}$:

$\times$	a	b	c
a	a	c	b
b	a	b	c
c	c	c	a

Construct NFA's for the following languages:

    (a) $\{x \mid \text{value}(x) \neq \text{value}(x^R)\}$.

    (b) $\{xy \mid \text{value}(x) = \text{value}(y^R)\}$.

    (c) $\{xy \mid \text{value}(x) = \text{value}(y)\}$.

2.5 Finite Automata and Regular Expressions

In this section, we are going to show that DFA's accept exactly the class of regular languages. This result is to be established in three steps:

    (1) If L is a regular language, then it is accepted by an NFA.

    (2) If L is accepted by an NFA, then it is accepted by a DFA.

    (3) If L is accepted by a DFA, then it is a regular language.

In Section 1.3, we showed that a regular expression r has a labeled digraph representation $G(r)$ such that for each string x, $x \in L(r)$ if and only if there is a path in $G(r)$ from the initial vertex to the final vertex whose associated labels are exactly the string x. Furthermore, each edge of $G(r)$ is labeled by exactly one symbol from $\{\varepsilon\} \cup \Sigma$. Thus, it is clear that $G(r)$ is the transition diagram of an NFA, with the initial vertex denoting the initial state and the final vertex denoting the unique final state. That is, part (1) above has been proven in Section 1.3.

Next, we note that part (2) has already been done in Section 2.4. Therefore, by combining parts (1) and (2), we can construct a DFA from any given regular expression. Before we prove part (3), let us see some examples of constructing an NFA or a DFA from a given regular expression.

Example 2.29 *Find a DFA accepting the language* $10 + (0 + 11)0^*1$.

Solution. First, we find an NFA to accept this language by using the method of Section 1.3. Then we transform this NFA to a DFA. The result is shown in Figure 2.34. □

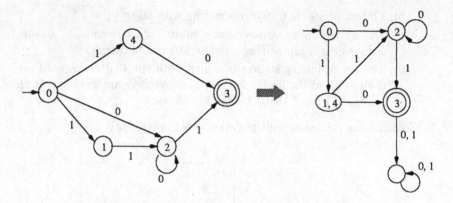

Figure 2.34:   Solution to Example 2.29.

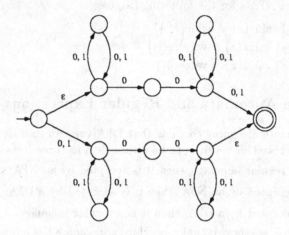

Figure 2.35:   Solution to Example 2.30.

Example 2.30 *Construct an NFA accepting the set L of binary strings of an odd length which contain the substring* 00.

Solution. A string x having a substring 00 can be written as $x = y00z$, for some $y, z \in \{0,1\}^*$. This string x is of an odd length either if $|y|$ is even and $|z|$ is odd, or if $|y|$ is odd and $|z|$ is even. Thus, L can be represented as

$$((0+1)\,(0+1))^*00((0+1)(0+1))^*(0+1)$$
$$+(0+1)((0+1)(0+1))^*00((0+1)(0+1))^*.$$

By using the method of Section 1.3, we obtain an NFA as shown in Figure 2.35.   □

Next, we prove part (3) by showing how to construct a regular expression from a given DFA. Our method actually works even if the given automaton is

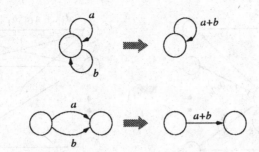

Figure 2.36: Multiple edges can be removed.

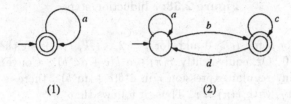

(1)   (2)

Figure 2.37: Basis step.

an NFA. In fact, we will prove this result on the labelled digraphs introduced in Section 1.3.

Recall that a labelled digraph G is a digraph with two special vertices, the initial vertex v_1 and the final vertex v_f, in which each edge is labelled by a regular expression. For each path π from v_1 to v_f in such a digraph G, we let $r(\pi)$ be the regular expression associated with π; that is, if π is

$$v_1 \xrightarrow{r_1} v_{i_1} \xrightarrow{r_2} v_{i_2} \xrightarrow{r_3} \cdots \xrightarrow{r_k} v_{i_k} = v_f,$$

then $r(\pi) = r_1 r_2 \cdots r_k$. Then, for each labelled digraph G, we let

$$L(G) = \bigcup \{L(r(\pi)) \mid \pi \text{ is a path from } v_1 \text{ to } v_f\}.$$

We now show, by induction on the number of vertices in G other than v_1 and v_f, that for each labelled digraph G, $L(G)$ is a regular set.

Basis Step: For $n = 0$, the digraph G has only two vertices v_1 and v_f, or only one vertex $v_1 = v_f$. We first eliminate all multiple edges in G by combining multiple edges with labels $r_1, r_2, \ldots, r_m$ from a vertex u to a vertex v into a single edge from u to v with the label $r_1 + r_2 + \cdots + r_m$ (see Figure 2.36). Then, the resulting digraph are of two types, as shown in Figure 2.37, in which a, b, c, d denote four regular expressions.

It is clear that a type (1) digraph G has $L(G) = a^*$. For a type (2) digraph G, consider a path π from v_1 to v_f. Assume that π passes through v_f for $k \geq 1$ times. Then, we can write π as $\pi_1 \pi_2 \cdots \pi_k$, where π_1 is a path from v_1 to v_f, and $\pi_2, \ldots, \pi_k$ are paths from v_f to v_f, with v_f not occurring as an intermediate vertex in any path π_j, $1 \leq j \leq k$. Then, it is clear that

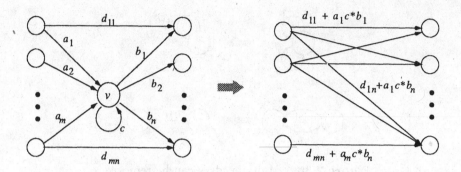

Figure 2.38: Induction step.

$r(\pi_1) = a^{i_1}b$ for some $i_1 \geq 0$ and, for $j = 2, \ldots, k$, $r(\pi_j)$ is either c or $da^{i_j}b$ for some $i_j \geq 0$. Or, equivalently, $r(\pi) \in a^*b(c + da^*b)^*$. Conversely, we can see that, for any regular expression r in $a^*b(c + da^*b)^*$, there is a path π in G from v_1 to v_f, with $r(\pi) = r$. Thus, it follows that

$$L(G) = a^*b(c + da^*b)^*,$$

and the basis step is proven.

Induction Step: For $n \geq 1$, we can choose a vertex v other than v_1 and v_f and remove it by the following transformation: First, by the method used in the basis step, we may eliminate multiple edges and assume that there is at most one edge from any vertex u to any vertex w. Now, assume that v has a self-loop with label c; that is, G has an edge $v \xrightarrow{c} v$. We remove v along with this edge. For any pair (u, w) of vertices in G, with edges $u \xrightarrow{a} v$, $v \xrightarrow{b} w$ and $u \xrightarrow{d} w$, we remove the edges $u \to v$ and $v \to w$ and replace the label d of the edge $u \to w$ with a new label $d + ac^*b$. (If there was no edge $u \to w$ in G, we treat it as having an edge $u \to w$ with label $\emptyset$.) We show this transformation in Figure 2.38. (To make the figure readable, we omit some edges from vertices on the left to vertices on the right. We assume that the edge from the ith vertex on the left to the jth vertex on the right has the label d_{ij}.) Note that this transformation does not change the associated language. Thus, by the induction hypothesis, the language accepted by G is regular.

The above completes the proof that the languages associated with labelled digraphs are all regular. Finally, we show that for any NFA M, $L(M)$ is regular. For any NFA M, we first convert it to an equivalent NFA M' with a single final state by changing all final states in M into nonfinal states, and adding a new final state and a new ε-move from each old final state to it (see Figure 2.39). Now the transition diagram of this NFA M' is exactly a labelled digraph G with the property that each edge is labelled by a single symbol from $\{\varepsilon\} \cup \Sigma$. It is also clear that $L(G) = L(M')$. Thus, by the above proof, $L(M')$ is a regular language.

We have just proved the following theorem:

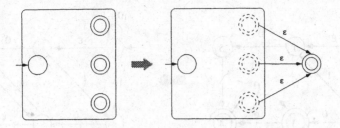

Figure 2.39: NFA with a single final state.

Theorem 2.31 *Let L be a language. The following are equivalent:*
(a) L is a regular language.
(b) There is a DFA M such that $L(M) = L$.
(c) There is an NFA M such that $L(M) = L$.

Example 2.32 *Find a regular expression for the language accepted by NFA in Figure 2.29(a).*

Solution. By using the above method, we can compute a regular expression for the language accepted by NFA in Figure 2.29(a) as shown in Figure 2.40. First, we create a new unique final state and then eliminate state q_5. Then, we eliminate states q_1, q_2, q_3 and q_4, one at a time. Finally, we use the basis step to get the regular expression $(0 + 1)^*(01 + 10)0^*$ from the last digraph. □

Exercise 2.5

1. For each of the following regular expressions r, construct a DFA that accepts $L(r)$:

   (a) $(0 + 10)^*(1 + 01)^*$.

   (b) $(0 + 1)^*0(0 + 1)(0 + 1)0(0 + 1)$.

   (c) $0(0 + 1)^*0 + 1(0 + 1)^*1$.

2. For each of the following languages, find an NFA that accepts it:

   (a) $\{x\#y \mid x, y \in (0 + 1)^*, |x| \equiv |y| \pmod 2\}$.

   (b) $\{x\#y \mid x, y \in (0 + 1)^*, |x| + |y| \geq 5\}$.

   (c) $\{x\#y \mid x, y \in (0 + 1)^*, |x| \cdot |y| \text{ is dividable by } 5\}$.

3. Figure 2.41 shows an NFA accepting 0^*, constructed based on the method of Example 2.22. The four ε-moves cannot be eliminated by the rule of Theorem 1.25. Apply the method in the proof of Theorem 2.31 to reduce some of its ε-moves. Can you find, from this example, a more general rule (than Theorem 1.25) to eliminate redundant ε-transitions?

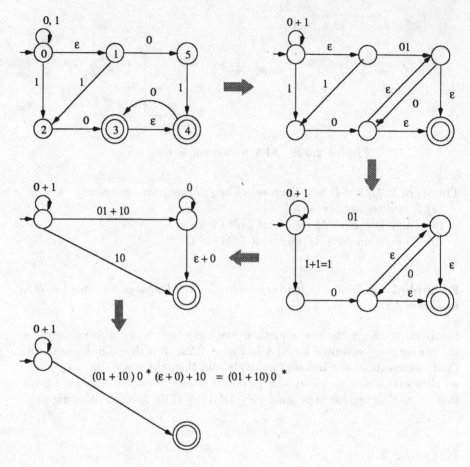

Figure 2.40: Finding a regular expression from an NFA.

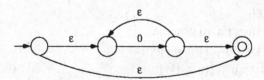

Figure 2.41: An NFA accepting 0^*.

4. For each of the languages accepted by NFA's of Figure 2.42, find a regular expression for it.

2.6   Closure Properties of Regular Languages

In Theorem 2.31, we have shown that a regular language has three types of representations: regular expressions, DFA's and NFA's. This equivalence

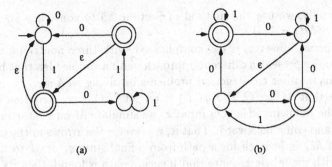

Figure 2.42: Two NFA's for Exercise 4.

result provides us with useful tools to manipulate regular expressions or finite automata to get new regular expressions or finite automata. In this section, we apply these tools to prove that regular languages are *closed* under many language operations Φ, in the sense that if a given language L is regular then the language $\Phi(L)$ is also a regular language. Furthermore, most results are proved by constructive methods.

We start with the most common language operations introduced in Section 1.1.

Theorem 2.33 *The class of regular languages is closed under union, intersection, subtraction, complementation, concatenation, Kleene closure and reversal.*

Proof. We showed in Section 2.2 how to construct, from two given DFA's M_1 and M_2, new DFA's to accept the union, the intersection and the difference of languages $L(M_1)$ and $L(M_2)$, as well as the complement of $L(M_1)$. Furthermore, we showed in Examples 2.21 and 2.22 how to construct, from two given NFA's M_3 and M_4, NFA's to accept the concatenation and the Kleene closure of $L(M_3)$ and $L(M_4)$.

Finally, we can prove by induction that if L is regular then L^R is regular (cf. Example 1.21). First, for the basis step, we check that $\emptyset^R = \emptyset$, $\{\varepsilon\}^R = \{\varepsilon\}$ and $\{a\}^R = \{a\}$. Next, for the induction step, we recall from Example 1.8 that $(AB)^R = B^R A^R$ and $(A \cup B)^R = A^R \cup B^R$. Furthermore, use a similar proof of Example 1.8, we can prove that $(A^*)^R = (A^R)^*$. Thus, the induction step is complete. $\square$

The following example presents a more constructive mehtod for proving that regular languages are closed under reversal.

Example 2.34 *Let M be an NFA. Construct an NFA M' such that $L(M') = L(M)^R$.*

Solution. From the last example, we can first find a regular expression r such that $L(r) = L(M)$. Next, we get a regular expression s such that $L(s) =$

$L(r)^R$. Finally, we use the method of Section 2.5 to construct an NFA M' such that $L(M') = L(s)$.

This process, however, is too complicated, with three nontrivial constructions. Here, we present a different approach, with a simple idea that has many applications in other construction problems involving NFA's.

Assume that $M = (Q, \Sigma, \delta, q_0, F)$ is an NFA. Our construction of M' is based on the following idea: On input x, we simulate M on x, starting from a final state and going backward. That is, we reverse the arrows in the transition diagram of M, and search for a path from a final state q_f of M to the initial state q_0, with the labels x. Note that if such a path is found, then its reversed path is an accepting path for x^R. Also, if there is a computation path of M on x^R, then its reversal is a such a path for x. Thus, M accepts x^R if and only if the reversed machine M' accepts x.

Formally, assume that $Q = \{q_0, q_1, \ldots, q_n\}$. We add a new starting state s and let $M' = (Q \cup \{s\}, \Sigma, \delta', s, \{q_0\})$, where

$$\delta'(s, \varepsilon) = F,$$
$$\delta'(q_i, a) = \{q_j \in Q \mid q_i \in \delta(q_j, a)\}, \text{ for } q_i \in Q \text{ and } a \in \Sigma \cup \{\varepsilon\}.$$

Finally, we remark that the machine M' obtained from this reversal construction is, in general, not a DFA even if M itself is a DFA: It is possible that, for some state q_i and some symbol a, there are more than one states q_j such that $\delta(q_j, a) = q_i$. In other words, the reversal simulation requires the ability of *nondeterministic search* for the right path from a final state to the initial state. □

Next, we consider a new language operation called substitution. Let f be a mapping which maps each symbol $a \in \Sigma$ to a language L_a over an alphabet Γ. We extend function f to the domain of Σ^* by $f(\varepsilon) = \{\varepsilon\}$ and $f(a_1 a_2 \cdots a_k) = f(a_1) f(a_2) \cdots f(a_k)$, for $a_1, \ldots, a_k \in \Sigma$. Then, for any language $L \subseteq \Sigma^*$, we obtain a new language by applying the *substitution* function f to L:

$$f(L) = \bigcup_{x \in L} f(x).$$

For example, suppose that $L = \{01, 10\}$ and $f(0) = 0(0+1)^*$, $f(1) = (0+1)^*1$. Then,

$$f(L) = 0(0 + 1)^*1 \cup 1(0 + 1)^*0.$$

A substitution f is called a *homomorphism* if for any $a \in \Sigma$, $f(a)$ is a language with a single string.

Example 2.35 *Let f be a substitution over Σ. Assume that $L \subseteq \Sigma^*$ is a regular language, and that $f(a)$ is a regular language for each $a \in \Sigma$. Then, $f(L)$ is also a regular language.*

Proof. Let r be a regular expression for language L and, for each $a \in \Sigma$, r_a be the regular expression for language $f(a)$. Replace each occurrence of symbol a in r by $f(a)$. Then, we obtain a new regular expression r'.

Now, we observe the following simple facts:

(a) For any two sets $A \subseteq \Sigma^*$ and $B \subseteq \Sigma^*$, we have $f(A \cup B) = f(A) \cup f(B)$, $f(AB) = f(A)f(B)$, and $f(A^*) = f(A)^*$.

(b) For any two regular expressions r and s, $(r+s)' = r' + s'$, $(rs)' = r' \cdot s'$, and $(r^*)' = (r')^*$.

Using these facts, we can prove by a simple induction that $L(r') = f(L)$ (cf. Examples 1.21 and 1.22). Thus, $f(L)$ is regular. □

Define the *quotient* of two languages L_1 and L_2 as

$$L_1/L_2 = \{x \mid (\exists y \in L_2)[xy \in L_1]\}.$$

For instance, if $L_1 = \{w \in \{0,1\}^* \mid w$ has an even number of occurrences of symbol $0\}$, $L_2 = \{0\}$ and $L_3 = \{0, 00\}$, then $L_1/L_2 = \{w \in \{0,1\}^* \mid w$ has an odd number of occurrences of symbol $0\}$, and $L_1/L_3 = \{0,1\}^*$.

Example 2.36 *Show that for any language L_2, if L_1 is regular then L_1/L_2 is also regular.*

Proof. Suppose that L_1 is accepted by a DFA $M = (Q, \Sigma, \delta, q_0, F)$. For any string $x \in L_1/L_2$, there exists a string $y \in L_2$ such that $\delta(q_0, xy) = \delta(\delta(q_0, x), y) \in F$. In other words, suppose that we run M on x and reach a state $q_i = \delta(q_0, x)$. If there exists $y \in L_2$ such that $\delta(q_i, y) \in F$, then x should be accepted; that is, q_i should be considered as a final state for L_1/L_2. Therefore, we can simply define

$$F' = \{q \in Q \mid (\exists y \in L_2) [\delta(q, y) \in F]\},$$

and let $M' = (Q, \Sigma, \delta, q_0, F')$. It is clear that M' accepts L_1/L_2. □

Example 2.37 *Let L be a regular language over Σ, k a positive integer and ϕ a mapping from Σ^k to Σ. Prove that*

$$L_1 = \{\phi(a_1 a_2 \cdots a_k) \cdots \phi(a_{(n-1)k+1} a_{(n-1)k+2} \cdots a_{nk}) \mid a_1 a_2 \cdots a_{nk} \in L\}$$

is regular.

Proof. Assume that L be accepted by a DFA $M = (Q, \Sigma, \delta, s, F)$. Then, the required NFA can be defined as $M' = (Q, \Sigma, \delta', s, F)$, where for each $q \in Q$ and each $a \in \Sigma$,

$$\delta'(q, a) = \{\delta(q, a_1 a_2 \cdots a_k) \mid \phi(a_1, a_2, \cdots, a_k) = a\}.$$ □

For any language L, let

$$\mathrm{MIN}(L) = \{x \in L \mid \text{no proper prefix of } x \text{ belongs to } L\}.$$

Example 2.38 *Prove that if L is regular, so is $\mathrm{MIN}(L)$.*

Proof. Assume that $M = (Q, \Sigma, \delta, q, F)$ is a DFA which accepts L. Then, $\mathrm{MIN}(L)$ is accepted by the NFA M' obtained from M by deleting all out-edges from final states.   □

For any two bits $a, b \in \{0, 1\}$, $a \vee b$ denotes the disjunction of a and b; that is, $0 \vee 0 = 0$ and $0 \vee 1 = 1 \vee 0 = 1 \vee 1 = 1$. For any two binary strings x and y with $|x| = |y|$, $x \vee y$ denotes the bitwise disjunction of x and y. For example, if $x = 0011$ and $y = 0101$, then $x \vee y = 0111$.

Example 2.39 *Show that if A and B are regular languages over $\{0, 1\}$, then*

$$A \vee B = \{x \vee y \mid x \in A, y \in B, |x| = |y|\}$$

is also regular.

Proof. Assume that DFA's $M_A = (Q_A, \{0, 1\}, \delta_A, s_A, F_A)$ and $M_B = (Q_B, \{0, 1\}, \delta_B, s_B, F_B)$ accept sets A and B, respectively. To accept language $A \vee B$, we build a product DFA M' to simulate M_A and M_B. At each move, if the input symbol is 0, then we simulate them in a normal way. If the input symbol is 1, then this symbol may come from $0 \vee 1$, $1 \vee 0$ or $1 \vee 1$; we simulate all three possible computation paths in M_A and M_B. More precisely, we let $M' = (Q_A \times Q_B, \{0, 1\}, \delta', [s_A, s_B], F_A \times F_B)$, where

$$\delta'([p, q], 0) = \{[\delta_A(p, 0), \delta_B(q, 0)]\}$$
$$\delta'([p, q], 1) = \{[\delta_A(p, 0), \delta_B(q, 1)], [\delta_A(p, 1), \delta_B(q, 0)], [\delta_A(p, 1), \delta_B(q, 1)]\}. \quad □$$

$\star$ **Example 2.40** *Show that if L is a regular language, so is*

$$\{xy \mid yx \in L\}.$$

Proof. Let $M = (Q, \Sigma, \delta, q_0, F)$ be a DFA accepting L. Assume that $Q = \{q_0, q_1, \ldots, q_n\}$. Intuitively, we can simulate M to decide whether an input w is in $\{xy \mid yx \in L\}$ or not as follows:

(1) We nondeterministically divide w into two parts $w = xy$.

(2) Then, we nondeterministically jump to a state q_i, and simulate M on x starting from state q_i.

(3) Suppose that $\delta(q_i, x) = q_j$ is not in F, then this simulation fails. Otherwise, we simulate M on y starting from state q_0, and accept w if $\delta(q_0, y) = q_i$.

How do we implement the *nondeterministic guess* of state q_i in step (2)? We create many copies of M and each copy implements one choice. The following is a more formal construction:

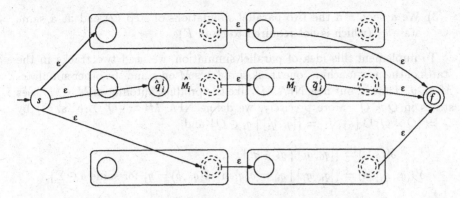

Figure 2.43: Solution to Example 2.40.

For each state q_i of M, we make two copies of M: $\widehat{M_i}$ and $\widetilde{M_i}$. We connect all final states of $\widehat{M_i}$ to the initial state of $\widetilde{M_i}$ with ε-edges. For a state q_j in M, we denote the corresponding states in $\widehat{M_i}$ and $\widetilde{M_i}$ by $\hat{q}_j^i$ and $\tilde{q}_j^i$, respectively. Now, we create a new initial state s and a new final state f, and connect s to state $\hat{q}_i^i$ for every $\widehat{M_i}$ and connect state $\tilde{q}_i^i$ for every $\widetilde{M_i}$ to f with ε-edges. Also, all final states in $\widehat{M_i}$ and $\widetilde{M_i}$ are changed to nonfinal states. (See Figure 2.43.)

We let M' be the resulting NFA, and claim that $L(M') = \{xy \mid yx \in L\}$. First, if $yx \in L$, then there exist states $q_i \in Q$ and $q_j \in F$ such that $\delta(q_0, y) = q_i$ and $\delta(q_i, x) = q_j$. Therefore, the following path in M' accepts xy:

$$s \xrightarrow{\varepsilon} \hat{q}_i^i \xrightarrow{x} \hat{q}_j^i \xrightarrow{\varepsilon} \tilde{q}_0^i \xrightarrow{y} \tilde{q}_i^i \xrightarrow{\varepsilon} f.$$

Conversely, we can see that any accepting path in M' must be of the above form, with $q_j \in F$. Thus, the original DFA accepts yx by the following path:

$$q_0 \xrightarrow{y} q_i \xrightarrow{x} q_j.$$

That means M' only accepts strings of the form xy with $yx \in L$. □

⋆ **Example 2.41** *Show that if L is a regular language, so is*

$$L_{\frac{1}{2}} = \{x \mid (\exists y)\,[|x| = |y|, xy \in L]\}.$$

Proof 1. Let $M = (Q, \Sigma, \delta, q_0, F)$ be a DFA accepting L, with $Q = \{q_0, q_1, \ldots, q_n\}$. We will construct an NFA accepting $L_{\frac{1}{2}}$. Intuitively, we can simulate M on x to decide whether $x \in L_{\frac{1}{2}}$ as follows:

(1) We nondeterministically guess a final state $q_j \in F$ and a string y with $|y| = |x|$.

(2) We simulate M, in parallel, on x from q_0 *forward*, and on y from q_j *backward*. (As demonstrated in Example 2.34, we reverse the direction of the arrows in the transition diagram of M to simulate it backward.)

(3) We accept x if the two parallel simulations of step (2) end at a same state q_k (which is not required to be in F).

To implement this idea of parallel simulation, we need two tracks in the states of the new machine, one track simulates M on x and the other simulates M on y. That is, our new NFA M', like the product automaton $M \times M$, uses states in $Q \times Q$. More precisely, we define NFA $M' = (Q', \Sigma, \delta', s, F')$ by $Q' = (Q \times Q) \cup \{s\}$, $F' = \{[q_i, q_i] \mid q_i \in Q\}$ and

$$\delta'(s, \varepsilon) = \{[q_0, q_k] \mid q_k \in F\},$$
$$\delta'([q_i, q_j], a) = \{[q_u, q_v] \mid q_u = \delta(q_i, a), \delta(q_v, b) = q_j \text{ for some } b \in \Sigma\}.$$

Note that, in an NFA, we actually cannot guess a string y and verify that $|x| = |y|$, but we can guess the symbols of y one at a time. This guessing technique is implemented above in the definition of $\delta'([q_i, q_j], a)$. From the above discussion, it follows that M' accepts $L_{\frac{1}{2}}$.   □

Proof 2. Let $M = (Q, \Sigma, \delta, q_0, F)$ be a DFA accepting L, with $Q = \{q_0, q_1, \ldots, q_n\}$. The idea of this construction is a combination of the product automaton method and the simulation idea of Example 2.40. That is, we need to nondeterministically guess a state q_i and a string y, then we simulate M, in parallel, on x from state q_0 and on y from state q_i. We accept x if the first simulation ends at state q_i and the second simulation ends at a state in F. Since we simulate them in parallel, the guessed string y must have $|y| = |x|$.

To implement this idea, we define, for each state $q_i \in Q$, an NFA $M_i = (Q, \Sigma, \widehat{\delta}, q_i, F)$ by

$$\widehat{\delta}(q_j, a) = \{\delta(q_j, b) \mid b \in \Sigma\}.$$

(All NFA's M_i have the same transition function $\widehat{\delta}$.) The NFA M_i then simulates M on all strings y, starting from state q_i.

Then, we combine machine M and machines M_i into a new NFA M' with $|Q| + 1$ tracks, with the first track simulating M on x and the $(i+1)$st track simulating M_i on y. Formally, $M' = (Q', \Sigma, \delta', s, F')$, where $Q' = Q^{n+2}$, $s = [q_0, q_0, q_1, \ldots, q_n]$, $F' = \{[q_i, q_{j_0}, q_{j_1}, \ldots, q_{j_n}] \mid 0 \le i \le n, q_{j_i} \in F\}$, and

$$\delta'([q_i, q_{j_0}, q_{j_1}, \ldots, q_{j_n}], a)$$
$$= \{[\delta(q_i, a), q_{k_0}, q_{k_1}, \ldots, q_{k_n}] \mid q_{k_t} \in \widehat{\delta}(q_{j_t}, a), \text{ for } t = 0, \ldots, n\}.   □$$

The second proof above, though creating an NFA with more states than that in the first proof, is a more general proof technique with many applications. The following is another example.

★ Example 2.42 *Show that if L is a regular set, so is*

$$L_{\frac{1}{3}} = \{z \mid (\exists x, y)\, [|x| = |y| = |z|, xyz \in L]\}.$$

Proof. We use the second proof technique of the last example to solve this problem.

Let $M = (Q, \Sigma, \delta, q_0, F)$ be a DFA accepting L, with $Q = \{q_0, q_1, \ldots, q_n\}$. For every $q_i \in Q$, define a DFA $\widehat{M_i} = (Q, \Sigma, \delta, q_i, F)$ and an NFA $\widetilde{M_i} = (Q, \Sigma, \widetilde{\delta}, q_i, F)$ by

$$\widetilde{\delta}(q, a) = \{\delta(q, b) \mid b \in \Sigma\}.$$

Also let $\overline{M} = \widetilde{M_0}$.

Now, we construct an NFA M' that contains $2n + 3$ tracks simulating, in parallel, $\overline{M}$ and $\widehat{M_i}, \widetilde{M_j}$ for $i = 0, 1, \ldots, n$. Intuitively, we use $\overline{M}$ to simulate M on x, use $\widehat{M_0}, \ldots, \widehat{M_n}$ to simulate M on y, and use $\widetilde{M_0}, \ldots, \widetilde{M_n}$ to simulate M on z. Therefore, after the machine M' reads input z, if $\overline{M}$ is in state q_i, $\widehat{M_i}$ is in state q_j, and $\widetilde{M_j}$ is in a final state, then M' accepts input z. That is, $M' = (Q', \Sigma, \delta', s, F')$, where $Q' = Q^{2n+3}$, $s = [q_0, \ldots, q_n, q_0, q_0, \ldots, q_n]$,

$$\delta'([q_{j_0}, \ldots, q_{j_n}, q_i, q_{k_0}, \ldots, q_{k_n}], a)$$
$$= \{[\delta(q_{j_0}, a), \ldots, \delta(q_{j_n}, a), t, t_0, \ldots, t_n] \mid$$
$$t \in \widetilde{\delta}(q_i, a), t_\ell \in \widetilde{\delta}(q_{k_\ell}, a), \ell = 0, \ldots, n\},$$

and

$$F' = \{[q_{j_0}, \ldots, q_{j_n}, q_i, q_{k_0}, \ldots, q_{k_n}] \mid q_{j_{k_i}} \in F]\}.$$

(In the above implementation, the first $n+1$ tracks simulate $\widehat{M_0}, \widehat{M_1}, \ldots, \widehat{M_n}$, the $(n + 2)$nd track simulates $\overline{M}$, and the last $n + 1$ tracks simulate $\widetilde{M_0}, \widetilde{M_1}, \ldots, \widetilde{M_n}$. So, q_{j_t} denotes the state of DFA $\widehat{M_t}$, q_i denotes the state of $\overline{M}$, and q_{k_ℓ} denotes the state of NFA $\widetilde{M_\ell}$. The condition for the final states F' reads as follows: we accept the input z if $\overline{M}$ ends at state q_i, $\widetilde{M_i}$ ends at some state q_{k_i} and $\widehat{M_{k_i}}$ ends at a state $q_{j_{k_i}} \in F$.) □

Using the above proof techniques, we can show that for any rational number $0 < r < 1$, if L is regular then the language

$$L_r = \{x \mid (\exists y) [|x| = r \cdot |xy|, xy \in L\}$$

is also regular. Can we prove this type of closure properties for L_r when r is not a constant but is a nonlinear function of the length of $|xy|$? The answer is yes for some simple functions r. However, the proof for such a result depends on certain structural properties of the DFA M that accepts L, and is not a direct construction from M. In the following, we show a simple example, and leave the general cases as an exercise (see Exercise 10 of this section).

⋆ **Example 2.43** *Let A and B be two regular languages. Show that the language defined by*

$$C(A, B) = \{x \in A \mid (\exists y)[|y| = |x|^2, y \in B]\}$$

is also regular.

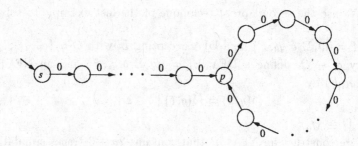

Figure 2.44: A DFA over a singleton alphabet has exactly one cycle.

Proof. We prove this result in four steps. First, we consider a simple case where $A = 0^*$ and $B \subseteq 0^*$. Assume that B is accepted by a DFA M_B. Since M_B operates on only one symbol 0, each state in the transition diagram of M_B has exactly one out-edge. It follows that the transition diagram of M_B contains exactly one cycle, as shown in Figure 2.44. Suppose that this cycle contains c edges and that the path from the initial state s to the first state p in the cycle contains a edges, where $c \geq 1$ and $a \geq 0$. We claim that for all integers m, with $m^2 \geq a$, $0^m \in C(0^*, B)$ if and only if $0^{m+c} \in C(0^*, B)$.

To prove our claim, we first note that $0^m \in C(0^*, B)$ if and only if $0^{m^2} \in B$, and $0^{m+c} \in C(0^*, B)$ if and only if $0^{(m+c)^2} \in B$. Since $m^2 \geq a$, the computation path of M_B on input 0^{m^2} starts from the initial state s and ends at a state q in the cycle. It is clear that, for any $k \geq 0$, the computation path of M_B on input 0^{m^2+kc} also ends at state q. That is, $0^{m^2} \in B$ if and only if $0^{m^2+kc} \in B$ for all $k \geq 0$. It follows that

$$0^m \in C(0^*, B) \Longleftrightarrow 0^{m^2} \in B \Longleftrightarrow 0^{m^2+(2m+c)c} \in B \Longleftrightarrow 0^{m+c} \in C(0^*, B).$$

From this claim, we can construct a DFA M_C accepting $C(0^*, B)$ as follows: M_C is a single-cycle DFA as shown in Figure 2.44, with $\lceil \sqrt{a} \rceil$ edges from state s to state p, and with c edges in the cycle. A state q is a final state if and only if $0^{j^2} \in B$ where j is the number of edges in the shortest path from s to q. This completes the proof of the first case.

Next, we consider the case where $A = \Sigma^*$ for some alphabet Σ and $B \subseteq 0^*$. Using the same argument as above, we can see that $x \in C(\Sigma^*, B)$ if and only if $xz \in C(\Sigma^*, B)$ for all z of length $|z| = c$. Furthermore, $x \in C(\Sigma^*, B)$ if and only if $w \in C(\Sigma^*, B)$ for all strings w of length $|w| = |x|$. Therefore, we can construct M_C for set $C(\Sigma^*, B)$ as in the first case above, except that we replace each edge $\xrightarrow{0}$ by a family of edges $\xrightarrow{a}$ over all symbols $a \in \Sigma$.

In the third step, we assume that $A = \Sigma^*$ and $B \subseteq \Gamma^*$ for some alphabets Σ and Γ. Let $B_0 = \{0^{|x|} \mid x \in B\}$. We note that B_0 can be obtained from B by replacing each symbol $a \in \Sigma$ by symbol 0, and so, by Example 2.35, B_0 is regular. In addition, it is easy to verify that $C(\Sigma^*, B_0) = C(\Sigma^*, B)$. It follows from the second case that $C(\Sigma^*, B)$ is regular.

Finally, we consider the general case of $A \subseteq \Sigma^*$ and $B \subseteq \Gamma^*$ for some alphabets Σ and Γ. We observe that $C(A,B) = A \cap C(\Sigma^*, B)$. From the third case, we know that $C(\Sigma^*, B)$ is regular. Since A is also regular, we conclude that $C(A,B)$ is regular. $\qquad\qquad\qquad\qquad\qquad\qquad\qquad\square$

⋆ **Example 2.44** *Show that if L is regular, so is*

$$\mathrm{SQRT}(L) = \{x \mid (\exists y)\,[|y| = |x|^2, xy \in L]\}.$$

Proof. Since L is regular, there exists a DFA $M = (Q, \Sigma, \delta, s, F)$ accepting L. For each state $q \in Q$, let A_q be the set of strings x whose computation path in M starts from s and ends at q, and B_q the set of strings x whose computation path in M, when started at state q, ends at a final state. That is,

$$A_q = \{x \in \Sigma^* \mid \delta(s, x) = q\},$$
$$B_q = \{x \in \Sigma^* \mid \delta(q, x) \in F\}.$$

Then, we can see that

$$\mathrm{SQRT}(L) = \bigcup_{q \in Q} \{x \in A_q \mid (\exists y)\,[|y| = |x|^2, y \in B_q]\}.$$

It is clear that all sets A_q and B_q are regular. Therefore, by Example 2.43, the set $\{x \in A_q \mid (\exists y)\,[|y| = |x|^2, y \in B_q]\}$ is regular for all $q \in Q$. We conclude that $\mathrm{SQRT}(L)$ is also regular. $\qquad\qquad\qquad\qquad\qquad\qquad\square$

Exercise 2.6

1. Prove the following identity:

   (a) $\mathrm{MAX}(L) = L \setminus (L/\Sigma^+)$, where $\mathrm{MAX}(L) = \{x \in L \mid x \text{ is not a proper prefix of any string in } L\}$.

   (b) $\mathrm{MIN}(L) = L \setminus (L\Sigma^+)$.

2. For any two bits $a, b \in \{0, 1\}$, $a \oplus b$ denotes the exclusive-or of a and b; that is, $0 \oplus 0 = 1 \oplus 1 = 0$ and $0 \oplus 1 = 1 \oplus 0 = 1$. For any two binary strings x and y with $|x| = |y|$, $x \oplus y$ denotes the bitwise exclusive-or of x and y. For example, if $x = 0011$ and $y = 0101$, then $x \oplus y = 0110$. Let $A = 001(0+1)^*$ and $B = (0+1)^*100$. Find a regular expression for each of the following languages:

   (a) $A \vee B$.

   (b) $A \oplus B = \{x \oplus y \mid x \in A, y \in B, |x| = |y|\}$.

   (c) $\{a_1 b_1 a_2 b_2 \cdots a_n b_n \mid a_1 a_2 \cdots a_n \in A, b_1 b_2 \cdots b_n \in B\}$.

3. Show that if A and B are regular languages, so are the following languages:

   (a) $\{x \mid xx^R \in A\}$.

   (b) $\{x \mid x \in A, xx \in A\}$.

   (c) $A_x = \{y \mid xy \in A\}$, where x is a fixed string.

   (d) $\{a_1 a_2 \cdots a_{2n} \mid a_2 a_1 a_4 a_3 \cdots a_{2n} a_{2n-1} \in A\}$.

   (e) $\{a_1 a_3 \cdots a_{2n-3} a_{2n-1} \mid a_1 a_2 \cdots a_{2n} \in A\}$.

   (f) $\{a_1 b_1 a_2 b_2 \cdots a_n b_n \mid a_1 a_2 \cdots a_n \in A, b_1 b_2 \cdots b_n \in B\}$.

   (g) $A \oplus B$.

$\star$ **4.** Give an alternative proof for Example 2.42 based on the following idea: We may simulate NFA $\overline{M}$ on xy together with $\widehat{M_i}$ on z by simulating two moves of $\overline{M}$ and one move of $\widehat{M_i}$ at each step. (Thus, the new NFA for $L_{\frac{3}{3}}$ has only $n + 2$ tracks.)

$\star$ **5.** Show that if A and B are regular languages, so are the following:

   (a) $\{xyz \mid zyx \in A\}$.

   (b) $\{xyz \mid zyx \in A, y \in B\}$.

   (c) $\{y \mid (\exists x) [|x| = |y|, xy \in A]\}$.

   (d) $\{x \mid (\exists y, z) [|x| = |y| = |z|, xyz \in A]\}$.

   (e) $\{y \mid (\exists x, z), [|x| = |y| = |z|, xyz \in A]\}$.

   (f) $\{yz \mid (\exists x) [|x| = |y| = |z|, xyz \in A]\}$.

   (g) $\{xy \mid (\exists z) [|x| = |y| = |z|, xyz \in A]\}$.

   (h) $\{x \mid (\exists w, y, z) [x = wyz \text{ and } wy^R z \in A]\}$.

6. Consider a Boolean function $f(a_1, a_2, \cdots, a_n)$. For any n binary strings $x_1, x_2, \cdots, x_n$ of equal length, denote by $f(x_1, x_2, \cdots, x_n)$ the bitwise function f on $x_1, x_2, \cdots, x_n$. That is, if $x_i = x_{i_1} x_{i_2} \ldots x_{i_k}$ for $i = 1, 2, \ldots, n$, where each x_{i_j} is a bit in $\{0, 1\}$, then $f(x_1, x_2, \ldots, x_n)$ is equal to

$$f(x_{11}, x_{21}, \ldots, x_{n1}) \cdot f(x_{12}, x_{22}, \ldots, x_{n2}) \cdots f(x_{1k}, x_{2k}, \ldots, x_{nk}).$$

Show that if languages $A_1, A_2, \cdots, A_n$ are regular, then language

$$\{f(x_1, x_2, \cdots, x_n) \mid |x_1| = |x_2| = \cdots = |x_n|,$$
$$x_1 \in A_1, x_2 \in A_2, \cdots, x_n \in A_n\}$$

is also regular.

7. In Exercise 3(c) above, show that, for any regular language A, the number of distinct A_x's is finite. Find an upper bound for this number, assuming that A is accepted by a DFA with s states.

8. Are the following statements true? Prove or disprove your answer.

   (a) If A is regular and $A \subseteq B$, then B is regular.

   (b) If A is regular and $B \subseteq A$, then B is regular.

   (c) If A^2 is regular, then A is regular.

(d) If A and AB are regular, then B is regular.

(e) If A and B are regular, then $\bigcup_{i=0}^{\infty}(A^i \cap B^i)$ is regular.

9. Show that every regular language in 0^* can be represented in the form

$$0^{a_1} + 0^{a_2} + \cdots + 0^{a_k} + (0^{b_1} + 0^{b_2} + \cdots + 0^{b_h})(0^c)^*,$$

for some integer constants $a_1, a_2, \cdots, a_k, b_1, b_2, \cdots, b_h$, and c.

$\star$ **10.** A subset P of nonnegative integers is *ultimately periodic* if there exists two positive integers b, p such that, for all $m \geq b$, $m \in P$ implies $m + p \in P$. Prove the following statements:

(a) For any regular language L, $\{|x| \mid x \in L\}$ is ultimately periodic.

(b) A language L over $\{0\}$ is regular if and only if $\{|x| \mid x \in L\}$ is ultimately periodic.

(c) If f is a mapping from integers to integers such that $f^{-1}(P)$ is ultimately periodic for every ultimately periodic set P, then the set $\{x \in A \mid (\exists y)\,[|y| = f(|x|), y \in B]\}$ is regular for every pair of regular sets A and B.

(d) If f is a mapping from integers to integers such that $f^{-1}(P)$ is ultimately periodic for every ultimately periodic set P, then the set $\{x \mid (\exists y)\,[|y| = f(|x|), xy \in L]\}$ is regular for every regular set L.

$\star$ **11.** Apply Exercise 10(d) above to prove the following results:

(a) If L is a regular language, then so is $\{x \mid (\exists y)\,[|y| = 2^{|x|}, xy \in L]\}$. [*Hint*: Use Fermat's theorem, which states that for any odd integer $m \geq 3$, there exists an integer $\varphi(m)$ such that $2^{\varphi(m)} \equiv 1 \bmod m$.]

(b) If L is a regular language, then so is $\{x \mid (\exists y)\,[|y|^2 = |x|, xy \in L]\}$.

2.7 Minimum Deterministic Finite Automata

In the past few sections, we have introduced a number of ways to construct a DFA for a given regular language. These methods, however, often result in DFA's with a large number of states. For instance, if we are given a regular expression r, we can find a DFA for $L(r)$ by first finding an NFA M_1 from r, using the method developed in Section 1.3, and then converting M_1 to a DFA M_2 by the subset construction method of Section 2.4. What is the size of the DFA M_2 compared with the size of r or M_1? In general, the first step creates an NFA of $O(n)$ states from a regular expression of n symbols, and the second step creates a DFA of up to 2^n states from an NFA of n states (cf. Example 2.27). Apparently, such a DFA is too big for a reasonably big number n.

As another example, consider the NFA M' constructed from a given DFA M in Example 2.40. Suppose the given DFA M has n states, then M' has

$2n^2 + 2$ states. If we convert this NFA to an equivalent DFA, the new DFA would have, in the worst case, $2^{O(n^2)}$ states.

Whereas this large size of DFA's is unavoidable in some cases, many DFA's constructed this way can be reduced to smaller, equivalent DFA's. In this section, we show how to find, for a given regular language, a DFA with the minimum number of states. Such a DFA is called a *minimum DFA*.

To begin with, we define, for any language $L \subseteq \Sigma^*$, a relation R_L on Σ^* as follows:

$$x \, R_L \, y \quad \text{if and only if} \quad (\forall w)\,[xw \in L \Leftrightarrow yw \in L].$$

This relation R_L is an equivalence relation. That is, it satisfies the following properties:

(1) *Reflexivity*: $(\forall x \in \Sigma^*)\,[x \, R_L \, x]$;

(2) *Symmetry*: $(\forall x, y \in \Sigma^*)\,[x \, R_L \, y \Rightarrow y \, R_L \, x]$;

(3) *Transitivity*: $(\forall x, y, z \in \Sigma^*)\,[x \, R_L \, y, y \, R_L \, z \Rightarrow x \, R_L \, z]$.

Recall that for any equivalence relation R on a set S and for any $x \in S$, the class

$$[x]_R = \{y \in S \mid x \, R \, y\}$$

is called an *equivalence class* containing x. Every equivalence relation R on a set S divides S into disjoint equivalence classes. The number of equivalence classes is called the *index* of R, and is denoted by $\mathrm{Index}(R)$.

Example 2.45 *Let* $L = \{x \in (0+1)^* \mid |x| \text{ is odd}\}$. *Find all equivalence classes of* R_L.

Solution. Note that $x R_L y$ if and only if $|x| - |y|$ is even. Therefore, there are two equivalence classes

$$[\varepsilon]_{R_L} = \{x \in (0+1)^* \mid |x| \text{ is even}\}$$
$$[0]_{R_L} = \{x \in (0+1)^* \mid |x| \text{ is odd}\}. \qquad \square$$

Example 2.46 *Let L be the set of nonempty binary strings starting and ending with the same symbol. Find all equivalence classes of* R_L.

Solution. We first show that $x R_L y$ if and only if x and y start with the same symbol and end with the same symbol.

For the forward direction, we first assume that x and y start with different symbols; for instance, x starts with 0 and y starts with 1. Then, $x0 \in L$ and $y0 \notin L$. This implies that x and y do not satisfy the relation $x \, R_L \, y$. Or, equivalently, $x \, R_L \, y$ implies that x and y start with the same symbol. Next, note that $x \, R_L \, y$ implies that $x \in L \Leftrightarrow y \in L$. Since x and y start with the same symbol, they must end with the same symbol.

For the backward direction, we assume that x and y start with the same symbol and end with the same symbol. Since x and y start with the same symbol, $xw \in L \Leftrightarrow yw \in L$ for all $w \in (0+1)^+$. Moreover, since x and y also end with the same symbol, $x \in L \Leftrightarrow y \in L$. Therefore, for any $w \in (0+1)^*$, $xw \in L \Leftrightarrow yw \in L$. That is, xR_Ly.

From the above characterization of the relation R_L, we can easily see that R_L has five equivalence classes:

$$[\varepsilon]_{R_L} = \varepsilon,$$
$$[0]_{R_L} = 0 + 0(0+1)^*0, \qquad [1]_{R_L} = 1 + 1(0+1)^*1,$$
$$[01]_{R_L} = 0(0+1)^*1, \qquad [10]_{R_L} = 1(0+1)^*0. \qquad \square$$

The following lemma relates, for a regular language L, Index(R_L) with the number of states in a DFA M that accepts L.

Lemma 2.47 *Assume that L is accepted by a DFA $M = (Q, \Sigma, s, \delta, F)$. Then, for any strings $x, y \in \Sigma^*$, if $\delta(s, x) = \delta(s, y)$ then $x R_L y$.*

Proof. Suppose that $\delta(s, x) = \delta(s, y)$ in M. Then, for any $w \in \Sigma^*$,

$$\delta(s, xw) = \delta(\delta(s, x), w)) = \delta(\delta(s, y), w)) = \delta(s, yw).$$

Therefore, for any $w \in \Sigma^*$, $xw \in L$ if and only if $yw \in L$. $\qquad \square$

The above lemma shows that if L is accepted by a DFA M of n states, then all strings with the same ending state are in the same equivalence class of R_L. Therefore, Index(R_L) is bounded by n and is finite. Thus, if we can find a DFA accepting language L with exactly Index(R_L) states, then this DFA must be a minimum DFA. The following theorem shows that, in fact, this property characterizes the minimum DFA's.

Theorem 2.48 *For any regular language L, its minimum DFA has exactly* Index(R_L) *states.*

Proof. Assume that L is a language over alphabet Σ. Define a DFA $M = (Q, \Sigma, \delta, s, F)$ as follows:

(1) $Q = \{[x]_{R_L} \mid x \in \Sigma^*\}$;

(2) $\delta([x]_{R_L}, a) = [xa]_{R_L}$;

(3) $s = [\varepsilon]_{R_L}$;

(4) $F = \{[x]_{R_L} \mid x \in L\}$.

From the discussion above, we know that if L is regular then Index$(R_L) < \infty$. It follows that Q is a finite set. In addition, the function δ is well defined because

$$[x]_{R_L} = [y]_{R_L} \implies [xa]_{R_L} = [ya]_{R_L}$$
$$\implies \delta([x]_{R_L}, a) = [xa]_{R_L} = [ya]_{R_L} = \delta([y]_{R_L}, a).$$

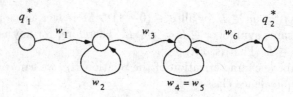

Figure 2.45: Computation path of a string w.

By a simple induction, we can extend this property to $\delta([\varepsilon]_{R_L}, x) = [x]_{R_L}$, for all $x \in \Sigma^*$. This shows that $L(M) = L$:

$$x \in L \Longleftrightarrow [x]_{R_L} \in F \Longleftrightarrow \delta([\varepsilon]_{R_L}, x) \in F \Longleftrightarrow M \text{ accepts } x.$$

Since M has $\text{Index}(R_L)$ states, it is, by Lemma 2.47, a minimum DFA for L.
□

Corollary 2.49 *A language L is regular if and only if* $\text{Index}(R_L) < \infty$.

Proof. Note that, in the proof of Theorem 2.48, we did not use the fact that L is regular. That is, we can construct the minimum DFA for any language L as long as $\text{Index}(R_L) < \infty$. Thus, such languages L must be regular. □

Example 2.50 *Show that L is regular if and only if there exists a positive integer k such that $x\,R_L\,y$ if and only if for every $z \in \Sigma^*$ with $|z| \leq k$, $xz \in L \Leftrightarrow yz \in L$.*

Proof. First, assume that L is regular and is accepted by a DFA $M = (Q, \Sigma, \delta, s, F)$. Let $k = |Q|^2 - 1$. We claim that if $xz \in L \Leftrightarrow yz \in L$ for all z of length $|z| \leq k$, then $x\,R_L y$. To see this, let us consider the product DFA $M^* = M \times M$. For every string w of length $|w| > k$, the computation path of M^* on w, starting from state $q_1^* = [\delta(s, x), \delta(s, y)]$ to $q_2^* = [\delta(s, xw), \delta(s, yw)]$, contains at least $|Q|^2 + 1$ states. Therefore, it contains some cycles in the transition diagram of M^*. Let us eliminate these cycles and keep only a simple path from q_1^* to q_2^*. This simple path corresponds to the computation path of M^* on a string z of length $|z| \leq k$, from q_1^* to q_2^*. (E.g., we show in Figure 2.45 the computation path of a string $w = w_1 w_2 w_3 w_4 w_5 w_6$, with w_2, w_4 and w_5 associated to the two cycles. We eliminate these cycles to form a new string $z = w_1 w_3 w_6$ which is associated with the simple path.) That is, $q_2^* = [\delta(s, xz), \delta(s, yz)]$; or, $\delta(s, xw) = \delta(s, xz)$ and $\delta(s, yw) = \delta(s, yz)$. Now, by the assumption, $xz \in L \Leftrightarrow yz \in L$; that is, two states $\delta(s, xz)$ and $\delta(s, yz)$ both are in F or both are not in F. Therefore, $xw \in L \Leftrightarrow yw \in L$. It follows that $x\,R_L\,y$.

Conversely, suppose there exists such a constant k. Note that each z can divide Σ^* into at most two parts: $\{x \mid xz \in L\}$ and $\{x \mid xz \notin L\}$. Therefore, R_L has at most $2^{1 + |\Sigma| + \cdots + |\Sigma|^k}$ equivalence classes. Hence, by Corollary 2.49, L is regular. □

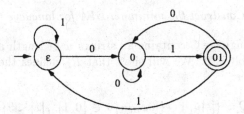

Figure 2.46: Solution to Example 2.51.

Example 2.51 *Find the minimum DFA for language* $(0 + 1)^*01$.

Solution. Let us denote this language by L, and study the equivalence classes of R_L. First, we consider the class $[\varepsilon]_{R_L}$. Note that

$$[\varepsilon]_{R_L} = \{x \in \{0,1\}^* \mid (\forall w)\, [xw \in (0 + 1)^*01 \Leftrightarrow w \in (0 + 1)^*01]\}.$$

Therefore, if $x \in [\varepsilon]_{R_L}$, then x must not end with 0 or 01, for otherwise $x1$ or $x\varepsilon$ would be in $(0 + 1)^*01$, which would imply that 1 or ε is in $(0 + 1)^*01$. Conversely, if x does not end with 0 or 01, then it is clearly in $[\varepsilon]_{R_L}$. So, we know that $[\varepsilon]_{R_L}$ contains strings ε, 1 and all strings ending with 11; or,

$$[\varepsilon]_{R_L} = \varepsilon + 1 + (0 + 1)^*11.$$

Next, we consider

$$[0]_{R_L} = \{x \in \{0,1\}^* \mid (\forall w)\, [0w \in (0 + 1)^*01 \Leftrightarrow xw \in (0 + 1)^*01]\}.$$

Since, for $w = 1$, $0w \in (0 + 1)^*01$, we know that $x \in [0]_{R_L}$ must end with 0. Conversely, it is clear that if x ends with 0, then $x \in [0]_{R_L}$. So, we get

$$[0]_{R_L} = (0 + 1)^*0.$$

Now, we note that $1 \in [\varepsilon]_{R_L}$ and so $[1]_{R_L} = [\varepsilon]_{R_L}$; and $00 \in [0]_{R_L}$ and so $[00]_{R_L} = [0]_{R_L}$. Therefore, we jump to

$$[01]_{R_L} = \{x \in \{0,1\}^* \mid (\forall w)\, [01w \in (0 + 1)^*01 \Leftrightarrow xw \in (0 + 1)^*01]\}.$$

By the same argument as that for $[0]_{R_L}$, we can see that $[01]_{R_L}$ contains all strings x which end with 01; or,

$$[01]_{R_L} = (0 + 1)^*01.$$

Finally, we note that $[10]_{R_L} = [0]_{R_L}$, $[11]_{R_L} = [\varepsilon]_{R_L}$ and, for all strings w of length $|w| \geq 3$, $w\,R_L\,x$ for some x of length $|x| \leq 2$. Therefore, there are only three equivalence classes: $[\varepsilon]_{R_L}$, $[0]_{R_L}$ and $[01]_{R_L}$, and the minimum DFA for L has only three states. We show it in Figure 2.46. $\square$

Example 2.52 *Construct the minimum DFA for language* $(0+1)^*0(0+1)^9$.

Solution. This language L contains all strings w of length at least 10 whose tenth rightmost bit is 0. We will show that R_L defines the following set of equivalence classes:

$$Q = \{[\varepsilon]_{R_L}\} \cup \{[0x]_{R_L} \mid x \in \{0,1\}^*, |x| \le 9\}.$$

First, we show that all equivalence classes in Q are distinct. Since, for any x with $|x| \le 9$, $0^{9-|x|} \notin L$ and $0x0^{9-|x|} \in L$, the strings ε and $0x$ are not in the same equivalence class. Now, we look at $0x$ and $0y$ with $x \ne y$. We consider three cases:

Case 1. $|x| < |y|$. Since $0x0^{9-|y|} \notin L$ and $0y0^{9-|y|} \in L$, strings $0x$ and $0y$ are not in the same equivalence class.

Case 2. $|x| > |y|$. Symmetric to Case 1.

Case 3. $|x| = |y|$. We can write $x = x_1 x_2 \cdots x_k$ and $y = y_1 y_2 \cdots y_k$ for some $k \ge 1$, where each x_i and each y_j is a bit in $\{0,1\}$. Since $x \ne y$, there exists an integer i, $1 \le i \le k$, such that $x_i \ne y_i$. Without loss of generality, assume that $x_i = 0$ and $y_i = 1$. In this case, $0x0^{9-k+i} \in L$ and $0y0^{9-k+i} \notin L$. Thus, $0x$ and $0y$ are not in the same equivalence class.

Next, we show that every binary string is in one of the equivalence classes in Q. For each string $w \in (0+1)^*$, consider its suffix u of length $\min(|w|, 10)$. First, if $u \in 1^*$, then we observe that $wy \in L$ for some $y \in \{0,1\}^*$ if and only if $|y| \ge 10$ and the tenth rightmost bit of y is 0. (If $|y| < 10$, then either $|wy| < 10$ or the tenth rightmost bit of wy is a bit in u and, hence, equal to 1.) It follows that for any string $y \in \{0,1\}^*$, $wy \in L$ if and only if $y \in L$, and so $w R_L \varepsilon$. Next, if $u = 1^j 0x$ for some $j \ge 0$ and $x \in \{0,1\}^*$ then, by following the same argument as above, we can see that $wy \in L$ if and only if $0xy \in L$. Thus, $w R_L 0x$.

Now, we can use the above analysis to construct the minimum DFA $M = (Q, \{0,1\}, \delta, [\varepsilon]_{R_L}, F)$ for L, where Q is the set defined above,

$$F = \{[0x]_{R_L} \in Q \mid |x| = 9\},$$

and the transition function δ can be described as follows:

(1) $\delta([\varepsilon]_{R_L}, 0) = [0]_{R_L}$, $\delta([\varepsilon]_{R_L}, 1) = [\varepsilon]_{R_L}$.

(2) If $|x| < 9$ then, for $a \in \{0,1\}$, $\delta([0x]_{R_L}, a) = [0xa]_{R_L}$.

(3) If $x = 1^9$ then $\delta([0x]_{R_L}, 0) = [0]_{R_L}$, $\delta([0x]_{R_L}, 1) = [\varepsilon]_{R_L}$.

(4) If $|x| = 9$ and $x = 1^i 0y$ for some y, with $0 \le i \le 8$, then $\delta([0x]_{R_L}, a) = [0ya]_{R_L}$, for $a \in \{0,1\}$. $\square$

From the above example, we can see that the minimum DFA for language $(0+1)^*0(0+1)^{n-1}$ must contain 2^n states. However, it is easy to construct an NFA for the same language with $n+1$ states. Thus, the exponential size increase of the subset construction is unavoidable in these cases. It also shows that, although NFA's and DFA's have the same computational power for recognizing languages, they are different in term of computational complexity.

In general, finding the equivalence classes of R_L for a given language L (from its regular expression or an informal description) may not be easy. However, if we are given a DFA M for L, then there is a simple method to find the equivalent minimum DFA.

The basic idea of this method is the simple observation of Lemma 2.47: For any DFA M, two input strings which end at the same state of M must belong to the same equivalence class of R_L. That is, for any DFA $M = (Q, \Sigma, \delta, s, F)$ accepting L, if we define, for each $q \in Q$, $S_q = \{x \in \Sigma^* \mid \delta(s, x) = q\}$, then every S_q is contained in a single equivalence class of R_L. Thus, we may define a new equivalence relation R_L^* on Q as follows:

$$p\, R_L^*\, q \iff S_p \text{ and } S_q \text{ are in the same equivalence class of } R_L$$
$$\iff (\forall w)\,[\delta(p, w) \in F \Leftrightarrow \delta(q, w) \in F].$$

Each equivalence class of R_L corresponds to an equivalence class of R_L^* in the following way:

$$[x]_{R_L} = \bigcup \{S_q \mid q \in [\delta(s, x)]_{R_L^*}\}.$$

From this relation, we can build the minimum DFA $M^* = (Q^*, \Sigma, \delta^*, s^*, F^*)$ for L as follows:

(1) $Q^* = \{[q]_{R_L^*} \mid q \in Q\}$;

(2) $\delta^*([q]_{R_L^*}, a) = [\delta(q, a)]_{R_L^*}$;

(3) $s^* = [s]_{R_L^*}$;

(4) $F^* = \{[f]_{R_L^*} \mid f \in F\}$.

Thus, to construct the minimum DFA M^* which is equivalent to a given DFA M, all we need to do is to compute the equivalence classes of R_L^*. We demonstrate three different methods in the next example.

Example 2.53 *Find the minimum DFA equivalent to the DFA M of Figure 2.47.*

Solution 1. Let $M = (Q, \Sigma, \delta, q_0, F)$, where $Q = \{q_0, q_1, \ldots, q_5\}$, and let $L = L(M)$. We note that states q_i and q_j are equivalent under R_L^* if and only if for all strings w, $\delta(q_i, w)$ and $\delta(q_j, w)$ both are in F or both are not in F. Therefore, to find the relation R_L^* between any two states, we construct a graph G as follows: Each vertex is an *unordered* pair (q_i, q_j) of states. Let U be the set of vertices (q_i, q_j) with one vertex $q_i \in F$ and the other vertex $q_j \notin F$. For each vertex $(q_i, q_j) \notin U$, with $i \neq j$, we draw edges

$$(q_i, q_j) \xrightarrow{a} (\delta(q_i, a), \delta(q_j, a))$$

for all $a \in \Sigma$. Then, it is clear that $q_i\, R_L^*\, q_j$ if and only if there is no path in G from (q_i, q_j) to a vertex in U.

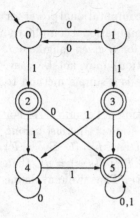

Figure 2.47: DFA M.

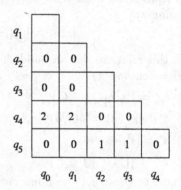

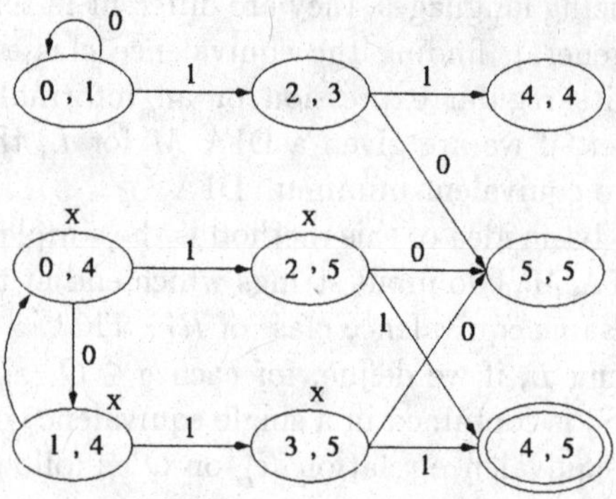

Figure 2.48: Graph G.

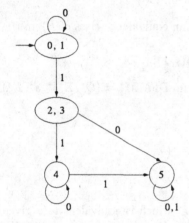

Figure 2.49: Minimum DFA of
Example 2.53.

	q_0	q_1	q_2	q_3	q_4
q_1					
q_2	0	0			
q_3	0	0			
q_4	2	2	0	0	
q_5	0	0	1	1	0

Figure 2.50: The table buildup
method for Example 2.53.

For this example, we show the corresponding graph G in Figure 2.48. (We only show vertices which are reachable from vertices not in U.) The vertex (q_4, q_5) is in U and is denoted by double circles. All vertices from which there are paths going to a vertex in U have been marked with X. Thus, we have $q_0 \, R_L^* \, q_1$ and $q_2 \, R_L^* \, q_3$. The resulting minimum DFA is shown in Figure 2.49.

□

Solution 2. In the above solution, the critical step is to determine, from a given pair (q_i, q_j) of states, whether there is a path in G from it to a vertex in U. This question can be solved using a table buildup method. We create a table of pairs (q_i, q_j). Initially, we mark all pairs in U with value 0. At stage $k > 0$, we mark each unmarked pair (q_i, q_j) with value k if there is an edge from it to a pair with mark $k - 1$; that is, we mark pair (q_i, q_j) with value k if

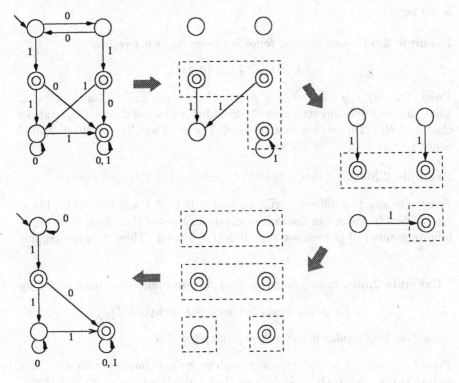

Figure 2.51: The third method.

there is an $a \in \Sigma$ such that $(\delta(q_i, a), \delta(q_j, a))$ has the value $k - 1$. We repeat this process until no new pairs are marked in a stage. The pairs (q_i, q_j) which remain unmarked must then satisfy $q_i \, R_L^* \, q_j$.

For this example, the above table buildup process is shown in Figure 2.50. The pairs of states which remain unmarked are (q_0, q_1) and (q_2, q_3).   □

Solution 3. Instead of building a table to check the relation R_L^*, we can also do it directly on the transition diagram of M. Initially, we divide all states into two blocks F and $Q - F$. Then, at each subsequent stage, we check every block S of states. For every $a \in \Sigma$, we consider $\delta(q_i, a)$ for all $q_i \in S$. If they do not all belong to the same block, then we divide S into smaller blocks according to their destination blocks; that is, if $\delta(q_i, a)$ and $\delta(q_j, a)$ belong to the same block but $\delta(q_k, a)$ belongs to a different block, then q_i and q_j remain in the same smaller block and q_k belongs to a different smaller block. We repeat this process until no block of states can be divided further.

The whole process on this example is shown in Figure 2.51.   □

Corollary 2.49 gives us a simple characterization of regular languages. It is very useful in the analysis of the structure of regular languages. In the following two examples, we show how to apply it to prove that a given language is *not* regular.

Example 2.54 *Show that the following language is not regular:*

$$L = \{xx^R \mid x \in \{0,1\}^*\}.$$

Proof. For any $x, y \in 0^*1$ with $x \neq y$, we know that $xx^R \in L$ and $yx^R \notin L$. Thus, any two different strings in 0^*1 must belong to two different equivalence classes of R_L. This means that $\text{Index}(R_L) = \infty$. Thus, by Corollary 2.49, L is not regular. $\square$

Example 2.55 *Show that $L = \{0^m 1^n \mid gcd(m,n) = 1\}$ is not regular.*

Proof. For any two different primes p and q, $0^p 1^p \notin L$ and $0^q 1^p \in L$. Therefore, 0^p and 0^q are not in the same equivalence class of R_L. Since there are an infinite number of primes, we have $\text{Index}(R_L) = \infty$. Thus, L is not regular.
$\square$

* Example 2.56 *For any language L, define an equivalence relation D_L by*

$$x \, D_L \, y \iff (\forall u)\,(\forall w)\,[uxw \in L \Leftrightarrow uyw \in L].$$

Show that L is regular if and only if $\text{Index}(D_L) < \infty$.

Proof. Clearly, for any strings x and y, $x \, D_L \, y$ implies $x \, R_L \, y$. Thus, $\text{Index}(R_L) \leq \text{Index}(D_L)$. It follows that $\text{Index}(D_L) < \infty$ implies that L is regular.

Conversely, assume that L is regular. To show that $\text{Index}(D_L) < \infty$, we consider a DFA $M = (Q, \Sigma, \delta, q_0, F)$ accepting L and define an equivalence relation D_M on Σ^* as follows:

$$x \, D_M \, y \iff (\forall q_i \in Q)\,[\delta(q_i, x) = \delta(q_i, y)].$$

First, note that $x \, D_M \, y$ implies $x \, D_L \, y$. It follows that $\text{Index}(D_L) \leq \text{Index}(D_M)$. Assume that the state set Q of M is $\{q_0, q_1, \ldots, q_{n-1}\}$. We claim that D_M has at most n^n equivalence classes. To see this, we observe that every equivalence class $[x]_{D_M}$ can be represented in the following way:

$$[x]_{D_M} = \bigcap_{i=0}^{n-1} \{y \mid \delta(q_i, x) = \delta(q_i, y)\}.$$

That is, $[x]_{D_M}$ is uniquely determined by the following sequence of n states:

$$\widetilde{Q}_x = (\delta(q_0, x), \delta(q_1, x), \ldots, \delta(q_{n-1}, x)).$$

If two strings x and y have the same sequence $\widetilde{Q}_x = \widetilde{Q}_y$, then $x \, D_M \, y$. Thus, the number of equivalence classes of the relation D_M is the number of possible sequences $\widetilde{Q}_x$, which is bounded by n^n. Therefore, we have $\text{Index}(D_L) \leq \text{Index}(D_M) \leq n^n < \infty$. $\square$

Exercise 2.7

1. Find all equivalence classess of R_L for the following languages:

   (a) $(0+1)^*01(0+1)^*$.

   (b) $(00+11)(0+1)^*$.

   (c) $011(0+1)^*001$.

   (d) The set of binary strings in which each block of four symbols have at least two 0's.

   (e) $\{x \in \{0,1\}^* \mid \#_0(x) = \#_1(x)\}$, where $\#_a(w)$ is the number of occurrences of symbol a in w.

2. For each of the following languages L, show that $\text{Index}(L) = \infty$ and so L is not regular.

   (a) $\{0^m 1^n \mid 0 \le m \le n\}$.

   (b) $\{0^n 1^m 0^{n+m} \mid n, m \ge 0\}$.

   (c) $\{ww \mid w \in \{0,1\}^*\}$.

   (d) $\{xx^R w \mid x, w \in \{0,1\}^+\}$.

3. For each of the following languages L, show that no two strings can be in the same equivalence class of R_L.

   (a) $\{0^p \mid p \text{ is a prime}\}$.

   (b) $\{0^{n^2} \mid n \ge 0\}$.

4. Construct the minimum DFA's for languages accepted by DFA's in Figure 2.52(a) and 2.52(b).

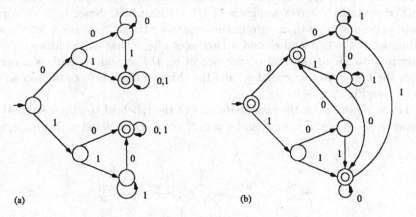

(a) (b)

Figure 2.52: Two DFA's for Exercise 4.

5. Construct a minimum DFA equivalent to the NFA of Figure 2.53.

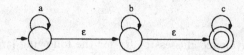

Figure 2.53: An NFA for Exercise 5.

2.8 Pumping Lemmas

Not all languages are regular. In fact, there are uncountably many languages
over an alphabet Σ (cf. Example 5.18), but only countably many of them are
regular (there are at most c^n possible regular expressions of length n for some
constant $c > 0$). Therefore, *most* languages are not regular.

In the last section, we have used the simple characterization of Corollary
2.49 for regular languages to prove that some languages are not regular. However, this method involves the analysis of equivalence classes of the relation
R_L, and is sometimes difficult to apply. In this section, we introduce another
necessary condition for regularity of languages which can be used to prove
that a language is nonregular. In the following, we write, for any string v, v^*
to denote the set $\{v\}^*$.

Lemma 2.57 (Pumping Lemma). *If a language L is accepted by a DFA M
with s states, then every string x in L with $|x| \geq s$ can be written as $x = uvw$
such that $v \neq \varepsilon$ and $uv^*w \subseteq L$.*

Proof. Consider the transition diagram of M. Since $x \in L$, the computation
path π of x starts from the initial state q_0 and ends at a final state q_f. The
concatenation of the labels over the path π is exactly the string x. The path
π has exactly $|x|$ edges because each edge is labeled by a symbol. Thus, the
path π contains a vertex sequence of $|x| + 1$ elements. Since $|x| \geq s$, some
state q_i occurs more than once in the sequence. Break the path π into three
subpaths at the first and second occurrences of q_i. That is, the first subpath
is from state q_0 to the first occurrence of q_i, the second subpath is a cycle
from the first q_i to the second q_i, and the third subpath is from the second q_i
to q_f (see Figure 2.54).

Let u, v, and w be the concatenations of the labels of the three subpaths,
respectively. Then, $x = uvw$, and $v \neq \varepsilon$. Since v is associated with a cycle, we

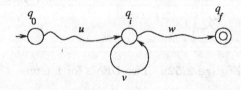

Figure 2.54: The path $(q_0, \cdots, q_i, \cdots, q_i, \cdots, q_f)$.

also have $uv^*w \subseteq L$. (E.g., uv^2w is in L because $\delta(q_0, uv^2w) = \delta(q_i, vvw) = \delta(q_i, vw) = \delta(q_i, w) = q_f$.)   □

Now, for a given langauge L, if we can prove that the necessary condition of the pumping lemma does not hold with respect to any $s > 0$, then L is not regular.

Example 2.58 $\{0^p \mid p \text{ is a prime}\}$ *is not a regular language.*

Proof. By way of contradiction, assume that $L = \{0^p \mid p \text{ is a prime number}\}$ is regular. Then, L is accepted by a DFA M. Let s be the number of states in M. Consider a prime number $p > s$. Note that $0^p \in L$ and $|0^p| = p > s$. Therefore, by the pumping lemma, 0^p can be written as $0^p = uvw$ such that $v \neq \varepsilon$ and $uv^*w \subseteq L$.

Let $i = |u| + |w|$ and $j = |v|$. Then, the condition $uv^*w \subseteq L$ means that, for any $k \geq 0$, $uv^kw = 0^{i+kj} \in L$. Or, equivalently, for any $k \geq 0$, $i + kj$ is a prime. In particular, when $k = 0$, it means that i is a prime. So, $i \geq 2$. When $k = i$, this means that $i(1 + j)$ is a prime. However, since $v \neq \varepsilon$, we have $j = |v| \geq 1$, and so $i(1 + j)$ is not a prime. This is a contradiction.   □

Note that in the above example, the underlying language is over a singleton alphabet $\{0\}$. For languages over an alphabet with more than one symbol, the above pumping lemma is not convenient and sometimes even not sufficient. For instance, consider the language $\{0^n1^n \mid n \geq 0\}$. When we follow the argument in the proof of the above example, we get $0^n1^n = uvw$ for some strings u, v, w. There are three possible cases for v: (1) v contains only symbol 0; (2) v contains only symbol 1; and (3) v contains both symbols 0 and 1. A complete proof needs to produce a contradiction for each case. This makes the proof more complicated and tedious. The following stronger pumping lemma is a nice tool to avoid this problem.

Lemma 2.59 (Pumping Lemma, Stronger Form). *If a language L is accepted by a DFA M with s states, then for any string $\alpha \in L$ with $|\alpha| \geq s$ and any way of breaking α into $\alpha = xyz$ with $|y| \geq s$, y can be written as $y = uvw$ such that $v \neq \varepsilon$ and $xuv^*wz \subseteq L$.*

Proof. Consider the transition diagram of M. Since $\alpha = xyz \in L$, the computation path π of α goes from the initial state q_0 to a final state q_f. The path π can be divided into three subpaths, associated with the strings x, y and z, respectively. Assume that the second subpath π_2, which is associated with y, is from state q_1 to state q_2. Then, π_2 has exactly $|y|$ edges and, by the same argument as in the proof of Lemma 2.57, π_2 can be further divided into three subpaths, with the middle one being a cycle (see Figure 2.55). Let u, v, and w be the strings associated with the three subpaths, respectively. Then, $y = uvw$ and $v \neq \varepsilon$. Since v is associated with a cycle, we also have $xuv^*wz \subseteq L$.   □

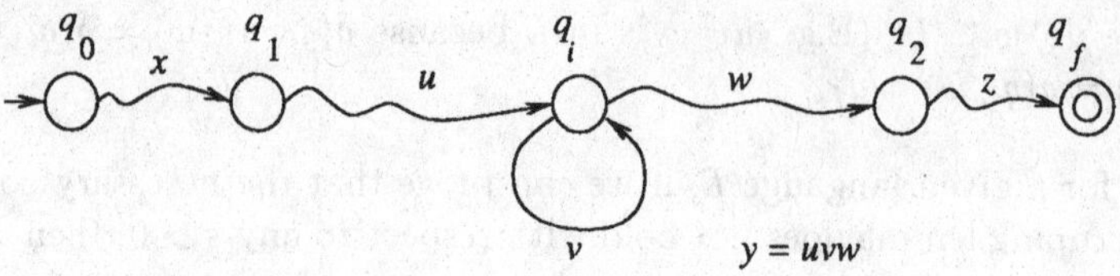

Figure 2.55: The path $(q_0, \cdots, q_1, \cdots, q, \cdots, q, \cdots, q_2, \cdots, f)$.

Example 2.60 $\{0^n 1^n \mid n \geq 0\}$ *is not a regular language.*

Proof. By way of contradiction, assume that $L = \{0^n 1^n \mid n \geq 0\}$ is regular. Then, L is accepted by a DFA M. Let s be the number of states in M. Consider a string $\alpha = 0^s 1^s \in L$. Choose $x = \varepsilon$, $y = 0^s$, and $z = 1^s$. Note that $|y| = |0^s| = s$. By the pumping lemma, α can be written as $\alpha = xuvwz$ such that $v \neq \varepsilon$ and $xuv^* wz \subseteq L$. This means that for any $k \geq 0$, $xuv^k wz \in L$. When $k = 0$, this means that $xuwz = 0^{s-|v|} 1^s \in L$. However, since $v \neq \varepsilon$, we have $s - |v| < s$, contradicting the definition of L. $\square$

From the above example, we can summarize in the following how to prove, by the pumping lemma, that a given language L is not regular:

(1) Assume that L is accepted by a DFA M of s states.

(2) Select a string $\alpha \in L$, with $|\alpha| \geq s$.

(3) Divide α into three parts $\alpha = xyz$ with $|y| \geq s$.

(4) For any way of dividing y into three parts $y = uvw$ with $v \neq \varepsilon$, argue that $xuv^k wz \notin L$ for some $k \geq 0$.

Since s is the size of the DFA M accepting L, and since the DFA M is unknown to us, we do not know how large s is. Therefore, steps (2), (3) and (4) must work for *all* positive integers s. Similarly, the breakdown of y into $y = uvw$ depends on the unknown DFA M, and so is unknown to us. Therefore, we must argue, in step (4), against *all* possible way of dividing y into uvw, as long as $v \neq \varepsilon$.

On the other hand, we are free to select the strings x, y, z, as long as $\alpha = xyz \in L$ and $|y| \geq s$. Indeed, the choice of $x = \varepsilon$, $y = 0^s$ and $z = 0^s$ in the above example made the proof simple. (The reader may verify this claim by trying the choice of $\alpha = 0^{2s} 1^{2s}$, $x = 0^s$, $y = 0^s 1^s$ and $z = 1^s$ to see how complicated the corresponding proof is.) In general, the main difficulty of using the pumping lemma to prove a language nonregular is to determine which strings x, y, z are to be used in the proof. The next two examples illustrate this point.

Example 2.61 *Show that* $L = \{\beta \beta^R \mid \beta \in \{0, 1\}^+\}$ *is not a regular language.*

Proof. By way of contradiction, assume that L is a regular language, accepted by a DFA M of $s > 0$ states. Following the idea of Example 2.60, we select a string $\alpha = 0^s 110^s \in L$, and let $x = \varepsilon$, $y = 0^s$, and $z = 110^s$. By the pumping lemma, y can be written as $y = uvw$ such that $v \neq \varepsilon$ and $xuv^*wz \subseteq L$. This means that for any $k \geq 0$, $xuv^k wz \in L$. When $k = 0$, this means that $xuwz = 0^{s-|v|} 110^s \in L$. However, we observe that $0^{s-|v|} 110^s$ is not of the form $\beta\beta^R$: Since $|v| \geq 1$, either the string $0^{s-|v|} 110^s$ is of an odd length (when $|v|$ is odd) or its first half contains two 1's and the second half has no 1. This is a contradiction. □

Example 2.62 *Show that* $L = \{\beta\beta^R\gamma \mid \beta \in \{0,1\}^+, \gamma \in \{0,1\}^*\}$ *is not regular.*

Proof. By way of contradiction, assume that L is a regular language, accepted by a DFA M of s states. We need to choose a string $\alpha \in L$ with $|\alpha| \geq s$ and divide it into three substrings $\alpha = xyz$ with $|y| \geq s$. Note that if we do it like in the last example, with $\alpha = 0^s 110^s$, $x = \varepsilon$, $y = 0^s$ and $z = 110^s$, then the proof does not work:

(1) The string $0^{s-|v|} 110^s$ is of the form $\beta\beta^R\gamma$, with $\beta = 0^{s-|v|} 1$ and $\gamma = 0^{|v|}$;

(2) The string $0^{s+k|v|} 110^s$, with $k \geq 2$, is of the form $\beta\beta^R\gamma$, with $\beta = 0$.

To fix this problem, we choose $\alpha = 010^s 110^s 10 \in L$ ($\beta = 010^s 1$ and $\gamma = \varepsilon$), and let $x = 01$, $y = 0^s$, and $z = 110^s 10$. Note that the only prefix of $x0^t z$ that is of the form $\beta\beta^R$ is the whole string, and it holds only for $t = s$.

More precisely, we check that, by the pumping lemma, y can be written as $y = uvw$ such that $v \neq \varepsilon$ and $xuv^*wz \subseteq L$. This means that for any $k \geq 0$, $xuv^k wz \in L$. In particular, $xuv^2 wz = 010^{s+|v|} 110^s 10 \in L$. Now, $xuv^2 wz \in L$ means $010^{s+|v|} 110^s 10 = \beta\beta^R\gamma$ for some $\beta, \gamma \in \{0,1\}^*$. Since there are only two occurrences of the substring 010 in this string (as the prefix and suffix), β must contain the prefix 010 and β^R must contain the suffix 010 and γ must be the empty string. In other words, $010^{s+|v|} 110^s 10 = \beta\beta^R$. However, this is obvious impossible, as explained in the proof of the last example. We have reached a contradiction. □

It is interesting to note that $\{\beta\gamma\beta^R \mid \beta \in \{0,1\}^+, \gamma \in \{0,1\}^*\}$ is equal to the language with the following regular expression:

$$0(0 \cup 1)^+ 0 \cup 1(0 \cup 1)^+ 1.$$

Thus, it *is* a regular language.

Example 2.63 *Show that the language* $L = \{0^n 10^m 10^p 10^q \mid n, m, p \geq 1, q \equiv nm \pmod{p}\}$ *is not regular.*

Solution. By way of contradiction, assume that L is a regular language, accepted by a DFA M of s states. Consider the string $\alpha = 010^{s+1} 10^{s+1} 10^{s+1}$. Apply the pumping lemma to string α, with $x = 010^{s+1} 10^{s+1} 10$, $y = 0^s$ and $z = \varepsilon$. Then, the suffix $y = 0^s$ can be written as uvw such that $v \neq \varepsilon$ and for any $k \geq 0$, $xuv^k w$ is in L. Take $k = 0$. We get $xuw = 010^{s+1}10^{s+1}10^t$, with $1 \leq t \leq s$. Since $t \not\equiv 1(s+1) \pmod{s+1}$, we get a contradiction.   □

Note that, for any fixed integer $p > 1$, the language $\{0^n 10^m 10^q \mid n, m, p \geq 1, q \equiv nm \pmod{p}\}$ is regular (see Exercise 3(f) of Section 2.3).

⋆ **Example 2.64** *Consider the following multiplication table on* $\{a, b, c\}$:

×	a	b	c
a	a	a	c
b	c	a	b
c	b	c	a

Recall, from Example 2.28, that for any string x in $\{a, b, c\}^+$, value(x) denotes the value obtained by multiplying symbols in x from left to right. Show that the set

$$L = \{xy \mid x, y \in \{a, b, c\}^*, |x| = |y|, \text{value}(x) = \text{value}(y)\}$$

is not regular.

Proof. Assume, by way of contradiction, that language L is a regular set and is accepted by a DFA M of $s > 0$ states. To find a contradiction, we select a string $\alpha = bc^s bc^s \in L$ and let $x = b$, $y = c^s$ and $z = bc^s$. Apparently, $\alpha \in L$. Now, we apply the pumping lemma to decompose y into $y = uvw$ with $v \neq \varepsilon$ and $xuv^* wz \subseteq L$. This means that, for any $k \geq -1$, $bc^{s+k|v|}bc^s \in L$; in particular, $bc^{s+2|v|}bc^s \in L$. It follows that $bc^{s+2|v|}bc^s = \beta\gamma$ for some β and γ in $\{a, b, c\}^*$ with $|\beta| = |\gamma|$ and value$(\beta) = $ value(γ). From $|\beta| = |\gamma|$, we know that $\beta = bc^{s+|v|}$ and $\gamma = c^{|v|}bc^s$. From the given multiplication table, we get value$(\beta) = b$ and value$(y) \in \{a, c\}$. This is a contradiction.   □

⋆ **Example 2.65** *Show that the set L of all strings over alphabet*

$$\Gamma = \left\{ \begin{pmatrix} 0 \\ 0 \\ 0 \end{pmatrix}, \begin{pmatrix} 1 \\ 0 \\ 0 \end{pmatrix}, \begin{pmatrix} 0 \\ 1 \\ 0 \end{pmatrix}, \begin{pmatrix} 0 \\ 0 \\ 1 \end{pmatrix}, \begin{pmatrix} 1 \\ 1 \\ 0 \end{pmatrix}, \begin{pmatrix} 1 \\ 0 \\ 1 \end{pmatrix}, \begin{pmatrix} 0 \\ 1 \\ 1 \end{pmatrix}, \begin{pmatrix} 1 \\ 1 \\ 1 \end{pmatrix} \right\}$$

that represent correct multiplication is not regular. For example, the relation

$$
\begin{array}{r}
0\ \ 0\ \ 1\ \ 1 \\
\times\ \ 0\ \ 1\ \ 0\ \ 1 \\
\hline
1\ \ 1\ \ 1\ \ 1
\end{array}
$$

implies that the following string is in L:

$$\begin{pmatrix} 0 \\ 0 \\ 1 \end{pmatrix} \begin{pmatrix} 0 \\ 1 \\ 1 \end{pmatrix} \begin{pmatrix} 1 \\ 0 \\ 1 \end{pmatrix} \begin{pmatrix} 1 \\ 1 \\ 1 \end{pmatrix}.$$

Proof. Assume, by way of contradiction, that L is regular and is accepted by a DFA M of $s > 0$ states. Consider the following string α:

$$\begin{pmatrix} 0 \\ 0 \\ 1 \end{pmatrix}^s \begin{pmatrix} 1 \\ 1 \\ 1 \end{pmatrix} \begin{pmatrix} 0 \\ 1 \\ 0 \end{pmatrix}^s.$$

The string α represents the multiplication of the following form:

$$\overbrace{10\cdots0}^{s} \times \overbrace{1\cdots1}^{s+1} = \overbrace{1\cdots1}^{s+1}\overbrace{0\cdots0}^{s},$$

and hence is in L. We let

$$x = \begin{pmatrix} 0 \\ 0 \\ 1 \end{pmatrix}^s \begin{pmatrix} 1 \\ 1 \\ 1 \end{pmatrix}, \quad y = \begin{pmatrix} 0 \\ 1 \\ 0 \end{pmatrix}^s, \quad z = \varepsilon.$$

By the pumping lemma, y can be written as $y = uvw$ such that $v \neq \varepsilon$ and $xuwz \in L$. This implies the following incorrect multiplication:

$$\overbrace{10\cdots0}^{s-|v|} \times \overbrace{1\cdots1}^{s-|v|+1} = \overbrace{1\cdots1}^{s+1}\overbrace{0\cdots0}^{s-|v|}.$$

Thus, we have reached a contradiction. $\qquad\square$

* **Example 2.66** *Show that the set L_2 of the binary expansions of the integers in set $A = \{2^n \mid n \geq 1\}$ is regular, but the set L_3 of the ternary expansions (base 3 representations) of the integers in A is not regular.*

Proof. It is clear that the set L_2 consists of all strings of the form 10^n for all $n \geq 1$; that is, $L_2 = 10^+$. Thus, L_2 is regular.

Next, we assume, for the sake of contradiction, that L_3 is regular and is accepted by a DFA M of $s > 0$ states. For any string $t \in \{0, 1, 2\}^*$, we let n_t be the integer whose ternary expansion is t (with possible leading zeros). We select an arbitrary x in L_3 with $|x| \geq s$. We apply the first pumping lemma (Lemma 2.57) to the string x to get $x = uvw$, with $v \neq \varepsilon$ and $uv^*w \in L_3$. Then, for any $k \geq 0$, the string $uv^k w \in L_3$; that is, $n_{uv^kw} \in A$. Let 2^{m_k} be the integer whose ternary expansion is equal to $uv^k w$. Since $v \neq \varepsilon$ and since $x > 0$, we know that $m_{k+1} > m_k$ for all $k \geq 0$. What is 2^{m_k} in terms of n_u, n_v and n_w? Assume that $|v| = p > 0$ and $|w| = q$. Then, for $k \geq 1$, we have

$$2^{m_k} = n_u \cdot 3^{kp+q} + n_v(3^{(k-1)p+q} + 3^{(k-2)p+q} + \cdots + 3^q) + n_w.$$

It follows that, for $k \geq 2$,

$$2^{m_k} - 2^{m_{k-1}} = n_u \cdot 3^{kp+q} + (n_v - n_u) \cdot 3^{(k-1)p+q}$$
$$= 3^{(k-1)p+q}(n_u(3^p - 1) + n_v).$$

Since $3^{(k-1)p+q}$ is an odd integer, and since $2^{m_{k-1}}$ divides $2^{m_k} - 2^{m_{k-1}}$, we must have that $2^{m_{k-1}}$ divides the integer $n_u(3^p-1)+n_v$. However, this cannot be true for $k \geq 3$, since

$$n_u(3^p - 1) + n_v \leq n_u \cdot 3^{p+q} + n_v \cdot 3^q + n_w = 2^{m_1} < 2^{m_2}.$$

So, we have reached a contradiction.   □

Sometimes, using the pumping lemma directly to prove a language non-regular takes some thinking to come up with the required string α. In these cases, we can often combine the pumping lemma with the closure properties of Section 2.6 to produce simpler proofs. The following are some examples. Let $\#_a(w)$ denote the number of occurrences of symbol a in string w.

Example 2.67 *Show that $L = \{w \in \{0,1\}^* \mid \#_0(w) \neq \#_1(w)\}$ is not regular.*

Proof. We may prove this by selecting $\alpha = 0^s 1^{(s!)+s}$, with $x = \varepsilon$, $y = 0^s$ and $z = 1^{(s!)+s}$, and arguing that for any way of dividing y into $y = uvw$ with $v \neq \varepsilon$, $xuv^k wz = 0^{s+(k-1)|v|}1^{(s!)+s} \notin L$ when $k = (s!)/|v| + 1$. (*Note*: Since $|v| \leq |y| = s$, k must be an integer.)

This proof, though somewhat inspiring, is not easy to find. A simpler proof is as follows:

(1) $L_1 = \{0^n 1^n \mid n \geq 0\}$ is not regular. (This can be proved by the pumping lemma easily as in Example 2.60.)

(2) $L_2 = \{w \in \{0,1\}^* \mid \#_0(w) = \#_1(w)\}$ is not regular, since $L_2 \cap 0^* 1^* = L_1$ is not regular. (If L_2 were regular then, by the property that regular languages are closed under intersection, L_1 would be regular.)

(3) L is not regular since $\overline{L} = L_2$ is not regular.   □

Example 2.68 *Show that $L = \{a^n b^m c^k \mid n, m, k \geq 0, n \neq m \text{ or } m \neq k \text{ or } k \neq n\}$ is not regular.*

Proof. It is easy to use the pumping lemma to prove that

$$\overline{L} \cap a^* b^* c^* = \{a^n b^n c^n \mid n \geq 0\}$$

is not regular. Thus, by the closure properties of the regular languages, L is not regular.   □

Example 2.69 *Let L be a regular language. Show that*

$$L' = \{xz \mid (\exists y) [|x| = |y| = |z| \text{ and } xyz \in L]\}$$

is not necessarily regular.

Proof. Consider the regular language $L = a^* bc^*$. For an arbitrary string $a^i bc^j$ in L with $i + j + 1 = 3n$, let $a^i bc^j = xyz$ with $|x| = |y| = |z| = n > 0$. There are three cases:

(1) Both i and j are greater than or equal to n. Then, $x = a^n$ and $z = c^n$ and so $a^n c^n \in L'$.

(2) The integer i is less than n. Then, $x = a^i bc^{n-i-1}$ and $z = c^n$ and so $a^i bc^{2n-i-1} \in L'$. Note that $i + (2n - i - 1) = 2n - 1$ is odd.

(3) The integer j is less than n. Similar to case (2), we get $a^{2n-j-1} bc^j \in L'$.

Thus, we can see that

$$L' = \{a^n c^n \mid n > 0\} \cup \{a^m bc^n \mid m + n \text{ is odd}\}.$$

It follows that L' is not regular, since $L' \cap a^* c^* = \{a^n c^n \mid n > 0\}$ is not regular (by Example 2.60). □

Exercise 2.8

1. Show that the following languages are not regular.

   (a) $\{0^{n^3 + 3n^2 - 2n} \mid n \geq 0\}$.

   (b) $\{0^p 1^q 0^m 1^n \mid p + q = m + n, p, q, m, n \geq 0\}$.

   (c) $\{0^m 1^n \mid m, n \geq 0 \text{ and } m \neq 2n + 1\}$.

   (d) $\{0^m 1^n \mid 2n \leq m \leq 3n, m, n \geq 0\}$.

   (e) $\{w \in \{0, 1, 2\}^* \mid \#_0(w) + \#_1(w) = \#_2(w)\}$.

   (f) $\{0^{pq} \mid p \text{ and } q \text{ are primes}\}$.

2. For each of the following languages, determine whether it is regular. Present a proof for your answer.

   (a) The set of binary strings having an equal number of 0's and 1's.

   (b) The set of binary strings having an equal number of 01's and 10's.

   (c) The set of binary strings having an equal number of 010's and 101's.

   (d) $\{xy \mid x, y \in \{0, 1\}^*, |x| = |y|, \#_0(x) \geq \#_0(y)\}$.

   (e) $\{xyz \mid x, y, z \in \{0, 1\}^*, |x| = |z| > 0, \#_0(x) \geq \#_0(z)\}$.

   (f) $\{x \# y \# z \mid x, y, z \text{ are binary expansions of positive integers satisfying } x + y = z\}$.

★ 3. Let Γ be the alphabet of Example 2.65.

   (a) Show that the set L of all strings over alphabet Γ that represent correct division is not regular. For example,

$$
\begin{array}{r}
1\ 1\ 1\ 1 \\
\div\ 0\ 1\ 0\ 1 \\
\hline
0\ 0\ 1\ 1
\end{array}
$$

implies that the following string is in L:

$$
\begin{pmatrix} 1 \\ 0 \\ 0 \end{pmatrix} \begin{pmatrix} 1 \\ 1 \\ 0 \end{pmatrix} \begin{pmatrix} 1 \\ 0 \\ 1 \end{pmatrix} \begin{pmatrix} 1 \\ 1 \\ 1 \end{pmatrix}.
$$

(b) Show that the set of all strings over Γ that represent correct multiplication, with the second multiplier equal to 3, is regular.

4. Is it true that for any regular language L over $\{0, 1\}$, the set $N(L) = \{0^{\#_0(x)}1^{\#_1(x)} \mid x \in L\}$ is also regular? Prove your answer.

5. Prove the following stronger form of the pumping lemma: For any regular language L and any positive integer k, there exists a positive integer s such that any string x in L with $|x| > s$ can be decomposed into $x = uvw$ such that $|v| > k$ and for any $i \geq 0$, $uv^i w \in L$.

$\star$ 6. Find a regular language L such that

$$\hat{L} = \{xz \mid (\exists y) [|x| = |y| = |z| \text{ and } xyzy \in L]\}$$

is not regular.

7. Let A and B be regular sets over alphabet Σ. Which of the following languages, if any, are necessarily regular?

(a) $\{x \mid x \in A \text{ and } x^R \in B\}$.

(b) $\{x \mid x \in A \text{ and } x^R \notin B\}$.

(c) $\{x \mid x = x^R \text{ and } x \in A\}$.

$\star$ (d) $\{a_1 b_n a_2 b_{n-1} a_3 b_{n-2} \cdots a_n b_1 \mid a_i, b_i \in \Sigma \text{ for } 1 \leq i \leq n, a_1 a_2 \cdots a_n \in A, b_1 b_2 \cdots b_n \in B\}$.

$\star$ (e) $\{a_1 a_n a_2 a_{n-1} a_3 a_{n-2} \cdots a_n a_1 \mid a_i \in \Sigma \text{ for } 1 \leq i \leq n, a_1 a_2 \cdots a_n \in A\}$.

$\star$ (f) $\{a_1 a_{2n} a_3 a_{2n-2} a_5 a_{2n-4} \cdots a_{2n-1} a_2 \mid a_i \in \Sigma \text{ for } 1 \leq i \leq 2n, a_1 a_2 \cdots a_n \in A\}$.

8. Consider the language

$$L = \{x0^n y1^n z \mid x \in P, y \in Q, z \in R\},$$

where P, Q and R are nonempty sets over alphabet $\{0, 1\}$. Can you find regular sets P, Q, R such that L is not regular? Can you find regular sets P, Q, R such that L is regular? What if P, Q, R must be infinite regular sets?

$\star$ 9. (a) Is the language $\{0^{3m+4n} \mid m, n \geq 0\}$ regular? Prove your answer.

(b) Let L be a language over alphabet $\{0\}$. Show that L^* is regular. [*Hint*: Prove and use the fact that if a and b are relatively prime natural numbers, then for any integer $n \geq ab$, there exist nonnegative integers u and v such that $n = ua + vb$.]

3

Context-Free Languages

3.1 Context-Free Grammars

In the study of natural languages, a grammar is a set of rules that govern how sentences in a language are generated. For instance, the English grammar contains, among others, the following rules:

$$\langle sentence \rangle \longrightarrow \langle subject \rangle \langle predicate \rangle$$
$$\langle subject \rangle \longrightarrow \langle noun \rangle$$
$$\langle predicate \rangle \longrightarrow \langle verb \rangle \langle adverb \rangle$$
$$\langle noun \rangle \longrightarrow \texttt{water}$$
$$\langle verb \rangle \longrightarrow \texttt{evaporates}$$
$$\langle adverb \rangle \longrightarrow \texttt{constantly}$$

To explain how these grammar rules work, let us call terms of the form $\langle \cdots \rangle$ *nonterminal symbols* and words in English *terminal symbols*. (Thus, an English sentence, in the terminology of formal languages, is a string over terminal symbols.) We call a string formed by nonterminal and terminal symbols a *sentential form*, and call a string formed by terminal symbols only a *sentence*. We can generate a sentence from the above given grammar rules as follows:

(1) First, we create a sentential form of a single symbol $\langle sentence \rangle$.

(2) We repeatedly preform the substitution of (2.1) until the sentential form contains only terminal symbols:

89

(2.1) We select a nonterminal symbol $\langle a \rangle$ in the sentential form and replace it by the right-hand side of a grammar rule whose left-hand side is $\langle a \rangle$.

For instance, we can use the above grammar rules to generate the sentence **water evaporates constantly** as follows:

$$
\begin{aligned}
\langle sentence \rangle \ &\Rightarrow \ \langle subject \rangle \, \langle predicate \rangle \\
&\Rightarrow \ \langle noun \rangle \, \langle predicate \rangle \\
&\Rightarrow \ \langle noun \rangle \, \langle verb \rangle \, \langle adverb \rangle \\
&\Rightarrow \ \textbf{water} \, \langle verb \rangle \, \langle adverb \rangle \\
&\Rightarrow \ \textbf{water vaporates} \, \langle adverb \rangle \\
&\Rightarrow \ \textbf{water vaporates constantly}
\end{aligned}
$$

The above grammar rules have the simple form

$$A \longrightarrow x,$$

where A is a nonterminal symbol and x is a string of nonterminal and terminal symbols. Grammar rules of this form can be used to generate a rich class of English sentences. We call a grammar with rules of this form a *context-free grammar*.

We remark that a grammar for a natural language contains both *syntactic* rules, which describe the structure of a sentence, and *semantic* rules, which describe the meanings of the words in a sentence. Context-free grammars are only an approximation to the syntactic rules of the natural language grammars, and do not deal with semantics in most cases.

Formally, we define a *context-free grammar* to be a quadruple (V, Σ, R, S) of the following four components:

V: a finite set of nonterminal symbols;

Σ: a finite set of terminal symbols;

R: a finite set of rules which are of the form $A \to x$, where $A \in V$ and $x \in (V \cup \Sigma)^*$;

S: a special symbol in V, called the *starting symbol*.

Let $G = (V, \Sigma, R, S)$ be a context-free grammar. Then, we call a string $x \in (V \cup \Sigma)^*$ a *sentential form*, and a string $y \in \Sigma^*$ a *sentence*. Let u, v be two strings in $(V \cup \Sigma)^*$ and $A \in V$. Then, we write

$$uAv \underset{G}{\Longrightarrow} uxv$$

(or, $uAv \Rightarrow uxv$, if G is understood), if $(A \to x)$ is a rule in R. That is, we can substitute string x for symbol A in a sentential form if $(A \to x)$ is a rule in R. For any two sentential forms x and y, we write

$$x \underset{G}{\overset{*}{\Longrightarrow}} y$$

(or, $x \stackrel{*}{\Rightarrow} y$, if G is understood), if there exists a sequence $x = x_0, x_1, x_2, \ldots,$
$x_n = y$ of sentential forms such that $x_i \underset{G}{\Rightarrow} x_{i+1}$ for all $i = 0, 1, \ldots, n-1$.

In the above, if $x \stackrel{*}{\Rightarrow} y$, with $x = S$ and $y \in \Sigma^*$, then we say the grammar
G *generates* the sentence y, and say the sequence

$$S = x_0 \Rightarrow x_1 \Rightarrow \cdots \Rightarrow x_n = y$$

is a *derivation* of the sentence y. The language $L(G)$ generated by G is the
set of all strings over Σ that are generated by G; that is,

$$L(G) = \{x \in \Sigma^* \mid S \underset{G}{\stackrel{*}{\Rightarrow}} x\}.$$

A language is called a *context-free language* if it is generated by a context-free
grammar.

Example 3.1 *Consider the context-free grammar* $G_1 = (\{S\}, \{0, 1\}, \{S \rightarrow \varepsilon,$
$S \rightarrow 0S1\}, S)$. *What is the language* $L(G_1)$?

Solution. There is only one nonterminal symbol in G_1 and the only rule that
retains that symbol is $S \rightarrow 0S1$. Thus, the only derivations of G_1 are of the
form

$$S \Rightarrow 0S1 \Rightarrow 00S11 \Rightarrow \cdots \Rightarrow 0^n S 1^n \Rightarrow 0^n 1^n.$$

Thus, $L(G_1) = \{0^n 1^n \mid n \geq 0\}$. □

When we have more than one grammar rule with the same left-hand side,
such as

$$A \longrightarrow x_1, \; A \longrightarrow x_2, \; \ldots, \; A \longrightarrow x_m,$$

we can combine them into one *multiple* rule:

$$A \longrightarrow x_1 \mid x_2 \mid \cdots \mid x_m.$$

For instance, the rules in the above example G_1 can be written as $S \rightarrow \varepsilon \mid 0S1$.

Example 3.2 *Consider the context-free grammar* $G_2 = (\{S, A, B\}, \{a, b\}, R,$
$S)$, *where* R *consists of the following rules:*

$$S \longrightarrow ABA, \qquad A \longrightarrow a \mid bb, \qquad B \longrightarrow bS \mid \varepsilon.$$

What is the language $L(G_2)$?

Solution. Since the nonterminal symbol A can only produce terminal symbols,
we may delay its substitution to the end. Therefore, the derivations of G_2
have the following general form:

$$S \Rightarrow ABA \Rightarrow AbSA \Rightarrow AbABAA \Rightarrow AbAbSAA$$
$$\Rightarrow A(bA)^2 BA^3 \Rightarrow \cdots \Rightarrow A(bA)^n BA^{n+1} \Rightarrow A(bA)^n A^{n+1}.$$

Now, if we replace each A by either a or bb, we get a sentence of the form

$$(a + bb)(ba + bbb)^n (a + bb)^{n+1}.$$

Thus, $L(G_2)$ consists of all these strings with $n \geq 0$. $\qquad\qquad$ □

There are many techniques for designing a context-free grammar to generate a given language. We first introduce two basic concepts: matching and recursive relation. More ideas will be studied in the next section.

Example 3.3 *Find a context-free grammar that generates the language*

$$L = \{0^n 1^{2n} \mid n \geq 0\}.$$

Solution. This language is like $L(G_1)$ of Example 3.1, in the sense that if we replace each 1 of G_1 by 11 then we get a grammar for L. So, the required grammar is $G = (\{S\}, \{0, 1\}, \{S \to \varepsilon \mid 0S11\}, S)$. $\qquad\qquad$ □

Starting from scratch, we may construct the above grammar in two ways. First, we observe that the rule $S \to 0S11$ always generates a matching pair of 0 and 11. Applying this rule n times, we get a sentential form $0^n S(11)^n$. This simple type of rules and their variations are very useful in the design of context-free grammars.

Another way to find the grammar is to try to get a recursive expression of the longer strings in L in terms of the shorter strings in L. Namely, a longer string $0^{n+1} 1^{2(n+1)}$ in L can be written as $0(0^n 1^{2n})11$. Thus, if there is a derivation $S \overset{*}{\Rightarrow} 0^n 1^{2n}$, then we need a rule $S \to 0S11$ to get a derivation $S \overset{*}{\Rightarrow} 0^{n+1} 1^{2(n+1)}$. We further demonstrate this idea in the next few examples.

Example 3.4 *Find a context-free grammar that generates the language*

$$L = \{x \in \{0, 1\}^* \mid x = x^R\}.$$

Solution. We may view this problem as a matching problem: the kth leftmost symbol of input x must be equal to the kth rightmost symbol of x. We can use the rules $S \to 0S0$ and $S \to 1S1$ to enforce this matching relation.

We can also view this problem as a recursive relation problem: a string $x \in L$ of length $2n + 2$ can be written as either $0y0$ or $1y1$ for some $y \in L$ of length $2n$. Thus, we need rules $S \to 0S0$ and $S \to 1S1$ to generate x recursively.

From the above ideas, it is easy to see that L can be generated by a grammar $G = (\{S\}, \{0, 1\}, R, S)$, where R contains the following rules:

$$S \longrightarrow \varepsilon \mid 0 \mid 1 \mid 0S0 \mid 1S1.$$ $\qquad\qquad$ □

Example 3.5 *Find a context-free grammar that generates the language*

$$L = \{x \in \{a, b\}^* \mid each\ prefix\ of\ x\ has\ at\ least\ as\ many\ a's\ as\ b's\}.$$

Solution. Using the matching approach, we need to match, in a string $x \in L$, each b with an a which occurs to its left (allowing some a not matched with any b). Since the order of the occurrences of a and b is only partially fixed, this matching idea appears hard to work out. Instead, we use the recursive method to construct the required grammar.

How can we express longer strings in L by shorter strings in L? First, if $x = \varepsilon$, then we know that $x \in L$. For nonempty string $x \in L$, we note that the first symbol of x must be a since the first symbol itself is a prefix of x. Therefore, we can write $x = ay$. Now, if $y \in L$, then $x = ay$ is the recursive expression we are looking for.

Next, let us consider the case when y is not in L. In this case, y must have a prefix which contains one more b than a. Let u be the shortest such prefix of y. Then, the last symbol of u must be b. Let us write $u = wb$ and $x = awbz$. Now, we argue that w and z must be in L. First, by the definition of u, each prefix of w has at least as many a's as b's. That shows $w \in L$. Furthermore, $u = wb$ has exactly one more b than a. So, awb has as many a's as b's. Now, assume that t is a prefix of z. Then, $awbt$ is a prefix of x and, so, has at least as many a's as b's. It follows that t has at least as many a's as b's. This shows that z is in L.

The above analysis shows that a nonempty string $x \in L$ can be expressed as either $x = ay$ for some $y \in L$ or $x = awbz$ for some $w, z \in L$. Using S as the starting symbol to generate all strings in L, we see that L can be generated by the grammar $G = (\{S\}, \{a, b\}, R, S)$ with the following rules:

$$S \longrightarrow \varepsilon \mid aS \mid aSbS.$$

For instance, the string $aababbab$ is generated as follows:

$$S \Rightarrow aSbS \Rightarrow aaSbSbS \Rightarrow aabSbS \Rightarrow aabaSbSbS$$
$$\overset{*}{\Rightarrow} aababbS \Rightarrow aababbaSbS \overset{*}{\Rightarrow} aababbab. \qquad \square$$

Example 3.6 *Find a context-free grammar that generates*

$$L = \{x \in \{a, b\}^* \mid x \text{ has as many } a\text{'s as } b\text{'s}\}.$$

Solution. Let us analyze how a string x in L looks like. First, for any string w in $\{a, b\}^*$, let $d(w)$ be the number of b's in w minus the number of a's in w. Thus, $L = \{x \in \{a, b\}^* \mid d(x) = 0\}$. Now, suppose that u is the shortest nonempty prefix of x having $d(u) = 0$. Assume that u starts with symbol b. Then, we claim that u must end with symbol a.

Proof of Claim. Let us assume that $|u| = k$ and, for $1 \le i \le k$, let u_i be the prefix of u of length exactly i. Consider the sequence $(u_1, u_2, \ldots, u_k)$ of the prefixes of u. In this sequence, since the lengths $|u_i|$ increase from one string to the next string by exactly one, the values of $d(u_i)$, from one to the next, also differ by exactly one. Now, we note that if u ends with symbol b, then $d(u_1) = 1$ and $d(u_{k-1}) = -1$ (since $d(u_k) = d(u) = 0$). It implies that $d(u_i) = 0$ for some i between 1 and $k - 1$. However, we assumed that u is the shortest nonempty prefix of x with $d(u) = 0$; thus, this is a contradiction and the claim is proven.

Now, from the above claim, we see that u can be written as $u = bya$ for some $y \in \{a, b\}^*$, and x can be written as $x = byaz$ for some $y, z \in \{a, b\}^*$. Furthermore, since $d(x) = d(u) = 0$, we see that $d(y) = d(z) = 0$. That is, we have a recursive expression for $x \in L$: $x = byaz$ with $y, z \in L$.

Similarly, if u starts with symbol a, then it must end with symbol b, and x can be written as $x = aybz$ for some $y, z \in L$.

From the above analysis, we conclude that L can be generated by a grammar $G = (\{S\}, \{a, b\}, R, S)$ with the following rules:

$$S \longrightarrow \varepsilon \mid aSbS \mid bSaS.$$

For instance, $a^4 b^8 a^4$ has the following derivation:

$$S \Rightarrow aSbS \Rightarrow aaSbSbS \overset{*}{\Rightarrow} a^4(Sb)^4 S \overset{*}{\Rightarrow} a^4 b^4 S$$
$$\overset{*}{\Rightarrow} a^4 b^4 b^4 (aS)^4 \overset{*}{\Rightarrow} a^4 b^8 a^4. \qquad \square$$

All of the languages studied in the above examples are not regular. Thus, it shows that a context-free language is not necessarily regular. The following theorem shows that, on the other hand, a regular language must be context-free. Thus, the class of regular languages is a proper subclass of the class of context-free languages.

Theorem 3.7 *For each regular language L, there exists a context-free grammar G such that $L = L(G)$.*

Proof. A regular language L is accepted by a DFA $M = (Q, \Sigma, \delta, q_0, F)$. Without loss of generality, we may assume that $Q \cap \Sigma = \emptyset$. Now, we construct a context-free grammar $G = (V, \Sigma, R, S)$ with $V = Q$, $S = q_0$ and

$$R = \{q \longrightarrow ap \mid \delta(q, a) = p\} \cup \{f \longrightarrow \varepsilon \mid f \in F\}.$$

Then, by a simple induction, we can prove that for any $p, q \in Q$ and any $x \in \Sigma^*$, $\delta(q, x) = p$ if and only if there is a derivation $q \overset{*}{\Rightarrow} xp$ in G. In particular, $x \in L$ if and only if there is a derivation

$$q_0 \overset{*}{\Rightarrow} xf \Rightarrow x,$$

for some state $f \in F$. This shows that $L \subseteq L(G)$. Moreover, since the only rules in R having a right-hand side with no nonterminal symbols are of the form $f \to \varepsilon$ with $f \in F$, the above derivations are the only ones in G. It follows that $L = L(G)$. $\qquad \square$

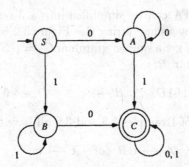

Figure 3.1: DFA for Example 3.8.

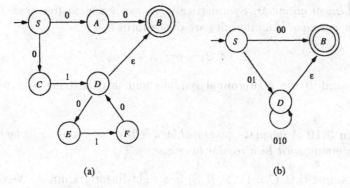

(a)   (b)

Figure 3.2: Two NFA's for Example 3.9.

Example 3.8 *Construct a context-free grammar that generates the regular language accepted by the DFA in Figure* 3.1.

Solution. From the proof of Theorem 3.7, we define a grammar $G = (V, \Sigma, R, S)$, with $V = \{S, A, B, C\}$, $\Sigma = \{0, 1\}$, and the following rules:

$$S \longrightarrow 0A \mid 1B, \quad A \longrightarrow 0A \mid 1C, \quad B \longrightarrow 0C \mid 1B, \quad C \longrightarrow 0C \mid 1C \mid \varepsilon. \quad \square$$

The method of Theorem 3.7 can also be applied to construct a context-free grammar directly from an NFA.

Example 3.9 *Construct a context-free grammar that generates the regular language accepted by the NFA in Figure* 3.2(a).

Solution. From the transition diagram of Figure 3.2(a), we can define the grammar $G_1 = (V, \{0, 1\}, R, S)$, with $V = \{S, A, B, C, D, E, F\}$ and rules

$$
\begin{aligned}
S &\longrightarrow 0A \mid 0C, & A &\longrightarrow 0B, & B &\longrightarrow \varepsilon, \\
C &\longrightarrow 1D, & D &\longrightarrow 0E \mid B, & E &\longrightarrow 1F, \\
F &\longrightarrow 0D.
\end{aligned}
$$

We note that the NFA can be simplified into a 3-vertex labeled digraph with each edge labeled by a single string (see Figure 3.2(b)). From this labeled digraph, we can actually get a simpler grammar $G_2 = (\{S, B, D\}, \{0, 1\}, R, S)$, with the following rules in R:

$$S \longrightarrow 00B \mid 01D, \qquad B \longrightarrow \varepsilon, \qquad D \longrightarrow 010D \mid B. \qquad \square$$

The grammar rules of Examples 3.8 and 3.9 all have the form

$$A \longrightarrow wB \quad \text{or} \quad A \longrightarrow w,$$

where A and B are nonterminal symbols and w is a string of terminal symbols. If a context-free grammar consists of rules of these forms only, then we call it a *right-linear grammar*. Symmetrically, we say a context-free grammar is a *left-linear grammar* if all its rules are of the form

$$A \longrightarrow Bw \quad \text{or} \quad A \longrightarrow w,$$

where A and B are nonterminal symbols and w is a string over terminal symbols.

Theorem 3.10 *A language generated by a left-linear grammar or by a right-linear grammar must be a regular language.*

Proof. Assume that $G = (V, \Sigma, R, S)$ is a right-linear grammar. We define a labeled digraph D as follows: The vertex set of D is $V \cup \{f\}$, where $f \notin V$. Let S be the initial state and f the unique final state. For each rule in G of the form $A \to wB$, where $A, B \in V$ and $w \in \Sigma^*$, draw an edge $A \xrightarrow{w} B$ (with w as the label) in D. For each rule of the form $A \to w$, where $A \in V$ and $w \in \Sigma^*$, draw an edge $A \xrightarrow{w} f$ in D.

It is not hard to show that each derivation $S \overset{*}{\Rightarrow} w$ of the grammar G corresponds to a path in D from the initial vertex S to the final vertex f whose label is w. Therefore, the language represented by this labeled digraph D is exactly $L(G)$. From the study of Chapters 1 and 2, we know that the language represented by the labeled digraph D is regular (indeed, it can easily be converted to an NFA) and, hence, $L(G)$ is regular.

Next, assume that $G_1 = (V, \Sigma, R_1, S)$ is a left-linear grammar. We construct a right-linear grammar $G_2 = (V, \Sigma, R_2, S)$, with

$$R_2 = \{A \to w^R B \mid (A \to Bw) \in R_1\} \cup \{A \to w^R \mid (A \to w) \in R_1\}.$$

Now, for any derivation in G_1

$$S \Rightarrow A_1 w_1 \Rightarrow A_2 w_2 w_1 \Rightarrow \cdots \Rightarrow A_{k-1} w_{k-1} \cdots w_1 \Rightarrow w_k \cdots w_1,$$

there is a corresponding derivation in G_2:

$$S \Rightarrow w_1^R A_1 \Rightarrow w_1^R w_2^R A_2 \Rightarrow \cdots \Rightarrow w_1^R \cdots w_{k-1}^R A_{k-1} \Rightarrow w_1^R \cdots w_k^R.$$

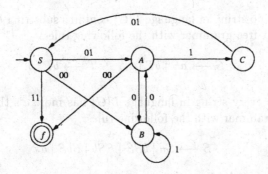

Figure 3.3: Solution to Example 3.11.

Thus, it is clear that $L(G_2) = L(G_1)^R$. From the first part of this proof, we know that $L(G_2)$ is regular. Thus, by Theorem 2.33, $L(G_1)$ is also regular. $\square$

From the above theorem, we say a context-free grammar is a *regular grammar* if it is either right-linear or left-linear.

Example 3.11 *Let G be a regular grammar with the following rules:*

$$S \longrightarrow 01A \mid 00B \mid 11, \qquad A \longrightarrow 0B \mid 1C \mid 00,$$
$$B \longrightarrow 0A \mid 1B, \qquad\qquad C \longrightarrow 01S.$$

Construct an NFA accepting $L(G)$.

Solution. From the construction in the proof of Theorem 3.10, we obtain a labeled digraph as shown in Figure 3.3. It can be converted to an NFA easily.
$\square$

Exercise 3.1

In the following exercises, each grammar is presented only with rules, with the convention that all upper-case letters denote nonterminal symbols, all lower-case letters and numerals denote terminal symbols, and S denotes the starting symbol.

1. Describe, in English and/or by regular expressions, the language that is generated by each of the following context-free grammars:

   (a) $S \longrightarrow aSa \mid bSb \mid a \mid b$.

   (b) $S \longrightarrow aS \mid bS \mid \varepsilon$.

   (c) $S \longrightarrow aS \mid Sb \mid a$.

   (d) $S \longrightarrow SS \mid a \mid b$.

   (e) $S \longrightarrow SS \mid aSb \mid \varepsilon$.

   (f) $S \longrightarrow aS \mid aSbS \mid \varepsilon$.

2. Show that no string in language $L(G)$ contains substring ba, where G is the context-free grammar with the following rules:

$$S \longrightarrow aS \mid bT \mid a, \qquad T \longrightarrow bT \mid b.$$

3. Show that every string in language $L(G)$ has more a's than b's, where G is the grammar with the following rules:

$$S \longrightarrow Sa \mid bSS \mid SSb \mid SbS \mid a.$$

4. (a) Show that the following grammar does *not* generate the language $\{x \in \{0,1\}^* \mid x \text{ has as many 0's as 1's}\}$:

$$S \longrightarrow 0S1 \mid 01S \mid 1S0 \mid 10S \mid S01 \mid S10 \mid \varepsilon.$$

   (b) Show that the following grammar generates the language $\{x \in \{0,1\}^* \mid x \text{ has as many 0's as 1's}\}$:

$$S \longrightarrow SS \mid 0S1 \mid 1S0 \mid \varepsilon.$$

5. For each of the following regular languages, construct a right-linear grammar and a left-linear grammar for it:

   (a) $10(0+1)^*10$.
   (b) $((0+11)^*10)^*$.
   (c) The set of binary strings that do not contain the substring 000.
   (d) The set of binary strings of which the suffix of length ten begins with 000.

6. For each of the following context-free grammar G, construct an NFA that accepts $L(G)$:

   (a) $S \longrightarrow baS \mid bS \mid \varepsilon$.
   (b) $S \longrightarrow Sab \mid Sb \mid ab \mid b$.
   (c) $S \longrightarrow A \mid B, \quad A \longrightarrow baA \mid bA \mid \varepsilon, \quad B \longrightarrow Bab \mid Bb \mid ab \mid b$.
   (d) $S \longrightarrow AB, \quad A \longrightarrow baA \mid bA \mid \varepsilon, \quad B \longrightarrow Bab \mid Bb \mid ab \mid b$.
   (e) $S \longrightarrow AA \mid BB, \quad A \longrightarrow baA \mid bA \mid \varepsilon, \quad B \longrightarrow Bab \mid Bb \mid ab \mid b$.

7. For each of the following context-free grammar G, find an equivalent regular grammar:

   (a) $S \longrightarrow AabB, \quad A \longrightarrow aA \mid bA \mid \varepsilon, \quad B \longrightarrow Bab \mid Bb \mid ab \mid b$.
   (b) $S \longrightarrow AB, \quad A \longrightarrow Aa \mid Ab \mid a \mid b, \quad B \longrightarrow aB \mid abB \mid \varepsilon$.
   (c) $S \longrightarrow AA \mid B, \quad A \longrightarrow aAa \mid bAb \mid a \mid b, \quad B \longrightarrow aB \mid bB \mid \varepsilon$.
   (d) $S \longrightarrow AB, \quad A \longrightarrow aAa \mid bAb \mid a \mid b, \quad B \longrightarrow aB \mid bB \mid \varepsilon$.

8. A context-free grammar $G = (V, \Sigma, R, S)$ is said to be *linear* if every rule of it is of the form $A \to xB$ or $A \to Bx$ or $A \to x$, where $A, B \in V$ and $x \in \Sigma^*$. Show that a language generated by a linear grammar is not necessarily regular.

9. For each of the following languages L, construct a context-free grammar that generates L:

   (a) $\{a^n b^m \mid m \geq n, m - n \text{ is even}\}$.
   (b) $\{xc^n \mid x \in \{a, b\}^*, \#_a(x) = n \text{ or } \#_b(x) = n\}$, where $\#_a(x)$ denotes the number of occurrences of symbol a in string x.
   (c) $\{xc^n \mid x \in \{a, b\}^*, \#_a(x) + \#_b(x) \geq n\}$.

3.2 More Examples of Context-Free Grammars

In this section, we study more techniques of constructing context-free grammars. Our first new idea is that in a context-free grammar $G = (V, \Sigma, R, S)$, each nonterminal symbol $A \in V$ represents a language, that is, the set of strings $x \in \Sigma^*$ with a derivation $A \stackrel{*}{\Rightarrow} x$. Therefore, when we design a context-free grammar, we may designate a few nonterminal symbols to represent some specific languages and use the grammar rules to express their relations.

Example 3.6 (Revisited) *Find a context-free grammar that generates*

$$L = \{x \in \{a, b\}^* \mid x \text{ has as many } a\text{'s as } b\text{'s}\}.$$

Solution 2. Let us use the notation $\#_a(x)$ to denote the number of occurrences of symbol a in a string x. For convenience, we will use a capital letter S, A or B to denote both a nonterminal symbol of the grammar and the set of strings for which there is a derivation from that symbol. We let the symbol S represent the language L, the symbol A represent the set of strings x with $\#a(x) = \#_b(x) + 1$, and the symbol B represent the set of strings x with $\#a(x) = \#_b(x) - 1$.

Now, let x be a string in S. Then, either $x = \varepsilon$ or $x = ay$ for some $y \in \{a, b\}^*$ or $x = bz$ for some $z \in \{a, b\}^*$. If $x = ay$ then $\#_a(y) = \#_b(y) - 1$, and so $y \in B$. If $x = bz$ then $\#_a(z) = \#_b(z) + 1$ and, so $z \in A$. Therefore, we get the relation $S = \varepsilon \cup aB \cup bA$. This relation can be expressed in grammar rules as $S \to \varepsilon \mid aB \mid bA$.

Next, we study strings represented by A and B. First, if a string x is in A, then either $x \in aS$ or $x \in bA'$, where A' represents the set of strings z with $\#_a(z) = \#_b(z) + 2$.

We claim that strings in A' can always be decomposed into the concatenation of two substrings in A. To see this, we use the same argument as in Solution 1: Let $d(w)$ denote $\#_b(w) - \#_a(w)$ and w_i denote the prefix of w of length i. Then, for a string w of length n, $w \in A'$ implies $d(w_0) = 0$ and

$d(w_n) = -2$. It follows that for some i, $1 \le i \le n - 1$, $d(w_i) = -1$. So, $w = w_i v$ and both w_i and v are in A.

By the above claim, $A = aS \cup bAA$. Similarly, we get $B = bS \cup aBB$.

From the above analysis, we obtain the following context-free grammar $G = (\{S, A, B\}, \{a, b\}, R, S)$, where R consists of the following rules:

$$S \longrightarrow \varepsilon \mid aB \mid bA, \qquad A \longrightarrow aS \mid bAA, \qquad B \longrightarrow bS \mid aBB. \qquad \square$$

Example 3.12 *Find a context-free grammar that generates the language*

$$L = \{x \in \{a, b\}^* \mid x \text{ has twice as many } b\text{'s as } a\text{'s}\}.$$

Solution. Let $f(x) = 2\#_a(x) - \#_b(x)$. Then $L = \{x \in \{a, b\}^* \mid f(x) = 0\}$. The values of f on the prefix sequence of any string change in the following ways:

(a) Each increasing is in value 2;

(b) Each decreasing is in value 1.

We define four nonterminal symbols S, A, B and C to represent four languages over $\{a, b\}$ as follows:

(i) S represents $L = \{x \mid f(x) = 0\}$;

(ii) $A = \{x \mid f(x) = 1\}$;

(iii) $B = \{x \mid f(x) = -1\}$;

(iv) $C = \{x \mid f(x) = 2\}$.

Then, it is easy to see that $S = \varepsilon \cup aB' \cup bA$, where $B' = \{x \mid f(x) = -2\}$. Now, every string $w \in B'$ of length n has $f(w_0) = 0$ and $f(w_n) = -2$, where w_i denotes the prefix of w of length i. By property (b) of the function f, we know that there must be a prefix w_j of w with $f(w_j) = -1$. Thus, we know that $B' = BB$. Or, equivalently, $S = \varepsilon \cup aBB \cup bA$.

Next, it is easy to see that $A = bC \cup aB$. Also, from the above analysis, we know that $B = bS \cup aBBB$.

Finally, we note that C can be expressed as $aS \cup bAC \cup bCA$. To see this, we let $C' = \{x \mid f(x) = 3\}$. Then, for any string $x \in C'$ with length n, we have $f(x_0) = 0$ and $f(x_n) = 3$, where x_i denotes the prefix of x of length i. Then, by property (a) of f, there must be a prefix x_j of x with either $f(x_j) = 1$ or $f(x_j) = 2$. In the first case, $x_j \in A$ and $y \in C$; and in the second case, $x_j \in C$ and $y \in A$, where y is the suffix of x such that $x = x_j y$.

Now, from the above analysis, we obtain the following context-free grammar: $G = (\{S, A, B, C\}, \{a, b\}, R, S)$ where R consists of the following rules:

$$S \longrightarrow \varepsilon \mid aBB \mid bA, \qquad A \longrightarrow aB \mid bC,$$
$$B \longrightarrow bS \mid aBBB, \qquad C \longrightarrow aS \mid bAC \mid bCA. \qquad \square$$

Example 3.13 *Find a context-free grammar for the language*

$$L = \{x \in \{a, b\}^* \mid \#_b(x) = 2\#_a(x) + 3\}.$$

Solution. From the analysis of Example 3.12, we know that every string x in L can be decomposed to be $x = yz$ with $y \in A$, $z \in C$, or with $y \in C$, $z \in A$. So, we obtain a grammar $G_1 = (\{S_1, S, A, B, C\}, \{a, b\}, R_1, S_1)$ for L, where R_1 contains all rules in G of Example 3.12, plus the rules

$$S_1 \longrightarrow AC \mid CA. \qquad \square$$

Example 3.14 *Find a context-free grammar that generates the language*

$$L = \{a^m b^n c^p d^q \mid m + n = p + q\}.$$

Solution. The equation $m + n = p + q$ suggests that we use the idea of matching to find the correct rules. That is, we need to match letters a and b with letters c and d, and we should do it in a recursive way. Since we do not know the exact relations between the sizes m, n, p, q, we will perform these matchings in stages. At each stage, we match the two outermost symbols and continue until we run out of one type of symbols.

(1) In stage S, we use the rule $S \to aSd$ to genearate a number of a's with the same number of d's. Then, depending on whether $m \geq q$, we move to stage A or stage B by the rules $S \to A \mid B$.

(2) In stage A, we deal with the case $m \geq q$. We generate some a's with the same number of c's, and then move to stage C. That is, we create rules $A \to aAc \mid C$.

(3) In stage B, we deal with the case $m \leq q$. We generate some b's with the same number of d's, and then move to stage C. That is, we have the rules $B \to bBd \mid C$.

(4) Finally, in stage C, we match symbols b with symbols c with the rules $C \to bCc \mid \varepsilon$.

The complete set of grammar rules are as follows:

$$S \longrightarrow aSd \mid A \mid B, \qquad A \longrightarrow aAc \mid C,$$
$$B \longrightarrow bBd \mid C, \qquad C \longrightarrow bCc \mid \varepsilon.$$

Note that if a string $x = a^m b^n c^p d^q$ in L has $m > q$, then the derivation of x starts from stage S then moves to stage A and then to stage C, while a string y with $m < q$ must go through stages S, B and C. A string z with $m = q$ can be derived in either way. $\qquad \square$

Example 3.15 *Find a context-free grammar that generates the language*

$$L = \{a^m b^n c^p \mid m + 2n \geq p\}.$$

Solution. First, let us consider the simpler language $L_1 = \{a^m b^n c^p \mid m+2n = p\}$. Based on the idea of the last example, we can easily get the following grammar for it:

$$S \longrightarrow aSc \mid A, \qquad A \longrightarrow bAcc \mid \varepsilon.$$

Next, we modify this grammar to allow the case $m + 2n > p$. This can happen if we have (i) at least one extra a, or (ii) at least one extra b, or (iii) at least one extra b together with one extra c. These extra symbols may occur in both matching stages of the derivation. Thus, we can add rules $S \to aS$, $A \to bA$ and $A \to bAc$ to the grammar for L_1. That is, the grammar for language L is as follows:

$$S \longrightarrow aSc \mid aS \mid A, \qquad A \longrightarrow bAcc \mid bAc \mid bA \mid \varepsilon. \qquad \square$$

* Example 3.16 *Find a context-free grammar that generates the language*

$$L = \{a^m b^n \mid 3m \leq 5n \leq 4m\}.$$

Solution. First, we consider a simpler language: $L_0 = \{a^m b^n \mid 3m \leq 5n \leq 4m, m \equiv 0 \pmod 5\}$. For any string $a^{5p} b^n$ in L_0, we must have $15p \leq 5n \leq 20p$, or, $3p \leq n \leq 4p$. Thus, we may rewrite L_0 as

$$L_0 = \{a^{5p} b^{3p+k} \mid 0 \leq k \leq p\}.$$

From this expression, it is easy to see that L_0 is generated by the grammar $G_0 = (\{A\}, \{a, b\}, R_0, A)$ with the following rules:

$$A \longrightarrow a^5 A b^3 \mid a^5 A b^4 \mid \varepsilon.$$

Intuitively, this grammar matches every five a's with either three b's or four b's. Therefore, the total number of b's is between $3/5$ and $4/5$ of the number of a's. More formally, we note that if a derivation $A \overset{*}{\Rightarrow} a^{5p} b^n$ applies the rule $A \to a^5 A b^4$ for k times, the rule $A \to a^5 A b^3$ for $p - k$ times, and the rule $A \to \varepsilon$ at the end, then we must have $n = 3p + k$. Thus, every string in L_0 can be generated by the grammar G_0. Conversely, it is obvious that these are the only possible derivations from symbol A. Thus, we have proved that $L(G_0) = L_0$.

The above idea of matching every five a's with either three or four b's is critical in this problem. We can actually apply this to other strings in L. Let us define, for each $i = 1, 2, 3, 4$, a language

$$L_i = \{a^m b^n \mid 3m \leq 5n \leq 4m, m \equiv i \pmod 5\}.$$

For each L_i, $1 \leq i \leq 4$, we can use this matching idea to construct a grammar for it.

First, consider L_4. A string in L_4 is of the form $a^{5p+4}b^n$, where $3(5p+4) \leq 5n \leq 4(5p+4)$, or $3p + 12/5 \leq n \leq 4p + 16/5$. Since n must be an integer, the above relation between p and n is equivalent to

$$3p + 3 \leq n \leq 4p + 3.$$

This relation tells us that we can generate L_4 by matching every five a's with three or four b's, and then generating four extra a's and three extra b's. That is, the grammar $G_4 = (\{S_4, A\}, \{a, b\}, R_4, S_4)$ with rules

$$S_4 \longrightarrow a^4 Ab^3, \qquad A \longrightarrow a^5 Ab^3 \mid a^5 Ab^4 \mid \varepsilon$$

generates the language L_4.

Langauge L_3 has a similar grammar. We note that $3(5p + 3) \leq 5n \leq 4(5p + 3)$ is equivalent to $3p + 2 \leq n \leq 4p + 2$. So, in addition to the rules in G_0, we also need the rule $S_3 \to a^3 Ab^2$ to make up the extra a's and b's.

For language L_2, the relation $3(5p + 2) \leq 5n \leq 4(5p + 2)$ is simplified to $3p + 2 \leq n \leq 4p + 1$. This relation creates some problem with our approach. Suppose that we match $5p$ copies of a's with j copies of b's, with $3p \leq j \leq 4p$. Then, we cannot match the extra two a's with any number of b's: If we generate extra two a's with extra two b's, then we may get as many as $4p + 2$ copies of b's, which number is too large. On the other hand, if we generate extra two a's with only one extra b, then we may get as few as $3p + 1$ copies of b's. To solve this problem, we change the above relation to

$$3(p - 1) + 5 \leq n \leq 4(p - 1) + 5.$$

Equivalently, strings in L_2 are of the form $a^{5(p-1)+7}b^{q+5}$, with $3(p - 1) \leq q \leq 4(p - 1)$. Therefore, all we need to do is to generate extra seven a's with extra five b's; or, equivalently, we need an extra rule $S_2 \to a^7 Ab^5$. (*Note*: When $p = 0$, there is no integer n satisfying the above inequality.)

Language L_1 is similar to L_2. The basic relation $3(5p+1) \leq 5n \leq 4(5p+1)$ is equivalent to $3p + 1 \leq n \leq 4p$. From that, we get

$$3(p - 1) + 4 \leq n \leq 4(p - 1) + 4.$$

So, in addition to the rules of G_0, we need an extra rule $S_1 \to a^6 Ab^4$.

Note that L is the union of languages L_i, for $0 \leq i \leq 4$. So, we can combine the above rules together into a grammar for L:

$$S \longrightarrow a^4 Ab^3 \mid a^3 Ab^2 \mid a^7 Ab^5 \mid a^6 Ab^4 \mid A,$$
$$A \longrightarrow a^5 Ab^3 \mid a^5 Ab^4 \mid \varepsilon. \qquad \square$$

We solved the above problem by dividing the given language L into five subproblems, finding a context-free grammar for each subproblem, and then combining the five grammars into one. This technique is very useful for complicated languages. The following theorem justifies this technique of combining simple grammars into a more complicated grammar.

Theorem 3.17 *The class of context-free languages are closed under union, concatenation, and Kleene closure.*

Proof. Let L_1 and L_2 be two context-free languages, generated by grammars G_1 and G_2, respectively. Assume that $G_i = (V_i, \Sigma_i, R_i, S_i)$ for $i = 1, 2$, and that $V_1 \cap V_2 = \emptyset$. (If $V_1 \cap V_2 \neq \emptyset$, we can simply rename all nonterminal symbols in V_2 to be different from those in V_1.) Also assume that $S_3, S_4 \notin V_1 \cup V_2$.

Then, it is easy to check the following:

(1) Language $L_1 \cup L_2$ is generated by grammar $G_3 = (V_1 \cup V_2 \cup \{S_3\}, \Sigma_1 \cup \Sigma_2, R_3, S_3)$, where

$$R_3 = R_1 \cup R_2 \cup \{S_3 \to S_1 \mid S_2\}.$$

(2) Language $L_1 L_2$ is generated by $G_4 = (V_1 \cup V_2 \cup \{S_4\}, \Sigma_1 \cup \Sigma_2, R_4, S_4)$, where

$$R_4 = R_1 \cup R_2 \cup \{S_4 \to S_1 S_2\}.$$

(3) Language L_1^* is generated by $G_5 = (V_1, \Sigma_1, R_5, S_1)$, where

$$R_5 = R_1 \cup \{S_1 \to S_1 S_1 \mid \varepsilon\}. \qquad \qquad \square$$

Recall the operation of substitution on languages, defined in Section 2.6.

Theorem 3.18 *Assume that $L \subseteq \Sigma^*$ is a context-free language, and that f is a substitution with the property that $f(a)$ is a context-free language for every $a \in \Sigma$. Then, $f(L)$ is context-free.*

Proof. Suppose that L is generated by the context-free grammar $G = (V, \Sigma, R, S)$ and, for every $a \in \Sigma$, the language $f(a)$ is generated by the context-free grammar $G_a = (V_a, \Sigma_a, R_a, S_a)$. Assume that $V_a \cap V = V_a \cap V_b = \emptyset$ for all $a \neq b \in \Sigma$.

Then, $f(L)$ is generated by $G^f = (V^f, \Sigma^f, R^f, S)$, where

$$V^f = V \cup \left(\bigcup_{a \in \Sigma} V_a \right), \quad \Sigma^f = \bigcup_{a \in \Sigma} \Sigma_a, \quad R^f = R' \cup \left(\bigcup_{a \in \Sigma} R_a \right),$$

and R' is the set of rules in R with each symbol $a \in \Sigma$ replaced by S_a. $\qquad \square$

We now apply these closure properties to construct context-free grammars.

Example 3.19 *Find a context-free grammar generating*

$$L = \{0^m 1^n \mid m \neq n, m, n \geq 0\}.$$

Solution. Note that $L = L_1 \cup L_2$, where $L_1 = \{0^m 1^n \mid m > n \geq 0\}$, and $L_2 = \{0^m 1^n \mid n > m \geq 0\}$. It is clear that L_1 can be generated by the following rules:

$$S_1 \longrightarrow 0 \mid 0 S_1 \mid 0 S_1 1,$$

and L_2 can be generated by

$$S_2 \longrightarrow 1 \mid S_2 1 \mid 0 S_2 1.$$

Thus, we can combine the above rules to get a grammar $G = (\{S, S_1, S_2\},$ $\{0, 1\}, R, S)$ that generates L, where

$$R = R_1 \cup R_2 \cup \{S \to S_1 \mid S_2\}. \qquad \square$$

⋆ **Example 3.20** *Find a context-free grammar generating*

$$L = \{x \in \{0,1\}^* \mid x \neq ww \text{ for any } w \in \{0,1\}^*\}.$$

Solution 1. Let us analyze what types of strings are in L. First, any string x of an odd length belongs to L. Next, assume that $|x|$ is even and $x \in L$. Write $x = y_1 y_2 \cdots y_m z_1 z_2 \cdots z_m$, where each y_i or z_j is a symbol in $\{0, 1\}$. Since $x \in L$, $y_i \neq z_i$ for some $i = 1, 2, \cdots, m$. There are two cases.

Case 1. $y_i = 0$ and $z_i = 1$. Then, x looks like this:

$$x = \underbrace{y_1 \cdots y_{i-1}}_{i-1} 0 \underbrace{y_{i+1} \cdots y_m z_1 \cdots z_{i-1}}_{(m-i)+(i-1)} 1 \underbrace{z_{i+1} \cdots z_m}_{m-i}.$$

That is, x is of the form $x = u0v1w$ for some u, v, w, satisfying $|v| = |u| + |w|$.

Case 2. $y_i = 1$ and $z_i = 0$. Similarly, x is of the form $x = u1v0w$ for some u, v, w, satisfying $|v| = |u| + |w|$.

In other words, we have $L = L_0 \cup L_1 \cup L_2$, where

$$L_1 = \{u0v1w \mid u, v, w \in \{0,1\}^*, |v| = |u| + |w|\},$$
$$L_2 = \{u1v0w \mid u, v, w \in \{0,1\}^*, |v| = |u| + |w|\},$$
$$L_3 = \{x \mid |x| \text{ is odd}\}.$$

It is interesting to note that L_1 is not disjoint from L_2. That is, a string $x \in L$ may belong to both L_1 and L_2. Furthermore, a string x in L_1 may be expressed as $u0v1w$ by several different triples (u, v, w). But, this fact is irrelevant. As long as $L = L_1 \cup L_2 \cup L_3$, we can apply Theorem 3.17 to solve this problem.

Now, it is easy to get grammars for languages L_1, L_2 and L_3. For instance, we can use the closure properties again: Define

$$X = \{u0v \mid u, v \in \{0,1\}^*, |u| = |v|\},$$
$$Y = \{u1v \mid u, v \in \{0,1\}^*, |u| = |v|\}.$$

Then, we have $L_1 = XY$, $L_2 = YX$ and $L_3 = X \cup Y$. Let $G_X = (\{A\}, \{0, 1\},$ $R_X, A)$, with

$$R_X = \{A \to 0 \mid 0A0 \mid 0A1 \mid 1A0 \mid 1A1\},$$

and $G_Y = (\{B\}, \{0, 1\} R_Y, A)$, with

$$R_Y = \{B \to 1 \mid 0B0 \mid 0B1 \mid 1B0 \mid 1B1\}.$$

Then, $X = L(G_X)$ and $Y = L(G_Y)$. Combining them together, we get the grammar $G = (\{S, A, B\}, \{0, 1\}, R, S)$ for language L, where

$$R = R_X \cup R_Y \cup \{S \to A \mid B \mid AB \mid BA\}. \qquad \square$$

Solution 2. In Solution 1, we have constructed grammars G_X and G_Y for sets X and Y, respectively. Now, define a new grammar $G' = (\{S\}, \{0, 1\}, R', S)$, with

$$R = \{S \to 0 \mid 1 \mid 01 \mid 10\}.$$

Then, using the substitution $f(0) = X$ and $f(1) = Y$, we have $f(L(G')) = L$, and the construction of Theorem 3.18 gives us the same grammar G for L as the one in Solution 1. $\qquad \square$

$\star$ **Example 3.21** *For $i \geq 1$, denote by b_i the binary representation of integer i (with no leading zeroes). Find a context-free grammar generating*

$$L = \{0, 1, \#\}^* - \{b_1 \# b_2 \# \cdots \# b_n \mid n \geq 1\}.$$

Solution. Note that a string $x = a_1 \# a_2 \# \cdots \# a_n$, with each $a_j \in \{0, 1\}^*$, belongs to the set $\{b_1 \# b_2 \# \cdots \# b_n \mid n \geq 1\}$ if and only if $a_1 = 1$, and for every j, $1 \leq j \leq n-1$, $a_j \# a_{j+1}$ is of the form $b_i \# b_{i+1}$ for some integer $i \geq 1$. In other words, a string $x \in \{0, 1, \#\}^*$ is in L if and only if it satisfies one of the following conditions:

(1) $[x = y]$ or $[x$ has a prefix $y\#]$ for some $y \in \{0, 1\}^* - \{1\}$.

(2) $[x = y\#z]$ or $[x$ has a prefix $y\#z\#]$ or $[x$ has a substring $\#y\#z\#]$ or $[x$ has a suffix $\#y\#z]$ for some $y, z \in \{0, 1\}^*$ such that $y\#z \neq b_i \# b_{i+1}$ for any integer $i \geq 1$.

The above conditions (1) and (2) may be expressed by the regular expression notation as follows:

$$L = L_1 (\#(0 + 1)^*)^* \cup ((0 + 1)^* \#)^* L_2 (\#(0 + 1)^*)^*,$$

where

$$L_1 = \{y \in \{0, 1\}^* \mid y \neq 1\},$$
$$L_2 = \{y\#z \mid y, z \in \{0, 1\}^*, y\#z \neq b_i \# b_{i+1} \text{ for any } i \geq 1\}.$$

The language L_1 is regular: $L_1 = \varepsilon + (0 + 10 + 11)(0 + 1)^*$, and it can be generated by the following rules, starting with S_1:

$$S_1 \longrightarrow \varepsilon \mid 0A \mid 10A \mid 01A, \qquad A \longrightarrow \varepsilon \mid 0A \mid 1A.$$

To find a context-free grammar for L_2, let us first analyze how the string b_{i+1} is related to b_i:

(a) If $b_i = 1^k$ for some $k > 0$ then $b_{i+1} = 10^k$.

(b) If $b_i = u01^k$ for some $u \in 1(0+1)^*$ and some $k \geq 0$, then $b_{i+1} = u10^k$.

It follows from (a) and (b) that $L_2 = L_3 \cup L_4 \cup L_5 \cup L_6$, where

$$L_3 = \{y\#z \mid y, z \in \{0,1\}^*, y \text{ or } z \text{ does not begin with } 1\},$$
$$L_4 = \{1^k\#z \mid z \in \{0,1\}^*, k \geq 1, z \neq 10^k\},$$
$$L_5 = \{u01^k\#v10^h \mid u, v \in \{0,1\}^*, h \neq k\},$$
$$L_6 = \{u01^k\#v10^h \mid u, v \in \{0,1\}^*, u \neq v\}.$$

To simplify our job, we can further express L_4 and L_6 as unions of simpler context-free languages:

$$L_4 = \{1^k\#0^h \mid k \geq 1, h \geq 0\} \cup \{1^k\#10^h \mid k \geq 1, k \neq h\}$$
$$\cup \{1^k\#v10^h \mid k \geq 1, v \in \{0,1\}^+\};$$

$$L_6 = \{u01^k\#v10^h \mid |u| \neq |v|\} \cup \{u_1 1 u_2 01^k\#v_1 0 v_2 10^h \mid |u_2| = |v_2|\}$$
$$\cup \{u_1 0 u_2 01^k\#v_1 1 v_2 10^h \mid |u_2| = |v_2|\}.$$

It is clear that each subset above is context-free. For instance, the language $\{u_1 1 u_2 01^k\#v_1 0 v_2 10^h \mid |u_2| = |v_2|\}$ can be generated by the following grammar rules, starting with S_6:

$$
\begin{aligned}
S_6 &\longrightarrow A1P1D, & A &\longrightarrow \varepsilon \mid 0A \mid 1A, \\
D &\longrightarrow \varepsilon \mid 0D, & E &\longrightarrow \varepsilon \mid 1E, \\
P &\longrightarrow 0P0 \mid 0P1 \mid 1P0 \mid 1P1 \mid 0E\#A0. &&
\end{aligned}
$$

Combining the context-free grammars for all the above sets, we can find a context-free grammar for L_2. Further combining it with grammar G_1, we obtain a context-free grammar G for language L. This grammar G uses variables $V = \{S, S_1, S_2, S_4, S_5, S_6, A, B, C, D, E, P, Q, U, V, W, T\}$, with S as the starting symbol. The nonterminal symbols A, D, E, B, C represent simple regular languages $(0+1)^*$, 0^*, 1^*, $(\#(0+1)^*)^*$ and $((0+1)^*\#)^*$, respectively. The nonterminal symbols S_1, S_2, S_4, S_5 and S_6 represent languages L_1, L_2, L_4, L_5 and L_6, respectively. (Language L_3 is a simple regular language that can be generated directly from S_2.) The symbols P, Q, U, V, W and T are auxiliary symbols for languages L_4, L_5 and L_6. (Nonterminals U and V are designed for the first subset of L_6, and P and Q for the other two subsets.) The rules of G are as follows:

$$S \longrightarrow S_1 B \mid C S_2 B,$$

$$S_1 \longrightarrow \varepsilon \mid 0A \mid 10A \mid 01A,$$

$$S_2 \longrightarrow \#A \mid A\# \mid 0A\#A \mid A\#0A \mid S_4 \mid S_5 \mid S_6,$$

$$S_4 \longrightarrow 1E\# \mid 1E\#0A \mid 1E\#1A1D \mid T,$$

$$T \longrightarrow 1T0 \mid 1E\#1 \mid 1\#100D,$$

$$S_5 \longrightarrow A0W,$$

$$W \longrightarrow 1W0 \mid 1E\#A1 \mid \#A10D,$$

$$S_6 \longrightarrow U1D \mid V1D \mid A1P1D \mid A0Q1D,$$

$$U \longrightarrow 0U0 \mid 0U1 \mid 1U0 \mid 1U1 \mid 0A0E\# \mid 1A0E\#,$$

$$V \longrightarrow 0V0 \mid 0V1 \mid 1V0 \mid 1V1 \mid 0E\#0A \mid 0E\#1A,$$

$$P \longrightarrow 0P0 \mid 0P1 \mid 1P0 \mid 1P1 \mid 0E\#A0,$$

$$Q \longrightarrow 0Q0 \mid 0Q1 \mid 1Q0 \mid 1Q1 \mid 0E\#A1,$$

$$A \longrightarrow \varepsilon \mid 0A \mid 1A, \quad B \longrightarrow \varepsilon \mid BB \mid \#A, \quad C \longrightarrow \varepsilon \mid CC \mid A\#,$$

$$D \longrightarrow \varepsilon \mid 0D, \qquad E \longrightarrow \varepsilon \mid 1E. \qquad \qquad \square$$

Exercise 3.2

1. For each of the following languages, construct a context-free grammar that generates the language:

   (a) $\{a^i b^j \mid 2i = 3j + 1\}$.
   (b) $\{a^i b^j \mid 2i \neq 3j + 1\}$.
   $\star$ (c) $\{a^i b^j \mid 2i \leq 3j \leq 4i\}$.
   $\star$ (d) $\{a^i b^j \mid 2i + 3 \leq 3j \leq 4i - 2\}$.

2. For each of the following languages, construct a context-free grammar that generates the language:

   (a) $\{a^i b^j c^k \mid i \geq k \text{ or } j \geq k\}$.
   (b) $\{a^i b^j c^k \mid i + j = k\}$.
   (c) $\{a^i b^j c^k \mid j = i + k\}$.
   (d) $\{a^i b^j c^k \mid j \geq i + k - 3\}$.
   (e) $\{a^i b^j c^k \mid i + j \neq k + 3\}$.
   (f) $\{a^i b^j c^k \mid i + 2j = k\}$.
   (g) $\{a^i b^j c^k \mid i + 2j \equiv k \pmod 3\}$.
   $\star$ (h) $\{a^i b^j c^k \mid i + 2j = 3k\}$.
   $\star$ (i) $\{a^i b^j c^k \mid i + 2k \geq 3j\}$.
   $\star$ (j) $\{a^i b^j c^k \mid i + 2k \leq 3j \leq 2i + 3k\}$.

3. For each of the following languages, construct a context-free grammar that generates the language:

   (a) $\{a^i b^j c^k d^\ell \mid i + k = j + \ell\}$.

    (b) $\{a^i b^j c^k d^\ell \mid i + k \leq j + \ell + 3\}$.

★ (c) $\{a^i b^j c^k d^\ell \mid i + 2k = j + 3\ell\}$.

★ (d) $\{a^i b^j c^k d^\ell \mid i + 2k \neq j + 3\ell\}$.

★ (e) $\{a^i b^j c^k d^\ell \mid i + 2\ell = j + 3k\}$.

★ (f) $\{a^i b^j c^k d^\ell \mid i + 2\ell \neq j + 3k\}$.

    (g) $\{b_i \# b_{i+1}^R \mid b_i$ is the binary representation of integer $i, i \geq 0\}$.

4. Construct a context-free grammar to generate all regular expressions over alphabet $\{a, b\}$.

5. For each of the following languages, construct a context-free grammar for it.

    (a) $\{x^R \# y \mid x, y \in \{0, 1\}^*, x$ is a substring of $y\}$.

    (b) $\{x^R \# y \mid x, y \in \{0, 1\}^*, x$ is a subsequence of $y\}$. (A string $x = x_1 x_2 \cdots x_k$ is a subsequence of a string $y = y_1 y_2 \cdots y_n$, where each x_i and each y_j is a single letter, if there exist $1 \leq j_1 < j_2 < \cdots < j_k \leq n$ such that $y_{j_\ell} = x_\ell$ for $1 \leq \ell \leq k$.)

    (c) $\{a^m b y \mid y \in (a + b)^{n-1}, n > m \geq 1\}$.

    (d) $\{a^m b y \mid y \in (a + b)^{n-1}, m > n \geq 1\}$.

    (e) $\{x_1 \# x_2 \# \cdots \# x_n \mid x_1, \ldots, x_n \in \{0, 1\}^*, (\exists 1 \leq i < j \leq n) [x_i = x_j^R]\}$.

    (f) $\{x_1 \# x_2 \# \cdots \# x_n \mid x_1, \ldots, x_n \in \{0, 1\}^*, (\exists 1 \leq i < j \leq n) [x_i \neq x_j]\}$.

★ (g) $\{0, 1\}^* - \{www \mid w \in \{0, 1\}^*\}$.

★ (h) $L = (0 + 1)^* - \{(0^n 1^n)^n \mid n \geq 1\}$. [*Hint*: The language $\bigcup_{m \neq n} 0^m (1^+ 0^+)^n 1^+$ is context-free.]

3.3 Parsing and Ambiguity

In Section 3.1, we defined that a string x is in $L(G)$ for some context-free grammar $G = (V, \Sigma, R, S)$ if and only if there is a derivation $S \overset{*}{\Rightarrow} x$ in G. Such a derivation demonstrates the step-by-step applications of the rules to generate x from the starting symbol S. We can also display a derivation by a tree, called a *parse tree*, or a *derivation tree*. For instance, consider the context-free grammar $G_1 = (\{S\}, \{a, b, c\}, R, S)$, with

$$R = \{S \rightarrow SbS \mid ScS \mid a\},$$

and the string $abaca \in L(G_1)$. The derivation

$$S \Rightarrow SbS \Rightarrow SbScS \Rightarrow abScS \Rightarrow abSca \Rightarrow abaca$$

can be represented by the tree of Figure 3.4(a), and the derivation

$$S \Rightarrow ScS \Rightarrow SbScS \Rightarrow abScS \Rightarrow abSca \Rightarrow abaca$$

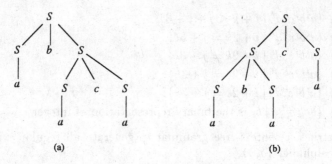

Figure 3.4: The sentence *abaca* has two parse trees.

can be represented by the tree of Figure 3.4(b).

In general, for a context-free grammar $G = (V, \Sigma, R, S)$, a parse tree can be constructed as follows:

(1) Let S be the root of the tree.

(2) Repeat the following until every leaf of the tree is either ε or a terminal symbol:

For any leaf $A \in V$ of the tree, select a rule $A \rightarrow x_1 x_2 \cdots x_n$, where $x_i \in V \cup \Sigma$ for $i = 1, \ldots, n$, and replace the node A in V by the following tree:

If the concatenation of the leaves of a parse tree is the string $x \in \Sigma^*$, then we say this is a parse tree of x.

It is clear that a parse tree of x corresponds to a derivation of x. In fact, a parse tree often represents more than one derivation of x. For instance, for the grammar G_1 defined above, there are 16 different derivations for $x = abaca$. Among them, the eight derivations that begin with $S \Rightarrow SbS$ are all represented by the same parse tree of Figure 3.4(a). The other eight derivations that begin with $S \Rightarrow ScS$ are all represented by the parse tree of Figure 3.4(b).

To make the relation between parse trees and derivations clearer, we define that a derivation of a string $x \in L(G)$ is a *leftmost derivation* if it always applies a rule to substitute for the leftmost nonterminal symbol in a sentential form. Then, it is easy to verify that each parse tree of a string x corresponds to a unique leftmost derivation of x. For instance, among the eight derivations for $x = abaca$ that begin with $S \Rightarrow SbS$, the following is the only leftmost derivation:

$$S \Rightarrow SbS \Rightarrow abS \Rightarrow abScS \Rightarrow abacS \Rightarrow abaca.$$

Thus, a parse tree of a string x demontrates the structure of the generation of x from the grammar rules, disregarding the order of applications of these rules.

Parsing Algorithms. The task of finding a parse tree for x from a given context-free grammar G is called *parsing*. Parsing is one of the most important issues in compiler design. By adding certain constraints to the grammar, people have developed a number of parsing techniques. Here, we only present a general (but often inefficient) *top-down* parsing method.

Let $G = (V, \Sigma, R, S)$ be a context-free grammar. A string $w \in (V \cup \Sigma)^*$ is called a sentential form if $S \stackrel{*}{\Rightarrow} w$, and it is called a *left sentential form* if there is a leftmost derivation from S to w. If w is a string of terminal symbols, then it has a leftmost derivation from S if and only if it has a derivation from S. This is not true for sentential forms. It is possible that a sentential form can only be obtained from S through a non-leftmost derivation.

For any context-free grammar G, we define the *leftmost graph* $g(G)$ of G as follows:

(a) The vertices of $g(G)$ are all left sentential forms of G.

(b) For any two left sentential forms w_1 and w_2, if there is a rule $r = (A \to x)$ of G such that $w_1 = uAv$ and $w_2 = uxv$ for some $u \in \Sigma^*$ and $v \in (V \cup \Sigma)^*$, then there is an directed edge from w_1 to w_2, with label r.

Thus, $g(G)$ is an edge-labeled directed graph, which is often infinite. Note that if all leftmost sentential forms of G have a unique leftmost derivation from the starting symbol S, then $g(G)$ is actually a tree, with the start symbol S as the root.

To find a parse tree of a string x of terminals, we can simply perform a search of the graph $g(G)$. Since the graph $g(G)$ might be infinite, the graph search is not guaranteed to halt on all inputs. Nevertheless, with a minor restriction to the grammar G, we can be sure that the graph search always halts. A grammar rule is called an *ε-rule*, if it is of the form $A \to \varepsilon$ for some $A \in V$. We observe that if a context-free grammar does not have an ε-rule, then the size of the sentential forms in a derivation must be nondecreasing. Thus, to determine whether $S \stackrel{*}{\Rightarrow} x$, we may simply restrict ourself to search the subgraph of $g(G)$ over vertices of length $\leq |x|$.

Example 3.22 *Determine whether $x = abaca$ belongs to $L(G)$ or not, where $G = (\{S\}, \{a, b, c\}, \{S \to SbS \mid ScS \mid a\}, S)$.*

Solution. We start with the starting symbol S, and perform a depth-first search of the graph $g(G)$, using the following ordering of the rules: $r_1 : (S \to a)$, $r_2 : (S \to SbS)$, $r_3 : (S \to ScS)$. During the search, we also use the following conditions to prune the graph:

(1) If a vertex has length ≥ 6, then we delete this vertex.

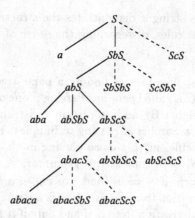

Figure 3.5: Depth-first top-down search.

(2) If a vertex has two occurrences of symbol b or two occurrences of symbol c, then we delete this vertex.

Figure 3.5 shows the depth-first search tree of the graph $g(G)$, with the above pruning condition. Note that we stop the search as soon as the sentence *abaca* is found. The dot lines in Figure 3.5 denote the search paths that are not yet performed.

We can also perform the graph search by a breadth-first search using the same pruning criteria. We leave it as an exercise.   □

The above method applies only to context-free grammars G which have no ε-rules. What about grammars with ε-rules? We note that there is a simple method to find, from a grammar G, a new grammar G' with no ε-rule such that $L(G') = L(G) - \{\varepsilon\}$. Namely, we first identify all symbols that can derive the empty string ε. Then, for each such symbol A, we replace all rules of the form $B \to uAv$ by $B \to uAv \mid uv$, if $uv \neq \varepsilon$. We also delete all rules of the form $A \to \varepsilon$. It can be easily checked that this new grammar G' generates all strings in $L(G) - \{\varepsilon\}$. Finally, if $\varepsilon \in L(G)$, then we can first follow the above step to eliminate all ε-rules, and then add a new start symbol S' and two new rules $S' \to S \mid \varepsilon$. The resulting grammar is then equivalent to G and has a single ε-rule $S' \to \varepsilon$ which does not affect our tree search algorithm.

Ambiguity. A context-free grammar G is *ambiguous* if there exists a string $x \in L(G)$ that has two different parse trees. Note that a parse tree for a string x not only tells us whether x is in $L(G)$, but also gives us the syntactic structure of x, which, in turn, may induce the semantic meaning of x. When x has two parse trees, it makes it hard to determine which structure is the correct one. Let us look at an example from a standard rule in many programming languages.

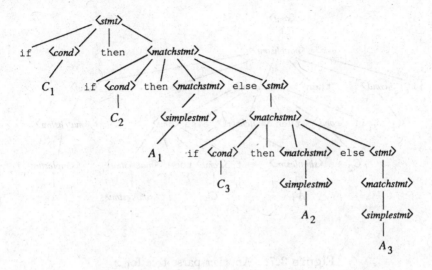

Figure 3.6: A parse tree for x.

Example 3.23 *Consider the following grammar G, in which a word of the form $\langle \cdots \rangle$ denotes a nonterminal, and other words denote terminals:*

$$\langle stmt \rangle \longrightarrow \text{if } \langle cond \rangle \text{ then } \langle matchstmt \rangle \mid \langle matchstmt \rangle$$
$$\langle matchstmt \rangle \longrightarrow \text{if } \langle cond \rangle \text{ then } \langle matchstmt \rangle \text{ else } \langle stmt \rangle \mid \langle simplestmt \rangle$$
$$\langle cond \rangle \longrightarrow C_1 \mid C_2 \mid C_3$$
$$\langle simplestmt \rangle \longrightarrow A_1 \mid A_2 \mid A_3.$$

Let x be the sentence

$$\text{if } C_1 \text{ then if } C_2 \text{ then } A_1 \text{ else if } C_3 \text{ then } A_2 \text{ else } A_3.$$

Find two different parse trees for x.

Solution. We show two parse trees for x in Figure 3.6 and Figure 3.7. They imply two different syntactic structures of the sentence x and, hence, two different semantic interpretations of x. For instance, if condition C_1 is false then, in the first parse tree (a), none of the simple statement A_1, A_2 or A_3 will be executed, while in the second parse tree (b), A_3 is to be executed. □

From the above example, we can see that if a context-free grammar is ambiguous, then it would be difficult to determine the meaning of the sentence from its different parse trees. Therefore, it is desirable to design unambiguous grammars whenever it is possible. In the following two examples, we show how to modify an ambiguous grammar into an equivalent unambiguous grammar.

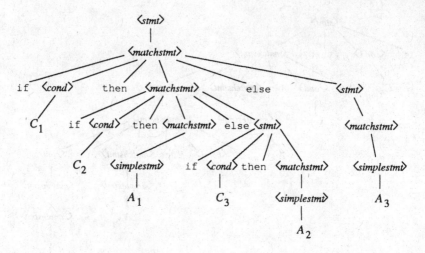

Figure 3.7: Another parse tree for x.

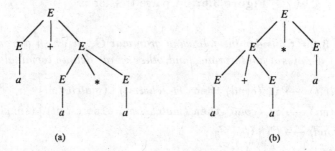

Figure 3.8: Two parse trees for $a + a * a$.

Example 3.24 *(a) Show that the following context-free grammar G for arithmetic expressions over variables a and b is ambiguous:*

$$E \longrightarrow E + E \mid E - E \mid E * E \mid E \div E \mid (E) \mid a \mid b.$$

(b) Find an equivalent unambiguous grammar for $L(G)$.

Solution. (a) The expression $a + a * a$ has two parse trees, as shown in Figure 3.8. Note that the two parse trees have different semantic interpretations. If we evaluate the expression following the order given by the parse tree, then the first tree Figure 3.8(a) gives us $a + a * a = a + (a * a) = a + a^2$, and the second tree Figure 3.8(b) gives us $a + a * a = (a + a) * a = 2a^2$.

(b) Usually, ambiguity comes from *parallel substitutions* for a nonterminal symbol in a sentential form. For instance, in grammar G, E can be replaced by either $E + E$ or $E * E$, and each sentential form can derive $E + E * E$. To avoid this problem, we use different nonterminal symbols to represent operands of different operators. In the following, we use symbol T (standing for *term*) to represent operands of operations $+$ and $-$, and use symbol F (standing for *factor*) to represent operands of $*$ and $\div$.

In addition, we note that the intended interpretation of an arithmetic expression follows the usual preference rules:

(i) The operators $+$ and $-$ have higher preference over $*$ and $\div$.

(ii) Within the operators of the same preference (e.g., $+$ and $-$) in an arithmetic expression, the one to the left has the preference over the one to the right.

We can enforce these rules in the following grammar:

$$E \longrightarrow E + T \mid E - T \mid T,$$
$$T \longrightarrow T * F \mid T \div F \mid F,$$
$$F \longrightarrow (E) \mid a \mid b.$$

For instance, $a - b * a + b$ has a unique parse tree as shown in Figure 3.9(a). We note that the symbols $-$ and $+$ must be generated first before we use T to generate $b * a$, because there is no way to generate $-$ or $+$ from T (without using parentheses). Thus, the preference rule (i) is followed. Second, if we start the derivation of $a - b * a + a$ by $[E \Rightarrow E - T]$, then the symbol $+$ cannot be generated without parentheses. Thus, we must generate the rightmost $+$ or $-$ symbol first, and this forces the parse tree to follow the preference rule (ii). (If we replace the first grammar rule by $[E \to T + E \mid T - E \mid T]$, then we force the parse tree to generate the leftmost $+$ or $-$ symbol first.) If we want to generate parse trees defying these preference rules, we must use parentheses. For instance, if we want to perform $a + b$ first in the expression $a - b * a + b$, then we must generate the expression $a - b * (a + b)$, whose unique parse tree is as shown in Figure 3.9(b). □

* Example 3.25 Let $\#_a(w)$ denote the number of occurrences of symbol a in a string w. Let $L = \{x \in \{a, b\}^* \mid \#_a(x) = \#_b(x)\}$.

(a) Show that both solutions of Example 3.6 for L are ambiguous:

$G_1:$ $S \longrightarrow aSbS \mid bSaS \mid \varepsilon$.

$G_2:$ $S \longrightarrow \varepsilon \mid aB \mid bA,$ $A \longrightarrow aS \mid bAA,$ $B \longrightarrow bS \mid aBB$.

(b) Find an unambiguous context-free grammar for the language L.

Solution. (a) In grammar G_1, the ambiguity comes from the two occurrences of the nonterminal symbol S in the sentential form $aSbS$ in the following two leftmost derivations for the string $abab$:

$$S \Rightarrow aSbS \Rightarrow abSaSbS \Rightarrow abaSbS \Rightarrow ababS \Rightarrow abab,$$
$$S \Rightarrow aSbS \Rightarrow abS \Rightarrow abaSbS \Rightarrow ababS \Rightarrow abab.$$

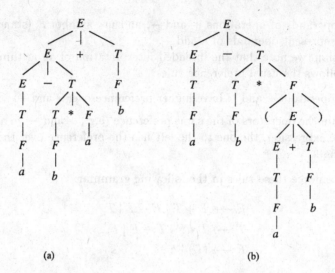

(a)   (b)

Figure 3.9: (a) The unique parse tree for $a - b * a + b$. (b) The unique parse tree for $a - b * (a + b)$.

For Grammar G_2, it comes from the occurrences of AA or BB in the sentential forms. Recall that A generates the set of all strings w with $\#_a(w) = \#_b(w) + 1$. Now, suppose $w = xyz$, with $\#_a(x) = \#_b(x) + 1$, $\#_a(y) = \#_b(y)$ and $\#_a(z) = \#_b(z) + 1$. Then, we have two ways to generate w from AA. One way is to use $A \overset{*}{\Rightarrow} xy$ and $A \overset{*}{\Rightarrow} z$. The other way is to use $A \overset{*}{\Rightarrow} x$ and $A \overset{*}{\Rightarrow} yz$. Based on this idea, we can construct two leftmost derivations for the string $bbabbaaa$:

$$S \Rightarrow bA \Rightarrow bbAA \Rightarrow bbaSA \Rightarrow bbabAA \Rightarrow bbabbAAA \overset{*}{\Rightarrow} bbabbaaa,$$

$$S \Rightarrow bA \Rightarrow bbAA \Rightarrow bbaSA \Rightarrow bbaA \Rightarrow bbabAA \Rightarrow bbabbAAA$$
$$\overset{*}{\Rightarrow} bbabbaaa.$$

(b) We show how to modify grammar G_1 into an unambiguous grammar, and leave the modification of G_2 into an unambiguous grammar as an exercise (Exercise 5).

We observe that if $x \in L$, then a parse of x must match each occurrence of a in x with a unique b in x. If there are more than one way to match an occurrence of a with some b then we have ambiguity. To eliminate this ambiguity, we read string x from left to right and try to match the most recently read unmatched occurrences of a and b. For instance, suppose $x = abaabb$, then the matching must be done as this:

$$a\ b\ a\ a\ b\ b$$

and the matching

$$\overbrace{a\ b}\ \overbrace{a\ a}\ \underbrace{b\ b}$$

is incorrect, since we should match the first two symbols a and b as soon as they are read. In the following, we will design a context-free grammar to enforce this matching policy.

For any string $w \in \{a,b\}^*$, let $c(w) = \#_a(w) - \#_b(w)$. We will use two extra nonterminals X and Y. The nonterminal X will generate the set

$$A = \{x \in \{a,b\}^* \mid c(x) = 0, (\forall y, y \text{ is a prefix of } x)[c(y) \geq 0]\}.$$

The nonterminal Y will generate the set

$$B = \{x \in \{a,b\}^* \mid c(x) = 0, (\forall y, y \text{ is a prefix of } x)[c(y) \leq 0]\}.$$

We now construct an unambiguous context-free grammar G_X for set A:

$$G_X : \quad X \longrightarrow aXbX \mid \varepsilon.$$

First, we show that $L(G_X) = A$. It is clear that each string $x \in L(G_X)$ has $c(x) = 0$. Furthermore, a simple induction on the length of x shows that each prefix y of x must have $c(y) \geq 0$: This is trivial if $|x| = 0$. If $|x| > 0$ and if x is derived from X via

$$X \Rightarrow aXbX \overset{*}{\Rightarrow} aubX \overset{*}{\Rightarrow} aubv,$$

with $X \overset{*}{\Rightarrow} u$ and $X \overset{*}{\Rightarrow} v$, then, by the inductive hypothesis on u, any prefix y of au has $c(y) \geq 1$ and $c(aub) = 0$. Thus, for any prefix z of v, $c(aubz) = c(z) \geq 0$. It follows that $L(G_X) \subseteq A$.

Conversely, we prove, by induction on the length of x, that each $x \in A$ is in $L(G_X)$. Again, this is trivial for $x = \varepsilon$. For any nonempty string $x \in A$, it is easy to see that x must begin with a and end with b. Write $x = aubv$, where au is the longest prefix of x with the following property:

P_1: All the nonempty prefixes z of au, including au itself, have $c(z) > 0$.

We claim that both u and v are in A. Indeed, for any prefix w of u, we have $c(w) = c(aw) - 1 \geq 0$, since property P_1 implies $c(aw) \geq 1$. Also, by the definition of au, we must have $c(aub) = 0$ and, hence, $c(u) = 0$. Therefore, $u \in A$. We can also verify that $c(v) = 0$ since $c(x) = 0$ and $c(aub) = 0$, and that all prefixes z of v satisfy $c(z) \geq 0$, since $c(aub) = 0$ implies $c(z) = c(aubz) \geq 0$.

From the claim and the inductive hypothesis, we have $X \overset{*}{\Rightarrow} u$ and $X \overset{*}{\Rightarrow} v$. Together, we get a derivation for x:

$$X \Rightarrow aXbX \overset{*}{\Rightarrow} aubX \overset{*}{\Rightarrow} aubv = x. \tag{3.1}$$

This completes the proof of $A \subseteq L(G_X)$.

Finally, we observe that if x is generated by X from the derivation (3.1), then au must be the longest prefix of x having property P_1, since $c(u) = 0$ implies $c(aub) = 0$ and, for every prefix w of u, $c(w) \geq 0$ implies $c(aw) \geq 1$. Thus, the matching of the first a in x with the symbol b right after u is unique. It follows from an induction argument that the parsing of x in G_X is unique.

Next, we define a grammar G_Y:

$$Y \longrightarrow bYaY \mid \varepsilon.$$

By a symmetric argument, we know that G_Y is an unambiguous grammar for set B.

We are now ready to define the unambiguous context-free grammar G_3 for L:

$$S \longrightarrow aXbS \mid bYaS \mid \varepsilon, \quad X \longrightarrow aXbX \mid \varepsilon, \quad Y \longrightarrow bYaY \mid \varepsilon.$$

It is obvious that $L(G_3) \subseteq L$. Conversely, we prove, by induction on the length of x, that if $x \in L$ then x has a unique parse tree in G_3. This is trivial for $x = \varepsilon$. For the inductive step, let $x \in \{a,b\}^+$ be a string that begins with a. Then, we can write $x = aubv$, where au is the longest prefix of x satisfying property P_1. By the same argument above, there is a unique way to parse $X \stackrel{*}{\Rightarrow} u$. Furthermore, we have $c(u) = 0$ and so $c(v) = 0$. By induction, we also have a unique way to parse $S \stackrel{*}{\Rightarrow} v$. Thus, there is a derivation of x:

$$S \Rightarrow aXbS \stackrel{*}{\Rightarrow} aubS \stackrel{*}{\Rightarrow} aubv = x.$$

Furthermore, we argue that this is the unique parsing of x; that is, in the first step of a derivation $S \Rightarrow aXbS \stackrel{*}{\Rightarrow} x$, the first symbol a must be matched with the symbol b after u.

First, we show that a cannot be matched with any b in u: If $u = u_1bu_2$ for some u_1, u_2, then we must have $c(u_1) > 0$, since, by property P_1, $c(au_1b) > 0$. Thus, u_1 cannot be derived from X. Second, we argue that a cannot be matched with any b in v: If $v = v_1bv_2$, then $c(ub) = c(aub) - 1 = -1$ and, hence, ubv_1 has a prefix with a negative value of c. Thus, $ubv_1 \notin A$ and so X cannot generate it.

The same argument works for strings x beginning with b. This concludes our proof that G_3 is an unambiguous grammar for L.   □

The above examples showed that some ambiguous context-free grammars can be modified into an unambiguous one. This is, however, not always possible. A context-free language is called *inherently ambiguous* if every grammar generating it is ambiguous. A typical example of an inherently ambiguous context-free language is $L = \{a^i b^j c^k \mid i = j \text{ or } j = k\}$. Intuitively, for any context-free grammar G that generates L, there must be a method to generate strings of the form $a^i b^i c^k$, and a separate method to generate strings of the form $a^i b^k c^k$. Then, for strings of the form $a^i b^i c^i$, there would be two different ways to generate it. The formal proof of this fact requires more careful analysis of context-free grammars. We delay it until Secion 3.5 (see Example 3.54).

Lookahead Sets. In general, it is difficult to determine whether a given context-free grammar is ambiguous or not. Indeed, this problem is *undecidable*, meaning that there is no general procedure to solve this problem for all context-free grammars (see Example 5.47). In the following, we present a sufficient condition for the unambiguity of a context-free grammar. This condition is based on the depth-first top-down parsing algorithm of Example 3.22.

Let $G = (V, \Sigma, R, S)$ be a context-free grammar. We write $\alpha \underset{L}{\overset{*}{\Rightarrow}} \beta$ to denote that the leftmost derivation from a sentential form α to a sentential form β. For any nonterminal A, we say a rule $A \to x$ is an A-rule. We define the *lookahead set* of nonterminal A as

$$\mathrm{LA}(A) = \{w \in \Sigma^* \mid S \underset{L}{\overset{*}{\Rightarrow}} uAv \underset{L}{\overset{*}{\Rightarrow}} uw \in \Sigma^*, \text{ for some } u, v \in (V \cup \Sigma)^*\}.$$

That is, if we have reached, in a leftmost derivation, a sentential form α whose leftmost nontermial is A, then the suffixes of all sentences that can be derived from α, starting from symbol A, are in the lookahead set of A. For each A-rule $A \to x$ in R, the *lookahead set* of the rule $A \to x$ is defined by

$$\mathrm{LA}(A \to x)$$
$$= \{w \in \Sigma^* \mid S \underset{L}{\overset{*}{\Rightarrow}} uAv \underset{L}{\Rightarrow} uxv \underset{L}{\overset{*}{\Rightarrow}} uw \in \Sigma^*, \text{ for some } u, v \in (V \cup \Sigma)^*\}.$$

Suppose $A \to x_1$, $A \to x_2$, $\cdots$, $A \to x_k$ are all the A-rules in grammar G. Then, it is easy to see that

$$\mathrm{LA}(A) = \bigcup_{i=1}^{k} \mathrm{LA}(A \to x_i).$$

Lemma 3.26 *A context-free grammar G is unambiguous if, for every nonterminal A, the sets $\mathrm{LA}(A \to x)$ over all A-rules $A \to x$ form a partition of $\mathrm{LA}(A)$, that is, if $\mathrm{LA}(A \to x) \cap \mathrm{LA}(A \to y) = \emptyset$ for any two distinct A-rules $(A \to x)$ and $(A \to y)$.*

Proof. For the sake of contradiction, suppose that G is ambiguous. Then, there exists a string $w \in \Sigma^*$ such that $S \overset{*}{\Rightarrow} w$ has two leftmost derivations. Since the two leftmost derivations start with the same sentential form S, there exists a sentential form uAv, with $u \in \Sigma^*$, such that the two leftmost derivations are identical from S to uAv but different at the next derivation step. That is, the two leftmost derivations are of the form

$$S \overset{*}{\Rightarrow} uAv \Rightarrow uxv \overset{*}{\Rightarrow} uw' = w$$

and
$$S \overset{*}{\Rightarrow} uAv \Rightarrow uyv \overset{*}{\Rightarrow} uw' = w,$$

where $(A \to x)$ and $(A \to y)$ are two distinct A-rules. This implies that w' belongs to both $LA(A \to x)$ and $LA(A \to y)$, contradicting the assumption. □

The above lemma gives us a sufficient condition for unambiguity. For most grammars, however, this condition is not easy to check. A simple remedy is to truncate the lookahead sets to a fixed size.

For any language L and any constant $k \geq 1$, define the operation $trunc_k$ by

$$trunc_k(L) = \{x \mid [x \in L, |x| \leq k] \text{ or } [xy \in L \text{ for some } y, |x| = k]\}.$$

Denote
$$LA_k(A) = trunc_k(LA(A))$$
$$LA_k(A \to x) = trunc_k(LA(A \to x)).$$

We say a context-free grammar G is a *strong* $LL(k)$ *grammar* if it satisfies the following *strong* $LL(k)$ *condition*: For every nonterminal A in G, the sets $LA_k(A \to x)$ over all A-rules $(A \to x)$ form a partition of $LA_k(A)$. It is clear that the strong $LL(k)$ condition implies the condition given in Lemma 3.26 and, therefore, a strong $LL(k)$ grammar is unambiguous. Intuitively, a grammar G is a strong $LL(k)$ grammar if, in the parsing of a string x to get its leftmost derivation, we can look at the next k symbols of x to determine which grammar rule to apply to the leftmost nonterminal in the current sentential form. This is a simple and yet very useful notion in compiler design.

Example 3.27 *Show that the context-free grammar G with rules*

$$S \longrightarrow aA, \qquad A \longrightarrow BA \mid a, \qquad B \longrightarrow bS \mid cS$$

is unambiguous.

Proof. Since there is only one S-rule, we have $LA_1(S) = LA_1(S \to aA)$. Next, it is easy to see that the two lookahead sets for B are $LA_1(B \to bS) = \{b\}$ and $LA_1(B \to cS) = \{c\}$, and are disjoint. Finally, the two lookahead sets of A are $LA_1(A \to BA) = \{b, c\}$ and $LA_1(A \to a) = \{a\}$, and they are disjoint. Therefore, G is a strong $LL(1)$ grammar and, hence, is unambiguous. □

Exercise 3.3

1. Let G be the context-free grammar with rules

$$S \longrightarrow aSaa \mid B, \qquad B \longrightarrow bbBcc \mid C, \qquad C \longrightarrow bc.$$

(a) Draw a parse tree for $a^3 b^3 c^3 a^6$.

(b) Show that this grammar is unambiguous.

2. Let G be the context-free grammar with rules

$$S \longrightarrow AaSbB \mid \varepsilon, \qquad A \longrightarrow aA \mid a, \qquad B \longrightarrow bB \mid \varepsilon.$$

(a) Show that G is ambiguous.

(b) Find an unambiguous context-free grammar equivalent to G.

3. Consider grammar G with rules

$$S \longrightarrow aAcaa \mid bAbcc, \qquad A \longrightarrow a \mid ab \mid \varepsilon.$$

Find the minimum k such that G is a strong LL(k) grammar.

4. (a) Show that grammar G_3 of Example 3.25(b) is a strong LL(1) grammar.

(b) Does the grammar of Example 3.24(b) satisfy the condition of Lemma 3.26? Does it satisfy a strong LL(k) condition for any $k \geq 0$?

5. Modify grammar G_2 of Example 3.25 into an equivalent, unambiguous grammar.

6. *Left-factoring* in a grammar G is the operation of replacing rules $A \rightarrow a\alpha_1 \mid \cdots \mid a\alpha_k$ by $A \rightarrow aA'$ and $A' \rightarrow \alpha_1 \mid \cdots \mid \alpha_k$, where $a \in \Sigma$ and $\alpha_1, \ldots, \alpha_k \in (V \cup \Sigma)^*$. Prove the following statements:

(a) Grammar G is ambiguous if and only if the grammar G' resulted from a left-factoring operation on G is ambiguous.

(b) If, after a left-factoring operation, a grammar G becomes a strong LL(k) grammar, then G must be a strong LL($k+1$) grammar. Is the converse true?

7. For each of the following context-free grammars, determine whether it is a strong LL(1) grammar. If not, find a strong LL(1) grammar which is equivalent to it.

(a) $S \longrightarrow S_1\$, \quad S_1 \longrightarrow aaS_1b \mid bb \mid ab.$

(b) $S \longrightarrow S_1\$, \quad S_1 \longrightarrow aA \mid S_1b \mid S_1c, \qquad A \longrightarrow bAc \mid \varepsilon.$

8. Show that the following grammars are not strong LL(k) grammars for any $k > 0$, but they are unambiguous.

(a) $S \longrightarrow aSb \mid A, \quad A \longrightarrow aAc \mid \varepsilon.$

(b) $S \longrightarrow A \mid B, \quad A \longrightarrow aAb \mid ab, \quad B \longrightarrow aBc \mid ac.$

3.4   Pushdown Automata

Context-free grammars are *generators* for context-free languages, from which
we can obtain sentences in the language by repeatedly applying the grammar
rules. Using a context-free grammar to parse a given string is, though possible,
not easy. In this section, we introduce a model of *recognizers*, called *pushdown
automata*, to recognize strings in a given context-free language.

A *pushdown automaton* (PDA) is a nondeterministic finite automaton
equipped with an additional storage device called a *stack*, and a stack head
which reads from and writes to the top of the stack (see Figure 3.10). The
stack is a first-in last-out storage device with no predetermined size limit. The
stack head always scans the top element of the stack. It performs two basic
stack operations: *push* (add a new symbol at the top of the stack) and *pop*
(read and remove the top symbol from the stack).

More formally, we define a PDA as a 6-tuple $M = (Q, \Sigma, \Gamma, \delta, s, F)$, where
Q, Σ, s and F are the same as those in an NFA, Γ is a finite alphabet of stack
symbols, and δ is a transition function

$$\delta : Q \times (\Sigma \cup \{\varepsilon\}) \times (\Gamma \cup \{\varepsilon\}) \to 2^{Q \times (\Gamma \cup \{\varepsilon\})}.$$

For $q \in Q$, $a \in \Sigma$ and $u \in \Gamma$, an instruction $(p, v) \in \delta(q, a, u)$ means that if the
PDA M is in state q, reading a tape symbol a and a stack symbol u, then one
of its possible moves is to replace the top symbol u of the stack by v, move
the tape head one cell to the right and then move into state p. It is possible
that u or v is equal to ε. When $v = \varepsilon$, that is, $(p, \varepsilon) \in \delta(q, a, u)$, it means that
the PDA M may simply delete the top symbol u of the stack without writing
a new symbol to the stack (this is a simple pop operation). When $u = \varepsilon$,
that is, $(p, v) \in \delta(q, a, \varepsilon)$, it means that the PDA M performs this operation
without reading what the top symbol of the stack is (this is a simple push
operation). It is also allowed to have $a = \varepsilon$, that is, $(p, v) \in \delta(q, \varepsilon, u)$. This
type of instructions is like the ε-move of an NFA; that is, the PDA M performs

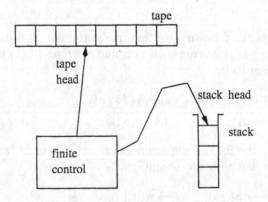

Figure 3.10:   A pushdown automaton.

the operation as in the case of $(p, v) \in \delta(q, a, u)$, except that it does not read a tape symbol (and so its tape head does not move).

At the beginning, a PDA $M = (Q, \Sigma, \Gamma, s, F, \delta)$ is in state s, having an empty stack, and its tape head is scanning the leftmost symbol of the input tape. At the end, we say a PDA *accepts* the input if, in one of its computation paths, it reads all input symbols, has an empty stack, and reaches a final state $q \in F$. We let $L(M)$ be the set of all strings accepted by M.

Example 3.28 *Consider the PDA* $M = (\{q, p\}, \{a, b, c\}, \{a, b\}, \delta, q, \{p\})$, *where δ is defined as follows:*

$$\delta(q, a, \varepsilon) = \{(q, a)\}, \quad \delta(p, a, a) = \{(p, \varepsilon)\},$$
$$\delta(q, b, \varepsilon) = \{(q, b)\}, \quad \delta(p, b, b) = \{(p, \varepsilon)\},$$
$$\delta(q, c, \varepsilon) = \{(p, \varepsilon)\}.$$

Determine what $L(M)$ is.

Solution. This machine works in the following way: At the initial state q, it pushs the input symbols a and b to the stack until it reads a tape symbol c. After reading c, it moves to state p. In state p, M compares each symbol on the tape with the top symbol of the stack. If they are all equal, then the machine accepts the input.

Let $w \in \{a, b\}^*$ be the prefix of the input before the first occurrence of symbol c, and x be the suffix of the input after the first occurrence of c. We note that, at the time of PDA M moving to state p, the string w is stored in the stack in the reverse order (the first symbol of w is at the bottom of the stack, and the last symbol of w is at the top). So, when it compares the suffix x with the stack symbols, it compares the first symbol of x with the last symbol of w, and so on. Therefore, it accepts only if $x = w^R$. That is, $L(M) = \{wcw^R \mid w \in \{a, b\}^*\}$. □

To better understand how a pushdown automaton works, we need to define the concept of configurations of a PDA. A configuration of a PDA M is a record of information of M at a certain stage of computation, including the state it is in, the tape symbols which it has yet to read, and the stack symbols in the stack. That is, a *configuration* of a PDA $M = (Q, \Sigma, \Gamma, \delta, s, F)$ is a member in $Q \times \Sigma^* \times \Gamma^*$. A configuration (q, x, γ) denotes that the PDA M is in state q, its tape symbols to be read are x, with the tape head scanning the leftmost symbol of x, and the stack currently holds symbols γ (with the leftmost symbol of γ representing the top symbol of the stack).

For any two configurations (q, x, β) and (p, y, γ), we say (p, y, γ) is a *successor configuration* of (q, x, β), and write $(q, x, \beta) \vdash (p, y, \gamma)$, if there is an instruction $(p, v) \in \delta(q, a, u)$ such that $x = ay$ and $\beta = u\alpha$, $\gamma = v\alpha$ for some $\alpha \in \Gamma^*$, where a, u, v may be equal to ε. We write $(q, x, \beta) \vdash^* (p, y, \gamma)$ if there exists a sequence of configurations $C_0, C_1, \ldots, C_n$ such that $C_0 = (q, x, \beta)$,

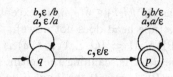

Figure 3.11: Transition diagram of PDA M of Example 3.28.

$C_n = (p, y, \gamma)$ and $C_i \vdash C_{i+1}$ for all $i = 0, 1, \ldots, n - 1$. A sequence $(C_0, C_1, \ldots, C_n)$ of configurations of M is a *computation path* of M if C_0 is an initial configuration (s, x, ε), C_n does not have a successor configuration, and $C_i \vdash C_{i+1}$ for all $i = 0, 1, \ldots, n - 1$. We recall again that M is, in general, nondeterministic and so it may have more than one computation path starting from the same initial configuration. In addition, a configuration (q, x, β) may have no successor configuration, even if $x \neq \varepsilon$.

Now, we can define formally the notion of a PDA M accepting a string $x \in \Sigma^*$ as follows: M accepts x if and only if there is a computation path of M that starts with the initial configuration (s, x, ε) and ends at a configuration $(f, \varepsilon, \varepsilon)$ for some $f \in F$; that is,

$$L(M) = \{x \in \Sigma^* \mid (\exists f \in F) \, [(s, x, \varepsilon) \vdash^* (f, \varepsilon, \varepsilon)]\}.$$

For instance, the following are three computation paths of the machine M of Example 3.28 on inputs $abcba$, $abcb$, and $abcbab$.

$(q, abcba, \varepsilon) \vdash (q, bcba, a) \vdash (q, cba, ba) \vdash (p, ba, ba) \vdash (p, a, a) \vdash (p, \varepsilon, \varepsilon);$

$(q, abcb, \varepsilon) \vdash (q, bcb, a) \vdash (q, cb, ba) \vdash (p, b, ba) \vdash (p, \varepsilon, a);$

$(q, abcbab, \varepsilon) \vdash (q, bcbab, a) \vdash (q, cbab, ba) \vdash (p, bab, ba) \vdash (p, ab, a) \vdash (p, b, \varepsilon).$

Note that in the second computation path, the machine M rejects since the stack is not empty when M finishes reading the input symbols. In the third computation path, it rejects because the configuration (p, b, ε) does not have a successor configuration, and yet the input is not completely read.

A pushdown automaton may also be represented, as an NFA, by its transition diagram. In the transition diagram of a PDA, each vertex represents a state and each edge from vertex q to p with label "$a, u/v$" represents a transition $(p, v) \in \delta(q, a, u)$. For example, the PDA M of Example 3.28 can be represented by the transition diagram of Figure 3.11.

It is worth mentioning that in the transition diagram of a DFA or an NFA, a path from the initial state to a final state represents an accepting computation path, but it is not the case for PDA's. It is easy to find a path from the initial state q to the final state p in Figure 3.11 which does not represent an accepting computation path. Actually, such a path in the transition diagram may not even represent a legal computation path. A legal computation path of a PDA must take into account the correct stack information.

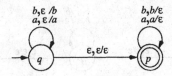

Figure 3.12:   Solution to Example 3.29.

Example 3.29 *Construct a PDA accepting the language* $\{ww^R \mid w \in \{a, b\}^*\}$.

Solution. This example is similar to the last one, except that the input does not have a middle separator c, and so we do not know when to start the comparison between the input and the stack. How do we attack this problem? We recall that PDA's are nondeterministic machines. Thus, we may nondeterministically start the comparison at any point. An input string is then accepted as long as the remaining input symbols match correctly with the stack symbols with respect to *some* separating point.

According to this idea, a PDA is constructed in Figure 3.12. We show three computation paths on input $abba$; the first one accepts, and the other two move to state p at the wrong time and reject.

$$(q, abba, \varepsilon) \vdash (q, bba, a) \vdash (q, ba, ba) \vdash (p, ba, ba) \vdash (p, a, a) \vdash (p, \varepsilon, \varepsilon);$$
$$(q, abba, \varepsilon) \vdash (q, bba, a) \vdash (q, ba, ba) \vdash (q, a, bba) \vdash (p, a, bba);$$
$$(q, abba, \varepsilon) \vdash (q, bba, a) \vdash (p, bba, a). \qquad \square$$

Example 3.30 *Construct a PDA that accepts the language*

$$\{a^i b^j c^k \mid i, j, k \geq 0, i + k = j\}.$$

Solution. The basic idea for this problem is to use different states to enforce the order of the occurrences of the letters a, b and c, and use the stack to meet the requirement of $i + k = j$. Therefore, we construct a PDA M with three states s, q, p, where s is the initial state and p is the unique final state. At state s, M pushes each input symbol a into the stack. At state q, M reads each input symbol b and either matches the symbol b with a symbol a in the stack or pushes the symbol b into the stack. At state p, it reads a symbol c and matches it with a symbol b in the stack. The transition diagram of the complete PDA is shown in Figure 3.13.

Like the last example, this PDA M moves nondeterministically from state s to state q and from state q to state p. Therefore, there may be many different computation paths for the same input. There is, however, at most one accepting path which changes states when input changes symbols. $\square$

Example 3.31 *Construct a PDA that accepts the language*

$$L = \{a^i b^j \mid 2i \neq 3j\}.$$

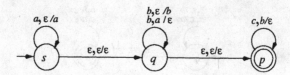

Figure 3.13:   Solution to Example 3.30.

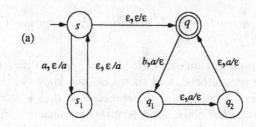

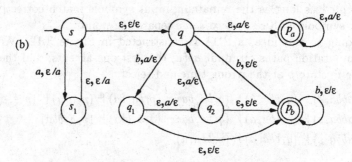

Figure 3.14:   Solution to Example 3.31.

Solution. First, we consider the language $L_1 = \{a^i b^j \mid i, j \geq 0, 2i = 3j\}$. For a
string $a^i b^j$ to be in L_1, it must be true that $i = 3k$ and $j = 2k$ for some $k \geq 0$.
Thus, for each symbol a of the input, we can push two copies of symbol a into
the stack. Then, for each symbol b we read from the input, we match it with
three a's in the stack. How do we push two symbols aa into the stack? We
can push one a into the stack and then move to a temporary state in which we
push another a into the stack. Similarly, we can match each input symbol b
with one stack symbol a first, and then move to another two temporary states
to pop up two more symbols a. A PDA based on this idea is constructed in
Figure 3.14(a).

Next, we consider the language L. The idea here is to use the above PDA
to match every b with *one and a half* a's. After that, we nondeterministically
move to state p_a or state p_b to handle the case of $2i > 3j$ or $2i < 3j$, respectively. To get to state p_a, we need to pop up at least one more symbol a
from the stack without a matching b. When we reach state p_a, we clean up
the stack and accept the input. To get to state p_b, we need to read at least
· one more symbol b. When we reach state p_b, we read off all symbols b on the

input tape and accept the input.

There is a subtle problem with the second case. That is, it is possible that i is not a multiple of 3, and M might be stuck at state q_1 or q_2, trying to pop a symbol a from an empty stack. To solve this problem, we note that if M has an empty stack at state q_1 or q_2, it means that M has recognized the condition of $2i < 3j$. Thus, we can move directly to the final state p_b from these two states without popping up any more symbols a from the stack. (There is no problem with the first case, since we can always match all input symbols b with the symbols a in stack when $2i > 3j$.)

The PDA for L is shown in Figure 3.14(b). The following is an accepting path for input $a^4 b^4$:

$$
\begin{aligned}
(s, a^4 b^4, \varepsilon) &\vdash (s_1, a^3 b^4, a) \vdash (s, a^3 b^4, aa) \vdash^* (s, b^4, a^8) \\
&\vdash (q, b^4, a^8) \vdash (q_1, b^3, a^7) \vdash (q_2, b^3, a^6) \vdash (q, b^3, a^5) \\
&\vdash^* (q, bb, aa) \vdash (q_1, b, a) \vdash (q_2, b, \varepsilon) \vdash (p_b, b, \varepsilon) \vdash (p_b, \varepsilon, \varepsilon). \qquad \Box
\end{aligned}
$$

$\star$ **Example 3.32** *Construct a PDA that accepts the language*

$$L = \{x \in \{a, b\}^* \mid 2\#_a(x) \neq 3\#_b(x)\}.$$

Solution. This problem looks like the last one, but there is a critical difference that, in this problem, the symbols a and b may occur in any order. Therefore, we may read a symbol b before we meet any matching symbol a. In this case, we need to push the symbol b into the stack in order to perform the matching later. The general rules here are:

(1) Each input symbol a is worth two stack symbols a, each input symbol b is worth three stack symbols b.

(2) Each stack symbol a needs to match a stack symbol b.

(3) We need to perform a matching if the new input symbol is different from the one at the top of the stack.

(4) If the new input symbol is the same as the top of the stack symbol, then we always push the new symbol into the stack.

There are some exceptional cases we need to take care of before we can complete the design of the PDA: If there are not enough stack symbols to match the new input symbol, then we push the extra worth of stack symbols into the stack. For instance, if we read an input symbol b and the stack has only one symbol a, then we pop off this symbol a and then push in two stack symbols b. We implement these ideas in the PDA M shown in Figure 3.15.

In this PDA, we use state s_1 to handle the input symbol a. When an input symbol a is read, we either match it with a stack symbol b or push a stack symbol a into the stack. Then, we move to state s_1. At state s_1, we pop off another stack symbol b or push another stack symbol a into the stack; and then we move back to state s. We use states q_1 and q_2 to handle the input symbol b in a similar way.

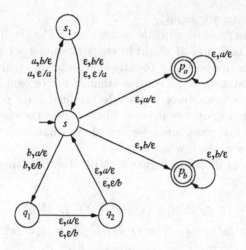

Figure 3.15: Solution of Example 3.32.

To see that this PDA M correctly accepts the language L, we notice that if we always follow the above rules, there is a computation path of M in which the stack always contains at most one type of stack symbols. Therefore, for any $x \in \{a, b\}^*$, we have

$$(s, x, \varepsilon) \vdash^* (s, \varepsilon, a^m)$$

if $2\#_a(x) - 3\#_b(x) = m \geq 0$, or

$$(s, x, \varepsilon) \vdash^* (s, \varepsilon, b^m)$$

if $2\#_a(x) - 3\#_b(x) = -m \leq 0$. Thus, if $m \neq 0$, M can move to the final state p_a or the final state p_b, accordingly. This shows that if $x \in L$ then M must have an accepting computation path.

Conversely, suppose that we have an accepting computation path on an input x that ends at state p_a. Then, this computation path looks like this:

$$(s, x, \varepsilon) \vdash^* (s, \varepsilon, a^{j+1}) \vdash (p_a, \varepsilon, a^j) \vdash (p_a, \varepsilon, \varepsilon),$$

for some $j \geq 0$, since we do not read any input symbol in state p_a, and can only pop off symbols a in state p_a. (In other words, computation paths that do not follow rule (3) and, hence, leave some symbol b in the stack when we reach state p_a do not accept.) Since we always enforce the matching rules (1) and (2) before we reach state p_a, we must have $2\#_a(x) = 3\#_b(x) + j + 1$ and, hence, $x \in L$. Similar argument works for the case in which M halts in p_b. (See Exercise 4(b) of this section for a different implementation which enforces rule (3) more carefully.)

In the following, we show two computation paths of M on the same input $ababaab$, the first an accepting path and the second rejecting.

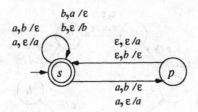

Figure 3.16: Solution of Example 3.33.

$(s, ababaab, \varepsilon) \vdash (s_1, babaab, a) \vdash (s, babaab, aa) \vdash (q_1, abaab, a)$

$\vdash (q_2, abaab, \varepsilon) \vdash (s, abaab, b) \vdash (s_1, baab, \varepsilon) \vdash (s, baab, a)$

$\vdash (q_1, aab, \varepsilon) \vdash (q_2, aab, b) \vdash (s, aab, bb) \vdash (s_1, ab, b)$

$\vdash (s, ab, \varepsilon) \vdash (s_1, b, a) \vdash (s, b, aa) \vdash (q_1, \varepsilon, a) \vdash (q_2, \varepsilon, \varepsilon)$

$\vdash (s, \varepsilon, b) \vdash (p_b, \varepsilon, \varepsilon).$

$(s, ababaab, \varepsilon) \vdash^* (s, aab, bb) \vdash (s_1, ab, abb) \vdash (s, ab, aabb)$

$\vdash (s_1, b, aaabb) \vdash (s, b, aaaabb) \vdash (q_1, \varepsilon, aaabb) \vdash (q_2, \varepsilon, aabb)$

$\vdash (s, \varepsilon, abb) \vdash (p_a, \varepsilon, bb) \vdash?.$ $\square$

Example 3.33 *Construct a PDA M that accepts the following language:*

$$\{w \in \{a, b\}^* \mid \#_a(w) \le \#_b(w) \le 2\#_a(w)\}.$$

Solution. In this problem, we need to match symbols a and b such that each symbol a is matched with at least one and at most two symbols b. This presents a new problem: for each symbol a, should we push in one stack symbol a or two stack symbols aa? If we push in only one stack symbol a, then we may not be able to check whether $\#_b(w) \le 2\#_a(w)$ when we find that there are extra b's. Likewise, if we push in two stack symbols aa, then we have no way to verify whether $\#_a(w) \le \#_b(w)$. The solution here is to use the nature of nondeterminism of PDA's to push in *either* one a *or* two a's. That is, we nondeterministically divide all occurrences of symbol a into two parts. Each symbol a in the first part is to be matched with one symbol b, and each symbol a in the second part is to be matched with two symbols b. It is obvious that if this matching succeeds for any partition of symbols a, we must have $\#_a(w) \le \#_b(w) \le 2\#_a(w)$. Conversely, if $\#_a(w) \le \#_b(w) \le 2\#_a(w)$, then there is such a partition of symbols a that will match a's and b's evenly.

Based on the above idea, we present the PDA in Figure 3.16. An accepting computation path for input $baabbabb$ is as follows:

$(s, baabbabb, \varepsilon) \vdash (s, aabbabb, b) \vdash (p, abbabb, \varepsilon) \vdash (s, abbabb, a)$

$\vdash (s, bbabb, aa) \vdash (s, babb, a) \vdash (s, abb, \varepsilon) \vdash (p, bb, a) \vdash (s, bb, aa)$

$\vdash (s, b, a) \vdash (s, \varepsilon, \varepsilon).$ $\square$

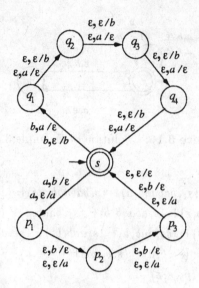

Figure 3.17: Solution of Example 3.34.

Example 3.34 *Construct a PDA M that accepts the language*

$$L = \{w \in \{a, b\}^* \mid 3\#_a(w) \le 5\#_b(w) \le 4\#_a(w)\}.$$

Solution. This problem is similar to the last one. We follow the following rules to match symbols a with symbols b:

(1) Each input symbol a is worth either three or four stack symbols a, and each input symbol b is worth five stack symbols b.

(2) Each stack symbol a needs to match a stack symbol b.

(3) We perform the matching whenever it is possible.

We show this PDA M in Figure 3.17. Note that we have added a transition $(s, \varepsilon) \in \delta(p_3, \varepsilon, \varepsilon)$ that allows M to move from state p_3 to state s without changing the stack. Therefore, M can treat an input symbol a as either three stack symbols a or four stack symbols a.

To see that this PDA works correctly, first assume that $w \in L$. Let $\#_a(w) = i$, $\#_b(w) = j$. Then, we must have $3i \le 5j \le 4i$. Equivalently, there must be an integer k, $0 \le k \le i$, such that $5j = 3k + 4(i - k)$. (E.g., if $i = 18$, then $11 \le j \le 14$. We check that $5 \cdot 11 = 3 \cdot 17 + 4 \cdot 1$, $5 \cdot 12 = 3 \cdot 12 + 4 \cdot 6$, $5 \cdot 13 = 3 \cdot 7 + 4 \cdot 11$, and $5 \cdot 14 = 3 \cdot 2 + 4 \cdot 16$.) Therefore, there is a computation path of M accepting w. Conversely, it is clear that if $w \notin L$, then there is no way to match stack symbols a and b evenly and so M does not accept w. $\square$

Exercise 3.4

1. For each of the following languages L, construct a PDA to accept L. In addition, for each given string $x \in L$, show an accepting computation

path of your PDA on x.

(a) $\{a^n b^m \mid m, n \geq 0, m \neq 3n\}$; $x = a^2 b^4$.

(b) $\{a^n b^m \mid 0 \leq 2n \leq m \leq 3n\}$; $x = a^2 b^5$.

(c) $\{a^n b^m \mid 0 \leq 2n \leq 3m \leq 4n - 2\}$; $x = a^3 b^3$.

(d) $\{a^i b^j c^k \mid i, j, k \geq 0, i + 2k = j\}$; $x = a^3 b^7 c^2$.

(e) $\{a^i b^j c^k \mid i, j, k \geq 0, 2i + 3k \leq 4j\}$; $x = a^4 b^4 c^2$.

(f) $\{a^i b^j c^k d^l \mid i, j, k \geq 0, i + k \leq j + l\}$; $x = a^2 b^4 c^5 d^3$.

(g) $\{a^i b^j c^k d^l \mid i, j, k \geq 0, 2i + 3k \leq 4j + l\}$; $x = a^3 b^4 c^4 d^5$.

(h) $\{w \in \{a, b\}^* \mid 2\#_a(w) + 5 \leq 3\#_b(w)\}$; $x = abbabba$.

(i) $\{w \in \{a, b\}^* \mid 2\#_a(w) \leq 3\#_b(w) \leq 4\#_a(w)\}$; $x = abbaaab$.

(j) $\{w \in \{a, b, c\}^* \mid \#_a(w) \leq \#_b(w) + 3\#_c(w)\}$; $x = aacabbbaa$.

$\star$ (k) $\{w \in \{a, b, c\}^* \mid 2\#_a(w) \leq \#_b(w) + 3\#_c(w) \leq 5\#_a(w)\}$; $x = acabcc$.

2. In Example 3.32, when we finished processing the input symbols, we move to one of the final states p_a or p_b if the stack is nonempty. Show that the two separate states are necessary. That is, suppose we merge states p_a and p_b of Figure 3.15 into a single final state p, with the instructions

$$\delta(s, \varepsilon, a) = \delta(s, \varepsilon, b) = \delta(p, \varepsilon, a) = \delta(p, \varepsilon, b) = (p, \varepsilon).$$

Show that, then, the new PDA would accept some strings not in L.

3. Show that each of the following variations of the pushdown automaton model is equivalent to our original definition of pushdown automata, in the sense that the class of languages accepted by pushdown automata remains the same.

(a) The PDA is allowed to push two stack symbols into the stack in one move; that is, the transition function δ is a function of the following form:

$$\delta : Q \times (\Sigma \cup \{\varepsilon\}) \times (\Gamma \cup \{\varepsilon\}) \to 2^{Q \times (\{\varepsilon\} \cup \Gamma \cup \Gamma^2)}.$$

(b) The PDA is allowed to push any number of stack symbols into the stack in one move; that is, the transition function δ is a function of the following form:

$$\delta : Q \times (\Sigma \cup \{\varepsilon\}) \times (\Gamma \cup \{\varepsilon\}) \to 2^{Q \times \Gamma^*}.$$

(c) The PDA is required to pop up the top element of the stack at each move and is allowed to push two stack symbols into the stack in one move; that is, the transition function δ is a function of the following form:

$$\delta : Q \times (\Sigma \cup \{\varepsilon\}) \times \Gamma \to 2^{Q \times (\{\varepsilon\} \cup \Gamma \cup \Gamma^2)}.$$

(We assume that the PDA starts with a special symbol $ in the
stack, i.e., the initial configuration is $(s, x, \$)$.)

(d) The PDA accepts an input string as long as it reaches a final state
after it finishes reading the input symbols (regardless of whether
the stack is empty or not); that is, the PDA accepts a string $x \in \Sigma^*$
if $(s, x, \varepsilon) \vdash^* (q, \varepsilon, \gamma)$ for some $q \in F$ and some $\gamma \in \Gamma^*$.

4. A PDA $M = (Q, \Sigma, \Gamma, \delta, s, F)$ is a *deterministic PDA* if no configuration
of M has more than one successor configuration (but a nonfinal configuration may have no successor). For each of Examples 3.28–3.33, do the
following:

(a) Determine whether the PDA given in the example is deterministic
or not.

(b) If the answer to (a) is *no*, then determine whether there is an
equivalent deterministic PDA accepting the same language. If
yes, present your deterministic PDA; if no, show why not. [*Hint*:
One way of eliminating (part of) nondeterminism in a PDA is to
use the PDA model of Exercise 3(c).]

3.5   Pushdown Automata and Context-Free Grammars

Many ideas in the design of pushdown automata used in the last section are
similar to those used in the design of context-free grammars. This observation suggests a close relation between these two language processors. Indeed,
we prove in this section that the class of languages accepted by pushdown
automata is exactly the class of context-free languages.

Theorem 3.35 *For every context-free grammar G, there is a PDA M such
that $L(M) = L(G)$.*

Proof. Given a context-free grammar $G = (V, \Sigma, R, S)$, we will construct a
PDA M to simulate grammar G such that $L(M) = L(G)$. The idea of the
PDA is simple: On input x, we first push the start symbol S of grammar G
into the stack. Then, we simulate the leftmost derivation of x by G. At each
step, if the top symbol of the stack is a nonterminal A, then we select a rule
$A \rightarrow w$ of G and replace A by w. If the top symbol is a terminal symbol a,
then we try to match it with the next input symbol. If they do not match,
then this computation path rejects; otherwise, we remove this symbol from
the stack and continue. Note that each terminal symbol at the top of the
stack belongs to the string generated in this derivation. Thus, if all those
symbols match correctly with those of the input, then the input is generated
by G and we accept it.

The only technical problem with the above idea is that the right-hand side
w of a rule $A \rightarrow w$ may have more than one symbol, but our PDA can only
push into the stack one symbol at a time. This problem can be easily resolved

by the technique of Example 3.31, using extra temporary states to push extra symbols into the stack (cf. Exercise 3(b) of Section 3.4).

More precisely, we can define the PDA as $M = (Q, \Sigma, V \cup \Sigma, \delta, s, \{q\})$, where Q contains s, q and other states to be defined below, and δ contains the following instructions:

(1) $\delta(s, \varepsilon, \varepsilon) = \{(q, S)\}$.

(2) For every terminal $a \in \Sigma$, $\delta(q, a, a) = \{(q, \varepsilon)\}$.

(3) For every rule $r_i = (A \to w_1 w_2 \cdots w_k)$ in R, where each w_j, $1 \leq j \leq k$, is a single symbol in $V \cup \Sigma$, we create $k - 1$ new states $q_{i,1}, q_{i,2}, \ldots, q_{i,k-1}$ and define

$$\delta(q, \varepsilon, A) \ni (q_{i,1}, w_k),$$
$$\delta(q_{i,j}, \varepsilon, \varepsilon) = \{(q_{i,j+1}, w_{k-j})\}, \quad \text{for } 1 \leq j \leq k - 2,$$
$$\delta(q_{i,k-1}, \varepsilon, \varepsilon) = \{(q, w_1)\}.$$

(If $k \leq 1$, i.e., $r_i = (A \to w_1)$, where $w_1 \in V \cup \Sigma \cup \{\varepsilon\}$, then we define $(q, w_1) \in \delta(q, \varepsilon, A)$.)

The idea of this construction is quite simple. In particular, the following two properties are easy to prove by induction on the length of computation or the length of derivation. We leave the formal proofs to the reader.

(1) Suppose that there is a computation path $(q, y, S) \vdash^* (q, \varepsilon, \gamma)$ by M for some $y \in \Sigma^*$ and $\gamma \in (V \cup \Sigma)^*$. Then, there is a leftmost derivation $S \underset{L}{\overset{*}{\Rightarrow}} y\gamma$ in G.

(2) Suppose $S \underset{L}{\overset{*}{\Rightarrow}} y\gamma$ in G, where $y \in \Sigma^*$ and $\gamma \in (V \cup \Sigma)^*$. Then, there is a computation path in M from (q, y, S) to (q, ε, γ).

Now, suppose that $x \in L(M)$. Then, there is a computation path $(q, x, S) \vdash^* (q, \varepsilon, \varepsilon)$. By property (1) above, we have $S \underset{L}{\overset{*}{\Rightarrow}} x$ and, hence, $x \in L(G)$. Conversely, if $x \in L(G)$ then, by property (2), $S \underset{L}{\overset{*}{\Rightarrow}} x$ implies $(q, x, S) \vdash^* (q, \varepsilon, \varepsilon)$. Thus, $x \in L(M)$. □

Example 3.36 *Consider the context-free grammar $G = (\{S\}, \{a, b\}, R, S)$, with the rules*

$$S \longrightarrow aS \mid aSbS \mid \varepsilon.$$

Construct a PDA M such that $L(M) = L(G)$.

Proof. We follow the construction of Theorem 3.35. The resulting PDA M is as shown in Figure 3.18.

Corresponding to the derivation

$$S \Rightarrow aS \Rightarrow aaSbS \Rightarrow aabS \Rightarrow aab,$$

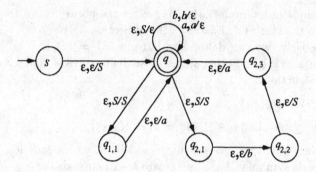

Figure 3.18:   PDA for Example 3.36

the accepting computation path of PDA M is

$$(s, aab, \varepsilon) \vdash (q, aab, S) \vdash (q_{1,1}, aab, S) \vdash (q, aab, aS) \vdash (q, ab, S)$$
$$\vdash (q_{2,1}, ab, S) \vdash (q_{2,2}, ab, bS) \vdash (q_{2,3}, ab, SbS) \vdash (q, ab, aSbS)$$
$$\vdash (q, b, SbS) \vdash (q, b, bS) \vdash (q, \varepsilon, S) \vdash (q, \varepsilon, \varepsilon). \qquad \square$$

★ Theorem 3.37 *For every PDA M, there is a context-free grammar G such that $L(G) = L(M)$.*

Proof. Let $M = (Q, \Sigma, \Gamma, \delta, q, F)$ be a PDA. First, we modify it to an equivalent PDA M' which always looks at the top symbol of the stack at each move (except the very first move). To do so, we need to make two adjustments on our PDA model:

(a) We push, at the first move, a special symbol $ into the stack to indicate the bottom of the stack. This prevents the possible stack underflow problem.

(b) We allow the new PDA M' to push two stack symbols into the stack at one move. This is necessary in order to push a new symbol into the stack. It is easy to see that this change does not increase the computational power of the PDA (see Exercise 3(c) of Section 3.4).

More precisely, we define a new PDA $M' = (Q \cup \{s_1, f\}, \Sigma, \Gamma \cup \{\$\}, \delta', s_1, \{f\})$, where s_1 and f are two new states, $ is a new stack symbol, and δ' contains the following instructions:

(1) $\delta'(s_1, \varepsilon, \varepsilon) = \{(s, \$)\}$.

(2) $\delta'(q, \varepsilon, \$) = \{(f, \varepsilon)\}$, for all $q \in F$.

(3) $(p, B) \in \delta'(q, a, A)$, if $(p, B) \in \delta(q, a, A)$, where $A \in \Gamma$ and $B \in \Gamma \cup \{\varepsilon\}$.

(4) $(p, BA) \in \delta'(q, a, A)$ for all $A \in \Gamma \cup \{\$\}$, if $(p, B) \in \delta(q, a, \varepsilon)$, where $B \in \Gamma \cup \{\varepsilon\}$.

It is clear that $L(M') = L(M)$.

Now, we construct a context-free grammar G to *simulate* the computation of M'. Grammar G contains the following nonterminal symbols:

$$V = \{\langle q, A, p \rangle \mid q, p \in Q \cup \{f\}, A \in \Gamma \cup \{\$\}\}.$$

Each nonterminal $\langle q, A, p \rangle$ will generate the following set:

$$\{x \in \Sigma^* \mid (q, x, A) \vdash^* (p, \varepsilon, \varepsilon)\}.$$

To do so, we define the following rules of G:

(1) For each instruction $(p, B) \in \delta'(q, a, A)$, where $|B| = 1$ and $a \in \Sigma \cup \{\varepsilon\}$, we define the rules

$$\langle q, A, r \rangle \longrightarrow a \langle p, B, r \rangle, \quad \text{for all } r \in Q \cup \{f\}.$$

(2) For each instruction $(p, BA) \in \delta'(q, a, A)$, where $|B| = 1$ and $a \in \Sigma \cup \{\varepsilon\}$, we define the rules

$$\langle q, A, r \rangle \longrightarrow a \langle p, B, r' \rangle \langle r', A, r \rangle, \quad \text{for all } r, r' \in Q \cup \{f\}.$$

(3) For each instruction $(p, \varepsilon) \in \delta'(q, a, A)$, where $a \in \Sigma \cup \{\varepsilon\}$, we define the rule

$$\langle q, A, p \rangle \longrightarrow a.$$

To see that the above construction works correctly, it suffices to show that

$$\langle q, A, p \rangle \overset{*}{\Rightarrow} x \text{ if and only if } (q, x, A) \vdash^* (p, \varepsilon, \varepsilon)$$

(so that $\langle s, \$, f \rangle \overset{*}{\Rightarrow} x$ if and only if $(s, x, \$) \vdash^* (f, \varepsilon, \varepsilon)$).

We first prove the forward direction by induction on the length of the derivation $\langle q, A, p \rangle \overset{*}{\Rightarrow} x$. First, if this derivation is of length 1. Then, it must use a rule created in Case (3) above, and it follows that $(q, x, A) \vdash^* (p, \varepsilon, \varepsilon)$. Next, assume that $\langle q, A, p \rangle \overset{*}{\Rightarrow} x$ has length ≥ 2. Then, the first step of the derivation may come from a rule created in Case (1) or in Case (2).

In Case (1), $\langle q, A, p \rangle \Rightarrow a \langle r, B, p \rangle \overset{*}{\Rightarrow} ay = x$, for some state $r \in Q \cup \{f\}$. By the inductive hypothesis, we have $(r, y, B) \vdash^* (p, \varepsilon, \varepsilon)$. Thus, by the condition of (1), $(q, x, A) \vdash (r, y, B) \vdash^* (p, \varepsilon, \varepsilon)$.

In Case (2), $\langle q, A, p \rangle \Rightarrow a \langle r, B, r' \rangle \langle r', A, p \rangle \overset{*}{\Rightarrow} ay = x$, for some states $r, r' \in Q \cup \{f\}$. Then, we have $\langle r, B, r' \rangle \overset{*}{\Rightarrow} y_1$, $\langle r', A, p \rangle \overset{*}{\Rightarrow} y_2$ for some y_1 and y_2 satisfying $y_1 y_2 = y$. By the inductive hypothesis, we know that $(r, y_1, B) \vdash^* (r', \varepsilon, \varepsilon)$ and $(r', y_2, A) \vdash^* (p, \varepsilon, \varepsilon)$. By the condition of (2), we have $(q, ay, A) \vdash (r, y, BA)$. Combining them together, we have a computation as follows:

$$(q, ay_1 y_2, A) \vdash (r, y_1 y_2, BA) \vdash^* (r', y_2, A) \vdash^* (p, \varepsilon, \varepsilon).$$

Thus, we have proved the forward direction.

For the backward direction, we assume that $(q, x, A) \vdash^* (p, \varepsilon, \varepsilon)$ in n moves. Suppose $n = 1$. Then, we must have an instruction $(p, \varepsilon) \in \delta'(q, a, A)$ and $x = a \in \Sigma \cup \{\varepsilon\}$. So, by Case (3), $\langle q, A, p \rangle \Rightarrow a = x$. Now, for $n > 1$, we assume that $(q, x, A) \vdash (r, y, \gamma) \vdash^* (p, \varepsilon, \varepsilon)$, where $x = ay$ for some $a \in \Sigma \cup \{\varepsilon\}$.

Then, we must have $1 \leq |\gamma| \leq 2$ (the PDA M' must read a symbol from the stack to operate, and so (r, y, ε) does not have a successor configuration).

If $\gamma = B \in \Gamma \cup \{\$\}$, then the first step must come from an instruction of the form $(r, B) \in \delta'(q, a, A)$. So, we have, from Case (1), $\langle q, A, p \rangle \Rightarrow a \langle r, B, p \rangle$. Also, by the inductive hypothesis, we have $\langle r, B, p \rangle \overset{*}{\Rightarrow} y$. Together, we get $\langle q, A, p \rangle \overset{*}{\Rightarrow} ay = x$.

Next, if $|\gamma| = 2$ then $\gamma = BA$ for some $B \in \Gamma \cup \{\$\}$, and the first step comes from an instruction $(r, BA) \in \delta'(q, a, A)$. That is, we have the following derivation:

$$(q, x, A) \vdash (r, y, BA) \overset{*}{\vdash} (p, \varepsilon, \varepsilon),$$

where $x = ay$. Then, there must be strings y_1, y_2 satisfying $y_1 y_2 = y$ and a configuration (r', y_2, A) such that $(r, y, BA) \overset{*}{\vdash} (r', y_2, A) \overset{*}{\vdash} (p, \varepsilon, \varepsilon)$. (The configuration (r', y_2, A) is the first configuration after (r, y, BA) with the original stack symbol A in (q, x, A) resurfaced as the top symbol of the stack.) By Case (2), we must have the following derivation step in G:

$$\langle q, A, p \rangle \Rightarrow a \langle r, B, r' \rangle \langle r', A, p \rangle.$$

By the inductive hypothesis, we have $\langle r, B, r' \rangle \overset{*}{\Rightarrow} y_1$ and $\langle r'A, p \rangle \overset{*}{\Rightarrow} y_2$. Thus, together we have $\langle q, A, p \rangle \overset{*}{\Rightarrow} ay_1 y_2 = x$. The above completes the proof of the correctness of the grammar G.   □

$\star$ **Example 3.38** *Construct a context-free grammar G such that $L(G) = L(M)$, where M is the PDA of Example 3.29.*

Solution. First, we transform M into M' with the following 13 instructions:

$\delta'(s, \varepsilon, \varepsilon) = \{(q, \$)\},$

$\delta'(q, a, \$) = \{(q, A\$)\}, \quad \delta'(q, a, A) = \{(q, AA)\}, \quad \delta'(q, a, B) = \{(q, AB)\},$

$\delta'(q, b, \$) = \{(q, B\$)\}, \quad \delta'(q, b, A) = \{(q, BA)\}, \quad \delta'(q, b, B) = \{(q, BB)\},$

$\delta'(q, \varepsilon, \$) = \{(p, \$)\}, \quad \delta'(q, \varepsilon, A) = \{(p, A)\}, \quad \delta'(q, \varepsilon, B) = \{(p, B)\},$

$\delta'(p, a, A) = \{(p, \varepsilon)\}, \quad \delta'(p, b, B) = \{(p, \varepsilon)\}, \quad \delta'(p, \varepsilon, \$) = \{(f, \varepsilon)\},$

where s is the new starting state and f is the new unique final state. (For clarity, we use stack symbols A and B instead of a and b, respectively.)

We now follow the proof of Theorem 3.37 to construct the context-free grammar G. From the construction, the set V of nontermials of G is $V = \{\langle r, C, t \rangle \mid r, t \in \{q, p, f\}, C \in \{\$, A, B\}\}$. However, we observe that many of these nonterminals are *useless*, in the sense that the set

$$\{x \in \Sigma^* \mid (r, x, C) \overset{*}{\vdash} (t, \varepsilon, \varepsilon)\}$$

is empty. We can eliminate these useless nonterminals to simplify the construction:

(1) We observe that the PDA M cannot move from p to q, nor from f to p or q. Therefore, we can eliminate all nonterminals $\langle p, C, q \rangle$, $\langle f, C, p \rangle$, $\langle f, C, q \rangle$ for all $C \in \{\$, A, B\}$.

(2) Since there is no action at state f, we can eliminate all nonterminals $\langle f, C, f \rangle$ for $C \in \{\$, A, B\}$.

(3) We observe that the stack symbol $\$$ is never used until we want to move to state f. Therefore, we can eliminate all nonterminals $\langle r, \$, t \rangle$ for $r, t \in \{q, p\}$.

(4) When we move to f, we must remove the stack symbol $\$$. So, the nonterminals $\langle r, C, f \rangle$ are useless for $r \in \{q, p\}$ and $C \in \{A, B\}$.

(5) We never pop up anything from the stack in state q. Therefore, $\langle q, A, q \rangle$ and $\langle q, B, q \rangle$ are useless.

After these eliminations, there are only six nonterminals left:

$$V = \{\langle q, \$, f \rangle, \langle p, \$, f \rangle, \langle q, A, p \rangle, \langle q, B, p \rangle, \langle p, A, p \rangle, \langle p, B, p \rangle\},$$

where $\langle q, \$, f \rangle$ is the starting symbol.

Now, for each instruction of M' (except $\delta'(s, \varepsilon, \varepsilon) = \{(q, \$)\}$), we construct corresponding grammar rules for G. For instance, from instruction $\delta'(q, a, \$) = \{(q, A\$)\}$, we get the following rule:

$$\langle q, \$, f \rangle \longrightarrow a \, \langle q, A, p \rangle \, \langle p, \$, f \rangle,$$

and from the instruction $\delta'(q, b, A) = \{(q, BA)\}$, we get

$$\langle q, A, p \rangle \longrightarrow b \, \langle q, B, p \rangle \, \langle p, A, p \rangle.$$

The complete grammar G is as follows:

$$\langle q, \$, f \rangle \longrightarrow \langle p, \$, f \rangle \mid a \, \langle q, A, p \rangle \, \langle p, \$, f \rangle \mid b \, \langle q, B, p \rangle \, \langle p, \$, f \rangle,$$
$$\langle q, A, p \rangle \longrightarrow \langle p, A, p \rangle \mid a \, \langle q, A, p \rangle \, \langle p, A, p \rangle \mid b \, \langle q, B, p \rangle \, \langle p, A, p \rangle,$$
$$\langle q, B, p \rangle \longrightarrow \langle p, B, p \rangle \mid a \, \langle q, A, p \rangle \, \langle p, B, p \rangle \mid b \, \langle q, B, p \rangle \, \langle p, B, p \rangle,$$
$$\langle p, A, p \rangle \longrightarrow a, \qquad \langle p, B, p \rangle \longrightarrow b, \qquad \langle p, \$, f \rangle \longrightarrow \varepsilon.$$

For instance, M' accepts the inupt $abba$ with the following computation path:

$$(s, abba, \varepsilon) \vdash (q, abba, \$) \vdash (q, bba, A\$) \vdash (q, ba, BA\$) \vdash (p, ba, BA\$)$$
$$\vdash (p, a, A\$) \vdash (p, \varepsilon, \$) \vdash (f, \varepsilon, \varepsilon).$$

The corresponding leftmost derivation of $abba$ by G is as follows:

$$\langle q, \$, f \rangle \Rightarrow a \, \langle q, A, p \rangle \, \langle p, \$, f \rangle \Rightarrow ab \, \langle q, B, p \rangle \, \langle p, A, p \rangle \, \langle p, \$, f \rangle$$
$$\Rightarrow ab \, \langle p, B, p \rangle \, \langle p, A, p \rangle \, \langle p, \$, f \rangle \Rightarrow abb \, \langle p, A, p \rangle \, \langle p, \$, f \rangle$$
$$\Rightarrow abba \, \langle p, \$, f \rangle \Rightarrow abba. \qquad \square$$

We observe that the construction in the proof of Theorem 3.37 is very tedious and the resulting context-free grammar is often too complicated to understand. For instance, in Example 3.34, we had a relatively simple PDA for the language $\{w \in \{a, b\}^* \mid 3\#_a(w) \le 5\#_b(w) \le 4\#_a(w)\}$, but an equivalent context-free grammar for this language is very difficult to construct (cf. Example 3.16). Nevertheless, this equivalence result is a useful tool for proving the closure properties of context-free languages. In Theorem 3.17, we have used simple constructions of context-free grammars to show that the class of context-free languages are closed under union, concatenation and Kleene closure. In the following, we use pushdown automata to prove more closure properties of context-free languages.

First, we consider the operation of intersection.

Example 3.39 *Show that if A is a regular language and B is a context-free language, then $A \cap B$ is a context-free language.*

Proof. Let $M_A = (Q_A, \Sigma, \delta_A, s_A, F_A)$ be a DFA accepting A and $M_B = (Q_B, \Sigma, \Gamma_B, \delta_B, s_B, F_B)$ a PDA accepting B. Similar to the product finite automaton, we can construct a *product pushdown automaton M* which simulates M_A and M_B in parallel. The PDA M accepts an input string x if both M_A and M_B accept it.

The detail is as follows: We define $M = (Q, \Sigma, \Gamma, \delta, s, F)$, where $Q = Q_A \times Q_B$, $\Gamma = \Gamma_B$, $s = [s_A, s_B]$, $F = F_A \times F_B$, and

$$\delta([p, q], a, \beta) = \begin{cases} \{([\delta_A(p, a), r], \gamma) \mid (r, \gamma) \in \delta_B(q, a, \beta)\} & \text{if } a \ne \varepsilon, \\ \{([p, r], \gamma) \mid (r, \gamma) \in \delta_B(q, a, \beta)\} & \text{if } a = \varepsilon, \end{cases}$$

where $\beta \in \Gamma \cup \{\varepsilon\}$. It is clear that $L(M) = A \cap B$. □

Can we use the above proof technique to show that context-free languages are closed under intersection? That is, can we construct a product pushdown automaton that simulates two pushdown automata in parallel? The answer is no, since we do not know how to simulate two stacks with only one stack. In fact, we will show, in Corollary 3.48, that the intersection of two context-free languages is not necessarily context-free. Thus, such a product pushdown automaton does not exist.

On the other hand, representing a language as an intersection of several context-free languages can still be helpful in determining whether its *complement* is context-free or not.

Example 3.40 *Show that $L = \{0, 1\}^* - \{(0^m 1^m)^n \mid m, n \ge 1\}$ is a context-free language.*

Proof. We first show that $\overline{L}$ is the intersection of two context-free languages. Let $A = \{0^m 1^m \mid m \ge 1\}^+$ and $B = \{0\}^+ \{1^m 0^m \mid m \ge 1\}^* \{1\}^+$. That is,

$$A = \{0^{m_1}1^{m_1}0^{m_2}1^{m_2}\cdots 0^{m_k}1^{m_k} \mid m_1, m_2, \ldots, m_k \geq 1, k \geq 1\},$$
$$B = \{0^{m_0}1^{m_1}0^{m_1}1^{m_2}0^{m_2}\cdots 1^{m_k}0^{m_k}1^{m_{k+1}} \mid m_0, m_1, \ldots, m_{k+1} \geq 1, k \geq 0\}.$$

It is clear that both A and B are context-free. In addition, we can check that $A \cap B = \overline{L}$.

It is not hard to see that both $\overline{A}$ and $\overline{B}$ are also context-free. More precisely, we note that

$$\overline{A} = (0^+1^+)^* \{0^m 1^n \mid m, n \geq 1, m \neq n\}(0^+1^+)^*$$
$$\cup \, 1^+(0+1)^* \cup (0+1)^*0^+$$

$$\overline{B} = 0^+(1^+0^+)^* \{1^m 0^n \mid m, n \geq 1, m \neq n\}(1^+0^+)^*1^+$$
$$\cup \, 1^+(0+1)^* \cup (0+1)^*0^+.$$

So, both $\overline{A}$ and $\overline{B}$ are context-free. It follows that $L = \overline{A} \cup \overline{B}$ is also context-free. □

Example 3.41 *Show that if L_1 is a context-free language and L_2 is a regular language, then the quotient L_1/L_2 is a context-free language.*

Proof. Recall that x is in L_1/L_2 if and only if there exists a string $y \in L_2$ such that $xy \in L_1$. To check the existence of such a string y, we can use the idea of parallel simulation again. That is, let M_1 be a PDA that accepts L_1 and M_2 a DFA accepting L_2. Then, we first simulate M_1 on x, and then, when x is done, we perform a parallel simulation of M_1 and M_2 on an unknown string y.

This approach has two problems:

(a) How do we know that we have reached the end of the input string?

(b) How do we find this unknown string y?

Problem (a) can be solved by adding an *end-of-string* symbol \$ to the input. That is, we first construct a PDA to accept $\{x\$ \mid x \in L_1/L_2\}$ instead of L_1/L_2, where \$ is a new symbol. This shows that the language $(L_1/L_2)\{\$\}$ is context-free. We then argue that it implies that L_1/L_2 is also context-free. For problem (b), we note that PDA's are nondeterministic and so we can simply use the ε-moves to *guess* and *check* the existence of y.

We now describe, based on the above idea, the detail of the product PDA M for $(L_1/L_2)\{\$\}$. Assume that $M_1 = (Q_1, \Sigma, \Gamma, \delta_1, s_1, F_1)$ and $M_2 = (Q_2, \Sigma, \delta_2, s_2, F_2)$. Then, $M = (Q_1 \cup (Q_1 \times Q_2), \Sigma \cup \{\$\}, \Gamma, \delta, s_1, F_1 \times F_2)$, where δ is defined as follows:

(1) For $q \in Q_1$ and $a \in \Sigma \cup \{\varepsilon\}$, $\delta(q, a, \beta) = \delta_1(q, a, \beta)$.

(2) For $q \in Q_1$, $\delta(q, \$, \varepsilon) = \{([q, s_2], \varepsilon)\}$.

(3) For $[q_1, q_2] \in Q_1 \times Q_2$ and $\beta \in \Gamma \cup \{\varepsilon\}$,

$$\delta([q_1, q_2], \varepsilon, \beta) = \{([p_1, p_2], \gamma) \mid (\exists a \in \Sigma \cup \{\varepsilon\})$$
$$[(p_1, \gamma) \in \delta_1(q_1, a, \beta), p_2 = \delta_2(q_2, a)]\}.$$

It is clear that the above PDA M accepts $x\$$ if and only if there exists a computation path of M_1 that accepts xy for some $y \in L_2$. Thus, $L(M) = (L_1/L_2)\{\$\}$. By Theorem 3.37, there exists a context-free grammar G generating $(L_1/L_2)\{\$\}$. Note that in G, $\$$ is a terminal symbol. Now, we change $\$$ from a terminal symbol to a nonterminal symbol and add a new rule $\$ \to \varepsilon$ to G. Then, we obtain a new context-free grammar generating L_1/L_2. □

⋆ **Example 3.42** *Show that if L is regular, then*

$$\widetilde{L} = \{xz \mid (\exists y)\, [|x| = |y| = |z|, xyz \in L]\}$$

is context-free.

Proof. Let $M = (Q, \Sigma, \delta, q_1, F)$ be a DFA accepting L, with $Q = \{q_1, q_2, \ldots, q_n\}$. We will construct a PDA to accept the language $\widetilde{L}$. The idea is to apply the multi-track simulation of Example 2.40 to PDA's:

(1) We nondeterministically divide the input w into two parts $w = xz$.

(2) We simulate M on x and also push x into the stack. Assume that it ends at state q_i, $1 \le i \le n$.

(3) We guess a string y and simulate M on y starting at state q_i; we simultaneously simulate M on z starting from state q_j for all $j = 1, \ldots, n$. During these simulations, we use string x in the stack to check that $|y| = |z| = |x|$.

(4) We accept the input if the simulation of y ends at a state q_j and the simulation of z starting at q_j ends at a final state.

To implement the above idea, we need the following NFA: We define an NFA $M' = (Q, \Sigma, \delta', q_1, F)$, where $\delta'(q_i, a) = \{\delta(q_i, b) \mid b \in \Sigma\}$, for $q_i \in Q$ and $a \in \Sigma$.

Now, we can define our new PDA as $\widetilde{M} = (\widetilde{Q}, \Sigma, \Sigma, \widetilde{\delta}, q_1, \widetilde{F})$, where $\widetilde{Q}$, $\widetilde{F}$ and $\widetilde{\delta}$ are defined as follows:

(i) $\widetilde{Q} = Q \cup Q^{n+1}$ (so that each state in $\widetilde{M}$ is either a state $q_i \in Q$ or a state of the form $[q_{i_0}, q_{i_1}, \ldots, q_{i_n}]$ with $q_{i_j} \in Q$ for $j = 0, 1, \ldots, n$).

(ii) $\widetilde{F} = \{[q_m, q_{i_1}, \ldots, q_{i_n}] \in Q^{n+1} \mid q_{i_m} \in F\}$.

(iii) At each state $q_j \in Q$, $\widetilde{\delta}(q_j, a, \varepsilon) = \{(\delta(q_j, a), a)\}$, for all $a \in \Sigma$.

(iv) At each state $q_j \in Q$, $\widetilde{\delta}(q_j, \varepsilon, \varepsilon) = \{([q_j, q_1, q_2, \ldots, q_n], \varepsilon)\}$.

(v) At state $[q_j, q_{i_1}, q_{i_2}, \ldots, q_{i_n}] \in Q^{n+1}$, $\widetilde{\delta}([q_j, q_{i_1}, q_{i_2}, \ldots, q_{i_n}], a, b)) =$

$$\{([q_k, \delta(q_{i_1}, a), \delta(q_{i_2}, a), \ldots, \delta(q_{i_n}, a)], \varepsilon) \mid q_k \in \delta'(q_j, a)\}.$$

Assume that $w = xz \in \widetilde{L}$, where $|x| = |z|$. Then, there is an accepting path of M on xyz for some $|y| = |x|$ as follows:

$$\delta(q_1, xyz) = \delta(q_j, yz) = \delta(q_k, z) = q_t \in F.$$

Correspondingly, the PDA $\widetilde{M}$ accepts w as follows: It begins with a simulation of M on x. At the end, it reaches the configuration (q_j, z, x^R). Next, it applies the instructions of type (iv) to get to the following configuration:

$$([q_j, q_1, q_2, \ldots, q_n], z, x^R).$$

Then, it applies instructions of type (v) to the above configuration. The computation path that guesses the correct y in the first track leads to the following configuration:

$$([q_k, q_{i_1}, q_{i_2}, \ldots, q_{i_n}], \varepsilon, \varepsilon),$$

where $q_{i_k} = q_t \in F$, because $\delta(q_k, z) = q_t$. Thus, this computation accepts w.

Conversely, it is easy to see that any accepting computation path of $\widetilde{M}$ must follow this pattern. In particular, it must move from a state q_i in Q to a state in Q^{n+1} after it reads $|w|/2$ symbols, for otherwise the stack size is different from the size of the remaining input and $\widetilde{M}$ cannot accept. In addition, when it finishes the input and gets the empty stack, the state in the first track must correspond to $\delta(q_j, y)$ for some y of length $|y| = |x|$. Therefore, the design of the final set $\widetilde{F}$ guarantees that there is a computation path in M accepting xyz. This proves that $\widetilde{M}$ accepts exactly set $\widetilde{L}$. $\qquad \square$

Exercise 3.5

1. For each of the following context-free grammars G, following the procedure of Theorem 3.35 to construct a PDA that accepts the language $L(G)$:

    (a) $S \longrightarrow \varepsilon \mid aSbS \mid bSaS$.
    (b) $S \longrightarrow \varepsilon \mid SS \mid aSb$.
    (c) The grammar of Solution 2 to Example 3.6.
    (d) The unambiguous grammar of Example 3.24(b).

2. For each of the following PDA's M, following the procedure of Theorem 3.37 to construct a context-free grammar that generates the language $L(M)$:

    (a) The PDA of Example 3.30.
    (b) The PDA of Figure 3.14(a) (for language $\{a^i b^j \mid 2i = 3j\}$).

3. Construct pushdown automata to accept the following languages:

    (a) $\{0^n 1^m \mid m \neq n, m \neq 2n, m \neq 3n\}$.
    (b) $\{a^i b^j c^k \mid i \neq j \text{ or } j \neq k \text{ or } i \neq k\}$.
    $\star$ (c) $\{0, 1\}^* - \{(0^n 1)^n \mid n \geq 1\}$.

$\star$ (d) $\{0,1\}^* - \{b_i \# b_{i+1} \mid b_i$ is the binary representation of $i, i \geq 1\}$.

4. Show that if L is a regular language, then each of the following languages is context-free:

    (a) $\{x \in L \mid x = x^R\}$.

$\star$ (b) $\{wy \mid (\exists x, z) \, [|w| = |x| = |y| = |z|, wxyz \in L]\}$.

$\star$ (c) $\{yx \mid (\exists w, z) \, [|w| = |x| = |y| = |z|, wxyz \in L]\}$.

$\star$ (d) $\{xz \mid |w| = |x| = |y| = |z|, wxyz \in L\}$.

5. Show that $L_1 \setminus L_2$ is a context-free language, if L_1 is context-free and L_2 is regular.

6. A *two-stack pushdown automaton (2-stack PDA)* is a PDA with two pushdown stacks. At each move, M can read, in addition to an input symbol, the top symbols of both stacks, and to write symbols to both stacks. Formally, a 2-stack PDA is a 6-tuple $M = (Q, \Sigma, \Gamma, \delta, s, F)$, where Q, Σ, Γ, s, F are the same as those of a PDA, and δ is a transition function

$$\delta : Q \times (\Sigma \cup \{\varepsilon\}) \times (\Gamma \cup \{\varepsilon\})^2 \to 2^{Q \times (\Gamma \cup \{\varepsilon\})^2}.$$

Let $a \in \Sigma \cup \{\varepsilon\}$, and $u_1, u_2, v_1, v_2 \in \Gamma \cup \{\varepsilon\}$. Then, an instruction $(p, v_1, v_2) \in \delta(q, a, u_1, u_2)$, indicates that the PDA M reads the input a, the top symbol u_1 of stack 1, the top symbol u_2 of stack 2, and then it moves to state p, repaces u_1 by v_1 and replaces u_2 by v_2.

    (a) Define formally the notion of configurations and successor configurations of a 2-stack PDA.

    (b) Construct a 2-stack PDA to accept the language $\{a^n b^n c^n \mid n \geq 0\}$.

    (c) Construct a 2-stack PDA to accept the language $\{a^n b^m c^n d^m \mid n \geq m\}$.

$\star$ 7. A pushdown automaton M is called a *linear-bounded PDA* if there is a constant $c > 0$ such that the size of the stack of M, during its computation on any input x, is bounded by $c|x|$. Show that the class of languages accepted by linear-bounded PDA's is exactly the class of context-free languages.

3.6   Pumping Lemmas for Context-Free Languages

In this section, we prove a pumping lemma for context-free languages which is analogous to the pumping lemma for regular languages. We demonstrate how to apply this lemma and its stronger forms to prove that a given language is *not* context-free.

Let $G = (V, \Sigma, R, S)$ be a context-free grammar. Assume that $|V| = m$ and that, for every rule $A \to x$ in R, $|x| \leq d$ for some constant $d > 0$. This means that, in any parse tree under grammar G, every vertex has at most d children. Thus, a parse tree of depth m has at most d^m leaves. (The *depth* of a parse tree is the length of the longest path from the root to a leaf.) In other words, a parse tree having more than d^m leaves must have a path longer than m and, hence, some nonterminal symbol of G must occur twice in this path. This simple observation leads to the following pumping lemma:

Lemma 3.43 (Pumping Lemma) *Let G be a context-free grammar. Then, there exists a constant $K > 0$, depending on G, such that every string w in $L(G)$ with $|w| \geq K$ can be decomposed as $w = uvxyz$ satisfying the following conditions:*

(1) $v \neq \varepsilon$ or $y \neq \varepsilon$.
(2) $|vxy| \leq K$.
(3) $uv^n xy^n z \in L(G)$ for all $n \geq 0$.

Proof. Let $G = (V, \Sigma, R, S)$, with $|V| = m$. Assume that, for every rule $A \to x$ in R, $|x| \leq d$. Choose $K = d^{m+1}$, and let $w \in L$ with $|w| \geq K$. Consider a shortest derivation for $S \overset{*}{\Rightarrow} w$. Let T be the parse tree corresponding to this derivation. In tree T, each internal node is labeled by a nonterminal symbol and each leaf is labeled by a terminal symbol or ε. Clearly, T has $|w| \geq d^{m+1}$ leaves. Thus, T has a path of length at least $m + 1$ from the root to a leaf.

Consider the longest path π from the root to a leaf in T. Then, the path π has at least $m + 1$ internal nodes, whose labels are nontermial symbols. Thus, there exists a pair of such nodes having the same label (i.e., the same nonterminal symbol). We choose such a pair (q_1, q_2) such that the higher node q_1 of the pair is the lowest one among the higher node of all such pairs. (A node t_1 is *higher* than a node t_2 if t_1 is closer to the root than t_2.) It follows that the subpath π' of π from q_1 to the leaf has only one pair of nodes of the same label, namely, (q_1, q_2). Therefore, π' has length at most $m + 1$. Let A be the label of the vertex q_1. We now decompose tree T into three parts T_1, T_2, T_3, at the nodes q_1 and q_2, as shown in Figure 3.19(a). That is, T_1 is the tree T with all the proper descendants of node q_1 (the higher A) removed; T_2 is the subtree of T rooted at q_1, with all the proper descendants of node q_2 (the lower A) removed; and T_3 is the subtree of T rooted at q_2. Then, the string w is decomposed into five parts correspondingly as $w = uvxyz$. More precisely, u is the string formed by the leaves of the subtree T_1 to the left of node q_1, and z is formed by those leaves to the right of q_1; v is the string formed by the leaves of the subtree T_2 to the left of node q_2, and y is formed by those leaves to the right of q_2; and x is the string of the leaves of the subtree T_3.

Now, we verify that this decomposition satisfies our need:

(1) Suppose $v = y = \varepsilon$, then w can be obtained by the parse tree T' which is the concatenation of T_1 and T_3 , by identifying the root q_2 of T_3 with vertex q_1 of T_1 (see Figure 3.19(b)). This new parse tree corresponds to a shorter derivation from S to w, contradicting the assumption that T corresponds to the shortest derivation. Thus, we must have $v \neq \varepsilon$ or $y \neq \varepsilon$.

(2) Note that the longest path in $T_2 \cup T_3$ has length $\leq m + 1$ (otherwise,

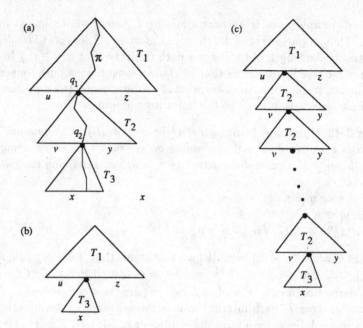

Figure 3.19: Proof of the pumping lemma.

this longest path plus the ancestors of q_1 would form a path longer than π). Therefore, $|vxy| \leq d^{m+1} = K$.

(3) For $n = 1$, $uv^n xy^n z$ is just $w \in L(G)$. For $n = 0$, we can obtain a parse tree T' for $uv^0 xy^0 z = uxz$ as described in part (1) above. For $n \geq 2$, we obtain a parse tree for $uv^n xy^n z$ by inserting $n-1$ extra copies of subtree T_2 between the original subtrees T_2 and T_3 (see Figure 3.19(c)). So, $uv^n xy^n z \in L(G)$ for all $n \geq 0$.   □

Example 3.44 *Show that* $\{a^n b^n c^n \mid n \geq 0\}$ *is not a context-free language.*

Solution. Suppose, to the contrary, that L is a context-free language, accepted by a context-free grammar G. Let K be the constant associated with G, as given in Lemma 3.43. Consider string $w = a^K b^K c^K$. By Lemma 3.43, w can be decomposed as $w = uvxyz$, satisfying conditions (1)–(3) of Lemma 3.43.

By condition (2), vxy is either a substring of $a^K b^K$ or a substring of $b^K c^K$. If vxy is a substring of $a^K b^K$ then, by condition (1), the string uxz has either less than K occurrences of a or less than K occurrences of b. However, since vxy is a substring of $a^K b^K$, we know that c^K is a substring of z and so uxz has K occurrences of symbol c. It follows that $uxz \notin L$, contradicting condition (3). Similarly, we can also get a contradiction in the case that vxy is a substring of $b^K c^K$. Thus, L cannot be context-free.   □

Example 3.45 *Show that* $L = \{ww \mid w \in \{0,1\}^*\}$ *is not a context-free language.*

Solution. Suppose, to the contrary, that L is a context-free language and G is a context-free grammar generating L. Let K be the constant associated with G, as given in Lemma 3.43. Consider string $ww = 0^K 1^K 0^K 1^K$ (with $w = 0^K 1^K$). By Lemma 3.43, ww can be decomposed as $ww = uvxyz$ such that conditions (1)–(3) of the lemma are satisfied by this decomposition.

By condition (2), vxy is a substring of the first half of ww ($0^K 1^K$), or a substring of the middle $2K$ letters of w ($1^K 0^K$), or a substring of the second half of ww ($0^K 1^K$). In each case, uxz contains a block of 0's (or 1's) that is shorter than K, and a block of 0's (or 1's, respectively) of length exactly K. It is obvious that such a string is not equal to $w'w'$ for any $w' \in \{0, 1\}^*$. This contradicts condition (3) and, hence, proves that L is not context-free. □

In Section 3.2, we have seen that sets like $\{0^n 1^m \mid \alpha m \leq \beta n\}$ for some positive constants α and β are context-free. When the inequality $\alpha m \leq \beta n$ is changed to a nonlinear inequality, the set becomes non-context-free.

Example 3.46 *Show that $L = \{0^n 1^m \mid m \leq n^2\}$ is not a context-free language.*

Proof. Suppose, to the contrary, that there is a context-free grammar G that generates L. Let K be the constant associated with G, as given in Lemma 3.43. Consider string $w = 0^t 1^{t^2}$, where $t = \max\{K, 2\}$. By Lemma 3.43, w can be decomposed as $w = uvxyz$, satisfying conditions (1)–(3) of the lemma.

We consider the following cases:

Case 1. vy contains at least one 0. Then, $uxz = 0^i 1^j$, with $i \leq t - 1$ and $j \geq t^2 - K$ (by condition (2)). Since $t = \max\{K, 2\}$, $t^2 - K > t^2 - 2t + 1 = (t - 1)^2$. We see that $j > i^2$ and so $uxz \notin L$. This is a contradiction to condition (3).

Case 2. $vy = 1^j$ for some j, $1 \leq j \leq K$. Then, $uv^2 xy^2 z = 0^t 1^{t^2 + j} \notin L$, also contradicting condition (3). □

Example 3.47 *Show that $L = \{a^i b^j c^k \mid k = \max\{i, j\}\}$ is not a context-free language.*

Proof. Suppose, to the contrary, that L is a context-free language. Then, L is generated by a context-free grammar G. Let K be the constant associated with this grammar G, as given in Lemma 3.43. Consider string $w = a^K b^K c^K$. By Lemma 3.43, w can be decomposed as $w = uvxyz$, satisfying conditions (1)–(3) of the lemma.

By condition (2), we know that vxy cannot contain both a and c.

Case 1. vy contains symbol c. In this case, the number of c's in uxz is less than K and the number of a's in uxz is equal to K. Hence, $uxz \notin L$, which contradicts condition (3).

Case 2. vy does not contain symbol c. In this case, either the number of a's or the number of b's in $uv^2 xy^2 z$ is greater than K and the number of c's in $uv^2 xy^2 z$ is equal to K. Hence, $uv^2 xy^2 z \notin L$, again a contradiction. □

Recall that for any language L, MAX(L) is the set of strings $x \in L$ such that x is not a proper prefix of any string in L. It was shown in Exercise 1(a) of Section 2.6 that regular languages are closed under the MAX operation.

Corollary 3.48 *The class of context-free languages is not closed under intersection, complementation, or the* MAX *operation.*

Proof. Note that $\{a^n b^n c^m \mid m, n \geq 0\}$ and $\{a^m b^n c^n \mid m, n \geq 0\}$ are two context-free languages. Their intersection is $\{a^n b^n c^n \mid n \geq 0\}$, which is not context-free, as proved in Example 3.44. Thus, context-free languages are not closed under intersection.

For complementation, we note that, by Example 3.20, the complement of $\{ww \mid w \in \{0,1\}^*\}$ is a context-free language. Thus, Example 3.45 showed that context-free languages are not closed under complementation. (This result also follows from De Morgan's Law, since we already know that context-free languages are closed under union, but not closed under intersection.)

Finally, for the MAX operation, we consider the language $L = \{a^i b^j c^k \mid i \geq k \text{ or } j \geq k\}$. It is easy to verify that L is context-free. Clearly, MAX(L) = $\{a^i b^j c^k \mid k = \max\{i, j\}\}$. Therefore, by Example 3.47, context-free languages are not closed under MAX.   □

Although context-free languages are not closed under intersection, we know, by Example 3.39, that the intersection of a context-free language and a regular language must be context-free. This weaker closure property is still helpful in proving a language not context-free.

Example 3.49 *Show that* $L = \{w \in \{a, b, c\}^* \mid \#_a(w) = \#_b(w) = \#_c(w)\}$ *is not context-free.*

Proof. We note that the language $L_1 = \{a^n b^n c^n \mid n \geq 0\}$ is equal to $L \cap a^* b^* c^*$. By Example 3.39, we know that L cannot be context-free, for otherwise L_1 would also be context-free, contradicting Example 3.44.   □

Example 3.50 *Show that if a set L has the property that every subset of L is context-free, then L must be a finite set.*

Proof. Suppose, for the sake of contradiction, that L is infinite. Then, there is an infinite subset A of L having the following property: For any $w \in A$, all strings x of length $|w| + 1 \leq |x| \leq 2|w|$ are not in A. Indeed, we can construct set A recursively as follows:

> Initially, we let $A = \emptyset$. At stage 0, we select a shortest nonempty string $w_0 \in L$ and add it in A. Assume that by the end of stage e, we have selected strings $w_0, w_1, \ldots, w_e$ in L with the properties $|w_i| > 2|w_{i-1}|$ for all $i = 1, \ldots, e$, and have added them to A. At stage $e + 1$, we select a string w_{e+1} in L with the property $|w_{e+1}| > 2|w_e|$ and add it to A.

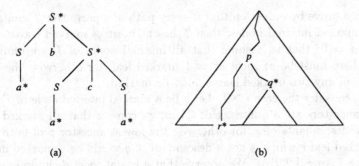

Figure 3.20: (a) A marked parse tree. (b) A leaf r outside the subtree rooted at q cannot be marked.

Since L is infinite, the above construction is well defined for all stages $e > 0$. From our assumption, we know that A is context-free, and so it is accepted by a context-free grammar G. Let $K > 0$ be the constant associated with grammar G, as given in Lemma 3.43. Now, choose a string w in A with $|w| > K$. Then, by Lemma 3.43, w can be decompsed as $w = uvxyz$, with $0 < |vy| \le |vxy| \le K$ and $uv^n xy^n z \in A$ for all $n \ge 0$. However, we observe that $|w| < |uv^2 xy^2 z| \le |w| + K < 2|w|$, and so, by the property of A, $uv^2 xy^2 z \notin A$. This gives us a contradiction, and so shows that L must be finite. □

For regular languages, we have established a stronger form of the pumping lemma, which allows us to "pump" a specific part of the string under consideration. This stronger form often simplifies the proofs using the pumping lemma. Can we also improve the pumping lemma for context-free languages to a similar form? The answer is a qualified yes: We can only require that the "pumping part" of the string must intersect with a predetermined specific substring, but not completely contained in that substring.

★ **Lemma 3.51** (Ogden's Lemma) *Let G be a context-free grammar. Then there exists a constant $K > 0$, depending on G, such that if we mark at least K symbols of a string w in $L(G)$, with $|w| \ge K$, then w can be decomposed as $w = uvxyz$ satisfying the following conditions:*
(1) String v or string y has at least one marked symbol;
(2) String vxy contains at most K marked symbols; and
(3) $uv^n xy^n z \in L(G)$ for all $n \ge 0$.

Proof. The proof follows the same line of arguments of the proof of Lemma 3.43. We follow the definiton of d, m and K of Theorem 3.43. Suppose that T is a parse tree of w, which has $\ge K$ marked symbols. We say an internal node in T is a *marked* node if it has at least two children, both of which contain a marked leaf as a descendant. For instance, Figure 3.20(a) shows a parse tree with marked and unmarked nodes.

We can prove by induction that if every path of a parse tree T contains at most i marked internal nodes, then T has at most d^i marked leaves. First, assume $i = 0$; that is, assume that all internal nodes of T are unmarked. Then, there must be at most $d^0 = 1$ marked leaf, for otherwise the lowest ancestor of any two marked leaves must be marked.

Next, consider the case $i \geq 1$. Let q be a marked internal node in T whose proper ancestors are all unmarked. Then, we can see that all marked leaves in T are descendants of q, for otherwise the lowest ancestor p of both q and any marked leaf r which is not a descendant of q would be a marked internal node (see Figure 3.20(b)). We observe that q has at most d children, each of which is the root of a subtree with at most $i - 1$ marked internal nodes in any path. So, by the inductive hypothesis, each of these subtrees has at most d^{i-1} marked leaves, and so there are totally at most d^i marked leaves in T. This completes the induction proof.

Now, since w has at least $K = d^{m+1}$ marked symbols, the maximum number of marked internal nodes in a path of T is $\geq m + 1$. Thus, such a path contains at least one pair of marked internal nodes with the same label. Let us choose a path π with the maximum number of marked internal nodes, and choose its lowest pair of marked nodes (q_1, q_2) with the same label. Then, we decompose tree T into subtrees T_1, T_2 and T_3, at these two nodes, as in Lemma 3.43. The corresponding decomposition of the leaves w into $uvxyz$ satisfies conditions (1)–(3). We leave the details to the reader.   □

Example 3.52 *Show that $L = \{a^n b^n c^i \mid i \neq n\}$ is not context-free.*

Proof. To prove this result by Lemma 3.43, we might start with the string $w = a^K b^K c^{K+K!}$ so that if $v = a^j$ and $y = b^j$, then $j \leq K$ and, so, we get a contradiction when we "pump" v and y for $K!/j$ times. The problem with this approach is that it fails in the case when $vxy = c^j$ for some $j > 0$. To avoid this problem, we might use Ogden's lemma and mark all letters a in w to force the case of $v = a^j$ and $y = b^j$. The detail is as follows:

Suppose, to the contrary, that there is a context-free grammar G generating L. Let K be the constant associated with this grammar G, as given in Ogden's lemma. Consider string $w = a^K b^K c^{K+K!}$ with all symbols a marked. Then, w can be decomposed as $w = uvxyz$ satisfying conditions (1)–(3) of Ogden's lemma.

First, we observe that neither v nor y contains more than one type of symbols. For instance, if v contains both symbols a and b, then string uv^2xy^2z has a symbol b occurring before a symbol a and, hence, is not in L, contradicting condition (3).

By the above observation and condition (1), either b or c is not in vy.

Case 1. b is not in vy, Then, uv^2xy^2z has more a's than b's and, hence, is not in L. This contradicts condition (3).

Case 2. c is not in vy. Let j be the number of a's in vy. Then, the string $uv^n xy^n$, with $n = 1 + K!/j$ has as many a's as c's and, hence, is not in L. Again, this is a contradiction.   □

Example 3.53 *Show that* $L = \{b_{i_1}\#b_{i_2}\#\cdots\#b_{i_k} \mid k \geq 2$, *each* b_{i_j} *is the binary representation of integer* $i_j > 0$, *and* $(i_1, i_2, \ldots, i_k)$ *contains an integer occurring exactly twice*} *is not context-free.*

Proof. Proving this directly using the pumping lemma would be tedious. By the closure property of Example 3.39, we can restrict our attention to the set

$$L_1 = L \cap 10^*\#10^*\#10^*$$
$$= \{10^i\#10^j\#10^k \mid i = j \neq k \text{ or } i = k \neq j \text{ or } j = k \neq i\}.$$

Now, by a proof similar to that of Example 3.52, we can prove that L_1 is not context-free and it follows that L is not context-free. $\qquad\square$

The following result was promised in Section 3.3, and is an interesting application of Ogden's lemma.

⋆ **Example 3.54** *Show that the language* $L = \{a^ib^jc^k \mid i = j \text{ or } j = k\}$ *is inherently ambiguous.*

Proof. Suppose, to the contrary, that G is an unambiguous context-free grammar for L. Let K be the constant associated with G, as given in Ogden's lemma. Now, consider a string $w = a^mb^mc^{m+m!}$ in L, where $m > K$ and $m! > 2m$. We mark all occurrences of letter a. By Ogden's lemma, we can write w as $w = uvxyz$ satisfying conditions (1)–(3) of Ogden's lemma. In fact, by the proof of Ogden's lemma, we can say more about the derivation of w. That is, there must be a nonterminal A such that

$$S \overset{*}{\Rightarrow} uAz \overset{*}{\Rightarrow} uvAyz \overset{*}{\Rightarrow} uvxyz.$$

That is, $A \overset{*}{\Rightarrow} vAy$ and $A \overset{*}{\Rightarrow} x$.

Let us study the string $\alpha = uv^2xy^2z$ in L. Recall that $\#_a(\alpha)$ denotes the number of occurrences of symbol a in a string α. First, as argued in the proof of Example 3.52, each of v and y can hold at most one type of symbols in $\{a, b, c\}$, for otherwise α is no longer of the form $a^ib^jc^k$. Next, we observe that v and y can have at most m occurrences of symbol b and so $\#_b(\alpha) \leq 2m < m + m! \leq \#_c(\alpha)$. It follows that $\#_a(\alpha) = \#_b(\alpha)$. By condition (1), we know that $\#_a(\alpha) > m$. It follows from the above discussion that $v = a^i$ and $y = b^i$ for some i, $1 \leq i \leq m$.

Now, let $n = m!/i + 1$, and we get a derivation of the string

$$\beta = uv^nxy^nz = a^{m+(n-1)i}b^{m+(n-1)i}c^{m+m!} = a^{m+m!}b^{m+m!}c^{m+m!}$$

by

$$S \overset{*}{\Rightarrow} uAz \overset{*}{\Rightarrow} uvAyz \overset{*}{\Rightarrow} uv^nAy^nz \overset{*}{\Rightarrow} uv^nxy^nz = \beta. \qquad (3.2)$$

Next, we consider the string $w' = a^{m+m!}b^mc^m$. Applying Ogden's lemma to w', with all letters c marked, we get $w' = u_1v_1x_1y_1z_1$ such that for some nonterminal B,

$$S \overset{*}{\Rightarrow} u_1Bz_1 \overset{*}{\Rightarrow} u_1v_1By_1z_1 \overset{*}{\Rightarrow} u_1v_1x_1y_1z_1.$$

By the same argument as above, we get $v_1 = b^j$ and $y_1 = c^j$ for some j, $1 \le j \le m$. Now, applying the derivation $B \overset{*}{\Rightarrow} b^j B c^j$ for t times, where $t = m!/j + 1$, we get a derivation of β as follows:

$$S \overset{*}{\Rightarrow} u_1 B z_1 \overset{*}{\Rightarrow} u_1 v_1 B y_1 z_1 \overset{*}{\Rightarrow} u_1 v_1^t B y_1^t z_1 \overset{*}{\Rightarrow} u_1 v_1^t x_1 y_1^t z_1 = \beta. \qquad (3.3)$$

Apparently, the parse tree of this derivation is different from the parse tree of the derivation (3.2): In the derivation (3.2), all but m occurrences of symbol b are generated together with matching letters a, while in the derivation (3.3), all but m occurrences of symbol b are generated together with matching letters c. Thus, the string w_n has two different parse trees, and G is ambiguous. This is a contradition.   □

Finally, we present another interesting property of context-free languages. Let α be a k-dimensional integer vector, and $\Gamma = \{\gamma_1, \gamma_2, \cdots, \gamma_j\}$ be a finite set of k-dimensional integer vectors. We write $\alpha + span(\Gamma)$ to denote the set

$$\left\{ \alpha + \sum_{i=1}^{j} m_i \gamma_i \mid m_1, m_2, \cdots, m_j \ge 0 \right\}.$$

A set of k-dimensional integer vectors is called *linear* if it is equal to $\alpha + span(\Gamma)$ for some α and Γ. A set of k-dimensional integer vectors is said to be *semilinear* if it is a union of finitely many linear sets.

For any string x over an alphabet $\{a_1, a_2, \cdots, a_k\}$, with a fixed ordering $a_1 \prec a_2 \prec \cdots \prec a_k$, define $\phi(x) = (n_1, n_2, \cdots, n_k)$, where n_i is the number of occurrences of symbol a_i in x. For any language L over alphabet $\{a_1, a_2, \cdots, a_k\}$, we let $\phi(L) = \{\phi(x) \mid x \in L\}$.

* Lemma 3.55 (Parikh's Lemma) *For any context-free language L, $\phi(L)$ is semilinear.*

Proof. Let $G = (V, \Sigma, R, S)$ be a context-free grammar generating L. Let $m = |V|$, and assume that each rule $A \to z$ in R has $|z| \le d$. Let $K = d^{m^2+1}$. Also let $L_0 = \{w \in \Sigma^* \mid |w| \le K\}$. Clearly, L_0 is finite. To show the lemma, it suffices to prove that for any string w in L, there exist $\alpha \in \phi(L_0)$ and $\Gamma \subseteq \phi(L_0)$ such that

$$\phi(w) \in \alpha + span(\Gamma) \subseteq \phi(L).$$

This will be done by showing the following claim. In the following, we generalize the term "parse tree" to include any subtree T' of a parse tree T. That is, the root of a parse tree could be any nonterminal symbol and the leaves of a parse tree could be either terminal or nonterminal symbols.

Claim. For any $w \in L$, let T be a parse tree for w, and let V_1 be the set of nonterminals which occur in T (called the *nonterminal set* of T). Then, there exist $\alpha \in \phi(L_0)$ and $\Gamma \subseteq \phi(L_0)$ satisfying the following properties:

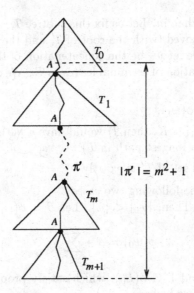

Figure 3.21: Decomposition of the tree T.

(1) $\phi(w) = \alpha + \sum_{\gamma \in \Gamma} \gamma$.

(2) There is a string w_α in L_0, which has a parse tree T_α whose nonterminal set is exactly V_1, such that $\phi(w_\alpha) = \alpha$.

(3) For each $\gamma \in \Gamma$, there is a nonterminal $A_\gamma \in V_1$ and a (generalized) parse tree T_γ, with root A_γ, and a leaf A_γ such that the concatenation of all other leaves is a string $w_\gamma \in L_0$ with $\phi(w_\gamma) = \gamma$.

Proof of Claim. We prove the claim by induction on $|w|$. For $|w| \leq K$, this is trivially true, with $w_\alpha = w$ and $\Gamma = \emptyset$. Assume that $|w| > K$ and that T is a parse tree for w, with the nonterminal set V_1. Since $|w| > K = d^{m^2+1}$, a longest path in T from the root to a leaf must have length at least $m^2 + 2$. Choose one of the longest paths π in T, and let π' be its subpath of the lowest $m^2 + 2$ nodes, including the leaf. So, π' has exactly $m^2 + 1$ internal nodes. Since there are at most m nonterminal symbols in V_1, one of them must occur in π' for at least $m + 1$ times. We choose such a nonterminal A in π', and decompose tree T into $m + 2$ subtrees $T_0, T_1, \ldots, T_{m+1}$, at the $m + 1$ nodes whose labels are A (see Figure 3.21). (Note that all these subtrees are nonempty.)

Let the nonterminal set of subtree T_i be U_i, for $i = 0, \ldots, m+1$. We observe that at least one intermediate subtree T_i, $1 \leq i \leq m$, has the property that

$$U_i \subseteq \bigcup_{j=0, j \neq i}^{m+1} U_j,$$

for otherwise each U_i would contain a nonterminal B_i which is not in any other subtree (and hence not equal to A), and the total number of nonterminals in tree T would be more than m. Let us fix this subtree T_i, and let T' be the tree T with subtree T_i removed (with the root of T_i and the root of T_{i+1} merged into a single node). We let w_0 be the concatenation of the leaves of T'. Also let w_1 be the concatenation of terminal leaves in T_i. We observe the following properties:

(a) $\phi(w) = \phi(w_0) + \phi(w_1)$.

(b) $|w_1| \leq K$. (If $|w_1| > K$, then T_i would have a path longer than π', and π would not be a longest path in T).

(c) The nonterminal set of T' is exactly V_1.

Now, we consider the following two cases:

Case 1. $|w_1| > 0$. Then, $|w_0| < |w|$. Let $\beta = \phi(w_1)$. By the inductive hypothesis,

$$\phi(w_0) = \alpha + \sum_{\gamma \in \Gamma} \gamma,$$

for some $\alpha \in \phi(L_0)$ and $\Gamma \subseteq \phi(L_0)$, which satisfy properties (2) and (3) of the Claim. Therefore, we have

$$\phi(w) = \alpha + \beta + \sum_{\gamma \in \Gamma} \gamma,$$

with $\alpha \in \phi(L_0)$ and $\Gamma \cup \{\beta\} \subseteq \phi(L_0)$ satisfying properties (2) and (3) of the Claim. (Note that β satisfies property (3).)

Case 2. $|w_1| = 0$. Then, T' is a parse tree of w, with at least one node smaller than T. We can repeat the above process on T' and, after a finite number of times, we must reach a case with $|w_1| > 0$.

This completes the proof of the Claim.

Finally we show that the lemma follows from the Claim. Assume that $w \in L$ and that T is a parse tree of w with the nonterminal set V_1. From the claim, we have $\phi(w) = \alpha + \sum_{\gamma \in \Gamma} \gamma$, for some $\alpha \in \phi(L_0)$ and $\Gamma \subseteq \phi(L_0)$, satisfying conditions (2) and (3). All we need to prove is that

$$\alpha + span(\Gamma) \subseteq \phi(L).$$

Let $\beta = \alpha + \sum_{j=1}^{k} m_j \gamma_j$, where $\gamma_1, \ldots, \gamma_k \in \Gamma$ and $m_1, \ldots, m_k > 0$. First, by property (2), there is a string $w_\alpha \in L_0$, satisfying $\phi(w_\alpha) = \alpha$, which has a parse tree T_α with the nonterminal set V_1. Now, for each γ_j, $1 \leq j \leq k$, let T_j be the (generalized) parse tree satisfying (3) with respect to γ_j, and let A_j be the root of T_j. By condition (3), $A_j \in V_1$, and so it occurs in tree T_α. For each j, $1 \leq j \leq k$, we insert m_j copies of tree T_j at the node A_j (cf. Figure 3.19(c)). Let w' be the concatenation of the leaves of the resulting tree. Then,

$$\phi(w') = \alpha + \sum_{j=1}^{k} m_j \gamma_j = \beta.$$

So, $\beta \in \phi(L)$. This completes the proof of the lemma. $\square$

⋆ **Example 3.56** *A language L over a singleton alphabet $\{0\}$ is context-free if and only if it is regular.*

Proof. Since a regular language is context-free, it suffices to show the forward direction. Suppose $L \subseteq \{0\}^*$ is context-free. By Parikh's lemma, $\phi(L)$ is semilinear; therefore $\phi(L)$ is a union of finitely many linear sets $T_1, \ldots, T_n$, where each T_i is a one-dimensional linear set. Let $L_i = \{0^m \mid m \in T_i\}$; that is, $\phi(L_i) = T_i$. Then, it is obvious that $L = \bigcup_{i=1}^n L_i$. Since a finite union of regular languages is still regular, it suffices to prove that each L_i is regular, for $i = 1, \ldots, n$.

Fix an $i \in \{1, \ldots, n\}$. Since $\phi(L_i)$ is linear, we can write

$$\phi(L_i) = \Big\{ u + \sum_{j=1}^k m_j v_j \ \Big| \ m_1, m_2, \cdots, m_j \geq 0 \Big\},$$

where $u, v_1, v_2, \cdots, v_k$ are positive integers. It follows that

$$L_i = 0^u (0^{v_1})^* (0^{v_2})^* \cdots (0^{v_j})^*,$$

and so it is regular. ◻

Example 3.57 *Show that $\{0^{n^2} \mid n \geq 1\}$ is not an intersection of k context-free languages over alphabet $\{0, 1\}$ for any k.*

Proof. First, we note that for any context-free language L over $\{0, 1\}$, $L \cap 0^*$ is a regular language: By Example 3.39, $L \cap 0^*$ is context-free and so, by Example 3.56, it is regular.

Now, for the sake of contradiction, suppose that $\{0^{n^2} \mid n \geq 1\}$ is an intersection of k context-free languages $L_1, L_2, \cdots L_k$ over alphabet $\{0, 1\}$ for some $k \geq 1$. Then it is also the intersection of $L_1 \cap 0^*, L_2 \cap 0^*, \ldots, L_k \cap 0^*$. Since each of $L_1 \cap 0^*, L_2 \cap 0^*, \ldots, L_k \cap 0^*$ is regular, we know that $\{0^{n^2} \mid n \geq 1\}$ is also regular. This is a contradiction (see Exercise 3(b) of Section 2.7). ◻

Parikh's lemma cannot replace the pumping lemma. For instance, the set $L_1 = (abc)^*$ and $L_2 = \{a^n b^n c^n \mid n \geq 0\}$ have the same counting set $\phi(L_1) = \phi(L_2)$, but one of them is context-free and the other is not. However, it sometimes gives us a stronger pumping property of a given language, allowing us to "pump" a specific part of a string to produce a contradiction. The following are some examples.

⋆ **Example 3.58** *Show that the language $L = \{a^m b^n \mid n \neq m^2\}$ is not context-free.*

Proof. This result is difficult to prove by the pumping lemma. For instance, suppose that we start with a string $w = a^m b^n$, with $n > m^2$. Then, when we apply the pumping lemma to w to get $w = uvxyz$, we cannot handle the case of $v = \varepsilon$ and $y = b^j$ with $j \neq n - m^2$. Suppose that we start with a string $w = a^m b^n$, with $n < m^2$. Then, we will have trouble with the case of $v = a^i$ and $y = b^i$. Using Ogden's lemma does not seem to help much. In the following, we show how to use Parikh's lemma to force the pumping of a substring of b^n only.

Suppose, to the contrary, that L is context-free. Then, by Parikh's lemma, $\phi(L)$ is a finite union of linear sets $T_1, \ldots, T_k$. Assume that, for each $1 \leq i \leq k$, $T_i = \alpha_i + span(\Gamma_i)$, for some two-dimensional integer vector α_i and some finite sets Γ_i of two-dimensional integer vectors. Note that the integers appearing in the integer vectors in $\Gamma = \bigcup_{i=1}^{k}(\{\alpha_i\} \cup \Gamma_i)$ are nonnegative. Let d_0 be the maximum integer appearing in any integer vector in Γ, and let $d = \max\{d_0, 3\}$. (Thus, for any $(d_1, d_2) \in \Gamma$, $d_1 \leq d$ and $d_2 \leq d$.)

Let $m = d!$ and $n = (d!)^2 - d!$. It is clear that $(m, n) \in \phi(L)$ and so $(m, n) \in T_i$ for some i, $1 \leq i \leq k$. We claim that Γ_i must contain a vector $(0, r)$, with $1 \leq r \leq d$. To see this, let us assume that all vectors (p, q) in Γ_i have $p \geq 1$. Since $(m, n) \in T_i$, we know that there are $m_1, \ldots, m_\ell > 0$ and $(p_1, q_1), \ldots, (p_\ell, q_\ell) \in \Gamma_i$ such that

$$(m, n) = \alpha_i + \sum_{j=1}^{\ell} m_j(p_j, q_j).$$

Since all p_j's are greater than 0, we see that $\sum_{j=1}^{\ell} m_j \leq m$. It follows that $n \leq (m+1)d$, since all integers q_j and the second component of α_i are bounded by d. However, since $d \geq 3$, we know that

$$n = (d!)^2 - d! > (d+2)d! - d! = (d+1)d! > d(d!+1) = d(m+1),$$

and we have a contradiction. This completes the proof of the claim.

Now, since $(0, r) \in \Gamma_i$, we know that $(m, n) + t(0, r) \in T_i \subseteq \phi(L)$ for all $t \geq 0$. For $t = d!/r$, we get $(m, n + tr) = (d!, (d!)^2) \in \phi(L)$, which is a contradiction. We conclude that L is not context-free. □

∗ Example 3.59 *Show that $L = \{a^p b^q \mid \gcd(p, q) = 1\}$ is not context-free.*

Proof. Suppose, to the contrary, that L is context-free. Then, by Parikh's lemma, $\phi(L)$ is a finite union of linear sets $T_1, \ldots, T_k$. Assume that, for each $1 \leq i \leq k$, $T_i = \alpha_i + span(\Gamma_i)$, for some two-dimensional integer vector α_i and some finite sets Γ_i of two-dimensional integer vectors. Let d be the maximum integer appearing in any integer vector in $\Gamma = \bigcup_{i=1}^{k}(\{\alpha_i\} \cup \Gamma_i)$. Now, let p be a prime number such that $p \geq 2d + 2$. Note that we must have $d \geq 1$, and so $p \geq 4$ and $p + 1 < 2(p - 1)$. Consider the vector (p, q), where $q = p + (p - 1)!$. It is clear that $\gcd(p, q) = 1$ and so $(p, q) \in T_i$ for some $i = 1, \ldots, k$.

By the same argument as given in Example 3.58, we can prove that there is a vector $(0, r)$ in Γ_i, with $1 \leq r \leq d$, because

$$q = p + (p - 1)! > (p - 1)(p - 2) > (p - 2)(p + 1)/2 \geq d(p + 1).$$

Therefore, we know that $(p, q + tr) \in T_i \subseteq \phi(L)$ for all $t \geq 0$. Note that $r \leq d \leq p - 1$. So, we can choose $t = (p-1)((p-1)!)/r$, and get $(p, q + tr) \in \phi(L)$. However,

$$q + tr = p + (p - 1)! + \frac{(p - 1) \cdot (p - 1)!}{r} \cdot r$$

$$= p + (p - 1)! \cdot (1 + (p - 1)) = p(1 + (p - 1)!),$$

and so $\gcd(p, q + kr) = p > 1$. This establishes a contradiction, and we conclude that L is not context-free. $\qquad\square$

Exercise 3.6

1. Prove the following variations of the pumping lemma for context-free languages:

   (a) For any context-free language L, there exists a constant $K > 0$ such that any string w in L with $|w| > K$ can be decomposed into $w = uv_1 v_2 x y_2 y_1 z$, satisfying the following conditions:

      (1) $|v_1 v_2 x y_2 y_1| \leq K$,

      (2) $|v_1 y_1| > 0, |v_2 y_2| > 0$, and

      (3) for any $n \geq 0$, $uv_1^n v_2^n x w y_2^n y_1^n z \in L$.

   (b) For any context-free language L, there exists a constant $K > 0$ such that any string w in L with $|w| > K$ can be decomposed into $w = uvxyz$, satisfying the following conditions:

      (1) $|vxy| \leq K$,

      (2) $|v| > 0, |y| > 0$, and

      (3) for any $n \geq 0$, $uv^n x y^n z \in L$.

   (c) For any context-free language L and any $k > 0$, there exists a constant $K > 0$ such that any string w in L with $|w| > K$ can be decomposed into $w = uvxyz$, satisfying the following conditions:

      (1) $|vy| \geq k$, and

      (2) for any $n \geq 0$, $uv^n x y^n z \in L$.

   (d) For any context-free language L and any $k > 0$, there exists a constant $K > 0$ such that any string w in L with $|w| > K$ can be decomposed into $w = uvxyz$, satisfying the following conditions:

      (1) $|v| \geq k, |y| \geq k$, and

      (2) for any $n \geq 0$, $uv^n x y^n z \in L$.

   (e) For any context-free language L and any $k > 0$, there exists a constant $K > 0$ such that any string w in L with $|w| > K$ can be decomposed into $w = uvxyz$, satisfying the following conditions:

      (1) $|vxy| \leq K$,

      (2) $|v| \geq k, |y| \geq k$, and

(3) for any $n \geq 0$, $uv^n xy^n z \in L$.

2. For each of the following languages, determine whether it is context-free, and present a proof for your answer.

   (a) $\{a^i b^j c^k \mid i < j < k\}$.
   (b) $\{a^i b^j c^k \mid i \neq j, j \neq k, k \neq i\}$.
   (c) $\{a^i b^j c^k \mid i < j \text{ or } k < j\}$.
   (d) $\{a^i b^j c^k \mid i < j \text{ and } k < j\}$.
   (e) $\{a^i b^j c^k \mid i < j \Rightarrow k < j\}$.
   (f) $\{a^i b^j c^k \mid i < j \Leftrightarrow k < j\}$.
   (g) $\{a^i b^i c^j d^j \mid i, j \geq 0\}$.
   (h) $\{a^i b^j c^i d^j \mid i, j \geq 0\}$.
   (i) $\{a^i b^j c^j d^i \mid i, j \geq 0\}$.

3. In the following, consider each binary string in $A = 1(0 + 1)^* + 0$ as a binary representation of a natural number. For each of the following languages, determine whether it is context-free, and present a proof for your answer.

   (a) $\{x \# y \mid x, y \in A, x = y + 3\}$.
   (b) $\{x \# y^R \mid x, y \in A, x = y + 3\}$.
   (c) $\{x \# y \mid x, y \in A, x = 3y\}$. [*Hint:* Consider a string $y = 1^K 0^K$, where K is the constant of the pumping lemma.]
   (d) $\{x \# y^R \mid x, y \in A, x = 3y\}$.
   (e) $\{x \# y \# z \mid x, y, z \in A, x = y + z\}$. [*Hint:* Use the closure property to reduce this problem to (a) above.]
   (f) $\{x \# y^R \# z^R \mid x, y, z \in A, x = y + z\}$.
   (g) $\{x \# y \# z \mid x, y, z \in A, x = y \cdot z\}$.
   (h) $\{x \# y^R \# z^R \mid x, y, z \in A, x = y \cdot z\}$.

$\star$ 4. For each of the following languages, determine whether it is context-free, and present a proof for your answer.

   (a) $\{xyz \mid xz = y \text{ for some } x, y, z \in \{0,1\}^*\}$. [*Hint:* Consider the intersection of this language with the regular language $10100^+ 11^+ 10100^+ 11^+$. Note that then y must begin with 101.]
   (b) $\{xyz \mid xz = y^R \text{ for some } x, y, z \in \{0,1\}^*\}$.
   (c) $\{xyz \mid xz = yx \text{ for some } x, y, z \in \{0,1\}^*\}$.
   (d) $\{xx^R ww^R \mid x, w \in \{0,1\}^*\}$.
   (e) $\{xwx^R w^R \mid x, w \in \{0,1\}^*\}$.
   (f) $\{xww^R x^R \mid x, w \in \{0,1\}^*\}$.

5. Recall that $\#_a(x)$ denotes the number of occurrences of the letter a in string x. For each of the following languages, determine whether it is context-free, and present a proof for your answer.

(a) $\{x \in \{a, b\}^* \mid \#_a(x) < \#_b(x) < 2\#_a(x)\}$.

(b) $\{x \in \{a, b\}^* \mid \#_a(x) \neq \#_b(x), \#_a(x) \neq 2\#_b(x)\}$.

(c) $\{x \in \{a, b\}^* \mid \#_a(x) \leq \#_b(x) \text{ or } \#_a(x) \geq 2\#_b(x)\}$.

(d) $\{x \in \{a, b\}^* \mid \#_a(x) = 2^{\#_b(x)}\}$.

(e) $\{x \in \{a, b\}^* \mid \#_a(x) \geq 2^{\#_b(x)}\}$.

(f) $\{x \in \{a, b, c\}^* \mid \#_a(x) \cdot \#_b(x) = \#_c(x)\}$.

$\star$ 6. Show that the language $\{a^i b^j c^k d^\ell \mid [i = j, k = \ell] \text{ or } [i = \ell, j = k]\}$ is inherently ambiguous.

$\star$ 7. Apply Parikh's lemma to show that the following languages are not context-free:

(a) $\{a^m b^n \mid n \neq 2^m\}$.

(b) $\{a^m b^n c^q \mid q \neq mn\}$. [*Hint*: Use the approach of Example 3.58. First prove that there must be a triple $(0, 0, r)$ in one of the generating set Γ_i.]

(c) $\{a^m b^n c^q \mid q^2 \neq m^3 \text{ or } q^2 \neq n^3\}$.

8. Let $(x)_r$ denote the string obtained from binary string x by changing 0 to 1 and 1 to 0. For each of the following languages, determine whether it is context-free, and present a proof for your answer.

(a) $\{x(x)_r \mid x \in \{0, 1\}^*\}$.

(b) $\{w \in \{0, 1\}^* \mid w \neq x(x)_r \text{ for any } x \in \{0, 1\}^*\}$.

(c) $\{x(x)_r^R \mid x \in \{0, 1\}^*\}$.

(d) $\{w \in \{0, 1\}^* \mid w \neq x(x)_r^R \text{ for any } x \in \{0, 1\}^*\}$.

9. (a) Recall the language operation $\oplus$ defined in Exercise 2 of Section 2.6. Show that context-free languages are not closed under the operation $\oplus$.

(b) Show that context-free languages are not closed under the operation MIN $(L) = \{x \in L \mid x \text{ does not have a proper prefix in } L\}$.

$\star$ (c) Consider operation $\text{REV}(L) = \{xy^R z \mid xyz \in L\}$ and language $L = \{0^m 1^n 0^n 1^m \mid m, n \geq 0\}$. Show that L is a context-free language, but $\text{REV}(L)$ is not.

$\star$ (d) Find a context-free language L such that $L_{\frac{1}{2}} = \{x \mid (\exists y) |x| = |y| \text{ and } xy \in L\}$ is not a context-free language.

$\star$ 10. Assume that L is a context-free language. Prove or disprove the following statements:

(a) If L_1 is regular, then $L_1 \setminus L$ is context-free.

(b) $\{x \mid xx^R \in L\}$ is context-free.

(c) $\{xx^R \mid x \in L \text{ or } x^R \in L\}$ is context-free.

(d) $\{xx^R \mid x \in L \text{ and } x^R \in L\}$ is context-free.

(e) $\{xx^R \mid x \in L \text{ or } x^R \notin L\}$ is context-free.

(f) $\{xx^R \mid x \in L \text{ and } x^R \notin L\}$ is context-free.

$\star$ **11.** Show that the set of all strings over alphabet

$$\left\{ \begin{pmatrix} 0 \\ 0 \\ 0 \end{pmatrix}, \begin{pmatrix} 1 \\ 0 \\ 0 \end{pmatrix}, \begin{pmatrix} 0 \\ 1 \\ 0 \end{pmatrix}, \begin{pmatrix} 0 \\ 0 \\ 1 \end{pmatrix}, \begin{pmatrix} 1 \\ 1 \\ 0 \end{pmatrix}, \begin{pmatrix} 1 \\ 0 \\ 1 \end{pmatrix}, \begin{pmatrix} 0 \\ 1 \\ 1 \end{pmatrix}, \begin{pmatrix} 1 \\ 1 \\ 1 \end{pmatrix} \right\}$$

that represent correct multiplication is not context-free (cf. Example 2.65).

12. A context-free grammar G is called a *linear grammar* if the right-hand side of each rule of G contains at most one nonterminal symbols. A language L is called a *linear language* if $L = L(G)$ for some linear grammar G. Show that for every linear language L, there exists a constant $K > 0$ such that every string w in L with length $|w| \geq K$ can be decomposed as $w = uvxyz$ satisfying the following conditions:

(1) $vy \neq \varepsilon$.

(2) $|uvyz| \leq K$.

(3) $uv^n xy^n z \in L$ for all $n \geq 0$.

13. Show that the following languages are not linear languages.

(a) $\{w \in \{0,1\}^* \mid \#_0(w) = \#_1(w)\}$.

$\star$ (b) $\{xy \in \{0,1\}^* \mid |x| = |y|, x \neq y\}$. [*Hint:* Apply the pumping lemma for linear languages (Exercise 12 above) to a string $w = a^m ba^k ba^m$ with $k > m \geq K$. Note that a string $a^i ba^j ba^\ell$ is not in the language if $j = i + \ell$.]

$\star$ (c) $\{xx^R ww^R \mid x, w \in \{0,1\}^*\}$.

4

Turing Machines

4.1 One-Tape Turing Machines

In the previous chapters, we have studied two types of computational models: finite automata and pushdown automata. A finite automaton is an abstract machine having a finite control but no run-time memory. The class of languages recognized by finite automata is characterized exactly as regular languages. A pushdown automaton also has a finite control and has, in addition, a single pushdown stack as the run-time memory, whose size may grow at the run time. The class of languages recognized by pushdown automata is characterized as context-free languages. It is clear that these machines are of limited computational power, compared with our real digital computers. For instance, the language $\{a^n b^n c^n \mid n \geq 0\}$ is not a context-free language but can be easily recognized by a short program in the real computers.

In this chapter, we introduce a new machine model, called the Turing machine, which has a finite control plus a tape as the run-time memory, whose size is unlimited. Furthermore, the tape head of the machine is allowed to move around the tape to read and write symbols, and so it behaves similarly to a real computer. Indeed, one of the main results of this chapter is to show that the computational power of Turing machines is the same as that of many other well-studied computational models.

There are many variations of Turing machines. We start with the simplest kind, the one-tape deterministic Turing machine. A *one-tape deterministic Turing machine* (also called *one-tape DTM*, *DTM* or, simply, *TM*), similar to a DFA, consists of three parts: a tape, a tape head, and a finite control

159

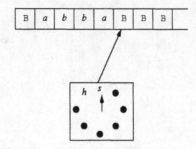

Figure 4.1: A one-tape DTM at the initial position.

(Figure 4.1). However, DTM's can perform more functions than DFAs:

(1) The tape of a DTM is divided into infinitely many cells such that it has a left end but is *infinite to the right*. Each cell can hold a symbol from a finite *tape alphabet* Γ. Symbols in Γ are divided into three groups: the input symbols, the blank symbol, and the auxiliary symbols. The set Σ of input symbols consists of all symbols that an input to the machine may have. The blank symbol $B \notin \Sigma$ represents an empty cell. The auxiliary symbols are other symbols in $\Gamma - \Sigma - \{B\}$.

(2) The tape head can move along the tape, one cell per move, either to the right or to the left. In addition to being able to read a symbol from the cell it scans, the head can also erase the symbol in the cell and write a new symbol there.

(3) The tape head is controlled by the finite control. The finite control has finitely many states. Among them, there are two special states, the *initial state* and the *final state*. The initial state is usually denoted by s, and the final state is usually denoted by h. All states other than the final state form the *state set* Q. After the head reads a symbol from the tape, the finite control will tell the head the action to excute (i.e., to write a new symbol and to move left or right) and change to a new state. These actions are described in a *transition function* (or, the *instructions*)

$$\delta : Q \times \Gamma \to (Q \cup h) \times \Gamma \times \{L, R\}.$$

An instruction $\delta(q, a) = (p, b, R)$ (or, $\delta(q, a) = (p, b, L)$) means that if at the beginning of a move, the head reads symbol a and the finite control is in state q, then the head changes the symbol a to b and moves to the right (or, respectively, to the left) and the finite control changes from state q to state p.

In summary, a one-tape DTM M can be described by a quintuple

$$M = (Q, \Sigma, \Gamma, \delta, s),$$

where Q is a finite set of states, Σ is a finite alphabet of input symbols, Γ is a finite alphabet of tape symbols with $\Sigma \cup \{B\} \subseteq \Gamma$, s is the initial state, and

δ is a transition function. (Because the blank symbol B and the final state h are common to every DTM, we do not need to define them here.)

Next, we explain how a DTM M accepts an input string x.

First, how does a DTM start? Initially, we assume that the machine is in the initial state s and the input x is stored in the second to $(n + 1)$st cells of the tape, where $n = |x|$, and the head is scanning the $(n + 2)$nd cell of the tape. The first cell as well as all cells to the right of the $(n + 1)$st cell are assumed to have the symbol B. Figure 4.1 shows the initial configuration of a DTM with input $w = abba$.

In order to explain how a DTM M operates on an input x, we need to establish a notation to describe the configurations of a one-tape DTM M. Assume that at some point, a DTM M is in a state q, its tape contains symbols $x_1 x_2 \cdots x_m BBB \cdots$, where $x_i \in \Gamma$ for $i = 1, \ldots, m - 1$, and $x_m \in \Gamma - \{B\}$, and its head is scanning the kth cell. Suppose that $m \geq k$, then we write

$$(q, x_1 x_2 \cdots x_{k-1}, x_k, x_{k+1} x_{k+2} \cdots x_m)$$

to denote this configuration. If $m < k$ then we write

$$(q, x_1 x_2 \cdots x_m \underbrace{B \cdots B}_{k-m-1}, B, \varepsilon)$$

to denote this configuration. In other words, a *configuration* of a DTM is a string in

$$Q \times \Gamma^* \times \Gamma \times (\Gamma^*(\Gamma - \{B\}) \cup \{\varepsilon\}).$$

A configuration $(q, x_1 \cdots x_{k-1}, a, y_1 \cdots y_m)$ denotes that the machine is in state q, its tape contains symbols $x_1 \cdots x_{k-1} a y_1 \cdots y_m BB \cdots$, and its head is scanning the kth cell (which contains symbol a). For instance, the configuration shown in Figure 4.1 can be represented by $(s, Babba, B, \varepsilon)$.

For each configuration (q, x, a, y), we also use the abbreviation $(q, x\underline{a}y)$ or $xq a y$ to represent it. (*Note*: If $Q \cap \Gamma = \emptyset$, then the second abbreviation presents no ambiguity.) So, $(s, Babba, B, \varepsilon)$, $(s, Babba\underline{B})$ and $Babbas\underline{B}$ all represent the same configuration of Figure 4.1.

Using this notation, the effect of each move of a DTM can be formally described as follows:

(1) At a configuration $(q, x\underline{a}y)$, if $\delta(q, a) = (p, b, R)$ and $y \neq \varepsilon$ then, after one move, its configuration becomes $(p, xb\underline{y_1}y_2)$ (called the *successor configuration* of $(q, x\underline{a}y)$), where $y = y_1 y_2$ and $|y_1| = 1$.

(2) At a configuration $(q, x\underline{a})$, if $\delta(q, a) = (p, b, R)$ then, after one move, its configuration becomes $(p, xb\underline{B})$.

(3) At a configuration $(q, x\underline{a}y)$, if $\delta(q, a) = (p, b, L)$ and $x \neq \varepsilon$ then, after one move, its configuration becomes $(p, x_1\underline{x_2}by)$ if $y \neq \varepsilon$ or $b \neq B$, or it becomes $(p, x_1\underline{x_2})$ if $y = \varepsilon$ and $b = B$, where $x = x_1 x_2$ and $|x_2| = 1$.

(4) At a configuration $(q, \underline{a}y)$, if $\delta(q, a) = (p, b, L)$ then the machine *hangs*, or, halts without accepting the input. This configuration does not have a successor configuration.

(5) At a configuration $(h, x\underline{a}y)$, machine halts and accepts the input. This configuration does not have a successor configuration.

If $\alpha_2 = (p, u\underline{b}v)$ is a successor configuration of $\alpha_1 = (q, x\underline{a}y)$, then we write $\alpha_1 \vdash_M \alpha_2$. If there is a sequence of configurations $\alpha_1, \alpha_2, \ldots, \alpha_n$, $n \geq 1$, such that $\alpha_i \vdash_M \alpha_{i+1}$ for all $i = 1, 2, \ldots, n-1$, then we write $\alpha_1 \vdash_M^* \alpha_n$. When the machine M is understood, we may simply write $\alpha_1 \vdash \alpha_2$ and $\alpha_1 \vdash^* \alpha_n$ to denote $\alpha_1 \vdash_M \alpha_2$ and $\alpha_1 \vdash_M^* \alpha_n$, respectively.

Formally, a string x is said to be *accepted* by a TM M if M halts at state h on input x, or, equivalently, if $(s, \text{B}x\underline{\text{B}}) \vdash^* (h, y\underline{a}z)$ for some $y, z \in \Gamma^*$ and $a \in \Gamma$. We say that the sequence of configurations in $(s, \text{B}x\underline{\text{B}}) \vdash^* (h, y\underline{a}z)$ is the *computation path* (or, simply, the *computation*) of M on x. A string x is not accepted by M if either M hangs on x or M does not halt on x.

Example 4.1 *Let M_1 be the one-tape DTM defined by the quintuple $(Q, \Sigma, \Gamma, \delta, s)$, where $Q = \{s, q_1, q_2, q_3, p\}$, $\Sigma = \{a, b\}$, $\Gamma = \{a, b, \text{B}\}$ and δ is given by the following table:*

δ	a	b	B
s	p, a, R	p, b, R	q_1, B, L
q_1	q_1, a, L	q_1, b, L	q_2, B, R
q_2	q_2, a, R	q_3, b, R	p, B, L
q_3	p, a, R	q_3, b, R	h, B, L
p	p, a, R	p, b, R	p, B, L

Then, the initial configuration of M_1 on input $abba$ is exactly the one shown in Figure 4.1. In our notation, it is $(s, \text{B}abba\underline{\text{B}})$. Starting from this initial configuration, the computation of M_1 can be described as follows:

$$(s, \text{B}abba\underline{\text{B}}) \vdash (q_1, \text{B}abb\underline{a}) \vdash (q_1, \text{B}ab\underline{b}a) \vdash (q_1, \text{B}a\underline{b}ba) \vdash (q_1, \text{B}\underline{a}bba)$$

$$\vdash (q_1, \underline{\text{B}}abba) \vdash (q_2, \text{B}\underline{a}bba) \vdash (q_2, \text{B}a\underline{b}ba) \vdash (q_3, \text{B}ab\underline{b}a) \vdash (q_3, \text{B}abb\underline{a})$$

$$\vdash (p, \text{B}abba\underline{\text{B}}) \vdash (p, \text{B}abb\underline{a}) \vdash (p, \text{B}abba\underline{\text{B}}) \vdash (p, \text{B}abb\underline{a}) \vdash \cdots$$

That is, M_1 will eventually enter state p and its head will move between the fifth and sixth cells of the tape forever. In other words, M_1 enters an infinite loop on input $abba$.

On the input a^3b the DTM M_1 behaves differently:

$$(s, \text{B}aaab\underline{\text{B}}) \vdash^* (q_1, \underline{\text{B}}aaab) \vdash (q_2, \text{B}\underline{a}aab) \vdash (q_2, \text{B}a\underline{a}ab) \vdash (q_2, \text{B}aa\underline{a}b)$$

$$\vdash (q_2, \text{B}aaa\underline{b}) \vdash (q_3, \text{B}aaab\underline{\text{B}}) \vdash (h, \text{B}aaa\underline{b}).$$

Thus, M_1 accepts the input a^3b.   □

In the above example, we see easily that once M_1 goes into the state p, it will be trapped in an infinite loop, that is, it never halts. In other words, the

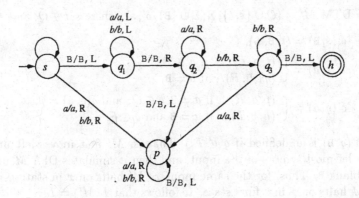

Figure 4.2: The transition diagram of the DTM M_1.

state p does nothing but introduces an infinite loop. For simplicity, we may eliminate the state p and present δ in the following form:

δ	a	b	B
s			q_1, B, L
q_1	q_1, a, L	q_1, b, L	q_2, B, R
q_2	q_2, a, R	q_3, b, R	
q_3		q_3, b, R	h, B, L

The blank entries in the above table ($\delta(s,a)$, $\delta(s,b)$, $\delta(q_2,\text{B})$ and $\delta(q_3,a)$) indicate that if the machine enters such a configuration (i.e., $(s, x\underline{a}y)$, $(s, x\underline{b}y)$, $(q_2, x\text{B}\underline{y})$ or $(q_3, x\underline{a}y)$ for some $x, y \in \Gamma^*$), it will enter an infinite loop and does not accept the input. In other words, we will allow the transition function δ to be left undefined on some input (q, a). If the value of $\delta(q, a)$ is undefined, then it means that the machine will move into an infinite loop.

Similar to DFA's and PDA's, a one-tape DTM can also be represented by a *transition diagram*. Each vertex in a transition diagram represents a state. Each edge in a transition diagram has a label of the form "$a/b, R$" or "$a/b, L$". An edge from state q to state p with label "$a/b, R$" (or, "$a/b, L$") represents the instruction $\delta(q, a) = (p, b, R)$ (or, respectively, $\delta(q, a) = (p, b, L)$). For example, the DTM M_1 of Example 4.1 can be represented by the transition diagram of Figure 4.2.

For any DTM M, we let $L(M) = \{x \in \Sigma^* \mid M \text{ accepts } x\}$. A language L is called *Turing-acceptable* if $L = L(M)$ for some DTM M. In the above example, it is not hard to see that $L(M_1) = \{a^m b^n \mid m \geq 0, n \geq 1\} = a^* b b^*$. It is a special case of the following theorem.

Theorem 4.2 *Every regular language is Turing-acceptable.*

Proof. Let L be accepted by a DFA $M = (Q, \Sigma, \delta, q_0, F)$. We construct a one-tape DTM $M' = (Q \cup \{s, t\}, \Sigma, \Sigma \cup \{B\}, \delta', s)$, where $s, t \notin Q$, and

$$\delta'(s, B) = (t, B, L),$$

$$\delta'(t, a) = \begin{cases} (t, a, L) & \text{if } a \in \Sigma; \\ (q_0, B, R) & \text{if } a = B, \end{cases}$$

$$\delta'(q, a) = \begin{cases} (p, a, R) & \text{if } a \neq B, q \in Q, \text{ and } \delta(q, a) = p, \\ (h, B, L) & \text{if } a = B \text{ and } q \in F. \end{cases}$$

(*Note*: $\delta'(q, B)$ is undefined if $q \notin F$.) That is, M' first moves left until it finds the leftmost symbol of the input, and then it simulates DFA M until it reads a blank B. Thus, for the same input x, M' halts on x in state h if and only if M halts on x in a final state. It follows that $L(M') = L$.   □

We observe that when a DTM M halts at state h, there may be some nonblank symbols left in the tape. We call these symbols the *output* of the machine M. Since a DTM can generate outputs, it can also be used as a model for computing functions. Note that a DTM may not halt on some inputs, and so the function computed by it may be undefined at some inputs. In general, we call a function $f : (\Sigma_1^*)^k \to \Sigma_2^*$ a *partial function* if f is allowed to be undefined at some $(x_1, \ldots, x_k) \in (\Sigma_1^*)^k$, that is, if the real domain of f is a subset of $(\Sigma_1^*)^k$. We call a function $f : (\Sigma_1^*)^k \to \Sigma_2^*$ a *total* function if it is defined at every $(x_1, \ldots, x_k) \in (\Sigma_1^*)^k$, that is, if the real domain of f is exactly $(\Sigma_1^*)^k$. We write $f(x_1, \ldots, x_k) \downarrow$ to denote that f is defined at $(x_1, \ldots, x_k)$, and $f(x_1, \ldots, x_k) \uparrow$ to denote that f is undefined at $(x_1, \ldots, x_k)$. Clearly, a total function is a special case of partial functions.

We say a partial function $f : (\Sigma_1^*)^k \to \Sigma_2^*$ is *computed by a one-tape DTM* M if for every $(x_1, x_2, \ldots, x_k) \in (\Sigma_1^*)^k$ such that $f(x_1, x_2, \ldots, x_k)$ is defined,

$$(s, Bx_1Bx_2B \cdots Bx_k\underline{B}) \vdash_M^* (h, By\underline{B}),$$

where $y = f(x_1, x_2, \ldots, x_k)$, and for every $(x_1, x_2, \ldots, x_k) \in (\Sigma_1^*)^k$ such that $f(x_1, x_2, \ldots, x_k)$ is undefined,

$$(s, Bx_1Bx_2B \cdots Bx_k\underline{B}) \vdash_M^* \cdots \qquad \text{(never halts)}.$$

A partial function $f : (\Sigma_1^*)^k \to \Sigma_2^*$ is called a *Turing-computable* function if it is computed by a one-tape DTM.

A language L is *Turing-decidable* if its characteristic function

$$\chi_L(x) = \begin{cases} 1 & \text{if } x \in L, \\ 0 & \text{otherwise} \end{cases}$$

is Turing-computable. In other words, a language L is Turing-decidable if there is a DTM M to decide whether a given input x is in L or is not in L. This is, in general, a stronger form of acceptance than that of a Turing-acceptable language, for which a DTM M only decides whether $x \in L$ and may not halt on $x \notin L$. The difference between Turing-acceptable and Turing-decidable languages is one of the main topics of Chapter 5.

Exercises 4.1

1. Trace DTM M_1 of Example 4.1 and show the computation of M_1 on inputs *aabba* and *bbbab*.

2. Consider the DTM $M_2 = (Q, \Sigma, \Gamma, \delta, s)$ with $Q = \{s, q_1, q_2\}$, $\Sigma = \{a, b\}$, $\Gamma = \{a, b, \text{B}\}$, and

δ	a	b	B
s			q_1, B, L
q_1	q_1, a, L	q_2, b, R	h, B, R .
q_2	h, a, L		

   (a) Trace M_2 on inputs *aaab*, *abaa* and *aaaa*.

   (b) What is $L(M_2)$?

3. Consider the DTM $M_3 = (Q, \Sigma, \Gamma, \delta, s)$, with $Q = \{s, q_1, q_2, q_3, q_4, q_5\}$, $\Sigma = \{a, b\}$, $\Gamma = \{a, b, \text{B}\}$, and

δ	a	b	B
s			q_1, B, L
q_1	q_1, a, L	q_1, b, L	q_2, B, R
q_2	q_3, a, R	q_4, b, R	q_5, B, L
q_3	q_3, a, R	q_4, a, R	q_5, B, L
q_4	q_3, a, R	q_4, b, R	q_5, B, L
q_5	h, a, R	h, B, R	

   (a) Trace M_3 on inputs *aaabba* and *bbbaba*.

   (b) What is the function computed by M_3?

4. Consider the DTM $M_4 = (Q, \Sigma, \Gamma, \delta, s)$, in which Q, Σ and Γ are the same as those of M_3, and δ is the same as δ of M_3 except for

δ	a	b	B
q_5	q_5, a, L		h, B, R .

   What is $L(M_4)$?

5. Show that every regular language is Turing-decidable.

6. Assume that $L \subseteq \{0, 1\}^*$ is Turing-decidable. Show that the language $\{0, 1\}^* - L$ is also Turing-decidable. That is, for a given DTM M that computes the characteristic function χ_L of L, describe in detail how to modify M to get a new DTM M' such that M' computes the characteristic function of $\{0, 1\}^* - L$. Can you do the same for Turing-acceptable languages?

4.2   Examples of Turing Machines

We present some examples of Turing-computable functions and Turing-acceptable and Turing-decidable languages.

Example 4.3 *Show that $A = \{ww^R \mid w \in \{0,1\}^*\}$ is Turing-acceptable.*

Solution. The general idea is simple. For each input $x = x_1 x_2 \cdots x_n$, where each x_i is a symbol 0 or 1, we compare x_1 with x_n, x_2 with x_{n-1}, and so on. To do such a comparison, the DTM reads x_n, remembers it and then moves to the cell containing x_1 and compares them. (By *remembering* a symbol, we mean that the DTM moves into a state, or a subset of states, associated with this particular symbol and performs the necessary action within it.) Based on this idea, we construct a DTM M_A for A whose transition function δ is as follows:

δ	0	1	B
s			q_1, B, L
q_1	q_2, B, L	q_4, B, L	h, B, R
q_2	$q_2, 0, L$	$q_2, 1, L$	q_3, B, R
q_3	q_6, B, R		
q_4	$q_4, 0, L$	$q_4, 1, L$	q_5, B, R
q_5		q_6, B, R	
q_6	$q_6, 0, R$	$q_6, 1, R$	q_1, B, L

We also present its transition diagram in Figure 4.3. Since this is our first example, we also include a detailed description of M_A:

(1) At state s, it moves left to find x_n and enters state q_1.

(2) It then enters a loop from state q_1 through either q_2, q_3, q_6 or through q_4, q_5, q_6 then back to q_1.

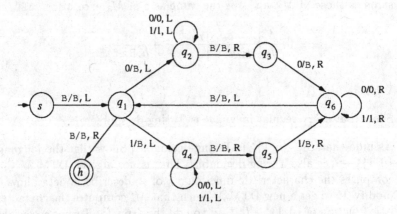

Figure 4.3:   Machine M_A of Example 4.3.

(3) In the ith iteration of the loop, M_A reads a symbol x_{n+1-i} at state q_1 and, depending on whether $x_{n+1-i} = 0$ or 1, enters state q_2 or q_4, respectively. Thus, state q_2 *remembers* that $x_{n+1-i} = 0$ and state q_4 *remembers* that $x_{n+1-i} = 1$. Also, M_A erases symbol x_{n+1-i} after reading it.

(4) In state q_2, it moves left until it finds the blank symbol B, then it moves right to find x_i and enters q_3.

(5) In state q_3, it checks whether $x_i = 0$. If $x_i \neq 0$, then it realizes that $x_i \neq x_{n+1-i}$ (since q_3 remembers that $x_{n+1-i} = 0$) and enters an infinite loop. If M_A finds that there is no symbol x_i left (i.e., it sees B at state q_3), then it means the input length is odd, and M_A also enters an infinite loop. If $x_i = 0$, then it erases it and goes to state q_6, in which it moves right until it sees the blank symbol B, and then changes back to state q_1, ready to compare x_{n-i} with x_{i+1}.

(6) Actions in states q_4 and q_5 are the same as those in q_2 and q_3, except that they remember that $x_{n+1-i} = 1$.

(7) When machine M_A, at state q_1, finds that no more symbol left to compare, it halts in state h.

In the following, we show the computation of M_A on input 0110:

$$(s, \text{B0110}\underline{\text{B}}) \vdash (q_1, \text{B011}\underline{0}) \vdash (q_2, \text{B01}\underline{1}) \vdash (q_2, \text{B0}\underline{1}1) \vdash^* (q_2, \underline{\text{B}}011)$$

$$\vdash (q_3, \text{B}\underline{0}11) \vdash (q_6, \text{BB}\underline{1}1) \vdash^* (q_6, \text{BB11}\underline{\text{B}}) \vdash (q_1, \text{BB1}\underline{1}) \vdash (q_4, \text{BB}\underline{1})$$

$$\vdash (q_4, \text{B}\underline{\text{B}}1) \vdash (q_5, \text{BB}\underline{1}) \vdash (q_6, \text{BBB}\underline{\text{B}}) \vdash (q_1, \text{BB}\underline{\text{B}}) \vdash (h, \text{BBB}\underline{\text{B}}). \qquad \square$$

Example 4.4 *Show that the following function is Turing-computable:*

$$f(x) = \begin{cases} w & \text{if } x = ww^R \text{ for some } w \in \{0,1\}^*, \\ \uparrow & \text{otherwise.} \end{cases}$$

Solution. This problem is similar to Example 4.3, except that it needs to output w when input x is found equal to ww^R. So, we modify M_A of Example 4.3 as follows:

> After M_A compares x_i with x_{n+1-i} in the ith iteration, we do not erase x_i. Instead, we replace x_i by x_i' (i.e., replace 0 by $0'$ and 1 by $1'$), where $0'$ and $1'$ are new auxiliary symbols. When all symbols have been compared and x is found to be of the form ww^R, we have w' left in the tape. We simply change it back to w and halt.

The complete machine is shown in Figure 4.4. The following is the trace of this machine on input 0110:

$$(s, \text{B0110}\underline{\text{B}}) \vdash (q_1, \text{B011}\underline{0}) \vdash (q_2, \text{B01}\underline{1}) \vdash (q_2, \text{B0}\underline{1}1) \vdash^* (q_2, \underline{\text{B}}011)$$

$$\vdash (q_3, \text{B}\underline{0}11) \vdash (q_6, \text{B0'}\underline{1}1) \vdash^* (q_6, \text{B0'11}\underline{\text{B}}) \vdash (q_1, \text{B0'1}\underline{1}) \vdash (q_4, \text{B0'}\underline{1})$$

$$\vdash (q_4, \text{B}\underline{0}'1) \vdash (q_5, \text{B0'}\underline{1}) \vdash (q_6, \text{B0'1'}\underline{\text{B}}) \vdash (q_1, \text{B0'}\underline{1}') \vdash (q_7, \text{B}\underline{0}'1)$$

$$\vdash (q_7, \underline{\text{B}}01) \vdash (q_8, \text{B}\underline{0}1) \vdash^* (q_8, \text{B01}\underline{\text{B}}) \vdash (q_9, \text{B01B}\underline{\text{B}}) \vdash (h, \text{B01}\underline{\text{B}}). \qquad \square$$

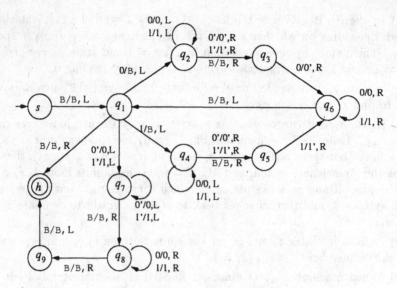

Figure 4.4: DTM of Example 4.4.

Example 4.5 *Show that $\{ww^R \mid w \in \{0,1\}^*\}$ is Turing-decidable.*

Solution. This time, we need to output 1 for x of the form ww^R and output 0 for x not of this form. We recall that if M_A of Example 4.3 finds $x_{n+1-i} = 0$ and $x_i = 1$ for some i, then it will enter the infinite loop at state q_3, and if it finds $x_{n+1-i} = 1$ and $x_i = 0$, then it will enter the infinite loop at state q_5. So, we only need to add new states in which the machine can erase all unprocessed symbols and output 0 from these configurations. The complete new machine is shown in Figure 4.5. Note that we replace each x_i by \$ after it is successfully matched with x_{n+1-i}. This allows us to locate the leftmost blank **B** and to put the output value 0 or 1 in the second cell.   □

Let **N** be the set of natural numbers. A natural number $n \in \mathbf{N}$ can be represented by string 1^n. Based on this representation, we say a partial function $f : \mathbf{N}^k \to \mathbf{N}$ is *Turing-computable* if the function $\tilde{f} : (\{1\}^*)^k \to \{1\}^*$, defined by $\tilde{f}(1^{n_1}, 1^{n_2}, \ldots, 1^{n_k}) = 1^{f(n_1, \ldots, n_k)}$, is Turing-computable.

Example 4.6 *Show that the function $\pi_2^2(n_1, n_2) = n_2$, for $n_1, n_2 \in \mathbf{N}$, is Turing-computable.*

Solution. The idea of the machine is to create a loop, each iteration of which moves the block 1^{n_2} one square to its left and reduces 1^{n_1} to 1^{n_1-1} so that the configuration changes from $(s, \mathbf{B}1^{n_1}\mathbf{B}1^{n_2}\underline{\mathbf{B}})$ to $(s, \mathbf{B}1^{n_1-1}\mathbf{B}1^{n_2}\underline{\mathbf{B}})$. We show the complete DTM in Figure 4.6, and its computation on inputs $(2,3)$ and $(2,0)$ as follows:

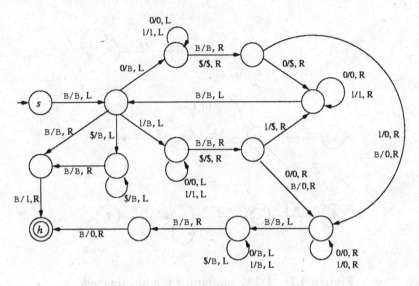

Figure 4.5: DTM of Example 4.5.

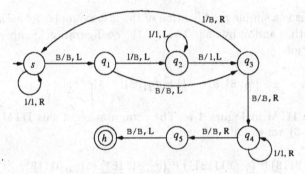

Figure 4.6: DTM computing the function π_2^2.

$(s,\ \text{B11B111}\underline{\text{B}}) \vdash (q_1, \text{B11B111}\underline{1}) \vdash (q_2, \text{B11B11}\underline{1}) \vdash^* (q_2, \text{B11}\underline{\text{B}}11)$

$\vdash (q_3, \text{B11}\underline{1}111) \vdash (s, \text{B1B}\underline{1}11) \vdash^* (s, \text{B1B111}\underline{\text{B}}) \vdash^* (s, \text{BB111}\underline{\text{B}})$

$\vdash (q_1, \text{BB111}\underline{1}) \vdash (q_2, \text{BB11}\underline{1}) \vdash^* (q_2, \text{BB}\underline{\text{B}}11) \vdash (q_3, \underline{\text{B}}111) \vdash (q_4, \text{B}\underline{1}11)$

$\vdash^* (q_4, \text{B111}\underline{\text{B}}) \vdash (q_5, \text{B111B}\underline{\text{B}}) \vdash (h, \text{B111}\underline{\text{B}}).$

$(s,\ \text{B11B}\underline{\text{B}}) \vdash (q_1, \text{B11}\underline{\text{B}}) \vdash (q_3, \text{B1}\underline{1}) \vdash (s, \text{B1B}\underline{\text{B}}) \vdash (q_1, \text{B1}\underline{\text{B}}) \vdash (q_3, \text{B}\underline{1})$

$\vdash (s, \text{BB}\underline{\text{B}}) \vdash (q_1, \text{B}\underline{\text{B}}) \vdash (q_3, \underline{\text{B}}) \vdash (q_4, \text{B}\underline{\text{B}}) \vdash (q_5, \text{BB}\underline{\text{B}}) \vdash (h, \text{B}\underline{\text{B}}).$ □

Example 4.7 *Find a Turing machine that computes the function*

$$sub(n, m) = \begin{cases} n - m & if\ n \geq m \geq 0, \\ 0 & if\ m > n \geq 0. \end{cases}$$

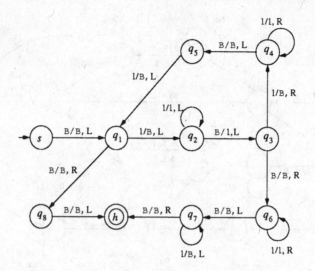

Figure 4.7: DTM computing the function *sub*.

Solution. This is a simple modification of the last example. At each iteration, we reduce both n and m by one. That is, the configuration changes as follows in each iteration:

$$(q_1, \text{B}1^i\text{B}1^{j-1}\underline{1}) \vdash^* (q_1, \text{B}1^{i-1}\text{B}1^{j-2}\underline{1}).$$

We show the DTM in Figure 4.7. The computation of this DTM on inputs $(3, 2)$ and $(2, 3)$ are as follows:

$$(s, \text{B}111\text{B}11\underline{\text{B}}) \vdash (q_1, \text{B}111\text{B}1\underline{1}) \vdash (q_2, \text{B}111\text{B}\underline{1}) \vdash (q_2, \text{B}111\underline{\text{B}}1)$$
$$\vdash (q_3, \text{B}11\underline{1}11) \vdash (q_4, \text{B}11\text{B}1\underline{1}) \vdash^* (q_4, \text{B}11\text{B}11\underline{\text{B}}) \vdash (q_5, \text{B}11\text{B}1\underline{1})$$
$$\vdash (q_1, \text{B}11\text{B}\underline{1}) \vdash^* (q_1, \text{B}1\underline{\text{B}}) \vdash (q_8, \text{B}1\text{B}\underline{\text{B}}) \vdash (h, \text{B}1\underline{\text{B}}).$$

$$(s, \text{B}11\text{B}111\underline{\text{B}}) \vdash (q_1, \text{B}11\text{B}11\underline{1}) \vdash^* (q_1, \text{B}1\text{B}1\underline{1}) \vdash^* (q_1, \text{B}\underline{\text{B}}1) \vdash (q_2, \text{B}\underline{\text{B}})$$
$$\vdash (q_3, \underline{\text{B}}1) \vdash (q_6, \text{B}\underline{1}) \vdash (q_6, \text{B}1\underline{\text{B}}) \vdash (q_7, \text{B}\underline{1}) \vdash (q_7, \underline{\text{B}}) \vdash (h, \text{B}\underline{\text{B}}).$$ □

Designing a Turing machine is just like designing a computer program, except that here the programming environment is more restrictive (so, it is similar to programming in assembly languages). In most programming environments, when we have a complicated program in which certain part of it is repeated many times, we can create a separate procedure for it and write its code only once. This technique of software design can also be used in the design of Turing machines. We illustrate this idea in the following example.

Example 4.8 *For $1 \leq i \leq k$, show that function $\pi_i^k(x_1, x_2, \cdots, x_k) = x_i$ on natural numbers is Turing-computable.*

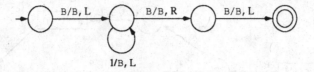

Figure 4.8: Procedure E.

Solution. We create two procedures. The first one, E, erases a block of 1's. That is, for any $x \in \{1, \mathbf{B}\}^*$ and $y \in \{1\}^*$, it has the effect of

$$(s, x\mathbf{B}y\underline{\mathbf{B}}) \vdash^* (h, x\underline{\mathbf{B}}).$$

The transition diagram of procedure E is shown in Figure 4.8.

The second procedure, P, erases the second rightmost block of 1's. That is, for any $x \in \{1, \mathbf{B}\}^*$ and $y, z \in \{1\}^*$, it works as follows:

$$(s, x\mathbf{B}y\mathbf{B}z\underline{\mathbf{B}}) \vdash^* (h, x\mathbf{B}z\underline{\mathbf{B}}).$$

Procedure P can be implemented exactly as shown in Figure 4.6.

Now, we can combine procedures E and P together to form a new machine M that computes π_i^k. The machine M looks like this:

$$\to \underbrace{E \longrightarrow E \longrightarrow \cdots \longrightarrow E}_{k-i} \longrightarrow \underbrace{P \longrightarrow P \longrightarrow \cdots \longrightarrow P}_{i-1}.$$

In the above, by $X \to Y$ we mean that the state h of procedure X is identified with state s of procedure Y (and is a new state of M which is neither the final state nor the initial state). So, the above picture means that machine M first erases the rightmost $k - i$ blocks of 1's, skips a block of 1's, and then erases $i - 1$ more blocks of 1's.

We express the machine M as $E^{k-i}P^{i-1}$. $\qquad\square$

The following example further demonstrates the technique of combining Turing machine procedures to create more complicated Turing machines. First, we extend the notion of Turing-computability to functions with more than one output. A partial function $f : (\Sigma^*)^m \to (\Sigma^*)^n$ is *Turing-computable* if there is a DTM M such that for every input $(x_1, x_2, \ldots, x_m) \in (\Sigma^*)^m$, if $f(x_1, x_2, \ldots, x_m)$ is defined and is equal to $(y_1, y_2, \ldots, y_n)$, we have

$$(s, \mathbf{B}x_1\mathbf{B}x_2\mathbf{B}\cdots\mathbf{B}x_m\underline{\mathbf{B}}) \vdash_M^* (h, \mathbf{B}y_1\mathbf{B}y_2\mathbf{B}\cdots\mathbf{B}y_n\underline{\mathbf{B}}),$$

and if $f(x_1, x_2, \ldots, x_m)$ is undefined, M does not halt when it starts from the initial configuration $(s, \mathbf{B}x_1\mathbf{B}x_2\mathbf{B}\cdots\mathbf{B}x_m\underline{\mathbf{B}})$.

Example 4.9 *Show that, for any $1 \le i \le k + 1$, the function*

$$insert_i^k(x_1, x_2, \cdots, x_k, y) = (x_1, \ldots, x_{i-1}, y, x_i, \ldots, x_k)$$

on strings over $\{a, b\}$ is Turing-computable.

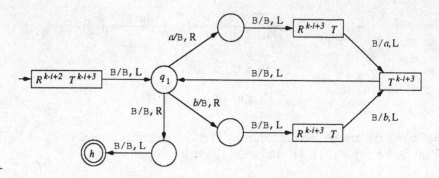

Figure 4.9:   DTM M computing the function $insert_i^k$.

Solution. We create two procedures:

Procedure R. This procedure moves a block of nonblanks to the right by one square. More precisely, it works as follows: for any $x, z \in \Gamma^*$ and $y \in (\Gamma - \{B\})^*$,

$$(s, xБy\underline{B}z) \vdash^* (h, x\underline{BB}yz).$$

Procedure T. This procedure finds the next blank to the right. That is, for any $x, z \in \Gamma^*$, $y \in (\Gamma - \{B\})^*$ and any $c \in \Gamma$, it has the effect of

$$(s, x\underline{c}yБz) \vdash^* (h, xcyБz).$$

We leave the implementations of procedures R and T as exercises. Using these two procedures, the DTM M for function f can be constructed as shown in Figure 4.9. This DTM M operates as follows:

(1) From state s to state q_1, M inserts a blank B between the block x_i and the blank to its left. That is,

$$(s, Bx_1B \cdots Bx_{i-1}Bx_iB \cdots Bx_kBy\underline{B})$$
$$\vdash^* (q_1, Bx_1B \cdots Bx_{i-1}BBx_iB \cdots Bx_kBy_1\underline{y_2}),$$

where $y = y_1y_2$ and $|y_2| = 1$. (If $y = \varepsilon$, then the head is scanning the blank to the right of x_k.)

(2) From state q_1, going through the loop once and back to state q_1, the configuration changes as follows:

$$(q_1, Bx_1B \cdots Bx_{i-1}Bz_4Bx_iB \cdots Bx_kBz_1z_2\underline{z_3})$$
$$\vdash^* (q_1, Bx_1B \cdots Bx_{i-1}Bz_3z_4Bx_iB \cdots Bx_kBz_1\underline{z_2}),$$

where $y = z_1z_2z_3z_4$ and $|z_2| = |z_3| = 1$.

(3) When y has been inserted between x_{i-1} and x_i, M reaches the configuration

$$(q_1, Bx_1B \cdots Bx_{i-1}ByBx_iB \cdots Bx_k\underline{B})$$

and it halts. $\square$

Read-Only Turing Machines. In Theorem 4.2, we showed that every regular language is Turing-acceptable. We note that the DTM M' in that proof never writes a new symbol over an original input symbol; that is, for any $q \in Q$ and any $a \in \Gamma$, $\delta'(q, a) = (p, a, D)$ for some $p \in Q$ and $D \in \{L, R\}$. We call such a DTM a *read-only DTM*. In the following, we show that read-only DTM's accept only regular languages.

$\star$ **Theorem 4.10** *Every language accepted by a one-tape, read-only DTM is regular.*

Proof. We first make a small change on our DTM model. We assume that the one-tape, read-only DTM $M = (Q, \Sigma, \Gamma, \delta, s)$ begins the computation with the tape head scanning the leftmost cell of the tape. In addition, if M accepts the input, then its tape head always moves from left to right when M enters the state h. That is, we assume that the initial configuration of M on x is $(s, \underline{\texttt{B}}x)$, and that the only instructions entering state h are of the form $\delta(q, a) = (h, a, R)$ for some $q \in Q$ and $a \in \Gamma$.

We note that this new DTM model is equivalent to the original model: Given a DTM M of the original model, we can create a DTM M' of the new model that accepts the same language as M. Namely, M' first moves to the right, passing through the input until it finds the first blank symbol to the right of the input. Then, it begins to simulate machine M. When M accepts, M' does not halt but makes one more move to the right and then halt in state h. Similarly, given a DTM M' of the new model, we can construct a DTM M'' of the original model such that $L(M'') = L(M')$. Therefore, this change on the model does not affect the class of languages accepted by one-tape, read-only DTM's.

Now, let us fix a one-tape, read-only DTM $M = (Q, \Sigma, \Gamma, \delta, s)$ of the new model. Since machine M cannot write new symbols on the tape, we may assume that $\Gamma = \Sigma \cup \{\texttt{B}\}$. We will design an NFA M' to simulate M. In order to describe the NFA M', we first need to define the notion of crossing sequences. Let us call the cells of the tape of a DTM $C_0, C_1, C_2, \cdots$, with C_0 indicating the leftmost cell of the tape. The *crossing sequence* between cells C_i and C_{i+1}, for $i \geq 0$, in a computation path of M, is the record of the *moving directions* and the *new states* when the tape head moves over the boundary between the cells C_i and C_{i+1}.

For instance, consider the following read-only DTM M:

δ	0	1	B
s			$p, \texttt{B}, R$
p	$q, 0, R$	$p, 1, R$	$h, \texttt{B}, R$
q	$q, 0, R$	$q, 1, R$	$r, \texttt{B}, L$
r	$p, 0, R$	$t, 1, L$	
t	$r, 0, L$	$t, 1, L$	

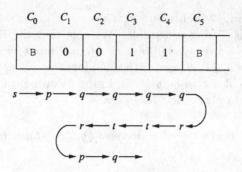

Figure 4.10: Crossing sequences.

For this DTM M, we show in Figure 4.10 the crossing sequences of the following computation path of M on input 0011:

$$(s, \underline{B}0011) \vdash (p, B\underline{0}011) \vdash (q, B0\underline{0}11) \vdash (q, B00\underline{1}1)$$
$$\vdash (q, B001\underline{1}) \vdash (q, B0011\underline{B}) \vdash (r, B001\underline{1}) \vdash (t, B00\underline{1}1)$$
$$\vdash (t, B0\underline{0}11) \vdash (r, B\underline{0}011) \vdash (p, B\underline{0}011) \vdash (q, B0\underline{0}11) \vdash \cdots$$

In Figure 4.10, the crossing sequence between cells C_i and C_{i+1} is written under the boundary between the two cells. For instance, the crossing sequence between cells C_1 and C_2 is $(\to q, r \leftarrow, \to p)$. For convenience, we write $(\langle q, R \rangle, \langle r, L \rangle, \langle p, R \rangle)$ to denote this crossing sequence. Thus, the pair $\langle q, R \rangle$ means that the tape head was moving from left to right when it crossed the boundary and the new state after that is q.

We observe the following two properties of the crossing sequences:

(a) If a computation path of M contains a crossing sequence in which the same pair $\langle q, D \rangle$, with $q \in Q$, $D \in \{L, R\}$, occurs twice, then this computation path contains two identical configurations and so it is in an infinite loop and does not accept. For instance, the crossing sequence between C_2 and C_3 in Figure 4.10 is $(\langle q, R \rangle, \langle t, L \rangle, \langle q, R \rangle)$, with two occurrences of the pair $\langle q, R \rangle$. They correspond to the two occurrences of the configuration $(q, B0\underline{0}11)$ in the computation path, and indicate that the computaion of M on input 0011 never halts.

(b) Any two consecutive pairs $\langle q, D_1 \rangle$, $\langle p, D_2 \rangle$ in a crossing sequence must have $D_1 \neq D_2$, since the tape head must move in different directions in two crossings over the same boundary.

Since we are only interested in the accepting paths of M, we define, formally, a *crossing sequence* to be a finite sequence of pairs $(\langle q_1, D_1 \rangle, \langle q_2, D_2 \rangle, \ldots, \langle q_m, D_m \rangle)$ in $(Q \cup \{h\}) \times \{L, R\}$, with the properties (i) $D_i \neq D_{i+1}$ for $1 \leq i \leq m-1$, and (ii) $\langle q_i, D_i \rangle \neq \langle q_j, D_j \rangle$ for $1 \leq i < j \leq m$.

Now, we go back to the design of the NFA M'. The idea of M' is to use the crossing sequences as the states to process the input. Assume that the input is x, with $|x| = n$. It starts with crossing sequence $S_0 = (\langle s, R \rangle)$ at the left boundary of cell C_0. At each step, M' looks at the current crossing sequence S_i between the boundary of C_{i-1} and C_i, reads the symbol a in cell C_i, and nondeterministically guesses the next crossing sequence S_{i+1} between C_i and C_{i+1}. After the guess, it then verifies that sequences S_i and S_{i+1} are *consistent* with respect to symbol a. It continues to the next step if S_i and S_{i+1} are indeed consistent. At the end, if the last pair of the crossing sequence S_{n+1} is $\langle h, R \rangle$, then it accepts the input.

To implement this idea by an NFA, we must decide, from the transition function δ, whether two crossing sequences S and T are consistent. That is, we need to check whether there exists a computation path in which S and T occur as the two crossing sequences around a symbol $a \in \Sigma \cup \{B\}$. This notion can be made more precise by the following recursive definition. First, let Q_R (and Q_L) be the collection of all crossing sequences whose first pair is $\langle q, R \rangle$ (and, respectively, $\langle q, L \rangle$) for some $q \in Q \cup \{h\}$. Consider a symbol $a \in \Gamma$. Then, two crossing sequences $S = (\langle q_1, R \rangle, \langle q_2, L \rangle, \ldots, \langle q_k, D_k \rangle)$ and $T = (\langle p_1, R \rangle, \langle p_2, L \rangle, \ldots, \langle p_\ell, D_\ell \rangle)$ in Q_R are consistent with respect to symbol a (denoted by $S \overset{a}{\rightleftharpoons} T$), if one of the following conditions holds:

(i) Both S and T are empty, or both S and T are the singleton sequence $(\langle h, R \rangle)$. In the latter case, we write $\langle q_1, R \rangle \to \langle p_1, R \rangle$.

(ii) $\delta(q_1, a) = (q_2, a, L)$, and $S'' = (\langle q_3, R \rangle, \ldots, \langle q_k, D_k \rangle)$ and T in Q_R have the relation $S'' \overset{a}{\rightleftharpoons} T$. In this case, we write $\langle q_1, R \rangle \to \langle q_2, L \rangle$.

(iii) $\delta(q_1, a) = (p_1, a, R)$, and $S' = (\langle q_2, L \rangle, \langle q_3, R \rangle, \ldots, \langle q_k, D_k \rangle)$ and $T' = (\langle p_2, L \rangle, \langle p_3, R \rangle, \ldots, \langle p_\ell, D_\ell \rangle)$ in Q_L have the relation $S' \overset{a}{\rightleftharpoons} T'$. In this case, we write $\langle q_1, R \rangle \to \langle p_1, R \rangle$.

Also, two crossing sequences $S = (\langle q_1, L \rangle, \langle q_2, R \rangle, \ldots, \langle q_k, D_k \rangle)$ and $T = (\langle p_1, L \rangle, \langle p_2, R \rangle, \ldots, \langle p_\ell, D_\ell \rangle)$ in Q_L are consistent with respect to symbol a (also denoted by $S \overset{a}{\rightleftharpoons} T$), if one of the following conditions holds:

(i′) Both S and T are empty.

(ii′) $\delta(p_1, a) = (p_2, a, R)$, and S and $T'' = (\langle p_3, L \rangle, \ldots, \langle p_\ell, D_\ell \rangle)$ in Q_L have the relation $S \overset{a}{\rightleftharpoons} T''$. In this case, we write $\langle p_1, L \rangle \to \langle p_2, R \rangle$.

(iii′) $\delta(p_1, a) = (q_1, a, L)$, and $S' = (\langle q_2, R \rangle, \langle q_3, L \rangle, \ldots, \langle q_k, D_k \rangle)$ and $T' = (\langle p_2, R \rangle, \langle p_3, L \rangle, \ldots, \langle p_\ell, D_\ell \rangle)$ in Q_R have the relation $S' \overset{a}{\rightleftharpoons} T'$. In this case, we write $\langle p_1, L \rangle \to \langle q_1, L \rangle$.

For instance, consider, in Figure 4.10, the crossing sequences $S = (\langle p, R \rangle)$ and $T = (\langle q, R \rangle, \langle r, L \rangle, \langle p, R \rangle)$ at the two sides of cell C_1. We can verify that $S \overset{0}{\rightleftharpoons} T$ as follows:

(1) Sequences $S_0 = \emptyset$ and $T_0 = \emptyset$ are consistent sequences in Q_L (by rule (i′)).

(2) Sequences S_0 and $T_1 = (\langle r, L \rangle, \langle p, R \rangle)$ are consistent sequences in Q_L, because $\delta(r, 0) = (p, 0, R)$ and S_0 and T_0 are consistent (from rule (ii′)).

(3) Sequences S and T are consistent sequences in Q_R, because $\delta(p, 0) = (q, 0, R)$ and S_0 amd T_1 are consistent (from rule (iii)).

From the above recursive definition of consistent sequences, we can construct the NFA M' as $M' = (Q_R, \{0, 1\}, \delta', (\langle s, R \rangle), (\langle h, R \rangle))$, where δ' is defined as follows: For each state $S_1 \in Q_R$ and each input $a \in \Sigma$,

$$\delta'(S_1, a) = \{S_2 \in Q_R \mid S_1 \overset{a}{\rightleftharpoons} S_2\},$$

and for each state $S_1 \in Q_R$,

$$\delta'(S_1, \varepsilon) = \{S_2 \in Q_R \mid S_1 \overset{B}{\rightleftharpoons} S_2\}.$$

To see that $L(M') = L(M)$, first assume that M accepts an input x. Also assume that in the computation of M on x, the rightmost cell it ever visits is C_m, and that it halts at cell C_j, $1 \leq j \leq m$ in state h. Without loss of generality, we may assume that $m \geq |x|$. Then, the computation path of M corresponds to a sequence of crossing sequences $S_0, S_1, \ldots, S_m$, that has the following properties:

(a) $S_0 = (\langle s, R \rangle)$. (*Note:* The tape head of M cannot move over the left boundary of C_0.)

(b) For each $0 \leq i \leq m - 1$, $S_i \overset{x_i}{\rightleftharpoons} S_{i+1}$, where x_i is the ith symbol of input x if $1 \leq i \leq n$, and $x_i = \text{B}$ otherwise.

(c) $\langle h, R \rangle$ occurs as the last pair in S_j.

Now, from property (c) and rules (i), (ii) and (iii), we know that $\langle h, R \rangle$ occurs as the last pair in each S_i, for $j \leq i \leq m$. (*Note:* If $\langle h, R \rangle$ is in S and $S \overset{a}{\rightleftharpoons} T$ for some a, then $\langle h, R \rangle$ must occur in T.) Furthermore, we know, from rule (i), that $S_m \overset{B}{\rightleftharpoons} S_{m+1}$, where $S_{m+1} = (\langle h, R \rangle)$. So, the computation path of M' that guesses the states $S_0, S_1, \ldots, S_{m+1}$ will accept input x.

Conversely, if M' accepts the input x, then the sequence of states $S_0, S_1, \ldots, S_{m+1}$, where $m \geq |x|$, must have the properties (a), (b) above, plus

(c') $S_{m+1} = (\langle h, R \rangle)$.

From these crossing sequences, we can reconstruct the computation path of M on x as follows: First, we change each pair $\langle q, R \rangle$ in S_i, $0 \leq i \leq m + 1$, to the configuration

$$(q, x_0 x_1 \cdots x_{i-1} \underline{x_i} x_{i+1} \cdots x_{m+1}),$$

where x_i is the ith symbol of input x if $1 \leq i \leq n$, and $x_i = \text{B}$, otherwise. (*Note:* This configuration contains extra trailing blank symbols B.) Also, change each pair $\langle q, L \rangle$ in S_i to the configuration

$$(q, x_0 x_1 \cdots x_{i-2} \underline{x_{i-1}} x_i \cdots x_{m+1}).$$

Next, we argue that these configurations, when arranged in the *right* order, form the computation path of M on x. What is the right order on these configurations? It is the order defined by the relation $\to$ on these pairs when they were matched by rules (i), (ii), (iii), (ii') and (iii') above. That is, if the two pairs $\langle p_1, D_1 \rangle$ and $\langle p_2, D_2 \rangle$ have the relation $\langle p_1, D_1 \rangle \to \langle p_2, D_2 \rangle$, then their two corresponding configurations α_1 and α_2 satisfy $\alpha_1 \vdash \alpha_2$. (We allow the special case of

$$(h, x_0 \cdots \underline{x_i} \cdots x_{m+1}) \vdash (h, x_0 \cdots \underline{x_{i+1}} \cdots x_{m+1}).)$$

For instance, suppose that $\langle p_1, R \rangle$ in S_i and $\langle p_2, R \rangle$ in S_{i+1} satisfy $\langle p_1, R \rangle \to \langle p_2, R \rangle$, and that $p_1 \neq h$. Then, by rule (iii), we know that $\delta(p_1, x_i) = (p_2, x_i, R)$. So, the corresponding configurations satisfy

$$(p_1, x_0 \cdots \underline{x_i} \cdots x_{m+1}) \vdash (p_2, x_0 \cdots \underline{x_{i+1}} \cdots x_{m+1}).$$

The other cases can be verified in a similar way.

Now, we observe that if $S_i \stackrel{x_i}{\rightleftharpoons} S_{i+1}$, then each pair $\langle p, R \rangle$ in S_{i+1} has either a predecessor $\langle q, R \rangle$ in S_i or a predecessor $\langle q, L \rangle$ in S_{i+1} (under relation $\to$). Also, each pair $\langle p, L \rangle$ in S_i has either a predecessor $\langle q, R \rangle$ in S_i or a predecessor $\langle q, L \rangle$ in S_{i+1} (under relation $\to$). This observation, together with the fact that S_0 has a unique pair $\langle s, R \rangle$ which does not have a predecessor, shows that every pair $\langle q, D \rangle$ in any crossing sequence S_i, $1 \leq i \leq m + 1$, has a predecessor. Furthermore, from the recursive rules (ii), (iii), (ii') and (iii'), it is clear that each pair has a unique predecessor. In other words, the configurations corresponding to these pairs $\langle q, D \rangle$ form a linear chain, starting from the initial configuration to the configuration $(h, x_0 \cdots \underline{x_{m+1}})$. We conclude that M accepts x. □

Exercises 4.2

1. For each of the following DTM's, trace the machine and show the computation on the given inputs:

   (a) The DTM M_A of Example 4.3 on inputs 0100 and 01010.
   (b) The DTM of Example 4.5 on inputs 0110 and 01010.
   (c) The DTM of Example 4.6 on inputs $(3, 0)$ and $(0, 3)$.
   (d) The DTM M of Example 4.9, with $k = 3$ and $i = 2$, from configuration $(q_1, \mathtt{BaaBBabBbbaBaba})$ to $(q_1, \mathtt{BaaBaBabBbbaBab})$.

2. Construct DTM's for procedures R and T of Example 4.9.

3. Construct DTM's to decide the following languages:

   (a) $\{ww \mid w \in \{0, 1\}^*\}$.
   (b) $\{ww^R w \mid w \in \{0, 1\}^*\}$.

(c) $\{a^m b^n c^k \mid m \geq n \geq k \geq 0\}$.

(d) $\{a^m b^n c^{n+m} \mid n, m \geq 0\}$.

(e) $\{w \in \{a, b\}^* \mid \#_a(w) > \#_b(w)\}$, where $\#_a(w)$ denotes the number of occurrences of letter a in string w.

(f) $\{a^{n_1} b a^{n_2} b \cdots b a^{n_k} \mid n_i = n_j$ for some $1 \leq i < j \leq k\}$.

4. Construct DTM's to compute the following functions:

(a) $f(m, n) = \max\{m, n\}$ over natural numbers m, n.

(b) $f(n_1, n_2, \ldots, n_k) = \max\{n_1, \ldots, n_k\}$ over natural numbers $n_1, \ldots, n_k$, where k is a fixed positive integer.

(c) $insert^k(x_1, \ldots, x_k, y, i) = insert_i^k(x_1, \ldots, x_k, y)$, where $x_1, \ldots, x_k$ and y are strings in $\{0, 1\}^*$ and i is a natural number represented by 1^i.

(d) $mult(n, m) = nm$ on natural numbers $n, m \geq 0$.

(e) $quot(n, m) = \lfloor \frac{n}{m} \rfloor$ on natural numbers $n \geq 0$ and $m \geq 1$.

(f) $lg(n) = \lceil \log_2 n \rceil$ on natural number n.

5. For any given DTM M, construct a new DTM M' such that M' accepts exactly the same set of strings as that of M (i.e., $L(M) = L(M')$) but when M' halts its tape is always empty (i.e., the final configuration is always $(h, \text{B}\underline{\text{B}})$).

$\star$ 6. Consider the regular language $L = \{0^{n_1} 1 0^{n_2} 1 \cdots 1 0^{n_k} \mid k \geq 5, n_1, \ldots, n_k \geq 0, n_j \equiv n_{j+1} \pmod 5$, where $j = (k \bmod 5) + 1\}$.

(a) Find a read-only DTM M accepting L. [*Hint*: M make two passes over the input. In the first pass, it checks that $k \geq 5$ and finds $j = (k \bmod 5) + 1$. In the second pass, it checks that $n_j \equiv n_{j+1} \pmod 5$.]

(b) Find all possible crossing sequences of M on any input.

(c) For any two crossing sequences S_1, S_2 of M, and for any symbol $a \in \{0, 1, \text{B}\}$, determine whether $S_1 \overset{a}{\rightleftharpoons} S_2$. Based on this relation between crossing sequences, construct an NFA M' that accepts L.

(d) Can you find an NFA with a smaller state set than M' that accepts L?

$\star$ 7. In the proof of Theorem 4.10, we observe that if the DTM M visits, during its computation on input x, some blank cells to the right of the input, then the NFA M' needs to move, after reading all input symbols, to other states by ε-moves to decide whether it accepts the input. Show that this is not necessary. That is, we can eliminate all ε-moves in δ' and change the set F of the final states to include all crossing sequences S which contain $\langle h, R \rangle$ as the last pair such that $S \overset{\text{B}}{\rightleftharpoons} S_1 \overset{\text{B}}{\rightleftharpoons} S_2 \overset{\text{B}}{\rightleftharpoons} \cdots \overset{\text{B}}{\rightleftharpoons} (\langle h, R \rangle)$. Explain how to determine the final set F.

⋆ **8.** We consider an extension of read-only DTM's. A *one-pebble, read-only DTM* (or, simply, *one-pebble DTM*) is a read-only DTM M with the additional capability that it can mark a specific cell of the input tape by putting a pebble on it. The machine M has only one pebble, and so at any time the tape can have at most one marked symbol. More precisely, a one-pebble DTM M is a DTM $M = (Q, \Sigma, \Gamma, \delta, s^*)$, where $Q = Q_1 \cup \{q^* \mid q \in Q_1\}$ for some finite set Q_1, $\Gamma = \Sigma \cup \{B\} \cup \{a^* \mid a \in \Sigma$ or $a = B\}$, $s \in Q_1$, and δ satisfies the following properties: For any $q \in Q_1$ and $a \in \Sigma \cup \{B\}$,

(i) $\delta(q, a) = (p, a, D)$ for some $p \in Q_1$ and $D \in \{L, R\}$.

(ii) $\delta(q, a^*)$ is either (p, a^*, D) or (p^*, a, D) for some $p \in Q_1$ and $D \in \{L, R\}$.

(iii) $\delta(q^*, a)$ is either (p^*, a, D) or (p, a^*, D) for some $p \in Q_1$ and $D \in \{L, R\}$.

(iv) $\delta(q^*, a^*)$ is undefined.

(In the above, the superscript * denotes the pebble. So, a state q^* indicates that M is holding the pebble at its finite control, and all tape symbols are unmarked; and a state $q \in Q_1$ indicates that the pebble is in an input cell. Note that property (i) indicates that M cannot mark a cell if it does not hold the pebble in its finite control now.)

(a) Construct a one-pebble DTM M such that on each input x of length $n \geq 2$, M halts in exactly n^2 moves.

(b) Show that for each read-only DTM M, there exist two constants c and d such that if M halts on an input x of length $n \geq 1$, then it must halt within $cn + d$ moves.

(c) Show that for each one-pebble DTM M, there exist two constants c and d such that if M halts on an input x of length $n \geq 1$, then it must halt within $cn^2 + d$ moves.

(d) Show that if L is a regular language, then there is a one-pebble DTM M that accepts the language SQRT(L). (Recall that SQRT(L) is defined in Example 2.44 as $\{x \mid (\exists y) \, |y| = |x|^2, xy \in L\}$.)

⋆ **9.** In this exercise, we prove that the language accepted by a one-pebble DTM must be regular. Assume that $M = (Q, \Sigma, \Gamma, \delta, s^*)$ is a one-pebble DTM with $Q = Q_1 \cup \{q^* \mid q \in Q_1\}$. Also assume that M operates on an input x and visits cells $C_0, C_1, \ldots, C_n$, with symbol s_i in cell C_i, for $i = 0, 1, \ldots, n$ (i.e., $s_0 s_1 \cdots s_n = BxB \cdots B$). For each i, $0 \leq i \leq n$, define a partial function $f_i : Q_1 \to Q_1$ as follows: If $\delta(q, s_i^*) = (p, s_i^*, D)$ for some $p \in Q_1$ and $D \in \{L, R\}$, then $f_i(q)$ is the next state $r \in Q_1$ $(r \neq h)$ at which M returns to cell C_i. Otherwise, $f_i(q)$ is undefined. That is, the function f_i encodes the states of M when it visits cell C_i with the pebble in cell C_i (similar to a crossing sequence of a read-only DTM). Note that f_i depends on both machine M and input x.

(a) Consider the language L_1 over the alphabet $(\Sigma \cup \{\mathtt{B}\}) \times F$, where F is the set of all partial functions from Q_1 to Q_1, with $w = [s_0, g_0][s_1, g_1] \cdots [s_n, g_n] \in L_1$ if and only if for all $i = 0, \ldots, n$, $g_i = f_i$, with respect to machine M and string $s_0 s_1 \cdots s_n$. (*Note*: If $|Q_1| = m$ then there are at most m^{m+1} symbols in F, each encodes one partial function from Q_1 to Q_1.) Show that there is a read-only DTM M_1 that accepts L_1; that is, show that a read-only DTM can check whether each symbol g_i stored at the second track of cell C_i encodes correctly the function f_i. [*Hint*: M_1 cannot simulate M step-by-step to check whether the values $f_i(q)$ are correct, because M_1 does not have a pebble and so once it leaves cell C_i, it cannot remember where it is. Instead, M_1 needs only to check the consistency of the function f_i with its neighbors f_{i-1} and f_{i+1}, similar to the problem of checking the consistency of neighboring crossing sequences in Theorem 4.10.]

(b) Let L_2 be the language over the alphabet $(\Sigma \cup \{\mathtt{B}\}) \times F$ such that $w = [s_0, g_0][s_1, g_1] \cdots [s_n, g_n] \in L_2$ if (1) $w \in L_1$ defined in part (a) above, and (2) the one-pebble DTM M accepts the input $t_0 t_1 \cdots t_n$, where $t_i = s_i$ if $s_i \neq \mathtt{B}$ and $t_i = \varepsilon$ if $s_i = \mathtt{B}$. Show that there is a read-only DTM M_2 accepting L_2. [*Hint*: M_2 uses the information g_i to simulate M as follows: If M holds the pebble in its state (i.e., if M is in a state q^*), then M_2 simulates M step-by-step. If M puts down the pebble in Cell C_i, then M_2 uses g_i at the second track to determine the state it will change to when it returns to cell C_i.]

(c) Show that if M is a one-pebble DTM, then $L(M)$ is regular. [*Hint*: Show that the language $L(M)$ is the image of a homomorphism ϕ on L_2; see Example 2.35.]

10. We consider another extension of read-only DTM's. A DTM M is called a *read/erase-only DTM* if it can, at each move, only read an input symbol and/or erase it (i.e., replace the original symbol by $\mathtt{B}$). That is, a DTM $M = (Q, \Sigma, \Gamma, \delta, s)$ is a read/erase-only DTM if $\Gamma = \Sigma \cup \{\mathtt{B}\}$, and the transition function δ satisfies the following property: For any $q \in Q$ and $a \in \Sigma \cup \{\mathtt{B}\}$, $\delta(q, a)$ is either (p, a, D) or $(p, \mathtt{B}, D)$ for some $p \in Q$ and $D \in \{L, R\}$.

(a) Show that there exists a read/erase-only DTM that accepts the language $L = \{a^n b^n c^n \mid n \geq 0\}$.

$\star$ (b) Show that there exists a Turing-decidable language that is not accepted by any read/erase-only DTM.

4.3 Multi-Tape Turing Machines

In this section, we extend one-tape Turing machines to multi-tape Turing machines and show that although these extended machines are more convenient

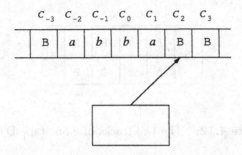

Figure 4.11: A two-way infinite one-tape DTM.

to use, the class of Turing-computable functions remains the same. The proof for this equivalence result amounts to a simulation of the multi-tape DTM by a standard one-tape DTM.

First, we extend a one-tape DTM to have a tape that is infinite to the both ends, called a *two-way-infinite one-tape DTM* (or, simply a *two-way DTM*). Figure 4.11 shows such a machine. A two-way infinite one-tape DTM $M = (Q, \Sigma, \Gamma, \delta, s)$ operates in the same way as a one-tape DTM except that its tape has no left end and so it is free to move to the left and never hangs.

Since the tape of a two-way DTM has no left end, its tape configuration has a different representation. Assume that the tape contains

$$\cdots \text{BBB} x \underline{a} y \text{BBB} \cdots$$

with the head scanning the symbol a, and that the leftmost symbol of x and the rightmost symbol of y are not B. Then, we write (x, a, y) or $x\underline{a}y$ to represent this tape configuration. For instance, the tape of Figure 4.11 can be represented by $abba\underline{\text{B}}$.

When a two-way DTM M computes a function, it writes the output *anywhere* in the tape and halts at state h with the head scanning the blank symbol to the right of the rightmost symbol of the output. In other words, M computes a function that maps input $(x_1, \ldots, x_n)$ to the output $(y_1, \ldots, y_m)$ if

$$(s, x_1 \text{B} x_2 \text{B} \cdots \text{B} x_n \underline{\text{B}}) \vdash_M^* (h, y_1 \text{B} y_2 \text{B} \cdots \text{B} y_m \underline{\text{B}}).$$

Let us see how a one-tape DTM M' can simulate this machine M. The main idea is to divide each tape cell of M' into two *tracks* and use these two tracks to simulate the two halves of the two-way tape of M. To be more precise, each cell of the tape of M', except the leftmost one, now contains two symbols from Γ, one called the *top symbol* and the other called the *bottom symbol*. The leftmost cell of the one-way tape of M' contains a special new symbol \$, which indicates that this is the left end of the tape.

Now, let us fix a specific cell of the two-way tape of machine M, and call this cell C_0. Call the cells to its right $C_1, C_2, \ldots$, and the cells to its left $C_{-1}, C_{-2}, \ldots$ (see Figure 4.11). Then, the bottom track of the tape of M'

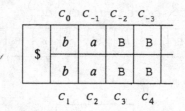

Figure 4.12: The two tracks of a one-tape DTM.

will simulate the right-hand part of the two-way tape of M, that is, cells $C_1, C_2, C_3, \ldots$, and the top track will simulate the left-hand part of the two-way tape of M, that is, cells $C_0, C_{-1}, C_{-2}, \ldots$. Note that the top track is of the reverse direction of left part of the two-way tape of M. That is, the two tracks together are like the two-way tape of M *folded* around the boundary between cells C_0 and C_1 (see Figure 4.12).

In addition to this setting of the tape, machine M' also has a larger state set Q'. In particular, for each state $q \in Q$, M' has two corresponding states q_b and q_t to simulate the state q. Additional states are also used for other purposes, and will be introduced later.

With this idea, the simulation is now straightforward. Let us call the cells of the tape of M', starting from the leftmost cell, $C'_0, C'_1, C'_2, \ldots$.

First, suppose that the input x to the machine M' is stored in cells C'_1, $C'_2, \ldots, C'_n$, and the head is scanning the cell C'_{n+1}. Then, the machine M' will replace each symbol a in cells $C'_1, C'_2, \ldots, C'_{n+1}$ by the symbol $[B, a]$, and replace the symbol B in cell C'_0 by \$. (We write $[B, a]$ to denote the symbol whose top part is B and the bottom part is a.) It then goes back to cell C'_{n+1} and changes its state to s_b. At this point, the configuration of M' is as follows:

$$(s_b, \$ \, [B, x_1] \, [B, x_2] \, \cdots \, [B, x_n] \, \underline{[B, B]}),$$

where x_i is the ith symbol of x for $i = 1, \ldots, n$. (*Note:* Cells $C'_{n+2}, C'_{n+3}, \ldots$ still hold the original blank symbol B.)

Next, M' begins to simulate machine M. If M' is in a *bottom* state q_b and reads a symbol $[a, b]$, then it simulates the action of $\delta(q, b)$. For instance, if M has an instruction $\delta(q, b) = (p, c, R)$, then M' has the following instructions:

$$\delta'(q_b, [a, b]) = (p_b, [a, c], R), \quad \text{for all } a \in \Gamma.$$

If M' is in a *top* state q_t and reads a symbol $[a, b]$, then it simulates the action of $\delta(q, a)$. For instance, if M has an instruction $\delta(q, a) = (p, c, R)$, then M' has the following instructions:

$$\delta'(q_t, [a, b]) = (p_t, [c, b], L), \quad \text{for all } b \in \Gamma.$$

Suppose that M' moves into a cell which has not been split into two tracks yet. It needs to split it. That is, for each $q \in Q$, M' has the following additional instructions:

$$\delta'(q_b, \text{B}) = (q_b', [\text{B}, \text{B}], R), \qquad \delta'(q_b', \text{B}) = (q_b, \text{B}, L),$$
$$\delta'(q_t, \text{B}) = (q_t', [\text{B}, \text{B}], R), \qquad \delta'(q_t', \text{B}) = (q_t, \text{B}, L),$$

where q_b' and q_t' are new states in $Q' - Q$. In addition, if machine M' reads the symbol $\$$, then it needs to *change track*. That is, for each $q \in Q$, M' has the following additional instructions:

$$\delta'(q_b, \$) = (q_t, \$, R), \quad \delta'(q_t, \$) = (q_b, \$, R).$$

Finally, if machine M reaches h_b or h_t, it restores the tape into the one-track form and halts. More precisely, it needs to first move all nonblank symbols (those in both the top track and the bottom track) to the bottom track starting from cell C_1', and then eliminate the top track (see Exercise 1 of this section).

From the above sketch, we have obtained the following theorem.

Theorem 4.11 *(a) Every function that is computed by a two-way infinite one-tape DTM is Turing-computable.*

(b) Every language that is accepted by a two-way infinite one-tape DTM is Turing-acceptable.

Next, we extend Turing machines to multi-tape DTM's. For each $k \geq 2$, a k-tape DTM is similar to a two-way DTM with the following exceptions:

(1) It has k two-way infinite tapes. Each tape has its own head. All heads are controlled by a common finite control. There are two special tapes, an input tape and an output tape. They hold the input string and the output string, respectively. The head of the input tape can only read and cannot erase or write symbols. (Such a tape is called a *read-only* tape.) The heads of other tapes can read, erase and write symbols. Figure 4.13 shows a three-tape DTM.

(2) In each move, a head in a multi-tape DTM can *stay* (denoted by S) at the same cell, without going to the right or to the left.

The transition function δ of a k-tape DTM is a function mapping $Q \times \Gamma^k$ to $(Q \cup \{h\}) \times \Gamma^k \times \{L, R, S\}^k$. An instruction

$$\delta(q, (a_1, a_2, \ldots, a_k)) = (p, (b_1, b_2, \ldots, b_k), (D_1, D_2, \ldots, D_k)),$$

where $D_i \in \{L, R, S\}$, for $i = 1, \ldots, k$, means that if the control is in state q and the head of the ith tape reads the symbol a_i, for $i = 1, \ldots, k$, then the head of the ith tape will write b_i over a_i, move in the direction D_i, and the control will change to state p.

A configuration of a k-tape DTM is just the state plus k tape configurations, each of the same form as that of a two-way DTM.

A multi-tape DTM can often reduce the work of a one-tape DTM dramatically. The following is an example.

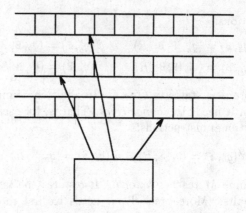

Figure 4.13:   A three-tape DTM.

Example 4.12 *Find a three-tape DTM M that computes the function $f(n,m) = n \cdot m$ on natural numbers n and m.*

Solution. Following the convention of Section 4.2, we assume that initially the tape configuration of the input tape is $1^n B 1^m \underline{B}$, and all other tapes have only blanks. That is, the initial configuration of M may be described as $(s, 1^n B 1^m \underline{B}, \underline{B}, \underline{B})$. We need to construct a DTM M such that the final configuration of tape 3 is $1^{nm} \underline{B}$. The algorithm of M is as follows:

(1) Copy 1^m to tape 2.

(2) For each symbol 1 in tape 2, delete it and copy 1^n from tape 1 to tape 3. When tape 2 is empty, halt with output in tape 3.

In the following, we present the transition function δ of M:

$\delta(s, (B, B, B)) = (q_1, (B, B, B), (L, S, S)),$

$\delta(q_1, (1, B, B)) = (q_1, (1, 1, B), (L, R, S)), \quad \delta(q_1, (B, B, B)) = (q_2, (B, B, B), (S, L, S)),$

$\delta(q_2, (B, 1, B)) = (q_3, (B, B, B), (L, S, S)), \quad \delta(q_2, (B, B, B)) = (h, (B, B, B), (S, S, S)),$

$\delta(q_3, (1, B, B)) = (q_3, (1, B, 1), (L, S, R)), \quad \delta(q_3, (B, B, B)) = (q_4, (B, B, B), (R, S, S)),$

$\delta(q_4, (1, B, B)) = (q_4, (1, B, B), (R, S, S)), \quad \delta(q_4, (B, B, B)) = (q_2, (B, B, B), (S, L, S)).$

We show its computation on input $(2, 3)$ as follows:

$(s, 11B111\underline{B}, \underline{B}, \underline{B}) \vdash (q_1, 11B11\underline{1}, \underline{B}, \underline{B}) \vdash (q_1, 11B1\underline{1}1, 1\underline{B}, \underline{B})$

$\quad \overset{*}{\vdash} (q_1, 11\underline{B}111, 111\underline{B}, \underline{B}) \vdash (q_2, 11\underline{B}111, 11\underline{1}, \underline{B}) \vdash (q_3, 1\underline{1}B111, 11\underline{B}, \underline{B})$

$\quad \vdash (q_3, \underline{1}1B111, 11\underline{B}, 1\underline{B}) \vdash (q_3, \underline{B}11B111, 11\underline{B}, 11\underline{B}) \vdash (q_4, \underline{1}1B111, 11\underline{B}, 11\underline{B})$

$\quad \overset{*}{\vdash} (q_4, 11\underline{B}111, 11\underline{B}, 11\underline{B}) \vdash (q_2, 11\underline{B}111, 1\underline{1}, 11\underline{B}) \overset{*}{\vdash} (q_2, 11\underline{B}111, \underline{1}, 1111\underline{B})$

$\quad \overset{*}{\vdash} (q_2, 11\underline{B}111, \underline{B}, 111111\underline{B}) \vdash (h, 11\underline{B}111, \underline{B}, 111111\underline{B}).$

We remark that the total number of moves by the above multi-tape DTM M to compute $n \cdot m$ is $O(nm)$, whereas a one-tape DTM using the same algorithm would take $O(m^2 n)$ moves.   □

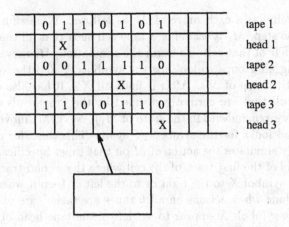

Figure 4.14: The TM M_1.

Next, we present a simulation of a multi-tape DTM by a two-way DTM.

Theorem 4.13 *Every function computed by a multi-tape DTM is Turing-computable.*

Proof. Assume that M is a k-tape DTM, where $k \geq 2$. We are going to describe how to construct a two-way one-tape DTM M_1 to simulate M. Suppose that the tape symbol set of M is Γ. Then we use the tape symbol set $\Gamma_1 = (\Gamma \times \{X, \mathtt{B}\})^k \cup \Sigma$ for M_1, where X is a symbol not in Γ. This means that we divide the single tape of M_1 into $2k$ tracks which form k groups. Each group contains two tracks: one uses the tape symbol set Γ, the other uses the tape symbol set $\{X, \mathtt{B}\}$. Thus, the *blank* symbol in Γ_1 is

$$\widetilde{\mathtt{B}} = \underbrace{[\mathtt{B}, \ldots, \mathtt{B}]}_{2k}.$$

Each group records the information about a tape of M, with the symbol X in the second track indicating the position of the tape head, and the first track containing the corresponding symbols in that tape of M. For instance, Figure 4.14 shows the machine M_1 that simulates a three-tape TM M. Its tape contains the information of the following tape configuration of M:

$$(0\underline{1}10101, 0011\underline{1}10, 110011\underline{0}).$$

Initially, we assume that the input is stored in the single-track form:

$$(s, x_1 x_2 \cdots x_n \widetilde{\mathtt{B}}),$$

where each x_i, $1 \leq i \leq n$, is a symbol in Σ. Machine M_1 first sets up the tape into the $2k$-track form to get the initial configuration

$$(s', [x_1, \mathtt{B}, \ldots, \mathtt{B}] [x_2, \mathtt{B}, \ldots, \mathtt{B}] \cdots [x_n, \mathtt{B}, \ldots, \mathtt{B}] [\mathtt{B}, X, \mathtt{B}, X, \ldots, \mathtt{B}, X] \underline{[\mathtt{B}, \ldots, \mathtt{B}]}).$$

Then, M_1 simulates each move of M as follows: We assume that after each simulation step, M_1 is scanning a tape cell such that all the symbols X appear to the left of that cell. To begin the simulation, M_1 moves from right to left scanning all groups to look for the symbols X and the symbols in Γ that appear at the top of X's. After it finds all X's, it has also collected all the tape symbols that are currently scanned by the tape heads of M (these tape symbols are *remembered* in the state of M_1). Next, M_1 moves back from left to right and looks for the symbols X again. This time, for each symbol X, M_1 properly simulates the action of M on that tape. Specifically, it writes over the symbol of the first track of the cell where the second track has an X, and moves the symbol X to the right or to the left or keep it where it is. The simulation is done when actions on all k tapes are taken care of. Note that, by then, all the symbols X appear to the left of the tape head of M_1.

At the end, when M reaches a halting configuration, M_1 erases all symbols in all groups except the output group, converts the tape into a single track form with outputs only, and leaves its head scanning the cell which contains X in the second track of the output group.

In the following, we present a more detailed description of how machine M_1 simulates one move of M. The rest of the machine M_1 is left as an exercise.

Assume that $M = (Q, \Sigma, \Gamma, \delta, s)$ is a three-tape DTM. Also assume that M_1 has already set up the tape in the six-track form, and that its tape head is scanning a cell to the right of all symbols X. We divide the simulation of one move of M into two stages. In the first stage, M_1 moves from right to left to collect the tape symbols currently scanned by M. In the second stage, M_1 moves from left to right to simulate the writing and moving of the tape heads of M. In the first stage, M_1 will use the following set of states:

$$\{ q_{x,y,z} \mid q \in Q, x, y, z \in \Gamma \cup \{?\} \},$$

where ? is a symbol not in Γ. A subscript $x \in \Gamma$ indicates that the tape symbol x has been collected, and the subscript ? indicates that this tape symbol is still unknown. For instance, $q_{?b?}$ denotes that M is currently in state q, and its second tape head is reading symbol b, and M_1 is yet to find out what the other two tape heads are reading.

The instructions of M_1 for the first stage can be described as follows, beginning with state $q_{???}$. (In the following, unless otherwise specified, each instruction applies to all $x, y, z \in \Gamma \cup \{?\}$ and all $a, b, c \in \Gamma$.)

$$\delta_1(q_{xyz}, [a, \mathsf{B}, b, \mathsf{B}, c, \mathsf{B}]) = (q_{xyz}, [a, \mathsf{B}, b, \mathsf{B}, c, \mathsf{B}], L)$$
$$\text{if } x =? \text{ or } y =? \text{ or } z =?,$$
$$\delta_1(q_{?yz}, [a, X, b, \mathsf{B}, c, \mathsf{B}]) = (q_{ayz}, [a, X, b, \mathsf{B}, c, \mathsf{B}], L),$$
$$\delta_1(q_{x?z}, [a, \mathsf{B}, b, X, c, \mathsf{B}]) = (q_{xbz}, [a, \mathsf{B}, b, X, c, \mathsf{B}], L),$$
$$\delta_1(q_{xy?}, [a, \mathsf{B}, b, \mathsf{B}, c, X]) = (q_{xyc}, [a, \mathsf{B}, b, \mathsf{B}, c, X], L),$$
$$\delta_1(q_{??z}, [a, X, b, X, c, \mathsf{B}]) = (q_{abz}, [a, X, b, X, c, \mathsf{B}], L),$$

$$\delta_1(q_{?y?}, [a, X, b, \mathsf{B}, c, X]) = (q_{ayc}, [a, X, b, \mathsf{B}, c, X], L),$$
$$\delta_1(q_{x??}, [a, \mathsf{B}, b, X, c, X]) = (q_{xbc}, [a, \mathsf{B}, b, X, c, X], L),$$
$$\delta_1(q_{???}, [a, X, b, X, c, X]) = (q_{abc}, [a, X, b, X, c, X], L).$$

The first stage is done when M_1 reaches a state q_{abc}, with $a, b, c \in \Gamma$. For the second stage, M_1 will use the following set of states:

$$\{q_{xyz} \mid q \in Q, x \in \{a, \bar{a}, \tilde{a}\}, y \in \{b, \bar{b}, \tilde{b}\}, z \in \{c, \bar{c}, \tilde{c}\}, a, b, c \in \Gamma\}.$$

It begins with q_{abc} and ends with $q_{\tilde{a}\tilde{b}\tilde{c}}$ if the instruction of M to be simulated is of the form:

$$\delta(q, (a, b, c)) = (p, (a', b', c'), (D_1, D_2, D_3)). \tag{4.1}$$

Here, we only present a more specific example. Instructions for other cases can be constructed in a similar way.

Assume that M_1 is in state q_{abc}, with $a, b, c \in \Gamma$, and is to simulate the instruction (4.1), with $D_1 = R$, $D_2 = D_3 = L$. In addition, assume that the relative positions of the three X's in tracks 2, 4, and 6 of the tape of M_1 are like those shown in Figure 4.14; that is, the symbol X in track 2 occurs to the left of the symbol X in track 4, and the symbol X in track 4 occurs to the left of the symbol X in track 6. For this type of tape configurations, M_1 has the following instructions. (The following instructions apply to all $u, v, w \in \Gamma$ and all $t_1, t_2, t_3 \in \{\mathsf{B}, X\}$.)

$$\delta_1(q_{abc}, [u, \mathsf{B}, v, \mathsf{B}, w, \mathsf{B}]) = (q_{abc}, [u, \mathsf{B}, v, \mathsf{B}, w, \mathsf{B}], R),$$
$$\delta_1(q_{abc}, [a, X, v, \mathsf{B}, w, \mathsf{B}]) = (q_{abc}, [a', \mathsf{B}, v, \mathsf{B}, w, \mathsf{B}], R),$$
$$\delta_1(q_{\bar{a}bc}, [u, \mathsf{B}, v, t_2, w, t_3]) = (q_{\bar{a}bc}, [u, X, v, t_1, w, t_2], L),$$
$$\delta_1(q_{\bar{a}bc}, [u, t_1, v, \mathsf{B}, w, \mathsf{B}]) = (q_{\bar{a}bc}, [u, t_1, v, \mathsf{B}, w, \mathsf{B}], R),$$
$$\delta_1(q_{\bar{a}bc}, [u, t_1, b, X, w, \mathsf{B}]) = (q_{\bar{a}\bar{b}c}, [u, t_1, b', \mathsf{B}, w, \mathsf{B}], L),$$
$$\delta_1(q_{\bar{a}\bar{b}c}, [u, t_1, v, \mathsf{B}, w, \mathsf{B}]) = (q_{\bar{a}\bar{b}c}, [u, t_1, v, X, w, \mathsf{B}], R),$$
$$\delta_1(q_{\bar{a}\bar{b}c}, [u, t_1, v, t_2, w, \mathsf{B}]) = (q_{\bar{a}\bar{b}c}, [u, t_1, v, t_2, w, \mathsf{B}], R),$$
$$\delta_1(q_{\bar{a}\bar{b}c}, [u, t_1, v, t_2, c, X]) = (q_{\bar{a}\bar{b}\bar{c}}, [u, t_1, v, t_2, c', \mathsf{B}], L),$$
$$\delta_1(q_{\bar{a}\bar{b}\bar{c}}, [u, t_1, v, t_2, w, \mathsf{B}]) = (q_{\bar{a}\bar{b}\bar{c}}, [u, t_1, v, t_2, w, X], R),$$
$$\delta_1(q_{\bar{a}\bar{b}\bar{c}}, [u, t_1, v, t_2, w, t_3]) = (p_{???}, [u, t_1, v, t_2, w, t_3], R). \qquad \square$$

A multi-tape DTM can have any large number of tapes, but the number k of tapes has to be a constant independent of the input size. What happens if we allow an arbitrarily large number k of tapes, without a predefined bound on k? This new type of machine is, then, more powerful than one-tape DTM's. In fact, such machines can accept any language.

Let us define such a machine more precisely: An *infinite-tape* DTM $M = (Q, \Sigma, \Gamma, \delta, s)$ has finitely many states and infinitely many tapes. Its transition function δ is a function from $Q \times \Gamma^+$ to $(Q \cup \{h\}) \times \Gamma^+ \times \{L, R, S\}^+$. An instruction of the form

$$\delta(q, a_1 a_2 \cdots a_k) = (p, b_1 b_2 \cdots b_m, D_1 D_2 \cdots D_n)$$

means that if M is in state q, and the tape heads of the first k tapes are reading symbols a_1, a_2, $\cdots$, a_k, respectively, and the other tape heads are reading B, then M changes the state to p, replaces the symbols scanned by the first m tape heads by b_1, b_2, $\cdots$, b_m, respectively, and moves the first n tape heads in the directions D_1, D_2, $\cdots$, D_n, respectively.

Example 4.14 *Prove that for any language $A \subseteq (0+1)^*$, there is an infinite-tape DTM M that accepts L.*

Proof. We note that the domain of the transition function δ is infinite; that is, δ may contain an infinite number of instructions. Thus, we can simply use one set of instructions to deal with one particular input. First, we copy the ith symbol x_i of input to the $(|x| - i + 2)$nd tape. Then, in a single move, we read all symbols of the input and decide to accept it or not. More precisely, the transition function δ for the machine M for A is defined as follows:

$$\delta(s, B) = (p, B, L),$$
$$\delta(p, a_1 \cdots a_k) = (p, Ba_1 \cdots a_k, L), \quad \text{for all } a_1, \ldots, a_k \in \Sigma,$$
$$\delta(p, Ba_1 \cdots a_k) = (h, B^{k+1}, S), \quad \text{if } a_k \cdots a_2 a_1 \in A,$$

where p is a state other than the initial state s and the final state h.   □

Exercises 4.3

1. Describe the details of the last part of the one-tape DTM M' of Theorem 4.11 which simulates a two-way DTM M. That is, show the instructions of M' that restore the output from the two-track form to the one-track form. For instance, it should change the tape configuration

   to the configuration BaBabbabB, and change the tape configuration

   to the configuration BabbB.

2. Describe the details of a simulation step of the two-way DTM M_1 of Theorem 4.13 that simulates a three-tape DTM M. That is, show the instructions of M_1 that move the head to left to collect the tape information of M and then move right to execute an instruction of M from this information.

3. Given a two-way infinite one-tape DTM M with $\Sigma = \{1\}$ and $\Gamma = \{0, 1, \mathbf{B}\}$, construct a multi-tape DTM M' that, on input $(1^n, 1^k)$, simulates M on input 1^n for at most k moves so that it halts if and only if M halts on input 1^n within k moves.

4. Construct multi-tape DTM's to accept the following languages. For each language, discuss how much time your machine saves over a one-tape DTM using the same algorithm.

   (a) $\{w \in \{a, b\}^* \mid w = w^R\}$.

   (b) $\{(x_1, x_2) \mid x_1, x_2 \in \{a, b\}^*, x_1 \text{ is a substring of } x_2\}$.

   (c) $\{a^n b^n c^n \mid n \geq 0\}$.

   (d) $\{a^m b^n c^k \mid m, n, k \geq 0, m \neq n \text{ or } n \neq k \text{ or } k \neq m\}$.

   (e) $\{w \in \{a, b, c\}^* \mid \#_a(w) = \#_b(w) = \#_c(w)\}$.

5. Construct multi-tape DTM's to compute the following functions. For each function, discuss how much time your machine saves over a one-tape DTM using the same algorithm.

   (a) $f(x) = x^R$ on strings $x \in \{a, b\}^*$.

   (b) $f(m, n) = n^m$ on natural numbers m, n.

   (c) $f(n_1, n_2, \ldots, n_k) = \max\{n_1, n_2, \ldots, n_k\}$ over positive integers $n_1, \ldots, n_k$, where k is not fixed.

   (d) $f(n_1, n_2, \ldots, n_k) = $ the maximum number of occurrences of a positive integer in $(n_1, \ldots, n_k)$, where k is not fixed. (E.g., $f(3, 5, 3, 6, 7) = 2$ and $f(3, 6, 3, 6, 6, 5, 6) = 4$.

   (e) $sort(n_1, n_2, \ldots, n_k) = $ the list $(n_1, \ldots, n_k)$ sorted in the increasing order, where $n_1, \ldots, n_k$ are positive integers and k is not fixed.

6. A two-dimensional DTM M is a TM whose "tape" is a two-dimensional plane divided into infinitely many cells (see Figure 4.15). A two-dimensional DTM M operates in a way similar to a two-way DTM except that in each move, it can move its head *up* (U), *down* (D), left (L), right (R) or stay (S). Initially, the input is stored in a horizontal row and the head is scanning the blank cell to its right. When it halts, the output is also stored in a horizontal row (but not necessarily the same row as the input) with the head pointing to the blank cell to its right. All other symbols not on this row are ignored.

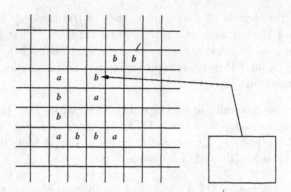

Figure 4.15: A two-dimensional DTM.

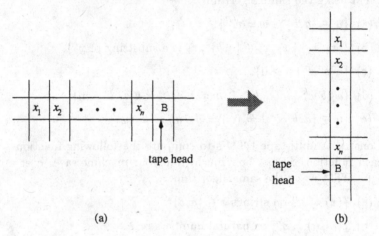

(a)   (b)

Figure 4.16: Configuration change of Exercise 6(b).

(a) Describe how to represent the machine configuration of a two-dimensional DTM. Use this notation to formally define the notion of a function computed by a two-dimensional DTM.

(b) Design a two-dimensional DTM to change from its initial tape configuration (a) to a new configuration (b), as shown in Figure 4.16.

(c) Show that a two-dimensional DTM can be simulated by a multi-tape DTM. Therefore, all functions computed by two-dimensional DTM's are Turing-computable.

7. We say that a pushdown automaton is *deterministic* if for any configuration, at most one instruction can be applied. Show that every deterministic pushdown automaton can be simulated by a two-tape DTM. (We will show in Section 4.7 that all context-free languages are Turing-acceptable.)

4.4 Church-Turing Thesis

From the equivalence results of the last section, it is plausible to conjecture that any other reasonable modifications of the Turing machine model will not change the computational power of Turing machines: In fact, it is commonly believed that almost all reasonable computational models can be simulated by multi-tape DTM's. For instance, consider *Random Access Machines* (RAM's) which are close to our real-world digital computers.

A RAM contains a read-only input tape, a write-only output tape and an infinite number of *registers*, named $R_0, R_1, \ldots$. Each cell of the tapes and each register can store a nonnegative integer of an arbitrary size. The control unit of the RAM can perform the following operations on integers stored in its registers: *read, write, add, subtract, multiply, divide, copy,* and *compare*. In addition, it can access a constant integer or to perform these operations by the indirect addressing scheme. For instance, in a program of an RAM, one may use an instruction like $\text{ADD}(5, R_3, R_{21}^*)$, in which integer 5 means using the constant 5 as the first operand, R_3 means using the content of register R_3 as the second operand, and R_{21}^* means to store the sum of constant 5 and the value v_3 in register R_3 in the register $R_{v_{21}}$ where v_{21} is the current content of R_{21} (thus, an indirect addressing is used here). It is not too hard to show how a multi-tape DTM can simulate a RAM. We now give a sketch.

First, we require that when a RAM begins the computation, all registers contain value zero. Thus, at any time during computation, a RAM has at most a finite number of nonzero registers. A multi-tape DTM can reserve one of its tapes, say tape 2, to simulate the contents of all nonzero registers. For instance, the following tape configuration represents the configuration of the RAM in which registers R_i has the values v_i, for $i = 0, 1, \ldots, m$, and all registers R_j, with $j > m$, have value 0:

$$\cdots \text{BB\$B}1^{v_0}\text{B}1^{v_1}\text{B}1^{v_2}\text{B}\cdots\text{B}1^{v_m}\text{BBB}\cdots$$

From this tape information, it is easy to find the content of register R_i: it is equal to the number of 1's between the $(i+1)$st and the $(i+2)$nd blank symbols B to the right of the special marker \$. Thus, to simulate an instruction of the RAM, for instance, $\text{ADD}(5, R_3, R_{21}^*)$, a multi-tape DTM first writes 5 and the contents of R_3 on tapes 3 and 4, respectively, and then adds them and puts the sum on tape 5. Next, it searches for the 22nd B in tape 2 to get v_{21} and puts it in tape 6. Then, it searches for the $(v_{21} + 1)$st B in tape 2 and replaces the following block of 1's by the block of 1's in tape 5. Note that if the sum is different from the original value in $R_{v_{21}}$, we need to move the rest of the contents of $R_{v_{21}+1}, \ldots, R_m$ to the right or to the left. This is similar to the function $insert^k$ of Exercise 4(c) of Section 4.2.

Historically, a number of different types of computational models have been proposed and studied. It turns out that almost all of them have been found to have the same computational power as Turing machines, in the sense that the class of computable functions defined by each proposed model is exactly the same as the class of Turing-computable functions. In general, we may call a computational model *reasonable* if it has the following properties:

1. The computation of a machine is given by a finite set of instructions.

2. Each instruction can be carried out in this model in a finite number of steps, or in a finite amount of time.

3. Each instruction can be carried out in this model in a deterministic manner so that the effect of the instruction is predictable.

Suppose a computational model is reasonable. Then, intuitively, we could simulate such a model by a Turing machine. This is called the Church-Turing Thesis.

Church-Turing Thesis. *A function computable in any reasonable computational model is computable by a Turing machine.*

Note that we cannot prove the Church-Turing Thesis as a theorem, as we cannot predict what types of computational devices people may invent and whether these new devices may be more powerful than Turing machines. So, we have to accept (or reject) the Church-Turing Thesis from the empirical studies. Once it is accepted on the empirical ground, however, we find it extremely useful in the theoretical study. Specifically, it provides a fixed computational environment to study the notion of *computable functions*. For instance, when we want to argue that a given function is computable, we do not need to prove this by constructing a Turing machine that computes it. We may simply use an algorithm in a more convenient model to describe how to compute it and rely on the Church-Turing Thesis to convince ourselves that this algorithm can be converted to an equivalent Turing machine. Conversely, if we want to prove that a function is not computable, we prove this in any reasonable model and argue, using the Church-Turing Thesis, that it is actually not computable at all, no matter which computational model is used.

In the above, we have seen that Turing machines can simulate multi-tape Turing machines and RAM's. These simulations provide some evidence for the Church-Turing Thesis. To further demonstrate the plausibility of the Church-Turing Thesis, we will consider, in the rest of this chapter, two other notions of computability based on machineries of very different natures and show that they are equivalent to the notion of Turing-computability.

Exercises 4.4

1. We present RAM's in more detail. A RAM is defined by a list of *instructions*, numbered from 1 to n. An instruction is of one of the types shown in Figure 4.17. (*Note*: We only list the instructions in the form of using direct addressing. As discussed in the text, they can also use constants or indirect addressing.) Initially, all registers of a RAM contain

Instruction	Meaning
READ(R_i)	read the next input integer into R_i
WRITE(R_i)	write $c(R_i)$ on the output tape
COPY(R_i, R_j)	write $c(R_i)$ to R_j
ADD(R_i, R_j, R_k)	write $c(R_i) + c(R_j)$ to R_k
SUB(R_i, R_j, R_k)	write $c(R_i) - c(R_j)$ to R_k
MULT(R_i, R_j, R_k)	write $c(R_i) \cdot c(R_j)$ to R_k
DIV(R_i, R_j, R_k)	write $\lfloor c(R_i)/c(R_j) \rfloor$ to R_k (write 0 if $c(R_j) = 0$)
GOTO(j)	go to the instruction j
IF-THEN(R_i, j)	if $c(R_i) \geq 0$ then go to the instruction j

Figure 4.17: Instructions of a RAM.

value 0, the output tape is "empty" (indicated by a special symbol, e.g., B), and the input tape contains a finite number of nonnegative integers $(n_1, \ldots, n_k)$, stored in cells 1 to k, and cell $k + 1$ is empty. The RAM begins with instruction 1 and, after finishing each instruction i, it goes to instruction $i + 1$ if instruction i is one of the first seven types, or it goes to the instruction j as defined in instruction i if instruction i is one of the last two types. The RAM halts when it reaches an instruction $k > n$.

For any RAM M, we let $L(M) = \{(n_1, \ldots, n_k) \mid M$ halts on input $(n_1, \ldots, n_k)\}$. We say M computes a function $f : \bigcup_{k=1}^{\infty} \mathbf{N}^k \to \bigcup_{k=1}^{\infty} \mathbf{N}^k$ if, on input $(n_1, \ldots, n_k)$, M halts with outputs $(m_1, \ldots, m_\ell) = f(n_1, \ldots, n_k)$.

(a) Design a RAM that computes the function *sort* of Exercise 5(e) of Section 4.3.

(b) Show the details of a multi-tape DTM that simulates the instruction ADD($5, R_3, R_{21}^*$) of a RAM.

(c) Show that every Turing-computable partial function $f : \mathbf{N}^k \to \mathbf{N}$, as defined in Section 4.2, is computable by a RAM.

4.5 Unrestricted Grammars

In this section, we extend context-free grammars to *unrestricted grammars*. An unrestricted grammar is like a context-free grammar, except that the left-hand side of a production rule is not restricted to a single nonterminal symbol, but could be any nonempty string formed by terminal or nonterminal symbols. That is, an *unrestricted grammar* (or, simply, a *grammar*) is a quadruple (V, Σ, R, S), where V is a finite set of nonterminal symbols, Σ is a finite set of terminal symbols, with $\Sigma \cap V = \emptyset$, $S \in V$ is the starting symbol, and R is a finite set of production rules each of the form

$$x \longrightarrow y$$

for some $x \in (V \cup \Sigma)^+$ and $y \in (V \cup \Sigma)^*$.

The notion of derivations $x \underset{G}{\Rightarrow} y$ and $x \underset{G}{\overset{*}{\Rightarrow}} y$ is the same as that of a context-free grammar G. Namely, for $x \in (V \cup \Sigma)^+$ and $y \in (V \cup \Sigma)^*$, we write $x \underset{G}{\Rightarrow} y$ if $x = uwv$, $y = uzv$ for some $u, v \in (V \cup \Sigma)^*$ and some rule $w \to z$ in R. For $x \in (V \cup \Sigma)^+$ and $y \in (V \cup \Sigma)^*$, we write $x \underset{G}{\overset{*}{\Rightarrow}} y$ if there exists a sequence of strings $x_0, x_1, \ldots, x_n \in (V \cup \Sigma)^*$ such that $x = x_0$, $y = x_n$, and $x_i \underset{G}{\Rightarrow} x_{i+1}$ for $i = 0, 1, \ldots, n-1$. When the grammar G is understood, we may write $x \Rightarrow y$ and $x \overset{*}{\Rightarrow} y$ for $x \underset{G}{\Rightarrow} y$ and $x \underset{G}{\overset{*}{\Rightarrow}} y$, respectively. We say a grammar G generates a string $w \in \Sigma^*$ if $S \underset{G}{\overset{*}{\Rightarrow}} w$. We let $L(G) = \{ w \in \Sigma^* \mid S \underset{G}{\overset{*}{\Rightarrow}} w \}$.

It is obvious that every context-free language can be generated by an unrestricted grammar, since context-free grammars are just special cases of unrestricted grammars. In general, unrestricted grammars can generate languages that are not context-free.

Example 4.15 *Find a grammar G such that $L(G) = \{ a^n b^n c^n \mid n \geq 0 \}$.*

Solution. The grammar G has nonterminals S, B, C, and the following rules:

$$
\begin{aligned}
S &\longrightarrow aSBC \mid \varepsilon, & CB &\longrightarrow BC, \\
aB &\longrightarrow ab, & bB &\longrightarrow bb, \\
bC &\longrightarrow bc, & cC &\longrightarrow cc.
\end{aligned}
$$

How does G generate $a^n b^n c^n$? It consists of three steps. First, it applies the first rule n times and the rule $S \to \varepsilon$ once to get a string $a^n (BC)^n$. Second, it applies the rule $CB \to BC$ for $n(n-1)/2$ times to move all B's to the left of all C's to get a string $a^n B^n C^n$. Finally, it uses the last four rules to change every B to b and every C to c. The following is the derivation of string $a^3 b^3 c^3$. We underline the substring of a sentential form that is to be replaced in the next step.

$$
\begin{aligned}
\underline{S} &\Rightarrow a\underline{S}BC \Rightarrow aa\underline{S}BCBC \Rightarrow aaa\underline{S}BCBCBC \Rightarrow aaaB\underline{CB}CBC \\
&\Rightarrow aaaBB\underline{CB}CC \Rightarrow aaaBB\underline{CB}CC \Rightarrow aaa\underline{aB}BBCCC \\
&\Rightarrow aaab\underline{B}BCCC \overset{*}{\Rightarrow} aaabbb\underline{C}CC \Rightarrow aaabbb\underline{cC}CC \overset{*}{\Rightarrow} aaabbbccc.
\end{aligned}
$$

Why don't we use the simpler rules $B \to b$ and $C \to c$ for the third step? That is because we do not want to let the grammar skip the second step and change all symbols B and C to b and c without first moving B's to the left of C's. Note that, using our grammar G, we are not able to change any B to b before moving it to the left of all C's. Thus, the grammar G does not generate any string not of the form $a^n b^n c^n$. □

Example 4.16 *Find a grammar G such that $L(G) = \{a^{2^n} \mid n \geq 0\}$.*

Solution. The grammar G has $V = \{S, L, L_h, R, [,]\}$ and rules

$$S \longrightarrow [\,Ra\,] \mid a,$$
$$Ra \longrightarrow aaR, \qquad\qquad R] \longrightarrow L] \mid L_h,$$
$$aL \longrightarrow La, \qquad\qquad [\,L \longrightarrow [\,R,$$
$$aL_h \longrightarrow L_h a, \qquad\qquad [\,L_h \longrightarrow \varepsilon.$$

The main idea of the grammar G is to use a loop to generate a sentential form $[Ra^{2^{k+1}}]$ from $[Ra^{2^k}]$. To do this, it first applies the second rule $Ra \to aaR$ to *move* the symbol R to the right and change, along the way, each a to aa. When R reaches the right end mark $]$, it changes to symbol L and moves back to the left end to get $[La^{2^{k+1}}]$ and then $[Ra^{2^{k+1}}]$. To get out of the loop, the symbol R may change to L_h instead of L when it meets the right end mark $]$. Then, the symbol L_h moves left to cancel off with the left end mark $[$. For instance, G generates $aaaa$ as follows:

$$\underline{S} \;\Rightarrow\; [\,\underline{Ra}\,] \;\Rightarrow\; [\,aa\underline{R}\,] \;\Rightarrow\; [\,a\underline{a}L\,] \;\overset{*}{\Rightarrow}\; [\,\underline{L}aa\,] \;\Rightarrow\; [\,\underline{R}aa\,]$$
$$\Rightarrow\; [\,aa\underline{Ra}\,] \;\Rightarrow\; [\,aaaa\underline{R}\,] \;\Rightarrow\; [\,aaaa\underline{L_h}\;\overset{*}{\Rightarrow}\;[\underline{L_h}aaaa \;\Rightarrow\; aaaa.$$

We note that, during an iteration of the loop, the nonterminal symbol R *cannot* move left until it meets $]$, and the nonterminal symbol L *cannot* change to R until it meets $[$. Therefore, each iteration of the loop has to double the number of a's. This shows that G cannot generate strings a^k if k is not a power of 2. □

Example 4.17 *Find a grammar G such that $L(G) = \{ww \mid w \in \{a, b\}^*\}$.*

Solution. The grammar G has $V = \{S, T, A, B, R, L_a, L_b, [,]\}$ and rules

$$S \longrightarrow T\,], \qquad\qquad T \longrightarrow aTA \mid bTB \mid [\,R,$$
$$RA \longrightarrow AR, \qquad\qquad RB \longrightarrow BR,$$
$$AR] \longrightarrow L_a\,], \qquad\qquad BR] \longrightarrow L_b\,],$$
$$AL_a \longrightarrow L_a A, \qquad\qquad AL_b \longrightarrow L_b A,$$
$$BL_a \longrightarrow L_a B, \qquad\qquad BL_b \longrightarrow L_b B,$$
$$[\,L_a \longrightarrow a\,[\,R, \qquad\qquad [\,L_b \longrightarrow b\,[\,R,$$
$$[\,R] \longrightarrow \varepsilon.$$

This grammar uses the same idea of moving a symbol R, L_a or L_b around to change the sentential forms. First, it uses the first two rules to get $S \overset{*}{\Rightarrow}$

$w\,[\,R\tilde{w}^R\,]$, where $\tilde{w}$ is the string w with symbol a replaced by A and symbol b replaced by B. Next, it uses symbol L_a or L_b to *carry* a terminal symbol a or b, respectively, to the left and put it to the left of the left-end mark $[$. This process reverses $\tilde{w}^R$ to w. The following is the derivation of *aabaaaba*:

$$S \Rightarrow \underline{T}\,] \overset{*}{\Rightarrow} aaba\underline{T}ABAA\,] \Rightarrow aaba\,[\,\underline{RAB}AA\,] \overset{*}{\Rightarrow} aaba\,[\,ABA\underline{AR}\,]$$

$$\Rightarrow aaba\,[\,AB\underline{AL_a}\,] \overset{*}{\Rightarrow} aaba\,[\,\underline{L_a}ABA\,] \Rightarrow aabaa\,[\,\underline{RAB}A\,]$$

$$\overset{*}{\Rightarrow} aabaa\,[\,AB\underline{AR}\,] \Rightarrow aabaa\,[\,AB\underline{L_a}\,] \overset{*}{\Rightarrow} aabaa\,[\,\underline{L_a}AB\,]$$

$$\Rightarrow aabaaa\,[\,\underline{RAB}\,] \overset{*}{\Rightarrow} aabaaaba\,[\,\underline{R}\,] \Rightarrow aabaaaba.$$

Again, it is easy to see that G cannot generate strings not of the form ww because each nonterminal has its fixed role and can only move around as designed.   □

Using the technique of carrying terminal symbols by nonterminals L or R, a grammar can essentially work like a DTM, with the symbols L and R playing the role of the tape head. The following example further demonstrates this technique.

★ **Example 4.18** *Find a grammar G such that $L(G) = \{a^n b^m c^{nm} \mid n, m \geq 0\}$.*

Solution. Grammar G has $V = \{S, A, B, \bar{b}, L, L_b, R, R_b, R_c, [\,,]\,\}$ and rules

$$
\begin{array}{lll}
S \longrightarrow [A], & A \longrightarrow aA \mid B, & B \longrightarrow bB \mid L, \\
aL \longrightarrow La, & bL \longrightarrow Lb, & \bar{b}L \longrightarrow Lb, \\
{[La} \longrightarrow a\,[R_b, & {[Lb} \longrightarrow bR, & {[L]} \longrightarrow \varepsilon, \\
R_b a \longrightarrow aR_b, & R_b b \longrightarrow \bar{b}R_c, & R_b\,] \longrightarrow L], \\
R_c b \longrightarrow bR_c, & R_c\,] \longrightarrow L_b\,]c, & \\
bL_b \longrightarrow L_b b, & \bar{b}L_b \longrightarrow \bar{b}R_b, & \\
Rb \longrightarrow bR, & R] \longrightarrow \varepsilon. &
\end{array}
$$

The grammar G generates $a^n b^m c^{nm}$ with a double loop structure. The inner loop uses symbols R_b, R_c and L_b to copy b^m to c^m, and the outer loop uses L to move each a to the left of the marker $[$ to control the number of times the inner loop is executed. One iteration of the outer loop is as follows:

$$a^k\,[La^{n-k}b^m]\,c^{km} \Rightarrow a^{k+1}[R_b a^{n-k-1}b^m]c^{km} \overset{*}{\Rightarrow} a^{k+1}[a^{n-k-1}R_b b^m]c^{km}$$

$$\Rightarrow a^{k+1}[a^{n-k-1}\bar{b}R_c b^{m-1}]c^{km} \overset{*}{\Rightarrow} a^{k+1}[a^{n-k-1}\bar{b}b^{m-1}R_c]c^{km}$$

$$\Rightarrow a^{k+1}[a^{n-k-1}\bar{b}b^{m-1}L_b]c^{km+1} \overset{*}{\Rightarrow} a^{k+1}[a^{n-k-1}\bar{b}L_b b^{m-1}]c^{km+1}$$

$$\Rightarrow a^{k+1}[a^{n-k-1}\bar{b}R_b b^{m-1}]c^{km+1} \overset{*}{\Rightarrow} a^{k+1}[a^{n-k-1}\bar{b}^m R_b]c^{(k+1)m}$$

$$\Rightarrow a^{k+1}[a^{n-k-1}\bar{b}^m L]c^{(k+1)m} \overset{*}{\Rightarrow} a^{k+1}[La^{n-k-1}b^m]c^{(k+1)m}.$$

The following is the complete derivation of $a^2 b^3 c^6$:

$$S \;\Rightarrow\; [A] \;\overset{*}{\Rightarrow}\; [aaA] \;\Rightarrow\; [aaB] \;\overset{*}{\Rightarrow}\; [aabbbB] \;\Rightarrow\; [aabbbL]$$
$$\overset{*}{\Rightarrow}\; [Laabbb] \;\Rightarrow\; a[R_b abbb] \;\Rightarrow\; a[aR_b bbb] \;\Rightarrow\; a[a\overline{b}R_c bb]$$
$$\overset{*}{\Rightarrow}\; a[a\overline{b}bbR_c] \;\Rightarrow\; a[a\overline{b}bbL_b]c \;\overset{*}{\Rightarrow}\; a[a\overline{b}L_b bb]c \;\Rightarrow\; a[a\overline{b}R_b bb]c$$
$$\Rightarrow\; a[a\overline{b}\,\overline{b}R_c b]c \;\Rightarrow\; a[a\overline{b}\,\overline{b}bR_c]c \;\Rightarrow\; a[a\overline{b}\,\overline{b}bL_b]cc$$
$$\overset{*}{\Rightarrow}\; a[a\overline{b}\,\overline{b}\,\overline{b}R_c]cc \;\Rightarrow\; a[a\overline{b}\,\overline{b}\,\overline{b}L_b]ccc \;\Rightarrow\; a[a\overline{b}\,\overline{b}\,\overline{b}R_b]ccc$$
$$\Rightarrow\; a[a\overline{b}\,\overline{b}\,\overline{b}L]ccc \;\overset{*}{\Rightarrow}\; a[Labbb]ccc \;\Rightarrow\; aa[R_b bbb]ccc$$
$$\overset{*}{\Rightarrow}\; aa[\overline{b}\,\overline{b}\,\overline{b}R_b]c^6 \;\Rightarrow\; aa[\overline{b}\,\overline{b}\,\overline{b}L]c^6 \;\Rightarrow\; aa[Lbbb]c^6$$
$$\Rightarrow\; aabRbb]c^6 \;\overset{*}{\Rightarrow}\; aabbbR]c^6 \;\Rightarrow\; a^2 b^3 c^6. \qquad\qquad \square$$

We now generalize the idea of the above examples to show that a grammar can *simulate* a DTM.

Theorem 4.19 *For any one-tape DTM $M = (Q, \Sigma, \Gamma, \delta, s)$, there exists a grammar $G_M = (V, \Sigma, R, S)$, with $V = Q \cup (\Gamma - \Sigma) \cup \{[,]\}$, such that for any configurations $(q, x\underline{a}y)$ and $(p, x'\underline{b}y')$, where $p, q \in Q$, $a, b \in \Gamma$, and $x, y, x', y' \in \Gamma^*$,*

$$(q, x\underline{a}y) \;\vdash^*_M\; (p, x'\underline{b}y') \quad \text{if and only if} \quad [xqay] \underset{G_M}{\overset{*}{\Longrightarrow}} [x'pby'].$$

Proof. The idea is to use a word $[xqay] \in (V \cup \Sigma)^*$ to represent a configuration $(q, x\underline{a}y)$ of the machine M, and to use the rules of the grammar G_M to simulate the instructions of TM M. More precisely, we define G_M as follows:

(1) For each instruction $\delta(q, a) = (p, b, L)$, where $b \neq$ **B**, G_M has the rules

$$cqa \longrightarrow pcb, \qquad \text{for all } c \in \Gamma.$$

(2) For each instruction $\delta(q, a) = (p, \mathbf{B}, L)$, G_M has the rules

$$cqad \longrightarrow pcBd, \qquad \text{for all } c, d \in \Gamma,$$

and the rules

$$cqa] \longrightarrow pc], \qquad \text{for all } c \in \Gamma.$$

(3) For each instruction $\delta(q, a) = (p, b, R)$, G_M has the rules

$$qac \longrightarrow bpc, \qquad \text{for all } c \in \Gamma,$$

and the rule

$$qa] \longrightarrow bpB].$$

It is clear that using these rules, we get $[xqay] \Rightarrow [x'pby']$ if and only if $(q, x\underline{a}y) \vdash (p, x'\underline{b}y')$. It follows that $[xqay] \overset{*}{\Rightarrow} [x'pby']$ if and only if $(q, x\underline{a}y) \vdash^* (p, x'\underline{b}y')$. $\qquad\qquad \square$

Theorem 4.20 *If a language $L \subseteq \Sigma^*$ is Turing-acceptable, then $L = L(G)$ for some grammar G.*

Proof. We assume that $L = L(M)$ for some TM M such that M always halts with the empty output. That is, when M halts, its configuration is always of the form $(h, \underline{BB})$ (cf. Exercise 5 of Section 4.2).

Now, we define G to be the grammar that contains all reversals of the rules of G_M (i.e., G contains a rule $v \to u$ if $u \to v$ is a rule in G_M), plus the rules

$$S \longrightarrow [BhB], \qquad sB] \longrightarrow L,$$
$$aL \longrightarrow La, \qquad [BL \longrightarrow \varepsilon,$$

for all $a \in \Sigma$, where L is a new nontermial symbol.

We note that if M accepts a string x, then $[BxsB] \underset{G_M}{\overset{*}{\Longrightarrow}} [BhB]$. Thus, we have

$$S \underset{G}{\Longrightarrow} [BhB] \underset{G}{\overset{*}{\Longrightarrow}} [BxsB] \underset{G}{\Longrightarrow} [BxL \underset{G}{\overset{*}{\Longrightarrow}} [BLx \underset{G}{\Longrightarrow} x.$$

Conversely, if M does not accept x then we cannot have $[BxsB] \underset{G_M}{\overset{*}{\Longrightarrow}} [BhB]$, and so there is no way to generate x in G.   □

Exercises 4.5

1. Consider the grammar G_1 with nonterminals $V = \{S, A, B, C\}$, terminals $\Sigma = \{a, b, c\}$, and rules

$$S \longrightarrow ASBC \mid \varepsilon,$$

$AB \longrightarrow BA,$	$AC \longrightarrow CA,$	$BA \longrightarrow AB,$
$BC \longrightarrow CB,$	$CA \longrightarrow AC,$	$CB \longrightarrow BC,$
$A \longrightarrow a,$	$B \longrightarrow b,$	$C \longrightarrow c.$

(a) Show a derivation of string $ccbaabcba$.

(b) What is $L(G_1)$? Give a brief argument for your answer.

2. Consider the grammar G_2 with nonterminals $V = \{S, A, L, L_h, R, [,]\}$, terminal $\Sigma = \{a\}$ and rules

$S \longrightarrow [ARa] \mid a,$	$RA \longrightarrow AR,$	$Ra \longrightarrow aaR,$
$R] \longrightarrow L] \mid L_h,$	$AL \longrightarrow LA,$	$aL \longrightarrow La,$
$[L \longrightarrow [AR,$	$aL_h \longrightarrow L_h a,$	$AL_h \longrightarrow L_h a,$
$[L_h \longrightarrow \varepsilon.$		

(a) Show a derivation of a^6.

(b) What is $L(G_2)$? Give a brief argument for your answer.

3. Construct grammars for each of the following languages. Also show (i) the derivation of the given string x and (ii) a proof of why your grammar does not generate any string not in the language.

   (a) $\{a^{n^2} \mid n \geq 0\}$, $x = a^9$. [*Hint*: Following the idea of Exercise 2 above, generate, at the kth iteration, a sentential form with k copies of A and $k^2 - k$ copies of a.]

   (b) $\{a^{2^n - n} \mid n \geq 0\}$, $x = a^5$.

   (c) $\{a^{n^2 + n} \mid n \geq 0\}$, $x = a^{11}$.

   (d) $\{a^{n^3 + 2n^2 - 5n + 4} \mid n \geq 0\}$, $x = a^{34}$. [*Hint*: Similar to part (a) above, generate, at the kth iteration, a sentential form with k copies of A, k^2 copies of B, and $k^3 + k^2 - 6k + 4$ copies of a.]

   (e) $\{a^n b^{2^n} a^n \mid n \geq 0\}$, $x = a^3 b^8 a^3$.

   (f) $\{a^n b^n a^n b^n \mid n \geq 0\}$, $x = a^4 b^4 a^4 b^4$.

   (g) $\{wcz \mid w, z \in \{a, b\}^*, w \neq z\}$, $x = aabcaaba$.

   (h) $\{w \in \{a, b, c\}^* \mid \#_a(w) > \#_b(w) > \#_c(w)\}$, $x = cbaabcbaa$.

   (i) $\{w^n \mid w \in \{a, b\}^*, |w| = n\}$, $x = aabaabaab$.

4. (a) Find a grammar G such that $w \overset{*}{\underset{G}{\Longrightarrow}} w^R$ for all $w \in \{a, b\}$.

   (b) Find a grammar G such that, for all $x, y \in \{a, b\}^*$ with $|x| = |y|$, $xy \overset{*}{\underset{G}{\Longrightarrow}} yx$.

5. We consider a new computational model called *Labeled Markov Algorithms* (LMA). An LMA M is defined as a triple (Σ, Γ, P), where Σ is the input alphabet, Γ is a working alphabet with $\Sigma \subseteq \Gamma$, and P is a program, consisting of a finite sequence $r_1, r_2, \ldots, r_n$ of instructions. Each instruction r_i in P is of the form

$$L_i : \alpha \to \beta; \text{ goto } L_j;$$

where $\alpha, \beta \in \Gamma^*$, and j is a positive integer ($\alpha \to \beta$ is called a *production rule* and L_j is called the *next instruction* label). An instruction ($L_i : \alpha \to \beta$; goto L_j;) can be applied to a string $w \in \Gamma^*$ if α is a substring of w. The application of this instruction to w produces a new string x by replacing the leftmost occurrence of α in w by β.

On an input $w \in \Sigma^*$, the LMA M operates as follows: At any time of computation, it maintains a current sentential form w and a current instruction label L_i. Initially, w is the input string and the current instruction label is L_1. At each step, it finds the least integer $k \geq i$, where L_i is the current instruction label, such that instruction r_k is applicable to w. Then, it applies r_k to w to obtain a new sentential form x. It resets w to be x, and resets the current instruction label L to be the the next instruction label of r_k. If no instruction r_k, with $k \geq i$, is applicable to the current sentential form w, then the machine halts with output w. (In particular, if the current instruction label is L_i, with i greater than the number n of instructions in P, then the machine halts.)

For any LMA M, we let $L(M) = \{x \in \Sigma^* \mid M \text{ halts on } x\}$, We say M computes a partial function $f : \Sigma^* \to \Gamma^*$, if M halts on each input $x \in \text{Domain}(f)$ with the final sentential form $w = f(x)$, and M does not halt on any $x \notin \text{Domain}(f)$.

(a) Design an LMA M that computes the function $f(x) = x^R$ for $x \in \{a, b\}^*$.

⋆ (b) Show that every Turing-computable function f is computable by an LMA.

⋆ (c) Show that for any LMA M, $L(M)$ is Turing-acceptable.

⋆ (d) Show that every partial function f computed by an LMA M is Turing-computable.

4.6   Primitive Recursive Functions

In this section, we consider only integer functions $f : \mathbf{N}^k \to \mathbf{N}$, for $k \geq 1$. We will build a class of integer functions from three types of initial functions and two operations on functions.

Initial Functions. The following functions are called initial functions:

1. (Zero function) $\zeta(n) = 0$, for $n \in \mathbf{N}$.

2. (Successor function) $\sigma(n) = n + 1$, for $n \in \mathbf{N}$.

3. (Projection functions) $\pi_i^k(n_1, \cdots, n_k) = n_i$.[1]

Composition: Let m, k be two positive integers. Given functions $g : \mathbf{N}^m \to \mathbf{N}$ and $h_i : \mathbf{N}^k \to \mathbf{N}$ for $i = 1, 2, \cdots, m$, define $f : \mathbf{N}^k \to \mathbf{N}$ by

$$f(n_1, \cdots, n_k) = g(h_1(n_1, \cdots, n_k), \cdots, h_m(n_1, \cdots, n_k)).$$

Function f is called the composition of functions g and $h_1, \ldots, h_m$. We write $g \circ (h_1, \ldots, h_m)$ to denote the function f.

Primitive Recursion: Let $k \geq 0$. Given $g : \mathbf{N}^k \to \mathbf{N}$ and $h : \mathbf{N}^{k+2} \to \mathbf{N}$, (when $k = 0$, g is just a constant), define $f : \mathbf{N}^{k+1} \to \mathbf{N}$ by

$$f(n_1, \cdots, n_k, 0) = g(n_1, \cdots, n_k),$$
$$f(n_1, \cdots, n_k, m + 1) = h(n_1, \cdots, n_k, m, f(n_1, \cdots, n_k, m)), \ m \geq 0.$$

---

[1] A remark about notation: when we write an integer i as a subscript in the function name, such as π_i^k, it means that i is a fixed integer. For instance, the fact that π_i^k are computable by Turing machines for any fixed k and any fixed i, $1 \leq i \leq k$, does not imply *directly* that the function $f^k(n_1, \ldots, n_k, i) = \pi_i^k(n_1, \ldots, n_k)$ is computable by a Turing machine. See also Exercise 2 of this section.

We say f is the function obtained from g and h by the operation of primitive recursion.

The class of *primitive recursive functions* over natural numbers can be defined as follows:

(1) An initial function is a primitive recursive function.

(2) If $g : \mathbf{N}^m \to \mathbf{N}$ and $h_1, \ldots, h_m : \mathbf{N}^k \to \mathbf{N}$ are primitive recursive functions, then $g \circ (h_1, \ldots, h_m)$ is also a primitive recursive function.

(3) If $g : \mathbf{N}^k \to \mathbf{N}$ and $h : \mathbf{N}^{k+2} \to \mathbf{N}$ are primitive recursive functions, then the function f obtained from g and h by primitive recursion is also a primitive recursive function.

(4) No other function is a primitive recursive function.

In other words, a primitive recursive function is a function that can be obtained from the initial functions by a finite number of applications of composition and primitive recursion operations.

Example 4.21 *Show that* $add(m, n) = m + n$ *is primitive recursive.*

Solution. The function add can be defined by

$$add(m, 0) = \pi_1^1(m),$$
$$add(m, n+1) = \sigma(\pi_3^3(m, n, add(m, n))).$$

Thus, add can be obtained from π_1^1 and $\sigma \circ \pi_3^3$ by the operation of primitive recursion, and so it is primitive recursive. □

Example 4.22 *Show that* $mult(m, n) = mn$ *is primitive recursive.*

Solution. The function $mult$ can be defined by

$$mult(m, 0) = \zeta(m),$$
$$mult(m, n+1) = add(\pi_1^3(m, n, mult(m, n)), \pi_3^3(m, n, mult(m, n))).$$

So, $mult$ is primitive recursive, since it can be obtained from ζ and $add \circ (\pi_1^3, \pi_3^3)$ by the operation of primitive recursion. □

Example 4.23 *Show that constant functions* $K_j^k(n_1, \cdots, n_k) = j$, $k, j \geq 1$, *are primitive recursive.*

Solution. Function K_j^k can be defined by

$$K_j^k(n_1, \cdots, n_k) = \underbrace{\sigma(\sigma \cdots (\sigma(\zeta(\pi_1^k(n_1, \cdots, n_k)))) \cdots)}_{j}.$$

(Note that the integer j is a fixed constant here.) □

Example 4.24 *Show that the function minus* $: \mathbf{N}^2 \to \mathbf{N}$, *defined by*

$$minus(m, n) = m \overset{.}{-} n = \begin{cases} 0 & if\, m \le n, \\ m - n & if\, m > n, \end{cases}$$

is primitive recursive.

Solution. It suffices to show that $pred(m) = m \overset{.}{-} 1$ is a primitive recursive function, because *minus* can be defined by

$$minus(m, 0) = \pi_1^1(m),$$
$$minus(m, n + 1) = pred(minus(m, n)).$$

To see that *pred* is primitive recursive, we note that $pred(0) = 0$ and

$$pred(m + 1) = m = \pi_1^2(m, pred(m)). \qquad \square$$

Remark. Note that, in the above, a more formal proof for *minus* should be

$$minus(m, n + 1) = pred(\pi_3^3(m, n, minus(m, n))).$$

For clarity, we omitted the function π_3^3 and used $minus(m, n)$ directly. In general, the projection functions π_i^k allow us to use any input anywhere in the definition of a primitive recursive function, and the constant functions K_j^k allow us to use any constant anywhere we want. So, we can omit these functions and simply write the inputs and constants wherever we need them.

Example 4.25 *Assume that* $f : \mathbf{N} \to \mathbf{N}$ *is primitive recursive. Then, the function* $g : \mathbf{N}^2 \to \mathbf{N}$, *defined by*

$$g(m, n) = f^{(n)}(m) \overset{\text{def}}{=} \underbrace{f(f(\cdots(f(m))\cdots))}_{n},$$

is also primitive recursive.

Solution. We note that

$$\begin{aligned} g(m, 0) &= \pi_1^1(m), \\ g(m, n + 1) &= f(g(m, n)). \end{aligned}$$

So, g is defined from π_1^1 and f using primitive recursion, and hence is primitive recursive. $\qquad \square$

Our goal of this and the next sections is to show that primitive recursive functions are a very rich class of functions. To achieve this goal, we first show that some control mechanisms of certain high-level programming languages are primitive recursive. We first consider some Boolean operations and Boolean relations. We use 1 to represent TRUE and 0 to represent FALSE.

Example 4.26 *Show that the following functions are primitive recursive:*

(a) $neg(x) = \begin{cases} 0 & if\ x \geq 1, \\ 1 & if\ x = 0. \end{cases}$

(b) $and(x, y) = \begin{cases} 1 & if\ x \geq 1\ and\ y \geq 1, \\ 0 & otherwise. \end{cases}$

(c) $or(x, y) = \begin{cases} 1 & if\ x \geq 1\ or\ y \geq 1, \\ 0 & otherwise. \end{cases}$

(d) $if\text{-}then\text{-}else(x, y, z) = \begin{cases} y & if\ x \geq 1, \\ z & otherwise. \end{cases}$

Solution. (a) $neg(x) = minus(1, x)$.

(b) $and(x, y) = neg(neg(mult(x, y)))$.

(c) $or(x, y) = neg(and(neg(x), neg(y)))$.

(d) $if\text{-}then\text{-}else(x, y, z) = add(mult(neg(neg(x)), y), mult(neg(x), z))$.   □

We often write "x and y" for $and(x, y)$, "x or y" for $or(x, y)$, and "if x then y else z" for $if\text{-}then\text{-}else(x, y, z)$.

Example 4.27 *Show that the following functions are primitive recursive:*

(a) $eq(x, y) = \begin{cases} 1 & if\ x = y, \\ 0 & if\ x \neq y. \end{cases}$

(b) $gr(x, y) = \begin{cases} 1 & if\ x > y, \\ 0 & if\ x \leq y. \end{cases}$

(c) $geq(x, y) = \begin{cases} 1 & if\ x \geq y, \\ 0 & if\ x < y. \end{cases}$

(d) $ls(x, y) = \begin{cases} 1 & if\ x < y, \\ 0 & if\ x \geq y. \end{cases}$

(e) $leq(x, y) = \begin{cases} 1 & if\ x \leq y, \\ 0 & if\ x > y. \end{cases}$

Solution. (a) $eq(x, y) = neg(add(minus(x, y), minus(y, x)))$.

(b) $gr(x, y) = neg(neg(minus(x, y)))$.

(c) $geq(x, y) = gr(x, y)\ or\ eq(x, y)$.

(d) $ls(x, y) = neg(geq(x, y))$.

(e) $leq(x, y) = neg(gr(x, y))$.   □

Example 4.28 *For every $k \geq 1$, the function $max^k(n_1, n_2, \ldots, n_k) = \max\{n_1, n_2, \ldots, n_k\}$ is primitive recursive.*

Solution. We can prove this by induction. When $k = 1$, $max^1(n_1) = \pi_1^1(n_1)$. For $k > 1$,

$$max^k(n_1, \ldots, n_k) = if\ n_k > max^{k-1}(n_1, \ldots, n_{k-1})$$
$$then\ n_k\ else\ max^{k-1}(n_1, \ldots, n_{k-1}).   □$$

We now define three more operations on functions that preserve primitive recursiveness. We call a total function $R : (\{0,1\}^*)^k \to \{0,1\}$ a *Boolean function* or a *predicate*. Recall that we identify the integer 1 with TRUE and 0 with FALSE. Therefore, if $R(n_1, \ldots, n_k)$ is a predicate, then the expression $R(n_1, \ldots, n_k)$ is equivalent to the expression $[R(n_1, \ldots, n_k) = 1]$. In addition, if a formula defines a predicate, we often write the formula, instead of the name of the predicate, to represent the predicate. For instance, we write $(\exists n)[n^2 = m]$ to denote the value of the predicate

$$g(m) = \left\{ \begin{array}{ll} 1 & \text{if } (\exists n)[n^2 = m], \\ 0 & \text{otherwise.} \end{array} \right.$$

Theorem 4.29 *Suppose that* $f : \mathbf{N}^{k+1} \to \mathbf{N}$ *is a primitive recursive predicate. Then, the following functions are also primitive recursive.*

(a) $g(n_1, \ldots, n_k, m) = (\forall i)_{i \leq m} f(n_1, \ldots, n_k, i)$. *(We say g is defined from f by the operation of* bounded universal quantifier.*)*

(b) $h(n_1, \ldots, n_k, m) = (\exists i)_{i \leq m} f(n_1, \ldots, n_k, i)$. *(We say h is defined from f by the operation of* bounded existential quantifier.*)*

$$(c)\ t(n_1, \ldots, n_k, m) = \left\{ \begin{array}{ll} (\min i)_{i \leq m} f(n_1, \ldots, n_k, i) \\ \qquad\qquad \text{if } (\exists i)_{i \leq m} f(n_1, \ldots, n_k, i), \\ 0 \qquad\qquad \text{otherwise,} \end{array} \right.$$

(We say t is defined from f by the operation of bounded minimization.*)*

Proof. All three functions can be defined by primitive recursion from f:

(a) $g(n_1, \ldots, n_k, 0) = f(n_1, \ldots, n_k, 0)$, and

$$g(n_1, \ldots, n_k, m+1) = [f(n_1, \ldots, n_k, m+1) \text{ and } g(n_1, \ldots, n_k, m)].$$

(b) $h(n_1, \ldots, n_k, 0) = f(n_1, \ldots, n_k, 0)$, and

$$h(n_1, \ldots, n_k, m+1) = [f(n_1, \ldots, n_k, m+1) \text{ or } h(n_1, \ldots, n_k, m)].$$

(c) $t(n_1, \ldots, n_k, 0) = 0$, and

$$t(n_1, \ldots, n_k, m+1) = [\text{if } (\exists i)_{i \leq m} f(n_1, \ldots, n_k, i) \text{ then } t(n_1, \ldots, n_k, m)$$
$$\text{else if } f(n_1, \ldots, n_k, m+1) \text{ then } m+1 \text{ else } 0]. \qquad \square$$

The above three operations are very useful for proving functions being primitive recursive.

Example 4.30 *The following functions are primitive recursive.*

(a) $quot(m, n) = \left\{ \begin{array}{ll} \lfloor \frac{m}{n} \rfloor & \text{if } n > 0, \\ 0 & \text{otherwise.} \end{array} \right.$

(b) $mod(m, n) = \left\{ \begin{array}{ll} m - \lfloor \frac{m}{n} \rfloor \cdot n & \text{if } n > 0, \\ 0 & \text{otherwise.} \end{array} \right.$

(c) $prime(n) = \left\{ \begin{array}{ll} 1 & \text{if } n \text{ is a prime,} \\ 0 & \text{otherwise.} \end{array} \right.$

Solution. (a) $quot(m, n) = [$*if* $n > 0$ *then* $(\min i)_{i \le m}[(i+1) \cdot n > m]$ *else* $0]$.

(b) $mod(m, n) = [$*if* $n > 0$ *then* $(\min i)_{i \le m}[quot(m, n) \cdot n + i = m]$ *else* $0]$.

(c) $prime(n) = [(n \ge 2)$ *and* $(\forall j)_{2 \le j \le n \div 1}[mod(n, j) > 0]]$. □

Remark. In the above proof of part (c), we used a more general quantifier $(\forall j)_{2 \le j \le n \div 1}$ than the one introduced in Theorem 4.29. More formally, we should first define a new predicate

$$prime'(n, k) = [n \ge 2 \text{ and } (\forall j)_{j \le k}[j \le 1 \text{ or } mod(n, j) > 0].$$

Then, we observe that $prime(n) = prime'(n, pred(n))$, and so *prime* is primitive recursive. From this example, we see that we can extend the basic quantifiers used in Theorem 4.29 to quantifiers of the form $(\exists j)_{\ell(n) \le j \le u(n)}$ and $(\forall j)_{\ell(n) \le j \le u(n)}$ and still preserve primitive recursiveness, as long as $\ell(n)$ and $u(n)$ are primitive recursive functions.

Example 4.31 *Let* $f(0) = 1$ *and, for* $n \ge 1$, $f(n) = $ *the* n*th digit to the right of the decimal point of the decimal expansion of* $\sqrt{2}$. *Prove that* f *is primitive recursive.*

Solution. Let $g(n)$ be the integer m whose decimal expansion is equal to $f(0)f(1)f(2) \ldots f(n)$ (e.g., $g(3) = 1414$). Then,

$$g(n) = (\min k)_{k \le 10^{n+1}} [(k+1)^2 > 2 \cdot 10^{2n}],$$

and $f(n) = mod(g(n), 10)$. □

Exercises 4.6

1. Show that the following functions are primitive recursive:

   (a) $factorial(n) = n!$.

   (b) $f_1(n) = n^{n^{\cdot^{\cdot^{n}}}} \Big\} n$ levels. [*Hint*: First consider a more general function $g_1(n, m) = n^{n^{\cdot^{\cdot^{n}}}} \Big\} m$ levels.]

   (c) $f_2(n) = \lfloor \log_2 n \rfloor$.

   (d) $f_3(n) = \begin{cases} 1 & \text{if } n \text{ is the sum of two primes,} \\ 0 & \text{otherwise.} \end{cases}$

   (e) $\phi(n) = $ the number of primes less than or equal to n.

   (f) $lcm(n, m) = $ the least common multiple of n and m.

   (g) $s(n) = $ the number of digits in the decimal representation of n.

   (h) $h(n, m) = $ the mth most significant digit of the decimal representation of n if $1 \le m \le s(n)$ (and $h(n, m) = 0$ if $m = 0$ or $m > s(n)$).

2. What is wrong with the following proof of Example 4.25?

> We prove it by induction on n, as in Example 4.28. When $n = 0$, $g(m, n) = \pi_1^1(n)$; so, $g(m, 0)$ is primitive recursive. For $n \geq 0$, $g(m, n+1) = f(g(m, n))$. Since f is primitive recursive and, by the inductive hypothesis, $g(m, n)$ is primitive recursive, we get that $g(m, n+1)$ is also primitive recursive. It follows that $g(m, n)$ is primitive recursive for all $n \geq 0$ and, hence, g is primitive recursive.

3. Assume that $R : \mathbf{N}^{k+1} \to \mathbf{N}$ is a primitive recursive predicate. Show that the following function $f : \mathbf{N}^{k+1} \to \mathbf{N}$ is also primitive recursive:

$$
f(n_1, \ldots, n_k, m) = \begin{cases} (\max i)_{i \leq m} R(n_1, \ldots, n_k, i) \\ \qquad\qquad \text{if } (\exists i)_{i \leq m} R(n_1, \ldots, n_k, i), \\ 0 \qquad\qquad \text{otherwise.} \end{cases}
$$

4. Assume that $f : \mathbf{N}^{k+1} \to \mathbf{N}$ is primitive recursive. Show that the following functions are also primitive recursive:

   (a) $g(n_1, \ldots, n_k, m) = \sum_{i=0}^{m} f(n_1, \ldots, n_k, i)$.

   (b) $h(n_1, \ldots, n_k, m) = \prod_{i=0}^{m} f(n_1, \ldots, n_k, i)$.

5. Assume that $f : \mathbf{N} \to \mathbf{N}$ is primitive recursive and satisfies $f(0) = 0$ and $f(n) < f(n+1)$ for all $n \geq 0$. Show that the function $h(m) = $ [the integer n such that $f(n) \leq m < f(n+1)$] is also primitive recursive.

6. Assume that both $f : \mathbf{N} \to \mathbf{N}$ and $g : \mathbf{N} \to \mathbf{N}$ are primitive recursive. Show that the following function $h : \mathbf{N}^2 \to \mathbf{N}$ is also primitive recursive:

$$
h(n, 0) = f(n),
$$
$$
h(n, m + 1) = g(h(n, \lfloor \tfrac{m+1}{2} \rfloor)).
$$

7. Assume that $f : \mathbf{N} \to \mathbf{N}$ is primitive recursive. Show that the following function $g : \mathbf{N}^2 \to \mathbf{N}$ is also primitive recursive:

$$
g(n, 0) = f(n),
$$
$$
g(n, m + 1) = g(g(n, m), m).
$$

4.7   Pairing Functions and Gödel Numberings

In this section, we extend the operation of primitive recursion to more general recursion operations. For instance, we would like to prove that the Fibonacci function $F : \mathbf{N} \to \mathbf{N}$, defined by the double recursion below, is primitive recursive:

$$
F(0) = 0,
$$
$$
F(1) = 1,
$$
$$
F(n + 2) = F(n) + F(n + 1).
$$

To do this, we introduce coding functions that encode several integers into one and use these functions to show that the seemingly more general recursion operations actually preserve primitive recursiveness.

A function $f : \mathbf{N}^2 \to \mathbf{N}$ is called a *pairing function* if it satisfies the following properties:

(i) (*Bijectivity*) f is one-to-one and onto.

(ii) (*Primitive recursiveness*) f is primitive recursive.

(iii) (*Monotonicity*)[2] $f(i,j) < f(i+1,j)$ and $f(i,j) < f(i,j+1)$, for all $i,j \in \mathbf{N}$.

Suppose that f is a pairing function. Then, the functions $l_f, r_f : \mathbf{N} \to \mathbf{N}$, defined by $f(l_f(n), r_f(n)) = n$, are well defined and are primitive recursive:

$$l_f(n) = (\min i)_{i \leq n} (\exists j)_{j \leq n} [f(i,j) = n],$$
$$r_f(n) = (\min j)_{j \leq n} [f(l_f(n), j) = n].$$

There are many pairing functions. We will use only one of them. (See Exercise 1 of this section for others.)

Example 4.32 *Show that the function* $\pi : \mathbf{N}^2 \to \mathbf{N}$, *defined by*

$$\pi(i,j) = \frac{(i+j)(i+j+1)}{2} + j,$$

is a pairing function.

Solution. It is obvious that π is primitive recursive. Figure 4.18 shows that π is indeed one-to-one and onto and satisfies the conditions that $\pi(i,j) < \pi(i+1,j)$ and $\pi(i,j) < \pi(i,j+1)$. □

We write $\langle i,j \rangle$ to denote $\pi(i,j)$, and $l(n)$ and $r(n)$ to denote $l_\pi(n)$ and $r_\pi(n)$, respectively.

Example 4.33 *Show that the Fibonacci function is primitive recursive.*

Solution. First, we transfer the double recursive definition of the Fibonacci function into a single recursive definition of a more general function G. Define $G(n) = \langle F(n), F(n+1) \rangle$. Then,

$$G(0) = \langle 0, 1 \rangle,$$
$$G(n+1) = \langle r(G(n)), l(G(n)) + r(G(n)) \rangle,$$

---

[2] In the literature, pairing functions are usually defined to be functions satisfying conditions (i) and (ii) only, though most implementations also satisfy condition (iii).

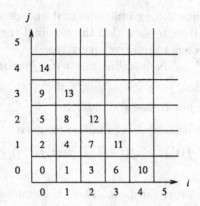

Figure 4.18:   The pairing function $\pi(i,j)$.

and, hence, G is primitive recursive. It follows that $F(n) = l(G(n))$ is also primitive recursive. $\Box$

We say a function $f : \bigcup_{k>1} \mathbf{N}^k \to \mathbf{N}$ is a *Gödel numbering* (of integer sequences) if f satisfies the following properties:

(i) (*Bijectivity*) f is one-to-one, onto.

(ii) (*Primitive recursiveness*) $f|_{\mathbf{N}^k}$, the function f restricted to the domain $\mathbf{N}^k$, is primitive recursive, for all $k \geq 1$.

(iii) (*Monotonicity*) $f(n_1, \ldots, n_{i-1}, n_i, n_{i+1}, \ldots, n_k) < f(n_1, \ldots, n_{i-1}, n_i+1, n_{i+1}, \ldots, n_k)$, for all $1 \leq i \leq k$.

Example 4.34 *Show that the function*

$$\tau(n_1, \ldots, n_{k-1}, n_k) = \langle k \doteq 1, \langle n_1, \langle \cdots \langle n_{k-1}, n_k \rangle \cdots \rangle \rangle \rangle$$

is a Gödel numbering.

Solution. We first verify that τ is one-to-one. Suppose that $\tau(n_1, n_2, \ldots, n_{k_1}) = \tau(m_1, m_2, \ldots, m_{k_2})$. By the one-to-oneness of π, we see that k_1 must be equal to k_2. Next, we can prove that τ is one-to-one on $\mathbf{N}^k$ for each fixed $k \geq 1$ by induction: If $k = 1$, then $\tau(n) = \langle 0, n \rangle$ is one-to-one. If $k > 1$, then $\tau(n_1, n_2, \ldots, n_k) = \langle k \doteq 1, \langle n_1, r(\tau(n_2, \ldots, n_k)) \rangle \rangle$. It follows from the one-to-oneness of $\tau|_{\mathbf{N}^{k-1}}$ and π that $\tau|_{\mathbf{N}^k}$ is also one-to-one.

Next, we check that for any integer $n \geq 0$, there is a unique sequence $(n_1, n_2, \ldots, n_k)$ such that $\tau(n_1, n_2, \ldots, n_k) = n$. First, we know that $k = l(n) + 1$. Next, for each $1 \leq i \leq k$, define

$$item(n, i) = \begin{cases} l(r^{(i)}(n)) & \text{if } 1 \leq i \leq k-1, \\ r^{(k)}(n) & \text{if } i = k. \end{cases}$$

Then, it is clear that $\tau(item(n,1), item(n,2), \ldots, item(n,k)) = n$. Thus, τ is onto. Note that we have shown in addition that we can decode τ by a primitive recursive function *item*. That is, $item(n, i)$ is the unique n_i such that for some $n_1, \ldots, n_{i-1}, n_{i+1}, \ldots, n_k$, $\tau(n_1, \ldots, n_k) = n$, if $1 \leq i \leq l(n)+1$.

Finally, from the primitive recursiveness of π, we get that $\tau|_{\mathbf{N}^k}$ is primitive recursive and, from the monotonicity property of π, we know that τ also satisfies the monotonicity property. □

We write $\langle n_1, n_2, \ldots, n_k \rangle$ to denote $r(\tau(n_1, n_2, \ldots, n_k))$ and $[n_1, n_2, \ldots, n_k]$ to denote $\tau(n_1, n_2, \ldots, n_k)$. We also write $size(n)$ to denote $l(n)+1$; thus, if $n = [n_1, n_2, \ldots, n_k]$, then $size(n) = k$.

· The following are some more primitive recursive operations on sequences of integers.

Example 4.35 *Show that the following functions are primitive recursive:*

(a) $list(m, 0) = 0$ *and* $list(m, k) = [\underbrace{m, m, \ldots, m}_{k}]$, *if* $k \geq 1$.

(b) $find([n_1, \ldots, n_k], m) = \begin{cases} \min\{i \mid 1 \leq i \leq k, n_i = m\} \\ \qquad \qquad \text{if such an } i \text{ exists,} \\ 0 \qquad \qquad \text{otherwise.} \end{cases}$

(c) $replace([n_1, \ldots, n_k], m, i) = \begin{cases} [n_1, \ldots, n_{i-1}, m, n_{i+1}, \ldots, n_k] \\ \qquad \qquad \text{if } 1 \leq i \leq k, \\ [n_1, \ldots, n_k] \quad \text{otherwise.} \end{cases}$

(d) $conseq([n_1, \ldots, n_k], [m_1, \ldots, m_\ell]) = [n_1, \ldots, n_k, m_1, \ldots, m_\ell]$.

(e) $subseq([n_1, \ldots, n_k], i, \ell)$

$= \begin{cases} [n_i, n_{i+1}, \ldots, n_{i+\ell-1}] & \text{if } 1 \leq i \leq k, \ 1 \leq \ell \leq k - i + 1 \\ 0 & \text{otherwise.} \end{cases}$

Solution. (a) We note that $list(m, 0) = 0$, $list(m, 1) = \langle 0, m \rangle$ and, for $k \geq 1$, $list(m, k+1) = \langle k, \langle m, r(list(m, k)) \rangle \rangle$.

(b) $find(n, m) = (\min i)_{1 \leq i \leq size(n)}[item(n, i) = m]$.

(c) Note that if $1 \leq i \leq size(n)$, then

$replace(n, m, i) = (\min t)_{t \leq list(n+m, size(n))}[size(t) = size(n)$

$\qquad \qquad \text{and } (\forall j)_{j \leq size(n)}[j = i \text{ or } item(t, j) = item(n, j)]$

$\qquad \qquad \text{and } item(t, i) = m].$

(*Note*: If $n = [n_1, \ldots, n_k]$ then $n \geq n_i$ for all $1 \leq i \leq k$ and so, by the monotonicity property of Gödel numberings, $list(n + m, size(n))$ is an upper bound of the output of $replace(n, m, i)$.)

(d) We observe that $conseq(n, m)$ can be expressed as follows:

$(\min t)_{t \leq list(n+m, size(n)+size(m))}[size(t) = size(n) + size(m)$

$\qquad \qquad \text{and } (\forall i)_{1 \leq i \leq size(n)}[item(t, i) = item(n, i)]$

$\qquad \qquad \text{and } (\forall j)_{1 \leq j \leq size(m)}[item(t, n + j) = item(m, j)].$

(e) If $1 \leq i \leq size(n)$ and $1 \leq \ell \leq size(n) - i + 1$, then we have

$$subseq(n, i, \ell) = (\min t)_{t \leq list(n, \ell)}[size(t) = \ell$$
$$\text{and } (\forall j)_{1 \leq j \leq \ell}[item(t, j) = item(n, i + j - 1)]].   \square$$

Note that all the proofs above, except for the function *list*, use only the fact that *size*, *item* and *list* are primitive recursive and do not depend on the particular Gödel numbering used. In other words, they hold for all Gödel numberings.

Example 4.36 *Show that the function* $f : \mathbf{N} \to \mathbf{N}$, *defined by* $f(0) = 1$, $f(n + 1) = f(0)^{n+1} + f(1)^n + \ldots + f(n)^1$, *is primitive recursive.*

Solution. Define $\tilde{f}(n) = [f(n), f(n - 1), \ldots, f(0)]$. We observe that

$$\tilde{f}(0) = [f(0)] = list(f(0), 1),$$
$$\tilde{f}(n + 1) = conseq(list(f(n + 1), 1), \tilde{f}(n)).$$

Note that $f(n + 1)$ can be written in terms of $\tilde{f}(n)$ as follows:

$$f(n + 1) = \sum_{i=0}^{n} (item(\tilde{f}(n), i + 1))^{i+1},$$

because $item(\tilde{f}(n), i + 1) = f(n - i)$. Therefore, $\tilde{f}(n + 1)$ can be expressed in terms of $\tilde{f}(n)$ (cf. Exercise 4(a) of Section 4.6). So, we conclude that $\tilde{f}$ is primitive recursive. It follows that $f(n) = item(\tilde{f}(n), 1)$ is also primitive recursive. $\square$

The above example can be easily generalized to the general recursion operations. We omit the proof.

Theorem 4.37 *Assume that*

$$f(n_1, \ldots, n_k, 0) = g(n_1, \ldots, n_k),$$
$$f(n_1, \ldots, n_k, m + 1) = h(n_1, \ldots, n_k, m, [f_0, f_1, \ldots, f_m]),$$

where f_i *is the abbreviation of* $f(n_1, \ldots, n_k, i)$, *for* $0 \leq i \leq m$. *If* g *and* h *are primitive recursive, then* f *is primitive recursive.*

We remark that the primitive recursion operation is equivalent to the recursive calls in a high-level programming language which limits a procedure $F(x)$ to recurisvely call itself $F(y)$ only if $y = x - 1$. This type of recursive calls can be easily converted to a bounded-iteration loop structure. For instance, if f is defined from g and h by primitive recursion, then it can be computed by the following segment of a pseudo-Pascal program (where the inputs to f are $(n_1, \ldots, n_k, m)$ and the output is f):

$$f := g(n_1, \ldots, n_k);$$
$$\text{for } i = 1 \text{ to } m \text{ do}$$
$$f := h(n_1, \ldots, n_k, i-1, f);$$

The general recursion operation considered in Theorem 4.37 above is equivalent to the recursive calls that allow a procedure $F(x)$ to call itself $F(y)$ with any $y < x$. The above theorem shows that this type of recursive calls can also be converted to a bounded-iteration loop structure. In practice, this type of recursive calls can be implemented in a nonrecursive procedure with a stack to store the values of $F(0), F(1), \ldots, F(x-1)$. (The role of the stack is like the function $\tilde{f}$ of Example 4.36.) The more general types of recursive calls which allow $F(x)$ to call $F(y)$ for any y may lead, in the worst case, to infinite loops and hence do not preserve primitive recursiveness. Several other types of recursions that preserve primitive recursiveness are studied in the exercises.

Example 4.38 *The function* $sort : \mathbf{N} \to \mathbf{N}$ *maps a number* $[n_1, n_2, \ldots, n_k]$ *to the number* $[n_{p_1}, n_{p_2}, \ldots, n_{p_k}]$, *where* $(p_1, p_2, \ldots, p_k)$ *is a permutation of* $(1, 2, \ldots, k)$ *such that* $n_{p_1} \leq n_{p_2} \leq \cdots \leq n_{p_k}$. *Show that* sort *is primitive recursive.*

Solution 1 (Selection sort). First, we define $maxindex([n_1, \ldots, n_k])$ to be the least index $1 \leq i \leq k$ such that $n_i \geq n_j$ for all $1 \leq j \leq k$. We note that

$$maxindex(n) = (\min i)_{1 \leq i \leq size(n)} (\forall j)_{1 \leq j \leq size(n)} [item(n, j) \leq item(n, i)].$$

Thus, *maxindex* is primitive recursive.

Next, we define $g([n_1, \ldots, n_k])$ to be the list $[n_1, \ldots, n_k]$ with the maximum item of $[n_1, \ldots, n_k]$ removed. Let $m^* = maxindex(n)$. Then, $g(n)$ can be expressed as follows:

(i) If $size(n) = 1$, then $g(n) = 0$;

(ii) If $size(n) > 1$ and $m^* = 1$ then $g(n) = subseq(n, 2, size(n) \dot{-} 1)$;

(iii) If $size(n) > 1$ and $m^* = size(n)$ then $g(n) = subseq(n, 1, size(n) \dot{-} 1)$;

(iv) If $size(n) > 1$ and $1 < m^* < size(n)$, then

$$g(n) = conseq(subseq(n, 1, m^* - 1), subseq(n, m^* + 1, size(n) - m^*)).$$

It follows that g is primitive recursive. In addition, it is easy to see that $g(n) < n$ for all $n > 0$ (see Exercise 3 of this section).

Now, we observe that $sort(0) = 0$, and $sort(n + 1)$ can be expressed as

if size $(n+1) = 1$ *then* $n + 1$

    else $conseq(sort(g(n + 1)), list(item(n + 1, maxindex(n + 1)), 1))$.

Thus, from Theorem 4.37, *sort* is primitive recursive. (See also Exercise 4 of this section.)   □

Solution 2. We simply search for a new sequence which has the desired properties. First, we define the predicate $perm(q)$ to mean that $q = [q_1, q_2, \ldots, q_k]$ is a permutation of $[1, 2, \ldots, k]$. That is,

$$perm(q) = (\forall i)_{1 \leq i \leq size(q)}(\exists j)_{1 \leq j \leq size(q)}[item(q, j) = i]].$$

Therefore, *perm* is primitive recursive.

Then, we observe that

$$sort(n) = (\min t)_{t \leq list(n,n)}[size(t) = size(n) \text{ and } sorted(t) \text{ and } perm_2(t, n)],$$

where $sorted(t)$ is the predicate [t is sorted], and $perm_2(t, n)$ is the predicate [t is a permutation of n]. We note that

$$sorted(t) = (\forall i)_{1 \leq i \leq size(t) \dot{-} 1}[item(t, i) \leq item(t, i + 1)],$$

and

$$perm_2(t, n) = (\exists q)_{q \leq list(size(n), size(n))}[perm(q) \text{ and } size(q) = size(n)$$
$$\text{and } (\forall i)_{1 \leq i \leq size(n)}[item(t, i) = item(n, item(q, i))]].$$

Therefore, both *sorted* and $perm_2$ are primitive recursive. It follows that *sort* is primitive recursive.

We remark that the simpler expression

$$(\forall i)_{1 \leq i \leq size(n)}(\exists j)_{1 \leq j \leq size(t)}[item(t, j) = item(n, i)]$$

for $perm_2(t, n)$ does not work if the list n has duplicate elements $n_i = n_j$ for some $i \neq j$.   □

Exercises 4.7

1. Show that the following functions are pairing functions.

(a) $f_1(n, m) = 2^n(2m + 1) - 1$.

(b) $f_2(n, m) = \max(n, m)^2 + m + g(m, n)$, where $g(m, n) = n$ if $m \geq n$, and $g(m, n) = 0$ if $n > m$.

2. Let $\tau_1 : \bigcup_{k=1}^{\infty} \mathbf{N}^k \to \mathbf{N}$ be defined by $f(n_1, \ldots, n_k) = 2^{n_1} 3^{n_2} \cdots p_k^{n_k}$, where p_k is the kth prime.

(a) Show that the τ_1 is onto, primitive recursive and monotone. Also show that τ_1 is *almost* one-to-one in the sense that if $\tau_1(n_1, \ldots, n_k) = \tau_1(m_1, \ldots, m_\ell)$, and if $k \leq \ell$, then $n_i = m_i$ for all i, $1 \leq i \leq k$, and $m_j = 0$ for all j, $k < j \leq \ell$.

(b) Verify that if we use τ_1 as a Gödel numbering, then the functions *size*, *item* and the functions of Example 4.35 all remain primitive recursive. (Here, $size(n)$ is the number of items in the sequence n, excluding the trailing zeros.)

3. Let $n_1, n_2, \ldots, n_k$ are k nonnegative integers. Prove that if $1 \le i_1 < i_2 < \cdots < i_\ell \le k$, then $[n_{i_1}, n_{i_2}, \ldots, n_{i_\ell}] \le [n_1, n_2, \ldots, n_k]$.

4. Assume that $f(n, 0) = g(n)$ and $f(n, m+1) = h(n, f(n, k(m)))$ for some primitive recursive g, h and k. Also assume that $k(m) \le m$ for all $m > 0$. Prove that f is also primitive recursive. (Note that Solution 1 of Example 4.38 actually used this result.)

5. Show that the following functions are primitive recursive:

   (a) $f(n, m) =$ the number of occurrences of integer m in the sequence $n = [n_1, \ldots, n_k]$.

   (b) $g(n) = [d_k, d_{k-1}, \ldots, d_0]$, where $d_k d_{k-1} \cdots d_0$ is the decimal representation of n (e.g., $g(2801) = [2, 8, 0, 1]$).

6. We may extend the notion of primitive recursive functions to functions from $\mathbf{Z}^k$ to $\mathbf{Z}$, where $\mathbf{Z}$ is the set of integers. All we need is to treat a pair $\langle n_1, n_2 \rangle$ as a representation of an integer in $\mathbf{Z}$: If $n_1 > 0$, then it represents n_2, otherwise it represents $-n_2$. Show that the following functions on integers are primitive recursive:

   (a) $inner(n, m) =$ the inner product of two k-dimensional vectors n and m, if $size(n) = size(m) = 2k$ (and it is 0, otherwise). (We treat a list $[n_1, n_2, \ldots, n_{2k}]$ as a k-dimensional integer vector whose ith element is the integer represented by $\langle n_{2i-1}, n_{2i} \rangle$; that is, it is n_{2i} if $n_{2i-1} > 0$, and is $-n_{2i}$ if $n_{2i-1} = 0$.)

   (b) $det(n) =$ the determinant of the matrix n if $size(n) = 2k^2$ for some $k \ge 1$ (and it is 0 otherwise). (We treat $[n_1, n_2, \ldots, n_{2k^2}]$ as a $k \times k$ integer matrix M with M_{ij} equal to the integer represented by the pair $\langle n_{2(i-1)k+2j-1}, n_{2(i-1)k+2j} \rangle$.)

7. We say a sequence $n = [n_1, \ldots, n_k]$ is *balanced* if there exists a partition of $\{1, 2, \ldots, k\}$ into two subsets B and C (i.e., $B \cup C = \{1, 2, \ldots, k\}$ and $B \cap C = \emptyset$) such that $\sum_{i \in B} n_i = \sum_{j \in C} n_j$. Prove that the predicate [n is balanced] is primitive recursive.

8. (a) Show that the function $merge(n, m)$ that merges two sorted sequences into a single sorted sequence (and output 0 if any of the two inputs is not sorted) is primitive recursive.

   (b) Prove that *sort* is primitive recursive using the algorithm of merge sort.

$\star$ 9. Assume that $g : \mathbf{N} \to \mathbf{N}$ and $h : \mathbf{N}^2 \to \mathbf{N}$ are two primitive recursive functions. Show that the following function f is primitive recursive:

$$f(0, n) = g(n),$$
$$f(m + 1, n) = f(m, h(m, n)).$$

[*Hint*: Introduce a third parameter and then apply the operation of primitive recursion on the third parameter.]

$\star$ **10.** Assume that g_1, g_2 and h are all primitive recursive. Show that the following function f is primitive recursive:

$$f(0, n) = g_1(n),$$
$$f(m + 1, 0) = g_2(m),$$
$$f(m + 1, n + 1) = h(m, n, f(m + 1, n), f(m, n + 1)).$$

[*Hint*: Use the pairing function to encode the two inputs into a single input.]

$\star$ **11.** Assume that g_1, g_2 and h are all primitive recursive. Show that the following function f is primitive recursive:

$$f(0, n) = g_1(n),$$
$$f(m + 1, 0) = g_2(m),$$
$$f(m + 1, n + 1) = h(m, n, f(m, n), f(n, m), f(m, m), f(n, n)).$$

[*Hint*: Use the pairing function f_2 defined in Exercise 1(b) of this section to encode the two inputs into a single input.]

12. Assume that g_1, g_2, h_1 and h_2 are all primitive recursive. Let f_1 and f_2 be functions defined by the following formulas:

$$f_1(m, 0) = g_1(m),$$
$$f_2(m, 0) = g_2(m),$$
$$f_1(m, n + 1) = h_1(m, n, f_1(m, n), f_2(m, n)),$$
$$f_2(m, n + 1) = h_2(m, n, f_1(m, n), f_2(m, n)).$$

Show that both f_1 and f_2 are primitive recursive:

4.8   Partial Recursive Functions

All primitive recursive functions are *total* functions; that is, they are defined on every possible input. In this section, we extend the class of primitive recursive functions to the class of *partial recursive functions* by adding a new operation, called unbounded minimization, which may produce nontotal functions from total functions. Recall that $f(n) \uparrow$ denotes the fact that f is undefined at input n.

Unbounded Minimization: Given a *total* predicate $g : \mathbf{N}^{k+1} \to \{0, 1\}$, define function $f : \mathbf{N}^k \to \mathbf{N}$ by

$$f(n_1, \cdots, n_k) = \begin{cases} (\min m)g(n_1, \cdots, n_k, m) & \text{if } (\exists m)g(n_1, \cdots, n_k, m), \\ \uparrow & \text{otherwise.} \end{cases}$$

We say f is obtained by unbounded minimization operation from function g, and simply write $f(n_1, \cdots, n_k) = (\min m)g(n_1, \cdots, n_k, m)$.

Partial Recursive Functions: A partial function f defined on $\mathbf{N}^k$ is called *partial recursive* if it is an initial function or if it can be obtained from initial functions by a finite number of applications of composition, primitive recursion, and unbounded minimization. A partial recursive function f is also called a *recursive* function if f is a total function.

Remarks. (1) Note that, in the above definition of unbounded minimization, we required that this operation can only be applied to total functions. Indeed, it is easy to obtain a nonrecursive function by applying the unbounded minimization operation on a nontotal recursive function (see, e.g., Exercise 7 of Section 5.4).

(2) In the definition of partial recursive functions, we implicitly extended the operation of composition to nontotal functions. For instance, if f is a partial function on $\mathbf{N}$ and $g(n) = 2n + 1$, then the composition of g and f is

$$h(n) = \begin{cases} 2f(n) + 1 & \text{if } f(n) \downarrow, \\ \uparrow & \text{if } f(n) \uparrow. \end{cases}$$

For convenience, we often simply write $h(n) = 2f(n) + 1$. Similarly, for two partial functions f, g on $\mathbf{N}$, we write $f = g$ to mean that, for each $n \in \mathbf{N}$, either both $f(n)$ and $g(n)$ are undefined, or both $f(n)$ and $g(n)$ are defined and their values are equal.

There are two classes of computable sets related to the notion of partial recursive functions.

Recursive Sets: A set $A \subseteq \mathbf{N}^k$ is *recursive* if its *characteristic* function

$$\chi_A(n_1, n_2, \ldots, n_k) = \begin{cases} 1, & \text{if } (n_1, n_2, \ldots, n_k) \in A \\ 0, & \text{if } (n_1, n_2, \ldots, n_k) \notin A \end{cases}$$

is a (total) recursive function.

Recursively Enumerable Sets. A set $A \subseteq \mathbf{N}^k$ is *recursively enumerable* (or, simply, *r.e.*) if its *semi-characteristic* function

$$\sigma_A(n_1, n_2, \ldots, n_k) = \begin{cases} 1, & \text{if } (n_1, n_2, \ldots, n_k) \in A \\ \uparrow, & \text{if } (n_1, n_2, \ldots, n_k) \notin A \end{cases}$$

is a partial recursive function.

In addition, we say a set $A \subseteq \mathbf{N}^k$ is *primitive recursive* if χ_A is primitive recursive.

Example 4.39 *Show that if a set A can be expressed as $A = \{n \mid (\exists m)R(n, m)\}$ for some recursive predicate R, then A is r.e. As a consequence,*

(a) $F = \{n \mid n \geq 2, (\exists a, b, c \geq 1)\, a^n + b^n = c^n\}$ *is r.e.*[3]

(b) *For any recursive function f, the set $J_f = \{n \mid n \geq 1, (\exists m)f^{(m)}(n) = 1\}$ is r.e.*[4]

Proof. This result follows from

$$\sigma_A(n) = neg(neg(1 + (\min m)R(n, m))). \qquad \square$$

To compare partial recursive functions with Turing-computable functions, we need to extend the notion of partial recursive functions to functions defined on strings.

For any fixed alphabet $\Sigma = \{s_1, s_2, \ldots, s_k\}$, with a fixed ordering $s_1 \prec s_2 \prec \cdots \prec s_k$ on its elements, the *lexicographic ordering* $\prec$ on strings in Σ^* can be defined as follows: Let $x = x_1 x_2 \cdots x_m$ and $y = y_1 y_2 \cdots y_n$, where each x_i and each y_j, $1 \leq i \leq m$, $1 \leq j \leq n$, is a letter in Σ. We say $x \prec y$ if

(a) $|x| < |y|$ (i.e., $m < n$), or

(b) $|x| = |y|$ and $(\exists i)_{1 \leq i \leq n}[x_1 = y_1, \ldots, x_{i-1} = y_{i-1}, x_i \prec y_i]$.

Then, the set Σ^*, written in the lexicographic ordering, is

$$\{\varepsilon, s_1, s_2, \ldots, s_k, s_1 s_1, s_1 s_2, \ldots, s_1 s_k, s_2 s_1, \ldots, s_k s_k, s_1 s_1 s_1, \ldots\}.$$

From this ordering on Σ^*, we define a one-to-one, onto function $\iota_\Sigma : \mathbf{N} \to \Sigma^*$ such that $\iota_\Sigma(n)$ is the nth string in Σ^* under the lexicographic ordering (starting with $\iota_\Sigma(0) = \varepsilon$). When the alphabet Σ is understood, we simply write ι for ι_Σ.

Theorem 4.40 *Assume that $\Sigma = \{s_1, s_2, \ldots, s_k\}$ and $s_1 \prec s_2 \prec \ldots \prec s_k$. Then, for each string $x = s_{i_n} s_{i_{n-1}} \ldots s_{i_1} s_{i_0}$, we have*

$$\iota^{-1}(x) = i_n \cdot k^n + i_{n-1} \cdot k^{n-1} + \cdots + i_1 \cdot k + i_0.$$

Proof. We can prove this relation by induction on strings x. First, if $x = \varepsilon$ then $\iota^{-1}(x) = 0$ and if $x = s_1$ then $\iota^{-1}(x) = 1$.

Next, assume that $x = s_{i_n} s_{i_{n-1}} \ldots s_{i_1} s_{i_0}$, with $n \geq 0$, and $\iota^{-1}(x) = i_n \cdot k^n + i_{n-1} \cdot k^{n-1} + \cdots + i_1 \cdot k + i_0$, and consider the successor y of x in Σ^* under the lexicographic ordering $\prec$. There are two possible cases.

---

[3] The famous Fermat's Last Theorem states that $F = \{2\}$ and so F is actually recursive.

[4] Let $f(n) = 3n + 1$ if n is odd, and $f(n) = n/2$ if n is even. The $(3n + 1)$-conjecture states that J_f consists of all positive integers.

Case 1. There exists an integer j, $0 \leq j \leq n$, such that $i_j < k$ and $i_\ell = k$ for all $\ell = 0, 1, \ldots, j-1$. That is, $x = s_{i_n} \cdots s_{i_{j+1}} s_{i_j} s_k \cdots s_k$. Then, $y = s_{i_n} \cdots s_{i_{j+1}} s_{i_j+1} s_1 \cdots s_1$. We verify that

$$
\begin{aligned}
\iota^{-1}(x) &= \sum_{\ell=j}^{n} i_\ell \cdot k^\ell + \sum_{\ell=0}^{j-1} k \cdot k^\ell \\
&= \sum_{\ell=j}^{n} i_\ell \cdot k^\ell + \sum_{\ell=1}^{j} k^\ell = \sum_{\ell=j}^{n} i_\ell \cdot k^\ell + \sum_{\ell=0}^{j} 1 \cdot k^\ell - 1.
\end{aligned}
$$

It follows that

$$
\iota^{-1}(y) = \sum_{\ell=j+1}^{n} i_\ell \cdot k^\ell + (i_j + 1) \cdot k^j + \sum_{\ell=0}^{j-1} 1 \cdot k^\ell.
$$

Case 2. $x = s_k s_k \cdots s_k$ (of length $|x| = n+1$). Then, we have $y = s_1 s_1 \cdots s_1$ (of length $|y| = n+2$). By the inductive hypothesis,

$$
\iota^{-1}(x) = k \cdot \sum_{\ell=0}^{n} k^\ell = \sum_{\ell=0}^{n+1} k^\ell - 1,
$$

and so

$$
\iota^{-1}(y) = \sum_{\ell=0}^{n+1} 1 \cdot k^\ell. \qquad \square
$$

In practice, we may view the string $s_{i_n} s_{i_{n-1}} \cdots s_{i_1} s_{i_0}$ as a *new base-k representation* of the integer $m = \iota_\Sigma^{-1}(x)$. We illustrate this idea in the following example.

Example 4.41 (a) Suppose $\Sigma = \{1, 2, \ldots, 8, 9, X\}$ with the ordering $1 \prec 2 \prec \cdots \prec 8 \prec 9 \prec X$. Then, we may treat every word in Σ^* that contains no X as the ordinary decimal expansion of an integer. For instance, let x be the string 3897. Then, from the above theorem, $\iota^{-1}(x) = 3 \cdot 10^3 + 8 \cdot 10^2 + 9 \cdot 10 + 7 = 3897$. If a string $x \in \Sigma^*$ contains symbol X, we can still easily calculate $\iota^{-1}(x)$ by treating X as 10. For instance, $\iota^{-1}(3XX7) = 3 \cdot 10^3 + 10 \cdot 10^2 + 10 \cdot 10 + 7 = 4107$.

(b) Suppose $\Sigma = \{0, 1\}$ and $0 \prec 1$. Then, $\iota(n)$ is just the ordinary binary expansion of $n+1$ with the leading 1 removed. For instance, let $n = 89$. Then the ordinary binary expansion of $n+1$ is 1011010 (i.e., $n+1 = 1 \cdot 2^6 + 1 \cdot 2^4 + 1 \cdot 2^3 + 1 \cdot 2 = 90$). By identifying 0 as s_1 and 1 as s_2, we can verify that

$$
\begin{aligned}
\iota^{-1}(011010) &= 1 \cdot 2^5 + 2 \cdot 2^4 + 2 \cdot 2^3 + 1 \cdot 2^2 + 2 \cdot 2 + 1 \\
&= 1 \cdot 2^5 + 1 \cdot 2^4 + 1 \cdot 2^3 + 1 \cdot 2^2 + 1 \cdot 2 + 1 \\
&\quad + 1 \cdot 2^4 + 1 \cdot 2^3 + 1 \cdot 2 \\
&= 1 \cdot 2^6 + 1 \cdot 2^4 + 1 \cdot 2^3 + 1 \cdot 2 - 1 = n. \qquad \square
\end{aligned}
$$

Based on the notion of lexicographic ordering and the function ι_Σ, we can extend the notion of partial recursive functions to functions on strings over Σ. A partial function $f : (\Sigma^*)^k \to \Sigma^*$ is called a *primitive recursive* (or, a *partial recursive*) function, if the function $\tilde{f} : \mathbf{N}^k \to \mathbf{N}$, defined by

$$\tilde{f}(n_1, n_2, \ldots, n_k) = \iota_\Sigma^{-1}(f(\iota_\Sigma(n_1), \ldots, \iota_\Sigma(n_k)))$$

is primitive recursive (or, respectively, partial recursive). A set $A \subseteq (\Sigma^*)^k$ is called a *recursive* (or, *r.e.*) set if the set

$$\tilde{A} = \{(n_1, n_2, \ldots, n_k) \in \mathbf{N}^k \mid (\iota_\Sigma(n_1), \ldots, \iota_\Sigma(n_k)) \in A\}$$

is recursive (or, respectively, r.e.).

In the following, when the alphabet Σ is understood, we will simply treat each string $x \in \Sigma^*$ as a representation of the integer $\iota_\Sigma^{-1}(n)$, and will write x to denote both the string x and the integer it represents. For instance, for $\Sigma = \{a, b, c\}$, with $a \prec b \prec c$, we may write $bac + 1$ to denote both the string immediately following the string bac in the lexicographic ordering $\prec$ (i.e., the string bba) and the integer $\iota_\Sigma^{-1}(bac) + 1$ (i.e., the integer $24 + 1 = 25$). In addition, we note that for $x, y \in \Sigma^*$, $x \prec y$ if and only if $\iota^{-1}(x) < \iota^{-1}(y)$. So, we will simply use a single symbol $<$ for both the integer ordering $<$ and the string ordering $\prec$, when there is no confusion.

We first show that some of the basic operations on strings are primitive recursive.

Example 4.42 *Assume that $\Sigma = \{s_1, s_2, \ldots, s_k\}$ and $s_1 \prec s_2 \prec \cdots \prec s_k$. Show that the following functions are primitive recursive:*

(a) *$leng_\Sigma(x) = |x|$.*

(b) *$concat_\Sigma^k(x_1, x_2, \ldots, x_k) = x_1 x_2 \cdots x_k$, $k \geq 1$.*

(c) *$substr_\Sigma(x, i, \ell) = $ the substring y of x starting from the ith symbol with length ℓ, if $1 \leq i \leq |x|$ and $1 \leq \ell \leq |x| - i + 1$; and 0, otherwise.*

(d) *$sub_\Sigma(x, y) = [x$ is a substring of $y]$.*

(e) *$head_\Sigma(x, y) = [x$ is a prefix of $y]$.*

(f) *$tail_\Sigma(x, y) = [x$ is a suffix of $y]$.*

Proof. First, let us repeat that we treat each of the above functions as an integer function with each $x \in \Sigma^*$ representing an integer $\iota_\Sigma^{-1}(x)$. For instance, in part (a), the function $leng_\Sigma$ maps an integer n to the integer $|\iota_\Sigma(n)|$; and in part (d), the function sub_Σ maps two integers n and m to 1 if $\iota_\Sigma(n)$ is a substring of $\iota_\Sigma(m)$, and to 0, otherwise.

(a) It is easy to see that the least string of length $n + 1$ is $w = s_1 s_1 \cdots s_1$ (with $n + 1$ symbols s_1) and $\iota_\Sigma^{-1}(w) = k^n + k^{n-1} + \cdots + 1$. Thus, for any $m > 0$, $|\iota_\Sigma(m)| = (\min n)_{n \leq m}[k^n + k^{n-1} + \cdots + 1 > m]$.

(b) This can be proved by induction. For $k = 1$, $concat_\Sigma^1$ is just the identity function. For $k > 1$,

$$concat_\Sigma^k(x_1, \ldots, x_k) = concat_\Sigma^{k-1}(x_1, \ldots, x_{k-1}) \cdot k^{|x_k|} + x_k.$$

(c) If $1 \leq i \leq |x|$ and $1 \leq \ell \leq |x| - i + 1$, then

$$substr_\Sigma(x, i, \ell) = (\min y)_{y \leq x}[|y| = \ell \text{ and}$$
$$(\exists u)_{u \leq x}(\exists v)_{v \leq x}[|u| = i - 1 \text{ and } uyv = x]].$$

(In the above, $[uyv = x]$ means $[concat_\Sigma^3(u, y, v) = x]$.)

(d) $sub_\Sigma(x, y) = (\exists u)_{u \leq y}(\exists v)_{v \leq y}[uxv = y]$.

(e) $head_\Sigma(x, y) = (\exists v)_{v \leq y}[xv = y]$.

(f) $tail_\Sigma(x, y) = (\exists u)_{u \leq y}[ux = y]$.   □

We are ready to prove that the notions of Turing-computability and partial recursiveness are equivalent. We first show that the *computation* by a grammar, as describe by Theorem 4.19, is partial recursive.

Lemma 4.43 *For any grammar G, the predicate*

$$derive_G(u, v, k) = [u \overset{*}{\Rightarrow} v \text{ in exactly } k \text{ steps}]$$

is primitive recursive.

Proof. First, the predicate $rule(x, y) = [x \to y$ is a rule of $G]$ is primitive recursive: Suppose G has rules $x_1 \to y_1$, $x_2 \to y_2$, ..., $x_m \to y_m$. Then,

$$rule(x, y) = [x = x_1 \text{ and } y = y_1] \text{ or } [x = x_2 \text{ and } y = y_2]$$
$$\text{or } \cdots \text{ or } [x = x_m \text{ and } y = y_m].$$

Next, we observe that the predicate $[u \Rightarrow v]$ is primitive recursive:

$$[u \Rightarrow v] = (\exists w_1)_{|w_1| \leq |u|}(\exists w_2)_{|w_2| \leq |u|}(\exists x)_{|x| \leq |u|}(\exists y)_{|y| \leq |v|}$$
$$[rule(x, y) \text{ and } u = w_1 x w_2 \text{ and } v = w_1 y w_2].$$

(*Note*: $|w| \leq m$ is equivalent to $w \leq k^m + k^{m-1} + \cdots + k$.)

Finally, we observe that

$$derive_G(u, v, 0) = eq(u, v),$$
$$derive_G(u, v, k+1) = (\exists w)_{|w| \leq |v| + \ell}[derive_G(u, w, k) \text{ and } w \Rightarrow v],$$

where ℓ is the length of the longest string in the left-hand side of any rule in G. Therefore, $derive_G$ is primitive recursive.   □

Theorem 4.44 *Every Turing-computable function is partial recursive.*

Proof. From Theorem 4.19, we know that if a function $f : (\Sigma^*)^k \to \Sigma^*$ is computable by TM M, then there is a grammar G_M that simulates the machine M such that

$$f(x_1, x_2, \ldots, x_k) = y \iff (\exists t)\, derive_{G_M}([\mathsf{B}x_1\mathsf{B}x_2\mathsf{B}\ldots\mathsf{B}x_k s\mathsf{B}], [\mathsf{B}yh\mathsf{B}], t).$$

We could then, as demonstrated in Example 4.39, use this relation between f and $derive_{G_M}$ to show that f is partial recursive.

We note, however, that f and $derive_{G_M}$ are two functions defined on two different alphabets: f on Σ and $derive_{G_M}$ on $\Lambda = \Gamma \cup Q \cup \{[,]\}$, where $\Sigma \subseteq \Lambda$ (see Theorem 4.19). Assume that $\Sigma = \{s_1, s_2, \ldots, s_m\}$ and $\Lambda = \{s_1, \ldots, s_m, s_{m+1}, \ldots, s_n\}$, with the ordering $s_1 \prec \cdots \prec s_m \prec s_{m+1} \prec \cdots \prec s_n$. Then, a string $x \in \Sigma^*$ represents the integer $\iota_\Sigma^{-1}(x)$ when we deal with function f and it represents the integer $\iota_\Lambda^{-1}(x)$ when we deal with grammar G_M. Therefore, to use the above relation, we must first "change base" to convert them into the same base Λ.

We define an integer function $base_{\Sigma,\Lambda}(i) = \iota_\Lambda^{-1}(\iota_\Sigma(i))$. For instance, if $m = 5$ and $n = 10$, then the string $s_2 s_1 s_3$ in Σ^* represents $2 \cdot m^2 + 1 \cdot m + 3 = 58$, and $s_2 s_1 s_3$ in Λ^* represents $2 \cdot n^2 + 1 \cdot n + 3 = 213$. The function $base_{\Sigma,\Lambda}$ then maps 58 to 213.

Using Theorem 4.40, it is not hard to see that $base_{\Sigma,\Lambda}$ is primitive recursive:

$$base_{\Sigma,\Lambda}(i) = (\min j)_{j \le n^{leng_\Sigma(i)+1}}[leng_\Lambda(j) = leng_\Sigma(i)$$
$$\text{and } (\forall \ell)_{1 \le \ell \le leng_\Lambda(j)}[subseq_\Lambda(j, \ell, 1) = subseq_\Sigma(i, \ell, 1)]].$$

Now we can complete the proof that f is partial recursive. Formally, we need to show that the function $\tilde{f} : \mathbf{N}^k \to \mathbf{N}$, defined by $\tilde{f}(n_1, \ldots, n_k) = \iota_\Sigma^{-1}(f(\iota_\Sigma(n_1), \ldots, \iota_\Sigma(n_k)))$, is primitive recursive. To do this, we first change base to set up the initial and final strings of G_M. That is, we define

$$g_1(n_1, \ldots, n_k) = concat_\Lambda^{2k+4}([, \mathsf{B}, base_{\Sigma,\Lambda}(n_1), \mathsf{B}, \ldots, \mathsf{B}, base_{\Sigma,\Lambda}(n_k), s, \mathsf{B},]),$$

and

$$g_2(m_1) = concat_\Lambda^6([, \mathsf{B}, base_{\Sigma,\Lambda}(m_1), h, \mathsf{B},]).$$

Then, we get

$$\tilde{f}(n_1, \ldots, n_k) = m_1 \iff (\exists t)\, \widetilde{derive}_{G_M}(g_1(n_1, \ldots, n_k), g_2(m_1), t),$$

where $\widetilde{derive}_{G_M}$ is the integer function associated with the string function $derive_{G_M}$ over the alphabet Λ. By combining m_1 and t into a single integer $m_2 = \langle m_1, t \rangle$, we can express $\tilde{f}$ as

$$\tilde{f}(n_1, \ldots, n_k) = l((\min m_2)\, \widetilde{derive}_{G_M}(g_1(n_1, \ldots, n_k), g_2(l(m_2)), r(m_2)).$$

This shows that $\tilde{f}$ is partial recursive. $\qquad\square$

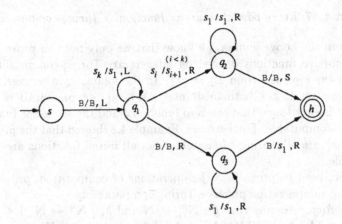

Figure 4.19: The Turing machine for *succ*.

Theorem 4.45 *For any grammar G over Σ, $L(G)$ is r.e.*

Proof. For any string $x \in \Sigma^*$, $x \in L(G)$ if and only if $(\exists k)\,derive_G(S, x, k)$. $\quad\square$

Next, we show that partial recursive functions are Turing-computable. First, we show that *changing of base* is Turing-computable. The basic representation for nonnegative integers is $\Sigma_1 = \{1\}$, with the string 1^n representing the integer n.

Lemma 4.46 *For any fixed Σ, let $\tau_\Sigma : \Sigma_1^* \to \Sigma^*$ be the function $\tau_\Sigma(1^n) = \iota_\Sigma(n)$. Then, both τ_Σ and τ_Σ^{-1} are Turing-computable.*

Proof. First, we note that the function *succ* : $\Sigma^* \to \Sigma^*$ which maps a string x to its successor in the lexicographic ordering is Turing-computable. The machine M_{succ} for *succ* is shown in Figure 4.19.

Next, we design a three-tape TM M that computes the function τ_Σ, using tape 1 as the input tape, tape 2 as the work tape and tape 3 as the output tape. We only describe the basic structure of the machine and omit the precise instructions:

(1) M copies the input to tape 2.

(2) M repeats step 3 until tape 2 has no symbol 1 left.

(3) M removes a symbol 1 from tape 2 and then simulates the machine M_{succ} on tape 3.

It is clear that when tape 2 has no symbol 1 left, tape 3 will have the nth string of Σ^* under the lexicographic ordering.

For the function τ_Σ^{-1}, we can design a TM M_1 that performs just the inverse of the above machine M. That is, M_1 first copies the input x to tape 2. Then, it simulates a machine that computes the inverse function of *succ* on tape 2 and writes a symbol 1 on tape 3, and it repeats this until tape 2 has no symbol in Σ left. We leave the details to the reader as an exercise. $\quad\square$

Theorem 4.47 *Every partial recursive function is Turing-computable.*

Proof. From the above lemma, we know that we only need to prove that all partial recursive functions defined on integers are Turing-computable, with respect to the representation $\Sigma_1 = \{1\}$. In the following, whenever there is no confusion, we do not distinguish integer n from its representation 1^n.

First, it is easy to see that the zero function ζ and the successor function σ are Turing-computable. Furthermore, Example 4.8 showed that the projection functions π_i^k are all Turing-computable. So, all initial functions are Turing-computable.

Next, we need to prove that the operations of composition, primitive recursion and minimization preserve Turing-computability.

Composition. Assume that $g : \mathbf{N}^m \to \mathbf{N}$ and $h_i : \mathbf{N}^k \to \mathbf{N}$, $1 \leq i \leq m$, are computed by 3-tape TM's M_i, $0 \leq i \leq m$, respectively. We design a new four-tape TM M that computes function

$$f(n_1, \ldots, n_k) = g(h_1(n_1, \ldots, n_k), \ldots, h_m(n_1, \ldots, n_k))$$

as follows:

(1) M repeats step 2 for $i = 1, 2, \ldots, m$.

(2) M simulates TM M_i on input $(n_1, \ldots, n_k)$, using tape 1 as the input tape, tape 2 as the output tape and tape 3 as the work tape. More precisely, for each simulation of machine M_i, it starts with the tape configuration

$$(B1^{n_1}B1^{n_2}B\cdots B1^{n_k}\underline{B}, B1^{t_1}B\cdots B1^{t_{i-1}}\underline{B}, B\underline{B}),$$

and ends with the tape configuration

$$(B1^{n_1}B1^{n_2}B\cdots B1^{n_k}\underline{B}, B1^{t_1}B\cdots B1^{t_{i-1}}B1^{t_i}\underline{B}, B\underline{B}),$$

where $t_j = h_j(n_1, \ldots, n_k)$, for $j = 1, \ldots, m$.

(3) M simulates TM M_0 on input $(t_1, t_2, \ldots, t_m)$, using tape 2 as the input tape, tape 3 as the output tape and tape 4 as the work tape.

Note that when M finishes the simulation of M_m, the configuration of tape 2 is

$$B1^{t_1}B\cdots B1^{t_2}B\cdots B1^{t_m}\underline{B},$$

and so the set up of the input to M_0 is correct.

Primitive Recursion. Assume that $g : \mathbf{N}^k \to \mathbf{N}$ and $h : \mathbf{N}^{k+2} \to \mathbf{N}$ are computed by 3-tape TM's M_g and M_h, respectively, and assume $f : \mathbf{N}^{k+1} \to \mathbf{N}$ is defined from g and h by primitive recursion. We can design a new multi-tape TM M to compute f in a bottom-up fashion: it first computes $t_0 = g(n_1, \ldots, n_k)$, and then uses this t_0 to compute $t_1 = h(n_1, \ldots, n_k, 0, t_0)$, and repeatedly computes $t_{i+1} = h(n_1, \ldots, n_k, i, t_i)$ for $i = 1, 2, \ldots, m$ (cf. the remark after Theorem 4.37). The detail of the machine M is left as an exercise.

Minimization. Assume that $g : \mathbf{N}^{k+1} \to \mathbf{N}$ is a total predicate and that

$$f(n_1, \ldots, n_k) = (\min m)\, g(n_1, \ldots, n_k, m).$$

Also assume that there is a 3-tape TM M_g computing g. We design a new 4-tape TM M to compute f. The idea of the machine M is to simulate M_g with inputs $(n_1, \ldots, n_k, m)$ for $m = 0, 1, \ldots$ until it outputs 1.

(1) M copies the inputs $(n_1, \ldots, n_k)$ to tape 2, and then adds an input 0 to tape 2.

(2) M repeats step 3 until tape 3 has the value 1. If tape 3 has the value 1, then M erases it and copies the last block of 1's of tape 2 to tape 3 as the output.

(3) M simulates machine M_g, using tape 2 as the input tape, tape 3 as the output tape and tape 4 as the work tape. When M_g halts and has an output not equal to 1, then M erases the output and adds 1 to the last input of tape 2.   □

Corollary 4.48 *A partial function* $f : (\Sigma^*)^k \to \Sigma^*$ *is partial recursive if and only if it is Turing-computable.*

Corollary 4.49 *A set* $A \subseteq (\Sigma^*)^k$ *is recursive if and only if it is Turing-decidable.*

Corollary 4.50 *Let* A *be a subset of* $(\Sigma^*)^k$, $k \geq 1$. *The following are equivalent:*

(a) *A is Turing-acceptable.*
(b) *$A = L(G)$ for some unrestricted grammar G.*
(c) *A is r.e.*

Proof. The direction (a) $\Rightarrow$ (b) is proved in Theorem 4.20, (b) $\Rightarrow$ (c) is Theorem 4.45, and (c) $\Rightarrow$ (a) follows immediately from Theorem 4.47.   □

Exercises 4.8

1. Design a multi-tape Turing machine that "adds" two strings over $\Sigma = \{1, 2, \ldots, X\}$; that is, on inputs $x, y \in \Sigma^*$, compute $z \in \Sigma^*$ such that $\iota_\Sigma^{-1}(z) = \iota_\Sigma^{-1}(x) + \iota_\Sigma^{-1}(y)$.

2. Complete the proof of the primitive recursion part of Theorem 4.47. That is, given multi-tape DTM's M_g and M_h computing functions g and h, design a multi-tape DTM M that computes the function f which is defined from functions g and h by primitive recursion.

3. Prove that every partial recursive function can be obtained from initial functions with a finite number of applications of composition and primitive recursion operations and a *single* application of unbounded minimization operation.

4. Show that the following functions defined on $\{a, b\}^*$ are primitive recursive:

    (a) $f_1(x, y) = [x$ is a subsequence of $y]$, where $x = x_1 x_2 \cdots x_k$ is a subsequence of $y = y_1 y_2 \cdots y_m$ if there exists a sequence of integers $1 \leq n_1 < n_2 < \cdots < n_k \leq m$ such that $y_{n_i} = x_i$ for $i = 1, \ldots, k$.

    (b) $f_2(x, y) =$ the number of occurrences of x as a substring in y.

    (c) $f_3(x) =$ the string obtained from x by replacing each occurrence of ba in x by ab. For instance, $f_3(babab) = ababb$.

    (d) $f_4(x) =$ the length of the longest w such that both w and w^R occur as substrings of x.

5. Show that every context-free language is primitive recursive.

6. Let $f(k, 0) = \lfloor e^k \rfloor$, and $f(k, n) =$ the nth digit to the right of the decimal point of the decimal expansion of e^k, where $e = \sum_{n=0}^{\infty} 1/n!$. Show that f is a recursive function. Is f a primitive recursive function?

7. Let G be a grammar over alphabet Σ. Show that the following functions g_1, g_2, g_3 are partial recursive:

    (a) $g_1(x) =$ the minimum number of steps in a derivation of x if $x \in L(G)$, and $g_1(x) \uparrow$, otherwise.

    (b) $g_2(x) =$ the minimum length (the number of symbols) of a derivation of x if $x \in L(G)$, and $g_2(x) \uparrow$, otherwise.

    (c) $g_3(x, y) = 1$ if there is a derivation of x that is shorter than any derivation of y, if both x and y are in $L(G)$, and $g_3(x, y) \uparrow$, otherwise.

    (d) Let $g_4(x, y) = \begin{cases} 1 & \text{if } g_3(x, y) \downarrow, \\ 0 & \text{otherwise.} \end{cases}$ Is g_4 a recursive function?

8. (*Ackermann function*) Define a function $A : \mathbf{N}^2 \to \mathbf{N}$ as follows:

$$A(0, n) = \begin{cases} n + 1 & \text{if } n \leq 1, \\ n + 2 & \text{otherwise,} \end{cases}$$
$$A(m + 1, 0) = 1,$$
$$A(m + 1, n + 1) = A(m, A(m + 1, n)).$$

    (a) Let $A_m(n) = A(m, n)$. What is $A_2(n)$? $A_3(n)$? Show that each A_m is primitive recursive.

    (b) Show that A is a recursive function.

    $\star$ (c) Show that for every primitive recursive function $f : \mathbf{N} \to \mathbf{N}$, there exists an integer $k \geq 0$ such that $f(n) \leq A_k(n)$ for almost all $n \geq 0$ (i.e., for all but finitely many $n \geq 0$).

    $\star$ (d) Show that A is not primitive recursive.

5

Computability Theory

5.1 Universal Turing Machines

In this chapter, we study the general properties of computable functions and develop some basic proof techniques for proving the computability or noncomputability results of given problems. This theory of computability is presented in the Turing machine model. Based on the Church-Turing Thesis, however, it is, in general, independent of the particular machine model chosen. In particular, we will present a few basic properties of the Turing machine model and demonstrate that the computability theory of any programming system which has these properties remains the same.

We start with the first basic property of the Turing machine system: the enumerability of Turing machines. We fix a class $\mathcal{M}$ of two-way infinite one-tape DTM's, which has the following common form:

(1) The states of a DTM in $\mathcal{M}$ are $q_1, \ldots, q_n$, for some $n \geq 1$.

(2) The initial state is q_1 and the final state is q_n.

(3) The input alphabet is $\{0, 1\}$.

(4) The tape alphabet is $\{a_1, a_2, \ldots, a_m\}$, $m \geq 3$, with $a_1 = 0$, $a_2 = 1$ and $a_3 = \mathsf{B}$.

For every finite alphabet Σ with t elements, we can encode a symbol in Σ by a string x in $\{0, 1\}^*$ of length $\lceil \log_2 t \rceil$. (It is like using a *byte* or a *word* to encode a symbol.) For any string x in Σ^*, we write $\tilde{x}$ to denote the string in $\{0, 1\}^*$ that encodes the string x symbol by symbol. It is not hard to see that for every Turing-computable function $f : (\Sigma^*)^k \to \Sigma$, there exists a DTM M in $\mathcal{M}$ such that M computes $\tilde{f} : (\{0,1\}^*)^k \to \{0,1\}^*$, where $\tilde{f}(\tilde{x}_1, \tilde{x}_2, \ldots, \tilde{x}_k) = \tilde{y}$ if and only if $f(x_1, x_2, \ldots, x_k) = y$. Therefore, we may consider a computational system in which the only machines available are those in $\mathcal{M}$, and the class of Turing-computable functions (under the above coding system) remains the same.

Coding of Turing Machines. We can encode each DTM M in $\mathcal{M}$ itself by a string in $\{0,1\}^*$ in the following way: First, each instruction $\delta(q_i, a_j) = (q_k, a_\ell, D_h)$ is encoded by the string

$$10^i 10^j 10^k 10^\ell 10^h 1,$$

where $h = 1, 2$, with D_1 representing L and D_2 representing R. Then, a machine in $\mathcal{M}$ with t instructions can be encoded by the string

$$1^k code_1 code_2 \cdots code_t 11, \tag{5.1}$$

where $code_i$ is the code of the ith instruction and k is any integer greater than 1. We note that we do not need to encode any other information of M, since we can find the information from the above code:

(1) $Q = \{q_1, \ldots, q_n\}$, where n is the length of the longest third 0-block in an instruction code. (We require that each DTM M in $\mathcal{M}$ must contain a "halting instruction," even if the machine may never execute it. Also note that the final state q_n does not occur in the first 0-block of an instruction code.)

(2) $\Sigma = \{a_1, \ldots, a_m\}$, where m is the length of the longest second or fourth 0-block in an instruction code.

(3) The starting state is q_1.

(4) The final state is q_n.

(5) The blank is 0^3.

Note that the above coding system is not one-to-one. More precisely, some strings in $\{0,1\}^*$ do not encode any DTM, and many strings encode the same DTM. To simplify the coding system, we arbitrarily define that a string $x \in \{0,1\}^*$ represents a fixed *empty DTM* M_ε, if x does not have the above correct form of a DTM code (e.g., if it begins with 110). This machine M_ε is defined as $(\{q_1, q_2\}, \{a_1, a_2\}, \{a_1, a_2, \text{B}\}, \delta_\varepsilon, q_2)$, where δ_ε contains a single instruction $\delta_\varepsilon(q_1, a_1) = (q_2, a_1, R)$. Note that M_ε contains a halting instruction which will never be executed, since its initial configurations $(q_1, \text{B}x\underline{\text{B}})$ do not have a successor configuration. Thus, it halts and rejects any input $x \in \{0,1\}^*$ in zero move; that is, $L(M_\varepsilon) = \emptyset$. With this assumption, we see that every string in $\{0,1\}^*$ encodes a DTM in $\mathcal{M}$. Also, each DTM has an infinite number of codes. We say a string $x \in \{0,1\}^*$ is a *legal code* if it encodes a nonempty DTM in the form (5.1).

Example 5.1 *Show that the set* $L = \{x \in \{0,1\}^* \mid x$ *is a legal code*$\}$ *is primitive recursive.*

Proof. A string x is legal if and only if the following hold:

(i) It is of the form (5.1);

(ii) For each instruction code $10^i 10^j 10^k 10^\ell 10^h 1$ of x, h is either 1 or 2;

(iii) No two instruction codes start with the same substring $10^i 10^j 1$;

(iv) If the maximum state is q_n, then no instruction begins with $10^n 1$.

We first check that the set of strings of the form (5.1) is a regular set

$$11^+ (10^+ 10^+ 10^+ 10^+ 10^+ 1)^* 11.$$

In Exercise 5 of Section 4.8, we showed that all context-free languages are primitive recursive. Since a regular language is context-free, we see that condition (i) is primitive recursive.

Recall that $sub(u, v) = [u$ is a substring of $v]$, $head(u, v) = [u$ is a prefix of $v]$ and $tail(u, v) = [u$ is a suffix of $v]$ are all primitive recursive predicates (Example 4.42).[1] Define the predicate $instr(y, x)$ to mean that y is an instruction code of x; or, equivalently,

$$y \in 10^+ 10^+ 10^+ 10^+ 10^+ 1 \text{ and } sub(y, x).$$

Then, it is clear that $instr$ is primitive recursive.

We now check the other three conditions. For condition (ii), we note that it is equivalent to

$$(\forall y)_{|y| \leq |x|} (\forall h)_{1 \leq h \leq |x|} [[instr(y, x) \text{ and } tail(10^h 1, y)] \Rightarrow [h = 1 \text{ or } h = 2]].$$

Similarly, condition (iii) is equivalent to

$$(\forall y)_{|y| \leq |x|} (\forall z)_{|z| \leq |x|} [[instr(y, x) \text{ and } instr(z, x) \text{ and }$$
$$(\exists w)_{|w| \leq |y|} [w \in 10^+ 10^+ 1 \text{ and } head(w, y) \text{ and } head(w, z)]] \Rightarrow y = z].$$

For condition (iv), we note that the maximum state number of x is

$$maxstate(x) = (\max k)_{1 \leq k \leq |x|} (\exists i)_{1 \leq i \leq |x|} (\exists j)_{1 \leq j \leq |x|}$$
$$(\exists \ell)_{1 \leq \ell \leq |x|} (\exists h)_{1 \leq h \leq |x|} \, instr(10^i 10^j 10^k 10^\ell 10^h 1, x).$$

So, it is a primitive recursive function. (See Exercise 3 of Section 4.6 for the operation max.) Now, condition (iv) can be stated as

$$(\forall i)_{i \leq |x|} (\forall y)_{|y| \leq |x|} [instr(y, x) \text{ and } head(10^i 1, y) \Rightarrow i < maxstate(x)]. \quad \square$$

---

[1] When $\Sigma_1 = \{0, 1\}$ is understood, we write $sub(u, v)$ for $sub_{\Sigma_1}(u, v)$, etc.

Enumeration of Partial Recursive Functions and R.E. Sets. For each string $x \in \{0,1\}^*$, we let M_x be the DTM in $\mathcal{M}$ such that x is one of its codes. Recall that $\iota_{\{0,1\}}(n)$ is the nth string in $\{0,1\}^*$ under the lexicographic ordering. If $x = \iota_{\{0,1\}}(n)$, we also write M_n for M_x. In the rest of this chapter, we write ι for $\iota_{\{0,1\}}$ and do not distinguish the integer n from the string $\iota(n)$.

For each $k \geq 1$, we write ϕ_n^k or $\phi_{\iota(n)}^k$ to denote the partial function from $(\{0,1\}^*)^k$ to $\{0,1\}^*$ computed by M_n. That is, for every input $(x_1, x_2, \ldots, x_k)$, if M_n halts on it with the final configuration $(h, y\underline{\mathtt{B}})$ for some $y \in \{0,1\}^*$, then $\phi_n^k(x_1, x_2, \ldots, x_k) = y$; and if M_n does not halt on this input, then $\phi_n^k(x_1, x_2, \ldots, x_k)$ is undefined. (If M_n halts on input $(x_1, x_2, \ldots, x_k)$ with a final configuration $(h, u\underline{a}v)$ that is not of the form $(h, y\underline{\mathtt{B}})$ for some $y \in \{0,1\}^*$, we arbitrarily define its output to be u_1 where u_1 is the longest suffix of u that is in $\{0,1\}^*$.) The class $\{\phi_n^k \mid k \geq 1, n \geq 0\}$ is exactly the class of partial recursive functions over $\{0,1\}$.

Every machine M_n accepts a language

$$L(M_n) = \{x \in \{0,1\}^* \mid (q_1, x\underline{\mathtt{B}}) \vdash_{M_n}^* (q_n, u\underline{a}v) \text{ for some } a \in \Gamma, u, v \in \Gamma^*\},$$

or, equivalently, $L(M_n)$ is the domain of ϕ_n^1. We write W_n or $W_{\iota(n)}$ to denote the set $L(M_n)$. Then, $\{W_n \mid n \geq 0\}$ is exactly the class of r.e. sets over alphabet $\{0,1\}^*$.[2]

The above coding system shows that there are only countably many DTMs in $\mathcal{M}$ and hence there are only countably many Turing-computable functions. On the other hand, there are uncountably many functions from a countable domain Σ^* (see Example 5.18). Thus, *most* functions are noncomputable.

Proposition 5.2 *Let Σ be any finite alphabet.*
  (a) There exists a function $f : \Sigma^* \to \Sigma^*$ that is not partial recursive.
  (b) There exists a set $A \subseteq \Sigma^*$ that is not r.e. (and hence not recursive).

Universal Turing Machines. Once we have a coding system for DTM's in $\mathcal{M}$, we can construct a *universal Turing machine* that can read the code y of a DTM M_y and a string x and simulate M_y on input x. In other words, a universal DTM works, in the modern computer terminology, like an *interpreter* of the programs written in our coding system. In this programming system, a programmer does not have to build a specific DTM by hardware; instead, he/she needs only a single set of hardware, the universal DTM U, and can write a program for any DTM and submit the program together with its inputs to the machine U and let U simulate it. It is interesting to mention that this

---

[2] We may also define, for each $k \geq 2$, the set W_n^k to be $\{(x_1, \ldots, x_k) \mid M_n \text{ halts on input } (x_1, \ldots, x_k)\}$. However, since we can always use pairing functions to encode a finite number of strings into one, the computability theory of these sets are the same as that of sets W_n, and we will not discuss this separately.

concept of the universal Turing machine was conceived by Alan Turing well before the real digital computers were invented.

In the following, we present a brief description of how the universal DTM works. We will present it as a three-tape DTM over the tape alphabet $\{0, 1, B\}$. Theorem 4.13 showed that there is an equivalent one-tape DTM for it. Therefore, there is actually a universal DTM in $\mathcal{M}$.

First, we note that machine U uses only a fixed alphabet $\{0, 1, B\}$, whereas machines M_y in $\mathcal{M}$ may have a bigger alphabet $\{a_1, \ldots, a_m\}$. So, we need a fixed coding system to encode a string x in $\{a_1, \ldots, a_m\}^*$ by a string x' in $\{0, 1\}^*$. We do this by a simple scheme: the symbol a_i is represented by string 0^i, and a string $x = a_{i_1} a_{i_2} \ldots a_{i_n}$ is represented by the string $x' = 0^{i_1} 1 0^{i_2} 1 \cdots 1 0^{i_n}$.

The machine U uses tape 1 as the input tape. When it starts, the configuration of tape 1 is of the form

$$x'_1 B x'_2 B \cdots B x'_k B y \underline{B},$$

where y is to be interpreted as the code of machine M_y and $x_1, \ldots, x_k$ are the inputs to machine M_y. (*Note*: Here, B denotes the blank symbol of U. The blank symbol a_3 of M_y is represented by a string 0^3.) The machine U uses tape 2 to simulate the tape of machine M_y, and uses tape 3 to store the current state of machine M_y. So, tapes 2 and 3 together represent a configuration of machine M_y.

With this setting, the simulation of M_y can be described as follows:

(1) *Initialization*: First, U copies y to tape 3 and checks whether y is a *legal* code of a DTM in $\mathcal{M}$. By Example 5.1, this problem is primitive recursive and so can be done by a DTM. (*Note*: Tape 1 is read-only, and so we need to copy it to tape 3 to do the checking.)

If it is not legal, then machine U copies the inputs $(x'_1, \ldots, x'_k)$ to tape 2 and halts (i.e., it accepts the input and outputs the same values as the inputs).

If it is legal, the machine U copies the inputs to tape 2 and writes 0 on tape 3 (to indicate that M_y is in state q_1). The configuration after this initialization step is

$$(s, x'_1 B \cdots B x'_k B y \underline{B}, 1 x'_1 10^3 1 \cdots 10^3 1 x'_k \underline{1} 0^3 1, \underline{B} 0).$$

Again, in the above, B denotes the blank symbol of U and 0^3 denotes the code of the blank symbol a_3 of M_y. Note that the head of tape 2 is scanning the symbol 1 that lies to the left of the 0-block which represents the symbol in $\{a_1, \ldots, a_m\}$ currently scanned by machine M_y (called the *current* 0-block).

(2) *Simulation*: Each move of machine M_y can be simulated as follows: First, U scans the string y to find an instruction code starting with $10^i 10^j 1$ where 0^i is the current content of tape 3 and 0^j is the 0-block to the right of the head of tape 2.

If such an instruction $10^i 10^j 10^k 10^\ell 10^h 1$ is found, then U simulates the instruction accordingly. Namely, it changes the content of tape 3 to 0^k, changes the 0-block to the right of the head of tape 2 to 0^ℓ, and moves the head of tape 2 to the next 1 to the right (if $h = 2$) or to the left (if $h = 1$). When it moves right, it also checks if this is the rightmost 1; if so, it adds $0^3 1$ to its right. When it moves left, it checks whether it is currently scanning the leftmost 1; if so, it adds 10^3 to its left and moves the tape head to scan the leftmost 1.

If such an instruction is not found, then U determines whether the current state stored in tape 3 is the final state q_n or not (i.e., whether it is equal to $maxstate(y)$). If it is the final state, then it halts and accepts. Otherwise, it enters an infinite loop and never halts. (In practice, it halts and *rejects*.)

We leave the details of the simulation as an exercise (see Exercise 2 of this section).

We have just proved the following theorem:

Theorem 5.3 *For every $k \geq 1$, the partial function $\Phi^k : (\{0,1\}^*)^{k+1} \to \{0,1\}^*$, defined by*

$$\Phi^k(x_1, x_2, \ldots, x_k, y) = \phi_y^k(x_1, x_2, \ldots, x_k),$$

is partial recursive.

The coding of a DTM by a string and the existence of a universal DTM play an important role in computability theory. So, let us study the computation of the universal DTM in more detail. First, let us encode each configuration of M_y by a single string in $\{0,1\}^*$. That is, the configuration

$$(q_j, a_{i_1} a_{i_2} \cdots a_{i_{m-1}} \underline{a_{i_m}} a_{i_{m+1}} \cdots a_{i_n})$$

of the machine M_y is encoded by

$$1110^{i_1} 10^{i_2} 1 \cdots 10^{i_{m-1}} 110^j 110^{i_m} 1 \cdots 10^{i_n} 111.$$

We say a string u is a *legal* code of a configuration if u is of the above form.

Example 5.4 *Show that the following predicates are primitive recursive:*
   (a) $legal(u, y) = [u$ is a legal code of a configuration of $M_y]$.

   (b) $final(u, y) = [legal(u, y)$ and u is a final configuration$]$.

   (c) $next(u, v, y) = [$if $final(u, y)$ then $u = v$ else $u \vdash_{M_y} v]$.

Proof. For any string u of length greater than 5, let $u' = substr(u, 3, |u| - 4)$.
   (a) We observe that u is a legal code of a configuration of M_y if and only if
   (i) $u \in 11(10^+)^* 110^+ 11(0^+1)^* 11$,

   (ii) $(\forall i)_{1 \leq i \leq |u|}[sub(110^i 11, u') \Rightarrow i \leq maxstate(y)]$, and

   (iii) $(\forall j)_{1 \leq j \leq |u|}[sub(10^j 1, u')$ and $neg(sub(110^j 11, u')) \Rightarrow j \leq maxsym(y)]$, where $maxstate(y)$ is the maximum state number of M_y and $maxsym(y)$ is the maximum symbol number of M_y.

The function $maxstate$ has been shown to be primitive recursive in Example 5.1. The function $maxsym$ can be proved to be primitive recursive in a similar way. From these results, we see that $legal$ is primitive recursive too.

(b) $final(u, y)$ is true if and only if $legal(u, y)$ and $110^{maxstate(y)}11$ is a substring of u'.

(c) We note that the first condition is easily checked by (b) above. It is not hard to see that the condition $[u \vdash_{M_y} v]$ is also primitive recursive (see Exercise 2). Therefore, the predicate $next$ is also primitive recursive. $\square$

Example 5.5 *Show that the following functions are primitive recursive:*

(a) $init^k(x_1, \ldots, x_k, y) =$ *the initial configuration of M_y on inputs $(x_1, \ldots, x_k)$, encoded as described above.*

(b) $output(u, y) =$ *the output in u if u is a final configuration of M_y, and $= 0$ otherwise.*

Proof. (a) First, we recall that each input symbol 0 is encoded by 0, symbol 1 by 00, and symbol blank B is by 0^3. Thus, it is clear that the function $g(x) = x'$ is primitive recursive, and so

$$init^k(x_1, \ldots, x_k, y) = 1x_1'10^31x_2'1 \cdots 10^31x_k'110110^3111$$

is primitive recursive.

(b) Recall that the output of u is the longest tail in $\{0, 1\}^*$ of the substring to the left of the state symbol of u. So, let

$$left(u) = (\min v)_{|v| \leq |u|} (\exists w)_{|w| \leq |u|} (\exists k)_{k \leq |u|} [11v110^k11w111 = u],$$

and we have

$$output(u, y) = if\ final(u, y)\ then\ (\max z)_{|z| \leq |u|} [tail(g(z), left(u))]\ else\ 0. \quad \square$$

The following two predicates will be used in the next few sections.

Lemma 5.6 *The following predicates are primitive recursive:*

(a) *For each $k \geq 1$, $halt^k(x_1, \ldots, x_k, y, t) = [M_y$ halts on inputs $(x_1, \ldots, x_k)$ in at most t moves].*

(b) *For each $k \geq 1$, $print^k(x_1, \ldots, x_k, z, y, t) = [M_y$ halts on inputs $(x_1, \ldots, x_k)$ in at most t moves and outputs z].*

Proof. (a) Define function $f(u, v, y, t)$ to mean that there exists $u_0, u_1, \ldots, u_t$ such that $u = u_0$, $v = u_t$ and $next(u_i, u_{i+1}, y)$ for all $i = 0, 1, \ldots, t-1$. Then, f is primitive recursive:

$$f(u, v, y, 0) = [u = v],$$
$$f(u, v, y, t+1) = (\exists w)_{|w| \leq |u| + |y|} [next(u, w, y)\ and\ f(w, v, y, t)].$$

Now, we note that

$$halt^k(x_1, \ldots, x_k, y, t) = (\exists v)_{|v| \leq |u_0| + t|y|}[f(u_0, v, y, t) \text{ and } final(v, y)],$$

where $u_0 = init^k(x_1, \ldots, x_k, y)$. Thus, $halt^k$ is primitive recursive.

(b) We note that $print^k(x_1, \ldots, x_k, z, y, t)$ is the same as $halt^k(x_1, \ldots, x_k, y, t)$ above plus the extra condition that $output(v, y) = z$.   □

When $k = 1$, we write $halt$ for $halt^1$ and $print$ for $print^1$.

Exercises 5.1

1. Show that the following functions are primitive recursive:

   (a) $state(i, \ell, x) = [x$ is a legal code of a DTM $M]$ and $[substr_{\{0,1\}}(x, i, \ell + 2)$ is equal to $10^\ell 1$ and represents a state q_ℓ in $M]$.

   (b) $chstate(x, i, j) = $ the code of a DTM which is obtained from M_x by changing each state q_i to q_j, if x is a legal code of a DTM M_x; and it is $= 0$, otherwise.

   (c) $\infty\text{-}loop(i, x) = [x$ is a legal DTM code] and $[M_x$ is undefined at state q_i on any symbol in $\Gamma]$.

2. Complete the proof of Example 5.4(c).

3. Show the detail of how the universal DTM U simulates a DTM M_y. In particular, show the instructions that search for the instruction code that matches the current state in tape 3 and the current symbol in tape 2. Then, show how to change state, change tape symbol and move left or right according to the instruction code.

5.2   R.E. Sets and Recursive Sets

In this section, we study the general properties of the classes of r.e. sets and recursive sets. In particular, we present a few characterizations of r.e. sets. Based on the work of the last section, we consider only sets over alphabet $\{0, 1\}$. We follow the notation developed in Section 4.8 and identify each integer n with the nth string $\iota_{\{0,1\}}(n)$ in $\{0, 1\}^*$.

First, we list two important results obtained in the last section.

Theorem 5.7 (Enumeration Theorem)

(a) A function $f : (\{0,1\}^*)^k \to \{0,1\}$ is partial recursive if and only if $f = \phi_n^k$ for some $n \geq 0$.

(b) A set A is r.e. if and only if $A = W_n$ for some $n \geq 0$.

From the enumeration theorem, we say $\{W_n\}$ is an *effective enumeration* of all r.e. sets.

Theorem 5.8 (Projection Theorem) *Let $A \subseteq \{0,1\}^*$. The following are equivalent:*

(a) There exists a primitive recursive predicate R such that $A = \{x \mid (\exists y) R(x, y)\}$.

(b) There exists a recursive predicate R such that $A = \{x \mid (\exists y) R(x, y)\}$.

(c) A is r.e.

Proof. The direction (a) $\Rightarrow$ (b) is trivial. The direction (b) $\Rightarrow$ (c) is proved in Example 4.37. For (c) $\Rightarrow$ (a), we assume that $A = W_n$ and note that, from Lemma 5.6, $W_n = \{x \mid (\exists t) halt(x, n, t)\}$. $\square$

The above two theorems can often simplify our proofs about r.e. sets. Let us look at some examples.

Example 5.9 *Assume that sets A and B are r.e. Show that sets $A \cup B$ and $A \cap B$ are also r.e.*

Proof 1 (by the product DTM). Assume that $A = W_n$ and $B = W_m$. First, we consider $C = A \cup B$. The idea is to construct a new DTM M that simulates both machines M_n and M_m. The machine M halts when one of the machines M_n or M_m halts. An important point is that M needs to simulate the machines M_n and M_m *in parallel*, because if we simulate one machine first and if that machine does not halt then we will never be able to find out whether the other machine halts or not.

To do so, we design a DTM M as the product DTM of M_n and M_m, like the product automata introduced in Sections 2.2 and 3.5; that is, each state of M encodes two states, one from M_n and the other from M_m. Furthermore, M uses two separate tapes to simulate the tape configurations of the two machines.

More precisely, assume that M_n has states $Q_n = \{q_1, \ldots, q_s\}$ and M_m has states $Q_m = \{q_1, \ldots, q_t\}$. Then, M has states $Q = Q_n \times Q_m$ plus some auxiliary states, and it has two tapes. It first uses the auxiliary states to copy the input from tape 1 to tape 2. Then, it uses the following instructions to simulate M_n and M_m parallelly:

$$\delta([q_{i_1}, q_{j_1}], (a_1, b_1)) = ([q_{i_2}, q_{j_2}], (a_2, b_2), (D_1, D_2)),$$

if $\delta_n(q_{i_1}, a_1) = (q_{i_2}, a_2, D_1)$ and $\delta_n(q_{j_1}, b_1) = (q_{j_2}, b_2, D_2)$, where δ_n and δ_m are the transition functions of M_n and M_m, respectively.

Recall that, in the Turing machine system $\mathcal{M}$, the highest-indexed state is the halting state. So, M needs to halt when it reaches one of the following states:

$$[q_s, q_j], \ [q_i, q_t], \ 1 \leq i \leq s, 1 \leq j \leq t.$$

Since M should have a single halting state h, we add the following instructions to M:

(1) $\delta([q_s, q_j], (a, b)) = (h, (a, b), (S, S))$, for $1 \leq j \leq t$, and $a \in \Gamma_n$, $b \in \Gamma_m$,

(2) $\delta([q_i, q_t], (a, b)) = (h, (a, b), (S, S))$, for $1 \leq i \leq s$, and $a \in \Gamma_n$, $b \in \Gamma_m$,

where Γ_n and Γ_m are the sets of tape symbols of M_n and M_m, respectively.

Next, we construct a DTM M' for set $D = A \cap B$. The machine M' behaves like machine M, except that it needs to continue simulating M_n or M_m when the simulation of the other DTM halts. That is, M' contains all instructions of M, except for those in (1) and (2), plus the following additional instructions:

(3) For each instruction $\delta_n(q_{i_1}, a_1) = (q_{i_2}, a_2, D_1)$ of M_n, add a new instruction

$$\delta([q_{i_1}, q_t], (a_1, b_1)) = ([q_{i_2}, q_t], (a_2, b_1), (D_1, S)).$$

(4) For each instruction $\delta_m(q_{j_1}, b_1) = (q_{j_2}, b_2, D_2)$ of M_m, add a new instruction

$$\delta'([q_s, q_{j_1}], (a_1, b_1)) = ([q_s, q_{j_2}], (a_1, b_2), (S, D_2)).$$

Also, M' has a single halting state $[q_s, q_t]$.   □

Proof 2 (by dovetailing). In order to simulate M_n and M_m, we do not need to combine M_n and M_m together to form the product DTM. We may simply include two machines M_n and M_m as two *subprocedures* of a new DTM M, which can use them to simulate their computation. Since we do not know which one of the two machines halts first and how many moves it takes before it halts, the machine M needs to simulate both machines for an indefinite number of moves. How does it do that? It first simulates each machine for $t = 1$ move. If neither machine halts, it increases t by one and simulates each of them for 2 moves. If neither machine halts in 2 moves, it increases t again and continues the simulation until one of them halts. This technique is more general than the product DTM technique and has many other applications. We call it the *dovetailing* technique.

More precisely, for set $C = A \cup B$, the dovetailing algorithm M on an input x works as follows:

(1) Set $t := 1$.

(2) Simulate M_n on x for t moves. If it halts, then halt; otherwise, go to (3).

(3) Simulate M_m on x for t moves. If it halts, then halt; otherwise, go to (4).

(4) Increase t by one, and go to step (2).

It is clear that the above algorithm halts if at least one of M_n or M_m halts on x. Furthermore, the algorithm is quite simple, and we can easily see (by the Church-Turing Thesis) that it can be implemented by a DTM M. It follows that C is r.e.

For set $D = A \cap B$, we do not have to simulate M_n and M_m alternatingly, because we need to wait for both machines to halt anyway. So, the algorithm is simpler:

(1) Simulate M_n on x until it halts; then go to step (2).

(2) Simulate M_m on x. If it halts, then halt.   □

Proof 3 (by the projection theorem). Assume that $A = L(M_n)$ and $B = L(M_m)$. Then, by the projection theorem, $A = \{x \mid (\exists t_1)\, halt(x, n, t_1)\}$ and $B = \{x \mid (\exists t_2)\, halt(x, m, t_2)\}$. Now, observe that $x \in A \cup B$ if and only if

$$(\exists t)[halt(x, n, t) \text{ or } halt(x, m, t)].$$

It follows from the projection theorem that $A \cup B$ is r.e.

For set $A \cap B$, the proof is similar: $x \in A \cap B$ if and only if

$$(\exists t)[halt(x, n, t) \text{ and } halt(x, m, t)].$$ □

At first glance, it seems that Proof 3 is totally different from Proofs 1 and 2, since it avoids the construction of the DTM simulators completely. However, if we examine the proof more carefully, we can see that it actually uses the same idea of the dovetailing simulation, except that it uses the existential quantifier $(\exists t)$ and a simple operator *or* (and, in the case of $A \cap B$, the operator *and*) to *encode* the whole algorithm of Proof 2. In the following, we will see more examples of using the projection theorem to simplify the proofs.

Example 5.10 *Show that the set $\{y \mid W_y \neq \emptyset\}$ is r.e.*

Proof. The idea is, for a given input y, to simulate M_y on all possible inputs and halt whenever one of the simulations halts. This simulation algorithm is more complicated than that of Proof 2 of Example 5.9, since we need to dovetail through an infinite number of simulations. The algorithm may be described as follows:

(1) Set $t := 1$.

(2) Set $x := \varepsilon$.

(3) If $|x| \leq t$, then simulate M_y on x for t moves. If it halts, then halt; otherwise, go to step (4). If $|x| > t$, then go to step (5).

(4) Reset $x := x + 1$ (i.e, let x be the next string in the lexicographic ordering), and go to step (3).

(5) Reset $t := t + 1$, and go to step (2).

Note that if W_y is not empty then there must be a string w and a number n such that M_y halts on w in n moves. By the time the algorithm reaches the stage with $t = \max\{n, |w|\}$ and $x = w$, the simulation of M_y on x will halt (if the algorithm did not halt before this stage). Therefore, the above algorithm is correct.

The above dovetailing algorithm can be simplifed by the projection theorem as follows:

$$W_y \neq \emptyset \iff (\exists x)[x \in W_y]$$
$$\iff (\exists x)(\exists t)[halt(x, y, t)]$$
$$\iff (\exists z)[halt(l(z), y, r(z))].$$

(Recall that $\langle a, b \rangle$ is the pairing function developed in Section 4.7, and $l(z)$ and $r(z)$ are the inverse of the pairing function: $z = \langle l(z), r(z) \rangle$.)

We note that using the last line of the proof by the projection theorem, we can actually construct a simpler simulation algorithm because, by the use of the pairing function, we only need to search for one string z instead of two strings x and t:

(1) Set $z := 0$.

(2) Simulate M_y on input $x = l(z)$ for $t = r(z)$ moves. If it halts, then accept; otherwise, go to step (3).

(3) Reset $z := z + 1$, and go back to step (2).   □

Example 5.11 *Show that if A is r.e. then $B = \bigcup_{y \in A} W_y$ is also r.e.*

Proof. Assume that $A = M_n$. Intuitively, we need to simulate M_n on all possible inputs and then, for each y found in W_n, to simulate M_y on the given input x. All these simulations need to be dovetailed, and the algorithm does not seem simple at all (see Exercise 2).

On the other hand, the projection theorem gives us a very simple proof (and, hence, a simple simulation algorithm):

$$x \in B \iff (\exists y)[y \in W_n \text{ and } x \in W_y]$$
$$\iff (\exists y)(\exists t)[halt(y, n, t) \text{ and } halt(x, y, t)]$$
$$\iff (\exists z)[halt(l(z), n, r(z)) \text{ and } halt(x, l(z), r(z))].$$

It follows that B is r.e.   □

Example 5.12 *Show that the range of a partial recursive function f : $\{0, 1\}^* \to \{0, 1\}^*$ is an r.e. set.*

Proof. Assume that $f = \phi_y$ and let A be the range of f. Then, we have

$$z \in A \iff (\exists x)(\exists t) print(x, z, y, t)$$
$$\iff (\exists w) print(l(w), z, y, r(w)).$$ □

We say a tape of a DTM is a *one-way write-only* tape to mean that the DTM can only write on the tape and once a symbol is written, the tape head moves to the right and is not allowed to move left. We say an infinite set A is *Turing-enumerable* if there exists a two-tape DTM M, whose second tape is a one-way write-only tape, such that when it is given the empty string ε as the input, M prints an infinite sequence of strings $x_1, x_2, \ldots$ on the second tape, with every two strings separated by a blank, such that $A = \{x_1, x_2, \ldots\}$. Note that the strings printed by M does not have to follow any specific order, and they do not have to be distinct from each other. As long as M prints only strings in A and every string in A is eventually printed, then A is said to be *enumerated* by M.

Theorem 5.13 *Assume that A is an nonempty set. Then, the following are equivalent:*

  (a) A is Turing-enumerable.
  (b) A is the range of a primitive recursive function.
  (c) A is the range of a recursive function.
  (d) A is the range of a partial recursive function.
  (e) A is r.e.

Proof. The directions (b) $\Rightarrow$ (c) and (c) $\Rightarrow$ (d) are trivial. The direction (d) $\Rightarrow$ (e) is just Example 5.12. We need to prove (a) $\Rightarrow$ (c), (e) $\Rightarrow$ (a) and (e) $\Rightarrow$ (b).

(a) $\Rightarrow$ (c): Assume that machine M enumerates A. Then, we can design a new four-tape DTM M' that prints, on input n, the nth string enumerated by M:

> M' uses tape 1 as the input tape, treating the input n as a counter. It uses tape 4 as the output tape, and uses tapes 2 and 3 to simulate M. In the simulation, whenever M prints a string x followed by a blank on tape 2, M' examines tape 1. If the counter of tape 1 is 0, then M' copies the string x to tape 4 and halts; otherwise, it decreases the counter by 1, and continues the simulation of M.

We note that M enumerates an infinite number of strings, and so M' halts on every input n. Thus, the function computed by M' is recursive. In addition, its range is exactly the set A.

(e) $\Rightarrow$ (a): Assume that $A = W_y$. Then, we can design a DTM M that enumerates A as follows:

(1) Set $x := 0$.

(2) Simulate M_y on input $l(x)$ for $r(x)$ moves (on tape 1). If it halts, then print $l(x)$ on tape 2 and then print a blank **B**.

(3) Set $x := x + 1$ and go back to step (2).

(More precisely, we need to split tape 1 of M into two tracks, using one track to store the values of x, $l(x)$ and $r(x)$, and using the other to simulate M_y.)

It is clear that M prints only strings in A. In addition, if a string z is in A, then there exists an integer t such that $halt(z, y, t)$. It follows that z will be printed by M. Finally, we observe that if $halt(z, y, t)$, then M will print z for each $x = \langle z, t' \rangle$, with $t' > t$. Thus, M prints an infinite sequence of strings in A. This means that M enumerates set A.

(e) $\Rightarrow$ (b): Assume that $A = W_y$. Let x_0 be the least string in A. Then, define

$$f(x) = \begin{cases} l(x) & \text{if } halt(l(x), y, r(x)), \\ x_0 & \text{otherwise.} \end{cases}$$

It is clear that the range of f is set A. Furthermore, since $halt$ is a primitive recursive function, f is primitive recursive. $\square$

Theorem 5.14 *Assume that A is an infinite set. Then, A is r.e. if and only if*

(f) A is the range of a one-to-one, recursive function.

Proof. In the last theorem, we showed that the condition (e) of A being r.e. is equivalent to each of the conditions (a)–(d). It is clear that (f) $\Rightarrow$ (c). Therefore, we need only to prove that, for an infinite set A, (a) $\Rightarrow$ (f):

Assume that machine M enumerates A. Then, we can design a new four-tape DTM M' that works on input n as follows:

(1) M' uses tape 1 as the input tape, tape 4 as the output tape.

(2) M' uses tapes 2 and 3 to simulate M. When M prints a string followed by a blank on tape 3, M' checks whether the string has been printed before. If yes, M' erases it.

(3) If the string just printed is new, then M' checks whether this is the nth string remained on tape 3. If so, it copies this string to tape 4 and halts. Otherwise, it goes back to step (2). $\square$

Next we consider recursive sets. The following characterization of recursive sets is very useful. For every set $A \subseteq \{0,1\}^*$, we write $\overline{A}$ to denote the set $\{0,1\}^* - A$.

Theorem 5.15 *A set A is recursive if and only if both A and $\overline{A}$ are r.e.*

Proof. If A is recursive, then its characteristic function χ_A is recursive. That is, $\chi_A = \phi_n$ for some $n \geq 0$. So, we have

$$x \in A \iff (\exists t)\, print(x, 1, n, t),$$
$$x \in \overline{A} \iff (\exists t)\, print(x, 0, n, t).$$

By the projection theorem, both A and $\overline{A}$ are r.e.

Conversely, assume that $A = W_n$ and $\overline{A} = W_m$. Then, define

$$time(x) = (\min t)[halt(x, n, t) \text{ or } halt(x, m, t)].$$

Since x is either in W_n or in W_m, the function $time$ is a recursive function. Now, we see that $\chi_A(x) = halt(x, n, time(x))$ and it follows that A is recursive. $\square$

We will see in the next section (Corollary 5.20) that there exist sets that
are r.e. but not recursive.

Example 5.16 *Show that if A and B are recursive sets, then $A \cup B$, $A \cap B$
and $\overline{A}$ are all recursive.*

Proof. This result can be proved by simple simulation algorithms. Here, we
present the proof by the characterization of Theorem 5.15.

First, since $\chi_{\overline{A}}(x) = 1 \div \chi_A(x)$, we see that $\overline{A}$ is also recursive. Now, since
A, B, $\overline{A}$ and $\overline{B}$ are all r.e., it follows that $A \cup B$, $\overline{A \cup B} = \overline{A} \cap \overline{B}$, $A \cap B$ and
$\overline{A \cap B} = \overline{A} \cup \overline{B}$ are all r.e. It follows from Theorem 5.15 that $A \cup B$ and $A \cap B$
are recursive.   □

A total function $f : \{0,1\}^* \to \{0,1\}^*$ is *increasing* if $f(x) \leq f(x+1)$ for
all x.

Theorem 5.17 *A nonempty set A is recursive if and only if it is the range
of an increasing recursive function $f : \{0,1\}^* \to \{0,1\}^*$.*

Prove. Assume that A is recursive. Let x_0 be the least string in A under the
lexicographic ordering. Define $f(0) = x_0$ and

$$f(x+1) = \begin{cases} x+1 & \text{if } \chi_A(x+1) = 1, \\ f(x) & \text{otherwise.} \end{cases}$$

We can see that f is recursive, since $f(x)$ can be expressed as follows (to avoid
the recursive definition):

$$f(x) = \text{if } x \leq x_0 \text{ then } x_0 \text{ else } (\max y)_{y \leq x}[\chi_A(y) = 1].$$

Furthermore, it is easy to see that the range of f is A, and that f is increasing.

Conversely, assume that f is an increasing recursive function and A is the
range of f. Then, from Theorem 5.13, we know that A is r.e. Now, if A is
finite, then A is recursive and so $\overline{A}$ is r.e. Otherwise, if A is infinite, then we
have

$$\overline{A} = \{x \mid x < f(0) \text{ or } (\exists y)[f(y) < x < f(y+1)]\},$$

since f is increasing. So, $\overline{A}$ is also r.e. We conclude from Theorem 5.15 that
A is recursive.   □

Exercise 5.2

1. Assume that $A, B, C \subseteq \{0,1\}^*$ are r.e. sets. Let

$$D = (A \cap B) \cup (B \cap C) \cup (C \cap A).$$

   (a) Construct a DTM that simulates the three DTM's accepting sets
       A, B, and C in parallel and accepts set D.

(b) Construct a DTM that simulates the three DTM's accepting sets A, B, and C by the dovetailing method and accepts D.

(c) Find a recursive predicate R such that $D = \{x \mid (\exists y)\, R(x, y)\}$.

2. Design two dovetailing algorithms for set B of Example 5.11, the first based on the intuitive algorithm given in the solution, and the second based on the last line of the proof by the projection theorem.

3. Assume that $A, B, C \subseteq \{0, 1\}^*$ and $A \cap B = B \cap C = C \cap A = \emptyset$. Also assume that there exist three partial recursive functions f_1, f_2, f_3 that have the following properties:

$$f_1(x) = \begin{cases} 1 & \text{if } x \in A \cup B, \\ 2 & \text{if } x \in C, \\ \uparrow & \text{otherwise,} \end{cases} \qquad f_2(x) = \begin{cases} \uparrow & \text{if } x \in A \cup C, \\ 0 & \text{otherwise,} \end{cases} \quad \text{and}$$

$$f_3(x) = \begin{cases} \uparrow & \text{if } x \in B \cup C, \\ 0 & \text{otherwise.} \end{cases}$$

(a) Prove that sets A, B, C are all recursive.

(b) Let M_1, M_2 and M_3 be three DTM's that compute functions f_1, f_2 and f_3, respectively. Construct DTM's that simulate M_1, M_2 and M_3 to compute χ_A, χ_B and χ_C.

4. Show that every infinite r.e. set has an infinite subset that is recursive.

5. (a) Assume that $f : \{0, 1\}^* \to \{0, 1\}^*$ is a partial recursive function, and A is an r.e. set. Show that $f(A)$ and $f^{-1}(A)$ are r.e. (Recall that $f(A) = \{f(x) \mid x \in A, f(x) \downarrow\}$ and $f^{-1}(A) = \{x \mid f(x) \downarrow, f(x) \in A\}$.)

(b) Assume that f is a recursive function and A is a recursive set. Is $f(A)$ recursive? Is $f^{-1}(A)$ recursive?

6. A function $f : \{0, 1\}^* \to \{0, 1\}^*$ is *strictly increasing* if $f(x) < f(x + 1)$ for all $x \in \{0, 1\}^*$. Show that an infinite set A is recursive if and only if A is the range of a strictly increasing recursive function f.

7. Show that the following sets are r.e.

(a) $A_1 = \{n \mid \{0, 1, \ldots, n\} \subseteq W_n\}$.

(b) $A_2 = \{n \mid |W_n \cap \{0, 1, \ldots, n\}| \geq n/2\}$. [*Hint:* Use the Gödel numbering to encode $n/2$ strings into a single string.]

(c) $A_3 = \{\langle n, x \rangle \mid \text{there exist } n_1, \ldots, n_k, \ k \geq 1, \text{ such that } x \in W_{n_1}, n_1 \in W_{n_2}, \ldots, n_{k-1} \in W_{n_k}, n_k \in W_n\}$.

(d) $A_4 = \{x \mid \text{there exists an integer } n \text{ such that } \phi_x(y) = 0 \text{ for all } y \in \{0, 1\}^n\}$.

(e) $A_5 = \{n \mid \text{during the computation of } M_n(111), M_n \text{ has a configuration that contains a substring } 000\}$.

8. Recall that $AB = \{xy \mid x \in A, y \in B\}$. Define $A + B = \{n + m \mid n \in A, m \in B\}$.

    (a) Show that if A and B are r.e. sets then AB, $A + B$ and A^* are also r.e.

    (b) Show that if A and B are recursive sets then AB, $A + B$ and A^* are also recursive.

9. Define a set $C = \{\langle x, y \rangle \mid$ there exists a partial recursive function f such that $f(x)$ is defined and $f(x) = y\}$.

    (a) Prove that C is r.e.

    (b) Is C recursive? why?

10. Show that the following function is partial recursive:

$$g(i, j, k) = \begin{cases} k & \text{if } (\exists n)\,[\phi_i(n) = \phi_j(n) = k], \\ \uparrow & \text{otherwise.} \end{cases}$$

5.3 Diagonalization

In the last section, we studied how to prove that a set is r.e. or is recursive. The main tools are simulation algorithms and the projection theorem. In this and the next sections, we develop proof techniques to show that a set is not recursive or is not r.e.

The first proof technique is diagonalization. Suppose that we are given an infinite number of objects (sets or functions) $A_1, A_2, \ldots$ and want to construct a new object B that is different from each of the given objects. Also suppose that the object B consists of an infinite number of parts. The diagonalization technique constructs B one part at a time, making the ith part different from the corresponding part of A_i. When the infinite number of steps of construction are done, we obtain an object B that is different from every A_i, $i \geq 0$. The following is a simple example.

Example 5.18 *Show that the set F of functions from $\mathbf{N}$ to $\{0, 1\}$ is uncountable.*

Proof. Suppose otherwise that F is countable; that is, it can be listed as f_0, $f_1, f_2, \cdots$. Define a new function $f : \mathbf{N} \to \{0, 1\}$ by $f(n) = 1 \dotminus f_n(n)$. Then, $f \in F$ and $f \neq f_n$ for every $n \geq 0$, because $f(n) = 1 \dotminus f_n(n) \neq f_n(n)$. Thus, we have found a contradiction to the assumption that F consists of $f_0, f_1, \ldots$. $\square$

In the above example, we are given a list of functions $f_0, f_1, f_2, \ldots$, and need to find a new function $f \in F$ such that f is different from every f_n, $n \geq 0$. That is, we need to satisfy an infinite number of requirements:

$$R_i: f \neq f_i, \quad i = 0, 1, \ldots.$$

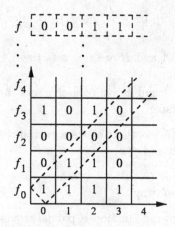

Figure 5.1:   The diagonalization.

Since a function f is defined by an infinite number of parts $f(0), f(1), f(2), \ldots$ and since these parts are independent of each other, we can satisfy the nth requirement by making the nth part $f(n)$ to be different from the corresponding part of the nth function f_n. This process can be seen more clearly in Figure 5.1. In this figure, the nth row contains the values of $f_n(0), f_n(1), \ldots$, and the function f is defined by taking the diagonal of the picture and changing every element of it (hence the term *diagonalization*).

We remark that the term diagonalization is a little misleading, since we do not have to define f to be the opposite of the diagonal. The construction works as long as for every $n \geq 0$, there is a point x_n such that $f(x_n) \neq f_n(x_n)$. For instance, we may let $x_n = n^2$ and let $f(n^2) = 1 \doteq f_n(n^2)$. Then, f still satisfies all the requirements R_i, $i \geq 0$. The values $f(m)$ for those m which are not perfect squares can be used to satisfy other requirements.

The next example shows that the construction of object B could be made by a machine as long as objects $A_0, A_1, \ldots$ can be presented to the machine in a uniform way.

We say a set A is *co-r.e.* if $\overline{A}$ is r.e.

Example 5.19 *Show that there exists a co-r.e. set that is not r.e.*

Proof. We are given a list $W_0, W_1, W_2, \ldots$, and need to find a set A that is different from each of them. We may simply construct A one element at a time: for each n, we let $n \in A$ if and only if $n \notin W_n$. That is, define $A = \{n \mid n \notin W_n\}$. Then, A is not r.e., since it is different from every W_n, $n \geq 0$. In addition, $\overline{A} = \{n \mid n \in W_n\} = \{n \mid (\exists t)halt(n, n, t)\}$, and so A is co-r.e.   □

Corollary 5.20 *(a) The set $K = \{n \mid n \in W_n\}$ is r.e. but not recursive.*
   (b) The set $K_0 = \{\langle y, x \rangle \mid M_x$ halts on input $y\}$ is r.e. but not recursive.

Proof. (a) K is the complement of set A of the above example. Since $\overline{K} = A$ is not r.e., K is not recursive (by Theorem 5.15).

(b) Suppose K_0 were recursive, then K would also be recursive since $\chi_K(x) = \chi_{K_0}(\langle x, x \rangle)$. Thus, by part (a), K_0 is not recursive. $\square$

A *decision problem* is a problem whose answer is either yes or no. Every decision problem corresponds to a language consisting of all inputs to which the answer is yes. We say a decision problem is *undecidable* (or, *unsolvable*) if the corresponding language is not recursive. So, from part (b) of Corollary 5.20, we say that the problem of determining whether a given Turing machine M halts on a given input string y (called the *halting problem*) is undecidable.

Example 5.21 *We say a partial recursive function* $f : \{0,1\}^* \to \{0,1\}^*$ *is* extendable *if there exists a recursive function* $g : \{0,1\}^* \to \{0,1\}^*$ *such that* $g(x) = f(x)$ *whenever* $f(x) \downarrow$. *Show that there exists a partial recursive function that is not extendable.*

Proof. If a partial recursive function f is extendable, then there exists an integer n such that ϕ_n is total and ϕ_n is the extension of f. So, we need to construct a partial recursive function f that is different from every total recursive function ϕ_n. To do this, define $f(n) = 1 - \phi_n(n)$.[3]

Then, f is partial recursive since $f(n) = 1 - \Phi^1(n, n)$. (Recall that Φ^1 is the two-input function computed by the universal TM.)

Now, for every recursive function ϕ_n, $f(n) \downarrow$ because $\phi_n(x) \downarrow$ for every $x \geq 0$. It follows that $f(n) = 1 - \phi_n(n)$ and ϕ_n is not the extension of f. $\square$

We have seen that $\{\phi_n\}$ is an enumeration of all partial recursive functions. Is there an enumeration of recursive functions? The answer is no. The following example shows that we cannot enumerate all DTM's that compute recursive functions. Exercise 4 of this section gives an even stronger negative result.

Example 5.22 *Show that* $\text{TOT} = \{n \mid W_n = \{0,1\}^*\} = \{n \mid \phi_n \text{ is recursive}\}$ *is not r.e.*

Proof. The proof is a simple modification of the Example 5.21. Suppose, for the sake of contradiction, that TOT is r.e. Then, by Theorem 5.13, there is a recursive function g whose range is TOT. We need to find a recursive function f such that $f \neq \phi_{g(n)}$ for all $n \geq 0$. Define $f(n) = 1 - \phi_{g(n)}(n)$.

Since $g(n) \in \text{TOT}$ for all $n \geq 0$, $\phi_{g(n)}(n)$ is always defined and so $f(n)$ is a total function. In addition, $f(n) = 1 - \Phi^1(n, g(n))$, and so f is recursive.

---

[3] Recall that when we write $f(n) = 1 - \phi_n(n)$, it means that if ϕ_n is defined on input n with output y, then $f(n)$ is equal to $1 - y$; otherwise, if ϕ_n is not defined on input n, then $f(n)$ is undefined.

Finally, we know that $f \neq \phi_{g(n)}$ for all $n \geq 0$, because $f(n) \neq \phi_{g(n)}(n)$. So, f provides us a contradiction to the assumption that TOT is r.e.   □

The above examples are straightforward applications of diagonalization. The following example is more involved. It shows how to modify the diagonalization requirements to create space for the object to be constructed to have some additional properties.

We say an r.e set S is *simple* if its complement $\overline{S}$ is infinite but does not contain any infinite r.e. subset.

⋆ **Example 5.23** *Show that there exists a simple set.*

Proof. The idea is to construct a set S such that for every $n \geq 0$, if W_n is infinite then we include an element of W_n in S. That is, the first set of requirements we need to satisfy is

$R_{1,n}$: If W_n is infinite, then $S \cap W_n \neq \emptyset$, $n \geq 0$.

If these requirements are satisfied, then the complement $\overline{S}$ of S does not contain any infinite W_n as a subset.

In addition to these requirements, we also need to make sure that S is not too *big*; that is, we need to make $\overline{S}$ infinite. So, we also need to satisfy

$R_{2,n}$: For every $n \geq 0$, $|\overline{S} \cap \{x \mid x < 2n\}| \geq n$, $n \geq 0$.

It is easy to see that these requirements imply that $\overline{S}$ is infinite.

There is, however, a problem with the above idea. Namely, the set INF $= \{n \mid W_n$ is infinite$\}$ is not an r.e. set (see Example 5.34), and so we will not be able to enumerate all infinite W_n, which appears necessary in order to satisfy the requirements $R_{1,n}$ by a Turing machine. The solution to this problem is that we will *pretend* that every W_n is infinite and *try* to include an element of W_n in S for all $n \geq 0$. This modification of requirements $R_{1,n}$ is acceptable since it does not hurt if we have $S \cap W_n \neq \emptyset$ for some finite W_n.

In the following, we construct set S by enumerating strings of S one at a time. This make S a Turing-enumerable set and, hence, an r.e. set.

Let $A = \{\langle n, x \rangle \mid x \in W_n, x \geq 2n\}$. Then, it is easy to see that A is an infinite r.e. set. From Theorem 5.13, it is the range of a recursive function g. We now describe an algorithm that enumerates the set S:

Algorithm for S. We maintain a finite set B in our construction. Before stage 0, we let the set B be empty. Then, we go to stage 0. At stage e, we compute $g(e)$ and let $n = l(g(e))$ and $x = r(g(e))$; that is, $g(e) = \langle n, x \rangle$. If $n \notin B$, then we print string x and add n to set B; else we do nothing. Then, we go to stage $e + 1$.

It is clear that each stage e ends in a finite number of steps since g is recursive. Therefore, by the Church-Turing Thesis, the above construction can be implemented by a Turing machine and so the output set S is Turing-enumerable.

To see that this construction satisfies all requirements, we first check that for each n such that W_n is infinite, the set $A_n = \{\langle n, x \rangle \mid \langle n, x \rangle \in A\}$ is infinite. Let $e_n = (\min e)[g(e) = \langle n, x \rangle$ for some $x]$. Then, at stage e_n, $n \notin B$ and $g(e_n) = \langle n, x \rangle$ for some x. Therefore, we will include x in S at stage e_n. It follows that S satisfies requirements $R_{1,n}$, for all $n \geq 0$.

For the second set of requirements $R_{2,n}$, we note that for any $n \geq 0$, set $S \cap \{x \mid x < 2n\}$ contains at most n strings since each of these strings x must come from $g(e) = \langle m, x \rangle$ for some $m < n$, and for each such m, we add at most one string x to S. Therefore, requirements $R_{2,n}$ are satisfied for all $n \geq 0$, and the construction works correctly. □

Exercises 5.3

1. Let A be any set (not necessarily countable). Show that there does not exist a one-to-one correspondence between set A and the set 2^A of all subsets of A.

2. Show that the set F_1 of all one-to-one, increasing functions from $\mathbf{N}$ to $\mathbf{N}$ is uncountable.

3. What are wrong with the following diagonalization proofs?

   (a) We show that there exists a partial recursive function $f : \{0, 1\}^* \to \{0, 1\}^*$ which is not enumerated in $\phi_0, \phi_1, \dots$. Define $f(n) = \phi_n(n) + 1$. Then, by the existence of the universal DTM, we can see that f is partial recursive. Thus, we have obtained a partial recursive function f that is different from every ϕ_n at input n, $n \geq 0$.

   (b) We show that the set $\text{REC} = \{x \mid W_x \text{ is recursive}\}$ is not r.e. Suppose, by way of contradiction, that REC is r.e. Then, there exists a recursive function g whose range is equal to REC. Define $A = \{x \mid x \notin W_{g(x)}\}$. Since each $W_{g(x)}$ is recursive, it is decidable whether $x \in W_{g(x)}$. Therefore, A is a recursive set. But this is a contradiction, since $A \neq W_{g(x)}$ for every $x \geq 0$.

4. Assume that $A \subseteq \mathbf{N}$ is a set with the following properties: (i) ϕ_n is recursive for all $n \in A$, and (ii) for all recursive functions f, $f = \phi_n$ for some $n \in A$. Show that A is not an r.e. set.

5. (a) Show that the class of primitive recursive functions is effectively enumerable (in the sense that there is an r.e. set B such that (i) ϕ_n is primitive recursive, for all $n \in B$, and (ii) for all primitive recursive function g, $g = \phi_n$ for some $n \in B$).

   (b) Show that there exists a recursive function that is not primitive recursive.

6. Show that set $A = \{n \mid \phi_n \text{ halts on } n \text{ and its output is greater than } n\}$ is not a recursive set.

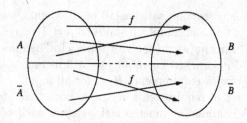

Figure 5.2: The reduction function f cannot cross the dotline.

7. Show that the set $\{\langle i, j \rangle \mid W_i = \overline{W_j}\}$ is not an r.e. set.

8. We say two sets A and B are *recursively separable* if there exists a recursive set C such that $A \subseteq C$ and $B \subseteq \overline{C}$. Show that for any $n \neq m \in \mathbf{N}$, sets K_n and K_m are not recursively separable, where $K_n = \{x \mid \phi_x(x) \text{ is defined and is equal to } n\}$.

9. Give a formal proof that set S defined in Example 5.23 is r.e. That is, let $h(e)$ be the string printed out in stage e by the algorithm for S ($h(e) \uparrow$ if it does not output any string in stage e). Prove that h is partial recursive (without using the Church-Turing Thesis).

$\star$ 10. Show that there exists a set A such that both A and $\overline{A}$ are infinite but neither has an infinite r.e. subset.

5.4 Reducibility

The second proof technique for proving languages not recursive or not r.e. is the technique of reducibility. Intuitively, we say a language A is reducible to a language B if the membership problems of the form "$x \in ? A$" can be reduced to the membership problems of the form "$y \in ? B$." Therefore, an algorithm for problem B could be converted to an algorithm for problem A. Technically, there are several different types of reducibility, with different applications. We will study only the simplest type of reducibility here, namely, the many-one reducibility.

Assume that A and B are two languages over the alphabet Σ. We say that A is *many-one reducible* to B, denoted by $A \leq_m B$, if there exists a recursive function $f : \Sigma^* \to \Sigma^*$ such that for every string $x \in \Sigma^*$,

$$x \in A \iff f(x) \in B.$$

The function f is called the *reduction function* (see Figure 5.2).

Proposition 5.24 *The following hold for all sets $A, B, C \subseteq \Sigma^*$:*
  (a) $A \leq_m A$.
  (b) $A \leq_m B, B \leq_m C \Rightarrow A \leq_m C$.

Proof. For part (a), the identity function is a reduction function for $A \leq_m A$ for all $A \subseteq \Sigma^*$.

For part (b), assume that $A \leq_m B$ by the reduction function f and $B \leq_m C$ by the reduction function g. Then, the function $h(x) = g(f(x))$ is a reduction function for $A \leq_m C$. $\qquad \square$

Example 5.25 *Assume that both A and B are nonempty proper subsets of Σ^*.*

(a) Show that if A is recursive then $A \leq_m B$.

(b) Show that if the set differences $A \setminus B$ and $B \setminus A$ of sets A and B are both recursive, then $A \leq_m B$.

Proof. (a) Let x_0 be a fixed string in $\overline{B}$ and x_1 a fixed string in B. Define

$$f(x) = \begin{cases} x_1 & \text{if } x \in A, \\ x_0 & \text{if } x \notin A. \end{cases}$$

Then, it is clear that $x \in A$ if and only if $f(x) \in B$. In addition, the predicate $[x \in A]$ is recursive and so f is recursive. Thus, f is a reduction function for $A \leq_m B$.

(b) Similarly to part (a), we choose two strings $x_0 \in \overline{B}$ and $x_1 \in B$ and define

$$g(x) = \begin{cases} x_1 & \text{if } x \in A \setminus B, \\ x_0 & \text{if } x \in B \setminus A, \\ x & \text{otherwise.} \end{cases}$$

Then, f is recursive since both $A \setminus B$ and $B \setminus A$ are recursive. In addition, if $x \in A$ then either $g(x) = x_1$, or $[g(x) = x$ and $x \notin A \setminus B]$; in either case, we have $g(x) \in B$. Similarly, if $x \notin A$ then either $g(x) = x_0$ or $[g(x) = x$ and $x \notin B \setminus A]$; in either case, $g(x) \notin B$. It follows that g is a reduction function for $A \leq_m B$. $\qquad \square$

Proposition 5.26 *Assume that $A \leq_m B$.*

(a) If B is recurisve then A is recursive.

(b) If B is r.e. then A is r.e.

Proof. Suppose $A \leq_m B$ by the reduction function f. Then, $\chi_A(x) = \chi_B(f(x))$ and $s_A(x) = s_B(f(x))$. Since f is recursive, it follows that χ_A is recursive if χ_B is recursive, and that s_A is partial recursive if s_B is partial recursive. $\qquad \square$

The above theorem allows us to prove a set B to be nonrecursive or non-r.e. by reducing a set A that is already proven to be nonrecursive or non-r.e. to set B. For instance, in Corollary 5.20, we showed that set $K_0 = \{\langle y, x \rangle \mid x \in W_y\}$ is not recursive by reducing set $K = \{x \mid x \in W_x\}$ to it. In that case, the reduction function is very simple: $f(x) = \langle x, x \rangle$. The following is another example.

Example 5.27 *Show that the set* EMP $= \{x \mid W_x = \emptyset\}$ *is not recursive.*

Proof. First, we note that

$$\text{EMP} = \{x \mid W_x = \emptyset\} = \{x \mid (\forall y)(\forall t)\,[halt\,(y, x, t) = 0]\}.$$

So, by the projection theorem, $\overline{\text{EMP}}$ is r.e. Thus, we try to show that EMP is not recursive by a reduction from the halting problem $K = \{x \mid x \in W_x\}$ to $\overline{\text{EMP}}$.

For any string $x \in \{0, 1\}^*$, we construct a DTM M' as follows:

> On input z, M' erases z and write $x\text{B}x$ on the tape. Then M' simulates the universal DTM U on input (x, x). If the simulation halts, then M' halts and accepts the input; otherwise, it does not halt.

Clearly, M' will accept any input if U accepts (x, x) or, equivalently, if M_x accepts x. Also, M' will not accept any input if M_x does not accept x. Let y be the code of the DTM M', then the function $f(x) = y$ is a reduction from K to $\overline{\text{EMP}}$.

It is left to show that f is a recursive function. For any fixed x, let M'' be the DTM that, on any input z, outputs x. That is, M'' computes the constant function $K_x^1(z) \equiv x$. Then, it is easy to see that the function $f_1(x) = [\text{code of } M'']$ is a primitive recursive function.

Next, we claim that the function $f_2(u, v) = [\text{the code of the DTM } M \text{ that computes the composition of } \phi_u \circ \phi_v]$ is primitive recursive. To see this, assume that $maxstate(v) = t$. Then, to get M, all we need to do is to change each state q_i in M_u to $q_{i+(t-1)}$, and combine the new TM with M_v. In Exercise 1 of Section 5.1, we showed that changing a state in the code of a DTM is a primitive recursive operation. Thus, f_2 is primitive recursive.

Now, we note that $f(x) = f_2(u, f_2(c, f_1(x)))$, where c is the code of the DTM that copies the input z into $z\text{B}z$, and u is the code of the universal DTM U. Therefore, f is primitive recursive. It follows that $K \leq_m \overline{\text{EMP}}$, and so $\overline{\text{EMP}}$ (and hence EMP) is not recursive since K is not recursive. $\square$

Let us examine the above proof of $K \leq_m \overline{\text{EMP}}$ more carefully. The proof can be divided into two steps. First, we need to prove that the DTM M' exists; that is, the function

$$g(z) = \begin{cases} 1 & \text{if } M_x \text{ halts on } x, \\ \uparrow & \text{otherwise} \end{cases}$$

is a partial recursive function. Second, we need to argue that the code y of M' can be computed from the code of M_x (by a DTM); or, equivalently, we need to show that the function $f(x) = y$ is recursive. In the above, we only gave an informal proof for the second step and relied on the Church-Turing Thesis to support its correctness. Since many other proofs use similar arguments, we formalize it below as a technical lemma, called the *s-m-n theorem.*

Theorem 5.28 (S-m-n Theorem). *For each pair of integers $m, n > 0$, there is a primitive recursive function $s^n_m : (\{0,1\}^*)^{n+1} \to \{0,1\}^*$ such that*

$$\phi^{m+n}_e(x_1, \ldots, x_m, y_1, \ldots, y_n) = \phi^m_{s^n_m(e, y_1, \ldots, y_n)}(x_1, \ldots, x_m).$$

Proof. Intuitively, s^n_m is a function that reads a TM code e and n strings $t_1, \ldots, t_n$ as inputs and outputs a new TM code e' such that $M_{e'}$ simulates M_e on $n + m$ inputs $(x_1, \ldots, x_m, y_1, \ldots, y_n)$ as follows: It reads m strings as the first m inputs to M_e and then uses the constants $t_1, \ldots, t_n$ as the last n inputs to M_e. It is probably easier to understand it in a high-level programming language environment: Assume the program e is of the form

$$read(x_1); \ read(x_2); \ \ldots; \ read(x_m);$$
$$read(y_1); \ read(y_2); \ \ldots; \ read(y_m);$$
$$w;$$

Then, the program $e' = s^n_m(e, t_1, \ldots, t_n)$ is as follows:

$$read(x_1); \ read(x_2); \ \ldots; \ read(x_m);$$
$$y_1 := t_1; \ y_2 := t_2; \ \ldots; \ y_n := t_n;$$
$$w;$$

It is easy to see that the mapping from the program e to e' is recursive. In the following, we show that this mapping is actually primitive recursive in the Turing machine programming system.

We prove the theorem by induction on n. First we consider the case $n = 1$. The function s^1_m takes as the input a DTM code e and a string $y \in \{0,1\}^*$ and outputs a DTM code z such that M_z on inputs $(x_1, \ldots, x_m)$ outputs the same value as M_e on inputs $(x_1, \ldots, x_m, y)$.

Assume that $|y| = k$ and $y = y_1 y_2 \cdots y_k$, where each y_j, $1 \leq j \leq k$, is a symbol in $\{0,1\}$. Also assume that M_e uses states $q_1, \ldots, q_t$ (i.e., $maxstate(e) = t$). Then, M_z contains the following instructions:

(i) All instructions of M_e, with q_1 changed to q_t and q_t changed to q_{t+k+1};

(ii) $\delta(q_1, \text{B}) = (q_{t+1}, \text{B}, R)$;

(iii) $\delta(q_{t+i-1}, \text{B}) = (q_{t+i}, y_{i-1}, R)$, $2 \leq i \leq k$;

(iv) $\delta(q_{t+k}, \text{B}) = (q_t, y_k, R)$.

Thus, the effect of instructions in groups (ii), (iii) and (iv) is to change the configuration from

$$(q_1, x_1 \text{B} x_2 \text{B} \cdots \text{B} x_m \underline{\text{B}})$$

to

$$(q_t, x_1 \text{B} x_2 \text{B} \cdots \text{B} x_m \text{B} y \underline{\text{B}}),$$

and the instructions in group (i) allow us to simulate M_e on this last configuration.

Define a function $g : (\{0,1\}^*)^3 \to \{0,1\}^*$ as follows:

(a) If $i = 0$, then $g(e, y, i)$ is the code of instructions of M_z in part (i);

(b) If $1 \leq i \leq k + 1$, then $g(e, y, i)$ is the code of the ith instruction in part (ii)–(iv);

(c) If $i \geq k + 2$, then $g(e, y, i) = 0$.

It is not hard to see that g is primitive recursive. For instance, for the case $2 \leq i \leq k$, $g(e, y, i)$ can be expressed as

$$\text{if } substr(y, i \dotminus 1, 1) = 0 \text{ then } 10^{t+i-1}10^3 10^{t+i}1010^2 1$$
$$\text{else } 10^{t+i-1}10^3 10^{t+i}10^2 10^2 1.$$

For case (a), $g(e, y, 0)$ can be obtained from e by replacing each substring $10^t 1$ that represents state q_t by the string $10^{t+k+1}1$, and replacing each substring 101 that represents state q_1 by the string $10^t 1$. By Exercise 1(b) of Section 5.1, it is primitive recursive.

Using function g, we can show that $s^1_m(e, y)$ is primitive recursive. We first define a new function s' that concatenates all instructions of $g(e, y, i)$:

$$s'(e, y, 0) = substr(g(e, y, 0), 1, |g(e, y, 0)| \dotminus 2),$$
$$s'(e, y, i + 1) = concat^2(s'(e, y, i), g(e, y, i + 1)).$$

Then, it is clear that $s^1_m(e, y) = cancat^2(s'(e, y, |y| + 1), 11)$ and is primitive recursive.

The above proved the case $n = 1$ (with respect to arbitrary $m > 0$). For the general cases $n > 1$, we define

$$s^{n+1}_m(e, y_1, \ldots, y_{n+1}) = s^n_m(s^1_{m+n}(e, y_{n+1}), y_1, \ldots, y_n)$$

and verify that

$$\phi^{m+n+1}_e (x_1, \ldots, x_m, y_1, \ldots, y_n, y_{n+1})$$
$$= \phi^{m+n}_{s^1_{m+n}(e, y_{n+1})}(x_1, \ldots, x_m, y_1, \ldots, y_n)$$
$$= \phi^m_{s^n_m(s^1_{m+n}(e, y_{n+1}), y_1, \ldots, y_n)}(x_1, \ldots, x_m).$$

Therefore, the function s^{n+1}_m satisfies the desired property.   □

Using the s-m-n theorem, we can present a more complete, and more elegant, proof of the reduction $K \leq_m \overline{\text{EMP}}$:

Example 5.27 (Revisited) *Show, by the s-m-n theorem, that $K \leq_m \overline{\text{EMP}}$.*

Proof. First, define a function

$$g(y, x) = \begin{cases} 1 & \text{if } x \in K, \\ \uparrow & \text{otherwise.} \end{cases}$$

Then, g is partial recursive since $g(y, x) = \sigma_K(x)$. (Recall that σ_K is the semi-characteristic function of set K.)

By the enumeration theorem, $g = \phi_e^2$ for some $e \geq 0$. For this fixed e, define $f(x) = s_1^1(e, x)$. We check that if $x \in K$, then

$$\phi_{f(x)}(y) = \phi_{s_1^1(e,x)}^1(y) = \phi_e^2(y, x) = g(y, x) = 1,$$

for all $y \in \{0, 1\}^*$ and so $W_{f(x)} = \{0, 1\}^* \neq \emptyset$. Also, if $x \notin K$, then

$$\phi_{f(x)}(y) = \phi_e^2(y, x) = g(y, x) \uparrow,$$

for all $y \in \{0, 1\}^*$ and so $W_{f(x)} = \emptyset$. Thus, f is a reduction function for $K \leq_m \overline{\mathrm{EMP}}$. $\square$

The following is another simple example. We say an r.e. set A is *complete* (with respect to the many-one reducibility) if $B \leq_m A$ for all r.e. sets B. A complete r.e. set is not recursive, for otherwise all r.e. sets would be recursive.

Example 5.29 *The halting problem K is complete.*

Proof. Let B be an r.e. set. We need to construct a reduction $B \leq_m K$. Define

$$g(y, x) = \begin{cases} 1 & \text{if } x \in B, \\ \uparrow & \text{otherwise.} \end{cases}$$

Then, g is partial recursive since $g(y, x) = \sigma_B(x)$.

By the enumeration theorem, $g = \phi_e^2$ for some $e \geq 0$. For this fixed e, define $f(x) = s_1^1(e, x)$. We check that if $x \in B$, then $\phi_{f(x)}(y) = \phi_e^2(y, x) = g(y, x) = 1$ for all $y \in \{0, 1\}^*$ and, in particular, $\phi_{f(x)}(f(x)) = 1$ and so $f(x) \in K$. Also, if $x \notin B$ then $\phi_{f(x)}(y) = \phi_e^2(y, x) = g(y, x) \uparrow$ for all $y \in \{0, 1\}^*$ and so $f(x) \notin K$. Thus, f is a reduction function for $B \leq_m K$. $\square$

By the transitivity of the reducibility $\leq_m$, an r.e. set A is complete if $K \leq_m A$. For instance, Example 5.27 showed that $\overline{\mathrm{EMP}}$ is a complete r.e. set.

Index Sets. We say a set $A \subseteq \{0, 1\}^*$ is a *function-index set* if for any $x, y \in \{0, 1\}^*$, $\phi_x = \phi_y$ implies $\chi_A(x) = \chi_A(y)$; a set $A \subseteq \{0, 1\}^*$ is a *set-index set* (or, simply, an *index set*), if for any $x, y \in \{0, 1\}^*$, $W_x = W_y$ implies $\chi_A(x) = \chi_A(y)$. In other words, A is a function-index set (or, a set-index set) if the membership question "$x \in ? A$" depends only on the *function* ϕ_x (or, respectively, on the set W_x), and does not depend on the machine M_x that computes ϕ_x. Note that each set-index set is also a function-index set.

Each function-index set (or, a set-index set) corresponds to a *property* of partial recursive functions (or, respectively, r.e. sets). We say the problem of determining whether a partial recursive function f has the property P is *undecidable* (from the code of a DTM that computes f) if the corresponding function-index set $A_P = \{x \mid P(\phi_x)\}$ is not recursive. Similarly, the problem of determining whether an r.e. set A has the property P is undecidable (from the code of a DTM that accepts A) if the corresponding set-index set $A_P = \{x \mid P(W_x)\}$ is not recursive.

For instance, the set EMP of Example 5.27 is a set-index set since the question "$x \in$?EMP" depends only on whether the set W_x is empty or not, and we say that the problem of determining whether an r.e. set is empty is undecidable. Similarly, set $A_1 = \{x \mid \phi_x(0) > 5\}$ is a function-index set (but not a set-index set). Rice's theorem below shows that A_1 is not recursive and so the problem of determining whether a partial recursive function f has value $f(0) > 5$ is undecidable.

On the other hand, the set $K = \{x \mid x \in W_x\}$ is not an index set since the question of whether $x \in K$ not only depends on the set W_x but also on the membership of x itself in W_x. (For a formal proof that K is not an index set, see, e.g., Exercise 11 of Section 5.5.) Similarly, the set $B_1 = \{x \mid M_x(0)$ halts in at most 200 moves$\}$ is not an index set since we can easily design two DTM's M_y and M_z computing the same function but one is in B_1 and the other not in B_1.

We say an index set A is *nontrivial* if it is neither empty nor equal to $\{0,1\}^*$. Then, by the *s-m-n* theorem, we can prove that all nontrivial index sets are nonrecursive. Thus, all nontrivial properties of partial recursive functions are undecidable.

Theorem 5.30 (Rice's Theorem) *All nontrivial function-index sets are non-recursive.*

Proof. Let A be a nontrivial function-index set. First, assume that all indices x such that $W_x = \emptyset$ are in $\overline{A}$. We show that $K \leq_m A$. Choose a fixed x_0 in A, and define

$$g(y,x) = \begin{cases} \phi_{x_0}(y) & \text{if } x \in K, \\ \uparrow & \text{otherwise.} \end{cases}$$

Then, g is partial recursive since $g(y,x) = \sigma_K(x) \cdot \phi_{x_0}(y)$.

By the enumeration theorem, $g = \phi_e^2$ for some $e \geq 0$. For this fixed e, define $f(x) = s_1^1(e,x)$. We check that if $x \in K$, then $\phi_{f(x)}(y) = g(y,x) = \phi_{x_0}(y)$ for all $y \in \{0,1\}^*$. Since A is a function-index set and $x_0 \in A$, it implies that $f(x) \in A$. On the other hand, if $x \notin K$ then $\phi_{f(x)}(y) = g(y,x) \uparrow$ for all $y \in \{0,1\}^*$ and so $W_{f(x)} = \emptyset$ and it follows that $f(x) \in \overline{A}$. Therefore, f is a reduction function for $K \leq_m A$, and it follows that A is not recursive.

Now, suppose that all indices x such that $W_x = \emptyset$ are in A. Then, by the same argument (with $x_0 \in \overline{A}$), we can prove that $K \leq_m \overline{A}$ and so A is not recursive. $\square$

Corollary 5.31 *The following sets are not recursive.*

(a) $A_1 = \{x \mid \phi_x(0) > 5\}$.

(b) TOT $= \{x \mid W_x = \{0,1\}^*\}$.

(c) FIN $= \{x \mid W_x$ *is finite*$\}$.
(d) REC $= \{x \mid W_x$ *is recursive*$\}$.
(e) REG $= \{x \mid W_x$ *is a regular set*$\}$.
(f) REV $= \{x \mid W_x = W_x^R\}$.

Next, we apply the technique of reducibility to prove that some index sets are not r.e. Our first result is a simple application of the proof of Rice's theorem.

Example 5.32 *Let A be a nontrivial function-index set. Show that if* EMP $\subseteq$ *A, then A is not r.e. Thus, the following index sets are not r.e:* $\overline{A_1}$, EMP, $\overline{\text{TOT}}$, FIN, REC, REG *and* REV.

Proof. From the proof of Rice's theorem, we see that if EMP $\subseteq A$, then $K \leq_m \overline{A}$, or, equivalently, $\overline{K} \leq_m A$. It follows from Proposition 5.26 that A is not r.e.

Since sets $\overline{A_1}$, EMP, $\overline{\text{TOT}}$, FIN, REC, REG and REV all contain EMP as a subset, they are not r.e.

For set $\overline{A_1}$, there is another simple way to show that $\overline{A_1}$ is not r.e. We observe that

$$x \in A_1 \iff (\exists t)(\exists w)\,[print(0, w, x, t) \text{ and } w > 5]$$
$$\iff (\exists z)\,[print(0, l(z), x, r(z)) \text{ and } l(z) > 5].$$

So, by the projection theorem, A_1 is r.e. Also, by Rice's theorem, A_1 is not recursive. It follows from Theorem 5.15 that $\overline{A_1}$ is not r.e. □

* Example 5.33 *Let A be an r.e. index set. Show that if $x \in A$ and $W_x \subseteq W_y$ then $y \in A$. Thus, the following sets are not r.e.:* $\overline{\text{REC}}$, $\overline{\text{REG}}$, $\overline{\text{REV}}$.

Proof. Assume that A is an index set and that there exist $x_0 \in A$ and $y_0 \notin A$ such that $W_{x_0} \subseteq W_{y_0}$. We show that, then, $K \leq_m \overline{A}$ and hence A is not r.e.

Define

$$g(z, x) = \begin{cases} 1 & \text{if } z \in W_{x_0} \text{ or } [z \in W_{y_0} \text{ and } x \in K], \\ \uparrow & \text{otherwise.} \end{cases}$$

Then, g is partial recursive since $g(z, x) \downarrow$ and equals 1 if and only if

$$(\exists t)[halt(z, x_0, t) \text{ or } [halt(z, y_0, t) \text{ and } halt(x, x, t)]].$$

By the enumeration theorem, there exists $e \geq 0$ such that $\phi_e^2(z, x) = g(z, x)$. Let $f(x) = s_1^1(e, x)$. If $x \in K$, then $\phi_{f(x)}(z) = g(z, x)$, and so $W_{f(x)} = W_{y_0} \cup W_{x_0} = W_{y_0}$. Thus, $x \in K$ implies $f(x) \in \overline{A}$. On the other hand, if $x \notin K$, then $W_{f(x)} = W_{x_0}$ and so $f(x) \in A$. This shows that f is a reduction function for $K \leq_m \overline{A}$ and, hence, A is not r.e.

For the second part of the question, we choose, for set $\overline{\text{REC}}$, x_0 and y_0 to be any indexes such that $W_{x_0} = K$ and $W_{y_0} = \{0,1\}^*$. Then, $x_0 \in \overline{\text{REC}}$, $y_0 \in \text{REC}$ and $W_{x_0} \subseteq W_{y_0}$. So, $\overline{\text{REC}}$ is not r.e.

The same x_0 and y_0 also work for $\overline{\text{REG}}$.

For set $\overline{\text{REV}}$, use any x_0 and y_0 such that $W_{x_0} = \{10\}$ and $W_{y_0} = \{10,01\}$.
□

$\star$ **Example 5.34** *Let A be an r.e. function-index set. Show that if $x \in A$ then there exists $y \in A$ such that W_y is a finite subset of W_x. Thus, the following sets are not r.e.: TOT, $\overline{\text{FIN}}$.*

Proof. Assume that A is a function-index set and that there exists an index $x_0 \in A$ such that $(\forall y)[W_y$ is a finite subset of $W_{x_0} \Rightarrow y \notin A]$. We need to show that $K \leq_m \overline{A}$ and so A is not r.e.

Define

$$g(z,x) = \begin{cases} \phi_{x_0}(z) & \text{if } halt(x,x,z) = 0 \text{ and } z \in W_{x_0}, \\ \uparrow & \text{otherwise.} \end{cases}$$

Then, g is partial recursive since $g(y,x) \downarrow$ and equals $\phi_{x_0}(z)$ if and only if

$$(\exists t)[halt(z,x_0,t)] \text{ and } [halt(x,x,z) = 0].$$

By the enumeration theorem, there exists $e \geq 0$ such that $\phi_e^2(z,x) = g(z,x)$. Let $f(x) = s_1^1(e,x)$. Suppose $x \notin K$. Then, $halt(x,x,z) = 0$ for all $z \geq 0$ and so $\phi_{f(x)}(z) = g(z,x) = \phi_{x_0}(z)$ for all $z \geq 0$. It follows that $f(x) \in A$. On the other hand, suppose $x \in K$. Let $z_0 = (\min z)halt(x,x,z)$. Then, we have $halt(x,x,z) = 0$ if and only if $z < z_0$. Therefore, $W_{f(x)} = W_{x_0} \cap \{z \mid z < z_0\}$ is a finite subset of W_{x_0}, and so $f(x) \in \overline{A}$. The above proved that f is a reduction function for $K \leq_m \overline{A}$.
□

The above examples showed either $K \leq_m A$ or $\overline{K} \leq_m A$ for many index sets A. In addition, the s-m-n theorem can also be used to establish the reductions between other index sets. For instance, the next example shows that problems TOT and $\overline{\text{FIN}}$ are *equivalent* under the many-one reducibility. It means that they have the same *degree of unsolvability*, in the sense that each problem is solvable using the other problem as an *oracle*, although neither is r.e. nor co-r.e.

$\star$ **Example 5.35** *Show that* TOT $\leq_m \overline{\text{FIN}}$ *and* $\overline{\text{FIN}} \leq_m$ TOT.

Proof. Before we give the formal proof, we present an informal analysis of the sets TOT and $\overline{\text{FIN}}$. We note that

$$x \in \text{TOT} \iff W_x = \{0,1\}^*$$
$$\iff (\forall y)[y \in W_x] \iff (\forall y)(\exists t) \cdot [halt(y,x,t)],$$

and

$$x \in \overline{\text{FIN}} \iff W_x \text{ is infinite}$$
$$\iff (\forall z)(\exists y)\,[y \geq z \text{ and } y \in W_x]$$
$$\iff (\forall z)(\exists y)\,[y \geq z \text{ and } (\exists t)\,[halt(y,x,t)]]$$
$$\iff (\forall z)(\exists w)\,[l(w) \geq z \text{ and } halt(l(w),x,r(w))].$$

Therefore, both sets TOT and $\overline{\text{FIN}}$ have the form

$$\{x \mid (\forall y)(\exists z)\,R(x,y,z)\}$$

for some recursive predicate R. Furthermore, we know from earlier examples that they are neither r.e. nor co-r.e. Therefore, they do not have a simpler form of $\{x \mid (\exists y)\,Q(x,y)\}$ or $\{x \mid (\forall y)\,Q(x,y)\}$ for any recursive predicate Q. This suggests that these two sets have the same *degree of unsolvability*.

Now, we present the reductions between them. First, we prove TOT $\leq_m$ $\overline{\text{FIN}}$. Define a function

$$g(x,y) = \begin{cases} 1 & \text{if } (\forall z)_{z \leq y}\,[z \in W_x], \\ \uparrow & \text{otherwise.} \end{cases}$$

Then, g is partial recursive since $g(x,y) \downarrow$ if and only if

$$(\exists t)[(\forall z)_{z \leq y}\, halt(z,x,t)].$$

(*Note*: $(\forall z)_{z \leq y}$ is a bounded quantifier, and so $[(\forall z)_{z \leq y}\, halt(z,x,t)]$ is a recursive predicate.)

By the enumeration theorem and the *s-m-n* theorem, there exists a recursive function f such that for all $x, y \geq 0$, $\phi_{f(x)}(y) = g(x,y)$. Now we observe that if $x \in$ TOT, then $W_x = \{0,1\}^*$ and so the condition $(\forall z)_{z \leq y}\,[z \in W_x]$ holds for all $y \geq 0$. It follows that $W_{f(x)} = \{0,1\}^*$ and is infinite. Conversely, if $x \notin$ TOT, then $W_x \neq \{0,1\}^*$. Let y_0 be the least string in $\overline{W}_x$. Then, $g(x,y) \uparrow$ for all $y \geq y_0$. That is, $W_{f(x)} = \{y \mid g(x,y) \downarrow\}$ is finite. Therefore, f is a reduction function for TOT $\leq_m \overline{\text{FIN}}$.

Next, we prove $\overline{\text{FIN}} \leq_m$ TOT. We define a function

$$h(x,y) = \begin{cases} 1 & \text{if } (\exists z)_{z \geq y}\,[z \in W_x], \\ \uparrow & \text{otherwise.} \end{cases}$$

Then,

$$h(x,y) = (\exists w)\,[l(w) \geq y \text{ and } halt(l(w),x,r(w))],$$

and so h is partial recursive.

By the enumeration theorem and the *s-m-n* theorem, there is a recursive function k such that for all $x, y \geq 0$, $\phi_{k(x)}(y) = h(x,y)$. Now, if $x \in \overline{\text{FIN}}$ then for every $y \geq 0$, the condition $(\exists z)_{z \geq y}\,[z \in W_x]$ holds and so $W_{k(x)} = \{0,1\}^*$. Conversely, if $x \in$ FIN, then W_x is finite. Let y_0 be the greatest integer in W_x (or, let $y_0 = 0$ if $W_x = \emptyset$). Then, the condition $(\exists z)_{z \geq y}\,[z \in W_x]$ does not hold for all $y > y_0$. It follows that $W_{k(x)}$ is finite and is not equal to $\{0,1\}^*$. This shows that k is a reduction function for $\overline{\text{FIN}} \leq_m$ TOT. $\square$

Exercises 5.4

1. Assume that $A \cup B = \{0,1\}^*$ and $A \cap B \neq \emptyset$. Show that if A and B are r.e., then $A \leq_m A \cap B$.

2. If $g : \{0,1\}^* \to \{0,1\}^*$ is one-to-one, then we define $g^{-1}(x) = (\min y)$ $[g(y) = x]$. Show that there exists a recursive function f such that for all one-to-one functions ϕ_m, $\phi_{f(m)} = \phi_m^{-1}$.

3. Show that there exists a recursive function $c(x,y)$ such that $\phi_{c(x,y)}(z) = \phi_x(\phi_y(z))$.

4. (a) Show that for every partial recursive function f, there exists a recursive function g such that $W_{g(x)} = f^{-1}(W_x)$.

   (b) Show that there is a recursive function g such that for all x, y,

   $$W_{g(x,y)} = \phi_x^{-1}(W_y) = \{z \mid \phi_x(z) \in W_y\}.$$

★ 5. (*Rice's theorem for r.e. index sets*) For any finite set $D = \{x_1, \ldots, x_n\}$, we say $[x_1, \ldots, x_n]$ (in any order) is a code of D. Show that an index set A is r.e. if and only if

   (i) $x \in A$ and $W_x \subseteq W_y$ imply $y \in A$;

   (ii) $x \in A$ implies that there exists $y \in A$ such that W_y is a finite subset of W_x; and

   (iii) There exists an r.e. set B that contains codes of all and only finite sets W_x such that $x \in A$ (i.e., for each $x \in A$ such that W_x is finite, B contains at least one of its code, and for every $[x_1, \ldots, x_n] \in B$ and every x such that $W_x = \{x_1, \ldots, x_n\}$, $x \in A$).

6. For any partial recursive function $f : \{0,1\}^* \to \{0,1\}^*$, we write D_f to denote its domain $\{x \mid f(x) \downarrow\}$. Let $f, g, h : \{0,1\}^* \to \{0,1\}^*$ be three partial recursive functions.

   (a) Show that there exists a partial recursive function $p : \{0,1\}^* \to \{0,1\}^*$ such that $D_p = D_f \cup D_g \cup D_h$, and for each $x \in D_p$, $p(x) = f(x)$ or $p(x) = g(x)$ or $p(x) = h(x)$.

   (b) Show that there does not always exist a partial recursive function $q : \{0,1\}^* \to \{0,1\}^*$ such that $D_q = D_f \cup D_g \cup D_h$, and for each $x \in D_q$, $q(x) = f(x)$ or $q(x) = g(x)$ or $q(x) = h(x)$, and for each $x \in D_f \cap D_g \cap D_h$, $q(x) = \min\{f(x), g(x), h(x)\}$.

7. Define

   $$f(n) = \begin{cases} \min\{W_n\} & \text{if } W_n \neq \emptyset, \\ \uparrow & \text{otherwise.} \end{cases}$$

   Is f a partial recursive function? Prove your answer.

★ 8. (a) Show that there exists an r.e. set B such that $\bigcap_{n \in B} W_n$ is not r.e.

(b) Show that if B is an r.e. index set then $\bigcap_{n \in B} W_n$ is also r.e.

9. Let C_1 be the class of all recursive sets, C_2 the class of all r.e. sets which are not recursive, C_3 the class of all co-r.e. sets which are not r.e., and C_4 the class of all sets that are neither r.e. nor co-r.e. For each of the following sets, determine in which class C_i, $i \in \{1, 2, 3, 4\}$, it belongs to.

(a) $B_1 = \{x \mid M_x(x)$ halts in at most 200 moves$\}$.

(b) $B_2 = \{x \mid \phi_x(x) > x\}$.

(c) $B_3 = \{x \mid |W_x| \geq 5\}$.

(d) $B_4 = \{x \mid |W_x| \geq x\}$.

(e) $B_5 = \{\langle x, y \rangle \mid y \in range(\phi_x)\}$.

(f) $B_6 = \{\langle x, y \rangle \mid \phi_x(y)$ is defined or $\phi_y(x)$ is undefined$\}$.

(g) $B_7 = \{n \mid \phi_n = \phi_{n_0}\}$, where n_0 is a fixed positive integer.

(h) $B_8 = \{x \mid$ range of ϕ_x is finite$\}$.

(i) $B_9 = \{n \mid W_n \subseteq P\}$, where P is the set of primes.

(j) $B_{10} = \{n \mid W_n = P\}$, where P is the set of primes.

(k) $B_{11} = \{n \mid W_n \subseteq K\}$.

10. A set A is called *single-valued* if for each y, there exists at most one z such that $\langle y, z \rangle \in A$. Let $B_{12} = \{x \mid W_x$ is single-valued$\}$. Show that $\text{EMP} \leq_m B_{12}$ and $B_{12} \leq_m \text{EMP}$,

11.   (a) Show that there is a recursive predicate R such that

$$x \in \text{REC} \iff (\exists y)(\forall z)(\exists w)\, R(x, y, z, w).$$

(b) Let $\text{COINF} = \{x \mid \overline{W}_x$ is infinite$\}$. Show that there exists a recursive predicate Q such that

$$x \in \text{COINF} \iff (\forall y)(\exists z)(\forall w)\, Q(x, y, z, w).$$

⋆ 12. Prove the following reductions:

(a) $\text{TOT} \leq_m \text{REC}$.

(b) $\text{TOT} \leq_m \text{COINF}$.

13. Let $B_{13} = \{x \mid W_x = K\}$.

(a) Show that there exists a recursive predicate R such that

$$x \in B_{13} \iff (\forall y)(\exists z)\, R(x, y, z).$$

⋆ (b) Show that $B_{13} \leq \text{TOT}$ and $\text{TOT} \leq_m B_{13}$.

14. Let $B_{14} = \{x \mid (\exists y \in W_x)\, [W_y$ is infinite$]\}$.

(a) Show that there exists a recursive predicate R such that

$$x \in B_{14} \iff (\exists y)(\forall z)(\exists w)\, R(x, y, z, w).$$

$\star$ (b) Show that REC $\leq_m B_{14}$.

$\star$ **15.** A set $B \subseteq \{0,1\}^*$ is called *productive* if there exists a partial recursive function f such that for every x, if $W_x \subseteq B$ then $f(x) \downarrow$ and $f(x) \in B - W_x$.

    (a) Show that if B is productive then B has an infinite r.e. subset.

    (b) Show that if $K \leq_m A$ then $\overline{A}$ is productive.

    (c) Conclude from (a) and (b) above that a simple set cannot be a complete r.e. set.

$\star$ **16.** Show that there exist two r.e. sets A and B such that $A \not\leq_m B$ and $B \not\leq_m A$. [*Hint*: construct A and B simultaneously by diagonalization.]

$\star$ 5.5 Recursion Theorem

In the past few sections, we presented a few proof techniques, including dovetailing, diagonalization, the *s-m-n* theorem and reducibility, which may be viewed as summaries of some intuitive algorithmic analysis of computable and noncomputable objects. In this section, we introduce one more technique, the recursion theorem, which is more abstract and more powerful than other techniques.

Theorem 5.36 (Recursion Theorem) *For any partial recursive function* f : $(\{0,1\}^*)^{k+1} \to \{0,1\}^*$, *there exists a constant* $e \geq 0$ *such that*

$$\phi_e^k(x_1, \ldots, x_k) = f(x_1, \ldots, x_k, e).$$

Proof. The interesting point here is that M_e is a DTM that can use its own code e like an input. How do we get such a machine that can access its own code as an input? The main tool here is the *s-m-n* theorem. We recall that, for any $y, z \in \{0,1\}^*$,

$$\phi_{s_k^1(y,z)}^k(x_1, \ldots, x_k) = \phi_y^{k+1}(x_1, \ldots, x_k, z).$$

Therefore, if we set $y = z$, we get a machine $M_{s_k^1(z,z)}$ which simulates the function ϕ_z^{k+1} on its own code:

$$\phi_{s_k^1(z,z)}^k(x_1, \ldots, x_k) = \phi_z^{k+1}(x_1, \ldots, x_k, z).$$

Now, let us apply this to the function f. Assume that f is computed by a DTM M^f and its machine code is e_1; that is, $f = \phi_{e_1}^{k+1}$. From the above observation, we see that the DTM $M_{s_k^1(e_1,e_1)}$ simulates f on its code e_1.

Unfortunately, this index $e = s_k^1(e_1, e_1)$ is not quite the index we are looking for, since the machine M_e only simulates f on e_1, not on e itself. In other words, what we did above is the following: We tried to create a machine that works just like M^f except that it also takes its own code e_1 as the last input. However, when we apply the s-m-n theorem to create this machine, the machine code has been changed from e_1 of M^f to $e = s_k^1(e_1, e_1)$ of the new machine. So, the last input e_1 is no longer its own machine code.

To fix this problem, we need to make two adjustments: First, we need to compute the new machine code e from e_1, and then simulate M^f on e instead of e_1. This can be done by simulating a DTM M^s that computes the function s_k^1 to get $e = s_k^1(e_1, e_1)$. Next, we note that now the new machine has been changed again (it now needs to simulate both M^f and M^s), and so the original code e_1 has to be modified accordingly. What is the correct new e_1? We note that the output $e = s_k^1(e_1, e_1)$ is to be used as the last input to M^f. Therefore, e_1 should be the code of a machine that computes the function $f(x_1, \ldots, x_k, s_k^1(x_{k+1}, x_{k+1}))$.

In summary, the new DTM M_e works as follows:

(1) It contains three components: the code of DTM M^f that computes f, the code of DTM M^s that computes s_k^1, and the constant e_1.

(2) It first computes its own code e by simulating M^s on (e_1, e_1).

(3) It then simulates M^f on inputs $(x_1, \ldots, x_k, e)$.

The following is the formal proof using the above ideas:

First, by the enumeration theorem, there exists a constant e_1 such that

$$\phi_{e_1}^{k+1}(x_1, \ldots, x_k, x_{k+1}) = f(x_1, \ldots, x_k, s_k^1(x_{k+1}, x_{k+1})).$$

Let $e = s_k^1(e_1, e_1)$. Then, we verify that e satisfies the requirement:

$$\phi_e^k(x_1, \ldots, x_k) = \phi_{s_k^1(e_1, e_1)}^k(x_1, \ldots, x_k)$$
$$= \phi_{e_1}^{k+1}(x_1, \ldots, x_k, e_1)$$
$$= f(x_1, \ldots, x_k, s_k^1(e_1, e_1)) = f(x_1, \ldots, x_k, e). \qquad \square$$

It is interesting to note that the above proof does not rely on specific properties of the Turing machine model. It works for any computational model in which the enumerability theorem and the s-m-n theorem hold true. To demonstrate this fact, and also to get more insight into the proof of the recursion theorem, let us prove it in the context of a more practical high-level programming environment (using a pseudo-Pascal language).

The question is to find, from a given program P_f, a new program P_e that, on input $(x_1, \ldots, x_k)$, can generate its own program code e and simulate program P_f on input $(x_1, \ldots, x_k, e)$, treating e as a character string. Our first attempt of such a program P_1 is to let e be the code of a program that simulates P_f on $(x_1, \ldots, x_k, e)$, as shown in Figure 5.3(a). (In program P_1, we use single quotes ' and ' to define a constant string; for example, 'string' denotes the constant string of length 6: **string**.) Note, however, that the constant e defined in the first statement of program P_1 is *not* the correct program code of itself since it does not include the first statement. Since the real code of the program needs to refer to itself (i.e., it is *self-referential*), this approach

Program P_1 :

$e :=$ 'read$(x_1, \ldots, x_k)$;
    $x_{k+1} := e$;
    $P_f(x_1, \ldots, x_k, x_{k+1})$;';
read$(x_1, \ldots, x_k)$;
$x_{k+1} := e$;
$P_f(x_1, \ldots, x_k, x_{k+1})$;

(a)

Program P_2 :

$e := {}'e := {}$"read$(x_1, \ldots, x_k)$;
    $x_{k+1} := e$;
    $P_f(x_1, \ldots, x_k, x_{k+1})$;" ;
read$(x_1, \ldots, x_k)$;
$x_{k+1} := e$;
$P_f(x_1, \ldots, x_k, x_{k+1})$;' ;
read$(x_1, \ldots, x_k)$;
$x_{k+1} := e$;
$P_f(x_1, \ldots, x_k, x_{k+1})$;

(b)

Figure 5.3: Two attempts for a self-referential program.

of directly creating the program code e does not work. For instance, if we change the first statement of program P_1 to define e as the program code of the whole program P_1, including the first statement, it still does not work as the new statement one has been changed. This new program P_2 is shown in Figure 5.3(b). (We follow the convention that the double quotes " and " within two enclosing single quotes really denote the single quotes ' and ', respectively; e.g., 'ab"cd"' denotes the constant string of length 6: ab'cd'.)

Now, let us try to use the idea of the proof of Theorem 5.36 to construct the program P_e. As we discussed in the proof, this program P_e has three components: the program P_f, the program P_s which computes the function s_k^1, and the code e_1. Here, e_1 is the constant string that includes the codes of both P_f and P_s. Thus, based on this idea, we come up with the program P_3 of Figure 5.4(a).

But, what exactly is the function $s_k^1(e_1, e_1)$ in the high-level language form? Suppose that u is a program code and v is a string. Then, $s_k^1(u, v)$ outputs the program code of the following form (assuming that the $(k+1)$st input is called e_1):

$$e_1 := v;$$
$$u;$$

Therefore, the correct program code $e = s_k^1(e_1, e_1)$ should be the concatenation of four strings:

(1) The constant string '$e_1 :=$ "',

(2) The string e_1 (the content of e_1, not the name 'e_1'),

(3) The constant string '";' and

(4) The string e_1.

Program P_3:

$$e_1 := {}^`e := s_k^1(e_1, e_1);$$
$$\qquad read(x_1, \ldots, x_k);$$
$$\qquad x_{k+1} := e;$$
$$\qquad P_f(x_1, \ldots, x_k, x_{k+1}); {}^`;$$
$$e := s_k^1(e_1, e_1);$$
$$read(x_1, \ldots, x_k);$$
$$x_{k+1} := e;$$
$$P_f(x_1, \ldots, x_k, x_{k+1});$$

(a)

Program P_4:

$$e_1 := {}^`e := concat({}^{``}e_1 := {}^{````}\text{ ''},$$
$$\qquad\qquad e_1, {}^{``}{}^{''};{}^{''}, e_1);$$
$$\qquad read(x_1, \ldots, x_k);$$
$$\qquad x_{k+1} := e;$$
$$\qquad P_f(x_1, \ldots, x_k, x_{k+1}); {}^`;$$
$$e := concat({}^`e_1 := {}^`{}^{''}, e_1, {}^`;{}^`, e_1);$$
$$read(x_1, \ldots, x_k);$$
$$x_{k+1} := e;$$
$$P_f(x_1, \ldots, x_k, x_{k+1});$$

(b)

Figure 5.4: Self-referential programs.

We show the expanded version of our program, program P_4, in Figure 5.4(b). It can be checked that, after the execution of statements 1 and 2, the content of variable e is exactly the code of program P_4.

Note that this is just an outline since we used, in program P_4, the procedure names *concat* and P_f instead of their program codes (see also Exercise 1 of this section).

The recursion theorem allows us to build programs that use their own program codes as inputs. The following are some simple applications.

Example 5.37 *(a) Show that there exists a constant e such that $\phi_e(x) = e$ for all $x \in \{0, 1\}^*$.*
(b) Show that there exists a constant e such that $W_e = \{e\}$.
(c) Show that there exists a constant n such that $\phi_n = \phi_{n+1}$.

Proof. (a) Let $f(x, e) = e$. By the recursion theorem, there exists a constant e such that $\phi_e(x) = f(x, e) = e$ for all $x \in \{0, 1\}^*$.

(b) Let

$$f(x, e) = \begin{cases} 1 & \text{if } x = e, \\ \uparrow & \text{otherwise.} \end{cases}$$

It is obvious that f is partial recursive. By the recursion theorem, there exists a constant e such that $\phi_e(x) = f(x, e)$. The domain of the function ϕ_e is $W_e = \{e\}$.

(c) Let $f(x, n) = \phi_{n+1}(x)$ and, then, apply the recursion theorem to f. □

Note that part (c) of the above example implies that no matter how we encode Turing machines (or machines in any reasonable computational model), there must be two consecutive machines that compute the same function, as

$$e_1 := \text{ 'write}(\text{"}e_1 := \text{""""});$$
$$\text{write}(e_1);$$
$$\text{write}(\text{""""}; \text{"});$$
$$\text{write}(e_1); \text{'} ;$$
$$\text{write}(\text{'}e_1 := \text{"'});$$
$$\text{write}(e_1);$$
$$\text{write}(\text{'"}; \text{'});$$
$$\text{write}(e_1);$$

Figure 5.5: A self-reproducing program.

long as the encoding of the machines admits a universal machine and satisfies the *s-m-n* theorem,

Example 5.38 *Write a program (in pseudo-Pascal) that, on any input, prints its own program code as the output (this is called a* self-reproducing *program).*

Solution. This is just part (a) of Example 5.37 in a high-level language environment. We can obtain a self-reproducing program by expanding the procedure P_f in program P_4. We note that the program P_f here is just the program that prints the last input as the output. In fact, the last input is just e, the output of the procedure $s_k^1(e_1, e_1)$. So, we may directly write the value of e out and skip the third and fourth statements of program P_4. The resulting program is shown in Figure 5.5. (See also Exercise 1 of this section.)   □

The recursion theorem can also simplify some proofs by the method of reducibility. For instance, we can combine the diagonalization techinique and the recursion theorem to prove Rice's theorem.

Example 5.30 (Revisited) *Prove Rice's theorem by the recursion theorem.*

Proof. Assume that A is a nontrivial index set. Let $n_1 \in A$ and $n_0 \notin A$. Suppose, by way of contradiction, that A is recursive. Then, define a function

$$f(x, e) = \begin{cases} \phi_{n_0}(x) & \text{if } e \in A, \\ \phi_{n_1}(x) & \text{if } e \notin A. \end{cases}$$

Since A is recursive, f is partial recursive.

By the recursion theorem, there exists a constant e such that $\phi_e(x) = f(x, e)$. Now, consider two cases:

Case 1. $e \in A$. Then, $\phi_e(x) = f(x, e) = \phi_{n_0}(x)$. However, since A is an index set and since $n_0 \notin A$, we get $e \notin A$. This is a contradiction.

Case 2. $e \in \overline{A}$. Then, $\phi_e(x) = f(x, e) = \phi_{n_1}(x)$ and, hence, $e \in A$. This is also a contradiction.

From the above analysis, we conclude that A cannot be recursive. □

The following are some more examples of combining the diagonalization technique with the recursion theorem to prove negative results.

Example 5.39 Let $f : \mathbf{N} \to \mathbf{N}$ be a recursive function. Show that there exists an integer n such that W_n is a recursive set and the least integer m such that $W_m = \overline{W}_n$ is greater than $f(n)$.

Proof. First, we use diagonalization to construct a recursive set A (depending on n) that is different from each $\overline{W}_m$, for all $m \leq f(n)$. Next, we apply the recursion theorem to find some n such that $A = W_n$.

Formally, define

$$g(m, n) = \left\{ \begin{array}{ll} 1 & \text{if } m \leq f(n) \text{ and } \phi_m(m) \downarrow, \\ \uparrow & \text{otherwise.} \end{array} \right.$$

It is easy to see that g is partial recursive. By the recursion theorem, there is a constant n such that $\phi_n(m) = g(m, n)$. That is,

$$W_n = \{m \mid m \leq f(n), m \in W_m\}.$$

So, W_n is a finite set and, hence, a recursive set. For each $m \leq f(n)$, $m \in W_m$ if and only if $m \in W_n$, and so $W_n \neq \overline{W}_m$. It follows that if $\overline{W}_m = \overline{W}_n$, then m must be greater than $f(n)$. □

Example 5.40 (Busy beaver) Let $f(x) = \min\{n \mid \phi_n(\varepsilon) = x\}$. Show that f is not a recursive function.

For each string $x \in \{0, 1\}^*$, $f(x)$ is the minimum Turing machine (in our standard enumeration) that prints x from the empty input. Intuitively, we may regard $f(x)$ as a string that encodes the *minimum information* of x that is necessary in order to recover x by the universal DTM U. (*Note:* By definition, $U(f(x), \varepsilon) = x$.) The idea of the proof is that if f were recursive, then we could use the DTM M^f that computes f to search for strings y whose "minimum information codes" are much larger than the size of M^f, and print such a string y. However, since we could get y by simulating M^f, M^f would be essentially its minimum information code. Thus, this provides us a contradiction. In the following, we present two proofs. The first one is an informal construction and the second one is a formal proof by the recursion theorem.

Proof 1. Assume that f is a recursive function and is computed by a DTM M^f. For any fixed integer m, construct a DTM T_m, which, on the empty input ε, finds and prints the minimum x such that $f(x) > 2^m$. More precisely, T_m operates as follows:

(1) Set $x := \varepsilon$.

(2) If $f(x) \leq 2^m$ then go to step (3); otherwise, halt with output x.

(3) Let $x := x + 1$ and go to step (2).

By the Church-Turing Thesis, this DTM T_m exists. Note that the functions f and $exp(m) = 2^m$ are fixed and so T_m depends only on m. Let $s(m)$ be the code of T_m; that is, $T_m = M_{s(m)}$. We claim that for large m, $s(m) < 2^m$, and this leads to a contradiction: If $s(m) < 2^m$ and if $M_{s(m)}(\varepsilon) = x$, then, by the definition of f, $f(x) \leq s(m) < 2^m$. However, by the construction of $M_{s(m)}$, we know that the output x of $M_{s(m)}(\varepsilon)$ must satisfy $f(x) > 2^m$.

To complete the proof, we need to prove the claim. We note that the machine $M_{s(m)}$ can be constructed in the following way:

(1) It contains two subprocedures M^f and M^{exp} that compute the functions f and exp, respectively. (*Note*: These subprocedures are independent of m.)

(2) It stores m as a constant in the binary form by $\lceil \log_2 m \rceil$ states. (More precisely, machine $M_{s(m)}$ first uses $\lceil \log_2 m \rceil$ special states to write down m on the tape before it begins the simulation of exp and f.)

(3) It uses a fixed number of tape symbols (independent of m).

The above shows that the size (the number of states) of machine T_m is bounded by $c_1 + \log_2 m$ for some constant $c_1 > 0$. Note that a DTM of k states and using ℓ symbols has at most $k \cdot \ell$ instructions and so the length of its code is bounded by $c_2 k \ell (k + \ell)$ for some constant $c_2 > 0$. Therefore, the code $s(m)$ of $M_{s(m)}$ is bounded by $2^{c_3 (c_1 + \log_2 m)^2}$ for some constant $c_3 > 0$. It is easy to see that for large integers m, $s(m) < 2^m$. This completes the proof of the claim. □

Proof 2. Assume that f is recursive. Define a function

$$g(y, m) = (\min x)[f(x) > m].$$

Note that f is a one-to-one function and so is unbounded (i.e., for any constant k, there exists some x such that $f(x) > k$). Therefore, g is a recursive function. By the recursion theorem, there exists a constant e such that

$$\phi_e(y) = g(y, e) = (\min x)[f(x) > e].$$

Since g is recursive, ϕ_e is also recursive. Suppose $\phi_e(\varepsilon) = x_0$. Then, by the definition of g, we know that $f(x_0) > e$. However, by the definition of f, we must have $f(x_0) \leq e$. This is a contradiction. □

The above question is closely related to the theory of *program-size complexity*, or, *Kolmogorov complexity*. Namely, define the program-size complexity $K(x)$ of a string $x \in \{0, 1\}^*$ to be the size of the minimum-size Turing machine M that prints x on the input ε. Then, it is easy to adopt the above proof technique to prove that the function $K(x)$ is nonrecursive. The theory of program-size complexity has many interesting applications to computability theory and computational complexity theory. The reader is referred to Li and Vitányi [1997] for further study.

Exercises 5.5

1. If we look at the self-reproducing program of Figure 5.5 (and program P_4 of Figure 5.4(b)) more carefully, we can see that it is still not completely correct, because all the double quotes in the program are printed as single quotes in the output. More precisely, each double-quote in the right-hand side of the first assignment statement "$e_1 := \cdots$" is stored in e_1 in the form of a single quote and so the third statement "write(e_1);" prints the right-hand side of the first statement with each double-quote replaced by a single quote. Fix this problem to make the program print exactly its own program code.

2. Write a computer program (in your favorite high-level language) that prints the reversal of its own code.

3. Write a computer program (in your favorite high-level language) that reads an input n and prints its own code n times.

4. Write a computer program (in your favorite high-level language) that reads an input x and outputs 1 if x is exactly its own program code, and outputs 0 otherwise. (This is called a *self-recognizing program*.)

5. Prove that there exists an integer $e \geq 0$ such that $W_e = W_{e \dot- 1} \cup W_{e+1}$.

6. Prove that for every recursive function f there exists a constant e such that $\phi_{f(e)} = \phi_e$.

7. Prove that there exists a recursive function f such that $\phi_{\phi_e(f(e))}(x) = \phi_{f(e)}(x)$ for all x.

8. Prove that there exist two integers $m \neq n$ such that $W_m = \{n\}$ and $W_n = \{m\}$. [*Hint*: Note that in the proof of the s-m-n theorem, the function $s^1_m(e, y)$ satisfies the property $s^1_m(e, y) > y$.]

9. (a) Prove that the s-m-n theorem can be improved so that each s^n_m is a one-to-one function in the sense that if $e_1 \neq e_2$ then $s^n_m(e_1, y_1, \ldots, y_n) \neq s^n_m(e_2, y_1, \ldots, y_n)$ for all $y_1, \ldots, y_n \in \mathbf{N}$.

   (b) Show that for any partial recursive function g and any constant n, there exists a constant $e > n$ such that $\phi_e(x) = g(x, e)$.

10. Does there exist an integer m such that $W_m = \{x \mid \phi_x(m) \text{ is defined}\}$? Does there exist an integer n such that $W_n = \{x \mid \phi_x(n) \text{ is undefined}\}$? Prove your answers.

11. Show that there exist integers m and n such that $W_m = W_n = K$ and $m \in K$ and $n \notin K$.

12. Use the recursion theorem to prove that the following sets are not r.e.: FIN, REC, $\overline{\text{REC}}$.

13. Let f be the function defined in Example 5.40. Define f^* to be its *inverse function*: $f^*(n) = (\max x)[f(x) \leq n]$. Prove that f^* grows to infinity faster than any recursive function g. That is, for any recursive function g, there exists n_0 such that $f^*(n) > g(n)$ for all $n \geq n_0$. (The function f^* is called the *busy beaver function*, which grows even faster than the Ackermann function.)

5.6   Undecidable Problems

In Section 5.4, we used Rice's theorem to establish many undecidability results about partial recursive functions, r.e. sets and Turing machines. For instance, the result that EMP is not recursive implies that the problem of determining whether a given DTM M halts on any input is undecidable. The application of Rice's theorem is, however, limited to the problems whose corresponding languages are index sets. In this section, we present some undecidability results for problems involving Turing machines and grammars whose corresponding languages are not index sets. Our main tool is the reducibility technique. We first present a few simple examples using reductions from index sets.

Example 5.41 *Show that the following problems are undecidable:*

(a) *Given a DTM M and a string y, determine whether M halts on some input z which is greater than or equal to y.*

(b) *Given two DTM's M_x and M_y, determine whether they are equivalent (i.e., whether they compute the same function).*

(c) *Given a DTM M, an input y and a state q_i of M, determine whether M ever enters state q_i in the computation on input y.*

(d) *Given a DTM M, determine whether the computation of $M(111)$ contains a configuration in which the tape contains a substring 000.*

Proof. (a) We need to show that set $A_1 = \{\langle x, y \rangle \mid M_x \text{ halts on some input } z \geq y\}$ is not recursive. We reduce the problem $\overline{\text{EMP}}$ to it. We define $g(x) = \langle x, 0 \rangle$. If $x \in \overline{\text{EMP}}$, then M_x halts on some $y \geq 0$, and so $\langle x, 0 \rangle \in A_1$. If $x \in \text{EMP}$, then M_x does not halt on any $y \geq 0$, and so $\langle x, 0 \rangle \notin A_1$. Therefore, g is a reduction function for $\overline{\text{EMP}} \leq_m A_1$.

(b) We need to show that $A_2 = \{\langle x, y \rangle \mid W_x = W_y\}$ is not recursive. We reduce the set EMP to it. Let M_{x_0} be a fixed DTM that does not halt on any input. Define $g(x) = \langle x, x_0 \rangle$. Note that $x \in \text{EMP}$ if and only if M_x is equivalent to M_{x_0}, and so g is a reduction from EMP to A_2.

(c) We need to show that $A_3 = \{\langle x, y, i\rangle \mid M_x$ enters state q_i in its computation on input $y\}$ is not recursive. We reduce the halting problem $K_0 = \{\langle x, y\rangle \mid \phi_x(y) \downarrow\}$ to it. For any DTM M_x, we modify M_x into a new DTM M' as follows: Suppose M_x has states $q_1, q_2, \ldots, q_n$, where q_n is the halting state. Then, M' has states $q_1, q_2, \ldots, q_{n+1}$, where q_{n+1} is the halting state. M' has all the instructions of M_x plus the following additional instructions:

$$\delta'(q_n, a) = (q_{n+1}, a, R), \text{ for all } a \in \Gamma.$$

It is easy to verify that M_x halts on y if and only if M' enters state q_n in its computation on input y.

We observe that the program code z of M' can be computed from program code x of M_x, since the modification of the code is quite simple. (Indeed, it can be proved that this modification is a primitive recursive function.) Thus, there exists a recursive function f such that $M' = M_{f(x)}$. Now, $g(\langle x, y\rangle) = \langle f(x), y, maxstate(x)\rangle$ is a reduction for $K_0 \leq_m A_3$.

(d) We need to show that the set A_4 of all program codes x for which the computation of M_x on input 111 contains 000 in one of its tape configurations is not recursive. We reduce the halting problem K to A_4. For any string $y \in \Sigma^*$, we let $\tilde{y}$ denote the string that is obtained from y with each symbol $a \in \Sigma$ replaced by the string Ba. (E.g., if $y = 01100$ then $\tilde{y} = B0B1B1B0B0$.) For any DTM M_x, we construct a new DTM M' as follows:

(1) M' erases its input y and writes down $\tilde{x}BB\tilde{x}$ on its tape. (*Note*: $\tilde{x}$ is a fixed constant to machine M'.)

(2) M' simulates the universal DTM U on the initial configuration (q_1, xBx) with the modification that, at each move, it skips a blank symbol. That is, when U moves right, M' moves two cells to the right; and when U moves left, M' moves two cells to the left.

(3) If the simulation halts, then M' enters a new state and writes down three consecutive 0's and then halts.

By the Church-Turing Thesis, such a DTM M' exists and, furthermore, can be constructed effectively from a given x. That is, there is a recursive function f such that $M' = M_{f(x)}$. We note that if $x \in K$ then the computation of $M_{f(x)}$ on input $y = 111$ halts with 000 on its tape, and if $x \notin K$ then the computation of $M_{f(x)}$ on input 111 never halts and its tape never contains three consecutive 0's. □

The transformations between Turing machines, partial recursive functions and grammars as presented in Sections 4.5 and 4.8 can be used to obtain undecidability results on grammars from undecidability results on Turing machines. We present a few simple examples.

Example 5.42 *Show that the following problems are undecidable:*
(a) Given a grammar G and a string x, determine whether $x \in L(G)$.

(b) *Given a grammar G and two strings x and y, determine whether $x \overset{*}{\underset{G}{\Rightarrow}} y$.*

(c) *Given a grammar G and two strings $x, y \in L(G)$, determine whether there is a derivation of x that is longer than the shortest derivation of y. (The length of a derivation is the number of sentential forms in the derivation.)*

(d) *Given a grammar G, determine whether $L(G) = \emptyset$.*

(e) *Given two grammars G_1 and G_2, determine whether $L(G_1) \subseteq L(G_2)$.*

(f) *Given a grammar G, determine whether $L(G)$ is a context-free language (i.e, for a given unrestricted grammar G, determine whether there is an equivalent context-free grammar).*

Proof. (a) Let $A_1 = \{(G, x) \mid x \in L(G)\}$. We reduce the halting problem $K_0 = \{(M, x) \mid M \text{ halts on } x\}$ to A_1. For any DTM M, let G'_M be the grammar defined in the proof of Theorem 4.20. Then, the mapping $f(M, x) = (G'_M, x)$ is a reduction for $K_0 \leq_m A_1$.

(b) Let $A_2 = \{(G, x, y) \mid x \overset{*}{\underset{G}{\Rightarrow}} y\}$. The mapping $f(M, x) = (G'_M, S, x)$ where S is the starting symbol of G'_M, is a reduction for $K_0 \leq_m A_2$.

(c) Let $A_3 = \{(G, x, y) \mid x, y \in L(G) \text{ and there exists a derivation of } x \text{ that is longer than the shortest derivation of } y\}$. We reduce A_1 to A_3 as follows: For any grammar $G_1 = (V_1, \Sigma_1, S_1, R_1)$ and any string x, we map them to grammar $G_2 = (V_2, \Sigma_1, S_2, R_2)$ and strings x and xa, where a is a symbol in Σ_1, $V_2 = V_1 \cup \{S_2\}$ and R_2 contains all grammar rules of R_1, plus the following three rules: $S_2 \rightarrow S_1$, $S_2 \rightarrow x$, and $S_2 \rightarrow xa$.

Then, $x \in L(G_1)$ if and only if there is a derivation $S_2 \overset{*}{\underset{G_2}{\Rightarrow}} x$ of length greater than two. Since the shortest derivation of xa in G_2 is of length two, we see that $x \in L(G_1)$ if and only if $(G_2, x, xa) \in A_3$.

(d) Let $A_4 = \{G \mid L(G) = \emptyset\}$. The function $f(M) = G'_M$ is a reduction from EMP to A_4.

(e) Let $A_5 = \{(G_1, G_2) \mid L(G_1) \subseteq L(G_2)\}$. We can reduce A_4 to A_5 by the function $f(G) = (G, G_0)$, where G_0 is the grammar with a single rule $S \rightarrow S$, where S is the starting symbol of G_0 and $S \notin \Sigma$.

(f) Let $A_6 = \{G \mid L(G) \text{ is context-free}\}$. We observe, from Rice's theorem, that $B_6 = \{x \mid W_x \text{ is a context-free language}\}$ is undecidable. The function $f(x) = G'_{M_x}$ is a reduction from B_6 to A_6, and so A_6 is undecidable   □

As we have seen above, many undecidability results about Turing machines and grammars can be proved by simple reductions from problems that have been proved undecidable in Section 5.4. For problems involving other computational models that are not known to be equivalent to the Turing machine model (e.g., context-free grammars), the reductions for their undecidability are more difficult.

First, we consider context-free grammars. We note that the *membership problem* (given a context-free grammar G and a string x, determine whether $x \in L(G)$) and the *emptyness problem* (given a context-free grammar G, determine whether $L(G) = \emptyset$) for context-free grammars are decidable. The following result shows that the *totality problem* for context-free grammars is undecidable.

* Example 5.43 *Show that the problem of determining whether a given context-free grammar G over the alphabet $\{0,1\}$ has $L(G) = \{0,1\}^*$ is undecidable.*

Proof. We reduce the problem EMP to this problem. Let M be a DTM. Recall that, in Section 5.1, we have defined a coding scheme for a configuration of M. We make a minor modification here. We encode the configuration

$$(q_j, a_{i_1} a_{i_2} \cdots a_{i_{m-1}} \underline{a_{i_m}} a_{i_{m+1}} \cdots a_{i_n})$$

by

$$111010^{i_1}10^{i_2}1 \cdots 10^{i_{m-1}}110^j110^{i_m}10^{i_{m+1}}1 \cdots 10^{i_n}111.$$

Next, we say a string z is a *legal computation* of M if

$$z = \alpha_0 \, (\alpha_1)^R \, \alpha_2 \, (\alpha_3)^R \, \cdots \, (\alpha_{m-1})^R \, \alpha_m \tag{5.2}$$

for some even $m > 0$ (where $(\alpha_i)^R$ denotes the reversal of the string α_i), or if

$$z = \alpha_0 \, (\alpha_1)^R \, \alpha_2 \, (\alpha_3)^R \, \cdots \, \alpha_{m-1} \, (\alpha_m)^R \tag{5.3}$$

for some odd $m > 0$, with the following properties:

(i) α_0 is (the code of) an initial configuration of M;

(ii) For each i, $0 \leq i \leq m - 1$, $\alpha_i \vdash_M \alpha_{i+1}$;

(iii) α_m is a final configuration.

In other words, a legal computation here is a computation path of M with every other configuration reversed. The reason to reverse every other configuration is to get the following claim:

Claim. The set of all *illegal* computations of M is a context-free language.

Proof of the Claim. For any string $z \in \{0,1\}^*$, we say x is a *configuration-block* (or, simply, a *c-block*) of z if x is a substring of z of the form $1110y0111$, with y containing no substring 111. A string $z \in \{0,1\}^*$ is not a legal computation if and only if one of the following holds:

(a) z is not of the form (5.2) or (5.3), with each α_i encoding a configuration.

(b) The first c-block α_0 of z is not an initial configuration.

(c) For some even i, $0 \leq i < m$, the ith c-block x and the $(i+1)$st c-block y of z do not satisfy $x \vdash_M y^R$.

(d) For some odd i, $0 \leq i < m$, the ith c-block x and the $(i + 1)$st c-block y of z do not satisfy $x^R \vdash_M y$.

(e) z has an odd number of c-blocks and the last c-block x of z is not a final configuration.

(f) z has an even number of c-blocks and the last c-block x of z is not the reversal of a final configuration.

We will show that, for each of the above conditions, the set of strings satisfying the condition is context-free and so the set of illegal computations, the union of these sets, is also context-free.

First note that the strings of the form (5.2) are those in

$$(1110(10^+)^*110^+1(10^+)^+111\ 111(0^+1)^+10^+11(0^+1)^*0111)^*,$$

and hence form a regular set. Similarly, the set of strings of the form (5.3) is also a regular set. So, the set S_1 of strings satisfying condition (a) is regular.

For condition (b), we note that the initial configurations are those of the form $(1110(10^+)^*110110^3111)$ and form a regular set. (Recall that 0^3 represents the blank **B**.) So, the set of strings of the form $1110y0111$, with y having no substring 111, which are not initial configurations is also a regular set. Let R_2 be a regular expression for this set. Then, the set S_2 of strings satisfying condition (b) is $R_2(0 \cup 1)^*$ and, hence, is regular.

Next, we construct a PDA M_1 to accept strings satisfying condition (c). The PDA M_1 works like a PDA that recognizes the set $\{xcy \mid x, y \in \{a, b\}^*, x \neq y^R\}$. We only present a sketch of M_1 and leave the details as an exercise:

(1) It nondeterministically skips through an even number of substrings 1111110 to find the beginning of a configuration u (or, just find the beginning of the first configuration u).

(2) It reads the configuration u and stores its successor configuration v in the stack. (If u does not have a successor configuration, then M_1 rejects the input.)

(3) It reads the next c-block w of z and compares it with the string v in the stack and accepts the input z if $w \neq v^R$.

Thus, the set S_3 of strings satisfying condition (c) is context-free.

Condition (d) is similar to condition (c) and we can prove, in a similar way, that the set S_4 of all strings satisfying (d) is context-free.

For condition (e), we assume that the final state of M is q_h. Then, a configuration x is a final configuration if it is in

$$(1110(0 \cup 1)^*110^h11(0 \cup 1)^*111).$$

Therefore, the set of strings of the form $1110y0111$, with y having no substring 111, that do not represent a final configuration is also regular. Let R_5 be the regular expression of this set, and Q be the regular expression for the set of strings over $\{0, 1\}$ having no substring 111. Then, the set S_5 of strings satisfying condition (e) is

$$(1110Q0111\ 1110Q0111)^*\ 1110Q0111\ R_5.$$

Therefore, S_5 is regular.

Condition (f) is similar to condition (e). We can prove, in a similar way, that set S_6 of strings satisfying condition (f) is also regular. The above completes the proof that the set S of illegal computations of M is context-free.

Note that our proof actually shows how to construct a context-free grammar G from M such that $L(G) = S$. More precisely, for each $j = 1, 2, \ldots, 6$, our proof above shows we can construct either a regular expression or a PDA for set S_j. From the work of Chapter 3, there are uniform procedures to transform regular expressions and PDA's to equivalent context-free grammars. (For conditions (b), (e) and (f), we also need the procedures of Chapter 2 to transform a regular expression to the regular expression of its complement.) Therefore, we may construct, from M, context-free grammars G_j such that $L(G_j) = S_j$ and we can combine them together to form the desired grammar G.

Finally, we observe that if M does not halt on any string, then there is no legal computation and so all strings in $\{0, 1\}^*$ are illegal. That is, $L(G) = \{0, 1\}^*$. On the other hand, if M halts on some string, then there exists at least one legal computation, and so $L(G) \neq \{0, 1\}^*$. Therefore, the above construction of grammar G from DTM M is a reduction from EMP to the given problem.   □

Corollary 5.44 *The following problems about context-free grammars are undecidable:*

(a) *Given two context-free grammars G_1 and G_2, determine whether $L(G_1) \subseteq L(G_2)$.*

(b) *Given two context-free grammars G_1 and G_2, determine whether $L(G_1) = L(G_2)$.*

Proof. Let G_0 be a context-free grammar such that $L(G_0) = \{0, 1\}^*$. The function $f(G) = (G_0, G)$ is a reduction from the problem of determining whether $L(G) = \{0, 1\}^*$ to both problem (a) and problem (b).   □

Next, we introduce an undecidable combinatorial word problem, called the Post correspondence problem, and use it to prove additional undecidable problems about context-free grammars.

Post Correspondence Problem (PCP): Given a finite set of ordered pairs $(x_1, y_1), \ldots, (x_n, y_n)$ of strings over Σ, determine whether there is a finite sequence of integers $(i_1, i_2, \ldots, i_m)$, with each $i_j \in \{1, \ldots, n\}$, such that

$$x_{i_1} x_{i_2} \cdots x_{i_m} = y_{i_1} y_{i_2} \cdots y_{i_m}. \tag{5.4}$$

For a particular instance $\{(x_1, y_1), \ldots, (x_n, y_n)\}$ of the problem PCP, if there exists a sequence $(i_1, i_2, \ldots, i_m)$ satisfying (5.4), then we say the string $x_{i_1} x_{i_2} \cdots x_{i_m}$ is a *solution* to this instance.

An easy way to understand the problem PCP is to treat each pair (x_i, y_i) as a domino with string x_i at the top and string y_i at the bottom: $\dfrac{x_i}{y_i}$. The question here then is to select, from the given dominoes

$$\frac{x_1}{y_1} \;,\; \frac{x_2}{y_2} \;,\; \cdots \;,\; \frac{x_n}{y_n} \;,$$

with unlimited supply for each type, some dominoes and arrange them into a row so that the top part of the dominoes spells the same word as the bottom part of the dominoes. For instance, we can obtain a solution *baaaaa* from the following given dominoes

$$\frac{aa}{a} \;,\; \frac{ba}{baaa}$$

as follows:

$$\frac{ba}{baaa} \;\bigg|\; \frac{aa}{a} \;\bigg|\; \frac{aa}{a} \;.$$

★ **Example 5.45** *Prove that the problem* PCP *is undecidable (with respect to some alphabet Σ).*

Proof. Let M be a fixed DTM, with a *one-way tape* (i.e., the original one-tape DTM defined in Section 4.1), such that the problem of determining whether M halts on a given string $x \in \{0, 1\}^*$ is undecidable. (I.e., $L(M)$ is a nonrecursive set.) We construct a reduction from the halting problem of this fixed DTM M to the problem PCP. That is, for each string x, we need to produce an instance $P_x = \{(x_1, y_1), \ldots, (x_m, y_m)\}$ such that M halts on x if and only if P_x has a solution z.

Assume that the set of states in M is $Q = \{q_1, q_2, \ldots, q_n\}$, where q_1 is the initial state and q_n is the halting state, and that the set of tape symbols of M is $\Gamma = \{s_1, s_2, \ldots, s_k\}$. Also assume that $Q \cap \Gamma = \emptyset$. Let $Q' = \{\bar{q}_1, \bar{q}_2, \ldots, \bar{q}_n\}$ and $\Gamma' = \{\bar{s}_1, \bar{s}_2, \ldots, \bar{s}_k\}$. Then, we fix the alphabet of our PCP problem as

$$\Sigma = Q \cup Q' \cup \Gamma \cup \Gamma' \cup \{q_{n+1}, \bar{q}_{n+1}, *, \bar{*}, [,]\}.$$

The pairs of strings in P_x consists of the following groups (for the sake of clarity, we show them as dominoes):

(1) $\dfrac{[\quad]}{[\mathtt{B}xq_1\mathtt{B}*]}$.

(2) $\dfrac{a}{\bar{a}}$, $\dfrac{\bar{a}}{a}$, for each $a \in \Gamma \cup \{*\}$.

(3) $\dfrac{q_i a c}{\bar{b}\bar{q}_j\bar{c}}$, $\dfrac{\bar{q}_i\bar{a}c}{bq_jc}$, $\dfrac{q_i a*}{\bar{b}\bar{q}_j\bar{\mathtt{B}}\bar{*}}$, $\dfrac{\bar{q}_i\bar{a}\bar{*}}{bq_j\mathtt{B}*}$, for each instruction $\delta(q_i, a) = (q_j, b, R)$ of M and for each $c \in \Gamma$.

(4) $\dfrac{cq_i a}{\bar{q}_j\bar{c}\bar{b}}$, $\dfrac{\bar{c}\bar{q}_i\bar{a}}{q_jcb}$, for each instruction $\delta(q_i, a) = (q_j, b, L)$ of M and for each $c \in \Gamma$.

(5) $\dfrac{q_n a}{\bar{q}_n}$, $\dfrac{\bar{q}_n\bar{a}}{q_n}$, $\dfrac{q_n*}{\bar{q}_{n+1}\bar{*}}$, $\dfrac{\bar{q}_n\bar{*}}{q_{n+1}*}$, for each $a \in \Gamma$.

(6) $\dfrac{aq_{n+1}}{\bar{q}_{n+1}}$, $\dfrac{\bar{a}\bar{q}_{n+1}}{q_{n+1}}$, for each $a \in \Gamma$.

(7) $\dfrac{q_{n+1}*]}{]}$, $\dfrac{\bar{q}_{n+1}\bar{*}]}{]}$.

We need to prove that M halts on x if and only if P_x has a solution. First, assume that M halts on x. We modify the definition of the configuration of M to include all tape symbols in all cells that have ever been visited by the tape head in the computation of M on input x. That is, the rightmost blank symbols in a configuration are not removed in the representation of the configuration. Assume that the computation of M on x consists of the following configurations:

$$\alpha_0 \vdash \alpha_1 \vdash \cdots \vdash \alpha_\ell,$$

where $\alpha_0 = \mathtt{B}xq_1\mathtt{B}$ and $\alpha_\ell = y_1 \cdots y_p q_n z_1 z_2 \cdots z_q$, where each y_i and each z_j is a single symbol in Γ. Define $\alpha_{\ell+i} = y_1 y_2 \cdots y_p q_n z_{i+1} \cdots z_q$, for $1 \le i \le q$, $\alpha_{\ell+q+1} = y_1 y_2 \cdots y_p q_{n+1}$, and $\alpha_{\ell+q+j} = y_1 \cdots y_{p+1-j} q_{n+1}$, for $2 \le j \le p+1$. We claim that if $\ell + q + p + 1$ is odd, then

$$[\alpha_0 * \bar{\alpha}_1\bar{*}\alpha_2 * \cdots * \bar{\alpha}_{\ell+q+p+1}\bar{*}]$$

is a solution to P_x, and if $\ell + q + p + 1$ is even, then

$$[\alpha_0 * \bar{\alpha}_1\bar{*}\alpha_2 * \cdots \bar{*}\alpha_{\ell+q+p+1}*]$$

is a solution to P_x. (In the above, we write $\bar{\alpha}_i$ to denote the string obtained from α_i with each symbol a in α_i replaced by the symbol $\bar{a}$.)

To prove this claim, the critical observation is that if we use top strings x_i's in P_x to form a string α_k*, $0 \le k \le \ell + q + p$, that is, if

$$x_{i_1} x_{i_2} \cdots x_{i_t} = \alpha_k*,$$

then the corresponding bottom strings must form the string $\bar{\alpha}_{k+1}\bar{*}$, that is,

$$y_{i_1} y_{i_2} \cdots y_{i_t} = \bar{\alpha}_{k+1}\bar{*}.$$

Similarly, if $x_{i_1} x_{i_2} \cdots x_{i_t} = \bar{\alpha}_k\bar{*}$, then $y_{i_1} y_{i_2} \cdots y_{i_t} = \alpha_{k+1}*$. For instance, if $k < \ell$, then these x_i's must be from groups 2, 3 or 4 and it is easy to see that the strings in groups 3 and 4 force the corresponding y_i's to form the successor configuration.

From this observation, we can prove the claim by induction. More precisely, we first define a pair of strings $\boxed{\frac{u}{v}}$ to be a *partial solution* to P_x if there exists a sequence $(i_1, \ldots, i_t)$, with each $i_j \in \{1, \ldots, n\}$, such that $u = x_{i_1} x_{i_2} \cdots x_{i_t}$, $v = y_{i_1} y_{i_2} \cdots y_{i_t}$ and u is a prefix of v. We can then prove by induction that for each odd $i \le \ell + q + p$,

$$\begin{array}{|l|}
\hline
[\alpha_0 * \bar{\alpha}_1 \bar{*} \cdots * \bar{\alpha}_i \bar{*} \\
\hline
[\alpha_0 * \bar{\alpha}_1 \bar{*} \cdots * \bar{\alpha}_i \bar{*} \alpha_{i+1} * \\
\hline
\end{array}$$

is a partial solution, and for each even $i \le \ell + q + p$,

$$\begin{array}{|l|}
\hline
[\alpha_0 * \bar{\alpha}_1 \bar{*} \cdots \bar{*} \alpha_i * \\
\hline
[\alpha_0 * \bar{\alpha}_1 \bar{*} \cdots \bar{*} \alpha_i * \bar{\alpha}_{i+1} \bar{*} \\
\hline
\end{array}$$

is a partial solution. First, we observe that the first pair $\boxed{\begin{array}{l} [\\ [Bxq_1B* \end{array}}$ is a partial solution. Next, assume that for some even $i < \ell + q + p$,

$$\begin{array}{|l|}
\hline
[\alpha_0 * \bar{\alpha}_1 \bar{*} \cdots \bar{*} \alpha_i * \\
\hline
[\alpha_0 * \bar{\alpha}_1 \bar{*} \cdots \bar{*} \alpha_i * \bar{\alpha}_{i+1} \bar{*} \\
\hline
\end{array}$$

is a partial solution. Then, the only way for the top part of the partial solution to match the bottom part is to attach a string $\bar{\alpha}_{i+1}\bar{*}$ to it. From the observation we made above, we know that the corresponding bottom part must be $\alpha_{i+2}*$, and so

$$\begin{array}{|l|}
\hline
[\alpha_0 * \bar{\alpha}_1 \bar{*} \cdots * \bar{\alpha}_{i+1} \bar{*} \\
\hline
[\alpha_0 * \bar{\alpha}_1 \bar{*} \cdots * \bar{\alpha}_{i+1} \bar{*} \alpha_{i+2} * \\
\hline
\end{array}$$

is also a partial solution. The other case of odd i is similar.

So, from the above induction proof, we know that either

$$[\alpha_0 * \cdots \bar{*} \alpha_{\ell+q+p} *$$
$$[\alpha_0 * \cdots \bar{*} \alpha_{\ell+q+p} * \bar{\alpha}_{\ell+q+p+1} \bar{*}$$

or

$$[\alpha_0 * \cdots * \bar{\alpha}_{\ell+q+p} \bar{*}$$
$$[\alpha_0 * \cdots * \bar{\alpha}_{\ell+q+p} \bar{*} \alpha_{\ell+q+p+1} *$$

is a partial solution. Now, we can attach one of the pairs in group 7 to them to obtain the desired solution.

Conversely, assume that P_x has a solution z. We note that it must begin with $[\alpha_0*$, since the pair in group 1 is the only one whose top string and bottom string begin with the same symbol. The only way to extend this partial solution to z is to add α_0* to the top part and, from the observation above, we know that this will add to the bottom part an extra string $\bar{\alpha}_1\bar{*}$. Continuing this argument, we can see that the solution must contain prefixes of the form

$$[\alpha_0 * \bar{\alpha}_1\bar{*} \cdots \bar{*}\alpha_i *$$

for an even i, or

$$[\alpha_0 * \bar{\alpha}_1\bar{*} \cdots * \bar{\alpha}_i\bar{*}$$

for an odd i. Now, suppose M does not halt on x, then the computation of $M(x)$ never enters the state q_n, and so these partial solutions do not contain q_n or $\bar{q}_n$ and, hence, do not contain q_{n+1} or $\bar{q}_{n+1}$. However, the two pairs of group 7 are the only ones whose two strings have the same ending symbol, and they contain either q_{n+1} or $\bar{q}_{n+1}$. That is a contradiction. We conclude that M must halt on x. $\square$

Example 5.46 *Prove that the problem of determining whether two given context-free grammars G_1 and G_2 have the property $L(G_1) \cap L(G_2) = \emptyset$ is undecidable.*

Proof. Let $A = \{(G_1, G_2) \mid L(G_1) \cap L(G_2) = \emptyset\}$. We reduce the problem PCP to $\overline{A}$. Let Σ be a fixed alphabet with respect to which PCP is known to be undecidable. Let \$ be a symbol not in Σ. For any instance $\{(x_1, y_1), \ldots, (x_n, y_n)\}$ of PCP, we construct two grammars G_1 and G_2 over the alphabet $\Sigma \cup \{\$\}$ as follows:

Grammar G_1 consists of the following rules:

$$S \longrightarrow aSa \mid a\$a, \quad \text{for all } a \in \Sigma.$$

So, $L(G_1) = \{w\$w^R \mid w \in \Sigma^+\}$. Grammar G_2 consists of the following rules:

$$S \longrightarrow x_i S y_i^R \mid x_i \$ y_i^R, \quad \text{for all } i = 1, \ldots, n.$$

Then, $L(G_2) = \{x_{i_1}x_{i_2}\cdots x_{i_m}\$(y_{i_1}y_{i_2}\cdots y_{i_m})^R \mid i_1, i_2, \ldots, i_m \in \{1, \ldots, n\}, m \geq 1\}$.

Now, if the instance $\{(x_1, y_1), \ldots, (x_n, y_n)\}$ has a solution, then $L(G_2)$ contains at least a string of the form $w\$w^R$ and so $L(G_1) \cap L(G_2) \neq \emptyset$. If it has no sulution, then $L(G_2)$ does not contain any string of the form $w\$w^R$ and so $L(G_1) \cap L(G_2) = \emptyset$. Thus, this construction is a reduction from PCP to $\overline{A}$, and so A is undecidable. $\Box$

Recall that a context-free grammar G is ambiguous if there exists a string $x \in L(G)$ such that there are two distinct leftmost derivations $S \underset{L}{\overset{*}{\Longrightarrow}} x$ for x.

Example 5.47 *Prove that the problem of determining whether a given context-free grammar G is ambiguous is undecidable.*

Proof. We reduce PCP to the ambiguity problem of the context-free grammars. For each instance $\{(x_1, y_1), \ldots, (x_n, y_n)\}$ of PCP over alphabet Σ, define a context-free grammar G that has the following rules:

$$
\begin{aligned}
S &\longrightarrow S_1 \mid S_2, \\
S_1 &\longrightarrow x_i S_1 ba^i b \mid x_i ba^i b, \quad \text{for all } 1 \leq i \leq n, \\
S_2 &\longrightarrow y_i S_2 ba^i b \mid y_i ba^i b, \quad \text{for all } 1 \leq i \leq n,
\end{aligned}
$$

where $a, b \notin \Sigma$.

We observe that if the instance $\{(x_1, y_1), \ldots, (x_n, y_n)\}$ of PCP has a solution $x_{i_1} x_{i_2} \cdots x_{i_k}$, then the string

$$z = x_{i_1} x_{i_2} \cdots x_{i_k} ba^{i_k} b \cdots ba^{i_2} bba^{i_1} b$$

has two distinct leftmost derivations, one from S_1 and the other from S_2.

Conversely, we note that if $S_1 \overset{*}{\Rightarrow} z$ then it is easy to see that there must be a unique derivation from S_1 to z, and z must be of the form

$$x_{i_1} x_{i_2} \cdots x_{i_k} ba^{i_k} b \cdots ba^{i_2} bba^{i_1} b. \tag{5.5}$$

Similarly, if $S_2 \overset{*}{\Rightarrow} z$ then there must be a unique derivation from S_2 to z and z must be of the form

$$y_{j_1} y_{j_2} \cdots y_{j_\ell} ba^{j_\ell} b \cdots ba^{j_2} bba^{j_1} b. \tag{5.6}$$

So, suppose that $z \in L(G)$ has two distinct derivations, then they must be two derivations of the form $S \Rightarrow S_1 \overset{*}{\Rightarrow} z$ and $S \Rightarrow S_2 \overset{*}{\Rightarrow} z$. Furthermore, z must be of the form (5.5) and of the form (5.6). Since $a, b \notin \Sigma$, it must be true that $k = \ell$ and $i_1 = j_1, \ldots, i_k = j_k$. It follows that $x_{i_1} x_{i_2} \cdots x_{i_k}$ is equal to $y_{i_1} y_{i_2} \cdots y_{i_k}$, and is a solution to the instance $\{(x_1, y_1), \ldots, (x_n, y_n)\}$. $\Box$

Exercises 5.6

1. For each of the following problems about Turing machines, determine whether it is decidable or not:

   (a) Given a one-way, one-tape DTM M (defined in Section 4.1) and a string x, determine whether the tape head of M will ever visit the $(2n)$th cell in the computation of M on input x, where $n = |x|$ (we call the leftmost cell of the tape the 0th cell, and the one to its right the first cell, etc.).

   (b) Given a two-way, one-tape DTM M (defined in Section 4.3) and a string x, determine whether the tape head of M will ever visit the $(2n)$th cell in the computation of M on input x, where $n = |x|$ (we call the cell holding the leftmost symbol of x the first cell, and the cell to its right the second cell, etc.).

   (c) Given a two-way, one-tape DTM M and a string x, determine whether the tape head of M will move left for more than n times (not necessarily in consecutive moves) in the computation of M on input x, where $n = |x|$.

   (d) Given a two-way, one-tape DTM M whose tape symbol set is $\Gamma = \{a, b, \mathbf{B}\}$ and a string $x \in \{a, b\}^*$, determine whether M will ever overwrite a symbol a by a symbol b in its computation on input x.

   (e) Given two DTM's M_1 and M_2 and two strings x_1 and x_2, determine whether it is true that sometime during the computation of M_1 on input x_1 and the computation of M_2 on input x_2, the first three cells of their tapes contain the same symbols (i.e., whether there is a configuration α of the computation of $M_1(x_1)$ and a configuration β of the computation of $M_2(x_2)$ such that the first three tape symbols of α is the same as those of β).

2. For each of the following problems about unrestricted grammars, determine whether it is decidable or not:

   (a) Given a grammar G over the alphabet $\{a, b, c\}$, determine whether $L(G)$ contains a string x of which aaa occurs as a substring.

   (b) Given a grammar G and a string $x \in L(G)$, determine whether there is a derivation of x that does not contain a sentential form in which aAa occurs as a substring, where a is a terminal symbol and A is a nonterminal symbol in G.

   (c) Given a grammar G and a string $x \in L(G)$, determine whether there is a derivation of x in which the lengths of the sentential forms do not decrease.

   (d) Given a grammar G and a string $x \in L(G)$, determine whether there is a derivation of x in which the lengths of the sentential forms decrease at most n times, where $n = |x|$.

3. Complete the details of the PDA M_1 of Example 5.43. That is, construct a PDA M_2 which accepts the set $\{xy \mid x$ and y are two legal configuration codes of M, and $neg(x \vdash y^R)\}$.

$\star$ **4.** For each of the following problems about context-free grammars, determine whether it is decidable or not:

   (a) Given a context-free grammar G and a DFA M, determine whether $L(G) \subseteq L(M)$.

   (b) Given a context-free grammar G and a DFA M, determine whether $L(M) \subseteq L(G)$.

   (c) Given a context-free grammar G, determine whether $L(G)$ is regular.

   (d) Given a context-free grammar G, determine whether the complement of $L(G)$ is context-free.

   (e) Given two context-free grammars G_1 and G_2, determine whether $L(G_1) \cap L(G_2)$ is context-free.

$\star$ **5.** For each of the following variations of PCP, determine whether it is decidable or not:

   (a) The problem PCP over the alphabet $\Sigma = \{1\}$.

   (b) The problem PCP over the alphabet $\Sigma = \{0, 1\}$.

   (c) Given a finite set of ordered pairs $(x_1, y_1), \ldots, (x_n, y_n)$ of strings in Σ^*, determine whether there is an infinite sequence $(i_1, i_2, \ldots)$ of integers in $\{1, \ldots, n\}$ such that $x_{i_1} x_{i_2} \cdots = y_{i_1} y_{i_2} \cdots$.

   (d) Given a finite set of ordered pairs $(x_1, y_1), \ldots, (x_n, y_n)$ of strings in Σ^*, determine whether there exist two sequences of integers $(i_1, i_2, \ldots, i_k)$ and $(j_1, j_2, \ldots, j_\ell)$, with each element belonging to $\{1, \ldots, n\}$, such that $x_{i_1} x_{i_2} \cdots x_{i_k} = y_{j_1} y_{j_2} \cdots y_{j_\ell}$.

   (e) The same question as (d) above, except that the two sequences of integers must be of the same size, that is, $k = \ell$.

$\star$ **6.** In this question, we consider the tiling problem. In this problem, a *colored tile* is a square tile of size 1×1 whose four sides are colored by colors selected from a finite set C. The four sides of a colored tile is clearly marked to be the up, down, left and right sides. Two colored tiles can be put in the plane next to each other if the two neighboring sides have the same color.

   TILING. Given a finite number of types $t_0, t_1, \ldots, t_n$ of colored tiles, determine whether it is possible to cover the first quadrant of the plane by colored tiles of these types (with infinite supply of the tiles of each type), starting with a tile of type t_0 at the lower left corner (see Figure 5.6).

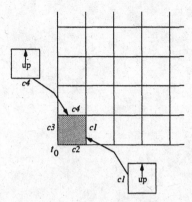

Figure 5.6: The problem TILING ($c_1, \ldots, c_4$ denote four colors of tile t_0).

Show that the problem TILING is undecidable. [*Hint*: Encode the Turing machine configurations by colors so that the colors of each row in the first quadrant represents one configuration, and the change of colors from one row to the next follows the instructions of a Turing machine.]

6

Computational
Complexity

6.1 Asymptotic Growth Rate

In the last two chapters, we have established a computability theory and, based on the Church-Turing Thesis, identified recursive functions as *the* class of computable functions. In this chapter, we extend this theory to a computational complexity theory, in which we study the computation time and space required to compute a recursive function by Turing machines. One of the goals of this computational complexity theory is to identify the class of *feasibly solvable problems*, that is, the class of functions that can be computed by a Turing machine within a reasonable amount of time and using a reasonable amount of memory space. To understand what "reasonable" means, we first look at a simple example.

Example 6.1 *Suppose we are given three pegs and n disks, with all n disks having different size. Initially, the n disks are stacked in decreasing size, from bottom to top, in the first peg (see Figure 6.1). The* TOWER OF HANOI *problem is to transfer the entire tower of n disks from the first peg to the second peg, moving one disk at a time and never putting a larger disk on top of a smaller disk. What is the fastest solution to this problem? Is the fastest solution feasible for size n = 64 (the size of the original Tower of Hanoi problem)?*

Solution. Suppose $n = 1$. Then, it is obvious that one move is all it takes. Now, suppose $n > 1$. Then, we can solve this problem recursively: We first move the top $n - 1$ disks to the third peg. Next, we move the bottom disk (the largest disk) to the second peg. After that, we move the other $n - 1$ disks

Figure 6.1:   The Tower of Hanoi problem.

from the third peg to the second peg.

Let $f(n)$ be the number of moves we need to move n disks from one peg to another peg by this recursive algorithm. Then, $f(n)$ satisfies the following recursive relation:

$$f(1) = 1$$
$$f(n) = 2f(n - 1) + 1, \quad n \geq 2.$$

It follows easily from this recursion that

$$f(n) = 2f(n - 1) + 1 = 2^2 f(n - 2) + 2 + 1$$
$$= \quad \cdots \quad = 2^{n-1} f(1) + 2^{n-2} + \cdots + 1 = 2^n - 1.$$

In addition, this is the minimum number of moves required to transfer n disks from one peg to another. Indeed, to do such a transfer, we must move the largest disk from one peg to the other. Before this move, we must first move all other disks to the third disk. Also, after the move of the largest disk, we must move all other disks to the top of the largest disk. Therefore, the minimum number $g(n)$ of moves satisfies the following inequality:

$$g(1) = 1$$
$$g(n) \geq 2g(n - 1) + 1, \quad n \geq 2.$$

Thus, $g(n) \geq f(n) = 2^n - 1$.

Finally, let us calculate how much time it takes to solve the problem for $n = 64$. Suppose that we can move one disk from one peg to another peg in one second. How long does it take to move the whole tower of 64 disks from the first peg to the third one? A year has either 365 or 366 days, and a day has 86,400 seconds. Therefore, a year has approximately 31,600,000 seconds. This means that we need about $(2^{64} - 1)/(31,600,000) \approx 584,000,000,000$ years to solve this problem. Even if we can build a robot to move one thousand disks in one second, it would still take 584 million years to solve the problem. Thus, we can confidently say that the problem is infeasible.   □

In the above example, we argued that the Tower of Hanoi problem is infeasible for input size $n = 64$. We note that for small size $n = 10$, the solution time $f(10) = 1023$ is definitely acceptable; however, when the input size grows to $n = 64$, it becomes unmanageable. The reason why this happens is that the solution time $f(n) = 2^n - 1$ grows too fast: its value doubles when the input value increases by only one. This suggests that we measure the computational complexity of an algorithm by the growth rate of its running time. If the running time of the fastest algorithm for a problem grows at such a fast rate, then this algorithm (and, hence, this problem) is considered infeasible. In the following, we present the general notations and techniques for measuring and comparing the growth rates of different functions.

A function $f(n)$ is said to *grow slower than* a function $g(n)$ (or, $g(n)$ *grows faster than* $f(n)$), denoted by $f(n) \prec g(n)$, if

$$\lim_{n \to \infty} \frac{f(n)}{g(n)} = 0.$$

For example, $g(n) = n^2$ grows faster than $f(n) = n$ since

$$\lim_{n \to \infty} \frac{n}{n^2} = \lim_{n \to \infty} \frac{1}{n} = 0.$$

The relation $\prec$ is a partial ordering:

Proposition 6.2 *If* $f(n) \prec g(n)$ *and* $g(n) \prec h(n)$, *then* $f(n) \prec h(n)$.

Proof. By definition, if $f(n) \prec g(n)$ and $g(n) \prec h(n)$, then

$$\lim_{n \to \infty} \frac{f(n)}{g(n)} = \lim_{n \to \infty} \frac{g(n)}{h(n)} = 0.$$

Therefore,

$$\lim_{n \to \infty} \frac{f(n)}{h(n)} = \lim_{n \to \infty} \frac{f(n)}{g(n)} \cdot \frac{g(n)}{h(n)} = 0.$$

This means that $f(n) \prec h(n)$. □

Two other commonly used notations are big-O and small-o: We write $f(n) = o(g(n))$ if $f(n) \prec g(n)$, and $f(n) = O(g(n))$ if for some constant K and for almost all $n \geq 0$, $f(n) \leq Kg(n)$.[1]

The following sequences of functions appear very often in the study of computational complexity:

Poly-log Sequence: $\{(\log n)^i \mid i = 1, 2, \cdots\}$.[2]

Polynomial Sequence: $\{n^i \mid i = 1, 2, \cdots\}$.

Subexponential Sequence: $\{n^{(\log n)^i} \mid i = 1, 2, \cdots\}$.

---

[1] "For almost all $n \geq 0$" means "for all but finitely many $n \geq 0$."
[2] For simplicity, we denote $\log = \log_2$ for the rest of this chapter.

Exponential Sequence: $\{2^{in} \mid i = 1, 2, \cdots\}$.

Superexponential Sequence: $\{2^{n^i} \mid i = 1, 2, \cdots\}$.

It is easy to check that these sequences satisfy the following properties. We leave the formal proof as an exercise to the reader.

(a) In each sequence, if $i < j$, then the ith function grows slower than the jth function. For instance, $n^{(\log n)^3} \prec n^{(\log n)^4}$.

(b) For any two sequences, every function in the former sequence grows slower than any function in the latter sequence (except for the first function of the last sequence). For instance, $(\log n)^{64} \prec n^{10} \prec n^{(\log n)^4} \prec 2^{3n} \prec 2^{n^2}$.

It is interesting to note that these five sequences do not contain all possible measurement for growth rates. The following are some examples not in these sequences.

Example 6.3 *Show that the function* $2^{\sqrt{\log n}}$ *grows slower than every function in the polynomial sequence, but faster than every function in the poly-log sequence.*

Proof. Using L'Hopital's rule, we check that, for any $i \geq 1$,

$$\lim_{n \to \infty} \frac{(\log n)^i}{2^{\sqrt{\log n}}} = \lim_{n \to \infty} \frac{i(\log n)^{i-1}(\log e)/n}{2^{\sqrt{\log n}}/(2n\sqrt{\log n})}$$

$$= \lim_{n \to \infty} \frac{(2\log e)\, i\, (\log n)^{i-1/2}}{2^{\sqrt{\log n}}}$$

$$= \lim_{n \to \infty} \frac{(2\log e)^{2i}\, i(i-1/2)(i-1)\cdots(1/2)}{2^{\sqrt{\log n}}} = 0.$$

Therefore, $(\log n)^i \prec 2^{\sqrt{\log n}}$ for any $i \geq 1$. Also,

$$\lim_{n \to \infty} \frac{2^{\sqrt{\log n}}}{n} = \lim_{n \to \infty} 2^{\sqrt{\log n} - \log n} = \lim_{n \to \infty} 2^{\sqrt{\log n}(1 - \sqrt{\log n})} = 0.$$

Therefore, $2^{\sqrt{\log n}} \prec n$.   □

Example 6.4 *Suppose* $f(n) \prec g(n)$. *Show that there exists a function* $h(n)$ *such that* $f(n) \prec h(n) \prec g(n)$.

Proof. Choose $h(n) = \sqrt{f(n)g(n)}$. Then,

$$\lim_{n \to \infty} \frac{f(n)}{h(n)} = \lim_{n \to \infty} \sqrt{\frac{f(n)}{g(n)}} = 0, \quad \text{and} \quad \lim_{n \to \infty} \frac{h(n)}{g(n)} = \lim_{n \to \infty} \sqrt{\frac{f(n)}{g(n)}} = 0. \quad □$$

In the following, we study a function that grows very slowly to infinity. For any $k \geq 1$, recall that

$$\log^{(k)} n = \underbrace{\log \cdots \log}_{k} n.$$

Define $\log^* n = \min\{k \mid k \geq 1, \log^{(k)} n \leq 1\}$.

Example 6.5 *Show that* $\log^* n \prec \log^{(m)} n$ *for any constant integer* $m \geq 1$.

Proof. We first prove that for any fixed $m \geq 2$ and sufficiently large n, $\log^* n < \log^{(m)} n$. To do so, we note that $2^n \geq 4n$ for $n \geq 4$. It follows that

$$n \geq 4 \implies 2 + \log n \leq n.$$

Repeatedly applying this inequality, we obtain

$$\log^{(i-1)} n \geq 4 \implies 2i + \log^{(i)} n \leq n.$$

Now, for $\log^* n > 4m$, substituting $\log^* n - 2m$ for i and $\log^{(m)} n$ for n, we get

$$2(\log^* n - 2m) \leq 2(\log^* n - 2m) + \log^{(\log^* n - m)} n \leq \log^{(m)} n.$$

(*Note*: $\log^{(h)}(\log^{(k)} n) = \log^{(h+k)} n$, and so

$$\log^{(i-1)} \log^{(m)} n = \log^{(\log^* n - m - 1)} n \geq 2^m \geq 4.)$$

That is, if n is so large such that $\log^* n > 4m$, then

$$\log^* n \leq 2 \log^* n - 4m \leq \log^{(m)} n.$$

Now, we note that for any fixed $m \geq 1$, $\log^{(m+1)} n \prec \log^{(m)} n$ (see Exercise 6). Together, we get $\log^* n \prec \log^{(m)} n$. $\square$

Exercise 6.1

1. Show that $2^{\ln n} = o(n)$ and $2^{\log(2n)} = O(n)$.

2. Show that $(\log n)^{10} \prec n^{10} \prec 2^{(\log n)^{10}}$.

3. Compare the following three functions using the $\prec$ notation:

$$2^{n^{\log n}}, \qquad n^{(\log n)^2}, \qquad (\log n)^{2^n}.$$

4. Compare $2^{\log^* n}$ with n using the $\prec$ notation.

5. Suppose that $f(n) \prec g(n)$. Is it true that for any increasing function $h(n)$ with $\lim_{n \to \infty} h(n) = \infty$, $h(f(n)) \prec h(g(n))$? Present a proof or a counterexample.

6. Prove that $\log^{(k+1)} \prec \log^{(k)} n$ for any $k \geq 0$.

7. Denote $\log^{**} n = \min\{k \mid (\log^*)^{(k)} n \leq 1, k \geq 1\}$. Compare $\log^{**} n$ with $\log^* n$.

8. Recall the Ackermann function A defined in Exercise 8 of Section 4.8.

  (a) Compare the function $f(n) = A(n, n)$ with 2^{2^n}.

  (b) Compare the function $g(n) = \max\{k \mid A(k, k) \leq n\}$ with $\log^* n$.

6.2   Time and Space Complexity

Computational complexity of a Turing machine studies the computational resources required for a Turing machine to solve a problem. Computation time and space are the two most important computational resources for Turing machines. Therefore, it is critical to study the class of Turing machines with limited running time and/or memory space.

For an input string x, the *running time* of a DTM M on x is the number of moves M takes to halt on input x, that is, the number of configurations in the computation from the initial configuration with x as the input to a halting configuration. We denote this number by $Time_M(x)$ (if M does not halt on x, then $Time_M(x) = \infty$). Based on the asymptotic view of Section 6.1, we group the inputs of the same length together and consider the running time on them as a single function. That is, assume that $t(n) \geq n + 1$ for sufficiently large n.[3] Then, we say M has a *time bound* $t(n)$ if for all inputs x with $|x| \leq n$,

$$Time_M(x) \leq \max\{n + 1, t(n)\}.$$

Recall that we defined several different models of Turing machines in Chapter 4. It is apparent that a single problem may have different running time when it is solved using different models of DTM's. In particular, a multi-tape DTM seems to have a lower time bound than an equivalent one-tape DTM (cf. Example 4.13). Therefore, when we compare the time complexity of two problems, we need to make sure that they are compared within the same model; that is, we need to be concerned with the implementation of an algorithm in a particular model of DTM's. Fortunately, the following theorem shows that the running time functions of different models of DTM's do not differ too much.

Theorem 6.6 *For any multi-tape DTM M, there exists a two-way, one-tape DTM M_1 computing the same function such that for all inputs x, we have $Time_{M_1}(x) \leq c \cdot (Time_M(x))^2$ for some constant $c > 0$.*

---

[3] We consider only DTM's that always read all its input symbols before it halts. Thus, we consider only functions $t(n) \geq n + 1$ as time bounds.

Proof. If we examine carefully the simulation of multi-tape DTM M by two-way, one-tape DTM M_1 of Theorem 4.13, we can see that each move of M is simulated by two passes over the entire tape configuration of M. Since the size of the tape configuration is bounded by $Time_M(x)$, each move of M takes $2Time_M(x) + c_1 k$ moves to simulate, where k is the number of tapes of M and c_1 is a constant. (The extra $c_1 k$ moves come from the adjustment of the new tape symbols in each track done in the second pass.) It can be checked that the initialization and ending stages take only time linear in the input size. Therefore, the total time $Time_{M_1}(x)$ is bounded by $c(Time_M(x))^2$ for some constant $c > 0$. □

The above theorem shows that the time complexity functions of equivalent DTM's do not differ too much. For the space complexity, however, we need to define the underlying model more carefully. A particular issue is that we do not usually count the space occupied by the input as the work space in the computation. Therefore, the space complexity of a one-tape DTM is difficult to measure since the machine may or may not use the input space for the computational purpose. So, in order to avoid this type of problem, we need to distinguish between the work tapes and the input/output tapes. We say a tape of a DTM M is an *input tape* if it is a read-only tape used to hold the input symbols. The machine M is allowed to read the inputs on this tape (more than once if it wants) but not to write over the input or blank symbols. We say a tape of a DTM M is an *output tape* if it is a write-only tape used to print the output symbols. The machine M is only allowed to write down the output symbol and then move the tape head to the right to the next blank cell. The tape head of an output tape is not allowed to move left. All other tapes are called *work tapes* or *storage tapes*. (A DTM may not have the input tape or the output tape. For instance, a one-tape DTM has only one work tape which is used to read inputs, to store temporary data, and to write outputs.)

For any input string x, the *memory space* that a DTM M uses on x is the number of cells on the work tapes which the tape head visits at least once during the computation. We let $Space_M(x)$ denote this number.

Similarly to the time complexity, we say a DTM M has a *space bound* $s(n)$ if for any input x,

$$Space_M(x) \leq \max\{1, \lceil s(|x|)\rceil\}.^4$$

Let us now fix a three-tape DTM model as a standard DTM model for space complexity measure. Such a DTM has an input tape and a work tape. It may or may not have the third output tape, depending on whether it needs to produce outputs or not. We call such a DTM a *standard one-worktape DTM*, or simply a *one-worktape DTM*. From the above definition, we only measure

---

[4] We consider only DTM's that visit at least one cell of the work tapes.

the tape cells in the work tape that are visited by the tape head for the space bound of such a DTM. The following theorem justifies our restriction to this specific model as far as the space complexity is concerned.

Theorem 6.7 *For any multi-tape DTM M, there is a standard one-worktape DTM M_2 computing the same function such that $Space_{M_2}(x) \leq Space_M(x)$ for all x.*

Proof. We can design a one-worktape DTM M_2 that simulates M as follows: It uses the work tape to encode all work tapes of M, in the manner described in Theorem 4.13. For each move of M, M_2 reads the symbol currently scanned by the input tape head, makes a pass over the work tape to collect the other symbols currently scanned by M, and makes another pass over the work tape to make changes on the work tape according to the instructions of M.

This is almost the same as DTM M_1 of Theorem 4.13, except that M_2 also reads an input symbol and moves the input tape head. It is clear that the space used by M_2 is bounded by the total space used by M.   □

Using the one-worktape DTM model, the following result is trivial:

Theorem 6.8 *For any one-worktape DTM M and any input x,*

$$Space_M(x) \leq Time_M(x) + 1.$$

We now consider the time and space complexity of a decision problem, based on the DTM model and the above defined time and space measures. Let $f : \mathbf{N} \to \mathbf{N}$ be an integer function. We say a language has *time complexity* $f(n)$ if it is accepted by a multi-tape DTM with time bound $f(n)$. We say a language has *space complexity* $f(n)$ if it is accepted by a multi-tape DTM with space bound $f(n)$. For any function $f(n)$, we define the following complexity classes:

$$DTIME(f(n)) = \{L \mid L \text{ has time complexity } f(n)\}.$$
$$DSPACE(f(n)) = \{L \mid L \text{ has space complexity } f(n)\}.$$

It is clear that, for any function $f(n)$, $DTIME(f(n))$ is a subclass of recursive sets. This fact also holds, but not so obviously, for $DSPACE(f(n))$ (see Exercise 1 of this section).

These time and space complexity classes have the following important properties. These properties allow us to use the standard asymptotic growth rates $f(n)$, such as $\log n$, n^2, 2^n, to define complexity classes without specifying the coefficients of $f(n)$.

⋆ **Theorem 6.9** (Tape Compression Theorem) *For any function $s(n)$ and any constant $c > 0$,*

$$DSPACE(s(n)) = DSPACE(c \cdot s(n)).$$

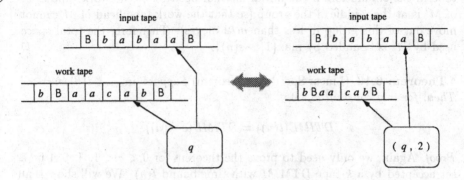

Figure 6.2: Tape compression.

Proof. It is clear that we only need to prove the theorem for $0 < c < 1$. Let $A \in DSPACE(s(n))$. By Theorem 6.7, we may assume that A is accepted by a standard one-worktape DTM M with space bound $s(n)$. We will show that A is accepted by another standard one-worktape DTM M' with space bound $c \cdot s(n)$. The basic idea is to group together a number of tape cells of M into a single cell and simulate the computation of M accordingly. To do this, we need to enlarge the character set and state set of M'.

Let m be a positive integer such that $m > 6/c$. We divide cells in the work tape of M into groups, each group containing exactly m cells. Each group of cells forms a single tape cell of M'. Thus, if the set of tape symbols of M is Γ, then the set of tape symbols of M' is $\Gamma \cup \Gamma^m$; that is, each tape symbol of M' in the input tape is a symbol $a \in \Gamma$, and each tape symbol of M' in the work tape is of the form $[a_{i_1}, a_{i_2}, \ldots, a_{i_m}]$, where each $a_{i_k} \in \Gamma$. In order to simulate machine M, M' records the internal position of the work tape head within a group of cells in its state. That is, if the set of states of M is Q, then the set of states of M' is $Q' = Q \times \{1, 2, \ldots, m\}$. A state (q, j) indicates that the machine M' is simulating M at state q, with its work tape head scanning the jth cell within the current group cell scanned by the work tape head of M'.

With this setting, it is easy to see that each configuration of M' corresponds to a unique configuration of M. For instance, Figure 6.2 shows the correspondence between two configurations (where $m = 4$). From this correspondence between configurations, it is clear how to simulate each move of M by M'. We omit the detail of the simulation.

Furthermore, we note that M' visits at most $\lfloor s(n)/m \rfloor + 2$ cells of the work tape (the worst case happens when $s(n) = km + 2$ for some $k \geq 1$, and M' encodes the middle km cells into k groups). Note that if $s(n) \geq 3/c$, then

$$\left\lfloor \frac{s(n)}{m} \right\rfloor + 2 \leq \frac{c \cdot s(n)}{6} + 2 \leq c \cdot s(n).$$

In the case of $s(n) < 3/c$, we note that M' visits only one cell of the work tape in the simulation, if the initial internal position of the work tape head of M' is at the middle of the group (so that the work tape head of M cannot move out of this group in less than $m/2$ moves). Therefore, the total space used by M' is bounded by $\max\{1, c \cdot s(n)\}$.   □

* Theorem 6.10 (Linear Speed-Up Theorem) *Suppose* $\lim_{n \to \infty} t(n)/n = \infty$. *Then, for any constant* $c > 0$,

$$DTIME(t(n)) = DTIME(c \cdot t(n)).$$

Proof. Again, we only need to prove the theorem for $0 < c < 1$. Let A be a set accepted by a k-tape DTM M with time bound $t(n)$. We will show that A is also accepted by a $(k+1)$-tape DTM M' with time bound $c \cdot t(n)$. The idea of the proof is to group together a sequnce of moves of M and simulate the effect of these moves in a constant number of moves. In order to do this, we need to group some tape cells into one, as we did in the tape compression theorem.

We descirbe the new DTM M' in the following. To simplify our explanation, we only consider the case of $k = 1$. The general cases are similar.

(1) Let m be a positive integer satisfying $m > 10/c$. We combine m tape cells in the tape of M into a single cell for M'. Thus, each tape symbol of M' is a member of Γ^m, where Γ is the set of tape symbols of M. In particular, M' first encodes each group of m input symbols into one tape symbol and puts them in the second tape. After this initialization step, M' only works on the second tape.

(2) Each state of M' is a pair of a local configuration and a local counter, where a *local configuration* consists of $3m$ cells of the tape of M, the head position within these $3m$ cells, and a state of M, and a *local counter* is a digit in $\{0, 1, \cdots, 9\}$. Thus, each state of M' is of the form

$$(q, a_1 a_2 \cdots a_{i-1}\underline{a_i}a_{i+1} \cdots a_{3m}; j),$$

where q is a state of M, $a_1, \ldots, a_{3m} \in \Gamma$, and $j \in \{0, 1, \ldots, 9\}$. For instance, $(q, 01\underline{1}001; 5)$ represents the state of M' whose local configuration is that shown in Figure 6.3 and its local counter is 5. Note that there are at most d^m local configurations for some constant d. Therefore, M' has a constant number of states.

(3) Each simulation step of M' consists of 10 moves, administered by the local counter. That is, in each move, M' changes its local counter from j to $j + 1$, if $0 \leq j \leq 8$, and from 9 to 0.

(4) In the first 4 moves (i.e., when the local counter is in $\{0, 1, 2, 3\}$), M' reads the symbols of the two neighbors of the cell it is scanning now. Let g denote the cell currently scanned by the tape head, r denote the right neighbor of g, and ℓ denote the left neighbor of g. M' reads symbols from these cells by a 4-move *bee-dance*: It moves to its right to read the symbol of cell r, then

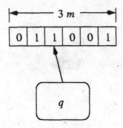

Figure 6.3: A local configuration.

moves left to cell g, then moves left to read the symbol of cell ℓ, and finally moves back to the original cell g. After the bee-dance, the local configuration of M' contains all symbols in the three cells of M' (corresponding to $3m$ cells of M).

(5) When the local counter of M' is equal to 4, M' simulates M on the local configuration for as many moves as possible. That is, it simulates M on the local configuration until one of the following conditions occurs: (a) M halts on the local configuration, (b) M enters a same local configuration the second time (thus, M enters an infinite loop), or (c) M tries to move out of the $3m$ cells of the local configuration. In case (a), M' simply halts. In case (b), M' enters an infinite loop. In case (c), M' changes its local configuration α to the configuration β right before the tape head of M moves out of the $3m$ cells. Note that the change from α to β takes only one move for M', since this change occurs internally in the local configuration and can be simply encoded in the transition function of M'. On the other hand, this change of configuration takes at least m moves for M since the tape head of M must move from group g to the right end of group r or to the left end of group ℓ.

(6) When the local counter of M' is in $\{5, 6, 7, 8\}$, M' does a second bee-dance to copy the new symols of its local configuration to the cells ℓ, r and g on its tape.

(7) Finally, when the local counter of M' is equal to 9, M' moves its tape head to one of its neighbor according to the tape position of its local configuration.

We show, in Figure 6.4, an example of such ten moves, which simulate the configuration change of M from $(q, 00\underline{0}111)$ to $(p, 111\underline{0}00)$.

It is clear that the above simulation is correct and so $L(M') = L(M)$. In addition, for $x \in L(M)$, M' uses ten moves to simulate at least m moves of M, before it halts. We note that, in the initialization stage, it takes n moves to copy the input to the second tape, in the group form, and it takes $\lceil n/m \rceil$ moves to reset the tape head at the rightmore input group. Also, in the halting stage, M' halts at the fifth move within that simulation step. Therefore, we see that M' has a time bound of

$$n + \left\lceil \frac{n}{m} \right\rceil + 5 + 10 \left\lceil \frac{t(n)}{m} \right\rceil \leq n + \frac{n}{m} + 10 \cdot \frac{t(n)}{m} + 16.$$

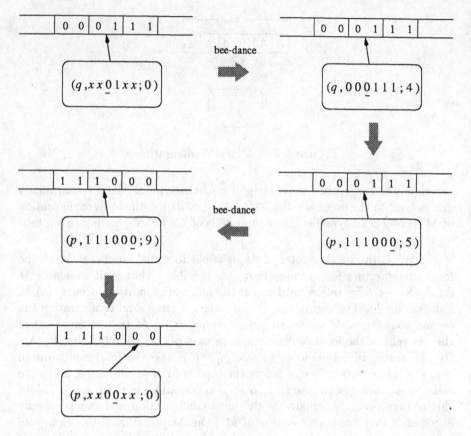

Figure 6.4: The ten moves.

Because $\lim_{n \to \infty} t(n)/n = \infty$, we have that, for sufficiently large n,

$$n + \frac{n}{m} + 10 \cdot \frac{t(n)}{m} + 16 \leq c \cdot t(n).$$

Thus, $A \in DTIME(c \cdot t(n))$.   □

To get a better understanding of Theorems 6.9 and 6.10, we study some examples in the following.

Example 6.11 *Suppose* $\lim_{n \to \infty} t_1(n)/n = \infty$. *If* $t_1(n) = t_2(n)$ *for sufficiently large* n, *then* $DTIME(t_1(n)) = DTIME(t_2(n))$.

Proof. Suppose $t_1(n) = t_2(n)$ for $n \geq n_0$. Then, for $n \geq n_0$, $\max\{n+1, t_1(n)\}$ $= \max\{n+1, t_2(n)\}$. Also, for $1 \leq n \leq n_0$, there exists a constant $c > 1$ such that $\max\{n+1, t_1(n)\} \leq c \cdot \max\{n+1, t_2(n)\}$. Thus, for any $n \geq 1$,

$$\max\{n+1, t_1(n)\} \leq c \cdot \max\{n+1, t_2(n)\}.$$

By Theorem 6.10, $DTIME(t_1(n)) \subseteq DTIME(c \cdot t_2(n)) = DTIME(t_2(n))$. Symmetrically, we have $DTIME(t_2(n)) \subseteq DTIME(t_1(n))$. It follows that $DTIME(t_1(n)) = DTIME(t_2(n))$. □

Example 6.12 *If $c > 1$, then for any $\epsilon > 0$, $DTIME(cn) = DTIME((1 + \epsilon)n)$.*

Proof. In the proof of Theorem 6.10, choose $m > 11c/\varepsilon$. Then

$$n + \frac{n}{m} + 10 \cdot \frac{cn}{m} + 16 \le n + (1 + 10c) \cdot \frac{n}{m} + 16 \le (1 + \varepsilon)n,$$

for sufficiently large n. □

Now that we have formally defined time and space complexity classes of languages, which of these classes are *feasible* classes? Unfortunately, this question again depends on the specific computational models we use. Although we have shown, in Chapter 4, that machines in different models can simulate each other so that the class of computable functions is the same for these machines, it is conceivable that one type of machine may run faster or use less work space than the other type. The empirical studies on these computational models, however, indicates that these simulations can often be done within a polynomial factor. That is, if one type of machines can accept a language in time $t(n)$, the other type of machines can accept it in time $(t(n))^c$ for some constant $c > 0$. For instance, Theorem 6.6 shows that one-tape DTM's can simulate multi-tape DTM's within a time factor of n^2. These studies support the following *extended* version of the Church-Turing Thesis, though the support is not as strong as that for the Church-Turing Thesis.

Extended Church-Turing Thesis. A function computable in polynomial time in any reasonable computational model using a reasonable time complexity measure is computable by a deterministic Turing machine in polynomial time.

Now, let us define the following complexity classes:

$$P = \bigcup_{c>0} DTIME(n^c).$$

$$EXP = \bigcup_{c>0} DTIME(2^{cn}).$$

$$EXPPOLY = \bigcup_{c>0} DTIME(2^{n^c}).$$

$$PSPACE = \bigcup_{c>0} DSPACE(n^c).$$

From the Extended Church-Turing Thesis, we see that these complexity classes are model-independent. Among these complexity classes, the class P is the most interesting one. We say a DTM M is a *polynomial-time DTM* if M has a time bound $t(n)$ for some polynomial function $t(n) = n^c$. We note that the composition of two polynomial functions is still a polynomial function. Therefore, if we have two polynomial-time DTM's M_1 and M_2, then the composition M of these two DTM's, in the sense that M first simulates M_2 on the input x and then simulates M_1 using the output y of M_2 as the input, is also a polynomial-time DTM. Therefore, the class P is closed under composition (of the polynomial-time machines). In addition, the class P is a robust class of languages, closed under the language operations union, intersection and complementation (see Exercise 3 of this section).

Based on the above observations and the empirical studies, people in general agree that the class P represents the class of *feasibly solvable languages*, or simply *feasible problems*. The following examples show that P is also closed under concatenation and the Kleene-star operation.

Example 6.13 *Show that if $A, B \in P$, then $AB \in P$.*

Proof. Assume that A is accepted by a multi-tape DTM M_1 with time bound $p_1(n)$, and B is accepted by a multi-tape DTM M_2 with time bound $p_2(n)$, where p_1 and p_2 are two polynomial functions. Consider an input x, with $|x| = n$, to the problem AB. For each partition of x into two substrings $x = x_1 x_2$, we check whether $x_1 \in A$ and $x_2 \in B$. We note that checking for each partition requires time at most

$$p_1(|x_1|) + p_2(|x_2|) + cn \le p_1(n) + p_2(n) + cn$$

for some constant c. (The term cn comes from the bookkeeping work to set up the partition for the machine to perform simulations on $M_1(x_1)$ and $M_2(x_2)$.) Since there are only $n + 1$ such partitions, the total computation time is $\le (n + 1)(p_1(n) + p_2(n) + cn)$, which is a polynomial function. □

Example 6.14 *Show that if $A \in P$, then $A^* \in P$.*

Proof. Assume that A is accepted by a DTM M_1 with time bound $p_1(n)$ for some polynomial p_1. For each input x, with $|x| = n > 0$, $x \in A^*$ if and only if there is a partition of x into nonempty substrings $x = x_1 x_2 \cdots x_m$, with $1 \le m \le n$, such that x_i is in A, for all $i = 1, 2, \ldots, m$. Note that if we try all such partitions, our algorithm would take an exponential amount of time, since there are 2^{n-1} such partitions.

So, how do we solve this problem in polynomial time? We note that x has at most $n(n + 1)/2$ nonempty substrings. Therefore, even though x has an exponential number of partitions, some substrings occur in many partitions. This observation suggests us to use the technique of *dynamic programming* to attack the problem A^*. More precisely, we note that a string x is in A^* if and only if

(a) $x \in A$; or

(b) There exists a partition $x = x_1 x_2$, where x_1 and x_2 are nonempty, such that $x_1 \in A$ and $x_2 \in A^*$.

So, we can build a table T of suffixes y of x, in the increasing order of the length of the suffix, indicating whether $y \in A^*$, and use this table to determine whether $x \in A^*$. The following is the algorithm:

(1) Let $T(n+1) := 1$.

(2) For each i, starting from n down to 1, do the following:

If, for some j, $i \leq j \leq n$, $substr(x, i, j-i+1) \in A$ and $T(j+1) = 1$, then let $T(i) := 1$; otherwise, let $T(i) := 0$.

(3) Accept x if $T(1) = 1$.

We observe that the above algorithm needs to simulate M for $O(n^2)$ times. Therefore, the total time of simulation and bookkeeping is bounded by $O(n^2(p_1(n) + n)) = O(n^3 \cdot p_1(n))$, which is bounded by a polynomial function $q(n)$. We conclude that $A^* \in P$.   □

Similar to class P, $PSPACE$ is a mathematical representation of the class of languages which are solvable by machines using a feasible amout of storage space. It is, however, not considered a faithful representation of feasibly solvable problems, since a TM using a polynomial amount of space may use more than a polynomial amount of time. The following example shows that a language in $PSPACE$ can be solved using an exponential amount of time. Whether this upper bound on time can be reduced is a major open question in complexity theory. In particular, it is not known whether $PSPACE = P$.

Example 6.15 $PSPACE \subseteq EXPPOLY$.

Proof. Suppose that $A \in PSPACE$; that is, A is accepted by a one-worktape DTM M with space bound n^c for some constant $c > 0$. Let us count how many different configurations M can have on an input of length n. First, since we are working on a decision problem, we can ignore the output tape of the machine M. Next, there are at most d^{n^c} possible different tape configurations in the work tape of M, where d is the number of tape symbols. (The input tape is read-only and so has a unique tape configuration.) For each tape configuration, there are n^c possible positions of the work tape head. In addition, there are $n + 2$ possible positions of the input tape head, and there are q possible states for some constant q. Thus, we have obtained an upper bound $q(n+2)n^c d^{n^c} = o(2^{n^{c+1}})$ for the number of configurations of M.

Now, we can construct a new 3-worktape DTM M' to simulate M as follows: M' uses the first work tape to simulate the work tape of M, and uses the second work tape to store the history of the computation of M. That is, M' stores all the configurations M ever had in the second work tape. Initially, all work tapes are empty. Then, M' simulates M one move at a time. After each simulation move, it writes down the current configuration of M on the third work tape. It compares this new configuration with each old configuration stored in the second work tape to see if it has occurred before. If so, then it halts and rejects the input (since this indicates that M has entered an infinite loop). Otherwise, it copies the configuration of the third work tape to the second work tape and resumes the simulation.

Note that each configuration is of size $O(n^c)$, and there are at most $o(2^{n^{c+1}})$ configurations in the second work tape. Therefore, each comparison takes $O(2^{n^{c+1}} \cdot n^c)$ moves, and the total time used by M' is at most $O((2^{n^{c+1}})^2 \cdot n^c)$. We conclude that $A \in DTIME(2^{n^{c+2}})$.   □

Exercise 6.2

1. Suppose that $s(n) \geq \log n$. Prove that if a Turing machine halts on all inputs and has a space bound $s(n)$, then it must have a time bound $c^{s(n)}$ for a constant c. Use this result to show that, for any $s(n)$, every set in $DSPACE(s(n))$ is a recursive set.

2. Show that every finite set of strings belongs to $DTIME(n)$.

3. Let $A \in DTIME(f(n))$ and $B \in DTIME(g(n))$. Prove that $A \cup B$ and $A \cap B$ are in $DTIME(\max\{f(n), g(n)\})$. Conclude from these results that the complexity classes P, $PSPACE$, EXP and $EXPPOLY$ are all closed under Boolean operations union, intersection and complementation.

4. In the proof of Theorem 6.10, we can actually use nine moves of M', instead of ten moves, to simulate at least m moves of M. This can be done by merging the fourth and fifth moves into one move. Can you use less than nine moves in M' to do the same job?

5. Estimate how many possible local configurations there are in the proof of Theorem 6.10.

⋆ 6. Show that every context-free language is in P (i.e., for every context-free grammar, there is a polynomial-time parsing algorithm).

7. Show that if A and B are in $PSPACE$, then AB and A^* are also in $PSPACE$.

8. Let $A, B \subseteq 1(0+1)^* + 0$ such that each string x in A or B is a binary representation of a natural number. We let $n(x)$ be the natural number whose binary representation is x.

   (a) Let $A + B = \{x \in 1(0+1)^* + 0 \mid n(x) = n(y) + n(z)$ for some $y \in A$ and $z \in B\}$. Show that if $A, B \in PSPACE$, then $A + B$ is also in $PSPACE$.

(b) Let $A \star B = \{x \in 1(0+1)^* + 0 \mid n(x) = n(y) \cdot n(z)$ for some $y \in A$ and $z \in B\}$. Show that if $A, B \in PSPACE$ then $A \star B$ is also in $PSPACE$.

$\star$ (c) Assume that $A, B \in P$. Is it true that $A + B$ is also in P? Is it true that $A \star B$ is also in P?

6.3 Hierarchy Theorems

Suppose that two functions $f(n)$ and $g(n)$ satisfy that $f(n) \prec g(n)$. Then, intuitively, Turing machines with the time bound $g(n)$ are more *powerful* than Turing machines with the time bound $f(n)$, in the sense that the machines with time bound $g(n)$ can compute some functions or languages that are not computable by machines with time bound $f(n)$. That is, we expect that $DTIME(g(n)) \setminus DTIME(f(n)) \neq \emptyset$. Likewise, we expect $DSPACE(g(n)) \setminus DSPACE(f(n)) \neq \emptyset$. This is, however, not always true. It is known that there are some ill-behaved functions f and g satisfying $f(n) \prec g(n)$ but $DTIME(g(n)) = DTIME(f(n))$ (called the *gap theorem*).

In this section, we show that this intuitive expectation is indeed correct, as long as the functions f and g are *well behaved* and that $g(n)$ grows faster than $f(n) \log f(n)$. In order to describe these results, we first need to define two classes of well-behaved functions. We say that a function $s(n)$ is *fully space-constructible* if there exists a DTM M such that for sufficiently large integers n and any input x with $|x| = n$, $Space_M(x) = s(n)$. Thus, if $s(n)$ is fully space-constructible, then we can simulate this DTM on any input x of length n to mark off exactly $s(n)$ cells in the work tapes. We call such a DTM a $s(n)$-*space marking machine*.

$\star$ **Theorem 6.16** (Space Hierarchy Theorem) *Let $s_2(n)$ be a fully space constructible function. Suppose that $\liminf_{n \to \infty} s_1(n)/s_2(n) = 0$ and $s_1(n) \geq \log n$. Then,*

$$DSPACE(s_2(n)) \setminus DSPACE(s_1(n)) \neq \emptyset.$$

Proof. We need to construct a language L which is in $DSPACE(s_2(n))$ but not in $DSPACE(s_1(n))$. The basic tool is a refined, space-bounded version of diagonalization. The setup for diagonalization is as follows:

Since any multi-tape DTM can be simulated by a standard one-worktape DTM within the same space, we need only consider all one-worktape DTM's. We enumerate all such DTM's M_w with space bound $s_1(n)$ (recall that M_w is the DTM whose code is w), and try to construct a new DTM M^* which has space bound $s_2(n)$ and satisfies $L(M^*) \neq L(M_w)$ for all M_w. That is, the DTM M^* needs to satisfy the following requirements:

R_w: $L(M^*) \neq L(M_w)$, for all $w \in \{0,1\}^*$ such that M_w has a space bound $s_1(n)$.

R': M^* has the space bound $s_2(n)$.

To satisfy these requirements, we design the machine M^* to simulate, on input w, the computation of $M_w(w)$ within space $s_2(|w|)$, and accept w if and only if M_w does not accept w.

There are several issues in this approach which did not occur before in the diagonalization proofs of Section 5.3:

(1) How do we make sure that M^* works within space bound $s_2(n)$?

(2) How do we enumerate all DTM's M_w with space bound $s_1(n)$?

(3) Is the space bound $s_2(n)$ large enough for M^* to simulate all M_w with space bound $s_1(n)$?

(4) What happens if M_w does not halt within space bound $s_1(n)$?

To solve question (1), we note that $s_2(n)$ is fully space-constructible, and so we can construct M^* in such a way that it first reads the input w, and then simulates a $s_2(n)$-space marking machine to mark off $s_2(|w|)$ cells in the work tape. It then begins to simulate M_w on w, using the input w as both the code of M_w and the input w, and using the $s_2(|w|)$ marked cells to simulate the work tape of M_w.

For question (2), we observe that the enumeration of DTM's presented in Section 5.1 can be easily modified to enumerate all standard one-worktape DTM's. More precisely, we note that each instruction of a one-worktape DTM is of the form

$$\delta(q_i, a_j, a_{j'}) = (q_k, a_\ell, D_h, D_{h'}),$$

which indicates that if the machine is in state q_i, reading a symbol a_j from the input tape and a symbol $a_{j'}$ from the work tape, then it changes to state q_k, writes a_ℓ over the symbol $a_{j'}$, moves the input tape head in the direction D_h, and moves the work tape head in the direction $D_{h'}$. This instruction can be encoded by the string

$$10^i 10^j 10^{j'} 10^k 10^\ell 10^h 10^{h'} 1.$$

Then, the whole DTM can be encoded as

$$1^m \; code_1 \; code_2 \; \cdots \; code_t \; 11$$

for any $m \geq 1$, if it has t instructions.

Now, suppose that $s_1(n)$ is also a fully space-constructible function, then we can also attach a $s_1(n)$-space marking DTM M with M_w to control its space usage. However, this is really not necessary, because we need to satisfy the requirement R_w only for those M_w which do have space bound $s_1(n)$. In other words, we can simply simulate M_w within space $s_2(|w|)$, and if M_w visits more than $s_1(|w|)$ cells, then the requirement R_w is automatically satisfied.

So, this brings us to question (3): Can we satisfy the requirement R_w when M_w does work within space bound $s_1(n)$? We first note that the set of tape symbols for M^* is fixed, but the set of tape symbols for M_w varies as w varies. Suppose that M^* uses tape symbols 0, 1 and B. Then, all tape symbols of

M_w have to be encoded by strings over $\{0, 1\}$. We recall that, in Section 5.1, the universal DTM U uses 01^i0 to encode the ith symbol of M_w. A more economical way is to use the ith binary string of length $\lceil \log t \rceil$ to encode the ith symbol of M_w, where t is the number of tape symbols in M_w. Thus, each symbol of M_w becomes a string of length $\lceil \log t \rceil$ in M^*. It means that M^* needs space $\lceil \log t \rceil s_1(|w|)$ to simulate the tape configuration of M_w.

In addition, we note that M uses input w both as the machine code of M_w and the input w and, hence, it cannot directly simulate M_w. Instead, M needs to store the current state and the current position of the input tape head of M_w in its work tape. This takes $\lceil \log q \rceil + \lceil \log n \rceil \leq 2\lceil \log n \rceil$ cells, where q is the number of states in M_w. Furthermore, M needs up to $\lceil \log n \rceil$ cells of scratch space in a separate work tape to compare a tape symbol or a state symbol in its work tape (written in the binary form) with a tape symbol or, respectively, a state symbol in its input tape (written in the unary form). Note that $\log n \leq s_1(n)$. Thus, altogether, we need to make sure that

$$(\lceil \log t \rceil + 3)s_1(|w|) \leq s_2(|w|). \tag{6.1}$$

We note that, although $\liminf_{n \to \infty} s_1(n)/s_2(n) = 0$, the above inequality does not always hold, since t varies as w varies. This problem is solved by the fact that each DTM has an infinite number of machine codes. Indeed, for sufficiently large n, each DTM has a code of length n. Now, from the assumption of $\liminf_{n \to \infty} s_1(n)/s_2(n) = 0$, we know that for any integer $t > 0$, there exists an integer n such that $\lceil \log t \rceil s_1(n) \leq s_2(n)$. Consider a machine code w' of length n such that $M_{w'} = M_w$. Then, inequality (6.1) holds with respect to w' and so the simulation of $M_{w'}$ by M^*, in stage w', can be done in space $s_2(|w'|)$, and requirement $R_{w'}$ can be satisfied. Since $L(M_w) = L(M_{w'})$, as long as the requirement $R_{w'}$ is satisfied, the requirement R_w is also satisfied.

Finally, let us consider question (4). Suppose that M_w does not halt on input w and it works within space $s_1(|w|)$. Then, it must eventually enter an infinite loop, and some configuration would occur more than once. However, we cannot find this infinite loop by checking the history of the computation as we did in Example 6.15, because that might take too much space.

An alternative way is to count the number of moves in the simulation. As shown in Example 6.15, if a DTM M works within space bound $s(n)$, then it has at most $f(s(n)) = q(n+1)s(n)t^{s(n)}$ different configurations. So, if M runs for more than $f(s(n))$ moves within space $s(n)$, some configuration must have occurred twice and we know that M does not halt. This means that M^* only needs to use at most $\log(f(s_1(n))$ cells to write down the number K of moves taken so far (in another separate tape) in order to determine whether M_w has entered an infinite loop or not. We note that $q \leq n$, and so

$$\log(f(s_1(n)) \leq \log s_1(n) + 2\log n + (\log t)s_1(n) \leq (\log t + 3)s_1(n),$$

since $s_1(n) \geq \log n$. Now, we can find, for each w, a code w' with large $|w'|$ such that $M_{w'}$ has exactly the same instructions as M_w and $\log(f(s_1(|w'|)) \leq$

$s_2(|w'|)$. For this w', M^* has enough space to simulate $M_{w'}$ on w' and to count the number of moves of simulation. When it counts more than $\log(f(s_1(|w'|))$ moves, M^* accepts w'.

In summary, M^* uses three work tapes and it works as follows:

(1) On input w with $|w| = n$, M^* first simulates a space-marking DTM to mark off $s_2(n)$ cells on each of the three work tapes. It then writes down a counter 0 on the third work tape.

(2) M^* then simulates M_w on w, using the first work tape as the work tape of M_w, and the second work tape for the extra scratch space. After each move of simulation, it adds one to the counter on the third tape.

(3) During the simulation, if the machine M_w or the counter of the third work tape needs more space or if M_w halts but rejects the input, then M^* halts and accepts the input. If M_w halts and accepts the input, then M^* rejects the input.

The above analysis shows that M^* works within space $3 \cdot s_2(n)$ and satisfies all requirements R_w. The theorem now follows from the tape compressioin theorem.   □

For time complexity, the hierarchy theorem is a little weaker than the space hierarchy theorem. We say a function $t(n)$ is *fully time-constructible* if there exists a DTM M such that for sufficiently large integers n and any input x with $|x| = n$, $Time_M(x) = t(n)$. We call such a DTM a $t(n)$-*clock machine*.

Theorem 6.17 (Time Hierarchy Theorem) *If $t_1(n) \geq n + 1$, $t_2(n)$ is fully time-constructible, and*

$$\liminf_{n \to \infty} \frac{t_1(n) \log(t_1(n))}{t_2(n)} = 0,$$

then

$$DTIME(t_2(n)) \setminus DTIME(t_1(n)) \neq \emptyset.$$

Proof (Sketch). The proof is similar to that of the space hierarchy theorem. Namely, we construct a new DTM M^* to simulate machine M_w on input w for at most $t_2(|w|)$ moves, and rejects the input if and only if M_w accepts w in time $t_2(|w|)$. To make sure that DTM M^* simulates M_w for at most $t_2(|w|)$ moves, it simulataneously simulates M_w and a $t_2(n)$-clock machine M^c and halts if either of them halts. The parallel simulation is to be done by dovetailing: It simulates M_w for one move and then simulates M^c for one move. The total time used by M^* is, thus, bounded by $c \cdot t_2(|w|)$ for some constant $c > 0$. By the linear speed-up theorem, $L(M^*)$ is still in $DTIME(t_2(n))$.

The only thing that needs extra attention is that the DTM M^* has a fixed number of tapes. However, the DTM M_w to be simulated by M^* may have an arbitrarily large number of tapes. So, M^* needs to use a small number of tapes to simulate a large number of tapes. This can be done as in Theorem

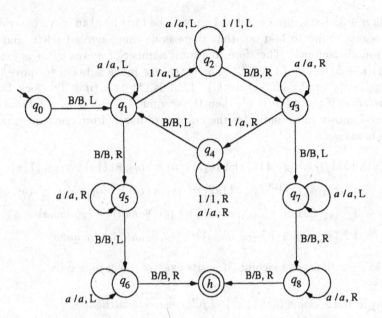

Figure 6.5: $(n+2)^2$ is fully time-constructible.

4.13, where we showed how to simulate a k-tape DTM by a one-tape DTM in time $O((t_1(n))^2)$, if the k-tape DTM halts in time $t_1(n)$. This simulation can be modified to run in time only $O(t_1(n)\log(t_1(n)))$, if we allow the simulator M^* to have two tapes. (The second tape can be used to move data around more efficiently. The exact simulation is too complicated, and we omit it here.) So, if we allow M^* to have at least two tapes and if its running time $t_2(n)$ grows faster than $t_1(n)\log(t_1(n))$, then M^* can simulate at least $t_1(n)$ moves of M_w, and the diagonalization works.   □

In order to apply the hierarchy theorems to specific complexity classes, we first need to know which functions are fully space or time constructible. It turns out that almost all familiar functions, including those in the five sequences defined in Section 6.1, are fully time and space constructible. In the following, we demonstrate this result on two simple functions.

Example 6.18 *Show that* $(n+2)^2$ *is fully time-constructible.*

Solution. We construct a one-tape DTM M which has a singleton input symbol set $\{1\}$ and the tape symbol set $\{1, \mathtt{B}, a\}$. It works as follows: It moves back and forth between the two blanks surrounding the nonblank symbols, each time changing one input symbol 1 into symbol a. After the last round in which it cannot find any symbol 1, it moves back and forth two more times.

The complete transition diagram of M is shown in Figure 6.5. Note that a complete trip from the blank at one end to the blank of the other end takes $n + 1$ moves. Also note that the total number of trips made by the tape head is $n + 3$: Each input symbol 1 causes the tape head to move one round; it takes one round to find out that there is no more symbol 1 left, and two more rounds to finish. Therefore, the total number of moves by M is exactly $(n + 1)(n + 3) + 1 = (n + 2)^2$. (The extra one move is taken to move from state q_6 or q_8 to the final state h.) That is, M is a $(n + 2)^2$-clock DTM. For instance, if the input is 1^4, then the computation of M is as follows (the number k shown in $\vdash^k$ indicates the number of moves from one configuration to the next):

$$(q_0, \ 1111\underline{B}) \vdash^1 (q_1, 111\underline{1}) \vdash^1 (q_2, 11\underline{1}a) \vdash^3 (q_2, \underline{B}111a) \vdash^1 (q_3, \underline{1}11a)$$

$$\vdash^1 (q_4, a\underline{1}1a) \vdash^3 (q_4, a11a\underline{B}) \vdash^1 (q_1, a11\underline{a}) \vdash^1 (q_1, a1\underline{1}a) \vdash^1 (q_2, a\underline{1}aa)$$

$$\vdash^2 (q_2, \underline{B}a1aa) \vdash^5 (q_4, aaaa\underline{B}) \vdash^5 (q_1, \underline{B}aaaa) \vdash^1 (q_5, \underline{a}aaa)$$

$$\vdash^4 (q_5, aaaa\underline{B}) \vdash^1 (q_6, aaa\underline{a}) \vdash^4 (q_6, \underline{B}aaaa) \vdash^1 (h, \underline{a}aaa).$$

We also note that the machine M visits exactly $n + 2$ tape cells.   □

Example 6.19 *Show that $\lceil \sqrt{n} \rceil$ is fully space-constructible.*

Solution. We construct a standard one-worktape DTM M' as follows:

(1) M' writes 1 on the work tape and moves its tape head to the right of this symbol 1. M' also moves its tape head of the input tape to the leftmost symbol of the input.

(2) M' uses the work tape to simulate the $(n+2)^2$-clock DTM M of Example 6.18. Meanwhile, the input tape head moves simultaneously from the leftmost input symbol toward right.

(3) If the input tape head is scanning a blank symbol when the simulation of M halts, then M' halts; otherwise, M' moves the head of the input tape to the leftmost symbol of the input, adds an extra symbol 1 to the work tape, moves the head of the work tape to scan the blank to the right of the rightmost symbol 1, and goes back to step (2).

Suppose M' halts when the work tape holds k symbols 1, then we know that the input length is less than or equal to $(k+2)^2$ and greater than $(k+1)^2$. In addition, we observe that the $(n+2)^2$-clock DTM M of Example 6.18 visits exactly $m + 2$ cells on input 1^m. Thus, M' visits exactly $\lceil \sqrt{n} \rceil$ cells.   □

Now we present some applications of the hierarchy theorems.

Example 6.20 $P \subsetneq EXP$.

Proof. Note that, for any fixed integer i, $n^i \prec 2^n$. That is, $n^i \leq 2^n$ for sufficiently large integers n. Therefore, by the linear speed-up theorem (and Example 6.11), $DTIME(n^i) \subseteq DTIME(2^n)$. Furthermore, if $t_1(n) = 2^n$ and

$t_2(n) = 2^{2n}$, then $t_2(n) = (t_1(n))^2$ and so $\lim_{n\to\infty} t_1(n)\log(t_1(n))/t_2(n) = 0$. It follows that

$$P \subseteq DTIME(2^n) \subsetneq DTIME(2^{2n}) \subseteq EXP. \qquad \square$$

We have shown in the last section that $P \subseteq PSPACE$, but it is not known whether the two classes are equal. It is interesting to note that we do know that $PSPACE \neq EXP$, but we do not know whether there exists a language in $EXP \setminus PSPACE$ or in $PSPACE \setminus EXP$.

Example 6.21 $EXP \neq PSPACE$.

Proof. Since, for any constant $c > 0$, $2^{cn} \leq 2^{n^2/2}$ for sufficiently large n, we have $DTIME(2^{cn}) \subseteq DTIME(2^{n^2/2})$. By the time hierarchy theorem, we have $EXP \subseteq DTIME(2^{n^2/2}) \subsetneq DTIME(2^{n^2})$.

Now, suppose, to the contrary, that $PSPACE = EXP$. We will show that $DTIME(2^{n^2}) \subseteq PSPACE$, and get a contradiction.

Let L be an arbitrary language in $DTIME(2^{n^2})$. Define $L' = \{x\$^t \mid x \in L, |x|+t = |x|^2\}$, where $\$$ is a symbol not used in L. Clearly, $L' \in DTIME(2^n)$, and so, by our assumption, $L' \in PSPACE$. This means that there exists an integer k such that $L' \in DSPACE(n^k)$. Let M be a DTM accepting L' in space bound n^k. Now, we construct a new DTM M' as follows.

> On input x of length n, M' copies x to a work tape and then adds $n^2 - n$ $\$$'s. M' then simulates M on $x\$^{n^2-n}$.

It is easy to see that the first step can be done using only n^2 cells. Then, the simulation uses n^{2k} cells. So, M' has space bound n^{2k} and $L(M') = L(M) = L$. Thus, $L \in PSPACE$. Since L is an arbitrary language in $DTIME(2^{n^2})$, this shows that $DTIME(2^{n^2}) \subseteq PSPACE$, and gives us a contradiction. $\qquad \square$

Exercise 6.3

$\star$ **1.** Describe the detail of the 3-worktape DTM M^* of Theorem 6.16. In particular, describe how M^* works using input w as both the machine code for M_w and as the input to M_w, while it is stored in the read-only input tape.

$\star$ **2.** In the proof of Theorem 6.17, we used the dovetailing technique to perform the parallel simulation of M_w and M^c. Can we use, instead, the product Turing machine method of Example 5.9 to perform the parallel simulation? [*Hint*: Note that M_w is not a fixed machine, and so we cannot build the product machine $M_w \times M^c$ directly.]

3. (a) Show that $\lceil \log n \rceil$ is fully space-constructible.

(b) Show that n^3 is fully time-constructible.

4. (a) Show that if $t(n)$ is fully time-constructible, then $DTIME(t(n)) \subseteq DSPACE(t(n))$.

(b) Show that if $s(n)$ is fully space-constructible and $s(n) \geq \log n$, then $DSPACE(s(n)) \subseteq DTIME(2^{c \cdot s(n)})$ for some constant $c > 0$.

5. Assume that $A \leq_m B$ by a reduction function f with time bound 2^n. Also assume that $B \in DTIME(2^n)$. What can you say about the time complexity of set A?

6. Show that $DSPACE(n(\log^* n)^{100}) \subsetneq DSPACE(n \log n)$.

7. Show that $EXP \subsetneq EXPPOLY$.

8. Show that $PSPACE \subsetneq \bigcup_{c>0} DSPACE(2^{cn})$.

6.4   Nondeterministic Turing Machines

In Chapters 2 and 3, we have seen that the notion of nondeterministic computation is useful in the study of regular and context-free languages. In this section, we introduce a new model of nondeterministic Turing machines, which is critical to the theory of computational complexity. A one-tape *nondeterministic Turing machine* (NTM) is like a one-tape DTM, except that at each step, the machine may have more than one choice of possible next moves. That is, the transition function δ of a one-tape NTM $M = (Q, \Sigma, \Gamma, \delta, q_0)$ is a mapping from $Q \times \Gamma$ to $2^{Q \times \Gamma \times \{R,L\}}$, where 2^S denotes the set of all subsets of S.

Since an NTM may have more than one possible next move at each step, a configuration may have more than one successor configuration. For instance, if an NTM has tape symbol set Γ, and an instruction

$$\delta(q, a) = \{(p_1, b_1, R), (p_2, b_2, L), (p_3, b_3, R)\},$$

then the configuration $(q, x c a d y)$, where $x, y \in \Gamma^*$ and $c, d \in \Gamma$, has three successor configurations: $(p_1, x c b_1 d y)$, $(p_2, x c b_2 d y)$, or $(p_3, x c b_3 d y)$. In other words, the computation of an NTM is no longer a single path, but is a *computation tree*. Similar to NFA's and PDA's, we define that an NTM M *accepts* an input x, if at least one computation path of the computation tree of M on x halts, that is, if the computation tree contains a leaf which is a halting configuration. Equivalently, an NTM M accepts x if and only if there exists a sequence of configurations $(\alpha_0, \alpha_1, \ldots, \alpha_m)$, starting from the initial configuration $\alpha_0 = (s, Bx B)$, ending at a halting configuration $\alpha_m = (h, u a v)$, such that $\alpha_i \vdash_M \alpha_{i+1}$ for all $i = 0, 1, \ldots, m - 1$. Note that an NTM, unlike NFA's and PDA's, may not halt on some inputs. It means that the computation tree of an NTM may be infinite. Nonetheless, we say it accepts the input x as long as the computation tree has a finite path whose leaf is a halting configuration. For an NTM M, we let $L(M)$ be the set of all strings accepted by M.

	a	b	c	B
s				q_0, B, L
q_0	q_0, a, L	q_1, b, L		
q_1		q_2, c, L		
q_2	q_3, a, L q_4, c, L	q_2, c, L		
q_3	q_3, a, L	q_2, c, L		q_5, B, R
q_4	q_4, c, L	q_2, c, L		q_5, B, R
q_5	q_6, B, R	q_9, B, R	q_5, B, R	
q_6	q_6, a, R	q_7, b, R	q_6, c, R	
q_7	q_8, c, L		q_7, c, R	(reject)
q_8	q_8, a, L	q_8, b, L	q_8, c, L	q_5, B, R
q_9	(reject)		q_9, B, R	h, B, R

Figure 6.6: The transition function of machine M.

Example 6.22 Let $L = \{a^{i_1} b a^{i_2} b \cdots b a^{i_k} b b a^j \mid i_1, \ldots, i_k, j > 0, \sum_{r \in A} i_r = j$ for some $A \subseteq \{1, 2, \ldots, k\}\}$. Find an NTM accepting the language L.

Proof. A string $a^{i_1} b a^{i_2} b \cdots b a^{i_k} b b a^j$ is in L if there are a number of a-blocks before bb whose total size is equal to the last a-block (after bb). A straightforward deterministic algorithm may have to check this condition over all possible subsets of a-blocks, which would take at least 2^k moves.

On the other hand, with a nondeterministic machine, we can just *guess* a subset $A \subseteq \{1, \ldots, k\}$ of a-blocks and then *verify* that the total size of the a-blocks in the subset A is equal to j. More precisely, we first move the tape head to the left passing the double-b mark. Then, for each block of symbols a, we nondeterministically decide either to keep it as it is or to change each symbol a in the block to the symbol c. When we reach the left-end blank, we move back toward right and behaves like a deterministic TM that compares the number of a's to the left of double-b with the number of a's to the right. It accepts the input if the two sides have an equal number of a's. We show the transition function of M in Figure 6.6. (For convenience, we actually change, in the first round, the double-b into a single b and all other b's into c's.)

Note that this algorithm creates 2^k paths in the computation tree, and most of them would reject the input. However, the input is considered accepted as long as one computation path accepts it. For instance, consider the input $x = aababaaabaabbaaaa$ (i.e., $i_1 = i_4 = 2$, $i_2 = 1$, $i_3 = 3$ and $j = 4$). If we select the first and fourth blocks to match with a^j, or if we select the second and third blocks to match with a^j, then these computation paths accept. All other 14 paths reject.

To be more precise, let us examine this computation tree more carefully. At first, the computation has a unique path:

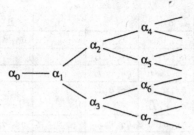

Figure 6.7: The computation tree of M on input x.

$$\alpha_0 = (s, a^2baba^3ba^2bba^4\underline{B}) \vdash (q_0, a^2baba^3ba^2bba^3\underline{a})$$
$$\vdash^* (q_1, a^2baba^3ba^2\underline{b}ba^4) \vdash (q_2, a^2baba^3ba\underline{a}cba^4) = \alpha_1.$$

At this point, α_1 has two successor configurations which lead to two different paths in the computation tree:

$$\alpha_1 \vdash (q_3, a^2baba^3b\underline{a}acba^4) \vdash^* (q_2, a^2baba^2\underline{a}ca^2cba^4) = \alpha_2,$$
$$\alpha_1 \vdash (q_4, a^2baba^3b\underline{a}c^2ba^4) \vdash^* (q_2, a^2baba^2\underline{a}c^4ba^4) = \alpha_3.$$

Similarly, α_2 has two successor configurations:

$$\alpha_2 \vdash (q_3, a^2baba\underline{a}aca^2cba^4) \vdash^* (q_2, a^2b\underline{a}ca^3ca^2cba^4) = \alpha_4,$$
$$\alpha_2 \vdash (q_4, a^2baba\underline{a}c^2a^2cba^4) \vdash^* (q_2, a^2b\underline{a}c^5a^2cba^4) = \alpha_5.$$

Also, α_3 has two successor configurations

$$\alpha_3 \vdash (q_3, a^2baba\underline{a}ac^4ba^4) \vdash^* (q_2, a^2b\underline{a}ca^3c^4ba^4) = \alpha_6,$$
$$\alpha_3 \vdash (q_4, a^2baba\underline{a}c^5ba^4) \vdash^* (q_2, a^2b\underline{a}c^8ba^4) = \alpha_7.$$

Each of α_4, α_5, α_6, and α_7 then has two successor configurations, and so on. We leave the rest of the computation tree to the reader. The general structure of the computation tree is as shown in Figure 6.7.   □

We make an important observation about the above nondeterministic algorithm. The algorithm consists of two stages: the guessing stage and the verification stage. In the guessing stage, it makes a number of nondeterministic guesses to create a specific configuration among many possible choices. For instance, with the input x defined in the above example, a specific configuration $(q_5, \underline{a}ac^7a^2cba^4)$ could be created by guessing that $A = \{1, 4\}$. In the verification stage, it verifies *deterministically* that the configuration obtained in the first stage satisfies the condition that there are an equal number of symbols a to the left and to the right of b. For instance, it accepts the configuration $(q_5, \underline{a}ac^7a^2cba^4)$ deterministically. Indeed, many useful nondeterministic algorithms can be devised using this two-stage construction method. We call such an algorithm a *guess-and-verify* algorithm. We will see more examples of such algorithms in Section 7.1.

In the above, we have defined one-tape NTM's. Multi-tape NTM's can be defined in a similar way. That is, a k-tape NTM operates just like a k-tape DTM, except that at one step, it may have more than one choice of next moves. We leave the detail of the definition to the reader.

Are NTM's more powerful than DTM's? The answer is no, in the sense that the class of languages accepted by NTM's is exactly the class of r.e. languages. This result could be considered as another support for the Church-Turing Thesis, even though we, in general, do not consider the NTM as a *reasonable* computatonal model, since there does not seem to be any physical devices that can be used to build such a machine.

Theorem 6.23 *Every set accepted by an NTM is an r.e. set.*

Proof. For simplicity, we consider only one-tape NTM's. The proof for the multi-tape NTM's is similar.

Assume that $M = (Q, \Sigma, \Gamma, \delta, q_0)$ is a one-tape NTM. Note that δ is mapping from $Q \times \Gamma$ to $2^{Q \times \Gamma \times \{R, L\}}$. Let k be the maximum size of sets $\delta(q, a)$ over all $(q, a) \in Q \times \Gamma$; that is, at each move, M has at most k choices of the next moves. Let $\eta_1, \eta_2, \cdots, \eta_k$ be k new symbols which are not in Γ. We construct a three-tape DTM M^* to simulate M as follows:

(1) M^* keeps a string y over the alphabet $\{\eta_1, \eta_2, \cdots, \eta_k\}$ in the second tape. Initially, $y = \eta_1$.

(2) M^* copies the input x from the first tape (the input tape) to the third tape and simulates M on input x on the third tape. During the simulation, it moves its tape head of the second tape toward right at each move. In other words, when M^* is simulating the jth move of M on x, it is also reading the jth symbol of the string y in the second tape. If the jth symbol of y is η_r, then M follows the rth choice for the next move of M (and if M has less than r choices for the next move, it follows the first choice). If $|y| < j$ (i.e., the head of the second tape is scanning a blank symbol), then go to step (3). The machine M^* halts if the simulation halts in state h within $|y|$ moves.

(3) Increment y of the second tape by one; that is, replace y by the next string over $\{\eta_1, \eta_2, \ldots, \eta_k\}$, in the lexicographic ordering. Then, go back to step (2).

We check that if there is an accepting computation path of M on x of length m, then this computation path corresponds to a sequence $(i_1, i_2, \ldots, i_m)$ of integers in $\{1, 2, \ldots, k\}$, in the sense that to get this path, the rth move of M follows the i_rth next-move among all choices. Therefore, M^* will halt when it reaches the string $y = \eta_{i_1} \eta_{i_2} \cdots \eta_{i_m}$ at the second tape. Conversely, it is obvious that M^* halts only when it finds an accepting computation path of M. Thus, we have $L(M) = L(M^*)$. ☐

Time and Space Complexity of NTM's. Now, we define the notion of time and space complexity of an NTM. Note that the computation of an NTM M on an input x may have many computation paths. Among these computation paths, which one should we use to measure its time and space complexity? We recall that the basic notion of a nondeterministic machine is that it accepts an input as long as at least one of the computation paths is an accepting path. So, following this spirit, we define that, if $x \in L(M)$, then $Time_M(x)$ is the number of moves in the shortest *accepting* computation path of M on x. That is, if the NTM M is able to find (nondeterministically) an accepting path for x in t moves, then $Time_M(x) \leq t$. What about the inputs x which are not in $L(M)$? We note that, in order to determine that $x \notin L(M)$, we need to examine all computation paths and be sure that all of them halt and reject the input. However, if M does not accept x, then some computation paths of M on x may be infinite. In that case, M cannot determine that $x \notin L(M)$ within any finite number of moves, as there are always some computation paths that are still *alive*. Therefore, we simply let $Time_M(x) = \infty$ if M does not accept x (even if all rejecting paths are finite).

To define the space complexity of NTM's, we restrict ourselves to one-worktape NTM's. Assume that M has one input tape and one work tape. If $x \in L(M)$, then we let $Space_M(x)$ be the number of tape cells in the work tape visited by M in the *accepting* computation path which uses the *least* amount of space. (*Note*: The shortest accepting path that defines $Time_M(x)$ and the least-space accepting path that defines $Space_M(x)$ are not necessarily the same path.) If $x \notin L(M)$, then again we let $Space_M(x) = \infty$.

We say M has a time bound $t(n)$ if $Time_M(x) \leq \max\{|x| + 1, t(|x|)\}$ for all $x \in L(M)$, and M has a space bound $s(n)$ if $Space_M(x) \leq \max\{1, s(|x|)\}$ for all $x \in L(M)$. Note that the above time and space bounds of an NTM M depend only on strings in $L(M)$. For instance, suppose that $L(M)$ is finite. Then, there exists a constant t_0 such that $Time_M(x) \leq t_0$ for all $x \in L(M)$. This implies that M has a time bound $\kappa(n)$, where $\kappa(n)$ is the constant function such that $\kappa(n) \equiv t_0$ (even though for sufficiently large n, $Time_M(x) = \infty$ for all x of length n, since they are all not in $L(M)$).

This definition can be justified as follows: Suppose that $Time_M(x) \leq t(|x|)$ for all $x \in L(M)$, and that $t(n)$ is a fully time-constructible function. Then, we can attach a (deterministic) $t(n)$-clock machine to M and stops the computation of $M(x)$ after $t(|x|)$ moves (and rejects if $M(x)$ does not halt in $t(|x|)$ moves). Now, this new machine M' accepts the same language as M and $Time_{M'}(x) \leq t(|x|)$ for all x. This shows that our definition of time complexity of NTM's is reasonable.

From the above complexity measures for NTM's, we can define the nondeterministic complexity classes as follows.

$NTIME(t(n)) = \{L(M) \mid M$ is an NTM with time bound $t(n)\}$.

$NSPACE(s(n)) = \{L(M) \mid M$ is an NTM with space bound $s(n)\}$.

$$NP = \bigcup_{c>0} NTIME(n^c).$$

$$NPSPACE = \bigcup_{c>0} NSPACE(n^c).$$

The following results are analogous to those for DTM's proved in Section 6.2. We omit the proofs.

Theorem 6.24 *Any multi-tape NTM M can be simulated by one-tape NTM's M_t and M_s, with the following properties:*

(a) $L(M) = L(M_t) = L(M_s)$.

(b) *For any $x \in L(M)$, $Time_{M_t}(x) \le c \cdot (Time_M(x))^2$ for some constant c.*

(c) *For any $x \in L(M)$, $Space_{M_s}(x) \le c \cdot Space_M(x)$ for some constant c.*

Theorem 6.25 *Suppose $\lim_{n \to \infty} t(n)/n = \infty$. Then, for any $c > 0$,*

$$NTIME(t(n)) = NTIME(c \cdot t(n)).$$

Theorem 6.26 *For any $c > 0$, $NSPACE(s(n)) = NSPACE(c \cdot s(n))$.*

Note that we did not list any hierarchy theorem for nondeterministic complexity classes. The reason is that the proofs of hierarchy theorems about nondeterministic classes are quite different from those for deterministic classes. Indeed, the diagonalization argument does not work well for nondeterministic machines. Recall the argument in the proof of Theorem 6.16: We constructed a DTM M^* such that M^* accepts w if and only if M_w rejects w. Now, suppose that M_w is an NTM. Then, in order to make sure that M_w rejects w, M^* has to check *all* computation paths of M_w on w, which would take an exponential amount of time even if M^* is an NTM. Thus, the straightforward application of diagonalization does not work for nondeterministic machines. In the following, we use a nice relation between deterministic and nondeterministic space complexity classes to show some weak hierarchy theorems for *NSPACE* classes.

Theorem 6.27 (Savitch's Theorem) *If $s(n) \ge \log n$, then*

$$NSPACE(s(n)) \subseteq DSPACE((s(n))^2).$$

Proof. Let $L = L(M)$, where M is an NTM with space bound $s(n)$. We note that the whole computation tree of M on an input x of length n contains at most $2^{c \cdot s(n)}$ different configurations for some constant c (cf. Example 6.15). Therefore, if M accepts x, then it must have an accepting computation path of length at most $2^{c \cdot s(n)}$ for some constant c (note that $s(n) \ge \log n$). We now construct a DTM M^* to simulate M to find this computation path in space $(s(n))^2$.

We note that the straightforward simulation which checks every branch of the computation tree of $M(x)$ does not work, because the tree has height

$2^{c \cdot s(n)}$ and so we need $2^{c \cdot s(n)}$ bits to record the current computation path under simulation. Instead, we use a divide-and-conquer algorithm to simulate M. To describe this algorithm, let us define some new notations. Let α_0 be the initial configuration of M on x. In order to check whether M accepts the input, it suffices for M^* to check that, for some acepting configuration α_f, M can move from α_0 to α_f in $2^{c \cdot s(n)}$ moves. Let $reach(\alpha_1, \alpha_2, k)$ denote the predicate that M can move from configuration α_1 to configuration α_2 within k moves. Then, what M^* needs to check is whether $reach(\alpha_0, \alpha_f, 2^{c \cdot s(n)})$ holds for some accepting configuration α_f.

The critical observation in the divide-and-conquer algorithm for M^* is that, for $i \geq 1$,

$$reach(\alpha_1, \alpha_2, 2^i) \iff (\exists \alpha_3)[reach(\alpha_1, \alpha_3, 2^{i-1}) \text{ and } reach(\alpha_3, \alpha_2, 2^{i-1})].$$

This relation suggests the following recursive algorithm to determine whether $reach(\alpha_1, \alpha_2, 2^i)$:

(1) If $i = 0$, then it returns YES if and only if $\alpha_1 \vdash \alpha_2$ or $\alpha_1 = \alpha_2$.

(2) If $i \geq 1$, then, for each configuration α_3, it recursively calls itself to check whether $reach(\alpha_1, \alpha_3, 2^{i-1})$ and $reach(\alpha_3, \alpha_2, 2^{i-1})$. It returns YES if and only if both recursive calls return YES for some α_3.

In order to estimate the space use of this recursive algorithm, let us see how we can use a stack to simulate this divide-and-conquer algorithm in a nonrecursive way:

(1) To determine whether $reach(\alpha_1, \alpha_2, 2^i)$, we need to go through all configurations α_3, and so we need $O(s(n))$ cells to store the current α_3.

(2) To determine whether $reach(\alpha_1, \alpha_3, 2^{i-1})$ and $reach(\alpha_3, \alpha_2, 2^{i-1})$, we need to push into the stack the information of the current setting. That is, we need to store the current α_1, α_2, α_3 and i in the stack, so that after we find out whether $reach(\alpha_1, \alpha_3, 2^{i-1})$ and $reach(\alpha_3, \alpha_2, 2^{i-1})$, we can continue the checking with respect to the next α_3. The space required to store the information is also $O(s(n))$.

(3) Since we start with $i = c \cdot s(n)$, the depth of the stack is at most $c \cdot s(n)$. Thus, the total space we need is $O((s(n))^2)$.

From the above analysis, we know that a DTM M^* can determine whether $reach(\alpha_0, \alpha_f, 2^{c \cdot s(n)})$, for any fixed α_f, within space $O((s(n))^2)$. Since the working space for simulation on different accepting configurations α_f can be re-used, the total space needed for the whole algorithm is still $O((s(n))^2)$. By the tape compression theorem, $L(M) \in DSPACE((s(n))^2)$.   □

Corollary 6.28 $PSPACE = NPSPACE$.

Corollary 6.29 $NP \subseteq PSPACE$.

Proof. $NP \subseteq NPSPACE = PSPACE$. □

We now apply Savitch's theorem to get some weak space hierarchy theorems for *NSPACE* complexity classes (see also Exercise 6 of this section).

Example 6.30 *Show that* $NSPACE(n) \subsetneq NSPACE(n^2 \log n)$.

Proof. By Savitch's theorem, $NSPACE(n) \subseteq DSPACE(n^2)$. By the space hierarchy theorem,

$$DSPACE(n^2) \subsetneq DSPACE(n^2 \log n).$$

Moreover, it is obvious that $DSPACE(n^2 \log n) \subseteq NSPACE(n^2 \log n)$. Therefore,

$$NSPACE(n) \subsetneq NSPACE(n^2 \log n). \qquad □$$

Lemma 6.31 *Let* $s_1(n)$, $s_2(n)$, *and* $f(n)$ *be fully space-constructible functions with* $s_2(n) \geq n$ *and* $f(n) \geq n$. *Then,*

$$NSPACE(s_1(n)) \subseteq NSPACE(s_2(n))$$

implies

$$NSPACE(s_1(f(n))) \subseteq NSPACE(s_2(f(n))).$$

Proof. For any $L \in NSPACE(s_1(f(n)))$, define

$$L' = \{x\$^{f(|x|)-|x|} \mid x \in L\},$$

where \$ is a symbol not in the alphabet of L. Then, it is obvious that L' is in $NSPACE(s_1(n))$. By our assumption, $L' \in NSPACE(s_2(n))$. This means that there exists an NTM M_2 with space bound $s_2(n)$ accepting L'. Now, construct a two-worktape NTM M_3 as follows:

(1) On input x, M_3 simulates an $f(n)$-space marking DTM to create the string $x\$^{f(|x|)-|x|}$ on the second tape.

(2) M_3 then simulates M_2 using the second tape as the input tape and the third tape as the work tape of M_2. M_3 accepts the input x if and only if M_2 accepts $x\$^{f(|x|)-|x|}$.

It is clear that M_3 accepts L in space bound $s_2(f(n))$. (*Note:* Since $s_2(n) \geq n$, the space used in the second tape is bounded by $s_2(f(n))$.) □

Example 6.32 *Show that* $NSPACE(n) \subsetneq NSPACE(n^{1.5})$.

Proof. By way of contradiction, suppose that $NSPACE(n^{1.5}) \subseteq NSPACE(n)$. Choose $f(n) = n^6$ and n^4, and apply Lemma 6.31 to the above relation. Then, we get

$$NSPACE(n^9) \subseteq NSPACE(n^6) \subseteq NSPACE(n^4).$$

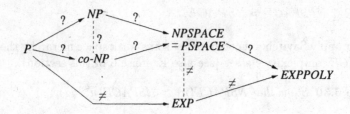

Figure 6.8: Inclusion relations between complexity classes

By Savitch's theorem and the space hierarchy theorem,

$$NSPACE(n^4) \subseteq DSPACE(n^8) \subsetneq DSPACE(n^9) \subseteq NSPACE(n^9).$$

This is a contradiction.   □

In Corollary 6.28, we have seen that $PSPACE = NPSPACE$. From this result, it is natural to ask whether the analogous result of $P = NP$ holds. If we examine the proof of Savitch's theorem, we can immediately see that the divide-and-conquer algorithm does not apply to polynomial-time NTM's. In fact, we do not know of any subexponential-time DTM's that can simulate polynomial-time NTM's. On the other hand, we also do not know of any proof technique that can separate NP from P. Indeed, the question of whether P is equal to NP has remained open since 1970, and is generally considered as *the* most important open question in complexity theory.

We are going to study the P versus NP question in Chapter 7. Here, let us just list the known and unknown relations between deterministic and nondeterministic complexity classes. First, we know that $P \subseteq NP$, and $NP \subseteq PSPACE = NPSPACE$. Next, let co-$NP$ denote the class of sets A whose complements $\overline{A}$ are in NP. Since the notion of an NTM M accepting an input x and the notion of M rejecting an input x are not symmetric, the nondeterministic time-bounded complexity classes are not known to be closed under complementation. In particular, it is not known whether $NP = co$-NP. These relations are summarized in Figure 6.8. In Figure 6.8, $A \xrightarrow{\neq} B$ means $A \underset{\neq}{\subseteq} B$, $A \xrightarrow{?} B$ means that $A \subseteq B$ but it is not known whether $A = B$, $A \cdots\overset{?}{\cdots} B$ means that it is not known whether $A = B$, and $A \cdots\overset{\neq}{\cdots} B$ means that $A \neq B$ but no inclusion relation between A and B is known.

Exercise 6.4

1. Construct multi-tape NTM's to accept the following languages in time $t(n) = 2n$:

   (a) $L_1 = \{a^{i_1}ba^{i_2}b\cdots ba^{i_k} \mid i_1, i_2, \ldots, i_k \geq 0, k \geq 3, i_r = i_s = i_t$ for some $1 \leq r < s < t \leq k\}$.

(b) $L_2 = \{x_1 c x_2 c \cdots c x_m c c y \mid x_1, \ldots, x_m, y \in \{a, b\}^*, (\exists i_1, \ldots, i_k) [1 \leq i_1 < \cdots < i_k \leq m, \ x_{i_1} x_{i_2} \cdots x_{i_k} = y]\}$.

$\star$ **2.** (a) A regular expression r is called a *starless regular expression* if it does not contain the symbol $*$ (the Kleene star). Show that the problem of determining whether two starless regular expressions r_1 and r_2 are not equivalent (i.e., whether $L(r_1) \neq L(r_2)$) is in *NP*.

     (b) Show that the problem of determining whether two regular expressions are not equivalent is in *NSPACE*(n).

     (c) An *extended regular expression* is a regular expression that can use an additional intersection operation (denoted by $\cap$). Show that the problem of determining whether two extended regular expressions are not equivalent is in $\bigcup_{c>0} NSPACE(2^{cn})$.

$\star$ **3.** In the proof of Theorem 6.27, the predicate $reach(\alpha_1, \alpha_2, 2^i)$ was solved by a deterministic recursive algorithm. Convert it to an equivalent non-recursive algorithm that uses space $O((s(n))^2)$.

4. Show that the complexity class *NP* is closed under union, intersection, concatenation and Kleene closure.

5. Show that, for any real numbers $r \geq 1$ and $0 < \epsilon < 1$,

$$NSPACE(n^r) \subsetneq NSPACE(n^{r+\epsilon}).$$

$\star$ **6.** (a) Show that Lemma 6.31 still holds if we replace the conditions $s_2(n) \geq n$ and $f(n) \geq n$ by $s_2(n) \geq \log n$ and $\log(f(n)) = O(s_2(n))$. [*Hint:* Note that NTM M_3 can simulate M_2 on input $y = x \$ f(|x|) - |x|$ without writing down the string y on the second tape. Instead, it may simply write down, in the second tape, the position k of the input tape head of M_2 and use k to determine what input symbol M_2's tape head is scanning.]

     (b) Show that, for any real numbers $r > 0$ and $0 < \epsilon < 1$,

$$NSPACE(n^r) \subsetneq NSPACE(n^{r+\epsilon}).$$

7. Show that if $t_1(n)$, $t_2(n)$, and $f(n)$ are fully time-constructible functions with $t_2(n) \geq n$ and $f(n) \geq n$, then $NTIME(t_1(n)) \subseteq NTIME(t_2(n))$ implies $NTIME(t_1(f(n))) \subseteq NTIME(t_2(f(n)))$.

8. (a) Show that $EXP \neq NP$.

     (b) Show that $EXP \neq \bigcup_{c>0} DTIME(2^{n^c})$.

9. Show that if $P = NP$, then

$$\bigcup_{c>0} DTIME(2^{n^c}) = \bigcup_{c>0} NTIME(2^{n^c}).$$

6.5   Context-Sensitive Languages

In this section, we study a restricted type of grammars and present a characterization of the space complexity of the corresponding languages. A *context-sensitive grammar* is a grammar in which the right-hand side of a rule is always at least as long as the corresponding left-hand side; that is, for any rule $\alpha \to \beta$ in this grammar, we must have $|\beta| \geq |\alpha|$. A language L is called a *context-sensitive language* if $L - \{\varepsilon\} = L(G)$ for some context-sensitive grammar G. For instance, the language $L(G)$ of Example 4.15 is context-sensitive, because we can change the rule $S \to \varepsilon$ to $S \to aBC$ to get a context-sensitive grammar for $L(G) - \{\varepsilon\}$. Indeed, it can be proved that the languages of all examples and exercises in Section 4.5 are context-sensitive. Their corresponding context-sensitive grammars can be obtained from simple modifications of their unrestricted grammars. We show some examples below.

Example 6.33 *Find a context-sensitive grammar for the language*

$$L = \{a^{2^n} \mid n \geq 0\}.$$

Solution 1. Recall the unrestricted grammar G for L given in Example 4.16:

(1)	$S \longrightarrow [Ra],$		(2)	$S \longrightarrow a,$
(3)	$Ra \longrightarrow aaR,$		(4)	$R] \longrightarrow L],$
(5)	$R] \longrightarrow L_h,$		(6)	$aL \longrightarrow La,$
(7)	$[L \longrightarrow [R,$		(8)	$aL_h \longrightarrow L_h a,$
(9)	$[L_h \longrightarrow \varepsilon.$			

It is clear that the only rules that violate the context-sensitive requirement that every rule $\alpha \to \beta$ must have $|\beta| \geq |\alpha|$ are rules (5) and (9). Now, suppose we replace them by

(5′) $R] \longrightarrow L_h\, a,$ and

(9′) $[L_h \longrightarrow a\, a,$

then it becomes a context-sensitive grammar G_1 with $L(G_1) = \{a^{2^n+3} \mid n \geq 0\}$.

Thus, all we have to do now is to modify grammar G_1 to always generate three less symbols a. This can be achieved by encoding a substring $aaaa$ of a sentential form by a single nonterminal symbol A_4. When we move the marker R to the right to *double* each symbol a to aa, we treat A_4 as $aaaa$; but, at the end, we only change A_4 to a single symbol a. That is, the following grammar G_2 is context-sensitive and it generates L:

$S \longrightarrow [RA_4] \mid a \mid aaaa,$		
$Ra \longrightarrow aaR,$	$RA_4 \longrightarrow aaaaA_4R,$	$R] \longrightarrow L] \mid L_h a,$
$aL \longrightarrow La,$	$A_4L \longrightarrow LA_4,$	$[L \longrightarrow [R,$
$aL_h \longrightarrow L_h a,$	$A_4L_h \longrightarrow L_h a,$	$[L_h \longrightarrow aa.$ □

Solution 2. A more general technique of converting an unrestricted grammar to a context-sensitive grammar is to "hide" the *auxiliary symbols* (which will eventually become ε), such as R, L, [and] here, by attaching them to their neighboring *real symbols* (which will eventually become terminal symbols). In the following, we use new nonterminal symbols $_XA_Y$ to replace a substring XaY in a sentential form of grammar G, where X and Y do not contain the symbol a. Whenever it is possible, we attach an auxiliary symbol X to the symbol a to its right. Therefore, new symbols $_XA_Y$ and A_Y are used only when Y ends with]. (To make the following grammar rules readable, we write $\boxed{_XA_Y}$ for $_XA_Y$ to emphasize that X and Y are attached to symbol A.)

Following the above idea, we replace rules (1) and (2) of grammar G by the following rules:

(1a) $S \longrightarrow \boxed{[_RA_]}$, (2a) $S \longrightarrow a$.

For rule (3), we replace it by the following six rules:

(3a) $\boxed{_RA}\,a \longrightarrow a\,a\,\boxed{_RA}$, (3b) $\boxed{_RA}\,\boxed{A_]} \longrightarrow a\,a\,\boxed{_RA_]}$,

(3c) $\boxed{_RA_]} \longrightarrow a\,\boxed{A_{R]}}$, (3d) $\boxed{[_RA}\,a \longrightarrow \boxed{[A}\,a\,\boxed{_RA}$,

(3e) $\boxed{[_RA}\,\boxed{A_]} \longrightarrow \boxed{[A}\,a\,\boxed{_RA_]}$, (3f) $\boxed{[_RA_]} \longrightarrow \boxed{[A}\,\boxed{A_{R]}}$.

It can be checked that these rules include all possible boundary cases that may happen.

Similarly, we replace rules (4)–(9) by the following corresponding rules, and the resulting grammar is context-sensitive and generates exactly the same language as grammar G:

(4a) $\boxed{A_{R]}} \longrightarrow \boxed{A_{L]}}$,

(5a) $\boxed{A_{R]}} \longrightarrow \boxed{A_{L_h}}$,

(6a) $a\,\boxed{_LA} \longrightarrow \boxed{_LA}\,a$, (6b) $\boxed{[A}\,\boxed{_LA} \longrightarrow \boxed{[_LA}\,a$,

(6c) $a\,\boxed{_LA_]} \longrightarrow \boxed{_LA}\,\boxed{A_]}$, (6d) $\boxed{[A}\,\boxed{_LA_]} \longrightarrow \boxed{[_LA}\,\boxed{A_]}$,

(6e) $\boxed{A_{L]}} \longrightarrow \boxed{_LA_]}$,

(7a) $\boxed{[_LA} \longrightarrow \boxed{[_RA}$,

(8a) $\boxed{A_{L_h}} \longrightarrow \boxed{_{L_h}A}$, (8b) $a\,\boxed{_{L_h}A} \longrightarrow \boxed{_{L_h}A}\,a$,

(8c) $\boxed{[A}\,\boxed{_{L_h}A} \longrightarrow \boxed{[_{L_h}A}\,a$,

(9a) $\boxed{[_{L_h}A} \longrightarrow a$. $\square$

Example 6.34 *Find a context-sensitive grammar for the language*

$$L = \{a^{n^2} \mid n \geq 1\}.$$

Solution. Following the hint of Exercise 3(a) of Section 4.5, we have the following unrestricted grammar for L:

$$S \longrightarrow [RA] \mid a,$$

$RA \longrightarrow AaaR,$	$Ra \longrightarrow aR,$	$R] \longrightarrow AL] \mid AL_h,$
$aL \longrightarrow La,$	$AL \longrightarrow LA,$	$[L \longrightarrow [R,$
$aL_h \longrightarrow L_h a,$	$AL_h \longrightarrow L_h a,$	$[L_h \longrightarrow \varepsilon.$

To see that this grammar is correct, we assume that we have a sentential form with n copies of A's and $n^2 - n$ copies of a's. Then, in the next round, we move R to the right to add one A and $2n$ copies of a's. Therefore, at the end of this round, we will have a sentential form with $n + 1$ copies of A's and $(n^2 - n) + 2n = (n+1)^2 - (n+1)$ copies of a's. The following is the derivation of string a^9:

$$S \;\Rightarrow [RA] \Rightarrow [AaaR] \Rightarrow [AaaAL] \Rightarrow [AaaLA]$$
$$\overset{*}{\Rightarrow} [LAaaA] \Rightarrow [RAaaA] \Rightarrow [AaaRaaA] \overset{*}{\Rightarrow} [Aa^4RA]$$
$$\Rightarrow [Aa^4Aa^2R] \Rightarrow [Aa^4Aa^2AL_h] \Rightarrow [Aa^4Aa^2L_h a \overset{*}{\Rightarrow} [L_h a^9 \Rightarrow a^9.$$

We note that only the last rule in this grammar does not have the property that the right-hand side is at least as long as the left-hand side. If we replace it by the rule

$$[L_h \longrightarrow aa,$$

then this new grammar is context-sensitive and generates the language $\{a^{n^2+2} \mid n \geq 1\}$. Now, all we have to do is to modify the grammar so that, at each round, the sentential form has n copies of A's and $n^2 - n - 2$ copies of a's. To do this, we only need to change the initial setting (and we still add, in each round, one extra A and two a's for each copy of A). That is, we only change rules of the first line to

$$S \longrightarrow [RAA] \mid a \mid a^4,$$

and our new grammar is context-sensitive and generates the language L. $\quad\square$

From Solution 2 of Example 6.33, we can see that almost all examples and exercises of unrestricted grammars in Section 4.5 can be converted to equivalent context-sensitive grammars. Is this true for all unrestricted grammars? In the following, we show that context-sensitive languages are exactly those acceptable by NTM's with a linear space bound. Thus, not all unrestricted grammars can be converted to equivalent context-sensitive grammars, since the unrestricted grammars generate exactly the class of r.e. languages.

Theorem 6.35 *The class of context-sensitive languages is exactly the class* $NSPACE(n)$.

Proof. First, assume that G is a context-sensitive grammar. We need to construct a standard one-worktape NTM M to accept all strings $w \in L(G)$ in space $O(n)$. Intuitively, the NTM M keeps a sentential form α on its work tape, and nondeterministically applies the rules of grammar G to derive the next sentential form until it is equal to the input. Since G is context-sensitive, the lengths of the sentential forms in a derivation are nondecreasing. Therefore, the successful computation of this NTM only uses n cells.

More formally, the NTM M works on a nonempty input w as follows:

(1) Write down S on the work tape. Let α be the string S.

(2) Repeat the following steps until one of the rejecting or accepting conditions is met:

    (a) Nondeterministically select a grammar rule $u \to v$ of G.

    (b) Find the first occurrence of the substring u in the string α currently on the work tape, and replace it by v. (If u does not occur in α, then this computation rejects.) Let β be the new string on the work tape.

    (c) Compare the string β with the input w. If $w = \beta$, then accept the input. If $|\beta| > |w|$, then this computation rejects. Otherwise, let $\alpha := \beta$ and continue.

We note that if $w \in L(G)$, then there is a leftmost derivation for w:

$$S = \alpha_0 \Rightarrow \alpha_1 \Rightarrow \cdots \alpha_m = w.$$

Correspondingly, there is a computation path of M on input w in which the strings α written on the work tape at step (2b) are exactly the strings α_0, $\alpha_1, \ldots, \alpha_m$ of the leftmost derivation of w. Furthermore, the sentential forms in the leftmost derivation never shrink, and so this computation path never rejects at step (2c), and will eventually accept when $\alpha = w$.

In addition, it is easy to check that the NTM M works within space bound $n + c$, where c is the maximum length of the right-hand side of any rule in G. Note that, in step (2b), where we substitute a string v for a substring u of α, if $|v| = |u|$, then this substitution is simple. If $|v| > |u|$, then we need to move the nonblank symbols to the right of α to the right to create extra space for v. This can be done by a DTM like the one studied in Example 4.9, which does not use extra space. Therefore, M never visits more than $n + c$ cells in the work tape. It follows from Theorem 6.26 that $L(G) \in NSPACE(n)$.[5]

---

[5] Actually, from the definition of the space complexity of an NTM, we only need to verify that the accepting computation path of M on w uses space n. The amount of space used in rejecting paths is irrelevant.

Conversely, let $L \in NSPACE(n)$. We may assume that there is a one-tape NTM M_1 that accepts L whose accepting computation path does not read any symbol beyond the two blanks surrounding the input w. (A one-worktape NTM M_2 which operates within space n can be easily converted to an equivalent one-tape NTM M_3, using two tracks to simulate the two tapes of M_2.) We need to construct a context-sensitive grammar to simulate the computation of M_1.

In Theorems 4.19 and 4.20, we showed how to construct, from a given DTM M, an unrestricted grammar G such that $L(G) = L(M)$. It is easy to verify that the same construction works for an NTM M. In the following, we further convert the grammar corresponding to NTM M_1 to an equivalent context-sensitive grammar. First, for each pair $(q, a) \in Q \times \Sigma$, we define a nontermial symbol $q\#a$. (For the sake of readability, we write $\boxed{q\#a}$ for the symbol $q\#a$.) Then, we define a grammar G_1 with the following rules:

(A) For each instruction $(p, b, L) \in \delta(q, a)$ of M_1, G_1 has the rules

$$c\,\boxed{q\#a} \longrightarrow \boxed{p\#c}\,b, \qquad \text{for all } c \in \Gamma.$$

(B) For each instruction $(p, b, R) \in \delta(q, a)$ of M_1, G_1 has the rules

$$\boxed{q\#a}\,c \longrightarrow b\,\boxed{p\#c}, \qquad \text{for all } c \in \Gamma.$$

That is, the grammar G_1 is just the grammar G_{M_1} of Theorem 4.19 without the boundary symbols [and], where rules in group (A) correspond to rules in groups (1) and (2) of G_{M_1}, and rules in group (B) correspond to rules in group (3) of G_{M_1}. We note that, since M_1 never reads any symbol beyond the leftmost blank or the first blank to the right of the input, the boundary symbols are unnecessary in our case. In other words, the second type of rules in group (3) of G_{M_1}, $\boxed{q\#a}\,] \longrightarrow b\,\boxed{p\#\text{B}}\,]$, will never be used.

In addition, in the proof of Theorem 4.19, the second type of rules in group (2), $c\,\boxed{q\#a}\,] \longrightarrow \boxed{p\#c}\,]$ (if $(p, \text{B}, R) \in \delta(q, a)$), is to allow the tape configurations of the machine M_1 to shrink. We eliminate these rules in grammar G_1 here. Thus, G_1 still simulates the computation of M, except that its sentential forms keep all trailing blanks we have ever visited.

From the above analysis, we can see that

$$(q, x\underline{a}y) \vdash^*_{M_1} (p, x'\underline{b}y') \quad \text{if and only if} \quad x\,\boxed{q\#a}\,y \underset{G_1}{\overset{*}{\Longrightarrow}} x'\,\boxed{p\#b}\,y',$$

where y' retains the trailing blanks.

Now, we define grammar G_2 as follows: It includes all reversals of the rules of G_1, plus the following rules:

$$\begin{aligned}
S &\longrightarrow \text{B}\,\boxed{h\#\text{B}}\,T, & T &\longrightarrow \text{B}\,T \mid \text{B}, \\
\boxed{s\#\text{B}} &\longrightarrow L_h, & a\,L_h &\longrightarrow L_h\,a, \\
\text{B}\,L_h &\longrightarrow \varepsilon,
\end{aligned}$$

for all $a \in \Sigma$, where L_h is a new nonterminal symbol. Then, grammar G_2 generates exactly the nonempty strings $w \in L$ as follows:

$$S \stackrel{*}{\Rightarrow} \text{B} \boxed{h\#\text{B}} \underbrace{\text{B} \cdots \text{B}}_{|w|} \stackrel{*}{\Rightarrow} \text{B} \, w \, \boxed{s\#\text{B}} \Rightarrow \text{B} \, w \, L_h \stackrel{*}{\Rightarrow} \text{B} \, L_h \, w \Rightarrow w.$$

Finally, the only rule in this grammar G_2 that violates the context-sensitive requirement is the rule $\text{B}L_h \to \varepsilon$. So, we can convert G_2 to an equivalent context-sensitive grammar G by the technique of Solution 2 of Example 6.33. That is, we can simply attach the leftmost and rightmost blanks to their neighboring symbols and make every rule satisfying the context-sensitive requirement. We leave the details to the reader as an exercise. □

Whether $NSPACE(n) = DSPACE(n)$ is, like the question of whether $NP = P$, a major open question in complexity theory. (Savitch's theorem only gives a weaker result: $NSPACE(n) \subseteq DSPACE(n^2)$.) We note, however, that, unlike the class NP, the class $NSPACE(n)$ is known to be closed under complementation. In the following, we prove a more general result that all classes $NSPACE(s(n))$ is closed under complementation, if $s(n)$ is fully space-constructible and $s(n) \geq \log n$.

In order to prove this result, we first define the notion of an NTM computing a function. We say that an NTM M with a write-only output tape *computes a partial function* $f : \Sigma^* \to \Sigma^*$, if the following conditions hold:

(i) For each $x \in Domain(f)$, there exists at least one accepting path of M on input x.

(ii) For each $x \in Domain(f)$, every accepting path of M on input x has the same output $y = f(x)$.

(iii) For each $x \notin Domain(f)$, there is no accepting path in the computation tree of M on input x.

In other words, an NTM M is considered as a transducer only if all of its accepting paths on an input x have the same output value.

$\star$ **Theorem 6.36** *For any fully space-constructible function $s(n) \geq \log n$,*

$$NSPACE(s(n)) = \text{co-}NSPACE(s(n)).$$

Proof. Let M be a one-worktape NTM with the space bound $s(n)$. Recall the predicate $reach(\alpha, \beta, k)$ defined in the proof of Savitch's theorem. In this proof, we further explore the concept of *reachable configurations*. Consider a fixed input x of length n. Let C_x be the class of all configurations of M on x that is of length $s(n)$. That is,

$$C_x = \{q\#j\#y\underline{b}z \mid q \in Q, 1 \leq j \leq n, |y\underline{b}z| \leq s(n)\},$$

where j indicates the position of the input tape head, and $y\underline{b}z$ is the tape configuration of the work tape. Note that each configuration in C_x is of length $\leq s(n) + \lceil \log n \rceil + \lceil |Q| \rceil + 2$. It is easy to see that we can define a linear ordering $\prec$ over configurations in C_x such that the relation $\alpha \prec \beta$ can be verified by a DTM in space $O(s(n))$.

The construction of the NTM that accepts $\overline{L(M)}$ is divided into three steps. First we observe that the predicate $reach(\alpha, \beta, k)$ is acceptable by an NTM M_1 in space $O(s(n) + \log k)$, if α and β are from C_x. The NTM M_1 operates as follows:

> *Machine M_1.* Let $\alpha_0 = \alpha$. For each $i = 0, \ldots, k - 2$, M_1 guesses a configuration $\alpha_{i+1} \in C_x$ and verifies that $\alpha_i = \alpha_{i+1}$ or $\alpha_i \vdash_M \alpha_{i+1}$. (If neither $\alpha_i = \alpha_{i+1}$ nor $\alpha_i \vdash_M \alpha_{i+1}$ holds, then M_1 rejects on this computation path.) Finally, M_1 verifies that $\alpha_{k-1} = \beta$ or $\alpha_{k-1} \vdash_M \beta$, and accepts if this holds.

Apparently, this NTM M_1 uses space $O(s(n) + \log k)$ and accepts (α, β, k) if and only if $reach(\alpha, \beta, k)$.

Next, we apply this machine M_1' to construct another NTM M_2 which, on any given configuration β, computes the exact number N of configurations in C_x that are reachable from β, using space $O(s(n))$. (*Note:* M_2 is an NTM transducer.)

Let m be the maximum length of an accepting path on input x. Then, $m = 2^{O(s(n))}$. To computer N, M_2 computes iteratively the number N_k of configurations in C_x that are reachable from β in at most k moves, for $k = 0, \ldots, m + 1$. When it finds, at stage $k + 1$, that $N_k = N_{k+1}$, it halts and outputs $N = N_k$.

To compute N_k, we first note that $N_0 = 1$, since β is the only configuration reachable from β in zero move. Next, for $k \geq 0$, N_{k+1} can be computed from N_k by the following nondeterministic transducer:

> *Nondeterministic algorithm for computing N_{k+1}:*
> Initialize the counter N_{k+1} to 0.
> For each configuration $\alpha \in C_x$, do the following:
> (1) Let r_α be FALSE.
> (2) For each $i = 1, \ldots, N_k$, do the following:
>   (a) Guess a configuration γ_i in C_x.
>   (b) Verify that (i) $\gamma_{i-1} \prec \gamma_i$ if $i > 1$, and (ii) $reach(\beta, \gamma_i, k)$ (by simulating machine M_1). (Reject this computation path if (i) or (ii) does not hold.)
>   (c) Set r_α to TRUE, if $reach(\gamma_i, \alpha, 1)$.
> (3) Add one to N_{k+1} if and only if $r_\alpha = $ TRUE.

Note that M_2 uses only space $O(s(n))$, because at each step corresponding to configuration α and integer i, it only needs to keep the following information in its work tape: i, k, N_k, the current N_{k+1}, r_α, α, γ_{i-1} and γ_i. Furthermore, it can be checked that M_2 computes correctly the number N of configurations reachable from β: Assume that N_k has been computed correctly. Then, in the computation of N_{k+1}, for each α, there exists exactly one nonrejecting path in step (2). Indeed, only the path that guesses, in the increasing order, the N_k configurations γ_i that are reachable from β in k moves survives the verifications (i) and (ii). All other paths are rejecting paths. For each α, this unique nonrejecting path must determine whether $reach(\beta, \alpha, k+1)$ correctly. Therefore, the value N_{k+1} must be correct too.

In the third step, we construct a third NTM M_3 for $\overline{L(M)}$ as follows:

> *Machine M_3.* First, M_3 simulates M_2 to compute the number N of reachable configurations from the initial configuration α_0. Then, it guesses N configurations $\gamma_1, \ldots, \gamma_N$, one by one and in the increasing order as in M_2 above, and checks that each is reachable from α_0 (by machine M_1) and none of them is an accepting configuration. It accepts if the above are checked; otherwise, it rejects this computation path.

We claim that this machine M_3 accepts $\overline{L(M)}$. First, it is easy to see that if $x \notin L(M)$, then all reachable configurations from α_0 are nonaccepting configurations. So, the computation path of M_3 that guesses correctly all N reachable configurations of α_0 will accept x. Conversely, if $x \in L(M)$, then one of the reachable configurations from α_0 must be an accepting configuration. So, a computation path of M_3 must guess either all reachable configurations that include one accepting configuration or guess at least one nonreachable configuration. In either case, this computation path must reject. Thus, M_3 accepts exactly those $x \notin L(M)$.

Finally, the same argument for M_2 verifies that M_3 uses space $O(s(n))$. The theorem then follows from the tape compression theorem for NTM's. $\square$

Corollary 6.37 *If A is a context-sensitive language, then $\overline{A}$ is also context-sensitive.*

Exercise 6.5

1. Construct context-sensitive grammars for the languages of Examples 4.17 and 4.18, and for the languages in Exercises 3(b)–3(i) of Section 4.5.

2. Complete the last part of the proof of Theorem 6.35. That is, describe how to attach the leftmost and rightmost blanks to their neighboring symbols to convert grammar G_2 to a context-sensitive grammar.

3. Show that the class of context-sensitive languages is closed under union, intersection, concatenation, and Kleene closure.

4. Find a recursive language L that is not context-sensitive.

⋆ **5.** What is wrong if we use the following simpler algorithm to compute N_k in the proof of Theorem 6.36?

> For each k, to compute N_k, we generate each configuration $\alpha \in C_x$ one by one and, for each one, nondeterministically verify whether $reach(\beta, \alpha, k)$ (by machine M_1), and increments the counter for N_k by one if $reach(\beta, \alpha, k)$ holds.

⋆ **6.** Recall, from Exercise 6 of Section 3.5, the notion of 2-stack PDA's. Show that each language accepted by a 2-stack PDA is a context-sensitive language.

7

NP-Completeness

7.1 NP

The complexity class *NP* contains thousands of natural problems, coming from diverse areas of graph theory, combinatorics, operations research, number theory and mathematical logic. We present a few examples in this section. In order to simplify the proofs of problems belonging to *NP*, we first give a simple characterization of the class *NP*, based on the notion of the guess-and-verify algorithm.

Theorem 7.1 *A language $A \subseteq \Sigma^*$ is in NP if and only if there exist a language $B \subseteq \Sigma^* \# \Lambda^*$ in P, where Λ is an alphabet and $\# \notin \Sigma \cup \Lambda$, and a polynomial function p, such that*

$$x \in A \iff (\exists y \in \Lambda^*) [|y| \le p(|x|), x \# y \in B]. \tag{7.1}$$

Proof. First, assume that $A = L(M)$ for a one-tape NTM $M = (Q, \Gamma, \Sigma, \delta, q_0)$ with time bound $p(n)$ for some polynomial p. Also, assume that for any configuration of M, there are at most k choices for the next move; that is, $|\delta(q, a)| \le k$, for any pair $(q, a) \in Q \times \Gamma$. Let $\Lambda = \{\eta_1, \eta_2, \ldots, \eta_k\}$. Recall that, in Theorem 6.23, we have constructed a DTM M^* to simulate an NTM M, using a string $y \in \Lambda^*$, written in the second tape, to decide which choice among the k possible next moves to take. We observe that if $x \in A$, then there is a string $y \in \Lambda^*$ of length $p(|x|)$ such that M^* accepts x with respect to the string y in the second tape. Conversely, if $x \notin A$, then M^* never accepts x. In other words, let B be the set of strings $x \# y \in \Sigma^* \# \Lambda^*$, with $|y| \le p(|x|)$,

323

such that M^* accepts x with respect to y. Then, set B is in P and satisfies (7.1).

Conversely, if sets A, B, and function p satisfy (7.1), then the following NTM M accepts set A:

(1) On input x, M guesses a string $y \in \Lambda^*$, with $|y| \leq p(|x|)$, in a separate tape.

(2) M verifies whether $x\#y \in B$ or not. It accepts x if $x\#y \in B$.

It is clear that the above NTM M works in time $r(p(n))$ for some polynomial r. Since the composition of two polynomial functions is still a polynomial function, M is a polynomial-time NTM. Therefore, A belongs to NP.   □

Suppose that sets A, B and polynomial function p satisfy (7.1), and that x is a string in A. Then, we call a string $y \in \Lambda^*$, with length $|y| \leq p(|x|)$, a *witness* or a *certificate* of $x \in A$, if $x\#y \in B$.

It is interesting to compare the above characterization of the class NP with the characterization of r.e. sets given in the projection theorem (Theorem 5.8). We have argued that the class P is a mathematical formulation of feasibly computable sets. Thus, it is the counterpart of the class of recursive sets in complexity theory. The above theorem, then, suggests that the class NP is the counterpart of the class of r.e. sets in complexity theory. Based on this analogy, people have attempted to apply the ideas and techniques of computability to attack the P versus NP problem.

Another interesting observation about the class NP is that a great number of puzzles and games are just special instances of some famous problems in NP, as their solutions are usually hard to find but easy to verify. We will also present some of these puzzles in this section.

Our first example is a fundamental problem in Boolean algebra, called the *satisfiability* problem. In order to define this problem, let us first review some basic concepts in Boolean algebra.

A *Boolean function* is a function whose variable values and function value all are in {TRUE, FALSE}. For convenience, we denote TRUE by 1 and FALSE by 0. In the following table, we show three basic Boolean functions: $\wedge$ (*conjunction*), $\vee$ (*disjunction*), and $\neg$ (*negation*), where $\wedge$ and $\vee$ are Boolean functions of two variables and $\neg$ is a Boolean function of one variable. Such a table is called a *truth-table*.

x	y	$x \wedge y$	$x \vee y$	$\neg x$
0	0	0	0	1
0	1	0	1	1
1	0	0	1	0
1	1	1	1	0

For simplicity, we also write xy for $x \wedge y$, $x + y$ for $x \vee y$ and $\bar{x}$ for $\neg x$. It is easy to see that conjunction and disjunction follow the commutative, associative, and distributive laws. An interesting and important law about negation is De Morgan's law: $\overline{x \cdot y} = \overline{x} + \overline{y}$ and $\overline{x + y} = \overline{x} \cdot \overline{y}$.

A *Boolean formula* is a formula over Boolean variables, with operations $\wedge$, $\vee$ and $\neg$. It represents a Boolean function in the same way that an arithmetic formula represents a function on numbers. It is not hard to see that all Boolean functions can be represented as a Boolean formula using these three basic operations.

We say a Boolean formula F over variables $x_1, x_2, \ldots, x_n$ is *satisfiable* if there is an assignment $t : \{x_1, \ldots, x_n\} \to \{0, 1\}$ that makes F true when we replace each variable x_i by $t(x_i)$. For instance,

$$F_1(x_1, x_2, x_3) = (x_1 x_2 + x_2 \overline{x}_3 + \overline{x}_1 x_3)(\overline{x}_1 \overline{x}_2 x_3 + x_1 \overline{x}_2 x_3)$$

is satisfiable, because $F_1 = 1$ by the assignment $t(x_1) = t(x_2) = 0$, and $t(x_3) = 1$; and

$$F_2(x_1, x_2, x_3) = (x_1 x_2 + x_2 \overline{x}_3 + \overline{x}_1 \overline{x}_3)(\overline{x}_1 \overline{x}_2 x_3 + x_1 \overline{x}_2 x_3)$$

is unsatisfiable, because $F_2 = 0$ for all eight different assignments to x_1, x_2 and x_3. We call an assignment t that makes F true a *truth assignment*.

Now, we define the satisfiability problem:

SATISFIABILITY (SAT): Given a Boolean formula F, determine whether F is satisfiable or not.

In the following, for each problem Π of the form "Given input x, determine whether x has property π," we let Π denote the set of inputs x having property π. For instance, SAT denotes the set of all satisfiable Boolean formulas.

Example 7.2 SAT *is in NP.*

Proof. A nondeterministic algorithm for SAT can be described in the guess-and-verify form as follows:

(1) On an input formula F over variables $x_1, \ldots, x_n$, guess an assignment $t : \{x_1, \ldots, x_n\} \to \{0, 1\}$.

(2) Check whether t satisfies F.

The above algorithm is obviously correct. We show that it can be implemented by a two-worktape NTM M in polynomial time. First, the guessing step (1) can be implemented by writing down n bits $t_1, t_2, \ldots, t_n \in \{0, 1\}$ in the second work tape. Then, in the verifying step (2), M copies the formula F to the first work tape, with each variable x_i replaced by the ith bit t_i in the second tape. It then evaluates the formula F', and accepts the input if $F' = 1$. It is easy to see that the set of legal Boolean formulas is, like the set of arithmetic formulas, context-free. Therefore, the evaluation of a formula F' with no variables can be done by parsing the formula and then evaluating the parse tree, and can be done in polynomial time (cf. Example 3.24 and Exercise 6 of Section 6.2).   □

Boolean formulas are a natural mathematical tool to encode logical statements. The following examples illustrate this idea.

Example 7.3 *Formulate the following puzzle as a Boolean formula F, and solve it by determining whether F is satisfiable:*

> *With five games left in the regular season, the team mathematician reported to the manager of the baseball team A: "We can still make the playoffs if we can beat team B, and in case team B beats team C then team C beats team D, and in case we lose to team C then team D also beats either team B or team C." Later, among the remaining five games, each team won at least one game, but no team won all its remaining games, and there was no tie game. Did team A have any chance to make the playoffs? If so, how?*

Solution. The five games left are apparently (1) A vs. B, (2) A vs. C, (3) B vs. C, (4) B vs. D, and (5) C vs. D. Let us use variable x_{uv} to denote the predicate "U beats V." Then, the condition reported by the team mathematician can be represented by the following Boolean formula F over five Boolean variables x_{ab}, x_{ac}, x_{bc}, x_{bd}, x_{cd}:

$$x_{ab} \cdot (x_{bc} \to x_{cd}) \cdot (\overline{x}_{ac} \to (\overline{x}_{bd} + \overline{x}_{cd})),$$

where $x \to y$ denotes "if x then y," which is equivalent to $\overline{x} + y$. The formula F can be simplified as follows:

$$
\begin{aligned}
x_{ab} \cdot &(x_{bc} \to x_{cd}) \cdot (\overline{x}_{ac} \to (\overline{x}_{bd} + \overline{x}_{cd})) \\
&= x_{ab} \cdot (\overline{x}_{bc} + x_{cd}) \cdot (x_{ac} + \overline{x}_{bd} + \overline{x}_{cd}) \\
&= x_{ab}\overline{x}_{bc}x_{ac} + x_{ab}\overline{x}_{bc}\overline{x}_{bd} + x_{ab}\overline{x}_{bc}\overline{x}_{cd} \\
&\quad + x_{ab}x_{cd}x_{ac} + x_{ab}x_{cd}\overline{x}_{bd} + x_{ab}x_{cd}\overline{x}_{cd}.
\end{aligned}
$$

The last formula is the sum of six terms, and so it is satisfiable if and only if at least one term in it is satisfiable. Among the six terms, we can see that the first one and the fourth one are not satisfied because A would have to win both games against B and C to satisfy them. The second term is also not satisfied since that would require B to lose all its three remaining games. The sixth term is logically unsatisfiable since it would require C beating D and also C losing to D. The third term is satisfiable with A beating B, B beating D, C beating both A and B, and D beating C. The fifth term can also be satisfied, with A beating B, B beating C, C beating A and D, and D beating B.

A more formal solution is to express the condition of "each team won at least one game, but no team won all its remaining games" in the following formula G:

$$(x_{ab} + x_{ac}) \left(\neg(x_{ab}x_{ac})\right) \left(\overline{x}_{ab} + x_{bc} + x_{bd}\right) \left(\neg(\overline{x}_{ab}x_{bc}x_{bd})\right)$$
$$\cdot \left(\overline{x}_{ac} + \overline{x}_{bc} + x_{cd}\right) \left(\neg(\overline{x}_{ac}\overline{x}_{bc}x_{cd})\right) \left(\overline{x}_{bd} + \overline{x}_{cd}\right) \left(\neg(\overline{x}_{bd}\overline{x}_{cd})\right).$$

Then, determine whether FG is satisfiable.   □

Example 7.4 *Formulate the following puzzle as a Boolean formula F, and solve it by determining whether F is satisfiable:*

> Three men named Lewis, Miller, and Nelson fill the positions of accountant, cashier, and manager in the leading department store in the City of NP. The following information about their jobs is known:
>
> - If Nelson is the cashier, Miller is the manager.
> - If Nelson is the manager, Miller is the accountant.
> - If Miller is not the cashier, Lewis is the manager.
> - If Lewis is the accountant, Nelson is the manager.
>
> What is each man's job?

Solution. Denote three men by L, M, N, and three jobs as a, c and m. Also write X_y to denote the predicate "X's job is y." Then, the given information implies that the following formula is satisfiable:

$$F = (\overline{N}_c + M_m)(\overline{N}_m + M_a)(M_c + L_m)(\overline{L}_a + N_m)$$
$$= (\overline{N}_c\overline{N}_m + \overline{N}_cM_a + M_m\overline{N}_m + M_mM_a)$$
$$\cdot (M_c\overline{L}_a + M_cN_m + L_m\overline{L}_a + L_mN_m).$$

Next, from the extra information that the three men fill the three positions, we know that $\overline{N}_c\overline{N}_m \to N_a$, $M_m \to \overline{N}_m$, $M_m \to \overline{M}_a$, and $M_aL_m \to N_c$, and so on. Therefore, F can be simplified as follows:

$$F = 1 \implies (N_a + \overline{N}_cM_a + M_m)(M_c\overline{L}_a + M_cN_m + L_m) = 1$$
$$\implies N_aM_c\overline{L}_a + N_aM_cN_m + N_aL_m + \overline{N}_cM_aM_c\overline{L}_a + \overline{N}_cM_aM_cN_m$$
$$+ \overline{N}_cM_aL_m + M_mM_c\overline{L}_a + M_mM_cN_m + M_mL_m = 1$$
$$\implies N_aM_c + N_aL_m = 1$$
$$\implies N_aM_cL_m = 1.$$

That is, Lewis is the manager, Miller is the cashier, and Nelson is the accountant.   □

Next, we consider problems about graphs. We have defined the notion of directed graphs in Chapter 1. We now introduce undirected graphs. An *undirected graph* (or, simply, a *graph*) is just like a directed graph, except that the edges have no direction; that is, each edge is a two-element subset of V. A graph has many different representations by a string. For instance, a graph G can be represented by its *adjacency matrix* A_G. First, we assume that the vertices in a graph are always named as $v_1, v_2, \ldots, v_n$, for some $n \geq 0$. Then, for each graph $G = (\{v_1, \ldots, v_n\}, E)$, its adjacency matrix is an $n \times n$ Boolean matrix A_G, with $A_G(i,j) = 1$ if and only if $\{v_i, v_j\} \in E$. Therefore, a graph of n vertices can be represented by a string $x \in \{0,1\}^*$ of length n^2, with $\{v_i, v_j\} \in E$ if and only if the $((i-1)n + j)$th bit of x is 1.[1]

Let $G = (V, E)$ be a graph, with $V = \{v_1, \ldots, v_n\}$. The notions of paths and cycles in a graph are the same as those of a digraph. A *Hamiltonian cycle* is a cycle that passes through each vertex of the graph exactly once (except for the starting and ending vertex, which is passed through twice). We now consider the following problem:

> HAMILTONIAN CYCLE (HC): Given a graph G, determine whether G has a Hamiltonian cycle.

Example 7.5 HC *is in NP.*

Proof. The problem HC can be solved by the following nondeterministic algorithm:

(1) On input $G = (\{v_1, \ldots, v_n\}, E)$, guess a permutation $(i_1, i_2, \cdots, i_n)$ of $\{1, 2, \ldots, n\}$.

(2) Check whether the permutation $(i_1, i_2, \cdots, i_n)$ determines a cycle in G; that is, check whether (i) for every $1 \leq j \leq n - 1$, $\{v_{i_j}, v_{i_{j+1}}\} \in E$, and (ii) $\{v_{i_n}, v_{i_1}\} \in E$. If the checking is successful, then halt and accept the input G.

We note that the guessing step (1) can be implemented by an NTM as follows: It writes down n integers between 1 and n, each of length $\lceil \log n \rceil$, and then deterministically checks that every integer between 1 and n occurs in the list. (In other words, step (1) itself has a guessing stage and a checking stage.) It is clear that the total time required is $O(n^2 \log n)$. In addition, it is clear that step (2) can be done in time $O(n^2)$. So, this is a polynomial-time nondeterministic algorithm, and it follows that HC $\in$ *NP*. □

Example 7.6 (KNIGHT'S TOUR) *Find a tour of the 8×8 chessboard by a knight which visits each square exactly once and comes back to the starting square.*

---

[1]Note that for an undirected graph G, A_G is symmetric in the sense that $A_G(i,j) = A_G(j,i)$, for all $i, j \in \{1, \ldots, n\}$, and so we can actually encode G by only $n(n - 1)/2$ bits. Nevertheless, as we are concerned only with polynomial-time computability of the underlying problems, this saving of the input size is irrelevant.

3	6	33	40	27	44	29	46
34	37	2	5	32	47	26	43
7	4	39	36	41	28	45	30
38	35	8	1	48	31	42	25
9	64	13	56	17	24	49	58
14	55	10	61	52	57	18	21
63	12	53	16	23	20	59	50
54	15	62	11	60	51	22	19

Figure 7.1: A knight's tour.

Solution. KNIGHT'S TOUR can be viewed as a special instance of the problem HC. Indeed, the problem KNIGHT'S TOUR on an $n \times n$ chessboard can be formulated as a subproblem of HC: For each $n \geq 1$, let $G_n = (V_n, K_n)$, where $V_n = \{v_{i,j} \mid 1 \leq i \leq n, 1 \leq j \leq n\}$, and

$$K_n = \{ \{v_{i,j}, v_{k,l}\} \mid i, j, k, l \in \{1, \ldots, n\},$$
$$[|k - i| = 1, |l - j| = 2] \text{ or } [|k - i| = 2, |l - j| = 1]\}.$$

Then, the graph G_n represents the moves of a knight in an $n \times n$ chessboard; that is, V_n representes the n^2 squares of an $n \times n$ chessboard, and two squares in the board are neighbors in G_n if and only if we can reach one square from the other by a knight's move. Therefore, KNIGHT'S TOUR on an $n \times n$ chessboard is exactly the problem of finding a Hamiltonian cycle in G_n. There are many solutions known to this problem, if n is an even integer greater than 5. (It is an interesting exercise to prove that KNIGHT'S TOUR has no solution for odd n's.) We show a solution in Figure 7.1 for the case of $n = 8$. (In Figure 7.1, the numbers in the squares indicate the order of the squares that are visited by the knight.) □

For our next problem, we say that a subset A of the vertex set V of a graph G is a *vertex cover* for G if every edge $e \in E$ contains a vertex in A.

VERTEX COVER (VC): Given a graph G and a positive integer k, determine whether G has a vertex cover of size at most k.

Example 7.7 VC *is in NP.*

Proof. Consider the following nondeterministic algorithm for VC:

(1) On input (G, k), guess a k-element subset C of vertices of G.

(2) Check that C is a vertex cover of G. If the checking is successful, then accept the input (G, k).

It is easy to see that this algorithm can be implemented by an NTM in polynomial time. First, step (1) can be done by writing down nondeterministically a string $c \in \{0, 1\}^*$ of length n, and then verifying that there are exactly k 1's in c. (This string c represents a subset C of $\{1, 2, \ldots, n\}$ with $i \in C$ if and only if the ith symbol of c is 1.)

For step (2), we need only go through each edge to verify that one of its vertices is in C. This can be done in time $O(n^2)$. So, this is a polynomial-time nondeterministic algorithm and, hence, VC is in NP. $\qquad\qquad\qquad$ □

The next problem is a generalization of the problem VC.

> HITTING SET (HS): Given subsets $A_1, A_2, \ldots, A_n$ of a set S and an integer k, determine whether there is a subset $A \subseteq S$ of size $|A| \leq k$ such that $A \cap A_i \neq \emptyset$ for all $i = 1, \ldots, n$.

Example 7.8 HS *is in NP*.

Proof. The following is a simple nondeterministic algorithm for HS:

(1) Guess a subset $A \subseteq S$ of size k.

(2) Verify that $A \cap A_i \neq \emptyset$ for all $i = 1, \ldots, n$. $\qquad\qquad\qquad$ □

Example 7.9 *Formulate the following logical puzzle as an instance of the problem HS and solve it by finding the correct subset.*

> *Three women, Joan, Michelle, and Tracy, made the following statements about their ages.*
>
> > *Joan:* "*I am 22 years old. I am two years younger than Michelle. I am one year older than Tracy.*"
> >
> > *Michelle:* "*I am not the youngest. I am three years different from Tracy. Tracy is 25 years old.*"
> >
> > *Tracy:* "*I am younger than Joan. Joan is 23 years old. Michelle is three years older than Joan.*"
>
> *If we know that, among three statements given by each person, exactly two are true. What are their ages?*

Solution. Let J, M, and T denote Joan, Michelle, and Tracy, respectively. Let X_i denote the ith statement of X. First, let us list all subsets of statements which result in a contradiction:

$$\{J_1, T_2\}, \qquad \{J_2, T_3\}, \qquad \{J_1, J_3, M_3\},$$
$$\{J_3, M_3, T_2\}, \quad \{J_1, T_1, M_3\}, \quad \{T_1, M_3, T_2\},$$
$$\{J_3, M_2, T_3\}$$

We also know that one statement in each of the following subsets is false:

$$\{J_1, J_2, J_3\}, \quad \{M_1, M_2, M_3\}, \quad \{T_1, T_2, T_3\}.$$

Altogether, each of the above subsets contains at least one false statement. Also, we know that there are totally three false statements. Thus, the above puzzle is equivalent to finding a hitting set of this family of subsets of size exactly three.

From the first two subsets, we know that these three statements must contain J_1 and T_3 or contain J_2 and T_2. By considering these two cases, we can find that $\{J_1, M_3, T_3\}$ is the only hitting set of size three. Therefore, they must be false statements, and other statements are all true. From these statements, we get that Joan is 23 (from T_2), Michelle is 25 (from J_2), and Tracy is 22 (from J_3). □

For any graph $G = (V, E)$, a subset $A \subseteq V$ is an *independent set* of G if for any two vertices u, v in A, $\{u, v\} \notin E$.

INDEPENDENT SET (IS): Given a graph G and a positive integer k, determine whether G has an independent set of size at least k.

Example 7.10 IS *is in NP.*

Proof. The following nondeterministic algorithm for IS is similar to that of VC:

(1) Guess a k-element subset A of the vertex set V of G.

(2) Check that, for any two vertices v_j, v_k in A, $\{v_j, v_k\} \notin E$. □

Example 7.11 (EIGHT-QUEEN PROBLEM) *Place eight queens in an 8×8 chessboard without them attacking each another. (In the chess game, a queen attacks another piece if they are located in the same row, or in the same column, or in the same diagonal.)*

Solution. This is a special instance of the problem IS. Let $H_n = (V_n, Q_n)$, where $V_n = \{v_{i,j} \mid 1 \le i \le n, 1 \le j \le n\}$, and

$$Q_n = \{\, \{v_{i,j}, v_{k,l}\} \mid i, j, k, l \in \{1, \ldots, n\},$$
$$[i = k] \text{ or } [j = l] \text{ or } [|k - i| = |l - j| \ne 0]\}.$$

Similar to Example 7.6, we can treat V_n as the n^2 squares of an $n \times n$ chessboard. Then, the graph H_n represents a queen's moves in an $n \times n$ chessboard. Thus, the EIGHT-QUEEN PROBLEM is exactly the problem of finding an independent set for H_8. In general, the problem IS on (H_n, n) is called the n-QUEEN PROBLEM. There are many solutions known to this problem for $n \ge 4$. We show a solution in Figure 7.2 for the case of $n = 8$. □

Our next example is a combinatorial problem.

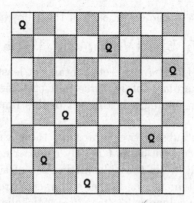

Figure 7.2: A solution to the eight-queen problem.

THREE-DIMENSIONAL MATCHING (3DM): Given three pairwisely disjoint sets A, B and C, each of n elements, and a set $W \subseteq A \times B \times C$, determine whether W has a subset W' of exactly n triples such that each element in $A \cup B \cup C$ appears in the n triples of W' exactly once. (Such a subset W' is called a *three-dimensional matching* of sets A, B and C.)

Example 7.12 3DM *is in NP.*

Proof. Consider the following nondeterministic algorithm:

(1) On input (A, B, C, W), guess a subset $W' \subseteq W$ of size $|A|$.

(2) Check that each element of $A \cup B \cup C$ occurs in W' exactly once. If the checking is successful, then accept the input.

It is easy to see that step (1) can be done by an NTM in time $O(m)$, where $m = |W|$, and step (2) can be done by a DTM in time $O(|A|)$.   □

Our next example is a famous problem in operations research. Suppose u and v are two n-dimensional integer vectors. We write $u \geq v$ to denote that the ith element of u is greater than or equal to the ith element of v for all $i = 1, 2, \ldots, n$.

INTEGER PROGRAMMING (IP): Given an $n \times m$ integer matrix A and an n-dimensional integer vector b, determine whether there exists an m-dimensional integer vector x such that $Ax \geq b$.

⋆ **Example 7.13** IP *is in NP.*

Proof (Sketch). It is natural to try the following nondeterministic algorithm for IP:

(1) Guess an m-dimensional integer vector x.

(2) Verify that $Ax \geq b$.

The correctness of the above algorithm is straightforward. However, it is not clear that it can be implemented by an NTM in polynomial time. We note that, in order to make this algorithm to work in polynomial time, we need to find a *witness* x of length polynomially bounded by the total size of the input (A, b). That is, we need the following lemma from linear algebra. (See Exercise 8 of this section for the proof.)

Lemma 7.14 *For any $n \times n$ integer matrix A and n-dimensional integer vector b, if there is an m-dimensional integer vector y satisfying $Ay \geq b$, then there is an m-dimensional integer vector x, satisfying $Ax \geq b$, such that the absolute value of each integer in x is bounded by $2(\alpha q)^{2q+2}$, where α is the maximum absolute value of elements in A and b, and $q = \max\{m, n\}$.*

With this lemma, we can modify step (1) of the above algorithm as follows:

(1′) Guess an m-dimensional integer vector x, with the absolute value of each integer in x bounded by $2(\alpha q)^{2q+2}$.

Note that the binary representation of an integer $t \leq 2(\alpha q)^{2q+2}$ is of length $\leq \log(2(\alpha q)^{2q+2}) = O(q \log q \log \alpha)$, which is polynomially bounded by the input size. So, after the modification, the algorithm runs in polynomial time. $\square$

Example 7.15 *Formulate the following logical puzzle as an instance of the problem IP, and solve it by solving the corresponding system of inequalities.*

> *Professor X presented a colloquium talk in the Department of Complexity. When he started to talk, he noticed that the 15 people of the audience satisfy the following conditions:*
>
> - *There were more students than professors.*
> - *There were more male professors than male students.*
> - *There were more male students than female students.*
> - *There was at least one female professor.*
>
> *Five minutes later, a person rushed into the room. However, the appearance of this person did not change the above four conditions. Is this person a man or a woman, a student or a professor?*

Solution. Let s_1, s_2, p_1, p_2 denote, respectively, the numbers of male students, female students, male professors, and female professors, both before and after the last person entering the room. From the given conditions, we have the following inequalities:

(1) $15 \leq s_1 + s_2 + p_1 + p_2 \leq 16$,

(2) $s_1 + s_2 \geq p_1 + p_2 + 1$,

(3) $p_1 \geq s_1 + 1$,

(4) $s_1 \geq s_2 + 1$,

(5) $p_2 \geq 1$.

From (1) and (2), we obtain

(6) $s_1 + s_2 \geq 8$,

(7) $p_1 + p_2 \leq 7$.

Furthermore, by (4) and (6), we have $s_1 \geq 5$. By (3), $p_1 \geq 6$. By (5) and (7), we obtain $p_1 = 6$ and $p_2 = 1$. It follows that $s_1 = 5$ and $8 \leq s_1 + s_2 \leq 9$. This implies that $3 \leq s_2 \leq 4$. We conclude that the last person coming into the room is a female student. $\qquad\square$

All the examples above have simple guess-and-verify algorithms. In the following, we show an example in NP, which does not have such a simple guess-and-verify algorithm. Instead, we prove that it is in NP by a nondeterministic *recursive* algorithm.

PRIMALITY TESTING (PRIME): Given a positive integer p, written in the binary form, determine whether p is a prime number.

To show that PRIME is in NP, we need the following result of number theory. We omit the proof of this lemma.

Lemma 7.16 *An odd integer $p > 2$ is a prime if and only if there exists an integer $a \in \{1, 2, \ldots, p-1\}$ such that*

(a) $a^{p-1} \equiv 1 \pmod{p}$, and

(b) $a^{(p-1)/q} \not\equiv 1 \pmod{p}$, for all prime factors q of $p-1$.

⋆ **Example 7.17** PRIME *is in NP.*

Proof. Lemma 7.16 suggests that to check whether p is a prime, we can guess an integer $a \in \{1, \ldots, p-1\}$ and then check conditions (a) and (b). So, we only need to show that conditions (a) and (b) can be done in polynomial time. We note, however, that condition (b) involves the checking of an inequality over all prime factors q of $p-1$, and so it seems to require a solution to the *integer factoring* problem, which asks, for a given integer n, to find all its prime factors. The integer factoring problem is apparently more difficult than the problem PRIME, and so this looks like a vicious cycle.

Fortunately, we note that since p is an odd integer, a prime factor q of integer $p-1$ must be less than $p/2$. This fact allows us to use a recursive, nondeterministic algorithm to solve the problem PRIME:

(1) For input p, guess an integer a, $1 \leq a \leq p-1$, and a sequence of distinct numbers $q_1, q_2, \ldots, q_k$, $1 \leq k \leq \log p$, with each q_i between 2 and $(p-1)/2$.

(2) Recursively check that each q_i, $1 \leq i \leq k$, is a prime number.

(3) Check that $q_1, q_2, \ldots, q_k$ are the only prime factors of $p - 1$.

(4) Check that $a^{p-1} \equiv 1 \pmod{p}$.

(5) Check that $a^{(p-1)/q_i} \not\equiv 1 \pmod{p}$, for all $1 \leq i \leq k$.

First, we claim that conditions (3), (4) and (5) can be verified by a DTM in time $O((\log p)^4)$. To see this, we note that the modulo exponentiation $x^y \bmod p$, with $x, y \leq p$, can be done by $O(\log p)$ modulo multiplications as follows: Write y in the binary form as $y = y_b y_{b-1} \cdots y_0$; that is, $y = \sum_{j=0}^{b} y_j 2^j$, with each $y_j \in \{0, 1\}$. Then,

$$x^y \bmod p = \prod_{0 \leq j \leq b, y_j = 1} (x^{2^j} \bmod p) \bmod p.$$

Since each $(x^{2^j} \bmod p)$ can be found by j modulo multiplications, x^y can be found by $2b$ modulo multiplications, where $b = \lfloor \log p \rfloor + 1$. Therefore, conditions (3), (4) and (5) can be done by $O((\log p)^2)$ modulo multiplications (or divisions). Since each modulo multiplication is over two integers of length $\log p$, it can be done in time $O((\log p)^2)$. Thus, the total checking time for conditions (3), (4) and (5) is $O((\log p)^4)$.

Next, we note that condition (2) can be done by applying the above algorithm recursively to $q_1, \ldots, q_k$. Note that each q_i is bounded by $(p-1)/2$, and so the depth of the recursive calls (the maximum number of nested recursive calls of the algorithm) is bounded by $\log p$. Let $m(p)$ denote the total computation time of the above algorithm on input p. Then, for the nondeterministic guess of step (1) which guesses the correct prime factors $q_1, \ldots, q_k$ of $p - 1$, we have the following recurrence relation on function m:

$$m(p) \leq c(\log p)^4 + \sum_{i=1}^{k} m(q_i),$$

for some constant $c > 0$. Note that each q_i, $1 \leq i \leq k$, is between 2 and $(p-1)/2$, and that $\sum_{i=1}^{k} \log q_i \leq \log p$. It follows that

$$\sum_{i=1}^{k} (\log q_i)^5 \leq (\log p)^5 - (\log p)^4$$

and, hence, $c(\log p)^5$ is an upper bound of $m(p)$ for the recurrence inequality. This means that the shortest accepting path of this nondeterministic algorithm takes time $O((\log p)^5)$ to accept the input p. So, the algorithm is a polynomial-time algorithm. □

The above example showed that for any prime p, there is a *short proof* for the fact that p is a prime. This short proof involves the correct guess at each step of the recursive nondeterministic algorithm and the corresponding verifications of conditions (3), (4) and (5).

Example 7.18 *Prove that 683 is a prime.*

Proof. We apply the recursive nondeterministic algorithm for PRIME on input $p = 683$. First, for input 683, we guess $a = 73$, $q_1 = 2$, $q_2 = 11$ and $q_3 = 31$. For this guess, we verify the following conditions:

(3) $p - 1 = 682 = 2 \cdot 11 \cdot 31$.

(4) $73^{682} \equiv 1 \pmod{683}$.

(5) $73^{341} \equiv 682 \pmod{683}$, $73^{62} \equiv 256 \pmod{683}$, and $73^{22} \equiv 3 \pmod{683}$.

Next, we need to prove that q_1, q_2 and q_3 are primes. For $q_1 = 2$, it is clearly a prime. For $q_2 = 11$, we may guess $(6; 2, 5)$ and verify the following conditions:

(3) $11 - 1 = 2 \cdot 5$.

(4) $6^{10} \equiv 1 \pmod{11}$.

(5) $6^5 \equiv 10 \pmod{11}$, and $6^2 \equiv 3 \pmod{11}$.

Also, we note that 2 and 5 are obviously primes. This proofs that 11 is a prime.

For $q_3 = 31$, we may guess $(3; 2, 3, 5)$ and verify that

(3) $31 - 1 = 2 \cdot 3 \cdot 5$.

(4) $3^{30} \equiv 1 \pmod{31}$.

(5) $3^{15} \equiv 30 \pmod{31}$, $3^{10} \equiv 25 \pmod{31}$, and $3^6 \equiv 16 \pmod{31}$.

Finally, we note that 2, 3 and 5 are obviously primes, and so we conclude that 31 is a prime.

This completes the proof that 683 is a prime. $\square$

An interesting fact about PRIME is that its complement, the set of nonprime numbers, is also in *NP*. In fact, it is easy to determine that an integer $n \geq 4$ is a composite number by the following straightforward guess-and-verify algorithm: Guess an integer m, $2 \leq m \leq n - 1$, and verify that m divides n. We recall that it is not known whether $NP = co\text{-}NP$, nor is it known whether $NP \cap co\text{-}NP = P$. Also, most natural examples of problems in *NP* are not known to be in *co-NP* unless they are actually in *P*. Thus, PRIME is one of very few candidates of problems in $(NP \cap co\text{-}NP) - P$.

Exercise 7.1

1. For any set A, let $A' = \{w\#0^n \mid w$ is a suffix of some x in A with $|x| = n\}$ and $A'' = \{w \mid w$ has a suffix x in $A\}$. Show that if A is in *NP*, then A' and A'' are also in *NP*.

2. For any set $B \subseteq \{0,1\}^*\#\{0,1\}^*$, let $prefix(B) = \{x\#u \mid x, u \in \{0,1\}^*, (\exists v \in \{0,1\}^*) \, x\#uv \in B\}$.

   (a) Assume that there is a polynomial function p such that $x\#y \in B$ implies $|y| \leq p(|x|)$. Show that if $B \in NP$, then $prefix(B) \in NP$.

   (b) Show that if $A = \{x \mid (\exists u)[|u| \leq p(|x|), x\#u \in B\}$ for some polynomial function p and if $prefix(B) \in P$, then $A \in P$.

3. A function $f : \{0,1\}^* \to \{0,1\}^*$ is *polynomial-time computable* if there is a polynomial-time DTM that computes the function f (i.e., on input x, it halts in $p(|x|)$ moves for some polynomial p, with the string $f(x)$ on the output tape). A function $f : \{0,1\}^* \to \{0,1\}^*$ is *polynomially honest* if there is a polynomial function p such that $|f(x)| \leq p(|x|)$ and $|x| \leq p(|f(x)|)$ for all $x \in \{0,1\}^*$. Assume that f is polynomial-time computable and is polynomially honest.

   (a) Assume that f is one-to-one and onto. Show that if $A \in NP$, then $f(A) \in NP$ and $f^{-1}(A) \in NP$.

   (b) Show that if $P = NP$, then the following functions are polynomial-time computable:

$$Max_f(u,v) = \max\{f(x) \mid u \leq_{\text{lex}} x \leq_{\text{lex}} v\},$$
$$Min_f(u,v) = \min\{f(x) \mid u \leq_{\text{lex}} x \leq_{\text{lex}} v\},$$

where $\leq_{\text{lex}}$ is the lexicographic ordering on $\{0,1\}^*$.

4. Formulate the following puzzles as instances of problems in *NP*, and then solve the puzzles by finding the witnesses to the instances:

   (a) Six men, A, B, C, D, E, and F, are the only members eligible for the offices of President, Vice-President, and Secretary in Club NP. The following preferences of these men are known:

- A won't be an officer unless E is President.
- B won't serve if he outranks C.
- B won't serve with F under any conditions.
- C won't serve with both E and F.
- C won't serve if F is President or B is Secretary.
- D won't serve with C or E unless he outranks them.
- E won't be Vice-President.
- E won't be Secretary if D is an officer.
- E won't serve with A unless F serves too.
- F won't serve unless either he or C is President.

How can the three offices be filled satisfying all above conditions?

   (b) Police arrested four men as the suspects of a murder case. They made the following statements when questioned:

     John: "Nick did it."
     Nick: "Bill did it."
     Dan: "I didn't do it."
     Bill: "Nick lied when he said I did it."

If exactly one of them is the real murderer and exactly one of the above statements is true, who is the murderer?

(c) Brown, Jones, and Smith are employed by the village of NP as fireman, policeman, and teacher, though not necessarily respectively. Someone in the village reported that:

- Brown and the teacher are neighbors.
- Jones and the teacher are neighbors.
- Both Brown and Smith are neighbors of the fireman.
- Both the policeman and the fireman are neightbors of Jones.
- The men are all neighbors.

However, the truth of the matter is that only two of these statements are true. Can you determine the job which each man holds?

(d) Both the Smiths and the Taylors have two young sons under eleven. The names of the boys, whose ages rounded off to the nearest year are all different, are Arthur, Bert, Carl, and David. Taking the ages of the boys only to the nearest year, the following statements are true:

- Arthur is three years younger than his brother.
- Bert is the oldest.
- Carl is half as old as one of the Taylor boys.
- David is five years older than the younger Smith boy.
- The total ages of the boys in each family differ by the same amount today as they did five years ago.

How old is each boy, and what is each boy's family name?"

5. The *threshold function* $T_{n,k}$ is a Boolean function defined as follows:

$$T_{n,k}(x_1, \cdots, x_n) = \begin{cases} 1 & \text{if there are at least } k \text{ 1's in } x_1, \cdots, x_n, \\ 0 & \text{otherwise.} \end{cases}$$

(a) Construct Boolean formulas $F_{n,k}$, using operations $\wedge$, $\vee$, $\neg$, and variables $x_1, x_2, \ldots, x_n$, such that it computes the function $T_{n,k}$.

(b) Show that there exist Boolean formulas $G_{n,k}$ using operations $\wedge$, $\vee$, $\neg$, variables $x_1, x_2, \ldots, x_n$, and some auxiliary variables $y_1, \ldots, y_m$, such that (i) the length of $G_{n,k}$ is bounded by n^c for some constant $c > 0$, and (ii) an assignment t satisfies $G_{n,k}$ if and only if t assigns value 1 to at least k variables in $\{x_1, \ldots, x_n\}$.

6. Prove that the following integers are primes: 293, 587, 65537, 214177.

7. Show that the following problems are in NP:

(a) LONGEST PATH (LP): Given a graph G and an integer $k > 0$, determine whether G has a simple path of at least k edges. (A path is *simple* if no vertex appears twice.)

(b) TRAVELING SALESMAN PROBLEM (TSP): Given a complete graph $G = (V, E)$ with a cost function $c : E \to \mathbf{N}$, and an integer k, determine whether there is a tour (i.e., a Hamiltonian cycle) of G with the total edge cost bounded by k.

(c) GRAPH ISOMORPHISM (GISO): Given two graphs G and H, determine whether G is isomorphic to H. (Two graphs $G = (V_1, E_1)$ and $H = (V_2, E_2)$ are *isomorphic* if $|V_1| = |V_2|$, and there is a one-to-one, onto mapping $f : V_1 \to V_2$ such that $\{u, v\} \in E_1$ if and only if $\{f(u), f(v)\} \in E_2$. The function f is called an isomorphism.)

(d) BOUNDED PCP: Given a finite set of ordered pairs $(x_1, y_1), \ldots, (x_n, y_n)$ of strings over an alphabet Σ, and an integer K (in the unary form 1^K), determine whether there is a finite sequence of integers $(i_1, i_2, \ldots, i_m)$, with each $i_j \in \{1, \ldots, n\}$ and $m \leq K$, such that

$$x_{i_1} x_{i_2} \cdots x_{i_m} = y_{i_1} y_{i_2} \cdots y_{i_m}.$$

(e) BOUNDED TILING: Given a finite number of types $t_0, t_1, \ldots, t_n$ of colored tiles and an integer K (in the unary form 1^K), determine whether it is possible to cover a $K \times K$ square by colored tiles of these types, starting with a tile of type t_0 at the lower left corner. (See Exercise 6 of Section 5.6 for the details of the definition.)

★ 8. Let A be an $n \times n$ integer matrix, and b an n-dimensional integer vector. Let α be the maximum absolute value of integers in A and b, and $q = \max\{m, n\}$.

(a) Show that if B is a square submatrix of A, then $|\det(B)| \leq (\alpha q)^q$, where $\det(B)$ denotes the determinant of matrix B.

(b) Show that if $\mathrm{rank}(A) = r < m$, then there exists a nonzero vector z such that $Az = 0$ and the maximum absolute value of integers in z is bounded by $(\alpha q)^q$.

(c) Assume that $Ax \geq b$ has an integer solution x. Let a_i denote the ith row of A, b_i the ith component of b, and e_j the jth m-dimensional unit vector (i.e., all components of e_j is 0, except that the jth component is 1). Let x be a solution for $Ax \geq b$ that maximizes the number of elements in the following set:

$$\mathcal{A}_x = \{a_i \mid b_i \leq a_i x \leq b_i + (\alpha q)^{q+1}, 1 \leq i \leq n\}$$
$$\cup \ \{e_j \mid |x_j| \leq (\alpha q)^q, 1 \leq j \leq m\}.$$

Prove that the rank of $\mathcal{A}_x$ is m.

(d) Use (c) above to prove Lemma 7.14.

7.2 Polynomial-Time Reducibility

We have seen, in Section 5.4, that the technique of reducibility is useful in proving a problem undecidable. Namely, suppose we know that A is undecidable and $A \leq_m B$, then B is also undecidable. In this section, we extend the notion of reducibility to a polynomial time-bounded version and apply it to show that many problems in *NP* have the *same* computational complexity, in the sense that their deterministic time complexity is within a polynomial factor of each other.

Let $A, B \subseteq \Sigma^*$ be two languages. We say set A is *polynomial-time many-one reducible* (or, simply, *polynomial-time reducible*) to B, and write $A \leq_m^P B$, if there exists a polynomial-time computable function $f : \Sigma^* \to \Sigma^*$ such that for every $x \in \Sigma^*$,

$$x \in A \iff f(x) \in B.$$

That is, $A \leq_m^P B$ if $A \leq_m B$ by a polynomial-time computable reduction function f. The following properties are analogous to Propositions 5.24 and 5.26:

Proposition 7.19 *(a)* $A \leq_m^P A$ *for all sets A.*

(b) If $A \leq_m^P B$ and $B \leq_m^P C$, then $A \leq_m^P C$.

(c) If $B \in P$ and $A \leq_m^P B$, then $A \in P$.

(d) If $B \in NP$ and $A \leq_m^P B$, then $A \in NP$.

(e) If $B \in PSPACE$ and $A \leq_m^P B$ then $A \in PSPACE$.

Proof. The proofs are essentially the same as Propositions 5.24 and 5.26. The main observation is that the composition of two polynomial functions is still a polynomial and, hence, that the composition of two polynomial-time computable functions is still polynomial-time computable.   □

We first present a few simple reductions among problems of similar forms to demonstrate the basic ideas of polynomial-time reductions. Recall the problem LP defined in Exercise 7(a) of Section 7.1.

Example 7.20 HC $\leq_m^P$ LP.

Proof. Let $G = (V, E)$ be an input instance of HC. We need to find a graph $G' = (V', E')$ and an integer $k > 0$ such that G contains a Hamiltonian cycle if and only if G' has a simple path of length k. In addition, the graph G' and integer k must be computable from graph G in polynomial time.

Note that a Hamiltonian cycle is a simple path except that the starting vertex and the ending vertex are the same. Thus, this construction is very simple: Assume that $V = \{v_1, \ldots, v_n\}$. Then, we let $V' = V \cup \{v_0, u_0, u_1\}$ and

$$E' = E \cup \{\{v_0, v_i\} \mid \{v_1, v_i\} \in E\} \cup \{\{u_0, v_0\}, \{u_1, v_1\}\}.$$

We also let $k = n + 2$.

Now, suppose that G has a Hamiltonian cycle $(v_1, v_{i_2}, \ldots, v_{i_n}, v_1)$, then the path $(u_1, v_1, v_{i_2}, \ldots, v_{i_n}, v_0, u_0)$ in G' has length $n + 2$. Conversely, we note that G' contains only $n + 3$ vertices, and so any simple path of length $n + 2$

in G' must pass through each vertex exactly once. Since both vertices u_1 and u_0 are of degree one, the path must be $(u_1, v_1, v_{i_2}, \ldots, v_{i_n}, v_0, u_0)$ for some permutation $(i_2, \ldots, i_n)$ of $\{2, 3, \ldots, n\}$. Furthermore, $(v_{i_n}, v_0) \in E'$ implies $(v_{i_n}, v_1) \in E$. Therefore, $(v_1, v_{i_2}, \ldots, v_{i_n}, v_1)$ is a Hamiltonian cycle in G.

The above proved that $G \in$ HC if and only if $(G', k) \in$ LP. In addition, it is clear the construction can be easily done in polynomial time. Therefore, this is a polynomial-time reduction from HC to LP.   □

We say two problems A and B are *polynomial-time equivalent* (under the reduction $\leq_m^P$), and write $A \equiv_m^P B$, if $A \leq_m^P B$ and $B \leq_m^P A$.

Example 7.21 VC $\equiv_m^P$ IS.

Proof. We observe that problems VC and IS have a very simple relation: A set $A \subseteq V$ is a vertex cover of the graph $G = (V, E)$ if and only if the set $V - A$ is an independent set of G. From this observation, we can see that the mapping from (G, k) to $(G, |V| - k)$ is a reduction for both IS $\leq_m^P$ VC and VC $\leq_m^P$ IS.   □

We have defined the problem GIso in Exercise 7(c) of Section 7.1. A variation of the problem GIso is the graph isomorphism problem over directed graphs.

DIGRAPH ISOMORPHISM (DGIso): Given two digraphs $G_1 = (V_1, A_1)$ and $G_2 = (V_2, A_2)$, determine whether there is a one-to-one, onto function $f : V_1 \to V_2$ such that $(u, v) \in A_1$ if and only if $(f(u), f(v)) \in A_2$.

Example 7.22 GIso $\equiv_m^P$ DGIso.

Proof. We first consider the reduction from GIso to DGIso: For any two undirected graphs $G_1 = (V_1, E_1)$ and $G_2 = (V_2, E_2)$, we construct two directed graphs $G_1' = (V_1, E_1')$ and $G_2' = (V_2, E_2')$, with

$$E_i' = \{(u, v), (v, u) \mid u, v \in V_i, \{u, v\} \in E_i\},$$

for $i = 1, 2$. Then, it is clear that G_1 and G_2 are isomorphic if and only if G_1' and G_2' are isomorphic.

For the reduction DGIso $\leq_m^P$ GIso, suppose that we are given two digraphs $G_1 = (V_1, E_1)$ and $G_2 = (V_2, E_2)$. For each digraph G_i, $i \in \{1, 2\}$, we construct an undirected graph $G_i' = (V_i', E_i')$ by replacing each edge $(u, v) \in E_i$ by a subgraph $H_{u,v}$ of nine vertices, with two of the vertices identified with u and v (see Figure 7.3). It is clear that if f is an isomorphism function between G_1 and G_2, then the corresponding mapping g which maps each $H_{u,v}$ to $H_{f(u),f(v)}$ is an isomorphism between G_1' and G_2'. On the other hand,

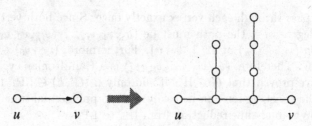

Figure 7.3: The subgraph $H_{u,v}$.

suppose that g is an isomorphism between G'_1 and G'_2. Then, it is easy to see that each subgraph $H_{u,v}$, with $u, v \in V_1$, must be mapped to a subgraph $H_{y,z}$, with $y, z \in V_2$. In addition, by the design of the subgraphs $H_{u,v}$, the corresponding mapping between G_1 and G_2 must be an isomorphism.

It is clear that the above reductions can be constructed in polynomial time. So, we conclude that GIso $\equiv_m^P$ DGIso.   □

Next, we introduce a subproblem of SAT, called 3SAT, which is very useful in the study of the *NP* theory. We first introduce more notations about Boolean formulas. In a Boolean formula, we define a *literal* to be a variable x_i or its negation $\overline{x}_i$. We say a Boolean formula F is an *elementary sum* if it is a sum of literals, and it is a *CNF (conjunctive normal form)* if it is a product of elementary sums. Each elementary sum C which occurs as a factor of a CNF F must have the property of $[C = 0 \Rightarrow F = 0]$. Such an elementary sum is called a *clause* of the Boolean function F. A CNF F is called a *3-CNF* if each clause of F contains exactly three literals about three distinct variables. That is, a 3-CNF formula must have the following form:

$$(z_{i_1} + z_{i_2} + z_{i_3})(z_{i_4} + z_{i_5} + z_{i_6}) \cdots (z_{i_{3m-2}} + z_{i_{3m-1}} + z_{i_{3m}}),$$

where each z_j is either a variable x_j or its negation $\overline{x}_j$.

The following are two subproblems of SAT:

CNF-SAT: Given a CNF F, determine whether F is satisfiable.

3SAT: Given a 3-CNF F, determine whether F is satisfiable.

Example 7.23 SAT $\leq_m^P$ CNF-SAT.

Proof. Define

$$c(x, y, z) = (x + y + \overline{z})(\overline{x} + z)(\overline{y} + z).$$

Then, it is easy to check that

(a) An assignment t satisfies $c(x, y, z)$ if and only if $t(x) + t(y) = t(z)$.

(b) An assignment t satisfies $c(\overline{x}, \overline{y}, \overline{z})$ if and only if $t(x) \cdot t(y) = t(z)$.

Now, for each Boolean formula F, we construct a CNF F^* as follows:

(1) Initially, set $F^* := 1$.

(2) While F contains at least one operator $+$ or $\cdot$, do the following:

    (2.1) Select a subformula $x + y$ (or, xy) of F, where x and y are two literals. Let G be the Boolean formula obtained by replacing the subformula $x + y$ (or, respectively, xy) in F by a new variable z. Also, Set $G^* := F^* \cdot c(x, y, z)$ (or, respectively, $F^* \cdot c(\overline{x}, \overline{y}, \overline{z})$).

    (2.2) Reset $F := G$, and $F^* := G^*$.

(3) Let $F^* := F^* \cdot F$. (*Note*: F must be a single literal.)

It is clear that the final F^* is a CNF formula. By the observations (a) and (b), it is easy to see that at the end of step (2.1), we must have the relation that FF^* is satisfiable if and only if GG^* is satisfiable. Note that, at the beginning, FF^* is just the original input formula F and, at the end, GG^* is the output formula F^*. Thus, we have that the input F is satisfiable if and only if the output F^* is satisfiable. Furthermore, the while loop will be executed at most $|F|$ times, and so it is a polynomial-time algorithm. It follows that the mapping from F to F^* is a polynomial-time reduction from SAT to CNF-SAT. $\qquad\square$

Note that the above reduction actually reduces a Boolean formula F to a CNF F^* with each clause in F^* having at most three literals. So, it is easy to modify this reduction to SAT $\leq_m^P$ 3SAT (see Exercise 1 of this section).

In the above examples, the two problems involved in the reductions have similar forms. Therefore, the reductions are just simple local changes on problem instances. When two problems in question are of different forms, the reduction between them are usually more complicated. However, there are some basic ideas we can apply. First, we note that a reduction function f for $A \leq_m^P B$ is an efficient way to transform a problem instance of A to a problem instance of B. Thus, if we know how to encode the data structures of problem A in terms of data structures of problem B, then the reduction f may become simple. For instance, we have seen, through the study of logical puzzles in the last section, that Boolean formulas and linear inqualities are useful tools to encode logical and numerical relations. Using this expressive power of Boolean formulas and linear inqualities, reductions from many problems in NP to SAT and IP are easy to construct.

Example 7.24 VC $\leq_m^P$ IP.

Proof. Let (G, k) be an instance of VC, where $G = (V, E)$ is a graph and k is a positive integer. Suppose $V = \{v_1, \cdots, v_n\}$. We need to define an instance of IP that encodes the condition of a vertex cover C of G. First, for each vertex v_i, $1 \leq i \leq n$, we define a variable x_i. Then, we define the following inequalities:

(1) $0 \leq x_i \leq 1$, for $i = 1, \ldots, n$.

(2) $x_i + x_j \geq 1$, for each $\{v_i, v_j\} \in E$.

(3) $x_1 + x_2 + \cdots + x_n \leq k$.

We note that with condition (1), a solution to the above system of inequalities encodes a subset C of V, with $x_i = 1$ indicating that $v_i \in C$. Under this interpretation, condition (2) means that each edge in E contains at least one vertex in C, and condition (3) means that $|C| \leq k$. Together, we see that the above system of inequalities has a solution $\{x_1, \ldots, x_n\}$ if and only if $C = \{v_i \in V \mid x_i = 1\}$ is a vertex cover of G of size $\leq k$. Therefore, this is a reduction from VC to IP.

Finally, we observe that the mapping from (G, k) to the above inequalities can be easily done in polynomial time. We conclude that VC $\leq_m^P$ IP. $\quad\square$

Example 7.25 3DM $\leq_m^P$ SAT.

Proof. Given an instance $W \subseteq A \times B \times C$ of the problem 3DM, we need to construct a Boolean formula F such that $F \in$ SAT if and only if $W \in$ 3DM. First, for each $w \in W$, we define a Boolean variable x_w. Then, we formulate the statement that W contains a three-dimensional matching W' as a Boolean formula F over variables x_w, with $x_w = 1$ indicating $w \in W'$. That is, under this interpretation, the formula F asserts:

(1) Each $a \in A \cup B \cup C$ occurs in some $w \in W'$; and

(2) An element $a \in A \cup B \cup C$ cannot occur in two different $u, v \in W'$.

For each $w \in W$ and each $a \in A \cup B \cup c$, we write $a \in w$ to denote that a is one of the three elements in w. Then, condition (1) can be formulated as

$$F_1 = \prod_{a \in A \cup B \cup C} \sum_{w \in W, a \in w} x_w,$$

and condition (2) can be formulated as

$$F_2 = \prod_{a \in A \cup B \cup C} \prod_{\substack{u, v \in W, u \neq v \\ a \in u \cap v}} (\overline{x}_u + \overline{x}_v).$$

The required formula is $F = F_1 F_2$.

For any $W' \subseteq W$, define an assignment $t_{W'}$, with $t_{W'}(x_w) = 1$ if and only if $w \in W'$. Then, under the above interpretation, we can see that W contains a three-dimensional matching W' if and only if $t_{W'}$ satisfies F. Furthermore, it is easy to see that formula F can be constructed from W in polynomial time. So, we conclude that 3DM $\leq_m^P$ SAT. $\quad\square$

Another idea for the construction of polynomial-time reductions among problems in *NP* is from Theorem 7.1. In Theorem 7.1, we showed that, for a set $A \in NP$, each instance $x \in A$ has a witness that certifies that this instance belongs to set A. Although two problems in NP may look very different, they must share this common property. Since a reduction function f for $A \leq_m^P B$ must map an instance x in A with witness w_x to an instance y in B with witness w_y, the idea of the construction, then, is to design the function f to *preserve* the witnesses of the two problems. That is, the function f not only maps x to y, but also maps w_x to w_y. We illustrate this idea in the following examples.

Example 7.26 $3\text{SAT} \leq_m^P \text{VC}$.

Proof. To show that $3\text{SAT} \leq_m^P \text{VC}$, we need to construct, from a 3-CNF formula F, a graph G_F and an integer K such that F is satisfiable if and only if G_F has a vertex cover of size K. The witness to a Boolean formula F in 3SAT is a truth assignment, and the witness to (G_F, K) in VC is a vertex cover $S \subseteq V$ of size K. So, the main idea of the design for G_F is to create a subgraph H_1 in G_F that corresponds to the variables in F such that a possible vertex cover of H_1 corresponds to an assignment of variables in F.

More precisely, suppose that F has m clauses $C_1, \ldots, C_m$ over n variables $x_1, \ldots, x_n$. For each variable x_i in F, we design two vertices v_i and $\overline{v}_i$ in H_1 with an edge between them. Then, any minimum vertex cover S_1 of H_1 must contain exactly one of these two vertices for every i, $1 \leq i \leq n$. In other words, each minimum cover S_1 corresponds to an assignment t on variables, with $t(x_i) = 1$ if and only if $v_i \in S_1$.

In addition to H_1, we also need a second part H_2 of G_F that relates the vertices in H_1 in a way like the clauses in F relate the variables $x_1, \ldots, x_n$. That is, we need to encode the clauses $C_1, \ldots, C_m$ in H_2, based on the above interpretation between vertex covers S_1 of H_1 and assignments t on variables $\{x_1, \ldots, x_n\}$. To do so, we create a triangle T_j for each clause C_j, $1 \leq j \leq m$, and connects T_j with H_1 in such a way that if variable x_i (or, its negation $\overline{x}_i$) is in C_j then T_j is connected to v_i (or, respectively, to $\overline{v}_i$).

Together, the whole graph G_F can be described as follows:

(1) G_F has $2n + 3m$ vertices: $v_i, \overline{v}_i$, for $1 \leq i \leq n$, and $u_{j,1}, u_{j,2}, u_{j,3}$ for $1 \leq j \leq m$.

(2) For each i, $1 \leq i \leq n$, there is an edge between vertices v_i and $\overline{v}_i$.

(3) For each j, $1 \leq j \leq m$, there are three edges between $u_{j,1}, u_{j,2}$ and $u_{j,3}$.

(4) For each pair (i, j), with $1 \leq i \leq n$ and $1 \leq j \leq m$, if x_i (or $\overline{x}_i$) is the kth literal of C_j, then there is an edge between v_i (or, $\overline{v}_i$) and $u_{j,k}$, where $k = 1, 2$ or 3.

Figure 7.4 shows the graph G_F with respect to the formula $F = (x_1 + x_2 + x_3)(\overline{x}_1 + \overline{x}_2 + x_3)$.

We observe that any vertex cover S of G_F must include at least one vertex in each pair v_i and $\overline{v}_i$, and at least two vertices in each triangle $\{u_{j,1}, u_{j,2}, u_{j,3}\}$. So, it includes at least $n + 2m$ vertices.

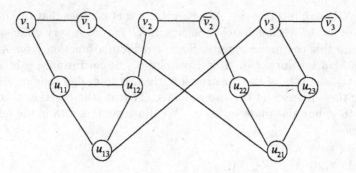

Figure 7.4: The graph G_F.

From this basic relation between F and G_F, it is easy to see that F is satisfiable if and only if G_F has a vertex cover of size at most $n + 2m$. First, suppose that F is satisfiable. Then, there exists a truth assignment t for F. From this t, we can find a vertex cover S for G_F as follows:

(a) For each i, $1 \leq i \leq n$, S contains v_i if $t(x_i) = 1$, and S contains $\overline{v}_i$ if $t(x_i) = 0$.

(b) For each j, $1 \leq j \leq m$, let k be the least integer in $\{1, 2, 3\}$ such that the kth literal of C_j is true under t. Add $u_{j,\ell}$ to S, for $\ell \in \{1, 2, 3\} - \{k\}$.

To check that S is indeed a vertex cover, we note that the only edges which are not obviously covered by S are edges between a vertex v_i (or, $\overline{v}_i$) and a vertex $u_{j,k}$. Note, however, that if such an edge exists, it means x_i (or, respectively, $\overline{x}_i$) is a literal of clause C_j. By the design (b) above, either this literal is true under t and, hence, x_i (or, respectively, $\overline{x}_i$) is in S, or it is false under t and then $u_{j,k}$ must be in S. This shows that S is a vertex cover of G_F.

Conversely, suppose that G_F has a vertex cover S of size at most $n + 2m$. From the basic observation, we know that S is of size exactly $n + 2m$ and includes exactly one vertex from each pair v_i and $\overline{v}_i$ and exactly two vertices from each triangle $u_{j,1}, u_{j,2}$ and $u_{j,3}$. Define an assignment t by $t(x_i) = 1$ if and only if $v_i \in S$, for $i = 1, \ldots, n$. We claim that t satisfies F. To see this, we note that for each j, $1 \leq j \leq m$, if $u_{j,k} \notin S$, and if the kth literal of C_j is x_i (or, $\overline{x}_i$), then there is an edge between v_i (or, respectively, $\overline{v}_i$) and $u_{j,k}$, and so we must have $v_i \in S$ (or, respectively, $\overline{v}_i \in S$). By the definition of t, the kth literal thus is satisfied. Since for each j, there is exactly one vertex $u_{j,k} \notin S$, we know that each clause is satisfied by t. Thus, t satisfies F.

Finally, we observe that the above construction from F to $(G_F, n + 2m)$ can clearly be done in polynomial time. Hence, we have proved that 3SAT $\leq^P_m$ VC. $\square$

Example 7.27 3SAT $\leq^P_m$ HC.

Proof. Let F be a 3-CNF formula of n variables $x_1, \ldots, x_n$ and m clauses

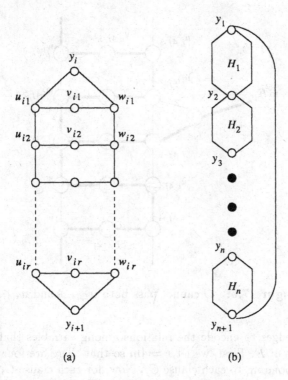

Figure 7.5: The graphs H_i and H.

$C_1, \ldots, C_m$. We need to construct a graph G_F such that $F \in 3\text{SAT}$ if and only if $G_F \in \text{HC}$. Again, we try to design a reduction f that preserves the witnesses. Here, a witness to a formula F in 3SAT is a truth assignment, and a witness to a graph G in HC is a Hamiltonian cycle in G. So, the basic idea is to divide the graph G_F into n subgraphs H_i, $1 \le i \le n$, each having two different Hamiltonian paths, corresponding to two assignments to variable x_i. Altogether, there are 2^n different Hamiltonian paths, corresponding to 2^n different assignments on variables $x_1, x_2, \ldots, x_n$.

To be more precise, our graph G_F contains n subgraphs $H_1, \ldots, H_n$. Each subgraph H_i is a ladder of $3r + 2$ vertices, as shown in Figure 7.5(a), where r is an integer parameter to be determined later. We identify the bottom vertex y_{i+1} of subgraph H_i with the top vertex of H_{i+1}, and join vertex y_1 with vertex y_{n+1} by an edge. Then, we obtain a graph H of G_F, as shown in Figure 7.5(b).

We note that each subgraph H_i has two Hamiltonian paths from y_i to y_{i+1}, one beginning with the edge from y_i to $u_{i,1}$, and the other beginning with the edge from y_i to $w_{i,1}$. They correspond to the two assignments to variable x_i. So, a Hamiltonian cycle from y_1 back to y_1 corresponds to an assignment to all variables.

To complete the construction of the graph G_F, we need to design some new

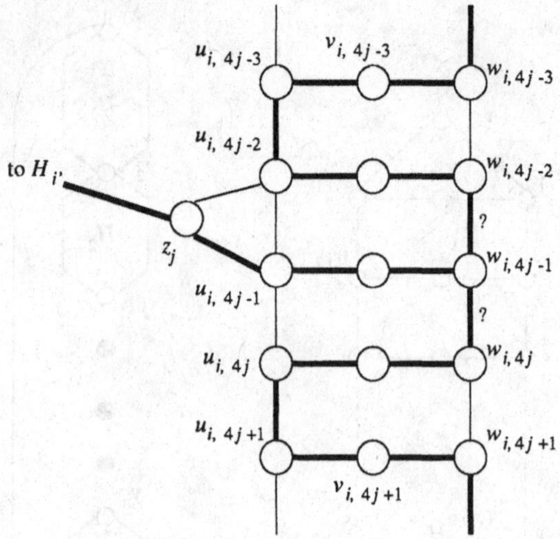

Figure 7.6: Q cannot pass both $w_{i,4j-2}$ and $w_{i,4j}$.

vertices and edges to encode the relations among variables that are defined by the clauses of F. First, we let $r = 4m$ so that there are four levels of the ladder corresponding to each clause C_j. Now, for each clause C_j, $1 \leq j \leq m$, we define a new vertex z_j. Then, we connect z_j to $u_{i,4j-1}$ and $u_{i,4j-2}$ if C_j contains literal x_i, and connect z_j to $w_{i,4j-1}$ and $w_{i,4j-2}$ if C_j contains literal $\overline{x}_i$. Thus, each z_j has degree 6.

We note that these new vertices and edges are designed in such a way that a Hamiltonian cycle of G_F must essentially follow the same path as a Hamiltonian cycle of H. That is, it must go from y_1 to y_2, passing through all vertices in H_1, then it goes from y_2 to y_3, passing through all vertices in H_2, and so on. The new vertices z_j must be visited between two vertices $u_{i,4j-1}$ and $u_{i,4j-2}$ or between two vertices $w_{i,4j-1}$ and $w_{i,4j-2}$ for some $i = 1, \ldots, n$. This fact can be verified as follows: Suppose otherwise that a Hamiltonian cycle Q contains edge $\{u_{i,4j-1}, z_j\}$ and then jumps to subgraph $H_{i'}$ for some $i' \neq i$. Since each vertex $v_{i,k}$ has only degree 2, Q must contain edges $\{u_{i,k}, v_{i,k}\}$ and $\{v_{i,k}, w_{i,k}\}$. This implies that Q must contain both edges $\{u_{i,4j-2}, u_{i,4j-3}\}$ and $\{u_{i,4j}, u_{i,4j+1}\}$. Furthermore, $w_{i,4j-1}$ and $w_{i,4j-2}$ are not connected to z_j since C_j cannot contain both x_i and $\overline{x}_i$. Thus, Q must contain both edges $\{w_{i,4j-1}, w_{i,4j}\}$ and $\{w_{i,4j-1}, w_{i,4j-2}\}$. These observations lead to a situation as shown in Figure 7.6, which is a contradiction. (In Figure 7.6, the thick lines denote the path Q.)

Now, we are ready to prove that F is satisfiable if and only if G_F has a Hamiltonian cycle. First, suppose that F is satisfiable and that t is a truth assignment for F. Let Q' be the Hamiltonian cycle of H, with the edge $\{y_i, u_{i,1}\}$ in Q' if and only if $t(x_i) = 1$, for $1 \leq i \leq n$. We then modify Q' as follows: For each vertex z_j, $1 \leq j \leq m$, find a literal in C_j which is assigned with value 1 by t. If this literal is x_i (or, $\overline{x}_i$), then Q' must contain edge $\{u_{i,4j-1}, u_{i,4j-2}\}$ (or, respectively, edge $\{w_{i,4j-1}, w_{i,4j-2}\}$); we replace this edge by two edges $\{u_{i,4j-1}, z_j\}$ and $\{z_j, u_{i,4j-2}\}$ (or, respectively, by edges $\{w_{i,4j-1}, z_j\}$ and $\{z_j, w_{i,4j-2}\}$). Clearly, after the modification, Q' becomes a cycle Q that passes through all vertices in G_F exactly once, that is, a Hamiltonian cycle of G_F.

Conversely, suppose that G_F has a Hamiltonian cycle Q. From the above analysis, we know that Q must pass through each vertex z_j *locally* through $u_{i,4j-1}$ and $u_{i,4j-2}$ or through $w_{i,4j-1}$ and $w_{i,4j-2}$. Let $t(x_i) = 1$ if and only if edge $\{y_i, u_{i,1}\}$ is in Q. Then, we claim that t satisfies every clause C_j, $1 \le j \le m$. To see this, we check that if Q contains edges $\{u_{i,4j-1}, z_j\}$ and $\{z_j, u_{i,4j-2}\}$, then x_i is a literal in C_j. In addition, Q must contain edge $\{y_i, u_{i,1}\}$ and so $t(x_i) = 1$. Similarly, if Q contains edges $\{w_{i,4j-1}, z_j\}$ and $\{z_j, w_{i,4j-2}\}$, then we must have $\overline{x}_i$ as a literal in C_j and $t(x_i) = 0$. Either way, C_j is satisfied by t.

Finally, we remark that the construction from F to graph G_F can be done in polynomial time and, hence, this is a polynomial-time reduction from 3SAT to HC. $\qquad\qquad\square$

Exercise 7.2

1. Prove that CNF-SAT $\le_m^P$ 3SAT.

2. In this exercise, we study an alternative proof for Example 7.25. Let us replace conditions (1) and (2) by condition (3): For every $a \in A \cup B \cup C$, there is a triple $w \in W'$ such that (i) $a \in w$, and (ii) if $w' \in W'$, $w' \ne w$ then $a \notin w'$. Translate this condition into a Boolean formula G over variables x_w and show that G is satisfiable if and only if W has a three-dimensional matching W'.

3. Construct the following reductions:

   (a) 3SAT $\le_m^P$ 3DM.
   (b) VC $\le_m^P$ HC.
   (c) HC $\le_m^P$ 3SAT.
   (d) VC $\le_m^P$ HS.

4. Consider the following variations of the problem 3SAT:

   3SAT-EXACTLY-ONE: Given a 3-CNF F, determine whether there is an assignment t on variables in F that assigns value TRUE to exactly one literal in each clause of F.

   3SAT-NOT-ALL: Given a 3-CNF F, determine whether there is an assignment t on variables in F that assigns value TRUE to either one or two literals (but not all three literals) in each clause of F.

Show that 3SAT, 3SAT-EXACT-ONE and 3SAT-NOT-ALL are polynomial time equivalent under $\leq_m^P$.

⋆ **5.** Consider the following problems:

SUBGRAPH ISOMORPHISM (SGIso): Given two graphs $G_1 = (V_1, E_1)$ and $G_2 = (V_2, E_2)$, determine whether there is a one-to-one mapping $f : V_1 \to V_2$ such that, for all $u, v \in V_1$, $\{u, v\} \in E_1$ implies $\{f(u), f(v)\} \in E_2$.

GRAPH AUTOMORPHISM (GAUTO): Given a graph $G = (V, E)$, determine whether there is a one-to-one function $f : V \to V$ other than the identity function such that, for all $u, v \in V$, $\{u, v\} \in E$ if and only if $\{f(u), f(v)\} \in E$.

Prove all the polynomial-time reductions you can find among the three problems GIso, SGIso and GAUTO.

7.3   Cook's Theorem

In Section 5.4, we have defined a complete r.e. set as an r.e. set A with the property that $B \leq_m A$ for all r.e. sets B. In a sense, a complete r.e. set A is the *hardest* r.e. set, meaning that if there were a TM solving problem A then every r.e. set B could be solved by a TM. We now extend this notion to the class *NP*. We say a set A is *NP-complete* if

(a) A is in *NP*; and

(b) $B \leq_m^P A$ for all $B \in NP$.

(A problem A satisfying condition (b) alone is called *NP-hard*.) So, an *NP*-complete set A is one of the hardest sets in *NP*, in the sense that if we have a deterministic polynomial-time algorithm for A, then every set in *NP* has such an algorithm and so $P = NP$. In other words, an *NP*-complete set A has the property that $A \in P$ if and only if $P = NP$.

Example 7.28 *Show that if $P = NP$, then all nonempty proper subsets A of Σ^* are NP-complete.*

Proof. Let $a_0 \in \Sigma^* - A$ and $a_1 \in A$ be two fixed string. If $P = NP$, then every set B in *NP* can be reduced to set A by the function

$$f(x) = \begin{cases} a_1, & \text{if } x \in B, \\ a_0, & \text{otherwise,} \end{cases}$$

because the question of whether $x \in B$ can be decided in polynomial time. □

Example 7.29 *If A is known to be NP-complete, is A^2 always NP-complete?*

Solution. The answer is NO if $P \neq NP$. Let $A \subseteq \{0,1\}^*$ be any *NP*-complete set. For every x, define $d(x)$ to be the string x with each symbol doubled (e.g., $d(0100) = 00110000$). Define

$$B = \{d(x) \mid x \in A\} \cup \{y \mid |y| \text{ is odd } \} \cup \{\varepsilon\}.$$

Then, B is still *NP*-complete: If $\varepsilon \in A$ then $A \leq_m^P B$ by function d; otherwise, if $\varepsilon \notin A$ then $A \leq_m^P B$ by function f, where $f(x) = d(x)$ if $x \neq \varepsilon$ and $f(\varepsilon) = d(x_0)$ for some fixed $x_0 \in \overline{A} - \{\varepsilon\}$. However, $B^2 = \{0,1\}^*$, because every string z of odd length is the concatenation of z and the empty string ε, and every nonempty string z of even length is the concatenation of two strings of odd length. □

We are going to see that most problems studied in Section 7.2 are *NP*-complete. In the following, we first show that SAT is *NP*-complete by presenting a generic reduction from a problem A in *NP* to SAT.

⋆ **Theorem 7.30** (Cook's Theorem) SAT *is NP-complete.*

Proof. We have shown in Example 7.2 that SAT is in *NP*. To prove this theorem, we need to prove that for every set A in *NP*, $A \leq_m^P$ SAT. Or, equivalently, we need to construct, from a given NTM M with a polynomial time bound $p(n)$, and a given input string $x \in \Sigma^*$, a Boolean formula F_x such that M accepts x if and only if F_x is satisfiable.

Before we describe how to construct F_x, let us study the computation of M on an input string x more carefully. First, let us assume that M is an NTM of the type defined in Section 4.1. That is, its initial state is s; its final state is h; and it has a single one-way infinite tape. (We call the leftmost cell of the tape the 0th cell, and the one to its right the first cell, etc.) Thus, its initial configuration on input x is $(s, \text{B}x\underline{\text{B}})$.

We note that if $x \in L(M)$, then there is an accepting computation path of M on x of length at most $p(n) + 1$ (i.e., containing at most $p(n) + 1$ configurations). In addition, since the tape head of M can move to the left or right at most one cell at a time, each configuration has length at most $p(n) + n + 2$.

Let $r(n) = p(n) + n + 1$. Then, $x \in L(M)$ if and only if there is a sequence of configurations $\alpha_0, \alpha_1, \ldots, \alpha_{r(n)}$ such that the following conditions hold:

(a) Each α_i contains exactly $r(n) + 1$ symbols. (We can pad extra blanks to the right, if necessary.)

(b) α_0 is the initial configuration of M on input x.

(c) $\alpha_{r(n)}$ is an accepting configuration.

(d) For any $i = 0, \ldots, r(n) - 1$, either $\alpha_i \vdash_M \alpha_{i+1}$, or α_i is an accepting configuration and $\alpha_i = \alpha_{i+1}$. (We use $\alpha_i \vdash \alpha_{i+1}$ to denote both conditions.)

To further simplify the above conditions, let us express each configuration using exactly $r(n) + 1$ symbols by attaching the state symbol q to the tape symbol a in the cell the tape head is scanning. Let Γ be the set of tape symbols used by M, and Q the set of states of M (including the halting state h). Then, each symbol in a configuration is a symbol in $\Gamma' = \Gamma \cup (Q\#\Gamma)$. That is, the configuration

$$(q, a_{i_1} a_{i_2} \cdots a_{i_{k-1}} \underline{a_{i_k}} a_{i_{k+1}} \cdots a_{i_m})$$

is expressed by exactly m symbols:

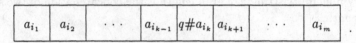

Let $s_{i,j}$ denote the jth symbol of the configuration α_i. Then, the above condition can be restated as follows: $x \in L(M)$ if and only if there exists $(r(n)+1)^2$ symbols $s_{i,j} \in \Gamma'$, $i, j \in \{0, 1, \ldots, r(n)\}$, such that

  (1) For each i, $0 \le i \le r(n)$, exactly one symbol of $s_{i,0}, s_{i,1}, \ldots, s_{i,r(n)}$ is in $Q\#\Gamma$. (So, each string $s_{i,0}s_{i,1} \cdots s_{i,r(n)}$ is a legal configuration.)

  (2) The string $s_{0,0}s_{0,1} \cdots s_{0,r(n)}$ is the initial configuration of M on input x.

  (3) $s_{r(n),j} = h\#a$ for some j, $0 \le j \le r(n)$, and some $a \in \Gamma$. (So, the string $s_{r(n),0}s_{r(n),1} \cdots s_{r(n),r(n)}$ is an accepting configuration.)

  (4) For each i, $0 \le i \le r(n) - 1$, either $s_{i+1,0}s_{i+1,1} \cdots s_{i+1,r(n)}$ is a successor configuration of $s_{i,0}s_{i,1} \cdots s_{i,r(n)}$, or they are an identical accepting configuration.

Let S be the $(r(n)+1) \times (r(n)+1)$ matrix with $s_{i,j}$ as its element in the ith row and jth column. Then, conditions (1)–(3) are just simple conditions on this matrix, which are easy to be translated to Boolean formulas. Condition (4) is, however, too complicated and needs to be replaced by more concrete subconditions. The main idea here is that we can check whether $\alpha_i \vdash \alpha_{i+1}$ by examining every four-square, ⊞-shaped window over the ith and $(i + 1)$st rows of the matrix S. In other words, if the matrix S satisfies condition (1), then condition (4) is equivalent to the following condition (4′):

  (4′) For every pair (i, j), with $0 \le i \le r(n) - 1$ and $0 \le j \le r(n)$, if $s_{i,j} = a$, $s_{i+1,j-1} = b$, $s_{i+1,j} = c$ and $s_{i+1,j+1} = d$, then (a, b, c, d) must satisfy one of the following conditions:

     (4.1) $a = q\#u \in (Q - \{h\})\#\Gamma$, $b = p\#v \in Q\#\Gamma$, $c, d \in \Gamma$, and $(p, c, L) \in \delta(q, u)$.

     (4.2) $a = q\#u \in (Q - \{h\})\#\Gamma$, $d = p\#v \in Q\#\Gamma$, $b, c, \in \Gamma$, and $(p, c, R) \in \delta(q, u)$.

     (4.3) $a = c \in \Gamma$.

     (4.4) $a \in \Gamma$ and $c = p\#a \in Q\#\Gamma$.

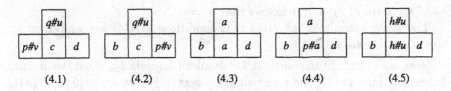

Figure 7.7: The five conditions.

(4.5) $a = c = h\#u$ for some $u \in \Gamma$.

(In the above, we assume that $s_{i,-1} = s_{i,r(n)+1} = \mathbf{B}$ for all i.)

The above five conditions are shown in Figure 7.7.

We now prove that (4) is equivalent to (4'), if condition (1) is satisfied. Assume that S satisfies condition (1); that is, each row of S is a configuration. We let α_i denote the ith row of S, for $i = 0,\ldots,r(n)$. We fix an $i \in \{0,\ldots,r(n) - 1\}$, and call a ⊞-shaped window *the jth window* if the top symbol of the window is the symbol $s_{i,j}$.

First assume that $\alpha_i \vdash \alpha_{i+1}$. Then, there are three possible cases:

Case 1. $\alpha_i \vdash \alpha_{i+1}$ by the application of an instruction of the form $(p, c, L) \in \delta(q, u)$ of M. Then, α_i contains a unique symbol $q\#u$ in $Q\#\Gamma$; for instance, $s_{i,j} = q\#u$. Then, we know that $s_{i,k} = s_{i+1,k}$ for $k \neq j - 1, j$. Therefore, the kth window is of the form (4.3), for $k \neq j - 1, j$. Furthermore, the jth window must be of the form (4.1), and the $(j - 1)$st window must be of the form (4.4). So, each window is of one of the five forms.

Case 2. $\alpha_i \vdash \alpha_{i+1}$ by the application of an instruction of the form $(p, c, R) \in \delta(q, u)$ of M. This case is similar to Case 1. Suppose that $s_{i,j} = q\#u$. Then, we can verify that all windows are of the form (4.3), except that the jth window is of the form (4.2), and the $(j + 1)$st window is of the form (4.4).

Case 3. α_i is an accepting configuration and $\alpha_i = \alpha_{i+1}$. Suppose that $s_{i,j} = h\#u$ for some $u \in \Gamma$. Then, all windows are of the form (4.3), except for the jth window, which is of the form (4.5).

Conversely, assume that every window over the ith and $(i + 1)$st rows of S is in one of the five forms. Assume that $s_{i,j} \in Q\#\Gamma$. Again, there are three cases.

Case 1. The jth window is of the form (4.1). From condition (1), we know that each row has exactly one state symbol. Therefore, the $(j - 1)$st window must be of the form (4.4), and all other windows must be of the form (4.3). By condition (4,3), we know that $s_{i,k} = s_{i+1,k}$ for $k \neq j, j - 1$. Also, by conditions (4.1) and (4.4), we know that the change from $(s_{i,j-1}, s_{i,j})$ to $(s_{i+1,j-1}, s_{i+1,j})$ follows an instruction $(p, c, L) \in \delta(q, u)$ in M. It follows that $\alpha_i \vdash \alpha_{i+1}$.

Case 2. The jth window is of the form (4.2). This is similar to Case 1.

Case 3. The jth window is of the form (4.5). Then, all other windows must be of the form (4.3), and it follows that $\alpha_i = \alpha_{i+1}$.

The above completes the proof that conditions (1)–(4) are equivalent to conditions (1)–(3) and (4′).

Now, we are ready to construct the Boolean formula F_x. First, we define, for each symbol a in Γ', and each pair of integers (i,j) with $i,j \in \{0,\dots,r(n)\}$, a Boolean variable $y_{i,j,a}$. In the design of the formula F_x, we will interprete an assignment $y_{i,j,a} = 1$ to mean that $s_{i,j} = a$. Based on this interpretation, the above four conditions on matrix S can be easily translated to the following five conditions on variables $y_{i,j,a}$:

(0) For each pair (i,j), with $i,j \in \{0,\dots,r(n)\}$, there exists exactly one $a \in \Gamma'$ such that $y_{i,j,a} = 1$. (This condition fixes the relation between variables $y_{i,j,a}$ and symbols $s_{i,j}$.)

(1) For each i, with $0 \le i \le r(n)$, there exists exactly one j, $0 \le j \le r(n)$, and one $a \in Q\#\Gamma$ such that $y_{i,j,a} = 1$.

(2) $y_{0,j,a} = 1$ if and only if the the jth symbol of the initial configuration is a.

(3) $y_{r(n),j,h\#a} = 1$ for some $j \in \{0,\dots,r(n)\}$ and some $a \in \Gamma$.

(4) For each pair (i,j), with $0 \le i \le r(n) - 1$ and $0 \le j \le r(n)$,

$$y_{i,j,a} \; y_{i+1,j-1,b} \; y_{i+1,j,c} \; y_{i+1,j+1,d} = 1$$

if and only if (a,b,c,d) satisfies one of the conditions (4.1)–(4.5).

For each condition (k), $k = 0,\dots,4$, we define, in the following, a Boolean formula f_k over variables $y_{i,j,a}$ such that f_k is satisfied if and only if condition (k) holds for variables $y_{i,j,a}$. (In f_2, we write x_t to denote the tth symbol of input x.)

$$f_0 = \prod_{i=0}^{r(n)} \prod_{j=0}^{r(n)} \left[\left(\sum_{a\in\Gamma'} y_{i,j,a} \right) \prod_{a,b\in\Gamma',a\neq b} (\overline{y}_{i,j,a} + \overline{y}_{i,j,b}) \right].$$

$$f_1 = \prod_{i=0}^{r(n)} \left[\left(\sum_{j=0}^{r(n)} \sum_{a\in Q\#\Gamma} y_{i,j,a} \right) \prod_{0\le j<j'\le r(n)} \prod_{a,b\in Q\#\Gamma} (\overline{y}_{i,j,a} + \overline{y}_{i,j',b}) \right].$$

$$f_2 = y_{0,0,\mathrm{B}} \; y_{0,1,x_1} \; y_{0,2,x_2} \cdots y_{0,n,x_n} \; y_{0,n+1,s\#\mathrm{B}} \; y_{0,n+2,\mathrm{B}} \cdots y_{0,r(n),\mathrm{B}}.$$

$$f_3 = \sum_{j=0}^{r(n)} \sum_{a\in\Gamma} y_{r(n),j,h\#a}.$$

$$f_4 = \prod_{i=0}^{r(n)-1} \prod_{j=0}^{r(n)} \sum_{(a,b,c,d)\in T} y_{i,j,a} \; y_{i+1,j-1,b} \; y_{i+1,j,c} \; y_{i+1,j+1,d},$$

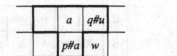

Figure 7.8: These two windows cannot detect the illegal transition.

where $T = \{(a, b, c, d) \in (\Gamma')^4 \mid (a, b, c, d) \text{ satisfies one of the conditions } (4.1)-(4.5)\}$, and $y_{i,-1,a}$ and $y_{i,r(n)+1,a}$ denote the constant 1 if $a = \mathbf{B}$, and denote the constant 0 if $a \neq \mathbf{B}$.

Now, we let $F_x = f_0\, f_1\, f_2\, f_3\, f_4$. From the above analysis, we see that F_x is satisfiable if and only if $x \in L(M)$. Thus, this is a reduction from $L(M)$ to SAT.

Finally, we remark that the construction can be done in polynomial time, as the lengths of the formulas f_k, for $k = 0, \ldots, 4$, are in $O(m^4 \cdot (r(n))^3)$, where m is the number of symbols in Γ', and the definition of each f_k is constructive. We conclude that $L(M) \leq_m^P$ SAT. □

The critical part of the above proof is the relation between condition (4) and condition (4'). In the following examples, we study some alternatives to condition (4').

Example 7.31 *In the proof of Cook's theorem, we have used conditions* (4.1) *– (4.5) on* ⊞*-shaped windows over matrix S to satisfy condition* (4). *Show that if we, instead, work with* ⊟*-shaped windows over matrix S, then no conditions on these windows can satisfy condition* (4). *In other words, show that the following relation does not hold for any subset* $T \subseteq (\Gamma')^4$:

$$\left(\prod_{j=0}^{r(n)} \sum_{(a,b,c,d)\in T} y_{i,j-1,a}\, y_{i,j,b}\, y_{i,j+1,c}\, y_{i+1,j,d}\right) = 1 \iff \alpha_i \vdash \alpha_{i+1},$$

where α_i denotes the ith configuration corresponding to the assignments to variables $y_{i,j,a}$.

Proof. Note that M is an NTM, and so $\delta(q, u)$ may contain more than one triple. Suppose that $\delta(q, u) = \{(p, v, L), (r, w, L)\}$, with $p \neq r$ and $v \neq w$. Then, consider the case where $s_{i,j-1} = a$, $s_{i,j} = q\#u$, $s_{i+1,j-1} = p\#a$ and $s_{i+1,j} = w$, for some $a \in \Gamma$. It is clear that $\neg(\alpha_i \vdash \alpha_{i+1})$. However, both the $(j-1)$st window and the jth window are clearly legal (see Figure 7.8). Thus, if the set T contains all legal windows, it cannot tell that $\neg(\alpha_i \vdash \alpha_{i+1})$. □

Example 7.32 *Show that, in the proof of Cook's theorem, function f_1 is necessary. That is, no definition of subset T can make the following true: $F'_x = f_0 f_2 f_3 f_4$ is satisfiable if and only if $x \in L(M)$.*

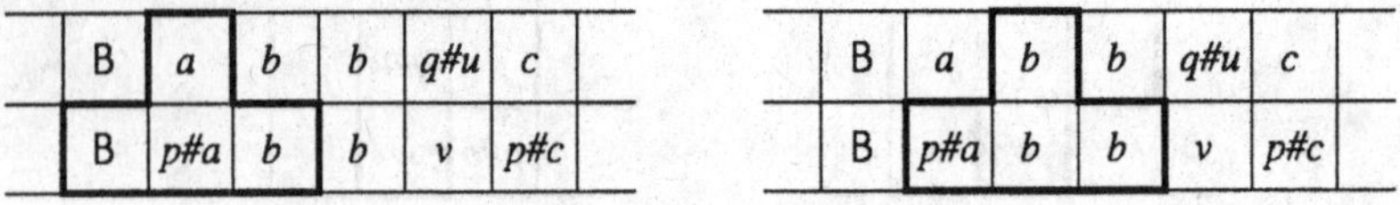

B	a	b	b	q#u	c
B	p#a	b	b	v	p#c

B	a	b	b	q#u	c
B	p#a	b	b	v	p#c

Figure 7.9:   Example 7.32

Proof. Without condition (1), conditions (4) and (4′) are not equivalent, no matter how we define subset T. We note that in order to satisfy f_4 when $\alpha_i \vdash \alpha_{i+1}$, we must define T to include conditions (4.1)–(4.5). Now, consider the case shown in Figure 7.9. It is apparent that the second row cannot be derived from the first row, since the second row has two symbols in $Q\#\Gamma$. However, all windows over this submatrix are legal according to T.   □

* **Example 7.33** *In the proof of Cook's theorem, it is possible to remove condition (1), as long as we replace condition (4′) by a new condition (4″) over six-square,* ⊞ *-shaped windows. Find the subconditions over the six-square,* ⊞ *-shaped windows that make (4″) equivalent to condition (4), without the assumption of condition (1).*

Solution. There are twelve possible legal, six-square windows with $s_{i,j-1} = a$, $s_{i,j} = b$, $s_{i,j+1} = c$, $s_{i+1,j-1} = d$, $s_{i+1,j} = e$ and $s_{i+1,j+1} = g$. We group them in three cases:

   Case 1.   There is an instruction $(p, v, L) \in \delta(q, u)$, and the window is consistent with this instruction. We show the four corresponding windows in the first row of Figure 7.10.

   Case 2.   There is an instruction $(p, v, R) \in \delta(q, u)$, and the window is consistent with this instruction. We show the four corresponding windows in the second row of Figure 7.10.

   Case 3.   All of a, b, c are in $\Gamma \cup (\{h\}\#\Gamma)$, and $a = d$, $b = e$ and $c = g$. We show the four corresponding windows in the third row of Figure 7.10.

   Now, define

(4″)   For every pair (i, j), with $0 \leq i \leq r(n)-1$ and $0 \leq j \leq r(n)$, if $s_{i,j-1} = a$, $s_{i,j} = b$, $s_{i,j+1} = c$, $s_{i+1,j-1} = d$, $s_{i+1,j} = e$ and $s_{i+1,j+1} = g$, then (a, b, c, d, e, g) must be in one of the twelve forms shown in Figure 7.10.

To see that condition (4″) is equivalent to condition (4), it suffices to show that if matrix S satisfies (4″), then matrix S satisfies condition (1), since these twelve windows are consistent with all five subwindows of Figure 7.7. We prove this by induction. First, we know from condition (2) that the first row of S contains exactly one symbol in $Q\#\Gamma$.

   Next, we assume that the ith row of S has exactly one symbol in $Q\#\Gamma$, and that it is $s_{i,j} = q\#u$. Let us call a window *the ℓth window* if the top middle symbol of the window is $s_{i,\ell}$. Then, the jth window is in the form of window

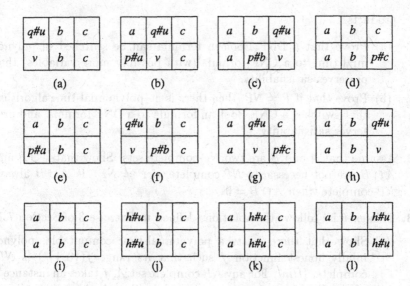

Figure 7.10: Twelve possible windows.

(b), (g) or (k) in Figure 7.10. If the jth window is of the form (b), then there must be an instruction $(p, v, L) \in \delta(q, u)$. It follows that the $(j - 2)$nd window must be of the form (d) in Figure 7.10, the $(j - 1)$st window must be of the form (c), and the $(j + 1)$st window must be of the form (a), since these are the only windows which are consistent with the jth window. (The $(j - 2)$nd window cannot be of the form (g), for otherwise there would be two symbols in $Q\#\Gamma$ in the ith row of S.)

We also claim that the kth window must be of the form (i) in Figure 7.10, if $k < j - 2$ or $k > j + 1$. To see this, we note that if k satisfies the above condition, then the top three symbols of the kth window must be all in Γ (by the inductive hypothesis). Therefore, the only possible window forms for it are (d), (e) and (i). However, if the kth window is of the form (d), then the $(k + 1)$st window must be of the form (c), and so $s_{i,k+2} \in Q\#\Gamma$, which is a contradiction. Similarly, we can see that the form (e) is not possible. So, the claim is proven. It follows that the $(i + 1)$st row of S contains exactly one symbol in $Q\#\Gamma$.

If the jth window is of the form (g) or (k), then the same argument can be applied to show that the $(i + 1)$st row of S contains exactly one symbol in $Q\#\Gamma$. We leave the detail to the reader. This completes the induction proof.

$\square$

Exercise 7.3

1. A Boolean formula which is a product of literals is called an *elementary product*. A *DNF (disjunctive normal form)* is a sum of elementary

products.

    (a) Prove that a DNF Boolean formula can be switched in polyno-
mial time to a CNF formula (with possibly more variables) that
preserves satisfiability.

    (b) Prove that if $P \neq NP$, then there is no polynomial-time algorithm
that switches a CNF Boolean formula to a DNF formula, and preserves satisfiability.

2. Assume that A and B are two NP-complete sets. Show that $A \cup B$ and
$A \cap B$ are not necessarily NP-complete, if $P \neq NP$. Is $A \cup B$ always
NP-complete when $A \cap B = \emptyset$?

3. This exercise follows the notations defined in Exercise 3 of Section 7.1.

    (a) Show that there exists a polynomial-time computable, polyno-
mially honest function f such that its range $f(\{0,1\}^*)$ is NP-
complete. [*Hint*: For any NP-complete set A, f takes an instance x
of A and a string y as the input and decides whether y is a witness
to $x \in A$.]

    (b) Define $S_f = \{\langle u, v, y \rangle \mid y \geq_{\text{lev}} Min_f(u, v)\}$. Show that there ex-
ists a polynomial-time computable, polynomially honest function
f such that S_f is NP-complete. [*Hint*: Design a function like part
(a), except that the problem A is a minimization problem.]

4. Assume that $P \neq NP$. Let A and B be two sets that are complete for
co-NP (i.e., $\overline{A}$ and $\overline{B}$ are NP-complete). Is AB necessarily in *co-NP*? Is
AB necessarily *co-NP*-complete? Is it possible that AB is in P? Justify
your answer.

⋆ 5. Suppose that, in the proof of Cook's theorem, we drop condition (1)
and replace condition (4′) by ($\overline{4}$), which specifies some subconditions
on five-square windows of one of the four shapes shown in Figure 7.11.
Show that no such subconditions on the five-square windows can make
($\overline{4}$) equivalent to (4′).

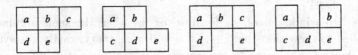

Figure 7.11: Five-square windows.

⋆ 6. Consider the alternative proof of Cook's theorem given in Example 7.33.
Let $T \subseteq (\Gamma')^6$ be the set corresponding to the twelve windows of Figure
7.10; that is, $(a, b, c, d, e, g) \in T$ if and only if (a, b, c, d, e, g) is in
one of the twelve forms in Figure 7.10, and satisfies the corresponding

conditions given in the three cases. Show that if there exists a mapping $\phi : (\Gamma')^3 \to (\Gamma')^3$ such that $(a, b, c, d, e, g) \in T$ if and only if $\phi(a, b, c) = (d, e, g)$, then $L(M)$ is in P.

⋆ 7. In this exercise, we consider a different setting for the proof of Cook's theorem. Instead of attaching the state symbol to the tape symbol currently scanned by the tape head, we may define separate Boolean variables to represent the state and the position of the tape head. That is, in addition to variables $y_{i,j,a}$ (for $a \in \Gamma$ only), we define, for each $i = 0, \ldots, r(n)$ and each $q \in Q$, a variable $Q_{i,q}$ to mean that the state symbol of α_i is q, and for each pair (i, j), with $i, j \in \{0, \ldots, r(n)\}$, a variable $H_{i,j}$ to mean that, in the configuration α_i, the tape head is scanning the jth symbol. To prove Cook's theorem in this setting, then we need to define six Boolean functions $g_1, \ldots, g_6$, such that, for $k = 1, \ldots, 6$, $g_k = 1$ if and only if the condition (k) below holds:

(1) For each $i = 0, \ldots, r(n)$, α_i is in exactly one state.

(2) For each $i = 0, \ldots, r(n)$, the head scans exactly one cell in α_i.

(3) For each $i = 0, \ldots, r(n)$ and each $j = 0, \ldots, r(n)$, the jth cell of α_i contains exactly one symbol.

(4) α_θ is the initial configuration of M on input x.

(5) $\alpha_{r(n)}$ is an accepting configuration.

(6) For each $i = 0, \ldots, r(n) - 1$, $\alpha_i \vdash \alpha_{i+1}$.

Assume that $g_1, \ldots, g_5$ satisfy the condition that $g_k = 1$ if and only if condition (k) holds. Also let g_6 be

$$
\prod_{i=0}^{r(n)} \prod_{j=0}^{r(n)} \prod_{q \in Q} \prod_{u \in \Gamma} \sum_{(p, v, D) \in \delta(q, u)} \Big[(\overline{H}_{i,j} + \overline{Q}_{i,q} + \overline{y}_{i,j,u} + H_{i+1, j+\Delta})
$$
$$
\cdot (\overline{H}_{i,j} + \overline{Q}_{i,q} + \overline{y}_{i,j,u} + Q_{i+1,p}) \cdot (\overline{H}_{i,j} + \overline{Q}_{i,q} + \overline{y}_{i,j,u} + y_{i+1,j,v}) \Big],
$$

where $\Delta = -1$ if $D = L$, and $\Delta = 1$ if $D = R$. Find a counterexample to disprove that $G_x = \prod_{i=1}^{6} g_i = 1$ if and only if M accepts x. Find a new function g_6 satisfying that $G_x = 1$ if and only if M accepts x.

7.4   More NP-Complete Problems

We have seen, from Cook's theorem, that SAT is NP-complete. In this section, we prove more NP-complete problems. First, we recall that $\leq_m^P$ is a transitive relation (Proposition 7.19(b)), and so we have:

Proposition 7.34 *If A is NP-complete, $B \in NP$ and $A \leq_m^P B$, then B is also NP-complete.*

From this proposition, we can prove a problem NP-complete by reducing a known NP-complete problem to it. Therefore, most problems we studied in Section 7.2 are, in fact, NP-complete.

Corollary 7.35 CNF-SAT, 3SAT, HC, LP, IS, VC, IP, *and* 3DM *are NP-complete.*

Proof. Example 7.23 established CNF-SAT as an NP-complete problem. Exercise 1 of Section 7.2 showed that 3SAT is NP-complete. The other examples of Section 7.2 showed that HC, LP, IS, VC, and IP are all NP-complete. Finally, Exercise 3(a) of Section 7.2 shows that $3\text{SAT} \leq_m^P 3\text{DM}$, and so 3DM is NP-complete.   □

To understand how difficult an NP-complete problem is, we often consider its subproblems by adding restrictions to the problem. Depending on how strong the restriction is, the new subproblem may remain NP-complete or may become polynomial-time solvable. For instance, for the problem VC, we may restrict the input graphs to be planar graphs, and the problem is still NP-complete (see Exercise 2(a) of this section). On the other hand, if we require the vertex cover to be also an independent set, then the problem VC becomes in P.

Example 7.36 *Does the problem* VC *remain NP-complete if each edge is to be covered by exactly one vertex?*

Solution. The answer is NO if and only if $P \neq NP$ (if $P = NP$, then all nontrivial sets in P are NP-complete; see Example 7.28).

Let EXACT-VC denote the set of pairs $(G = (V, E), k)$ for which there is a subset $A \subseteq V$ of size k such that every edge in E is covered by exactly one vertex in A. We note that if set $A \subseteq V$ covers every edge with exactly one vertex, then A is an independent set of G. In addition, we know, from Example 7.21, that the complement of a vertex cover is an independent set, and so, $V - A$ is also an independent set of G. This means that both A and $V - A$ are independent sets, and so the graph G is a bipartite graph (i.e., a graph whose vertex set can be partitioned into two subsets A and B such that its edges are all between a vertex in A and a vertex in B). Conversely, suppose $G = (V, E)$ is a bipartite graph with $V = A \cup B$, $A \cap B = \emptyset$ and each edge in E connects a vertex in A and a vertex in B. Then, G has a vertex cover A which covers exactly one vertex of each edge.

So, we have proved that $(G, k) \in$ EXACT-VC if and only if G is a bipartite graph with one of its vertex subset of size less than or equal to k. The latter property of a graph G is easily recognized in polynomial time (by, e.g., a breadth-first search over the graph). Therefore, the problem EXACT-VC is in P.   □

In the following, we present a few more famous NP-complete problems. For a graph $G = (V, E)$ and a set $A \subseteq V$, the *induced subgraph* $G|_A$ of G

on the vertex set A is the graph with the vertex set A and the edge set $E_A = \{\{u, v\} \in E \mid u, v \in A\}$.

> MINMUM CONNECTIVITY GRAPH (MCG): Given n subsets X_1, $X_2, \ldots, X_n$ of a set X and a positive integer k, find a graph G over the vertex set X, with at most k edges, such that every induced subgraph $G|_{X_i}$ of G, $1 \leq i \leq n$, is connected.

Example 7.37 *Prove that* MCG *is NP-complete.*

Proof. The problem MCG is in *NP*, since we can guess a graph G on X and check, in polynomial time, whether G has at most k edges and whether every $G|_{X_i}$ is connected. (To determine whether a given graph is connected, we can perform a standard depth-first search over the graph G, which visits each edge at most twice and so runs in linear time.)

To show that MCG is *NP*-hard, we reduce VC to it. For an instance (G, h) of VC, where $G = (V, E)$, we let $X = V \cup \{x\}$, where $x \notin V$, $k = |E| + h$, and construct, for each $e \in E$, two subsets of X: $X_{1,e} = e$, $X_{2,e} = e \cup \{x\}$. So, together, we have $2|E|$ subsets.

We say a graph H over the vertex set X is *feasible* if $H|_{X_{i,e}}$ is connected, for all $e \in E$ and $i = 1, 2$. Suppose that G has a vertex cover C of size $\leq h$. Then, $G \cup \{\{x, v\} \mid v \in C\}$ is a feasible graph with at most $|E| + h$ edges. Indeed, $G|_{X_{1,e}}$ contains exactly one edge e and so is connected; and $G|_{X_{2,e}}$ contains the edge e plus an edge between x and a vertex in $e \cap C$, and is also connected.

Conversely, suppose that there exists a feasible graph G' with at most $|E| + h$ edges on vertex set X. Then, it must contain all edges in G since $G'_{X_{1,e}}$ is connected for every $e \in E$. It follows that x has degree at most h. In addition, since $G'_{X_{2,e}}$ is connected for every $e \in E$, every edge e has at least one vertex connected to x in G'. This means that $C = \{v \mid \{x, v\} \in G'\}$ is a vertex cover for G. Furthermore, this vertex cover has size at most h, because each vertex in C is joined by an edge with x. It follows that $(G, h) \in$ VC. $\square$

In the next problem, we say (A, B) is a *partition* of a set S if $A \cup B = S$ and $A \cap B = \emptyset$.

> PARTITION: Given n positive integers $a_1, a_2, \cdots, a_n$, determine whether a partition (I_1, I_2) of $\{1, 2, \cdots, n\}$ exists such that
> $$\sum_{i \in I_1} a_i = \sum_{i \in I_2} a_i.$$

(Such a partition is called an *even partition* of the list $(a_1, \ldots, a_n)$.)

Example 7.38 PARTITION *is NP-complete.*

Proof. The problem PARTITION belongs to NP since we can guess a partition of the input instance and verify in polynomial time whether the partition is even. To show the NP-hardness of PARTITION, we reduce 3DM to it. For each instance $W \subseteq X \times Y \times Z$ of 3DM, we construct an instance of PARTITION as follows:

For each element x in $X \cup Y \cup Z$, denote by $\#(x)$ the number of occurrences of x in W. Note that if there is an element x in $X \cup Y \cup Z$ such that $\#(x) = 0$, then obviously W does not contain a three-dimensional matiching, and so the reduction is trivial. Therefore, we may assume, in general, $\#(x) \geq 1$ for all $x \in X \cup Y \cup Y$. Let $X = \{x_1, x_2, \cdots, x_n\}$, $Y = \{y_1, y_2, \cdots, y_n\}$, and $Z = \{z_1, z_2, \cdots, z_n\}$. For each vector $(x_i, y_j, z_k) \in W$, construct an integer a_{ijk} as follows:

$$a_{ijk} = m^i + m^{n+j} + m^{2n+k},$$

where $m = |W| + 1$. Define

$$s = \sum_{(x_i, y_j, z_k) \in W} a_{ijk} \quad \text{and} \quad t = \sum_{i=1}^{3n} m^i.$$

Note that, by the assumption that each $x \in X \cup Y \cup Z$ has $\#(x) \geq 1$, we have $s \geq t$. The instance of PARTITION corresponding to W consists of integers $b_1 = s + 1$, $b_2 = 2(s - t) + 1$, and a_{ijk} for $(x_i, y_j, z_k) \in W$. We note that the sum S of all these numbers is equal to

$$(s + 1) + 2(s - t) + 1 + s = 4s - 2t + 2.$$

In other words, these numbers have an even partition if and only if there is a subset of these numbers which sums to $2s - t + 1$.

Now, we observe that if W has a three-dimensional matching W', then

$$\sum_{(x_i, y_j, z_k) \in W'} a_{ijk} = t,$$

since each x_i occurs in W' exactly once, and so it contributes exactly m^i to the above sum, and similarly each y_j contributes m^{n+j} and each z_k contributes m^{2n+k} to the above sum. (An easy way to visualize the above claim it to view each number in its base-m representation. In this representation, $t = 1^{3n}$.) It follows that

$$b_2 + \sum_{(x_i, y_j, z_k) \in W'} a_{ijk} = 2s - t + 1 = \frac{S}{2},$$

and so this defines an even partition.

Conversely, assume that the instance of PARTITION corresponding to W has an even partition. Then, b_1 and b_2 must belong to the different sides of the partition, since $b_1 + b_2 = s + 1 + 2(s - t) + 1 > S/2$. Let

$$W' = \{(x_i, y_j, z_k) \in W \mid a_{ijk} \text{ belongs to the side of } b_2\}.$$

That is,

$$b_1 + \sum_{(x_i,y_j,z_k)\in W-W'} a_{ijk} = b_2 + \sum_{(x_i,y_j,z_k)\in W'} a_{ijk} = \frac{S}{2}.$$

Therefore, we get

$$\sum_{(x_i,y_j,z_k)\in W'} a_{ijk} = \frac{S}{2} - (2(s-t)+1) = t.$$

Note that, for all i, $1 \le i \le n$, $\#(x_i) \le m - 1$, and so all occurrences of x_i contribute at most $(m-1)m^i < m^{i+1}$ to the sum. Similarly, all occurrences of y_j (and z_k) contribute at most $(m-1)m^{n+j} < m^{n+j+1}$ (and, respectively, $(m-1)m^{2n+k} < m^{2n+k+1}$) to the sum. Therefore, to get the sum equal to t, there must be exactly one occurrence of each x_i, y_j and z_k in W'. This implies that W' is a three-dimensional matching.

Finally, we note that $S = 4s - 2t + 2$ is of length $O(n \log m)$, and so the total size of the constructed instance of PARTITION is $O(mn \log m)$. It follows that it can be constructed in time polynomial in $|W|$. $\square$

Because of its simple form, it is easy to reduce PARTITION to other problems to establish new NP-completeness results. The following are two packing problems.

KNAPSACK: Given $2n + 2$ nonnegative integers $c_1, c_2, \ldots, c_n$, $p_1, p_2, \ldots, p_n$, s, and k, determine whether there exists x_1, x_2, $\ldots, x_n \in \{0, 1\}$ satisfying

$$\sum_{i=1}^{n} c_i x_i \le s, \quad \text{and} \quad \sum_{i=1}^{n} p_i x_i \ge k. \tag{7.2}$$

(Intuitively, the problem KNAPSACK asks, for given costs $c_1, \ldots, c_n$ and profits $p_1, \ldots, p_n$ of n items, and a given bound s, to select a subset of items to maximize the profits, subject to the condition that the total cost does not exceed s.)

Example 7.39 KNAPSACK *is NP-complete.*

Proof. To show that KNAPSACK is in NP, we guess an assignment of values 0 and 1 to variables $x_1, \ldots, x_n$, and check that the assignment satisfies the constraint (7.2). It is clear that the checking of the constraint (7.2) can be done in deterministic polynomial time.

Next, we show that KNAPSACK is *NP*-hard by reducing PARTITION to it. For each instance $(a_1, a_2, \ldots, a_n)$ of PARTITION, we construct an instance $(c_1, \ldots, c_n, p_1, \ldots, p_n, s, k)$ of KNAPSACK as follows:

(1) $c_i = p_i = a_i$, for $1 \le i \le n$,

(2) $s = \left\lfloor \frac{1}{2} \sum_{i=1}^{n} a_i \right\rfloor$,

(3) $k = \left\lceil \frac{1}{2} \sum_{i=1}^{n} a_i \right\rceil$.

Clearly, $(a_1, a_2, \cdots, a_n)$ has an even partition (I_1, I_2) if and only if the corresponding assignment $(x_i = 1 \Leftrightarrow i \in I_1)$ satisfies the constraint (7.2).   □

> BIN PACKING (BP): Given $n + 2$ positive integers $a_1, a_2, \cdots, a_n$, c, and k, determine whether the list $(a_1, a_2, \cdots, a_n)$ can be partitioned into k sublists such that the sum of a_i's in each sublist is at most c.

(Intuitively, the problem BP asks, for n given items of size $a_1, a_2, \ldots, a_n$ and k given bins, each of size c, whether the n items can be packed in these k bins.)

Example 7.40 BP *is NP-complete.*

Proof. To show that BP is in *NP*, we can guess a partition of the input instance into k sublists and check that the total size of items in each sublist does not exceed c. This can apparently be done in polynomial time.

To show that BP is *NP*-hard, we reduce PARTITION to it. For each instance $(a_1, a_2, \cdots, a_n)$ of PARTITION, we construct an instance $(a_1, a_2, \cdots, a_n, c, k)$ of BP with

$$c = \left\lfloor \frac{1}{2} \cdot \sum_{i=1}^{n} a_i \right\rfloor$$

and $k = 2$. It is easy to see that $(a_1, a_2, \cdots, a_n)$ has an even partition if and only if the corresponding instance belongs to the set BP.   □

⋆ **Example 7.41** *Show that the following problem is NP-complete: Given positive integers $a_1, \ldots, a_n$, determine whether*

$$\int_0^{2\pi} \left(\prod_{i=1}^{n} \cos(a_i t) \right) dt \neq 0.$$

Proof. We first show by induction on n that

$$\prod_{i=1}^{n} \cos(a_i t) = \frac{1}{2^n} \sum_{(I_1, I_2) \in P_n} \cos \left(\sum_{i \in I_1} a_i t - \sum_{i \in I_2} a_i t \right), \qquad (7.3)$$

where P_n is the family of all possible partitions (I_1, I_2) of $\{1, 2, \cdots, n\}$, with (I_1, I_2) and (I_2, I_1) considered as two different partitions. For $n = 1$, there are two possible partitions $(\{1\}, \emptyset)$ and $(\emptyset, \{1\})$. In this case, the equality holds trivially. Now, consider $n \geq 2$. We recall the identity

$$\cos\alpha\cos\beta = \frac{1}{2}\big(\cos(\alpha+\beta) + \cos(\alpha-\beta)\big).$$

It follows that

$$
\begin{aligned}
\prod_{i=1}^{n}\cos(a_it) &= \frac{1}{2^{n-1}}\Bigg[\sum_{(I_1,I_2)\in P_{n-1}} \cos\Big(\sum_{i\in I_1} a_it - \sum_{i\in I_2} a_it\Big)\Bigg]\cos(a_nt) \\
&= \frac{1}{2^n}\sum_{(I_1,I_2)\in P_{n-1}}\Bigg[\cos\Big(\sum_{i\in I_1\cup\{n\}} a_it - \sum_{i\in I_2} a_it\Big) \\
&\qquad\qquad\qquad\qquad + \cos\Big(\sum_{i\in I_1} a_it - \sum_{i\in I_2\cup\{n\}} a_it\Big)\Bigg] \\
&= \frac{1}{2^n}\sum_{(I_1,I_2)\in P_n} \cos\Big(\sum_{i\in I_1} a_it - \sum_{i\in I_2} a_it\Big).
\end{aligned}
$$

Next, note that

$$\int_0^{2\pi}\cos(at)dt = \begin{cases} 0 & \text{if } a \neq 0 \\ 2\pi & \text{if } a = 0. \end{cases}$$

Thus, by (7.3), if $(a_1, a_2, \ldots, a_n) \in$ PARTITION, then there exists at least one partition $(I_1, I_2) \in P_n$ such that $\sum_{i\in I_1} a_i - \sum_{i\in I_2} a_i = 0$, and so

$$\int_0^{2\pi}\Big(\prod_{i=1}^n cos(a_it)\Big)dt \geq 2\pi.$$

Otherwise, if $(a_1, a_2, \ldots, a_n) \notin$ PARTITION, then all partitions $(I_1, I_2) \in P_n$ have $\sum_{i\in I_1} a_i - \sum_{i\in I_2} a_i \neq 0$, and so

$$\int_0^{2\pi}\Big(\prod_{i=1}^n cos(a_it)\Big)dt = 0.$$

In other words, this problem is equivalent to PARTITION. □

We next study an interesting geometric problem. A *tree* in the Euclidean plane is a connected graph with no cycles, whose vertices are points in the two-dimensional plane and edges are the line segments joining two vertices. The length of an edge connecting two points $x_1 = (a_1, b_1)$ and $x_2 = (a_2, b_2)$ is $d(x_1, x_2) = ((a_1 - a_2)^2 + (b_1 - b_2)^2)^{1/2}$. Let $x_1, x_2, \ldots, x_n$ be n points in the Euclidean plane. A *Steiner tree* over $x_1, \ldots, x_n$ is a tree T in the plane whose vertex set includes $\{x_1, \ldots, x_n\}$ as a subset. Vertices $x_1, x_2, \ldots, x_n$ are called the *terminal points* of tree T, and the other vertices in T are called the

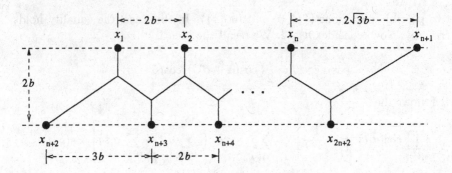

Figure 7.12: A basic Steiner minimum tree.

Steiner points of T. A *Steiner minimum tree* over $x_1, \ldots, x_n$ is the Steiner tree over $x_1, \ldots, x_n$ with the minimum total edge length. A decision version of the Steiner minimum tree problem can be formulated as follows:

> STEINER MINIMUM TREE (SMT): Given a set of n integer points in the Euclidean plane and a positive integer k, determine whether there exists a Steiner tree over terminal points $x_1, \ldots, x_n$ whose total edge length does not exceed k.

Example 7.42 SMT *is NP-complete.*

Proof (Sketch). We are going to present a reduction from PARTITION to SMT which depends on certain geometric properties of Steiner trees. Since the proofs of these geometric properties are tedious but not directly related to the idea of the reduction, we will omit these proofs here.

We first consider a special Steiner minimum tree as Shown in Figure 7.12. This is a Steiner minimum tree over $2n + 2$ terminal points $x_1, x_2, \ldots, x_{2n+2}$, which lie in two parallel lines of distance $2b$ for some positive integer b. We call these two parallel lines the base lines. More precisely, the coordinates of these points are

(1) $x_i = (2ib, 2b)$, for $1 \le i \le n$,

(2) $x_{n+1} = ((n + \sqrt{3})2b, 2b)$,

(3) $x_{n+2} = (0, 0)$, and

(4) $x_i = ((2(i - n - 2) + 1)b, 0)$, for $n + 3 \le i \le 2n + 2$.

By the minimality of the total length, it can be proved that every angle in this tree is of 120 degrees. Thus, this Steiner minimum tree consists of three families of parallel edges, with the edges passing through $x_1, x_2, \ldots, x_n$ and $x_{n+3}, x_{n+4}, \ldots, x_{2n+2}$ perpendicular to the two base lines.

This Steiner minimum tree has a key property: If we fix x_{n+1} and x_{n+2} and move other points along the two base lines, and also keep the directions

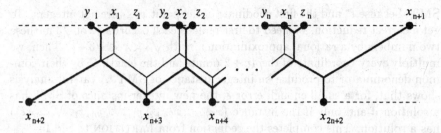

Figure 7.13:   The new Steiner minimum tree.

of all edges unchanged, then the total length of the tree does not change. This length is not hard to calculate:

$$\ell = (2 + \sqrt{3})nb + 4b.$$

Furthermore, it can be proved that this is actually the minimum total length of any Steiner tree over $x_1, \ldots, x_n$, even if we allow the edge directions to change.

Now, we use this basic Steiner minimum tree structure to construct a reduction from PARTITION to SMT. Let $a_1, \ldots, a_n$ be n given integers. We choose an integer $b \gg \sum_{i=1}^{n} a_i$ (i.e., b is much greater than the sum of a_i's), and create $2n + 2$ points $x_1, x_2, \ldots, x_{2n+2}$ as above. Next, for each x_i, with $1 \leq i \leq n$, on the upper base line, we add two points y_i and z_i on its left and its right, respectively, such that $d(y_i, x_i) = d(x_i, z_i) = a_i$. Over these $4n + 2$ points, we can define a class of Steiner trees, each corresponding to a partition (I_1, I_2) of $\{1, 2, \cdots, n\}$: For each partition (I_1, I_2), let $T(I_1, I_2)$ denote the tree that includes (i) the edges $\{x_i, y_i\}$ for $i \in I_1$, (ii) the edges $\{x_i, z_i\}$ for $i \in I_2$, and (iii) a Steiner minimum tree over the terminal points

$$\{x_i \mid 1 \leq i \leq 2n + 2\} \cup \{y_i \mid i \in I_2\} \cup \{z_i \mid i \in I_1\}.$$

(See Fig. 7.13.)

With $b \gg \sum_{i=1}^{n} a_i$, it can be proved that the shortest Steiner tree in the above class of trees $T(I_1, I_2)$ is actually the Steiner minimum tree over the $4n + 2$ points. In addition, this class of trees has the following properties:

(a) If there is an even partition (I_1, I_2) for $(a_1, \ldots, a_n)$, then $T(I_1, I_2)$ is the shortest one with length $\ell^* = \ell + (1 + \sqrt{3}/2) \sum_{i=1}^{n} a_i$. Actually, in this case, $T(I_1, I_2)$ has edges perpendicular to the two base lines.

(b) If (I_1, I_2) is not an even partition of $(a_1, \ldots, a_n)$, then $T(I_1, I_2)$ has length longer than ℓ^*.

That is, there exists an even partition of $(a_1, \ldots, a_n)$ if and only if there exists a Steiner tree with length at most ℓ^* that interconnects these $4n + 2$ points. However, we note that the mapping from the list $(a_1, \ldots, a_n)$ to $(x_1, \ldots, x_{2n+2}, y_1, \ldots, y_n, z_1, \ldots, z_n; \ell^*)$ is not a reduction from PARTITION to

SMT, because ℓ^* and the first coodinate of the point x_{n+1} are not integers. To get a correct reduction, we need to first replace each occurrence of $\sqrt{3}$ in these two numbers by a rational approximation r, with $\sqrt{3} < r < \sqrt{3} + \epsilon$. Then, we multiply every coordinate of the $4n + 2$ points and the length ℓ^* by their common denominator to produce an integer instance of SMT. A careful analysis shows that, for a small enough error ϵ, the new integer instance of SMT has a solution if and only if the instance $(x_1, \ldots, x_{2n+2}, y_1, \ldots, y_n, z_1, \ldots, z_n; \ell^*)$ has a solution. This completes the reduction from PARTITION to SMT.

Finally, we note that we still need to show that SMT is in NP. To do so, for every given instance of SMT, we guess an additional set of Steiner points, and verify that the total length of the tree interconnecting these points is bounded by the given length bound. Note that the additional Steiner points and the length of the tree may involve irrational numbers, and so approximations are required. It can be checked that the approximations can be calculated within polynomial time so that the result of calculation remains correct. We omit the detailed analysis.   □

Exercise 7.4

1. For each of the following problems, determine whether it is NP-complete or is in P. If it is NP-complete, find a reduction from a known NP-complete problem to it. If it is in P, find a polynomial-time algorithm for it.

   (a) Given a graph G, two vertices s and t in G and a positive integer k, determine whether there is a path between s and t of length less than or equal to k.

   (b) Given a graph G, two vertices s and t in G and a positive integer k, determine whether there is a path between s and t of length greater than or equal to k.

   ⋆ (c) Given a directed graph G, determine whether G has a cycle of an odd length.

   ⋆ (d) Given a directed graph G, determine whether G has a cycle of an even length.

   ⋆ (e) Given a graph G, determine whether G has a cycle of an odd length.

   (f) Given an edge-weighted complete graph G, three subsets X_1, X_2, X_3 of vertices and a positive integer k, determine whether there is a subgraph H of G of weight $\leq k$ that contains a spanning tree for each of X_1, X_2 and X_3. (A *spanning tree* for a subset $X \subseteq V$ is a connected subgraph H of G on the vertex set X that has no cycle.)

   (g) Given a graph $G = (V, E)$ and a positive integer k, determine whether there is a subset $T \subseteq E$ of at most k edges such that every vertex in V is incident with at least one edge in T.

⋆ (h) REGULAR EXPRESSION NONEQUIVALENCE: Given two regular expressions r_1 and r_2 without the Kleene-star operation, determine whether $L(r_1) \neq L(r_2)$.

(i) BOUNDED PCP (see Exercise 7(d) of Section 7.1).

(j) BOUNDED TILING (see Exercise 7(e) of Section 7.1).

2. Prove that the following variations of the problem VC are *NP*-complete:

(a) PLANAR VC: The problem VC restricted to planar graphs. (A *planar graph* is a graph that can be drawn on the two-dimensional plane such that no two edges cross each other at a non-vertex point.)

(b) CUBIC VC: The problem VC restricted to cubic graphs. (A *cubic graph* is a graph such that every vertex has degree three.)

⋆ (c) PLANAR CONNECTED-VC-4: Given a planar graph $G = (V, E)$ with each vertex in V having degree at most 4 and an integer $k > 0$, determine whether there is a vertex cover C of G of size k such that the induced subgraph $G|_C$ on vertex set C is connected.

⋆ (d) Given a graph G, determine whether G has a vertex cover C satisfying the following conditions:

(i) The subgraph $G|_C$ induced by C has no isolated point.

(ii) Every vertex in C is adjacent to a vertex not in C.

3. The *polar representation* of a CNF F is a bipartite graph $G_F = (V_1, V_2, E)$, where V_1 is the set of all variables and V_2 is the set of all clauses in F, and there is an edge in E between $x_i \in V_1$ and $c_j \in V_2$ if and only if the variable x_i appears in the clause c_j (in the form of x_i or $\overline{x}_i$). Prove the following statements:

(a) $(x + y + \overline{z})(\overline{x} + z + w)(\overline{x} + z + \overline{w})(\overline{y} + z + u)(\overline{y} + z + \overline{u})$ has a planar polar representation and it is satisfiable if and only if $x + y = z$.

(b) There exists a 3-CNF formula F with a planar polar representation and three variables x, y, and z, such that F is satisfiable if and only if $xy = z$.

(c) There exists a 3-CNF formula F with a planar polar representation and three variables x, y, and z, such that F is satisfiable if and only if $x \oplus y = z$. [*Hint*: $x \oplus y = x(\overline{x} + \overline{y}) + (\overline{x} + \overline{y})y$.]

(d) The following problem, called PLANAR POLAR-3SAT, is *NP*-complete: Given a 3-CNF formula F with a planar polar representation, determine whether F is satisfiable or not. [*Hint*: Applying the fact that $x \oplus (x \oplus y) = y$ and $(x \oplus y) \oplus y = x$ to the construction.]

4. The *nonpolar representation* of a CNF F is a graph $G_F = (V, E)$, with the vertex set V consisting of all literals and all clauses in F, and the edge set E consisting of all pairs $\{x, \overline{x}\}$ over all variables x in F plus

all literal-clause pairs $\{z, c\}$ such that z occurs in c. Prove the following statements:

(a) If the nonpolar representation of a CNF formula F is planar, then its polar representation must also be planar. However, the converse is not necessarily true.

(b) The following problem, called PLANAR NONPOLAR-3SAT, is *NP*-complete: Given a 3-CNF formula F with a planar nonpolar representation, determine whether F is satisfiable or not.

5. A (k, ℓ)-*CNF* F is a CNF such that each clause contains exactly k literals and each variable occurs in at most ℓ clauses. The problem (k, ℓ)-SAT is the problem 3SAT restricted to (k, ℓ)-CNF's. Prove the following results:

(a) For any $k > 0$, every (k, k)-CNF F is satisfiable.

(b) For any $\ell > 0$, $(2, \ell)$-SAT is polynomial-time solvable. (In fact, the problem 2SAT, which is the problem 3SAT restricted to CNF's with at most 2 literals in each clause, is polynomial-time solvable.)

$\star$ (c) $(3, 4)$-SAT is *NP*-complete.

7.5 NP-Complete Optimization Problems

In the last two sections, we have formally defined *NP*-complete problems as a class of *decision problems*. In the applications, we often deal with *search problems*, that is, problems whose answers are not simple *yes* or *no*. For instance, consider the vertex cover problem. The problem VC defined in Section 7.1 is a decision problem: For a given graph G and a given integer $k > 0$, determine whether there is a vertex cover of G of size at most k. A more natural formulation of this problem is the following search problem:

MIN-VC: For a given graph G, find a minimum vertex cover of G.

In fact, people often refer to MIN-VC as the vertex cover problem, and often say this search problem is *NP*-complete. So, what is the exact relation between these two problems, and is there a formal way to define *NP*-complete search problems? We try to clarify it here.

First, we can easily formulate a search problem as a function from strings to strings. For instance, MIN-VC is just the *multi-valued* function mapping graph G to one of its vertex cover of the minimum size. Then, with an appropriate coding of graphs and integers by binary strings, MIN-VC can be viewed as a multi-valued function from finite strings to finite strings. For a single-valued function f, we have defined its deterministic time complexity. In particular, f is said to be polynomial-time computable if there is a polynomial-time DTM M such that on each input x, M halts with the output $f(x)$. This definition can be easily extended to multi-valued functions. Namely, a multi-valued function f is *polynomial-time computable* if there is a polynomial-time

DTM M such that on each input x, M halts with an output y which is one of the values of $f(x)$.

To formally define the notion of an *NP*-complete multi-valued function, we need to define (a) how a nondeterministic TM computes a function, and (b) what is meant by a polynomial-time reduction between functions. Since the formal definition is tedious, we try to avoid it here. Instead, we content ourselves with an informal description and a practical example.

First, we define a new notion of reducibility between two functions that is more general than the many-one reduction between two sets (a decision problem can be considered as a function whose outputs are either 0 or 1). We say a function f is *polynomial-time Turing reducible* to g, denoted by $f \leq_T^P g$, if there is a polynomial-time DTM M such that for any x, M computes $f(x)$ with the *help* of the function g as an *oracle*. By using g as an oracle, we mean that M has a subprocedure M_g which, when asked for the value $g(z)$, can provide the answer $w = g(z)$ to M *free*, meaning that the computation from z to $g(z)$ does not count toward the time complexity of M (though the time to prepare the query string z is still counted toward its time complexity). Based on this new notion of reducibility, we say that a search problem f is *NP-complete* if the following conditions hold:

(a) A decision version S_f of f is an *NP*-complete set.

(b) This decision version S_f and the search version f are *polynomial-time Turing-reducible* to each other.

Example 7.43 *Show that* MIN-VC *is an NP-complete search problem.*

Proof. The problem VC is the natural decision version for MIN-VC. It is easy to see how to use MIN-VC as an oracle to solve problem VC in polynomial time: For any graph G and integer k, we first ask MIN-VC to find a minimum vertex cover C of G, and let k^* be the size of C. Then, we answer YES to the instance (G, k) if and only if $k^* \leq k$.

Next, we show how to reduce MIN-VC to VC. For any graph $G = (V, E)$, we show a polynomial-time algorithm that finds a minimum vertex cover C of G, with the help of the oracle VC:

(1) We ask $|V| + 1$ questions "Is $(G, j) \in$ VC?" for $j = 0, 1, \ldots, |V|$, to the oracle VC, and let $k^* = \min\{j \mid (G, j) \in$ VC$\}$.

(2) Set $U := V$ and $K := k^*$.

(3) Repeat the following until $K = 0$:

(3.1) For each $v \in U$, consider the induced subgraph $G|_{U - \{v\}}$ on the vertex set $U - \{v\}$, and ask the oracle whether $(G|_{U - \{v\}}, K - 1) \in$ VC.

(3.2) Select one $v \in U$ with $(G|_{U - \{v\}}, K - 1) \in$ VC. Reset $U := U - \{v\}$ and $K := K - 1$.

(4) Output the set $C := V - U$.

To see that this algorithm works correctly, we need to show the following two properties of the algorithm:

(a) At the beginning of each iteration of step (3.1), the induced subgraph $G|_U$ has a minimum vertex cover of size K.

(b) In each iteration of step (3), there always exists a vertex $v \in U$ satisfying $(G|_{U-\{v\}}, K-1) \in$ VC.

These properties can be proved easily by induction. It is clear that at the first iteration of step (3.1), $U = V$ and $K = k^*$, and so $G|_U$ is just G itself and its minimum vertex cover is of size K. So, property (a) is satisfied at the first iteration.

Now, assume that property (a) is satisfied at the jth iteration, for some $1 \le j \le k^*$. From property (a), we know that there is a set $V^* \subseteq V$ of size $K = k^* - j + 1$ which is a minimum vertex cover of $G|_U$. Then, for any $v \in V^*$, $V^* - \{v\}$ is a vertex cover of $G|_{U-\{v\}}$. Therefore, property (b) is also satisfied at the jth iteration of step (3). Furthermore, we note that, in the jth iteration, if we select a particular v satisfying $(G|_{U-\{v\}}, K-1) \in$ VC and reset U to be $U - \{v\}$ and K to be $K - 1$, then property (a) is satisfied at the $(j+1)$st iteration. This completes the induction proof of properties (a) and (b).

From property (a), it follows that the output C is a vertex cover of G, since the induced subgraph $G|_U$, with respect to the final U, has a vertex cover of size 0 (i.e., the final U is an independent set of G).

Finally, we note that step (3) runs for $k^* \le |V|$ iterations, and each iteration asks $|V|$ queries to the oracle and so this oracle algorithm works within polynomial time. (*Note*: The answers to the queries cost us nothing when we consider the Turing reduction.) $\square$

Proposition 7.44 *If $f \le_T^P g$ and g is polynomial-time solvable, then f is also polynomial-time solvable.*

Proof. If $f \le_T^P g$, then there is a polynomial-time DTM M_f that computes f with the help of the oracle g. Since M_f on any input x of length n runs in time $p(n)$ for some polynomial p, both the number of queries that can be asked by M_f and the length of each query y are bounded by $p(n)$ (M_f must take at least $|y|$ moves to write down the string y in order to ask for $g(y)$). Now, suppose that M_g is a DTM computing g in time $q(n)$ for some polynomial q. Then, we can compute $f(x)$ without using the oracle as follows:

On input x, we run DTM M_f on x and, when a query for $g(y)$ is made by M_f, we simulate M_g on input y to get the answer.

On an input of length n, M_f makes at most $p(n)$ queries, each of length at most $p(n)$. So, the total simulation time on M_g taken by the above algorithm to answer these queries is at most $p(n) \cdot q(p(n))$. Thus, the total running time $t(n)$ of the above deterministic algorithm is bounded by a function polynomial in n: $t(n) \le p(n)(q(p(n)) + 1)$. $\square$

From the above proposition, we see that if one of the problems VC or MIN-VC is solvable in polynomial time, then the other problem is also solvable in polynomial time. Therefore, the *NP*-completeness of VC implies that MIN-VC is solvable in polynomial time if and only if all *NP*-complete problems are solvable in polynomial time. This result thus justifies the use of the term *NP*-completeness on search problems such as MIN-VC.

Approximation to Optimization Problems. Many *NP*-complete search problems belong to the class of *optimization* problems, which ask for the maximum or the minimum solution to a given instance. These includes a number of problems we studied in the last few sections: VC, IS, KNAPSACK, SMT, and BIN PACKING. Note that, in practice, one does not really require the optimum solutions to these problems. A *nearly* optimum solution is sufficient for most applications. Thus, a reasonable approach to attack these problems is to consider their approximation versions. For instance, instead of finding the minimum-size vertex cover of a given graph, we may ask whether it is possible to find a vertex cover $C \subseteq V$ of a graph $G(V, E)$ such that $|C|$ is at most 20% larger than the size of the minimum vertex cover of G. In the following, we introduce a general framework to study the computational complexity of this type of approximation problem.

We formally define an *optimization problem* Π to consist of three components: $\Pi = (\Sigma, S, v)$, where Σ is an alphabet, $S \subseteq \Sigma^* \times \Sigma^*$ is a relation between strings, and v is a function from S to $\mathbf{N}$.[2] Intuitively, each string $x \in \Sigma^*$ represents a problem *instance* of Π. For each instance x, a string $y \in \Sigma^*$ is a *solution* to x if $(x, y) \in S$. For each solution y to instance x, there is an associated value $v(x, y) \in \mathbf{N}$. Thus, an optimization problem $\Pi = (\Sigma, S, v)$ is to find, for each $x \in \Sigma^*$, a solution y to x with

$$v(x, y) = \text{opt} \{v(x, z) \mid (x, z) \in S\},$$

where opt $=$ max if Π is a maximization problem, and opt $=$ min if Π is a minimization problem. For any instance $x \in \Sigma^*$ to Π, we also define $v^*(x)$ to denote the value of the optimum solution to x; that is, $v^*(x) = \text{opt} \{v(x, z) \mid (x, z) \in S\}$.

As a simple example, the minimization problem MIN-VC can be defined in this framework as follows: MIN-VC $= (\{0, 1\}^*, S_{\text{VC}}, v_{\text{VC}})$, where S_{VC} consists of all pairs $(x, y) \in (\{0, 1\}^*)^2$ such that (i) x encodes a graph $G = (V, E)$ (under a fixed coding scheme), (ii) y encodes a subset of V, and (iii) y is a vertex cover of x, and $v_{\text{VC}}(x, y) = |y|$.

An optimization problem $\Pi = (\Sigma, S, v)$ is *polynomially bounded* if it has the following properties:

---

[2] In general, the value of $v(x, y)$ may be a rational number (or a real number) instead of an integer. In most cases, though, it can be converted to an integer-valued function without changing the characteristic of the problem.

(i) There exists a polynomial function p such that for any $(x, y) \in S$, $|y| \leq p(|x|)$.

(ii) The set S is polynomial-time computable.

(iii) The function v is polynomial-time computable.

It is not hard to verify that the optimization problems we studied in the last few sections are all polynomially bounded.

Proposition 7.45 *If $P = NP$, then every polynomially bounded optimizaton problem $\Pi = (\Sigma, S, v)$ is solvable in polynomial time.*

Proof. First, assume that Π is a maximization problem. It has the following decision problem version:

$$\Pi_D = \{(x, q) \in \Sigma^* \times \mathbf{N} \mid (\exists y \in \Sigma^*) [(x, y) \in S, v(x, y) \geq q].$$

This decision problem is apparently in NP. So, by the assumption that $P = NP$, we can solve this decision problem in deterministic polynomial time.

For any instance $x \in \Sigma^*$, we can first use Π_D as an oracle to find $v^*(x)$ by a binary search. Note that v is polynomial-time computable, and so $0 \leq v(x, y) \leq 2^{p(|x|)}$ for some polynomial p. Therefore, the binary search must find $v^*(x)$ in $p(|x|)$ steps. By Proposition 7.44, there is a deterministic polynomial-time algorithm for function $v^*(x)$.

Next, we consider the decision problem

$$\Pi_D' = \{(x, w) \in (\Sigma^*)^2 \mid (\exists z \in \Sigma^*) [(x, wz) \in S, v(x, wz) \geq v^*(x)]\}.$$

Again, this problem is obviously in NP and, by the assumption, is in P. We can use Π_D' as an oracle to find a solution y such that $v(x, y) \geq v^*(x)$:

(1) Let $w = \varepsilon$.

(2) Ask the oracle whether $(x, w0) \in \Pi_D'$. If the answer is YES, then we reset $w := w0$, else we reset $w := w1$.

(3) If $|w| = p(|x|)$, then halt and output w; otherwise, go back to step (2).

It is easy to see that the above algorithm finds a solution y to x with value $v(x, y) = v^*(x)$. (The above method of searching for the maximum solution y is a variation of binary search, and is called *prefix search*.) In addition, it works within polynomial time and uses an oracle in P. (*Note*: If $(x, y) \in S$, then $|y| \leq p(|x|)$ for some polynomial function p.) It follows from Proposition 7.44 that Π is polynomial-time solvable.

The proof for the case of minimization problems Π is almost identical. $\square$

Now, we consider the approximation to optimization problems. Let r be a real number satisfying $r > 1$. For a maximization problem $\Pi = (\Sigma, S, v)$, its approximation version, with the approximation ratio r, is defined as follows:

r-APPROX-Π: For a given input $x \in \Sigma^*$, find a solution y such that $(x, y) \in S$, and $v(x, y) \geq v^*(x)/r$.

Similarly, for a minimization problem Π, its approximation version, with the approximation ratio r, is as follows:

r-APPROX-Π: For a given input $x \in \Sigma^*$, find a solution y such that $(x, y) \in S$, and $v(y) \leq r \cdot v^*(x)$.

The above problems may be further generalized to include the problems whose approximation ratio r is actually a function $r(n)$, depending on the input size n, instead of a constant real number. For instance, for a minimization problem Π, $\sqrt{n}$-APPROX-Π denotes the problem of finding a solution y to the input x such that $v(y) \leq \sqrt{n} \cdot v^*(x)$.

The approximation version of an NP-complete optimization problem is not necessarily NP-complete. In general, we may classify the approximation problems into three different classes, according to their computational complexity:

(1) The first class consists of approximation problems that are NP-complete for all approximation ratios $r > 1$. Among these problems, we may further divide them into subclasses, according to finer approximation ratios $r(n)$. For instance, a problem r-APPROX-Π_1 may be NP-complete for all constants $r > 1$, but is polynomial-time solvable for $r(n) = \log n$; whereas another problem r-APPROX-Π_2 may be NP-complete for $r(n) = c \cdot \log n$ for all $c > 0$. Then, we consider problem Π_2 as harder to approximate than problem Π_1.

(2) The second class consists of approximation problems that are NP-complete for some small approximation ratios, and are polynomial-time solvable for larger approximation ratios. That is, an approximation problem Π is in this class if there exists a constant $r_0 > 1$ such that r-APPROX-Π is NP-complete for $r < r_0$ and is polynomial-time solvable for $r > r_0$.

(3) The third class consists of all approximation problems that are polynomial-time solvable for all ratios $r > 1$. That is, a problem r-APPROX-Π belongs to the third class if, for each $k \geq 1$, there is a polynomial-time algorithm A_k for the problem $(1 + 1/k)$-APPROX-Π. We call such a sequence A_k of algorithms a *polynomial-time approximation scheme* (PTAS). Note that the run-time of each algorithm A_k of a PTAS is polynomial in the input size, but not necessarily polynomial in the parameter k. If, in addition, there is a single algorithm A that finds approximation solutions within the approximation ratio $r = 1 + 1/k$ in time polynomial in both the input length and k, then it is called a *fully polynomial-time approximation scheme* (FPTAS). A FPTAS is the best we can expect for an NP-complete optimization problem, short of proving $P = NP$.

To prove approximation problems belonging to the first or the second class, we need to construct *approximation-preserving reductions* between approximation problems. These reductions are usually modifications of the reductions between decision versions of the optimization problems and are often more complicated than the original reductions. We only present a few of them to demonstrate the general techniques.

We first consider a famous problem TSP (see Exercise 7(b) of Section 7.1).

Example 7.46 TSP *is NP-complete.*

Proof. There is a simple reduction from HC to TSP: For any graph $G = (V, E)$, we map it to a complete graph $G' = (V, E')$ with the costs $c(e) = 1$ if $e \in E$, and $c(e) = 2$ if $e \notin E$, and let $K = |V|$. Then, it is clear that G has a Hamiltonian cycle if and only if G' has a tour of total cost K.

The Turing reduction of the optimization version to the decision version is easy. We leave it to the reader as an exercise.   □

The optimization version of TSP is to find, for a given graph G with the cost function c on its edges, a minimum-cost tour of G. For each graph G with a cost function c on its edges, let $K^*(G, c)$ denote the minimum cost of a tour of G. The approximation version of TSP is as follows.

> r-APPROX-TSP: Given a complete graph $G = (V, E)$ with a cost function $c : E \to \mathbf{N}$, find a tour of G with the total cost less than or equal to $r \cdot K^*(G, c)$.

Example 7.47 *The problem* r-APPROX-TSP *is NP-complete for all* $r > 1$.

Proof. Let r be a fixed constant $r > 1$. We modify the reduction from HC to TSP as follows: For any graph $G = (V, E)$, we define a complete graph $G' = (V, E')$ with the costs $c(\{u, v\}) = 1$ if $\{u, v\} \in E$, and $c(\{u, v\}) = r|V|$ if $\{u, v\} \notin E$.

Assume that $|V| = n$. If G has a Hamiltonian cycle, then that tour in G' is of cost n; otherwise, a minimum-cost tour in G' is of cost $\geq (n - 1) + rn$. Thus, it is easy to see how to solve the question of whether $G \in HC$, using r-APPROX-TSP as an oracle:

> For a given graph G, construct graph G' and the cost function c as described above. Ask the oracle to find a tour T of G' with the cost at most $r \cdot K^*(G', c)$. Accept graph G (i.e., decide that $G \in HC$) if and only if the cost of T is $\leq rn$.

Notice that if G has a Hamiltonian cycle, then $K^*(G', c) = n$, and so the cost of the approximation solution T is $\leq rn$. On the other hand, if G does not have a Hamiltonian cycle, then the cost of T is $\geq K^*(G', c) \geq rn + (n-1)$. Thus, the above is a reduction for HC $\leq_T^P$ r-APPROX-TSP.   □

Another famous *NP*-compelte optimization problem belonging to the first class is the problem MAX-CLIQUE.

> MAX-CLIQUE: Given a graph $G = (V, E)$, find a complete sub-graph of the maximum size.

It is known that the problem $r(n)$-APPROX-CLIQUE is NP-complete for all functions $r(n) = n^c$, with $0 < c < 1$. In other words, if $P \neq NP$, then there is no polynomial-time algorithm that can find a clique of a given graph, guaranteed to have size $\geq \omega(G)/n^c$ for any $0 < c < 1$, where $\omega(G)$ is the size of the maximum clique of a graph G. This is the strongest nonapproximability result among all NP-complete optimization problems. The proof of this result requires a novel notion of *probabilistically checkable proofs* and algebraic coding theory, and is beyond our scope.

Now we turn our attention to the approximation problems in the second class. First, we formulate the problem 3SAT into an optimization problem.

> MAX-3SAT: Given a 3-CNF formula $F = C_1 C_2 \cdots C_m$, find a Boolean assignment t on its variables such that t satisfies the maximum number of clauses C_i in F.

It is clear that MAX-3SAT is NP-complete. Indeed, the approximation to MAX-3SAT is also NP-complete. The proof of the this result is, again, based on the study of probabilistically checkable proofs, and we omit it here.

Theorem 7.48 *The problem r-APPROX-3SAT is NP-complete for some $r > 1$.*

Note that this approximation problem is obviously solvable in polynomial time for $r = 2$ (see Exercise 5(b) of Section 7.4). Thus, r-APPROX-3SAT belongs to the second class.

In the last few sections, we have seen a number of polynomial-time reductions from 3SAT to the devision versions of other NP-complete optimization problems. Some of these reductions can be modifed to preserve approximability properties.

Example 7.49 *The problem r-APPROX-VC is NP-complete for some $r > 1$.*

Proof. We modify the polynomial-time reduction from 3SAT to VC constructed in Example 7.26 as follows: Assume that $F = C_1 C_2 \cdots C_m$ is a 3-CNF formula over n variables $x_1, x_2, \ldots, x_n$. We let l_{jk}, $k = 1, 2, 3$, to denote the three literals in each clause C_j. From this formula F, we define a graph $H_F = (V, E)$ as follows:

(1) V has $3m$ vertices u_{jk}, for $1 \leq k \leq 3$ and $\leq j \leq m$.

(2) For each j, $1 \leq j \leq m$, u_{j1}, u_{j2}, u_{j3} form a triangle.

(3) There is an edge $\{u_{jk}, u_{j'k'}\}$, if $j \neq j'$ and $l_{jk} = \neg l_{j'k'}$.

(Recall that in the graph G_F of Example 7.26, we used two vertices v_i and $\overline{v}_i$ to encode the literal x_i and $\overline{x}_i$, and connected each u_{jk} with v_i (or $\overline{v}_i$) if $l_{jk} = x_i$ (or, respectively $\overline{x}_i$). Here, we do not use vertices v_i and $\overline{v}_i$, and connect u_{jk} and $u_{j'k'}$ directly if they encode x_i and $\overline{x}_i$, respectively.)

We first observe two basic relations between the formula F and the graph H_F.

Claim 1. For any assignment t on $\{x_1, x_2, \ldots, x_n\}$, there is a vertex cover C of H_F with $|C| = 3m - s(t)$, where $s(t)$ is the number of clauses in F that are satisfied by t.

Proof. We define set C as follows:

(1) In each clause C_j that is satisfied by t, pick one literal l_{jk} with $t(l_{jk}) = 1$, and put two vertices $u_{jk'}$, with $k' \in \{1, 2, 3\} - \{k\}$, in C.

(2) If C_j is not satisfied by t, then put all three vertices u_{jk}, $k \in \{1, 2, 3\}$, in C.

It is clear that $|C| = 3m - s(t)$, and that the edges of the triangles over $\{u_{j1}, u_{j2}, u_{j3}\}$, for all $1 \leq j \leq m$, are covered by vertices in C. We note that if $\{u_{jk}, u_{j'k'}\} \in E$ and $j \neq j'$, then $l_{jk} = \neg l_{j'k'}$. Therefore, one of these literals is false under the assignment t, and hence the corresponding vertex u_{jk} or $u_{j'k'}$ must be in C. Therefore, C is a vertex cover of H_F.

Claim 2. For any vertex cover C of H_F, there is an assignment t of variables $\{x_1, x_2, \ldots, x_n\}$ such that $s(t) \geq 3m - |C|$.

Proof. We define the assignment t as follows: $t(x_i) = 1$ if there is a literal $l_{jk} = x_i$ such that $u_{jk} \notin C$; and $t(x_i) = 0$, otherwise. We check that if $|C \cap \{u_{j1}, u_{j2}, u_{j3}\}| < 3$, then t satisfies the clause C_j. To see this, assume that $u_{jk} \notin C$ for some $k = 1, 2, 3$. We check that if $l_{jk} = x_i$ for some $i = 1, \ldots, n$, then we have $t(x_i) = 1$ and, hence, t satisfies C_j. On the other hand, if $l_{jk} = \bar{x}_i$ for some $i = 1, \ldots, n$, then it is not possible to have $x_i = l_{j'k'}$ and $u_{j'k'} \notin C$, for that would leave the edge $\{u_{jk}, u_{j'k'}\}$ not covered by C. Therefore, we must have $t(x_i) = 0$ and, hence, t satisfies clause C_j.

Let $sat^*(F)$ denote the maximum $s(t)$ under any assignment t, and $vc^*(H_F)$ the size of the minimum vertex cover of H_F. The above Claims 1 and 2 imply that

$$sat^*(F) = 3m - vc^*(H_F).$$

Now, suppose that there is a polynomial-time algorithm that can find a vertex cover C of H_F of size $\leq r \cdot vc^*(H_F)$, with $1 < r < 7/6$. We claim that we can apply this algorithm to find an assignment t of F that satisfies at least $sat^*(F)/s$ clauses, where $s = 1/(7 - 6r)$. To see this, we first define t as in Claim 2 above. Then, we have

$$
\begin{aligned}
sat^*(F) - s(t) &\leq (3m - vc^*(H_F)) - (3m - |C|) \\
&= |C| - vc^*(H_F) \\
&\leq (r - 1) \cdot vc^*(H_F) \leq 3(r - 1)m.
\end{aligned}
$$

Next, by a simple greedy algorithm, we can find an assignment that satisfies at least $m/2$ clauses of F; and, hence, we have $sat^*(F) \geq m/2$. Together, we get

$$s(t) \geq sat^*(F) - 3(r - 1)m \geq (7 - 6r)sat^*(F) = \frac{sat^*(F)}{s}.$$

The above shows that s-APPROX-3SAT $\leq_T^P$ r-APPROX-VC. Now, from Example 7.48, there exists some $s > 1$ such that s-APPROX-3SAT is NP-complete.

Thus, for the corresponding $r = (7s - 1)/(6s)$, the problem r-APPROX-VC is also *NP*-complete.   □

The following subproblem of MAX-3SAT is useful in proving other nonapproximability results.

> MAX-3SAT-b: Given a 3-CNF formula $F = C_1 C_2 \cdots C_m$, with each variable x in F occurring in at most b clauses (in the form of x or $\bar{x}$), find a Boolean assignment t on its variables such that t satisfies the maximum number of clauses C_i in F.

Theorem 7.50 *The problem r-APPROX-3SAT-3 is NP-complete for some* $r > 1$.

The proof of the above result is an approximation-preserving reduction from r-APPROX-3SAT to r-APPROX-3SAT-3. We omit the proof (cf. Exercise 5(c) of Section 7.4).

We let VC-d denote the problem VC restricted to graphs of degree d.

Example 7.51 *For each $d \geq 3$, the problem r-APPROX-VC-d is NP-complete for some* $r > 1$.

Proof. In the proof of Example 7.49, we observe that if each variable x_i occurs in at most three clauses, then each vertex u_{jk} in H_F has degree at most four, since there are at most two vertices $u_{j'k'}$ whose corresponding literals $l_{j'k'}$ are equal to the negation of l_{jk}. Therefore, the reduction in Example 7.49 is actually a reduction from s-APPROX-3SAT-3 to r-APPROX-VC-4. In the following, we reduce the problem r-APPROX-VC-4 to t-APPROX-VC-3.

Given a graph $G = (V, E)$ in which every vertex has degree at most four, we construct a graph G' of degree at most three as follows: For each vertex x of degree d in G ($1 \leq d \leq 4$), construct a path p_x of $2d - 1$ vertices to replace it as shown in Figure 7.14. Among the $2d - 1$ vertices, let $\bar{c}_x$ be the set of d vertices which connect to the old neighbors of x (denoted by the black dots in Figure 7.14), and c_x the set of the other $d - 1$ vertices (denoted by the gray dots in Figure 7.14).

Note that this path p_x has a unique minimum vertex cover c_x of size $d - 1$. However, this vertex cover only covers edges in path p_x but not the original edges incident on x. The set $\bar{c}_x$ is also a vertex cover of p_x. It has size d, but it covers all edges in p_x plus all edges that are originally incident on x.

Assume that $|V| = n$ and $|E| = m$. We observe that if C is a vertex cover of graph G, then

$$C' = \left(\bigcup_{x \in C} \bar{c}_x \right) \cup \left(\bigcup_{x \notin C} c_x \right)$$

is a vertex cover of G'. In addition, $|C'| = |C| + 2m - n$. (*Note:* The set $\bigcup_{x \in V} \bar{c}_x$ has size $2m$.)

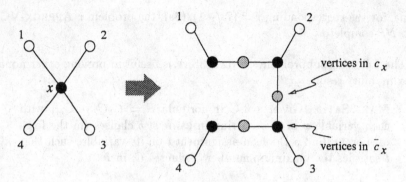

Figure 7.14: Path p_x.

Conversely, for each vertex cover C' of G', the set

$$C = \{x : \bar{c}_x \cap C' \neq \emptyset\}$$

is a vertex cover of G. Furthermore, $|C| \leq |C'| - 2m + n$.

Together, we have

$$vc^*(G') = vc^*(G) + 2m - n,$$

where $vc^*(G)$ is the size of the minimum vertex cover for G.

Now, assume that there is a polynomial-time algorithm A for the problem t-APPROX-VC-3 for some $t > 1$. Then, this algorithm on graph G' produces a vertex cover C' of size $\leq t \cdot vc^*(G')$. Correspondingly, we have a vertex cover C of G of size

$$\begin{aligned}
|C| &\leq |C'| - 2m + n \leq t \cdot vc^*(G') - 2m + n \\
&= t(vc^*(G) + 2m - n) - 2m + n \\
&= t \cdot vc^*(G) + (t-1)(2m - n).
\end{aligned}$$

Note that $m \leq 4 \cdot vc^*(G)$. It follows that

$$|C| \leq t \cdot vc^*(G) + 8(t-1)vc^*(G) = (9t - 8)vc^*(G).$$

That is, we have an algorithm for the problem $(9t - 8)$-APPROX-VC-4.

Thus, the above is a $\leq_T^P$-reduction from r-APPROX-VC-4 to t-APPROX-VC-3. Since r-APPROX-VC-4 is *NP*-complete for some $r > 1$, we conclude that t-APPROX-VC-3 is *NP*-complete for the corresponding $t = (r+8)/9 > 1$.
                                                                                                    □

Recall the notion of Steiner tress defined in Section 7.4. We consider a variation of the problem SMT.

> BOTTLENECK STEINER TREE (BST): Given a set $P = \{p_1, p_2, \ldots, p_n\}$ of n points in the Euclidean plane and a positive integer k, find a Steiner tree over the terminal points $p_1, p_2, \ldots, p_n$,

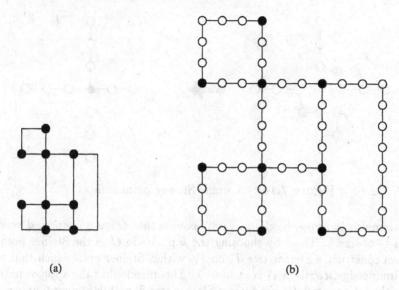

Figure 7.15: (a) A planar graph G. (b) The set P_G.

with at most k Steiner points, such that the length of the longest edges in the tree is minimized.

⋆ Example 7.52 *For* $1 < r < \sqrt{2}$, *r-APPROX-BST* *is NP-complete.*

Proof. Let r be a fixed real number, with $1 < r < \sqrt{2}$. Suppose that there exists a polynomial-time algorithm A for the problem r-APPROX-BST. We show how to apply algorithm A to solve the *NP*-complete problem PLANAR CONNECTED-VC-4 (see Exercise 2(c) of Section 7.4).

Let planar graph $G = (V, E)$ and integer k be an given instance of the problem PLANAR CONNECTED-VC-4. Then, we can embed graph G into the Euclidean plane so that all edges consist of horizontal and vertical segments of length at least $2k + 2$, so that every two edges meet at an angle of 90 degrees or 180 degrees. On any edge $\{u, v\}$ of length ℓ, we select $\ell' = \lceil \ell \rceil - 1$ interior points $x_1, \ldots, x_{\ell'}$ between u and v such that $|x_1 - u| = |x_{\ell'} - v| = 1$, and $|x_i - x_{i+1}| \leq 1$, for $1 \leq i \leq \ell' - 1$. Note that $\ell > 2k + 2$, and so $\ell' \geq 2k + 2$. We let P_G be the set of these interior points over all edges in G. (See Figure 7.15, in which the circles ○ denote the points in P_G, and the dark circles ● denote the vertices in G.)

We claim that G has a connected vertex cover of size k if and only if the algorithm A on input P_G produces a Steiner tree T with at most k Steiner points such that the maximum edge length in T is less than $\sqrt{2}$. From this claim, the problem PLANAR CONNECTED-VC-4 can be solved as follows: On input (G, k), apply algorithm A to input P_G and accept if the maximum edge length in the resulting tree is less than $\sqrt{2}$. In other words, PLANAR CONNECTED-VC-4 is $\leq_T^P$-reducible to r-APPROX-BST.

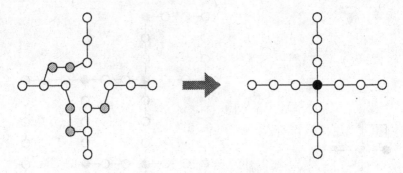

Figure 7.16:   A single Steiner point suffices.

It remains to prove the claim. First, assume that G has a connected vertex cover C of size k. Then, by choosing the k points in C as the Steiner points, we can construct a Steiner tree T_1 on P_G with k Steiner points such that the maximum edge length in T_1 is at most 1. This means that the approximation algorithm A on input P_G produces a Steiner tree T with k Steiner points such that the maximum edge length in T is at most $r < \sqrt{2}$.

Conversely, assume that the approximation algorithm A on input P_G produces a Steiner tree T with k Steiner points such that the maximum edge length in T is less than $\sqrt{2}$. We first note that the set P_G of terminal points has the following properties:

(a) Any two terminal points at two different edges of G have a distance at least $\sqrt{2}$.

(b) Any two terminal points at two nonadjacent edges of G have a distance at least $2k + 2$.

From (b), we know that we cannot connect terminal points at two nonadjacent edges by Steiner points only. Therefore, every Steiner point connects only terminal points at two adjacent edges. Furthermore, property (a) implies that two terminal points at two adjacent edges must be connected by at least one Steiner point in T. Now, for any two adjacent edges that are connected by some Steiner points, we can move one of these Steiner points to the location of the original vertex point in G that is the end point of these two edges. We connect this new Steiner point to all its original adjacent terminal points, and remove other Steiner points that connect the terminal points in these adjacent edges. (See Figure 7.16, in which all gray Steiner points are replaced by a single black Steiner point.) By this process, we create a Steiner tree T' with at most k Steiner points such that the maximum edge length in T' is at most 1. In addition, all Steiner points in T' are the original vertices of G. They form a connected vertex cover C of size at most k for G. This completes the proof of our claim.   □

Finally, we remark that a number of NP-complete optimization problems, including a large class of packing problems and geometric problems, are known to belong to the third class. We list some of them below without proofs, since the proof techniques involved are mainly those for the design of algorithms and are not directly related to the techniques we are studying in this book.

> KNAPSACK (optimization version): Given $2n + 1$ nonnegative integers $c_1, c_2, \ldots, c_n, p_1, p_2, \ldots, p_n$, and s, find $x_1, x_2, \ldots, x_n \in \{0, 1\}$ that maximize the value $\sum_{i=1}^{n} p_i x_i$, subject to the condition $\sum_{i=1}^{n} c_i x_i \leq s$.

Example 7.53 *The optimization version of* KNAPSACK *has a fully polynomial-time approximation scheme (FPTAS).*

Example 7.54 *The following optimization problems have polynomial-time approximation schemes (PTAS's):*

(a) BIN PACKING (optimization version): Given $n + 1$ positive integers $a_1, a_2, \cdots, a_n$, and c, find a partition of the list $(a_1, a_2, \cdots, a_n)$ into the minimum number of sublists such that the sum of a_i's in each sublist is at most c.

(b) STEINER MINIMUM TREE (SMT): Given n points $x_1, x_2, \ldots, x_n$ in the Euclidean plane, find the Steiner minimum tree over these points.

(c) RECTILINEAR SMT: The problem SMT with respect to the rectilinear distance instead of Euclidean distance. (In the two-dimensional plane, the rectilinear distance between two points $x = (a_1, b_1)$ and $y = (a_2, b_2)$ is $d_{rec}(x, y) = |a_1 - a_2| + |b_1 - b_2|$.)

(d) EUCLIDEAN TSP: Given n points $x_1, x_2, \ldots, x_n$ in the Euclidean plane, find a tour of these points of the minimum total edge length.

(e) PLANAR VC: The problem MIN-VC restricted to planar graphs.

(f) RECTANGULAR PARTITION: Given a rectilinear polygon that contains some rectilinear holes, partition it into hole-free rectangles with the minimum total edge length. (A *rectilinear polygon* is one whose edges are all horizontal or vertical.)

(g) CONVEX PARTITION: Given a convex polygon that contains some convex holes, partition it into hole-free convex polygons with the minimum total edge length. (A polygon is *convex* if the line segments connecting any two interior points of the polygon lie completely inside the polygon.)

(h) k-MINIMUM SPANNING TREE: Given n points $x_1, x_2, \ldots, x_n$ in the Euclidean plane, find k points from them to minimize the length of the minimum spanning tree on these k points.

Exercise 7.5

1. For each of the following search problems, formulate an appropriate decision version of it and show that the decision version and the search version are equivalent under polynomial-time Turing reduciblity.

(a) MAX-3SAT.

(b) The optimization version of KNAPSACK.

(c) LP (optimization version): Given a graph G, find a longest simple path in G.

(d) Given a positive integer n, find its largest prime factor.

2. For each of the following optimization problems, show that it is *NP*-complete:

(a) Given a directed graph, find a minimum subset of edges such that every directed cycle contains at least one edge in the subset.

(b) Given a directed graph, find a minimum subset of vertices such that every directed cycle contains at least one vertex in the subset.

(c) Given integers $a_1, a_2, \ldots, a_n, b_1, b_2, \ldots, b_n, s$ and t, find $x_1, x_2, \ldots, x_n \in \{0, 1\}$ that maximize the value $x_1 + x_2 + \cdots + x_n$, subject to the following constraints:

$$a_1 x_1 + a_2 x_2 + \cdots + a_n x_n \leq s,$$
$$b_1 x_1 + b_2 x_2 + \cdots + b_n x_n \leq t.$$

⋆ (d) Given a graph, find a wheel of the maximum size. (A *wheel* of size k is a subgraph of $k+1$ vertices, in which k vertices form a simple cycle and the other vertex is connected to all these k vertices.)

3. Show that for each of the following optimization problems Π, there exists an approximation ratio $r > 1$ such that r-APPROX-Π is *NP*-complete.

(a) NETWORK SMT: Given a graph $G = (V, E)$, an edge-weight function $w : E \rightarrow \mathbf{N}$ and a subset $P \subseteq V$, find a connected subgraph with the minimum total edge weight that interconnects vertices in P.

(b) CONNECTED-VC: Given a graph G, find a minimum vertex cover C such that the subgraph $G|_C$ induced by C is connected.

(c) TSP WITH TRIANGLE INEQUALITY: Given a complete graph G and an distance function $d : E \rightarrow \mathbf{N}$ that satisfies the triangle inequality, find a Hamiltonian cycle with the minimum total distance. (A distance function $d : E \rightarrow \mathbf{N}$ satisfies the *triangle inequality* if $d(\{a, b\}) + d(\{b, c\}) \geq d(\{a, c\})$ for any three vertices a, b, c.)

⋆ (d) TSP WITH $(1, 2)$-DISTANCE: Given a complete graph G and an edge-weight function $d : E \rightarrow \{1, 2\}$, find a Hamiltonian cycle with the minimum total distance.

⋆ 4. For a graph G, its *edge-square graph* G^2 is a graph obtained from G by replacing each edge $\{u, v\}$ by a copy of G, called $G_{u,v}$, and connecting both u and v to every vertex in $G_{u,v}$.

(a) Show that r-APPROX-LP is *NP*-complete for some $r > 1$.

(b) Show that if the longest simple path in G has length ℓ, then the longest simple path in G^2 has length at least ℓ^2. Moreover, given a path of length m in G^2, a path of length $\sqrt{m} - 1$ in G can be found in polynomial-time.

(c) Show that r-APPROX-LP is *NP*-complete for all $r > 1$.

⋆ **5.** Show that for each of the following optimization problems Π, there exists a constant $\varepsilon > 0$ such that n^ε-APPROX-Π is *NP*-complete.

(a) VERTEX COLORING: Given a graph $G = (V, E)$, find a coloring of V (i.e., a function $c : V \to \{1, 2, \ldots, m\}$) with the minimum number m of colors such that no two adjacent vertices have the same color.

(b) EDGE COLORING: Given a graph $G = (V, E)$, find a coloring of E (i.e., a function $c : E \to \{1, 2, \ldots, m\}$) with the minimum number m of colors such that no two adjacent edges (edges with a common vertex) have the same color.

References

Aho, A., Hopcroft, J. and Ullman, J. (1974), *The Design and Analysis of Computer Algorithms*, Addison-Wesley, Reading, MA.

Balcázar, J. L., Díaz, J. and Gabarró, J. (1988), *Structural Complexity I*, Springer-Verlag, Berlin, Germany.

Balcázar, J. L., Díaz, J. and Gabarró, J. (1990), *Structural Complexity II*, Springer-Verlag, Berlin, Germany.

Cohen, D. I. A. (1997), *Introduction to Computer Theory* (2nd edition), John Wiley & Sons, New York.

Cook, S. (1971), The complexity of theorem-proving procedures, *Proceedings of the 3rd ACM Symposium on Theory of Computing*, Association for Computing Machinery, New York, pp. 151–158.

Davis, M. D., Sigal, R. and Weyuker, E. J. (1994), *Computability, Complexity, and Languages*, Academic Press, San Diego.

Du, D.-Z. and Ko, K. (2000), *Theory of Computational Complexity*, John Wiley & Sons, New York.

Floyd R. W. and Beigel, R. (1994), *The Language of Machines*, Computer Science Press, New York.

Garey, M. R. and Johnson, D. (1979), *Computers and Intractability, a Guide to the Theory of NP-Completeness*, W.H. Freeman, San Francisco.

Ginzburg, A. (1968), *Algebraic Theory of Automata*, Academic Press, New York.

Hartmanis, J. (1976), *Feasible Computations and Provable Complexity Properties*, SIAM, Philadelphia.

Hopcroft, J. and Ullman, J. (1979), *Introduction to Automata Theory, Languages, and Computation*, Addison-Wesley, Reading, MA.

Karp, R. M. (1972), Reducibility among combinatorial problems, in *Complexity of Computer Computations*, Miller, R. and Thatcher, J., eds., Plenum Press, New York, pp. 85–103.

Kelley, D. (1995), *Automata and Formal Languages*, Prentice-Hall, Upper Saddle River, NJ.

Knuth, D. (1981), *The Art of Computer Programming, Vol. 2, Seminumerical Algorithms* (2nd Ed.), Addison-Wesley, Reading, MA.

Lawler, E. L. (1976), *Combinatorial Optimization: Networks and Matroids*, Holt, Rinehart and Winston, New York.

Lewis, H. R. and Papadimitriou, C. H. (1998), *Elements of the Theory of Computation* (2nd ed.), Prentice-Hall, Upper Saddle River, NJ.

Li, M. and Vitányi, P. (1997), *An Introduction to Kolmogorov Complexity and Its Applications* (2nd ed.), Springer-Verlag, Berlin.

Linz, P. (2001), *An Introduction to Formal Languages and Automata* (3rd Ed.), Jones and Bartlett, Sudbury, MA.

Machtey, M. and Young, P. (1978), *An Introduction to the General Theory of Algorithms*, North-Holland, Amsterdam.

Martin, J. C. (1991), *Introduction to Languages and the Theory of Computation*, McGraw-Hill, New York.

Minsky, M. L. (1967), *Computation: Finite and Infinite Machines*, Prentice-Hall, Upper Saddle River, NJ.

Papadimitriou, C. H. (1994), *Computational Complexity*, Addison-Wesley, Reading, MA.

Rogers, H., Jr. (1967), *Theory of Recursive Functions and Effective Computability*, Mc-Graw Hill, New York.

Salomaa, A. (1973), *Formal Languages*, Academic Press, New York.

Savage, J. E. (1998), *Models of Computation*, Addison-Wesley, Reading, MA.

Sipser, M. (1997), *Introduction to the Theory of Computation*, PWS Publishing Co., Boston.

Soare, R. I. (1987), *Recursively Enumerable Sets and Degrees*, Springer-Verlag, Berlin.

Sudkamp, T.A. (1997), *Languages and Machines*, Addison-Wesley, Reading, MA.

Taylor, R. G. (1998), *Models of Computation and Formal Languages*, Oxford University Press, New York.

Index

∨, 62, 324
∧, 324
¬, 324
⊕, 67
\, 3
≺, 216, 283
$(\exists i)_{i \leq m}$, 204
$(\forall i)_{i \leq m}$, 204
$\langle i, j \rangle$, 207
$\langle n_1, n_2, \ldots, n_k \rangle$, 209
$[n_1, n_2, \ldots, n_k]$, 209
$\leq_m$, 246
$\leq_m^P$, 340
$\leq_T^P$, 371
$\equiv_m^P$, 341
⊢, 123, 162
$\vdash_M$, 162
$\vdash^*$, 123, 162
$\vdash_M^*$, 162

$\overline{A}$, 3
A^*, 4
A^+, 5
A^k, 4
A^R, 6
$A \cdot B$, 3
$A \oplus B$, 67
$A \setminus B$, 3
$A \vee B$, 62

AB, 3
A-rule, 119
Ackermann function, 224
Adjacency matrix, 328
Alphabet, 1
    binary, 1
    Roman, 1
    Arabic digit, 1
Ambiguity, 112
Approximation problem, 374
Approximation ratio, 374
Arden's lemma, 6
Assignment, *see* Boolean function

BIN PACKING (BP), 364, 383
Binary string, 1
Boolean algebra, 324
Boolean formula, 325
    clause, 342
    conjunctive normal form (CNF), 342
    disjunctive normal form (DNF), 358
    literal, 342
    satisfiable, 325
Boolean function, 204, 324
    assignment, 325
        truth, 325
    associative law, 325
    commutative law, 324
    De Morgan's law, 325

389

distributive law, 325
BOTTLENECK STEINER TREE (BST), 380
BOUNDED PCP, 339
BOUNDED TILING, 339
BP, *see* BIN PACKING
BST, *see* BOTTLENECK STEINER TREE
Busy beaver function, 266
Busy beaver problem, 263

Certificate, 324
Changing base, 220
Characteristic function, 164, 215
χ_L, 164, 215
Church-Turing Thesis, 192
    extended, 293
Clause, 342
Clock machine, 300
CNF, *see* Conjunctive normal form
CNF-SAT, 342
co-NP, 336
co-r.e. set, 242
COINF, 257
Complementation, of a set, 3
Complete set, 251; *see also NP*-complete set
Composition, 200
Computation path, 124
Computational model, reasonable, 192
Concatenation, of lanuguages, 3
    of strings, 2
Conjunction, 324
Conjunctive normal form (CNF), 342; *see also* (k, ℓ)-CNF
    nonpolar representation, 369
    polar representation, 369
CONNECTED-VC, 384
Constant function, 201
Context-free grammar, 90
    ambiguous, 112, 276
    generating a sentence, 91
    left-factoring, 121
    leftmost graph, 111
    linear, 158
    nonterminal symbol, 89
    starting symbol, 90
    strong LL(k), 120

terminal symbol, 89
Context-free language, 91
    inherently ambiguous, 118
Context-sensitive grammar, 314
Context-sensitive language, 314
CONVEX PARTITION, 383
Cook's theorem, 351
Crossing sequence, 173, 174
CUBIC VC, 369

De Morgan's law, 325
Decision problem, 243, 370
Degree of unsolvability, 254
Derivation, 91
    leftmost, 110
Derivation tree, 109
Deterministic finite automata (DFA), 23
    accepting a language, 24
    accepting an input string, 24, 25
    computation path, 25
    final state, 24
    finite control, 23
    initial state, 24
    minimum, 70
    product automata, 33
    rejecting an input string, 24
    states, 23
    (state) transition function, 23, 25
    tape, 23
    tape head, 23
    transition diagram, 24
Deterministic Turing machine, *see* Turing machine
DFA, *see* Deterministic finite automata
DGISO, *see* DIGRAPH ISOMORPHISM
Diagonalization, 241, 242
    space-bounded, 297
Digraph, *see* Directed graph
DIGRAPH ISOMORPHISM (DGISO), 341
Directed graph, 16; *see also* Graph
    in-edge, 16
    labeled, *see* Labeled digraph
    out-edge, 16
Disjunction, 324

Disjunctive normal form (DNF), 14, 358; *see also* Regular expression

DNF, *see* Disjunctive normal form

Dovetailing, 234

DTM, *see* Turing machine

Dynamic programming, 294

ε, 2

ε-rule, 111

EDGE COLORING, 385

EIGHT-QUEEN PROBLEM, 331

Elementary product, 357

Elementary sum, 342

EMP, 248

Empty string, 2

Enumeration theorem, 232

Equivalence class, 70

Equivalence relation, 70

Existential quantifier, bounded, 204

Exponential functions, 284

EUCLIDEAN TSP, 383

$f^{(n)}$, 202

$f(n) \prec g(n)$, 283

Feasible problem, 294

Feasibly solvable language, 294

Fibonacci function, 206

FIN, 253

Finite automata, *see* Deterministic finite automata *and* Nondeterministic finite automata

FPTAS, *see* Polynomial-time approximation scheme

Fully space-constructible function, 297

Fully time-constructible function, 300

Function(s), *see also* Boolean function

    Ackermann, 224

    constant, 201

    exponential, 284

    growth rate, 283

    increasing, 239

    initial, 200

    multi-valued, *see* Multi-valued function

    pairing, 207

    partial, 164

    partial recursive, *see* Recursive function

    poly-log, 283

    polynomial, 283

    polynomial-time computable, 337, 370

    polynomially honest, 337

    primitive recursive, 201, 218

    projection, 200

    recursive, 215

    subexponential, 283

    successor, 200

    superexponential, 284

    threshold, 338

    total, 164

    Turing-computable, 164, 168, 171

    zero, 200

Function-index set, 251

$G|_A$, 360

$G(r)$, 17

Gap theorem, 297

GAUTO, *see* GRAPH AUTOMORPHISM

GISO, *see* GRAPH ISOMORPHISM

Gödel numbering, 208

Grammar, 90, 193

    context-free, *see* Context-free grammar

    context-sensitive, 314

    left-linear, 96

    linear, 99

    right-linear, 96

    unrestricted, 193

Graph(s), 16, 328; *see also* Directed graph

    isomorphic, 339

    adjacency matrix, 328

    cubic, 369

    cycle, 16

    edge, 16

    edge-square, 384

    loop, 16

    path, 16

    planar, 369

    vertex, 16

    vertex cover, 329

GRAPH AUTOMORPHISM (GAUTO), 350

GRAPH ISOMORPHISM (GISO), 339
Growth rate, 283
Guess-and-verify algorithm, 307, 323

Halting problem, 243
Hamiltonian cycle, 328
HAMILTONIAN CYCLE (HC), 328
HC, *see* HAMILTONIAN CYCLE
HITTING SET (HS), 330
Homomorphism, 60
HS, *see* HITTING SET

if-then-else, 203
Increasing function, 239
Independent set, 331
INDEPENDENT SET (IS), 331
Index(R), 70
Index set, *see* Set-index set *and*
      Function-index set
Induced subgraph, 360
Induction, mathematical, 13
Inductive definition, 13
INF, 244
Inherent ambiguity, 149
Initial functions, 200
Integer factoring, 334
INTEGER PROGRAMMING (IP), 332
Intersection, 3
ι_Σ, 216
IP, *see* INTEGER PROGRAMMING
IS, *see* INDEPENDENT SET
Isomorphic graphs, 339
Isomorphism function, 339
item(n), 208

K_j^k, 201
(k, ℓ)-CNF, 370
(k, ℓ)-SAT, 370
k-MINIMUM SPANNING TREE, 383
Kleene closure, 4
KNAPSACK, 363, 383
KNIGHT'S TOUR, 328
Kolmogorov complexity, 264

$L(G)$, 91
$L(M)$, 24, 25, 40
$L(r)$, 8
L_1/L_2, 61
$L_{\frac{1}{2}}$, 63

$l(n)$, 207
L'Hopital's rule, 284
Labeled digraph, 17, 55
    ε-edge, 18
    final vertex, 17
    initial vertex, 17
Labeled Markov algorithm (LMA),
    199
Language, 3
    context-free, *see* Context-free
        language
    context-sensitive, 314
    feasibly solvable, 294
    linear, 158
    quotient, 61
    regular, *see* Regular language
    reversal of a, 6
    Turing-acceptable, 163
    Turing-decidable, 164
Language equation, 6
Left-factoring, 121
Left-linear grammar, 96
Lexicographic ordering, 216
Linear grammar, 99
Linear language, 158
Linear set, 150
Linear speed-up theorem, 290
Literal, 342
LMA, *see* Labeled Markov algorithm
Lookahead set, 119
LONGEST PATH (LP), 338
LP, *see* LONGEST PATH

$\mathcal{M}$, 225
M_n, 228
M_x, 228
$M_1 \times M_2$, 33
Mathematical induction, 13
MAX(L), 67, 146
MAX-CLIQUE, 376
MAX-3SAT, 377
MAX-3SAT-b, 379
MCG, *see* MINIMUM CONNECTIVITY
    GRAPH
$(\min i)_{i \le m}$, 204
MIN(L), 61, 67
MIN-VC, 370
Minimization, bounded, 204

Minimum Connectivity Graph (MCG), 361
Minimum DFA, 70
Multi-valued function, 370
    polynomial-time computable, 370

N, 168
Negation, 324
Network SMT, 384
NFA, *see* Nondeterministic finite automata
Nondeterministic finite automata (NFA), 38
    accepting an input, 39, 40
    computation path, 38
    computation tree, 39
    ε-closure, 39
    ε-move, 38
    ε-transition, 38
    hanging, 38
    multiple-state transition, 38
    transition diagram, 38
Nondeterministic Turing machine (NTM), 304
    accepting an input, 304
    computation tree, 304
    computing a function, 319
    space complexity, 308
    time complexity, 308
Nonterminal symbol, 89
NP, 309, 323
NP-complete set, 350
    search problem, 371
NP-hard set, 350
NPSPACE, 309
NSPACE($t(n)$), 308
NTIME($t(n)$), 308
NTM, *see* Nondeterministic Turing machine

Ogden's lemma, 147
Optimization problem, 373
    approximation, *see* Approximation problem
    polynomially bounded, 373
Oracle, 371

Pairing function, 207
Parikh's lemma, 150

Parse tree, 109
Parsing, 111
    top-down, 111
Partial function, 164
Partial recursive function, *see* Recursive function
Partition, 361
Partition, 361
    even, 361
PCP, *see* Post Correspondence Problem
PDA, *see* Pushdown automata
ϕ_n^k, 228
π_i^k, 200
Planar Connected-VC-4, 369
Planar Nonpolar-3Sat, 370
Planar Polar-3Sat, 369
Planar VC, 369, 383
Poly-log functions, 283
Polygon, convex, 383
    rectilinear, 383
Polynomial functions, 283
Polynomial-time approximation scheme (PTAS), 375
    fully (FPTAS), 375
Polynomial-time computable function, 337, 370
Polynomial-time equivalence, 341
Polynomially honest function, 337
Positive closure, 5
Post Correspondence Problem (PCP), 272
Predicate, 204
Prefix, 2
prefix(B), 336
Primality Testing (Prime), 334
Prime, *see* Primality Testing
Primitive recursion, 200
Primitive recursive function, 201, 218
Primitive recursive set, 215
Probabilistically checkable proofs, 377
Product automata, 33
Productive set, 258
Program-size complexity, 264
Projection function, 200
Projection theorem, 233
PTAS, *see* Polynomial-time approximation scheme

Pumping lemma
    for regular languages, 80
        strong form, 81
    for context-free languages, 143
Pushdown automata (PDA), 122
    accepting an input, 123, 124
    configuration, 123
        successor, 123
    deterministic, 190
    linear-bounded, 142
    product, 138
    two-stack, 142

Quotient language, 61

R_L, 70
R_L^*, 75
r-APPROX-BST, 381
r-APPROX-LP, 385
r-APPROX-Π, 375
r-APPROX-3SAT, 377
r-APPROX-3SAT-3, 379
r-APPROX-TSP, 376
r-APPROX-VC, 377
r-APPROX-VC-d, 379
$r(n)$, 207
$r(n)$-APPROX-CLIQUE, 377
R. e. set, see Recursively enumerable
      set
RAM, see Random access machine
Random access machine (RAM), 191
REC, 245
RECTANGULAR PARTITION, 383
RECTILINEAR SMT, 383
Recursion theorem, 258
Recursive definition, 13
Recursive function(s), 215
    partial, 215, 218
        enumeration of, 228
        extendable, 243
    primitive, 201, 218
Recursive set, 215, 218
    primitive, 215
Recursively enumerable (r.e.) set(s),
      215, 218
    enumeration of, 228, 232
    complete, 251
Recursively separable sets, 246
Reducibility, 246

approximation-preserving, 375
many-one, 246
    polynomial-time, 340
polynomial-time, 340
Turing, polynomial-time, 371
Reduction function, 246
REG, 253
Regular expression, 8
    disjunctive normal form, 14
    distributive law, 9
    extended, 313
    preference rules, 9
    starless, 313
REGULAR EXPRESSION NONEQUIVA-
      LENCE, 369
Regular grammar, 97
Regular language, 8
Regular set, 8
REV, 253
Reversal, of a language, 6
    of a string, 2
Rice's theorem, 252
    for r. e. index sets, 256
Right-linear grammar, 96

S-m-n theorem, 248
SAT, see SATISFIABILITY
SATISFIABILITY (SAT), 325
Savitch's theorem, 309
Search problem, 370
    NP-complete, 371
Self-recognizing program, 265
Self-referential program, 259
Self-reproducing program, 262
Semi-characteristic function, 215
Semilinear set, 150
Sentence, 89, 90
Sentential form, 89, 90
    left, 111
Set-index set, 251
    nontrivial, 252
SGISO, see SUBGRAPH ISOMORPHISM
Σ^*, 3
σ, 200
σ_A, 215
Simple set, 244
$size(n)$, 209
SMT, see STEINER MINIMUM TREE
$Space_M(x)$, 308

Space complexity, 288
Space-constructible function, fully,
    297
Space hierarchy theorem, 297
    for *NSPACE*, 311
Space marking machine, 297
Spanning tree, 368
SQRT(L), 67, 179
Star closure, 4
Steiner minimum tree, 366
STEINER MINIMUM TREE (SMT),
    366
Steiner tree, 365
    Steiner points, 366
    terminal points, 365
String, 1
    binary, 1
    empty, 2
    length, 2
Subexponential functions, 283
SUBGRAPH ISOMORPHISM (SGISO),
    350
Subset construction, 46
Substitution, 60
Substring, 2
Subtraction, of sets, 3
Successor function, 200
Suffix, 2
Superexponential functions, 284
Symbol, 1

$T_{n,k}$, 338
Tape compression theorem, 288
Terminal symbol, 89
3DM, *see* THREE-DIMENSIONAL
    MATCHING
Three-dimensional matching, 332
THREE-DIMENSIONAL MATCHING
    (3DM), 332
3SAT, 342
3SAT-EXACTLY-ONE, 349
3SAT-NOT-ALL, 349
Threshold function, 338
TILING, 278
$Time_M(x)$, 286, 308
Time complexity, 288
Time-constructible function, fully,
    300
Time hierarchy theorem, 300

TM, *see* Turing machine
TOT, 243
Total function, 164
TOWER OF HANOI, 281
Transition diagram, 24
TRAVELING SALESMAN PROBLEM
    (TSP), 339, 376
    WITH (1, 2)-DISTANCE, 384
    WITH TRIANGLE INEQUALITY,
        384
Tree, 365
Truth assignment, 325
Truth table, 324
TSP, *see* TRAVELING SALESMAN
    PROBLEM
Turing-acceptable language, 163
Turing-computable function, 164,
    168, 171
Turing-decidable language, 164
Turing-enumerable set, 236
Turing machine(s) (TM, DTM), 159
    accepting an input, 162
    coding of, 226
    computation path, 162
    computing a function, 164
    configuration, 161
        successor, 161
    deterministic (DTM), 159
    enumeration, 225
    instructions, 160
    legal code of a, 226
    memory space, 287
    multi-tape, 183
        configuration, 183
        transition function, 183
    nondeterministic, *see* Nondeter-
        ministic Turing machine
    one-pebble, 179
    output, 164
    product, 233
    read/erase-only, 180
    read-only, 173
        crossing sequence, 173
    running time, 286
    space bound, 287
    standard one-worktape, 287
    state, 160
        final, 160
        initial, 160

    tape, 159
        input, 287
        one-way write-only, 236
        output, 287
        read-only, 183
        storage, 287
        tracks, 181
        work, 287
    tape alphabet, 160
    time bound, 286
    transition diagram, 163
    transition function, 160
    two-dimensional, 189
    two-way, 181
    two-way-infinite one-tape, 181
    universal, 228
2^S, 38
2SAT, 370

Ultimately periodic set, 69
Unbounded minimization, 215
Undecidable problem, 243, 251, 266
Undirected graph, 328
Union, 3
Universal quantifier, bounded, 204

Universal Turing machine, 228
Unrestricted grammar, 193
Unsolvability, degree of, 254
Unsolvable problem, 243

VC, *see* VERTEX COVER
$vc^*(G)$, 380
VERTEX COLORING, 385
Vertex cover, 329
VERTEX COVER (VC), 329

W_n, 228
Witness, 324
Word, 2
Word equation, 3
Word theory, 2

$x \cdot y$, 2
$x \vee y$, 62
x^R, 2
x^k, 2

ζ, 200
Zero function, 200